Code Centric: T-SQL Programming with Stored Procedures and Triggers

GARTH WELLS

Code Centric: T-SQL Programming with Stored Procedures and Triggers

Copyright ©2001 by Garth Wells

ISBN (pbk): 1-893115-83-6

Printed and bound in the United States of America 12345678910

Editorial Directors: Dan Appleman, Gary Cornell, Karen Watterson

Technical Editor: Diane Brockman

Projects Manager: Grace Wong

Developmental Editor: Martin Minner

Copy Editors: Kristen Brown, Kari Brooks

Production Editor: Kari Brooks

Page Composition: Tony Jonick, Rappid Rabbit Publishing

Indexer: Carol Burbo

Artist: Karl Miyajima

Part Opener Design: Tony Jonick, Rappid Rabbit Publishing

Cover: Derek Yee, Derek Yee Design

Distributed to the book trade in the United States by Springer-Verlag New York, Inc., 175 Fifth Avenue, New York, NY, 10010

and outside the United States by Springer-Verlag GmbH & Co. KG, Tiergartenstr. 17, 69112 Heidelberg, Germany

In the United States, phone 1-800-SPRINGER; orders@springer-ny.com; http://www.springer-ny.com

Outside the United States, contact orders@springer.de; http://www.springer.de; fax +49 6221 345229

For information on translations, please contact Apress directly at 901 Grayson Street, Suite 204, Berkeley, CA, 94710

Phone: 510-549-5937; Fax: 510-549-5939; info@apress.com; http://www.apress.com

For my daughter, Sara Nicole, who brings me an immeasurable amount of joy

Contents at a Glance

Contents

Foreword

BACK IN THE PALEOZOIC ERA, OR SO IT SEEMS, I began teaching Microsoft University students about a new OS/2 DBMS called SQL Server. While I had worked with databases big and small for years, this new Sybase/Microsoft/Ashton Tate product seemed intriguing. One of the most popular database classes taught Transact-SQL (T-SQL) programming to fledgling Microsoft and third-party developers. In those early days we had the luxury of SQL Server documentation which was actually printed on paper (you know, the stuff they print the Harry Potter books on). I still keep those old books at my home office (under lock and key). When I was asked to review and write a foreword for Garth's new book on T-SQL, I was anxious to see how well it stacked up to the (excellent) paper documentation from those early days of SQL Server. I was not disappointed.

SQL Server 2000 exposes a number of new (radically new) concepts—especially for developers working at the T-SQL level. For the first time we can execute user-written functions within a stored procedure. This feature alone is enough to encourage developers to create more structured procedures—procedures that are easier to code and debug. These new functions within stored procedures can pass the new Table object or the new SQL_Variant datatype as arguments. These innovations vastly expand T-SQL's power and flexibility. I think it's critical for all SQL Server developers (and trainers) to get up to speed on these innovations so they can best leverage their power in our applications.

Other innovations make it easier than ever to solve some of the tougher problems we face whether we're writing stored procedures or using ADO to execute queries. For example, anyone who has tried to get the current Identity value after an Insert operation knows how tough it is to capture the new integer or GUID value—especially in situations where additional rows are added by Insert triggers. SQL Server 2000 comes to the rescue by adding significant functionality that helps expose the *true* identity (value) of a newly inserted row.

Transact-SQL is not executed in a vacuum. It's often embedded in stored procedures or hard-coded into queries run from binary components or Active Server Pages. Any book or tutorial that does not address using T-SQL in the context of *programming* is missing the point. I was convinced Garth understood this concept when he advised his readers to avoid SELECT *. Anyone who has heard me speak knows why this is an evil habit. Better yet, his example queries show his attention to detail—they use correctly phrased and efficient code even when illustrating a simple point.

All too often we see cursory explanations of how a function or command works. You'll find that Garth takes you deeper into the inner workings of SQL Server so you understand not only what is happening at the surface, but also what's taking place behind the scenes. This way you are aware of the side effects of your SELECT or action query. You'll also gain a better understanding of how to tune your queries to improve not only your application's performance and your server's performance, but also your development performance. This book will not only serve as a good "programmer's guide," but as a good "language reference," as well.

Well done, Garth.

Bill Vaughn
President, Beta V Corporation

Preface

WHEN I FIRST STARTED WORKING WITH SQL SERVER some six years ago, there were no books or Web sites that a novice developer could use to learn how to program in T-SQL (Transact-SQL). In the early days I learned by experimenting with the simple examples in the SQL Server documentation and tips provided by the software vendor who supplied my employer's mission critical application. A few years later I discovered the SQL Server newsgroups, which opened my eyes to a new way to learn about SQL Server. In the newsgroups I was able to post problems I was having implementing solutions with T-SQL, and senior-level developers like SQL Server MVP (Most Valued Professional) Roy Harvey would take the time to explain the proper way to solve the problem.

Today, the SQL Server documentation is an outstanding reference, but it is very limited when it comes to presenting real-world examples. The newsgroups are still a great resource, but they provide little in terms of introductory-level material. This book provides both beginner-level material and real-world examples in an effort to give you the complete picture. For example, I not only show the basics of creating and altering a stored procedure, but also how they are used to implement solutions in real-world applications. In addition, I show you how to integrate the database with the client application using ASP/ADO.

The main goal of this book is to teach you how to use stored procedures and triggers to implement solutions on your programming projects. This goal is accomplished by demonstrating some of the ways I have used stored procedures and triggers on projects I have successfully implemented for my clients. Some of the examples are involved and require effort on your part, but the end result is that when you complete them, you will have a better understanding of T-SQL and will be better prepared to solve problems you encounter in your programming endeavors.

One aspect of the book that I am sure VB and ASP programmers will find helpful are the examples that demonstrate how to write ASP/ADO code needed to have their client applications interact with SQL Server. The sample browser-based application presented in Chapter 14 demonstrates numerous ways you are most likely to use these technologies to create applications for your clients.

Organization

The book is organized in three parts. Part I serves as an introduction to T-SQL and a reference for Parts II and III. It covers the main aspects of the language (e.g., data types, DML, and DDL) you need to know to understand and work through the extensive examples covered in the book. Part II concentrates on the different stored procedures available in SQL Server 2000. The extended, system, and user-defined procedures are covered, as well as triggers. In Part III, I present extensive examples to show you how procedures and triggers are used in real-world applications.

In an effort to make each chapter's topic easier to grasp, I include a "Before You Get Started" section. In some cases, the material presented gives you specific information about the technology discussed in the chapter. In others, though, I provide general information to help you understand a concept or give you insight based on my experiences.

If you are interested in Web development, you will find the material in the appendixes very useful. There are more than 90 pages that show you how to create HTML pages, use ASP to interact with a database, and implement XML integration with SQL Server 2000.

Real-World Examples

There are nine extensive examples presented in Chapter 13 that are based on my experience implementing database solutions with SQL Server. The examples vary in the type of solution demonstrated and include:

- Using cursors to dynamically apply permissions

- Creating dynamic, multi-parameter stored procedures

- Creating Crystal Reports whose data source is a stored procedure

- Using triggers to implement event-based notifications with email

- Executing DTS Packages via stored procedures

The code used to create the examples is available for download at http://www.apress.com and http://www.SQLBook.com, so you can have them working fairly quickly. As a matter of fact, each chapter has an associated sample file that contains all the code it references.

Sample Application

Chapter 14, the final chapter in the book, details a fully functioning browser-based application that is based on one currently in production for one of my clients. The application's specifications are detailed, and each procedure it uses is covered. The application includes 9 tables, 21 stored procedures, 4 triggers and an ASP interface that is composed of more than 25 .asp files.

Web Development Primers

Developing ASP-based database applications has been a hot topic in programming for a while now. Those of you interested in learning how to create these types of applications will really enjoy reading the HTML and ASP primers in the appendixes. I cover the basics of HTML and show how to use ASP technology to communicate with SQL Server. In addition to these topics, there is a primer on XML that is a must-read for those of you interested in the new data transfer technology. XML will be the data transfer language of the future, so the sooner you get up to speed on the language and how it interacts with SQL Server, the better positioned you will be to take advantage of the opportunities it generates.

Free SQL Server 2000 120-Day Evaluation CD

In addition to more than 5,000 lines of sample code, the book also comes with a free 120-day evaluation copy of SQL Server 2000, so there's no reason you can't start learning the proper way to program with T-SQL today!

Acknowledgments

WRITING A BOOK IS A CHALLENGING ENDEAVOR. I could not have successfully completed this project without the help of a number of individuals. Karen Watterson and Gary Cornell (Apress management) gave me their full support and the creative freedom needed to make changes and add content I thought would produce a better title. Grace Wong, Projects Manager, made sure the editing staff was qualified and that the project was well-organized. The book's editors, Diane Brockman, Martin Minner, Kari Brooks, and Kristen Brown, made sure the content was accurate and the manuscript well-written. Each editor did an excellent job, but I especially want to thank Diane for putting in extra effort as the technical editor. She not only fulfilled that role, but also pitched in to help with decisions concerning overall content and chapter organization.

In addition to these folks, there are a few colleagues who volunteered their time to help me with this project. They are: David Cantu, Tuan Nguyen, Robert Huis in 't Veld, and Jon Kilburn. I want to thank each of them for taking time out of their busy schedules to help me produce a better a book.

Garth Wells
President, DataDrivenWebSites.com, Inc.

Part I

Transact-SQL Basics

Transact-SQL Overview

THE MAIN GOAL OF THIS BOOK is to show how stored procedures and triggers are used to implement real-world solutions with SQL Server 2000. In order to accomplish this goal the reader must have a fundamental understanding of Transact-SQL (T-SQL). With this in mind, the book has been organized so that the material presented in Part One (Chapter 1 to 8) can serve as a reference for both Parts Two and Three. Part One not only covers the basics of T-SQL, but also contains a description of every programming concept (e.g., T-SQL built-in functions) used in the remainder of the book. If you see a code segment or reference that you do not understand in Parts Two and/or Three, be assured that it is explained in Part One.

This chapter begins a series of five whose purpose is to introduce you to the basic concepts of T-SQL. A general overview of the language is covered here, data types in Chapter 2, data definition language (DDL) in Chapter 3, and data manipulation language (DML) in Chapters 4 and 5. If you are a novice user of SQL Server, I encourage you to read these chapters thoroughly before taking on the rest of the book.

If you already have a good understanding of T-SQL you will probably want to jump ahead to Chapter 7 and read about user-defined functions, which are new to SQL Server 2000. If you are a frequent user of views, you will want to make sure you read Chapter 8 so you can understand the new indexing features that are now available. Otherwise, feel free to jump to Part Two and start reading about procedures.

NOTE Sample Code

The sample code for the book can be downloaded at either http://www.apress.com *or* http://www.SQLBook.com. *Download CodeCentric.zip and extract and access a chapter's sample file(s) as needed. For most chapters there is only a single .sql file, but for Chapters 10, 13, and 14, multiple files are used.*

Before You Get Started

This book uses a lot of examples to demonstrate the various functionality available in SQL Server 2000 and each one is included in the example file(s) that accompany each chapter. The example files were created so that you could more easily implement the examples as you read along. Query Analyzer is used extensively to execute the examples, so the various components and functionality available in the tool are discussed here.

Query Analyzer

Query Analyzer is an application that allows you to interact with the SQL Server database engine. It is not really a *part* of SQL Server, but simply a tool that comes with the product that makes it easier to use. Query Analyzer has been greatly enhanced in SQL Server 2000, so you can now use it to accomplish the following:

- Create and execute queries.

- Use templates that contain the basic syntax of commonly used database objects.

- Analyze and script database objects using Object Browser.

- Execute stored procedures using Object Browser.

- Perform query optimization analysis using the Show Execution Plan option.

- Locate database objects using Object Search.

- Debug stored procedures using the T-SQL Debugger.

Query Analyzer Components

When you launch Query Analyzer you are prompted to provide login information. Once you have provided a valid login and connected to the target server, the windows shown in Figure 1-1 are displayed.

Query Window is shown on the right and Object Browser is shown on the left.

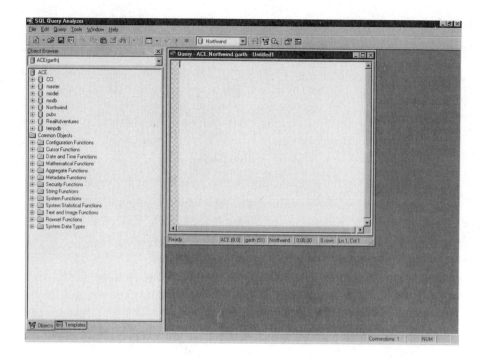

Figure 1-1. Query Analyzer

Query Window

The Query Window is where you will do most of your SQL programming so it is important that you understand the multiple panes of which it is composed. Table 1-1 describes the panes used in Query Window.

Table 1-1. Query Window Panes

PANE	DESCRIPTION
Editor	Where you type and execute SQL statements. Statements can be executed by clicking the Run button on the toolbar or by pressing CTRL+E. When the pane contains multiple statements, one or more can be executed in isolation by highlighting each and pressing CRTL+E.
Results	Where the results of the statements are displayed. By default, this pane is not displayed until a statement is executed. You can toggle the display of this pane by clicking the right-most icon on the toolbar.
Message	Where error messages are displayed. This pane simply overlays the Results Pane when an executed SQL Statement causes an error message to be displayed.

Table 1-1. Query Window Panes (Continued)

PANE	DESCRIPTION
Execution Plan	Where the graphical representation of the execution plan is displayed. This pane is not displayed by default, but can be activated by clicking Query on the main menu, selecting Show Execution Plan and then executing a SQL Statement. Once the statement has been executed a tab labeled Execution Plan will be displayed next to the Results tab. Simply click it to see a graphical representation of the execution plan.
Trace	Where server trace information is displayed. It is not displayed by default, but can be activated by clicking Query on the main menu, selecting Show Server Trace and then executing a SQL Statement. Once the statement has been processed a tab labeled Trace will be displayed to the right of the Results tab.
Statistics	Where statistics about the statements processed and the connection session are displayed. It is not displayed by default, but can be activated by clicking Query on the main menu, selecting Show Client Statistics and then executing a SQL Statement. Once the statement has been processed a tab labeled Statistics will be displayed to the right of the Results tab.

The last three panes described in Table 1-1 are optional for good reason. They display more advanced information that is used to optimize queries and/or troubleshoot performance problems. The Execution Plan Pane is used extensively in Appendix C, which discusses query optimization techniques. You should, however, postpone reading it until you complete Part Two of the book. The Trace and Statistics Panes are not used in this book, so if you would like to learn more about each one, see Books Online topics: Viewing and Analyzing Traces and Query Window Statistics Pane.

> **TIP Looking Up References in Books Online**
>
> *This book contains numerous references to topics in Books Online. To find a particular topic, simply open Books Online via the SQL Server program group, click the Search tab, type in the topic verbatim in the input box and click List Topics.*

Object Browser

Object Browser is new to SQL Server 2000, and it is an extremely useful tool. In pre-2000 versions of SQL Server I often needed both Query Analyzer and Enterprise Manager open at the same time in order to program. Object Browser includes the functionality (for example, easy access to a table's column names and data types) that formerly caused me to use Enterprise Manager, so I no longer need to have both applications open while developing.

Object Browser allows you to do the following:

- View all the objects in an instance of SQL Server.

- Create a script that shows the statements used to create an object.

- Create a script that allows you to modify or alter an object.

- View the data in a table or view.

- Execute a stored procedure.

- Add an extended property to an object. An extended property is used to add metadata to a database object.

- Delete a database object.

- View many of the built-in functions available in SQL Server 2000.

- View the available data types and their associated characteristics.

In order to use Object Browser to view all the objects in a database, simply expand the target database and expand the folder of the type of object you wish to view. You can place an object's name in the Editor Pane by clicking it and dragging it from the browser window into the pane. The various scripting options that are available for an object are accessed by right-clicking the target object and selecting the desired scripting option from the pop-up menu. To view the data in a table or view, simply right-click the object and select Open. In like manner, executing a stored procedure is as simple as right-clicking the target procedure and selecting Open. An extended property can be added to an object by right-clicking the object and selecting Extended Properties from the pop-up menu. To delete an object simply right-click it and select Delete. To get the syntax for a function shown in the Common Objects area into the Editor Pane, right-click the target and select the desired scripting option. To see the data types available in SQL Server 2000, simply expand the System Data Types folder. A description of the data type is displayed when you place your mouse over each item.

Object Search

Object Search, new to SQL Server 2000, allows you to search for an object in one or
more databases. You activate Object Search by clicking the database/magnifying
glass icon on the toolbar or by clicking Tools on the main menu and selecting Object
Search. The window displayed as a result of either action is shown in Figure 1-2.

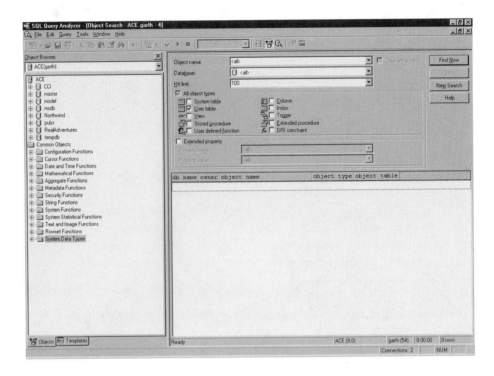

Figure 1-2. Object Search

Object Search gives you the ability to restrict a search by object name, database location, object type, or extended property name or value.

T-SQL Debugger

The T-SQL Debugger is new to SQL Server 2000, but there have been other stored
procedure debuggers available as add-ins to Visual C++, Visual Basic, and Visual
Interdev. This tool is described in detail in the "Debugging Stored Procedures"
section of Chapter 11.

General Comments on Query Analyzer

The following sections should help you better understand some of the additional features available in Query Analyzer.

Displaying Results

In pre-2000 versions of SQL Server the data displayed in the Results Pane was shown in plain text. In SQL Server 2000, the default behavior is to display the results in a grid. You also have the ability to pipe the results generated by a statement to a file. You can toggle these options by clicking Query on the main menu and selecting the desired option. Should you want to revert back to pre-2000 behavior and always display results in text, you change the default setting by completing the following:

1. Click Tools on the main menu and select Options.

2. Click the Results tab and change the option for the Default Results Target select box.

3. Click OK. Now the default is permanently changed.

Commenting Multiple Statements

As you build the statements used to create the various database objects required by your project, you often fill the Editor Pane with quite a bit of text. Should you have statements that you do not want to execute, but are not quite ready to delete from the pane, you can easily comment them out by completing the following:

1. Highlight the statement(s) you wish to comment out.

2. Click Edit on the main menu, highlight Advanced and select Comment Out.

This adds the inline comment marks double-dashes (--) to the start of each line. You can use the same Advanced option to remove the comment marks as well.

Add-In Tools

You can add shortcuts to commonly used programs to the Tools option from the main menu. For example, I often use the GWD Text Editor when writing ASP pages, so I added a shortcut to GWD using this approach. In order to add a program shortcut complete the following:

1. Click Tools on the main menu and select Customize.

2. Click the Tools tab and then click the Add icon (top-most icon with red arrow pointing to the right).

3. Type in a descriptor for the shortcut and press Enter.

4. Type in or select (using the Ellipsis button) the location and name of the file used to launch the application and click OK.

Once this process is complete, a shortcut to the application is available under the Tools option. Simply highlight Tools, select the shortcut and the program is launched.

Shortcuts to Stored Procedures

You can add shortcuts to commonly used stored procedures by associating the procedure with a defined key-combination. In order to create a hot-key combo shortcut to a stored procedure complete the following:

1. Click Tools on the main menu and select Customize.

2. Select an open key-combo, type in the stored procedure name, and click OK.

Once this is complete the stored procedure will be executed when both the Editor Pane is active and the key-combo is pressed. We will cover how this done in detail in the middle of Chapter 11 in the sidebar titled "Configure Hot-Key Combo in Query Analyzer."

Explore Query Analyzer

Query Analyzer contains quite a bit of functionality and has a number of configuration options. Since you will be spending so much time using this tool I encourage you to explore all the options available in the Tools, Options dialog. Understanding how Query Analyzer can work for you will make you a more efficient programmer.

Transact SQL

T-SQL is Microsoft's implementation of SQL (Structured Query Language) and includes both standards-dictated and extended functionality. In order to fully understand the last sentence you need to know that there is a *standard* SQL that is defined and published by ANSI (American National Standards Institute) and

ISO (International Organization for Standardization). The ANSI/ISO Standard is commonly referred to as ANSI SQL and includes all the functionality, syntax and data types that a software vendor's implementation of SQL must support in order to be ANSI-compliant. ANSI SQL (current version SQL-99) has three levels of compliance: entry, intermediate and full. To meet one of the levels of compliance a vendor's implementation of SQL must support all the functionality, syntax and data types of the particular level. SQL Server 2000 is entry-level compliant with SQL-92—the previous ANSI Standard—and, just so you know, there is no implementation of SQL (e.g., Oracle's PL/SQL) that is fully compliant with the ANSI Standard.

At this point you may be wondering two things:

1. Why is T-SQL only compliant with entry-level SQL-92?

2. Why would SQL 2000 provide extended functionality that is not required to be ANSI-compliant?

The answer to the first question is simple: it would have taken too much time to implement the new standard in the 2000 version of the product. According to Microsoft, it does plan to adhere to entry-level compliance of SQL-99 with the next major release of SQL Server. (I have no idea when this will be, and Microsoft isn't giving too many hints.) Don't worry about the lack of compliance with the new standard, though. Rest assured that you will be able to perform all the data definition and manipulation operations necessary to build world-class database applications with the current version of the product.

The answer to the second question is that Microsoft wants to make T-SQL easier to use than pure ANSI SQL. Let's face it, certain aspects of SQL are a little difficult to comprehend and not everyone has the time learn how to implement all their solutions using ANSI SQL. If Microsoft has the ability to simplify certain data definition and manipulation operations by extending the functionality of ANSI SQL, the company will produce a more marketable product and certainly make the lives (at least the programming aspect) of its customers a little easier.

There is, however, a group of professionals (let's call them SQL purists) who are against extending the functionality of ANSI SQL because using SQL that is not ANSI-compliant produces non-portable code. Non-portable means you cannot take the exact code that works in SQL Server and use it in another RDBMS (relational database management system) like Oracle or Informix. The purists make a valid point; but quite frankly, I don't think there are a lot of developers whose code will be used with more than one RDBMS. As far as I am concerned, the only time the extra effort required to use pure ANSI SQL is justified is when you are a software vendor (e.g., SAP) who supports multiple RDBMSs.

ANSI versus T-SQL Example

Let's take a look at an example that shows how a T-SQL extension of ANSI SQL can make programming a little easier. Most of you are familiar with columns whose value auto-increments when a new row is added to a table. Those of you with Access experience will know that the application uses an AutoNumber data type to implement this functionality. SQL Server does not have a data type that causes a column to auto-increment. Instead, it uses a property associated with a column's definition to indicate that the value will be incremented when a new row is added. The following CREATE TABLE statement shows how to create a column whose value increments by 1 when a new row is added to the table. Please note that the result of executing the statement in Query Analyzer is shown below the "--Results--" indicator.

```
USE tempdb
go
CREATE TABLE Customers
(
Cus_UniqueID int IDENTITY(1,1) PRIMARY KEY,
Cus_Name varchar(30)
)
--Results--
The command(s) completed successfully.
```

The **Cus_UniqueID** column is defined with an int (integer) data type and the IDENTITY property is what makes the column increment by 1 when a new row is added. The (1,1) after IDENTITY indicates the seed and increment value can be set when the table is created. If you wanted to have an initial value of 10 and increment it by 5 each time a record is added, you would use (10,5). You can also omit the (seed, increment value) part of the IDENTITY property, in which case the values default to one and one. If you use Enterprise Manager to create a table it is no more work than clicking a check box to add the property to a column. It is a little more work than Access, but still pretty easy.

The following code shows how to insert and review a row inserted into the **Customers** table.

```
USE tempdb
Go
INSERT Customers (Cus_Name) VALUES ( 'Big Red Machine Co.')

SELECT Cus_UniqueID, Cus_Name
FROM Customers
--Results--
(1 row(s) affected)
```

```
Cus_UniqueID Cus_Name
------------ ------------------------------
1            Big Red Machine Co.
```

When a column is defined with the IDENTITY property, it is not referenced in the INSERT statements executed on the table. SQL Server determines the next value and populates the column accordingly.

The ANSI SQL approach to implementing an auto-incrementing column does not involve setting any column-level properties. Instead, you modify the INSERT statement executed on the table so that a new value is calculated when a record is added. The following table structure is needed to demonstrate this approach.

```
USE tempdb
go
CREATE TABLE Customers_ANSI
(
 Cus_UniqueID int PRIMARY KEY,
 Cus_Name varchar(30)
)
--Results--
The command(s) completed successfully.
```

The following INSERT statement will calculate the next value dynamically when a new row is added to the **Customers_ANSI** table.

```
USE tempdb
go
INSERT Customers_ANSI
SELECT COALESCE(MAX(Cus_UniqueID)+1,1),
       'Big Red Machine Co.'
FROM Customers_ANSI

SELECT Cus_UniqueID, Cus_Name
FROM Customers_ANSI
--Results--
(1 row(s) affected)

Cus_UniqueID Cus_Name
------------ ------------------------------
1            Big Red Machine Co.
```

It is not important that you understand exactly *how* the INSERT statement works. The point here is to show that using a T-SQL extension is quite a bit easier than using pure ANSI SQL.

You must decide which approach to use in your applications. As for me, I am going to risk the wrath of the SQL purists and use the IDENTITY approach in both this book and my real-world applications.

TIP ANSI versus T-SQL Extension

There is no single resource that details what functionality available in T-SQL is not ANSI-compliant. There is, however, a configurable option that can be set to warn you when you are using code that does not adhere to the specified level of compliance. The option is called FIPS_Flagger and accepts the three levels of compliancy (entry, intermediate, and full) as arguments.

FIPS_Flagger is a very unusual name when compared to other configurable settings available in SQL Server 2000. The name is derived from the Federal Information Processing Standard (FIPS), which was written by the National Institute of Standards and Technology under the direction of Congress. FIPS defines the minimum functionality to which a product must adhere before the US Government can purchase it.

For more information on this option, see the Books Online topic: Set Fips_Flagger.

T-SQL Syntax Elements

Like any other programming language, T-SQL is composed of different syntax elements. The syntax elements of T-SQL are listed in Table 1-2.

Table 1-2. Syntax Elements of T-SQL

ELEMENT	DESCRIPTION
Identifiers	Names of the database objects within an instance of SQL Server. All objects (e.g., databases, tables, stored procedures, views) have an associated identifier. There are two types of identifiers available in SQL Server 2000: Regular and Delimited. Regular identifiers conform to the rules for specifying an identifier (e.g., no embedded spaces) while Delimited identifiers do not. When a Delimited identifier is referenced, it must be surrounded by either brackets or double-quotes (e.g., [Table Name]). For more information on the rules for identifiers, please see the Books Online topic: Using Identifiers.
Data Types	Types of data a column, variable or parameter can contain. The data types available in SQL Server 2000 are discussed in Chapter 2.
Functions	Code elements that accept zero, one or more parameters and return a value to the calling statement. SQL Server 2000 has both built-in and user-defined functions. The GETDATE() function (which returns the server's current system time) is an example of a built-in function. One might create a user-defined function to more easily calculate the number of business days in a given date range.
Expressions	SQL Statements or elements that can be resolved to a single value. A column, variable or IF statement are examples of statements or elements that resolve to a single value.
Comments	Text descriptions that allow code to be more easily understood. There are two methods of commenting code in SQL Server 2000. You can either use a double-dash (--) to comment a single line of code or the foreslash asterisk...asterisk foreslash (/*...*/) to comment one or more lines of code.
Keywords	Reserved words used by SQL Server 2000. There are more than 150 reserved keywords in this version of SQL Server and they are detailed in the Books Online topic: Reserved Keywords.

T-SQL DDL and DML

T-SQL is comprised of two types of statements: data definition language (DDL) and data manipulation language (DML). The statements that compose each are listed in the following sections.

DDL Statements

DDL statements are used to create, alter or delete a database object. These statements affect the *structure* of the object and no data is added, updated or deleted. The DDL statements in T-SQL follow. The text of each statement should make it obvious the function it performs.

CREATE DATABASE	ALTER DATABASE
DROP DATABASE	CREATE TABLE
ALTER TABLE	DROP TABLE
CREATE VIEW	ALTER VIEW
DROP VIEW	CREATE PROCEDURE
ALTER PROCEDURE	DROP PROCEDURE
CREATE TRIGGER	ALTER TRIGGER
DROP TRIGGER	CREATE FUNCTION
ALTER FUNCTION	DROP FUNCTION

DML Statements

DML statements are used to insert, update and delete data held in the objects defined with DDL statements. The DML statements available in T-SQL are:

SELECT	INSERT
UPDATE	DELETE
TRUNCATE TABLE	

In addition to the statements listed here there is another *class* of DML statements that are categorized as control-of-flow. The control-of-flow statements are discussed in detail in Chapter 4.

Naming Convention

A discussion on naming convention can often lead to harsh words from even the nicest developers. In my seven years of working with databases I have seen quite a few different naming conventions, and the ones that bothered me the most had little or no consistency. One could argue that a naming convention that is not consistent really is not a naming convention at all. I agree and think consistency should be maintained at all costs.

The naming convention you use is not dictated by SQL Server (other than, of course, the rules for identifiers), but by either personal preference or that mandated by your employer. The naming convention used for table and column names referenced in this book is described here. The naming convention used for other database objects is described when those objects are introduced if the convention is not intuitively obvious.

I use mixed-case plural descriptors for table names. A table that holds information about customers would be named **Customers**. A table that holds information about the orders a customer places would be named **CustomersOrders**.

I use the first three characters of the table name in which a column is located as a prefix for column names when a one-part name is used and the first three characters of each part when a multi-part table name is used. The primary keys for the **Customers** and **CustomersOrders** tables would be **Cus_UniqueID** and **CusOrd_UniqueID**, respectively. The "UniqueID" portion is not dictated by the table name, but by the value held in the column. The column that held the customers' names would be **Cus_Name** and the one that held the addresses would be **Cus_Address**. When a foreign key is placed in a table the original column name is used. A partial listing of the columns contained in **Customers** and **Customers-Orders** is shown in Figure 1-3.

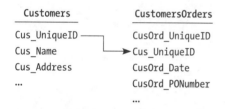

Figure 1-3. **Customers** *and* **CustomersOrders** *Table Layouts*

I have often seen naming conventions that attempt to embed the data type in a column name, but this has never appealed to me. From a relational database standpoint, I am more interested in foreign key references than the data type used to define a column. Plus, I do not see much value in knowing a column holds character data unless I also know the maximum allowable length. Column names like **strCustomerName** or **intCustomerID** only leave me wondering if the maximum length of the customer's name is 30, 40, or 50 characters and if the maximum value used to uniquely identify a customer is 255 or 32,767 or something larger.

Deja.com Power Search

I am a big fan of using the resources on the Internet to help me find better ways to implement solutions for my clients. One of the most helpful sites I have found is Deja.com at `http://www.deja.com`. Deja.com has a newsgroup search feature called Power Search that allows you to focus on a particular newsgroup (their terminology is Forum) and specify search criteria, such as Subject and Author.

You can access Power Search at `http://www.deja.com/home_ps.shtml` and use the available parameters to limit the scope of the search. When I want to research a SQL Server administrative issue, for example, I populate the Subject field with a keyword used to designate the topic and the Forum field with "microsoft.public.sqlserver.administration." I then execute the query by clicking Search.

If you are not sure which newsgroup is the most applicable for your issue, you can use the wildcard character for searching multiple newsgroups at the same time. For example, if you wanted to search all the Microsoft SQL Server newsgroups, you would populate Forum with "microsoft.public.sqlserver.*"

Using Power Search is a heck of lot faster than posting to a newsgroup and then waiting for someone to respond. Plus, it is highly likely that the particular problem you are trying to solve has been previously addressed in the newsgroups, so why waste bandwidth and other people's time by requesting help when the answer is only a few clicks away?

Before You Go

This chapter presented an introduction to Query Analyzer, a general overview of T-SQL, and the naming convention used for the tables and columns presented in this book. It also provided a very useful Internet-related tip to help you quickly find information, troubleshoot problems, or see how other developers are implementing similar solutions.

The next chapter provides a detailed description of the data types available in SQL Server 2000. It also covers a couple of topics that should allow you to better understand why there are so many different data types available and some of the advantages of using one over another.

CHAPTER 2
Data Types

THIS CHAPTER BUILDS ON the last by covering the data types available in SQL Server
2000. Understanding the available data types in SQL Server will ensure that your
table columns and variables are properly defined and can accommodate the full
range of values they are expected to hold. In addition, I'll cover some multi-lingual
issues and explain what data types are required to support international applications. The chapter concludes with a section that covers SQL Server's ability to
implicitly convert one data type to another. Understanding implicit conversion
should help you understand how SQL Server can perform what may seem like
illogical operations on certain data.

> **NOTE   Sample Code**
>
> *The sample code for this chapter can be downloaded at either*
> `http://www.apress.com` *or* `http://www.SQLBook.com`. *Download*
> *CodeCentric.zip and extract and access the Ch02.sql file.*

Before You Get Started

A couple of topics need to be covered before I present the data types available in
SQL Server 2000. The first is on Unicode, which is an integral part of creating international applications. The second concerns collation—a setting that dictates how
data is sorted and compared.

Unicode

SQL Server 2000 supports the Unicode 2.0 Standard (a.k.a. UCS 2) as defined by
the Unicode Consortium. Unicode 2.0 is an agreement set by the members of the
Consortium that specifies which character is related to an integer whose range of
values is 0–65,536. The Consortium's members are the major software and hardware vendors and governmental bodies throughout the world, so be assured no
major international issue is overlooked.

The 65,536 upper limit of the integer range is dictated by the fundamental storage unit for Unicode data, which is 2 bytes. The number of possible bit combinations for 2 bytes is 2^16, or 65,536. This large range of values allows for the character-to-integer mapping of the languages of Africa, the Americas, Asia, Europe, Middle East, and Pacifica as well as scientific symbols and a limited number of ancient scripts. The goal of Unicode is to provide a single character-to-integer mapping that can be used to develop international software applications. A software application based on Unicode can be used throughout the world with no modification as long as the client computer that is accessing the application supports Unicode.

Before the Unicode Standard was introduced, character data was defined on a regional basis using *code pages*. A code page defined the character-to-integer mapping for a particular geographical region of the world. For example, Code Page 932 defined character-to-integer mapping for the Japanese language. The code page approach used a 1-byte storage unit, which reduced the maximum number of characters to 256 (2^8).

This limited number of characters presented a big problem: not all characters for all languages could be represented with a single code page. The first 128 characters of all code pages (a.k.a. standard ASCII) have the same integer value, but this is not the case with the region-specific characters (e.g., accented characters) used by many languages. The code page used is a function of the operating system on a given computer; therefore, if you have a server using Code Page 932 (Japanese) sending data to a client using Code Page 1252 (Latin1), there is a potential for data loss because any characters encoded with a value above 128 may not represent the same character. Unicode will ensure there is no data loss because the character-to-integer mappings are all the same.

As the Internet grows and the world becomes smaller, developing Web sites and other applications that conform to UCS 2 will allow you to reach a larger target audience. The current challenge is not so much from a database standpoint because designing databases that are Unicode-compliant is fairly straightforward. The real challenge is ensuring that all the programming languages used to create the client-portion of the applications support Unicode and the operating system on which the applications are run support it as well.

Unicode Resources

If you would like to learn more about Unicode, please visit the Unicode Consortium's Web site at http://www.unicode.org. If you would like to learn more about how Unicode affects client applications, please go to http://msdn.microsoft.com/library/default.asp, click Books and then browse the various topics in Developing International Software for Windows 95 and Windows NT. The book is a little dated, but many of the topics (The Code-Page Model, for example) are fundamental and have not changed since it was published.

Collation in SQL Server 2000

In SQL Server 7, the term "Unicode collation" referred to the sort order used on Unicode data. Further, SQL 7 required you to specify the character set, sort order and Unicode collation separately. If you wanted to change any of these settings you had to rebuild the **master** database and unload/reload all the data in the user-defined databases.

SQL Server 2000 does not use the term "Unicode collation." It uses the more generic collation to refer to the set of rules that govern how data is compared, sorted and displayed. A default collation is specified during installation, but a different collation can be specified at the database or column level. You must specify three items to install a collation:

- Sort order used for Unicode data

- Sort order used for non-Unicode data

- Code page used to store non-Unicode data

If you want to change the default collation for an instance of SQL Server 2000, you are still required to rebuild the **master** database and unload/load the user-defined databases. You can, however, change the collation at the database level with the ALTER DATABASE statement and at the column level with the ALTER TABLE statement. For more information on collation in SQL Server 2000, please see the Books Online topic: SQL Collations.

Did you notice that I used the term "instance of SQL Server" in the previous paragraph? Starting with SQL Server 2000, you can install more than one copy of SQL Server on the same computer. So, you can install multiple *instances* of the software and configure each independently.

Data Types

A data type is the attribute of a column that restricts the type of data it can hold. Each data type has size requirements (in bytes), so the *proper* one should be used for each column. In my reading, most books dealing with SQL Server failed to use data types appropriate for the examples given. For that matter, I have seen numerous database designs used in production that simply used the int data type for all columns that hold numeric values and the char data type for all columns that hold character data. This type of database design results in wasted space, which could be significant if you are working with VLDBs (Very Large Databases). I will intentionally use appropriate data types in my examples, so your knowledge of their unique attributes is crucial to understanding the rationale for my selections.

Character Data Types (Non-Unicode)

DATA TYPE	DESCRIPTION
char[(n)]	Fixed-length data whose maximum length is 8,000 characters.
varchar[(n)]	Varying-length data whose maximum length is 8,000 characters.
text	Varying-length data whose maximum length is 2,147,483,647 characters.

The storage size for char is the specified length. A column defined as char(30) requires 30 bytes of storage space. The storage size for varchar is the actual number of characters in the column. The storage size of text varies with the amount data stored, but will never be less than 8,000 bytes (see the sidebar that follows).

As you can tell from the brackets, specifying the size for char and varchar is not required. When a size is not specified in a column definition or variable declaration, the length defaults to 1. When the CAST function (covered in Chapter 6) is used to convert a data type to char or varchar and n is not specified, the length defaults to 30.

I use the varchar data type in most of my columns that hold character data. Most of the character data I work with varies in length and you can save space by using varchar. The number of bytes required to store char data is the n specified in the definition, but the number of bytes required to store varchar data is the actual number of characters in the string.

Let's look at an example to see how much space could be wasted by using char when varchar is more appropriate. Assume you have a single-column table whose only column is defined as char(50) and holds 50,000 rows of data. You analyze the data in the column and determine that the average length is 25 characters. So the approximate number of bytes wasted (see sidebar) is equal to 1,250KB [((50-25) * 50,000)/1024] or 1.2MB(1,250KB/1,048KB). Keep in mind this is just one column. What if your database contained 100 or more tables and each of those contained columns defined with char instead of varchar? The space wasted adds up quickly when a large number of rows are inserted into a poorly designed table.

Space-Used Calculation

In order to understand why an estimate of space wasted by using char is approximate, you have to have a basic understanding of how data is stored in SQL Server 2000. SQL Server's fundamental data storage unit is called a page, and is 8KB in size. SQL Server allocates space in units called extents, each of which is made up of eight continuous pages. There are six different types of pages, but the one we are interested in is called a data page. A data page is composed of a 96-byte page header, one or more rows of data, and one or more row offsets. Figure 2-1 shows the layout of a data page.

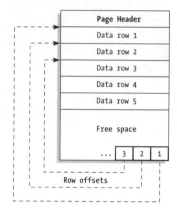

Figure 2-1. Data Page Layout

The page header contains general information about the data page—the page type, which database object owns it, and the free space available. The data rows are simply the rows that are inserted into the table to which the page belongs. A row offset is created for each row on the data page and it indicates how far (in bytes) the first byte of the row is from the start of page.

When the char(50) data type is used, each row occupies 50 bytes of storage space and a certain number of bytes for a row offset. When varchar(50) is used, and the average length of the data in the columns is 25, the number of rows per page (and subsequently the row offsets) will vary depending on the size of the character strings in each column. This could affect the total number of pages used depending on the order in which the data was inserted into the table—which could result in an 8-KB difference if an additional page is needed.

As you can see, getting the exact number of bytes saved is nearly impossible, but one thing's for sure: if you use the char(50) data type to define a column and the average length of the data stored in that column is less than 50, you are wasting space.

The text data type is used to store large amounts of character data. To be perfectly honest, I haven't had to use this data type since SQL Server 7 was introduced. Before version 7 the maximum length of char or varchar was 256. This was far too small to accommodate many description-type and comment columns, so you were required to use the text data type on a regular basis. If you never have to work with this data type consider yourself lucky. Manipulating data stored using text is a pain. For an example, please see the Books Online topic: WriteText.

> **TIP Text, Ntext, and Image Storage**
>
> *The* text, ntext *and* image *data types are all stored using one or more 8KB text/image pages. At a minimum, one text/image page is always used, so even if only one character is stored in a column defined with one of these data types, 8KB of storage is required.*

Character Data Types (Unicode)

DATA TYPE	DESCRIPTION
nchar[(n)]	Fixed-length Unicode data with a maximum length of 4,000 characters.
nvarchar[(n)]	Varying-length Unicode data with the maximum length of 4,000 characters.
ntext	Varying-length Unicode data with a maximum length of 1,073,741,823 characters.

The storage size for nchar is two times the specified length. A column defined as nchar(30) requires 60 bytes of storage space. The storage size for nvarchar is two times the actual number of characters in the column. The storage size of ntext varies with the amount of data stored, but will never be less than 8,000 bytes.

As with the non-Unicode character data types, when the length is not specified in a column definition or variable declaration, the default length is 1. When the CAST function is used to convert a data type to nchar and n is not specified, the default length is 30.

Data inserted into a column defined with either nchar or nvarchar is prefaced with an upper-case N to designate it as Unicode data. The following example shows the INSERT statement used with a column defined as either nchar or nvarchar.

```
INSERT Customers (Cus_Name) VALUES (N'SQLBook.com')
```

If the N is omitted, the default code page installed on the server will be used to store the integer representation of the data. If the data that is being inserted is not recognized by the server's code page, then a non-valid value will be stored in the database. This really only comes into play when you are working with extended characters that are not represented in the more- used code pages, but you should form the habit of specifying the N prefix when working with Unicode data.

You probably noticed that the only difference between the data type names used to represent non-Unicode versus Unicode data is that the latter is prefaced with an "n." This prefix is defined by the SQL-92 Standard, which was discussed in Chapter 1.

Binary String Data Types

DATA TYPE	DESCRIPTION
binary[(n)]	Fixed-length binary data with a maximum length of 8,000 bytes.
varbinary[(n)]	Varying-length binary data with a maximum length of 8,000 bytes.
image	Varying-length binary data with a maximum length of 2,147,483,647 bytes.

Although these data types are classified as strings in Books Online, you do not use quotes when inserting a value into a column defined with any one of them. The storage size is n + 4 bytes for binary and the length of data entered + 4 bytes for varbinary. The minimum data storage required for image data is 8KB. (See the previous Tip, "Text, Ntext, and Image Storage.")

Exact Numeric Data Types

Integers

DATA TYPE	DESCRIPTION	STORAGE SIZE (BYTES)
tinyint	Integer data whose range is 0 to 255.	1
smallint	Integer data whose range is –32,768 to 32,767.	2
int	Integer data whose range –2,147,483,648 to 2,147,483,647.	4
bigint[*]	Integer data whose range is –9,223,372,036,854,775,808 to 9,223,372,036,854,775,807.	8

*Please note this data type is new to SQL Server 2000.

The use of these data types is very straightforward. Simply define your columns and variables with the data that will accommodate the range of integers they will hold. Before moving on, however, look at another example that shows how much space would be wasted by choosing the incorrect data type. Assume you have a table with a column that is defined using int that will never hold a value greater than 50. Approximately how much space would be wasted by not using the tinyint data type if the table in which the column is located holds 50,000 rows of data? The answer is 0.14MB [(((4-1) * 50,000)/1024)/1048].

Decimal and Numeric

DATA TYPE	DESCRIPTION
dec[p[,(s)]]	Fixed precision and scale data whose range is –10^38-1 to 10^38-1. "dec" is a synonym for decimal, so decimal[p[,(s)]] can also be used.
num[p[,(s)]]	Same as dec[p[,(s)]]. "num" is a synonym for numeric, so numeric[p[(s)]] can also be used.

The p stands for precision and specifies the number of digits that can be stored in the column or variable. The maximum number of digits that can be stored is 38. The s stands for scale and is the maximum number of digits to the right of the decimal. The maximum number of digits to the right of the decimal is dependent on the precision specified. The storage size varies depending on the precision.

PRECISION	STORAGE SIZE (BYTES)
1–9	5
10–19	9
20–28	13
28–38	17

Money and Smallmoney

DATA TYPE	DESCRIPTION	STORAGE SIZE (BYTES)
smallmoney	Monetary data with the range of –214,748.3648 to 214,748.3647.	4

DATA TYPE	DESCRIPTION	STORAGE SIZE (BYTES)
money	Monetary data with the range of −922,337,203,685,477.5808 to 922,337,203,685,477.5807.	8

Using these data types is pretty straightforward, but there are a couple of things you'll want to keep in mind. Do not use comma separators when you INSERT or UPDATE monetary data because they will cause an error to be generated. The comma separators and money symbol will be displayed automatically when data of these types is retrieved from a table. If you have an existing set of values whose numbers contain separators and you want to INSERT them into a column that has been defined as money or smallmoney, use the CAST function to convert the source data to the appropriate type.

One more thing—the default money symbol is the dollar sign ($). If you work with a different currency, simply preface the dollar amount with that currency's symbol. The following INSERT statement uses the symbol for Lira in place of the dollar sign.

```
INSERT Product (Pro_UniqueID, Pro_Price) VALUES ('A100','£100.00')
```

Approximate Numeric Data Types

DATA TYPE	DESCRIPTION
float[(n)]	Floating point data with a range of −1.79E + 308 to 1.79E + 308.
real	Floating point data with a range of −3.40E + 38 to 3.40E + 38.

Floating point data is that which there is no fixed number of digits before or after the decimal point. This is in contrast to the previous section on exact numeric data types in which there were either no decimals used (int) or the precision and scale were specified (decimal). Floating point data is characterized as "approximate" because calculations performed with it are not as accurate as those performed with exact numeric data. The advantage, though, is that it is able to handle much larger values. Compare the range of the following data types with that shown in the section "Decimal and Numeric."

The n in float is used to specify the number of digits that will hold the mantissa (the number of digits to the left of the E). The value of n dictates both the precision (the number of digits to the right of the decimal point) and storage space required.

N	PRECISION	STORAGE SIZE (BYTES)
1–24	7 digits	4
25–53	15 digits	8

Date Data Types

DATA TYPE	RANGE	ACCURACY	STORAGE SIZE (BYTES)
smalldatetime	01/01/1900–06/06/2079	1 minute	4
datetime	01/01/1753–12/31/9999	3.33 milliseconds	8

The date data types available in SQL Server have been known to confuse developers new to the product. The main problem I have noticed in monitoring the newsgroups is that some developers do not understand that time is also stored with a date value. There really is no such thing as "1/1/90." You can insert this value into a column that is defined with a date data type, but what you are really doing is inserting "1/1/90 12:00:00:000 AM," midnight on January 1, 1990. When the time portion is not supplied, the system will default to midnight. Having the time stored presents some data display problems as well, but we'll cover those in the "Date Functions" section in Chapter 6.

Keep in mind when working with dates that if you do not specify the century portion of the year, SQL Server will use a default century based on the supplied year value. More specifically, any year value equal to or greater than 50 will default to 1900 (e.g., 1/1/50 = January 1, 1950) while any value less than 50 will default to 2000 (e.g., 1/1/49 = Janauary 1, 2049).

Identifier Data Types

DATA TYPE	DESCRIPTION	STORAGE SIZE (BYTES)
rowversion	A database-wide unique number that can be used to identify changes in a row.	8
unique-identifier	A globally unique identifier (GUID).	6

These data types are used to generate identification-type data and can be used to make programming easier. When you define a column with the rowversion data type, the column is updated each time a record is inserted or updated. If you're familiar with pre-2000 versions of SQL Server, you will recall that there is already a data type (timestamp) that provides the same functionality. In SQL Server 2000, both data types will be used for the exact same purpose, but in future versions the timestamp data type will be modified to conform to SQL-99—the current version of the ANSI Standard.

The uniqueidentifier (GUID) data type is used to create a unique identifier of the format "xxxxxxxx-xxxx-xxxx-xxxx-xxxxxxxxxxxv," where each x is a hexadecimal digit. As long as the host computer generates the value with the NEWID function (or an API that calls a function that generates a GUID), it is guaranteed to be unique to that computer. This does not, however, mean that the same value will not be regenerated on the same computer. In order to ensure the same GUID does not get inserted into the same column you use either a PRIMARY KEY or UNIQUE constraint.

The GUID value is generated by the combination of the unique ID of the NIC (Network Interface Card) and the CPU clock. When the value is generated on the server, it uses the *server's* NIC plus the server's CPU. When the value is generated from a client API call, it uses the *client's* NIC and the server's CPU.

Due to the storage size and general awkwardness of working with this type of data, you should not use it unless you need to ensure that the value contained in a column is globally unique. There are certain replication scenarios (e.g., merge replication) where this is helpful, but in most cases the IDENTITY property will allow you to create a column that will satisfy your needs.

Variant Data Types

DATA TYPE	DESCRIPTION
sql_variant	Holds data of any type except sql_variant, text, ntext, and image.

The sql_variant data type is new to SQL Server 2000. It can be used as a data type for columns, parameters, return values in user-defined functions, and variables and can hold data of any type except text, ntext, and image. You must, however, convert sql_variant data to numeric data type before it can be used in mathematical operations. For example, the SELECT statements shown here demonstrate that an error is generated if the variables are not CAST to an integer (int, smallint, or tinyint) data type before the mathematical operation is performed.

Correct

```
DECLARE @var1 sql_variant, @var2 sql_variant
SET @var1 = 65,000
SET @var2 = 34
SELECT CAST(@var1 AS int) + CAST(@var2 AS tinyint)

--Results--
-----------
65034
```

Incorrect

```
DECLARE @var1 sql_variant, @var2 sql_variant
SET @var1 = 65000
SET @var2 = 34
SELECT CAST(@var1 AS int) + @var2
--Results--
Server: Msg 403, Level 16, State 1, Line 4
Invalid operator for data type. Operator equals add, type equals sql_variant.
```

> **CAUTION sql_variant and ODBC**
>
> The sql_variant *data type is not fully supported by ODBC. Client applications that communicate with SQL Server and retrieve data of type* sql_variant *will not produce expected resultsets as the data is returned in a binary format.*

Other Data Types

DATA TYPE	DESCRIPTION
cursor	Used for variable or stored procedure output parameters that reference a cursor.
table	Used to temporarily store a set of rows.

The cursor data type is for use with variables or stored procedure output parameters and cannot be used to define a column. As you might have guessed by the name, the only time you will be using this data type is when you are creating or manipulating cursors. Don't worry if you are not familiar with the term cursor. You will learn about cursors in the "Control-of-Flow" section in Chapter 4.

The table data type is new to SQL Server 2000. If you work with a lot of temporary tables, you will definitely want to check into using this data type. It allows you to store a set of rows in a variable for processing. The only draw back to using the table data type is that you cannot populate it using SELECT INTO or the resultset returned by a stored procedure. Of course, if you run into one of these situations you can simply use the old tried and true temporary table approach. You will create and use a temporary table in the "Control-of-Flow" section in Chapter 4.

TIP No Arrays in T-SQL

One of the more frequently asked questions in the newsgroups concerns using arrays in SQL Server. SQL Server does not support arrays. You can either use a temporary table (defined with a single # for local scoping or a double ## for global scoping) or the table *data type that is new to SQL Server 2000. Simply create your table definition with the proper data type and use it just like an array. As a matter of fact, this approach can operate even more like an array in SQL Server 2000, because you can use the* sql_variant *data type so the columns can hold data of different types.*

User-Defined Data Types

The standard data types available in SQL Server 2000 are covered in the previous sections. This section focuses on how they can be extended by creating a user-defined data type. You do not *really* create a new data type, though, but simply alias an existing data type to a new name that is easier to remember and will help ensure that the same data type is used across multiple databases.

Let's take a simple example that will illustrate how user-defined data types can make development process more efficient. Assume we are developing a database application and the data elements: office phone, fax number and mobile phone need to be stored in multiple tables. Instead of having to type in char(10) each time you create a variable that is going to hold one of these data elements, you can create a user-defined data type called "phone" and reference it instead. Note that I use char(10) to define phone numbers because I do not like to store formatting characters with my data (e.g., XXXXXXXXX not XXX-XXX-XXXX). You can create user-defined data types via Enterprise Manager or with the system stored procedure **sp_addtype**. The system stored procedure approach follows:

```
USE tempdb
go
EXEC sp_addtype phone, 'CHAR(10)', 'NOT NULL'
(1 row(s) affected)

Type added.
```

Take a look at another practical example before we move on. A valid object (e.g., table, stored procedure, or view) identifier in SQL Server can hold up to 128 characters and is defined with the Unicode data type nvarchar. SQL Server 2000 comes with a user-defined data type for nvarchar(128) called sysname. When you want to create a variable that holds object identifier data, you can define the variable with sysname, which is a little easier to remember than nvarchar(128).

> **TIP Add User-Defined Data Types to the *model* Database**
>
> *If your company is going to create more than one database in SQL Server, you will want to establish a master list of the characteristics for certain data elements. This will prohibit, for example, the data element zip code from being defined in a different manner in each database. The way you do this is by adding a user-defined data type to the **model** database. When you create a new database in its contents are based on the **model** database, so any database object in **model** will automatically be created in your new database.*

Implicit Conversion

Implicit conversion concerns SQL Server's ability to convert one data type to another without user interaction. For example, a column defined as type tinyint can have its data stored in a variable of type smallint without user-interaction because SQL Server will understand that the base data can be stored in the target variable and implicitly convert it. When a data type cannot be implicitly converted you must use either the CAST or CONVERT functions (discussed in Chapter 6) to convert the data to the desired data type. Figure 2-2 shows the data type conversion rules used by SQL Server.

From: \ To:	char	varchar	nchar	nvarchar	datetime	smalldatetime	decimal	numeric	float	int(INT 4)	smallint(INT 2)	money	ntext	text	sql_variant
char		◉	◉	◉	◉	◉	◉	◉	◉	◉	◉	●	◉	◉	◉
varchar	◉		◉	◉	◉	◉	◉	◉	◉	◉	◉	●	◉	◉	◉
nchar	◉	◉		◉	◉	◉	◉	◉	◉	◉	◉	●	◉	◉	◉
nvarchar	◉	◉	◉		◉	◉	◉	◉	◉	◉	◉	●	◉	◉	◉
datetime	◉	◉	◉	◉		◉	●	●	●	●	●	●	○	○	◉
smalldatetime	◉	◉	◉	◉	◉		●	●	●	●	●	●	○	○	◉
decimal	◉	◉	◉	◉	◉	◉	*	*	◉	◉	◉	◉	○	○	◉
numeric	◉	◉	◉	◉	◉	◉	*	*	◉	◉	◉	◉	○	○	◉
float	◉	◉	◉	◉	◉	◉	◉	◉		◉	◉	◉	○	○	◉
int(INT 4)	◉	◉	◉	◉	◉	◉	◉	◉	◉		◉	◉	○	○	◉
smallint(INT 2)	◉	◉	◉	◉	◉	◉	◉	◉	◉	◉		◉	○	○	◉
money	●	●	●	●	◉	◉	◉	◉	◉	◉	◉		○	○	◉
ntext	●	●	◉	◉	○	○	○	○	○	○	○	○		●	○
text	◉	◉	●	●	○	○	○	○	○	○	○	○	●		○
sql_variant	●	●	●	●	●	●	●	●	●	●	●	●	○	○	

● Explicit conversion

◉ Implicit conversion

○ Conversion not allowed

* Requires explicit CAST to prevent the loss of precision or scale that might occur in an implicit conversion

Figure 2-2. Implicit Conversion Chart

Adapted from Microsoft SQL Server 2000 Books Online © Microsoft Corporation 1988-2000

Before You Go

This chapter provided some background information on Unicode data, detailed the available data types in SQL Server 2000, discussed user-defined data types and ended with a section on implicit conversion. Understanding what Unicode is and how it is used will help you design international applications that can be used throughout the world without modification. Understanding the available data types—and the range of values a column or variable defined with a particular type can hold—is key to designing applications that will function as expected. Properly using user-defined data types will help to ensure that the same data type is used to define and store similar data. Knowing about implicit conversion will help you better understand why *some* columns or variables can hold data from other columns or variables that are not defined with the same data type.

The next chapter covers DDL (data definition language)—the subset of T-SQL used to create, alter and delete database objects. If you have only used SQL Server's graphical design tools to create databases and database objects, you should find it very interesting. Understanding how the DDL statements are constructed will provide insight into how the graphical design tools create the various database objects.

CHAPTER 3

Data Definition Language

DDL (DATA DEFINITION LANGUAGE) is the subset of T-SQL that you use to create, alter, and delete database objects. This chapter will not provide complete coverage of all the DDL statements in T-SQL, but will instead concentrate on the ones you are most likely to use in your programming endeavors.

> **NOTE Sample Code**
>
> *The sample code for this chapter can be downloaded at either* `http://www.apress.com` *or* `http://www.SQLBook.com`. *Download CodeCentric.zip and extract and access the Ch03.sql file.*

Before You Get Started

Two topics need to be covered before you start on the DDL statements. The first topic is object ownership and referencing and the second is permissions.

Object Ownership and Referencing

Every table, view, stored procedure, trigger or function has an associated object owner. The general syntax of the SQL statements used to create these objects is shown here:

```
CREATE DatabaseObject [objectowner].objectidentifier
definition of object…
```

The brackets around `objectowner` indicate it is an optional argument. An object's owner is determined at create-time, but it can be changed post-creation. The main goal of this section is to explain which owner is assigned when you omit this optional argument or when the object is created by a member of the fixed-server role **sysadmin**. The rules that dictate who the object owner is can be a little confusing until you understand fixed-server and fixed-database roles and the system-created user **dbo**.

The SQL Server fixed-server and fixed-database roles are somewhat analogous to the group concept used in NT to implement security. These roles are a part of SQL Server's Security Model and allow you to more easily manage the actions users can perform. For example, a member of the fixed-server role **sysadmin** can perform any action within an instance of SQL Server, while a member of the fixed-database role **db_owner** can perform any action within a database. A member of the fixed-database role **db_ddladmin** can create, alter or delete all database objects within a database.

Each database in an instance of SQL Server has a special system-created user called **dbo** (database owner). The **dbo** user has implicit permission to perform any action in a database and cannot be deleted. When a member of **sysadmin** performs any action within a database, it is executed in the context of **dbo**. The **dbo** user is not explicitly associated with the fixed-database roles **db_owner** or **db_ddladmin**.

When you create a database object with a login that is a member of **sysadmin**, it automatically belongs to **dbo**. When an object is referenced in a SQL Statement the object owner portion of the reference can be omitted when it belongs to either **dbo** or the user who is executing the statement. The following two SELECT statements are equivalent when the **Customers** table is owned by **dbo**.

```
SELECT * FROM Customers
SELECT * FROM dbo.Customers
```

When you are not using a login that is member of **sysadmin**, two different scenarios can apply. The first is that you are member of the database roles **db_owner** or **db_ddladmin**. When you are a member of either one of these roles, all the database objects you create belong to your login unless you explicitly create the object with the owner name **dbo**. Here is an example so there is no misunderstanding of how this works.

Assume my login/user is "Garth," I am not a member of **sysadmin**, but I am a member of **db_owner** in the target database. I create a table called **Brokers** with the following statement:

```
CREATE TABLE Brokers
(
 Bro_UniqueID smallint IDENTITY PRIMARY KEY,
 Bro_Name varchar(30)
)
```

In order for another user to reference this table in a SQL statement, it must be qualified with the object owner name because I did not explicitly create it with **dbo** as the object owner. I (using the "Garth" login) can reference it without using an object owner name, but that's because I created it. In order for another user to retrieve the data in **Brokers** the following statement is used:

```
SELECT *
FROM Garth.Brokers
```

If I had used the statement shown here to create **Brokers** the object would belong to **dbo** and could be referenced without the object owner name.

```
CREATE TABLE dbo.Brokers
(
 Bro_UniqueID smallint,
 Bro_Name varchar(30)
)
go
SELECT *
FROM Brokers
```

The second scenario is when the user is not a member of either **db_owner** or **db_ddladmin**. Any object created by a user who is not a member of these roles must be qualified with the object owner's name when accessed by any user other than the owner.

Permissions

SQL Server provides two types of permissions:

- Statement permissions allow a user to do things like CREATE, ALTER and DROP database objects or perform administrative functions like backing up a database.

- Object permissions allow a user to SELECT, INSERT, UPDATE, DELETE, REFERENCE, and EXECUTE a database object.

Permissions can be managed on an individual user basis, but it is more efficient to *group* users and apply permissions to the group. Using this approach you simply add or remove users from a group that has the desired permissions for an individual user. SQL Server gives you the ability to create user-defined groups or select from a number of fixed-server and fixed-database roles. Tables 3-1 and 3-2 provide lists of the fixed-server and fixed-database roles and their associated permissions.

Table 3-1. Fixed-Server Roles

ROLE	PERMISSIONS
sysadmin	Performs all actions within an instance of SQL Server.
serveradmin	Configures server-wide settings.
setupadmin	Adds and removes linked servers, and executes a limited number of system stored procedures.
securityadmin	Manages server logins.
processadmin	Manages processes running in SQL Server.
dbcreator	Creates and alters databases.
diskadmin	Manages disk files.

Table 3-2. Fixed-Database Roles

ROLE	PERMISSIONS
db_owner	Performs all actions within the database.
db_accessadmin	Adds and removes NT groups, NT users, and SQL Server users in the database.
db_datareader	Views all data from all user tables in the database.
db_datawriter	Adds, updates or deletes data from all user tables in the database.
db_ddladmin	Adds, alters or drops objects in the database.
db_securityadmin	Manages roles and both statement and object permissions in the database.
db_backupoperator	Backs up the database.
db_denydatareader	Cannot view any data in the database.
db_denydatawriter	Cannot insert, update or delete any data in the database.

The fixed-server roles are used to grant server-wide permissions to a login, while the fixed-database roles are used to grant permissions within a database. Most of the fixed roles are used to grant administrative-related permissions

Unless you are a member one of the fixed-server roles, fixed-database roles or a user-defined group that has permission to perform the desired action, you will need another user to GRANT permission to perform the action. This chapter will indicate which roles have inherent permission to perform a particular action or access a particular database object and which ones have the ability to GRANT permissions to other users. If you would like to learn how to add a login/user to a fixed-server or fixed-database role, please read the Books Online topic: Adding a Member to a Predefined Role.

Data Definition Language (DDL)

DDL (data definition language) is the subset of SQL with which you define and manage all the objects (e.g., tables and views) that make up a database. The DDL for all database objects is not covered in this section because it is beyond the scope of the book; however, the DDL statements for all the objects used in the book's examples are explained. Please note that the CREATE FUNCTION, CREATE PROCEDURE, and CREATE TRIGGER statements will not be covered in this chapter, but instead in the chapters that are dedicated to each particular object.

If Enterprise Manager has been your sole means of creating database objects, I encourage you to read and experiment with the topics in this section. I'm not anti-GUI: it's just that understanding how to create database objects with T-SQL will give you a better understanding of what the GUI is doing for you and might even help you troubleshoot a problem or two if you don't like the way it created an object. Plus, the MCP (Microsoft Certified Professional) exams reference T-SQL in their questions, so if you want to become certified you'll have to learn it anyway.

In this chapter, the CREATE DATABASE and CREATE INDEX statements are covered in detail so you can examine SQL Server's data storage architecture. Limited coverage of the other statements' syntax is provided in order to minimize time spent on options that are not germane to this book. Brief coverage will also be given to the GUI method of creating these database objects. The GUI approach is fairly intuitive and the options offered using it should be obvious once you understand the T-SQL statements used to create a particular object.

CREATE DATABASE

When sending a database project to clients or other developers, you can ensure that it is created per specification by providing a script that creates the database and all the database objects. On many occasions I have seen projects and applications distributed with scripts that create all the objects within a database, but do not provide the statements for creating the actual database. Instead, instructions are provided that describe how the database should be created and identify any database settings that need to be implemented. This approach introduces human error, which can be avoided by taking some extra time to add statements that create and configure the database per the application's specifications. The complete syntax of CREATE DATABASE follows:

```
CREATE DATABASE database_name
 [ ON [PRIMARY]
        [ <filespec> [,...n] ]
        [, <filegroup> [,...n] ]
 ]
 [ LOG ON { <filespec> [,...n]} ]
 [ COLLATE collation_name ]
 [ FOR LOAD | FOR ATTACH ]

<filespec> ::=
  ( [ NAME = logical_file_name, ]
  FILENAME = 'os_file_name'
  [, SIZE = size]
  [, MAXSIZE = { max_size | UNLIMITED } ]
  [, FILEGROWTH = growth_increment] ) [,...n]

<filegroup> ::=
FILEGROUP filegroup_name <filespec> [,...n]
```

In order to fully understand the CREATE DATABASE syntax you have to be aware of the components that make up a database. A database is composed of

- One or more files (operating system files), and

- A transaction log.

The files that compose the data portion of the database reside in one or more filegroups. If you do not specify a filegroup, all the files listed in the `filespec` portion of statement will be associated with the PRIMARY filegroup. For most cases, having only a primary filegroup will be sufficient. You can, however, use some advanced file-placement techniques to ensure that a highly active database performs at an optimal level.

For example, assume your application is experiencing performance problems because numerous users are accessing a large table (located on the PRIMARY filegroup with all the other database objects) on a frequent basis. This causes the access speed for all the tables on the filegroup to be impacted because the large table requires substantial I/O resources. To alleviate the I/O contention, you could create another filegroup that is located on another hard drive (accessed by its own hard drive controller) and move the large table to the new filegroup. Data access speed for the large table should increase because it is isolated, and the access speed for the other objects on the PRIMARY filegroup should increase because they are no longer contending for I/O resources with the large table.

The other main component of a database is the transaction log. The transaction log records the modifications made to a database and is composed of one or more files. As you can see from the syntax, you have the ability to place the transaction log on a different drive than the one used for the data files. Placing the transaction log file(s) in a different location than the data files is a good idea. A common practice used on mission-critical servers that utilize a RAID 5 for data and a RAID 1 for operating system files is to place the transaction log on the RAID 1. That way, assuming your motherboard does not crash, you will always have access to either the data or the log, which will facilitate recovery if one of the RAID configurations experiences a failure.

Now that you have covered the components of a database, proceed to the individual arguments that are used with the CREATE DATABASE statement.

CREATE DATABASE Arguments

The CREATE DATABASE arguments are listed next.

database_name

The database identifier. The object identifier for a database operates differently than all other identifiers. More specifically, if you specify a file name in the LOG ON argument, the identifier can be 128 characters long: this correlates to the user-defined data type sysname. If you do not specify a file name in the LOG ON argument, the identifier can be only 123 characters long. The maximum length of the identifier is reduced because the statement will auto-generate a file name for LOG ON by appending a value to the database_name. I've never seen a database name that was even close to 128 characters long, but this information might prove handy if you are going to take the MCP exams.

ON

Optional argument that allows you to specify the files and filegroups that compose a database.

PRIMARY

Optional argument that allows you to differentiate between primary and secondary filegroups. The primary filegroup contains all the system tables (database catalog) and any object that is not explicitly created on a secondary filegroup.

n

Optional argument that serves as a placeholder to indicate more than one file can be specified.

LOG ON

Optional argument that allows you to explicitly list the files that compose the transaction log. If no file(s) is listed, one is automatically created and its size is 25 percent of that of the data files that make up the database.

COLLATE collation_name

Optional argument that allows you to specify a default collation for the database. If this argument is not specified, the database will use the default collation specified when SQL Server was installed.

FOR LOAD

Optional argument included for backward compatibility with pre-7 version of SQL Server. It sets the database option `dbo use only` to true, so the database can be restored. You are not required to set this database option when restoring databases in versions 7 and above.

FOR ATTACH

Optional argument that allows you to create a database from one or more files that composed an existing database. Use CREATE DATABASE…FOR ATTACH only when you are creating the database with 16 or more files. In all other cases use the system stored procedure **sp_attach_db**.

<filespec>

NAME logical_file_name   Specifies the logical name of the system file associated with the database. This argument is not required when you are creating a database from existing data files with the FOR ATTACH argument. The `logical_file_name` is used with SQL operations that act on the database and is quite a bit easier to remember than its associated database ID.

FILENAME = 'os_file_name'   The path and file name used to define the operating system file.

SIZE = size   Optional argument used to specify the size of a file. The default value when SIZE is not specified is the size of the primary file of the **model** database. When SIZE is specified it must be at least as large as the primary file of the **model** database. For secondary files the default size is 1MB. You can specify values in KB, MB, GB, or TB as long as the integer value (decimals are not allowed) has the appropriate associated unit. The minimum value allowed is 512KB.

MAXSIZE = { max_size | UNLIMITED }   Optional argument used to specify the maximum size to which a file can grow. If no value or UNLIMITED is used, the file can grow until all hard drive space is consumed. The `max_size` argument must be supplied in whole numbers: decimals are not allowed.

FILEGROWTH = growth_increment   Optional argument used to specify the rate at which the database grows when it needs more space. You can specify integer values using KB, MB, GB, or TB units or allow the growth to be a percentage of the current size by using the percent (%) sign. The default value is 10 percent when FILEGROWTH is not specified. The minimum growth value is 64KB and any value specified will be rounded to the nearest 64KB.

<filegroup>

FILEGROUP filegroup_name <filespec> [,...n]   Optional argument used to specify non-Primary filegroups and the associated file(s) that composes the filegroup.

Statement Permissions

In order to execute the CREATE DATABASE statement, you must be a member of the fixed-server roles **sysadmin** or **dbcreator** or have had execute permission explicitly granted to your login by a member of the either **sysadmin**, **dbcreator**, or **securityadmin**.

Creating a Database

The Query Analyzer and Enterprise Manager approaches to creating a database are described in this section.

Query Analyzer

The following statements will create a new database using default values.

```
USE master
go
CREATE DATABASE RealAdventures
--Results--
The CREATE DATABASE process is allocating 0.88 MB on disk 'RealAdventures'.
The CREATE DATABASE process is allocating 0.49 MB on disk 'RealAdventures_log'.
```

After you execute the statement in Query Analyzer, use the following SELECT statement to examine the row inserted in the **sysdatabases** table for RealAdventures (the results are too wide to display here).

```
USE master
go
SELECT *
FROM sysdatabases
WHERE name = 'RealAdventures'
```

Look at the **filename** column to see where the primary data file was created. My system created it in the C:\MSSQL7\Data subdirectory. If you upgraded to SQL Server 2000 from an earlier version of the product, then you should have the same value. If there was no existing version of SQL Server when you installed SQL Server 2000 (a clean install), then you will have a different value. SQL Server 2000 installs under the Program Files subdirectory, whereas the pre-2000 version's installed off the root of the C drive.

Use Explorer to examine the files created by the statement. After selecting the Data subdirectory, you will not only see RealAdventures.mdf, but RealAdventures_log.ldf as well. A log file name was not included in the statement, so one was automatically created by appending "_log.ldf" to the database's name. The size of my .mdf file is 896KB, which is the same size as model.mdf. The .ldf file is 504KB, which is not 25 percent of 896, but the minimum size allowed for a log file.

One more thing to note before we move on to the next example. The .mdf and .ldf file extensions used for primary data files and transaction log files are not required, but I strongly suggest that you stick with this standard. I also suggest that you use the .ndf extension when creating secondary files.

The last example was overly simple. Let's drop that database and create a new one that uses arguments you might use to create a real-world database. The following code deletes the existing **RealAdventures** database and creates another one using SIZE, MAXSIZE, and FILEGROWTH arguments for both the primary data file and the transaction log.

```
USE master
go
DROP DATABASE RealAdventures
go
CREATE DATABASE RealAdventures
ON
(NAME = 'RealAdventures',
 FILENAME = 'C:\MSSQL7\Data\RealAdventures.mdf',
 SIZE = 30 MB,
 MAXSIZE = 100 MB,
 FILEGROWTH = 15 MB)
LOG ON
(NAME = 'RealAdventures_Log',
 FILENAME = 'C:\MSSQL7\Data\RealAdventures.ldf',
 SIZE = 10 MB,
 MAXSIZE = 25 MB,
 FILEGROWTH = 2 MB)
--Results--
Deleting database file 'C:\MSSQL7\data\RealAdventures_log.LDF'.
Deleting database file 'C:\MSSQL7\data\RealAdventures.mdf'.
The CREATE DATABASE process is allocating 30.00 MB on disk 'RealAdventures'.
The CREATE DATABASE process is allocating 10.00 MB on disk 'RealAdventures_Log'.
```

Use Explorer to examine the characteristics of the files created by this statement.

TIP Use MAXSIZE

Specify a maximum size for a database whether you create it with T-SQL or via Enterprise Manager. If a maximum size is not specified and poor database administration occurs, there is the possibility the database will consume all available space on the hard drive on which it is located. Troubleshooting a database that has run out of space when there is still hard drive space available is a heck of lot easier than troubleshooting one where there is no space available.

Enterprise Manager

There are two options in Enterprise Manager for creating a database: the Database Properties dialog and the Database Creation Wizard. Both approaches are described here.

Database Properties Dialog   In order to create a database with the Database Properties dialog, complete the following:

1. Expand a Server, right-click the Databases folder and select New Database.

2. Populate the **Name** field and then click the Data Files tab. Notice that the value in the **File Name** field is the database name with a "_Data" suffix.

3. Change the Initial size (MB) value to the minimum required size.

4. Click the Restrict file growth (MB) radio button and then specify the maximum size for the database.

5. Click the Transaction Log tab and notice that the value in the **File Name** field is the database name with a "_Log" suffix. Specify the initial and maximum sizes for the transaction log file and then click OK.

Since all the options available in the dialog were covered in the previous section, I will leave it to you to determine the values for the fields. Once the database is created you can expand the Databases folder, right click on the new database and select Properties to change any of its default properties.

Database Creation Wizard   The following steps can be used to create a database with the Database Creation Wizard:

1. Click Tools on the main menu and select Wizards.

2. Expand the Database option, select Create Database Wizard and click OK.

3. Proceed through the wizard and populate the required fields.

Database options presented in the wizard are exactly the same as those in the Database Properties Dialog.

ALTER DATABASE

The ALTER DATABASE statement is used to modify the existing configuration of a database. In pre-2000 versions of SQL Server its primary purpose was to add existing files or filegroups to a database or change the characteristics of the files in use. In addition to those changes, you can now modify database options. For a complete listing of the database options that can be modified, see the Books Online topic: DATABASEPROPERTYEX.

In pre-2000 versions you changed database options with the system stored procedure **sp_dboption**. This method may not be supported in future versions of SQL Server, so use ALTER DATABASE to do this from now on. You can, of course, still use Enterprise Manager to change database options if you prefer the GUI approach.

The partial syntax of the ALTER DATABASE statement is shown here:

```
ALTER DATABASE database
| MODIFY FILE < filespec >
| SET < optionspec > [ ,...n ]
| COLLATE < collation_name >
}
```

ALTER DATABASE Arguments

The ALTER DATABASE arguments are listed here.

MODIFY FILE <filespec>

The MODIFY FILE <filespec> argument allows for the modification of the FILE-NAME, SIZE, FILEGROWTH, and MAXSIZE settings on an existing database file.

SET <optionspec> [,...n]

This argument allows one or more database options to be set. Listing and explaining the available database options could occupy an entire chapter, but as an example you can use this argument to mark a database as read-only.

COLLATE <collation_name>

This argument allows the default collation for the database to be changed. Specifying collation, as explained in Chapter 2, determines how data is sorted and compared. For more information on this, please see the Books Online topic: Collate.

Statement Permissions

Permission to execute ALTER DATABASE defaults to members of the fixed-server roles **sysadmin** and **dbcreator** and the fixed-database role **db_owner**. Permission to execute this statement is not transferable.

Altering a Database

You can alter a database via Query Analyzer or with the GUI tools available in Enterprise Manager. Both methods are described here.

Query Analyzer

Execute the following statement in Query Analyzer to change the file attributes of the **RealAdventures** database created in the previous section. The statement expands the size of the primary data file to 50MB and increases the maximum size to 150MB.

```
USE RealAdventures
go
ALTER DATABASE RealAdventures
MODIFY FILE
(
 NAME = 'RealAdventures',
 SIZE = 50 MB,
 MAXSIZE = 150 MB
)
--Results--
The command(s) completed successfully.
```

Use Explorer to examine the new file size of RealAdventures.mdf.

The following statement shows how to use the new syntax for ALTER DATABASE to mark the database as read-only.

```
USE RealAdventures
go
ALTER DATABASE RealAdventures SET READ_ONLY
--Results--
The command(s) completed successfully.
```

Enterprise Manager

In order to modify a database in Enterprise Manager, complete the following:

1. Expand a server and then expand the Databases folder.

2. Right-click the target database and select Properties.

Once the Database Properties Dialog is open, make the desired changes, and click OK.

DROP DATABASE

The DROP DATABASE statement is used to delete a database. This includes deleting the rows in the system tables that are used to define the database and its associated physical files. The full syntax follows:

```
DROP DATABASE database_name [ ,...n ]
```

Statement Permissions

Permission to execute DROP DATABASE defaults to members of the fixed-server roles **sysadmin** and **dbcreator** and the fixed database role **db_owner**. Permission to execute this statement is not transferable.

Dropping a Database

The two methods used to drop a database are described here.

Query Analyzer

The DROP DATABASE statement was used earlier to drop the **RealAdventures** database and the only functionality not shown was the ability to drop more than one (indicated by the n) database at a time. The following statements demonstrate how to delete multiple databases:

```
USE master
go
--Create two dummy database
CREATE DATABASE RealAdventures2
CREATE DATABASE RealAdventures3
```

```
go
--Delete dummy databases
DROP DATABASE RealAdventures2, RealAdventures3
--Results--
The CREATE DATABASE process is allocating 0.88 MB on disk 'RealAdventures2'.
The CREATE DATABASE process is allocating 0.49 MB on disk 'RealAdventures2_log'.
The CREATE DATABASE process is allocating 0.88 MB on disk 'RealAdventures3'.
The CREATE DATABASE process is allocating 0.49 MB on disk 'RealAdventures3_log'.
Deleting database file 'C:\MSSQL7\data\RealAdventures2_log.LDF'.
Deleting database file 'C:\MSSQL7\data\RealAdventures2.mdf'.
Deleting database file 'C:\MSSQL7\data\RealAdventures3_log.LDF'.
Deleting database file 'C:\MSSQL7\data\RealAdventures3.mdf'.
```

Enterprise Manager

In order to drop a database in Enterprise Manager, complete the following:

1. Expand a Server, and then expand the Databases folder.

2. Right-click the target database and select Delete.

3. Check the Delete back up and restore history for the database check box if
    you want to remove the back up and restore history from the related
    tables in the **msdb** database; then click Yes.

CREATE TABLE

The CREATE TABLE statement creates a table within a database. The partial syntax
of the statement follows:

```
CREATE TABLE [ database_name.[ owner ] . | owner. ] table_name
(
 column_name data_type  column_constraint
 | column_name AS computed_column_expression
 | table_constraint
)
column_constraint = [ NULL | NOT NULL ]
                           | [ { PRIMARY KEY | UNIQUE } [ CLUSTERED | NONCLUSTERED ]
                           | [ [ FOREIGN KEY ] REFERENCES ref_table [ ( ref_column ) ]
                           | CHECK ( logical_expression )
table_constraint = [ { PRIMARY KEY | UNIQUE }
                    [ CLUSTERED | NONCLUSTERED ]
                    { ( column [ ASC | DESC ] [ ,...n ] ) }
```

```
| FOREIGN KEY [ ( column [ ,...n ] ) ]
  REFERENCES ref_table [ ( ref_column [ ,...n ] ) ]
| CHECK ( search_conditions )
```

In short, the statement allows you to do the following:

- Create a table with a specified table name.

- Specify the table's column names, data types, and properties.

- Optionally create column-level constraints like assigning a default value when no value is supplied.

- Optionally create table-level constraints like specifying which columns will participate in a FOREIGN KEY relationship and whether it will enforce cascading deletes.

If you look closely at the column_constraint and table_constraint definitions, you will see that there is some overlap in the constraints you can create with each option. In the case of the PRIMARY KEY constraint, you can create it at the column-level if the primary key is only going to be composed of one field. For a multi-column primary key, use a table-level constraint. (See how the table-level section has the ,...n to indicate more columns can be included.) If you pay close attention to the OR symbol (|) in the table_constraint section, you will notice that it applies to three parts, so only one table-level constraint can exist per table. If you use up your one table-level constraint and need another constraint, you can use the column-level type.

If you want more details on each of the sections, see the Books Online topic: CREATE TABLE. Only the basics of the statement are used in this book, so extensive coverage is not provided.

Statement Permissions

Permission to execute the CREATE TABLE statement defaults to the fixed-server role **sysadmin** and the fixed-database roles **db_owner** and **db_ddladmin**. Members of **sysadmin** and **db_owner** can grant any user the ability to execute CREATE TABLE.

> **TIP   Temporary Tables**
>
> *A temporary table is one that exists for the duration of a user's session. It is created in the same manner as a permanent table, but the* table_name *is prefaced with either # or ##. A table created with # is called a local temporary table because it is only visible to the user session in which it was created. A table created with ## is called a global temporary table because it is visible outside the user session in which it was created.*
>
> *The use of temporary tables should be limited now that SQL Server 2000 supports the table data type (discussed in Chapter 2). I did, however, want to mention temporary tables in case you inherit some code in which they are used.*

Creating a Table

The Query Analyzer and Enterprise Manager approaches used to create a table are described here.

Query Analyzer

Next you will create some tables so you can get more comfortable with the CREATE TABLE syntax. Figure 3-1 shows the tables (and their relationships) you will learn to create.

The table layout in Figure 3-1 shows the relationship between real estate brokerage firms, the states in which the firms are located, the brokers who work for the firms, and the states in which the brokers are located. The following statements create a new database and the user-defined data types used to define the columns in the broker-related tables. User-defined data types were discussed in Chapter 2. Make sure you modify the FILENAME arguments per your system's configuration.

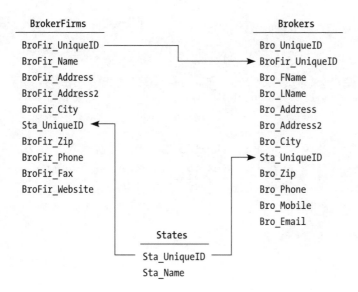

Figure 3-1. Real Estate Example Table Layout

```
USE master
go
CREATE DATABASE BrokerExample
ON
(NAME = 'BrokerExample',
 FILENAME = 'C:\MSSQL7\Data\BrokerExample.mdf',
 SIZE = 10 MB,
 MAXSIZE = 25 MB,
 FILEGROWTH = 5 MB)
LOG ON
(NAME = 'BrokerExample_Log',
 FILENAME = 'C:\MSSQL7\Data\BrokerExample.ldf',
 SIZE = 5 MB,
 MAXSIZE = 10 MB,
 FILEGROWTH = 2 MB)
go
USE BrokerExample
go
sp_addtype 'address', 'varchar(40)', 'NOT NULL'
go
sp_addtype 'address2', 'varchar(40)', 'NULL'
go
sp_addtype 'city', 'varchar(35)', 'NOT NULL'
```

```
go
sp_addtype 'zip', 'varchar(15)', 'NOT NULL'
go
sp_addtype 'phone', 'varchar(10)', 'NOT NULL'
go
sp_addtype 'mobile', 'varchar(10)', 'NULL'
go
--Results--
The CREATE DATABASE process is allocating 10.00 MB on disk 'BrokerExample'.
The CREATE DATABASE process is allocating 5.00 MB on disk 'BrokerExample_Log'.

(1 row(s) affected)


Type added.


(1 row(s) affected)


Type added.


(1 row(s) affected)


Type added.


(1 row(s) affected)


Type added.


(1 row(s) affected)


Type added.


(1 row(s) affected)


Type added.
```

Once the statements have successfully executed, right click on the Server in Object Browser and select Refresh. Expand the **BrokerExample** database and expand the User Defined Data Type folder. Figure 3-2 shows the results of these actions.

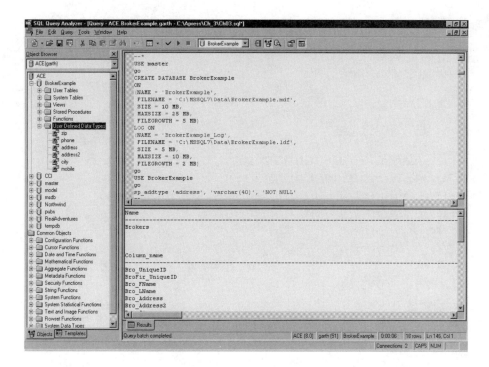

*Figure 3-2. Viewing **BrokerExample** database in Object Browser*

Now that the database and user-defined data types are created, use the following statements to create the tables shown in Figure 3-1:

```
USE BrokerExample
go
CREATE TABLE States
(
Sta_UniqueID tinyint PRIMARY KEY IDENTITY,
Sta_Name varchar(30)
)

CREATE TABLE BrokerFirms
(
BroFir_UniqueID tinyint PRIMARY KEY IDENTITY,
BroFir_Name varchar(40) NOT NULL,
BroFir_Address address,
BroFir_Address2 address2,
BroFir_City city NOT NULL,
Sta_UniqueID tinyint,
```

```
    BroFir_Zip zip,
    BroFir_Phone phone,
    BroFir_Fax phone,
    BroFir_WebSite varchar(50) NULL,
    )

    CREATE TABLE Brokers
    (
    Bro_UniqueID smallint PRIMARY KEY IDENTITY,
    BroFir_UniqueID tinyint NOT NULL,
    Bro_FName varchar(30) NOT NULL,
    Bro_LName varchar(30) NOT NULL,
    Bro_Address address2,
    Bro_Address2 address2,
    Bro_City city,
    Sta_UniqueID tinyint,
    Bro_Zip zip,
    Bro_Phone phone,
    Bro_Mobile phone,
    Bro_email varchar(40) NULL
    )
    --Results--
    The command(s) completed successfully.
```

Creating tables using this approach is fairly straightforward. Please note that the naming convention used for the column names is discussed in Chapter 1. Notice that I used the IDENTITY property to generate primary key values and applied no default or foreign key constraints to the tables. The foreign key constraints were omitted in order to make the statements easier to read. It is poor design to omit foreign key constraints so they will be added in the next section using the ALTER TABLE statement.

Enterprise Manager

In order to create a table in Enterprise Manager, complete the following:

1. Expand a Server and then expand the Databases folder.

2. Expand the database in which the table is to be created.

3. Right-click the Tables options and select New Table.

4. When the New Table dialog appears, specify the column names and associated column definitions. Use the icons on the toolbar to set a primary key and to manage relationships, indexes, and constraints.

5. Click the diskette icon to save the table, specify the table name in the Choose Name dialog and click OK.

ALTER TABLE

The ALTER TABLE statement is used to make the following changes to a table:

Add columns	Modify columns
Delete constraints	Disable constraints
Disable triggers	Delete columns
Add constraints	Modify constraints
Enable constraints	Enable triggers

The basic syntax of the statement follows:

```
ALTER TABLE table
 [ ALTER COLUMN column_name
    { new_data_type [ ( precision [ , scale ] ) ]
      [ NULL | NOT NULL ]
    ]
    | ADD
       { [ < column_definition > ]
    | DROP
       { [ CONSTRAINT ] constraint_name
           | COLUMN column } [ ,...n ]
}
```

In short, it allows you to modify the definitions of existing columns, add new columns, and add and drop constraints. The examples covered in this section will show you how to change the data type associated with a column, add a column to a table and add a foreign key constraint.

Statement Permissions

Permission to execute the ALTER TABLE statement defaults to the table owner and the database roles **db_owner** and **db_ddladmin** and is not transferable.

Altering a Table

The Query Analyzer and Enterprise Manager approaches used to alter a table are described here.

Query Analyzer

The following examples demonstrate how to use ALTER TABLE in Query Analyzer.

Changing a Column's Data Type   You might have already picked up on this, but I intentionally used the wrong data type for one of the columns in the **Brokers** table. Do you see it? I assigned the address2 data type to Bro_Address. This error won't cause my data modification statements to fail, but it will incorrectly allow NULL values to be inserted into the column. The following statement fixes the error by changing the data type from address2 to address:

```
USE BrokerExample
go
ALTER TABLE Brokers
ALTER COLUMN Bro_Address address
--Results--
(0 row(s) affected)
```

The results displayed show that zero rows were affected. This message leaves me wondering whether the change was actually made. Let's use the system stored procedure **sp_help** to verify the data type for **Bro_Address** was changed to address. Execute the following in Query Analyzer:

```
USE BrokerExample
go
sp_help 'Brokers'
--Results (Partial)--
Name          Owner    Type         Created_datetime
----------    -------- ----------   ------------------------
Brokers        dbo     user table   2000-08-13 22:08:46.767

Column_name        Type
----------------   ----------
Bro_UniqueID       smallint
BroFir_UniqueID    tinyint
Bro_FName          varchar
Bro_LName          varchar
Bro_Address        address
```

Bro_Address2	address2
Bro_City	city
Sta_UniqueID	tinyint
Bro_Zip	zip
Bro_Phone	phone
Bro_Mobile	phone
Bro_email	varchar

Even though the message indicated zero rows were affected, the data type for **Bro_Address** was changed as desired.

Adding a Column to a Table   Assume the broker-tracking tables have been in production for a while and the end-users want to add a column to **Broker** that holds a pager number. The statement used to add the column is shown here:

```
USE BrokerExample
go
ALTER TABLE Brokers
ADD Bro_Pager varchar(15)
--Results--
The command(s) completed successfully.
```

The varchar(15) data type was used instead of phone because some pager numbers require certain codes to be input before you can enter your message or number. When you execute the code in Query Analyzer a message is displayed that indicates the statement succeeded. This is good enough for me, but if you want to check the table's structure using **sp_help** feel free to do so.

Be aware that you cannot add a column defined as NOT NULL unless it is defined with a default constraint. For example, the following statement generates an error message:

```
USE BrokerExample
go
ALTER TABLE Brokers
ADD Bro_Pager2 varchar(15) NOT NULL
--Results--
Server: Msg 4901, Level 16, State 1, Line 1
```

ALTER TABLE can only be used to add columns that allow nulls or have a default constraint specified.

When you add a DEFAULT constraint, however, the code works as desired.

```
USE BrokerExample
go
ALTER TABLE Brokers
ADD Bro_Pager2 varchar(15) NOT NULL DEFAULT 'NONE'
--Results--
The command(s) completed successfully.
```

Adding a Foreign Key Constraint A foreign key constraint ensures that a *parent* record cannot be deleted as long as a *child* record exists. The table structure listed in Figure 3-1 should have foreign key constraints on the following relationships:

- **BrokerFirms.Sta_UniquedID → State.Sta_UniqueID**

- **Brokers.Sta_UniqueUD → State.Sta_UniqueID**

- **Brokers.BroFir_UniqueID → BrokerFirms.BroFir_UniqueID**

The following statements add the required foreign key constraints to the broker tables.

```
USE BrokerExample
go
ALTER TABLE BrokerFirms
ADD CONSTRAINT BrokerFirms_States
FOREIGN KEY (Sta_UniqueID) REFERENCES States (Sta_UniqueID)

ALTER TABLE Brokers
ADD CONSTRAINT Brokers_States
FOREIGN KEY (Sta_UniqueID) REFERENCES States (Sta_UniqueID)

ALTER TABLE Brokers
ADD CONSTRAINT Brokers_BrokerFirms
FOREIGN KEY (BroFir_UniqueID) REFERENCES BrokerFirms (BroFir_UniqueID)
--Results--
The command(s) completed successfully.
```

Note that I included constraint names in the statements. If you do not include a constraint name, one is automatically generated. Let's see what the format of an auto-generated constraint name looks like by dropping one we just created and re-creating it without supplying a name. The following statements drop the **Brokers_States** foreign key constraint and re-creates it using a system-generated name.

```
USE BrokerExample
go
ALTER TABLE Brokers
DROP CONSTRAINT Brokers_States

ALTER TABLE Brokers
ADD
FOREIGN KEY (Sta_UniqueID) REFERENCES States (Sta_UniqueID)
--Results--
The command(s) completed successfully.
```

You can use **sp_help** to look at the system-generated name. My computer generated the name **FK__Brokers__Sta_Uni__34C8D9D1**. If you are going to be dropping and re-creating constraints on a regular basis, I suggest you create a standard and use it in all your databases. Otherwise, you should let the system generate constraint names.

Enterprise Manager

To alter a table in Enterprise Manager, complete the following:

1. Expand a Server and then expand the Databases folder.

2. Expand the Database in which the table is located and select the Tables option.

3. Right-click the target table in the Detail pane and select Design Table.

4. Once the Design Table dialog is open, make the desired changes and click the diskette icon.

If the table to which the changes are being made participates in a foreign key relationship, you will be asked to confirm the changes to the database.

CREATE INDEX

An index is a structure that is used to efficiently find data in a table or view. More specifically, an index eliminates the need to scan all the rows in a table when looking for a particular row(s). Assume you have a table with 50,000 rows and you want to retrieve the data that resides in the row number 49,000. If no index is used, a table scan must be performed and 48,999 rows are traversed before the target row is found. When an index is used, SQL Server uses a B-tree structure to search through key index values to determine which row you are trying to find.

Implementing a sound indexing strategy is key to ensuring your database is performing at an optimal level. In order to implement a sound indexing strategy you must understand how the data is going to be accessed by the end users. The most common error I have seen with indexing strategies is index overuse. This is caused by a developer not knowing how the data is going to be accessed, so they index all columns that *may* participate in a join or a comparison operations. This strategy actually degrades database performance because every time a data modification statement is executed against the table, the associated indexes have to be updated. Each index requires a certain amount of overhead, so you want to make sure you have just the ones that are required to facilitate efficient data access.

Indexes can be created on a single column or a combination of columns. Indexes are automatically created when certain constraints are applied to a table. For example, when you define a column(s) with the PRIMARY KEY constraint, a UNIQUE NONCLUSTERED index is automatically created. The complete syntax of CREATE INDEX follows:

```
CREATE [ UNIQUE ] [ CLUSTERED | NONCLUSTERED ] INDEX index_name
    ON { table | view } ( column [ ASC | DESC ] )
[ WITH
        [ PAD_INDEX ]
        [ [ , ] FILLFACTOR = fillfactor ]
        [ [ , ] IGNORE_DUP_KEY ]
        [ [ , ] DROP_EXISTING ]
        [ [ , ] STATISTICS_NORECOMPUTE ]
        [ [ , ] SORT_IN_TEMPDB ]
]
[ ON filegroup ]
```

It's important that you understand all aspects of CREATE INDEX, so take the time to cover all the arguments.

CREATE INDEX Arguments

The arguments used with CREATE INDEX are described here.

UNIQUE

The UNIQUE argument allows you to specify that there are no repeating values in the index. Any attempt to INSERT or UPDATE a duplicate value in a column on which a UNIQUE index is based results in the transaction being rolled back. It is important for you to fully understand the last sentence. Let's say you are using a SELECT statement to insert values into a table and one of the 200 rows returned by the statement violates the UNIQUE index. An error message is generated and all INSERTs are rolled back, not just the one row that had the duplicate value. Another important point to understand is that NULLs are treated as the same value, so any attempt to insert more than one NULL into a column with a UNIQUE index will generate an error.

CLUSTERED

A CLUSTERED index is one in which the physical order of the rows is the same as the index. There can only be one CLUSTERED index per table or view. This makes perfect sense because you cannot have more than one physical ordering of the rows.

NONCLUSTERED

A NONCLUSTERED index is the default type created when type is not specified. It consists of a logical ordering of the column(s) that compose the index and point-ers to the physical location for each row. You can have up to 249 NONCLUSTERED indexes on a table or view, but a view must have a CLUSTERED index before a NONCLUSTERED index can be applied.

{ table | view }

The name of the table or view that contains the column to be indexed. There are no special requirements for creating an index on a table. A view, however, must be defined with SCHEMABINDING and be deterministic. Also, the key columns can-not be defined with the float data type. The ability to create an index on a view is new to SQL Server 2000.

column [ASC | DESC]

The column or columns that compose the index. Use ASC (default) or DESC to specify an ascending or descending sort order within the column. The maximum number of columns that can compose an index is sixteen and their fixed-value widths cannot exceed 900 bytes. If variable-width columns are included, their maximum widths are used to check the 900-byte limit. If the limit is exceeded, a warning message is displayed that informs the developer that all INSERTs or UPDATEs that cause the 900-byte limit to be exceeded will result in an error.

FILLFACTOR = *fillfactor*

Optional argument that allows you to specify how full SQL Server should make the leaf level of each index page when the index is created. The leaf level of an index consists of the pages that contain the key value(s) from the indexed column(s) and the pointer value to the row. When a query that utilizes an index is executed, the leaf level pages are searched to find the key value, and the key value's associated pointer is used to find the row in the table. The structure of an index is shown in Figure 3-3.

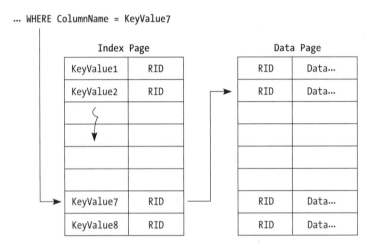

```
... WHERE ColumnName = KeyValue7
```

Figure 3-3. Index Structure

When an index is created, all the leaf level pages are also created and are completely filled with index data (key value/pointer) unless you use the FILLFACTOR argument. The negative ramification of using the default settings is that when INSERT or UPDATE statements are executed on the table, the leaf level pages have to be split (degrading performance) in order to hold the new index data. Using a FILLFACTOR allows the pages to *grow* without splitting and thus increases efficiency. The FILLFACTOR is only available at create-time and is not maintained post-creation.

IGNORE_DUP_KEY

Optional argument that allows you to control what happens when a duplicate value is inserted into a column with a UNIQUE index. This argument can only be used on UNIQUE CLUSTERED and UNIQUE NONCLUSTERED indexes. Using this argument will prohibit statements that attempt to insert or update duplicate key values from being rolled back. The rows that contain a duplicate key value will not be inserted into the table, but other rows will be inserted. An error message will be displayed notifying you that the duplicate values were referenced in the statement.

DROP_EXISTING

Optional argument that causes existing indexes to be deleted and re-created with the new arguments. This argument can provide performance benefits when CLUSTERED indexes are rebuilt because NONCLUSTERED indexes (which rely on the CLUSTERED index keys) will only be rebuilt if the key values change.

STATISTICS_NORECOMPUTE

Optional argument that prohibits the automatic recalculation of distribution statistics when they are determined to be out-of-date. Distribution statistics tell how the index key values are distributed across the range of values of which they are composed. The Query Optimizer uses this data to determine if an index should be used in a particular query operation. If the data is out-of-date, the Query Optimizer may make the wrong decision and thus negatively impact performance.

Starting with SQL Server 7, the distribution statistics were recalculated automatically when a certain threshold of data modification statements were executed on a table. This helps to ensure that the Query Optimizer has data that will allow it to make the best decisions about whether an index will reduce the cost of executing a query.

SORT_IN_TEMPDB

Optional argument that forces SQL Server to use **tempdb** to store the intermediate results of the index creation process. This argument can reduce the time it takes to create an index if **tempdb** is located on a separate hard drive configuration than the filegroup on which the index will reside.

ON *filegroup*

Optional argument that allows you to specify the filegroup on which the index will reside. When the argument is not supplied, all indexes are created on the primary filegroup.

Statement Permissions

Permission to execute the CREATE INDEX statement defaults to the fixed-server role **sysadmin**, the fixed-database roles **db_owner** and **db_ddladmin,** and the object owner. Permission to execute CREATE INDEX is not transferable.

Creating an Index

Creating an index with Query Analyzer and Enterprise Manager is described here.

Query Analyzer

There are two options available in Query Analyzer for creating an index. The first is by executing the CREATE INDEX statement in Editor Pane and the second involves using the Manage Indexes dialog. Both approaches are described below.

Editor Pane   Now that you know all about the CREATE INDEX statement, add one to the **Brokers** table so you can put your knowledge to work. Assume the end users are going to be looking up brokers by their last name on a regular basis and you want to ensure the lookups perform at optimal speed. In order to do this you need to create a NONCLUSTERED index on the **Bro_LName** column. The following statement shows how this is done:

```
USE BrokerExample
go
CREATE NONCLUSTERED INDEX ndx_Brokers_LName
ON Brokers (Bro_LName)
--Results--
The command(s) completed successfully.
```

You covered an awful lot of material to execute just two lines of code, but the code is really the simple part for this statement. The not-so-simple concept to understand about indexes is how they are used and when they are needed. You now know how they are used and how to create them, and you'll cover some techniques that show you how to determine when indexes are needed in Appendix C. Appendix C provides general coverage of query optimization and demonstrates how you can use one of the tools available in Query Analyzer to determine when an index will reduce the costs of executing a query (make the query execute faster).

Manage Indexes Dialog   The Manage Indexes dialog is accessed from the Tools option on the main menu. Simply click Tools and select Manage Indexes. Once the dialog appears, select the target database and table from the drop-down boxes and click New. The available options correspond to the CREATE INDEX arguments detailed above, so simply choose the appropriate options and click OK. Figure 3-4 shows the options available through the dialog.

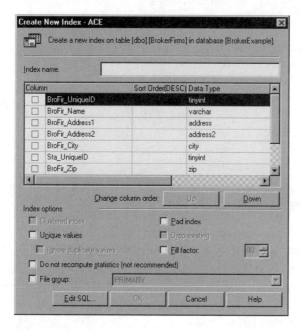

Figure 3-4. Create New Index dialog

Enterprise Manager

Enterprise Manager provides three options for creating an index:

- Manage Indexes dialog

- Manage Indexes/Keys icon in Table Designer

- Create Index Wizard

The three approaches are described here.

Manage Indexes Dialog   The Manage Indexes dialog available in Enterprise Manager is the same one available in Query Analyzer. Use the following steps to access the dialog:

1. Expand a Server and then expand the Databases folder.

2. Expand the database in which the index is to be created and select the Tables option.

3. Right-click the table to which the index is attached, highlight All Tasks, and select Manage Indexes.

Manage Indexes/Keys Icon   Complete the following to access the Manage Indexes/Keys icon in Table Designer:

1. Expand a Server and then expand the Databases folder.

2. Expand the database in which the index is to be created, right-click the Tables option, and select New Table.

3. Once the table's columns and their associated attributes have been added, click the Spreadsheet/Key icon (the second from the right on the toolbar).

4. Click New and modify the system-created name if it does not conform to your naming convention.

5. Select the desired index attributes and click Close.

6. Click the Diskette icon on the toolbar, and the table and associated indexes are created.

Create Index Wizard   The Create Index Wizard steps you through the process of creating an index. To access the wizard, complete the following:

1. Click Tools on the main menu and select Wizards.

2. Expand the Database option, select Create Index Wizard, and click OK.

3. Step through the wizard by selecting the target database and table and the attributes of the index.

4. Once you click Finish, the index is created.

TIP No ALTER INDEX

There is no ALTER INDEX statement. When you need to change the attributes of an index, use the CREATE INDEX statement with the DROP_EXISTING argument. Alternatively, you can delete the index with the DROP INDEX statement and re-create it with CREATE INDEX.

DROP INDEX

The syntax for the DROP INDEX statement is shown here.

```
DROP INDEX 'table.index | view.index' [ ,...n ]
```

You simply specify the table or view to which the index is attached and execute the statement.

There are multiple ways to drop an index, but the only one described here is the statement approach used in Query Analyzer. The other methods can be accessed via the dialogs described in the previous section. To drop the index created in the previous example, execute the following.

```
USE BrokerExample
go
DROP INDEX Brokers.ndx_Brokers_LName
--Results--
The command(s) completed successfully.
```

TIP Index Tuning Wizard

The Index Tuning Wizard (ITW), accessible through both Enterprise Manager and Query Analyzer, helps you determine the indexes that can be used to increase a database's performance. ITW is discussed in Appendix C.

Before You Go

You covered quite a bit of material in this chapter, but if you read it all and executed the examples in the Ch03.sql file you should have a good understanding of how to:

- Create, alter, and delete a database.

- Create, alter, and delete a table.

- Create and delete an index.

In addition to this you should have a good understanding of the effect of fixed security roles on object ownership and the files that compose a database.

The next chapter starts the first of two that cover DML (data manipulation language). Chapter 4 covers the SELECT statement, JOINs, and control-of-flow; Chapter 5 covers the INSERT, UPDATE, and DELETE statements.

DML: SELECT, JOINs, and Control-of-Flow

DML (DATA MANIPULATION LANGUAGE) is the subset of T-SQL that allows you to manipulate data stored in the database objects created with DDL (Data Definition Language) statements. DML is fundamental to working with SQL Server (and understanding the examples presented later in the book) so this chapter covers a lot of important material. The SELECT statement and some of the more useful clauses and operators are covered in detail and the various JOINs are presented and explained through a series of examples. The chapter completes with coverage of the control-of-flow statements available in T-SQL.

> **NOTE Sample Code**
>
> *The sample code for this chapter can be downloaded at either* http://www.apress.com *or* http://www.SQLBook.com. *Download CodeCentric.zip and extract and access the Ch04.sql file.*

Before You Get Started

When I first started working with SQL Server (version 4.2), I tried to do all complex data manipulation operations with a database object called a CURSOR. The T-SQL CURSOR allows you to create a resultset and traverse it one row at a time—similar to the way you might use a recordset object to process data. Operating on one row of data at a time using a DO WHILE or FOR construct is the procedural language approach to working with data and I had successfully used it many times before while working with FoxPro. (FoxPro is one of Microsoft's PC database development tools.)The problem, though, was that I knew this was not the proper way to use T-SQL. T-SQL is a set-oriented language and all RDBMSs are optimized for set operations. When you perform any data manipulation operation (assuming it can be completed with the set approach) using a procedural solution you are underutilizing the power of the database engine. When the set approach is used, you *tell* the database engine what you want, and it processes your SQL statement and returns a single set of data. Let's look at a simple example so you are clear on the difference between the two types of solutions. Assume you have a table named **Customers** that contains a **City** column—luckily there is a table that fits this description in the **Northwind** database—and you want to count the number of customers that are located in each city. A description of the procedural approach is shown here.

1. Create a cursor that contains the **City** value for each row (sorted in alphabetical order) in the table.

2. Set a variable equal to the first value in the cursor.

3. Start looping through the cursor.

4. Count the number of rows that equal the current **City** value.

5. When the **City** value changes, populate the variable with the new value and insert **City** and city count into a temporary table.

6. When all rows in the cursor have been processed, display the contents of the temporary table.

Even though the description above contains no code, you can see that it takes several statements to return the desired data. In contrast, the set approach (shown here) requires a single statement.

```
SELECT City, COUNT(City) AS CityCount
FROM   Customers
GROUP BY City
--Results (Partial)--
City            CityCount
--------------- -----------
Aachen          1
Albuquerque     1
Anchorage       1
...
Buenos Aires    3
...
Lisboa          2
London          6
Luleå           1
Lyon            1
Madrid          3
Mannheim        1
...
```

You are not expected to understand how the statement works (we have not covered the required material yet), but you do need to recognize that the set approach used one statement to return the desired data whereas the procedural approach used more than one (actually, more than five).

If you are new to SQL programming and encounter a complex data manipulation problem, the procedural approach will probably look like the *only* way to solve the problem. I encourage you to take the time to study the problem carefully to make sure a set solution is not possible. If your project's deadline does not afford you the opportunity to solve the problem the *right* way and you are forced to use a procedural solution, make sure you re-visit the problem when time permits.

The only way to increase your SQL programming skills is to fully understand how the set approach is used to solve complex data manipulation problems. One well-known SQL guru claims that it takes about a year to unlearn procedural programming concepts when you first start working with SQL. The time it takes you will be dependent on the types of problems you are asked to solve, the dedication you have to solving them the right way and the resources you have to help you understand the more difficult concepts.

SELECT

The SELECT statement allows you to retrieve data held in database objects like variables, views, user-defined functions and tables. The full syntax for SELECT is far too long and complex to list here. Instead, we will cover the basics so you will have a solid understanding of how it can be used to retrieve data. The components of a basic SELECT are shown here.

```
SELECT [ALL | DISTINCT] select_list
[ INTO new_table ]
FROM table_source
[ WHERE search_condition ]
[ ORDER BY order_expression [ ASC | DESC ] ]
```

SELECT Clauses

Descriptions of each of the clauses of the SELECT follow.

[ALL | DISTINCT]

Optional keywords that allow you to specify whether duplicate rows appear in the resultset. ALL, the default behavior, indicates duplicates are included. The DISTINCT argument removes duplicates rows from the resultset.

select_list

The select_list portion specifies the items (e.g., columns or variables) returned by the statement.

[INTO new_table]

Optional argument that allows you to create a table based on the items in the select_list. The structure of new_table is based on the data types of the items in select_list.

FROM table_source

The tables or views that contain the data needed to fulfill the request.

[WHERE search_condition]

Optional argument that allows you to filter the rows returned in the resultset.

[ORDER BY order_expression [ASC | DESC]]

Optional argument that allows you to order the resultset in either ascending or descending order

Selecting Data

Let's take a look at a series of examples that are based on the **Customers** and **Orders** tables in the **Northwind** database.

Simple SELECT

The following SELECT returns all the values in the **Country** column of the
Customers table.

```
USE Northwind
go
SELECT Country
FROM  Customers
--Results (Partial)--

Country
---------------
Germany
Mexico
Mexico
UK
Sweden
...
```

As you can see from the duplicate values for Mexico, the default of ALL rows is
used when DISTINCT is not specified. If you want to remove duplicate rows (an
easy way to determine the domain of **Country),** you can use the DISTINCT keyword as shown here.

```
USE Northwind
go
SELECT DISTINCT Country
FROM  Customers
--Results (Partial)--
Country
---------------
Argentina
Austria
Belgium
Brazil
Canada
...
UK
USA
Venezuela
```

The following is a simple SELECT that returns a resultset composed of two columns in a random order.

```
USE Northwind
go
SELECT CompanyName, Country
FROM Customers
--Results (Partial)--
CompanyName                                 Country
------------------------------------------- ----------------
Alfreds Futterkiste                         Germany
Ana Trujillo Emparedados y helados          Mexico
Antonio Moreno Taquería                     Mexico
Around the Horn                             UK
...
```

I specifically mention the random order of the resultset because many developers mistakenly think that when the ORDER BY clause is not used, the data is returned in the order in which it was inserted in the table. In most cases it will be returned in this order, but to ensure the order of the data you must use the ORDER BY clause (discussed in the next section).

Periodically, you will need to combine the values in two or more columns to produce a formatted resultset. This is a very straightforward process and is accomplished with the concatenation operator (+). The following shows how to combine the values in **CompanyName** and **Country** using a string constant for added formatting.

```
USE Northwind
go
SELECT CompanyName+'-->'+Country
FROM Customers
--Results (Partial)--
------------------------------------------------------------
Alfreds Futterkiste-->Germany
Ana Trujillo Emparedados y helados-->Mexico
Antonio Moreno Taquería-->Mexico
Around the Horn-->UK
...
```

As long as the data type for the columns is the same or can be implicitly converted, the columns can be joined as is. When the columns' data types cannot be implicitly converted, either the CAST or CONVERT functions must be used. Implicit conversion is covered in the "Implicit Conversion" section of Chapter 2, and CAST and CONVERT are discussed in Chapter 6.

ORDER BY

Let's apply a couple of different sorts to the data with the following statements. Please note that when ORDER BY is used without ASC or DESC, the data is returned in ascending order—alphabetically from A to Z.

```
--*Sort on CompanyName ascending
USE Northwind
go
SELECT CompanyName, Country
FROM Customers
ORDER BY CompanyName
--Results (Partial)--
CompanyName                              Country
---------------------------------------- ---------------
Alfreds Futterkiste                      Germany
Ana Trujillo Emparedados y helados       Mexico
Antonio Moreno Taquería                  Mexico
Around the Horn                          UK
...


--*Sort on Country descending
USE Northwind
go
SELECT CompanyName, Country
FROM Customers
ORDER BY Country DESC
--Results (Partial)--
CompanyName                              Country
---------------------------------------- ---------------
GROSELLA-Restaurante                     Venezuela
HILARION-Abastos                         Venezuela
LILA-Supermercado                        Venezuela
LINO-Delicateses                         Venezuela
Lonesome Pine Restaurant                 USA
...
```

The resultset can be ordered on any column or variable in the select_list or any column contained in the tables or views referenced in the FROM clause. The following shows how to order the previous example in ascending order on **Country** and descending on **CompanyName**.

```
USE Northwind
go
SELECT CompanyName, Country
FROM Customers
ORDER BY Country, CompanyName DESC
--Results (Partial)--
CompanyName                                Country
----------------------------------------   ---------------

Rancho grande                              Argentina
Océano Atlántico Ltda.                     Argentina
Cactus Comidas para llevar                 Argentina
Piccolo und mehr                           Austria
Ernst Handel                               Austria
Suprêmes délices                           Belgium
Maison Dewey                               Belgium
```

ORDER BY accepts both column names and the ordinal position of the columns that appear in the select_list as parameters. The previous example could be re-written using the ordinal position of **Country** and **CompanyName** as follows:

```
USE Northwind
go
SELECT CompanyName, Country
FROM Customers
ORDER BY 2, 1 DESC
--Results (Partial)
CompanyName                                Country
----------------------------------------   ---------------

Rancho grande                              Argentina
Océano Atlántico Ltda.                     Argentina
Cactus Comidas para llevar                 Argentina
Piccolo und mehr                           Austria
Ernst Handel                               Austria
Suprêmes délices                           Belgium
Maison Dewey                               Belgium
...
```

WHERE

The WHERE clause filters the resultset returned by a SELECT statement. The following example shows how to return only those companies that are located in Germany.

```
USE Northwind
go
SELECT CompanyName, Country
FROM Customers
WHERE Country = 'Germany'
--Results--
CompanyName                              Country
---------------------------------------- ---------------

Alfreds Futterkiste                      Germany
Blauer See Delikatessen                  Germany
Drachenblut Delikatessen                 Germany
Frankenversand                           Germany
Königlich Essen                          Germany
Lehmanns Marktstand                      Germany
Morgenstern Gesundkost                   Germany
Ottilies Käseladen                       Germany
QUICK-Stop                               Germany
Toms Spezialitäten                       Germany
Die Wandernde Kuh                        Germany

...
```

The various clauses of the SELECT can easily be combined, so if you wanted to sort the resultset by **CompanyName** you would use the following:

```
USE Northwind
go
SELECT CompanyName, Country
FROM Customers
WHERE Country = 'Germany'
ORDER BY CompanyName
--Results--
CompanyName                              Country
---------------------------------------- ---------------

Alfreds Futterkiste                      Germany
Blauer See Delikatessen                  Germany
Die Wandernde Kuh                        Germany
Drachenblut Delikatessen                 Germany
Frankenversand                           Germany
Königlich Essen                          Germany
Lehmanns Marktstand                      Germany
Morgenstern Gesundkost                   Germany
Ottilies Käseladen                       Germany
QUICK-Stop                               Germany
Toms Spezialitäten                       Germany

...
```

The WHERE clause can accept any number of search_conditions, so you can add additional filter criteria as needed. The following example shows how to filter the data on both the **Country** and **City** columns.

```
USE Northwind
go
SELECT CompanyName, Country, City
FROM Customers
WHERE Country = 'UK' AND
      City = 'London'
--Results--
```

CompanyName	Country	City
Around the Horn	UK	London
B's Beverages	UK	London
Consolidated Holdings	UK	London
Eastern Connection	UK	London
North/South	UK	London
Seven Seas Imports	UK	London

The examples covered so far have used the equality operator, but any comparison operator can be used to filter a resultset. The following shows how to use the inequality operator to return the companies in the U.K. that are not located in London.

```
USE Northwind
go
SELECT CompanyName, Country, City
FROM Customers
WHERE Country = 'UK' AND
      City <> 'London'
--Results--
```

CompanyName	Country	City
Island Trading	UK	Cowes

You can just as easily filter the resultset on numeric or datetime columns using equality operators. The following example uses the COUNT aggregate function to count the number of orders placed after 1/1/97. An aggregate function performs a calculation on a set of values and returns a single value. Aggregate functions are discussed in Chapter 6.

```
USE Northwind
go
SELECT COUNT(*)
FROM Orders
WHERE OrderDate > '1/1/97'
--Results--
-----------
676
```

If you recall from Chapter 2, the datetime data types in SQL Server store both date and time. In the previous example no time was specified, so midnight was used to filter the data. As you will see a little later, the same rule applies when data is inserted into a datetime column. When the time portion is not specified, midnight is used. The values in the **OrderDate** column were all entered with no time specified, so when you analyze them you will see "00:00:00.000" for the time portion of the data.

When the time portion of a column is populated with a value other than midnight and you want to filter the resultset accordingly, simply add the time portion to the WHERE clause. Assume the **OrderDate** column had the actual time the orders were entered, and you wanted to filter the resultset so only those entered after 2 PM on 1/1/97 were displayed. The following shows how to modify the WHERE clause to add the additional criteria.

```
USE Northwind
go
SELECT COUNT(*)
FROM Orders
WHERE OrderDate > '1/1/97 14:00:00'
--Results--
-----------
676
```

If you wanted to find all the orders entered in a particular date range you would simply add another comparison operator as follows:

```
USE Northwind
go
SELECT COUNT(*)
FROM Orders
WHERE OrderDate > '1/1/97' AND
      OrderDate < '1/31/97'
--Results--
-----------
30
```

So far, the examples have only included comparison operations of columns containing the same data type (both nvarchar or both datetime), but be assured columns of different data types can be included in the WHERE clause. The following example extends the previous by adding **ShipCountry** to the WHERE clause.

```
USE Northwind
go
SELECT COUNT(*)
FROM Orders
WHERE OrderDate > '1/1/97' AND
      OrderDate < '1/31/97'AND
      ShipCountry = 'France'
--Results--
-----------
3
```

INTO new_table

The INTO clause creates a new table using the items specified in the select_list. The following example shows how to create a new table named **Customers_NameAndCountry** that contains the **CustomerName** and **Country** columns and data.

```
USE Northwind
go
SELECT CompanyName, Country
INTO Customers_NameAndCountry
FROM Customers

SELECT CompanyName, Country
FROM Customers_NameAndCountry
--Results (Partial)--
(91 row(s) affected)
```

CompanyName	Country
Alfreds Futterkiste	Germany
Ana Trujillo Emparedados y helados	Mexico
Antonio Moreno Taquería	Mexico
...	

This example created a permanent table that will persist until it is explicitly deleted with the DROP TABLE statement (or via one of the GUI approaches). If you want to create a table that lasts for only the duration of the user session you can create a temporary table. The following shows how to create a temporary table.

```
USE Northwind
go
SELECT CompanyName, Country
INTO #Customers_NameAndCountry
FROM Customers

SELECT CompanyName, Country
FROM #Customers_NameAndCountry
--Results (Partial)--
(91 row(s) affected)


CompanyName                              Country
---------------------------------------- ----------------

Alfreds Futterkiste                      Germany
Ana Trujillo Emparedados y helados       Mexico
Antonio Moreno Taquería                  Mexico
...
```

Please note that if you close your connection to SQL Server (File>Disconnect) and then re-establish a connection and try to execute the previous SELECT, an error is generated.

```
SELECT CompanyName, Country
FROM #Customers_NameAndCountry
--Results--
Server: Msg 208, Level 16, State 1, Line 1
Invalid object name '#Customers_NameAndCountry'.
```

The **#Customers_NameAndCountry** table only exists for the duration of the user session and when the connection is closed the table is deleted.

> **TIP Avoid Using * With SELECT in Production Code**
>
> *In the previous examples individual column names were specified in the* select_list. *When you want to return all the columns in a table you can use an * in place of column names. The statement* SELECT * FROM Customers *returns all the columns in the* **Customers** *table. Although you can use this approach when doing development, it should not be used in production code. The main reason it should not be used is that the structure of the table the statement references can change over time and when this happens there is potential for breaking code that worked before the table was modified. Specifying the column names is also better for code maintenance. When the column names are specified you do not have to guess what the statement returns.*

Additional SELECT Clauses and Operators

The previous section only covered the basics of the SELECT statement. Let's take a few minutes to study some additional clauses that you will find useful when analyzing data stored in SQL Server.

GROUP BY Clause

The GROUP BY clause allows you to consolidate the rows that make up a group into a single row and, if you choose, apply aggregate calculations. This can best be demonstrated with an example. The following SELECT returns the **ShipCountry** values in the **Orders** table.

```
USE Northwind
go
SELECT ShipCountry
FROM Orders
GROUP BY ShipCountry
--Results (Partial)--
ShipCountry
---------------
Denmark
Norway
USA
Spain
Finland
...
```

This is the same resultset returned had you executed SELECT DISTINCT Ship-County, because the GROUP BY clause consolidates all members of a group to a single row—thus removing duplicates. This consolidation allows you to perform aggregate operations on the groups.

If you want to find out how many shipments were made to each country, simply add the COUNT function as follows:

```
SELECT ShipCountry,
       COUNT(ShipCountry)
FROM Orders
GROUP BY ShipCountry
--Results (Partial)--
ShipCountry
--------------- -----------
Denmark         18
Norway          6
USA             122
Spain           23
Finland         22
...
```

You should know that every column that appears in the select_list must also appear in the GROUP BY clause. Since all columns are consolidated to distinct values, you cannot have an *extra* column that traverses the groups. The following shows the error message generated when an extra column is in the select_list.

```
USE Northwind
go
SELECT ShipCountry,
       ShipCity,
       COUNT(ShipCountry)
FROM Orders
GROUP BY ShipCountry
--Results--
Server: Msg 8120, Level 16, State 1, Line 1
Column 'Orders.ShipCity' is invalid in the select list because it is not contained
in either an aggregate function or the GROUP BY clause.
```

This statement is supposed to calculate the number of shipments per city per country. To make it work, simply move the **ShipCity** to the GROUP BY as shown here.

```
USE Northwind
go
SELECT ShipCountry,
       ShipCity,
       COUNT(ShipCountry)
FROM Orders
GROUP BY ShipCountry, ShipCity
--Results (Partial)--
```

```
ShipCountry      ShipCity
---------------  ---------------  -----------
Germany          Aachen           6
USA              Albuquerque      18
USA              Anchorage        10
Denmark          Århus            11
Spain            Barcelona        5
...
```

You should note that either **ShipCity** or **ShipCountry** could be used with COUNT because the rows are simply grouped by distinct values in both columns.

HAVING Clause

The HAVING clause allows you to apply filter criteria to the GROUP BY clause. Let's say you want to extend the previous example so that you find the cities that have received more than five shipments. The following query uses HAVING to filter the resultset accordingly.

```
USE Northwind
go
SELECT ShipCountry,
       ShipCity,
       COUNT(ShipCountry)
FROM Orders
GROUP BY ShipCountry, ShipCity
HAVING COUNT(ShipCountry) > 5
--Results (Partial)--
ShipCountry      ShipCity
---------------  ---------------  -----------
Germany          Aachen           6
USA              Albuquerque      18
USA              Anchorage        10
Denmark          Århus            11
...
```

The HAVING clause can be used without GROUP BY, but then it simply mimics the behavior of the WHERE clause.

TOP N [PERCENT]

The TOP clause limits the numbers of rows returned from a resultset to N rows when PERCENT is not used and to N PERCENT of the resultset when PERCENT is specified. The following SELECT statement shows how to return **CustomerID** and the number of orders placed by the ten most active customers.

```
SELECT TOP 10 CustomerID,
              COUNT(CustomerID)
FROM Orders
GROUP BY CustomerID
ORDER BY COUNT(CustomerID) DESC
--Results --
CustomerID
---------- -----------
SAVEA       31
ERNSH       30
QUICK       28
FOLKO       19
HUNGO       19
BERGS       18
HILAA       18
RATTC       18
BONAP       17
FRANK       15
```

The resultset returned by this example is misleading because it is structured so that only ten rows can be returned, and it does not address ties for the tenth position. In other words, even if more than one company placed fifteen orders only one company will be returned.

In order to get the true top N companies use the WITH TIES option as shown here.

```
USE Northwind
go
SELECT TOP 10 WITH TIES CustomerID,
              COUNT(CustomerID)
FROM Orders
GROUP BY CustomerID
ORDER BY COUNT(CustomerID) DESC
```

```
--Results--
CustomerID
---------- -----------
SAVEA      31
ERNSH      30
QUICK      28
HUNGO      19
FOLKO      19
BERGS      18
HILAA      18
RATTC      18
BONAP      17
FRANK      15
LEHMS      15
WARTH      15
```

If you want to find the ten least active customers of those who have placed orders, simply reverse the order of the ORDER BY as follows:

```
USE Northwind
go
SELECT TOP 10 WITH TIES CustomerID,
            COUNT(CustomerID)
FROM Orders
GROUP BY CustomerID
ORDER BY COUNT(CustomerID) ASC
--Results--
CustomerID
---------- -----------
CENTC      1
GROSR      2
LAZYK      2
LAUGB      3
NORTS      3
FRANR      3
CONSH      3
BOLID      3
THECR      3
TRAIH      3
```

You should note that this resultset does not include those customers who have never placed an order. If a customer does not place an order, there is no row for the customer in the **Order** table. The method used to determine which customers have never placed an order will be covered in the JOIN section.

UNION [ALL] Operator

The UNION operator allows you to combine the resultset from two or more queries into one resultset. In a previous example, the INTO clause was used to create a
table named **Customers_NameAndCountry** that contained the values of the
CompanyName and **Country** columns of the **Customers** table. The following
example shows how UNION is used to combine the values of the columns from
both tables.

```
USE Northwind
go
SELECT CompanyName, Country
FROM Customers_NameAndCountry
UNION
SELECT CompanyName, Country
FROM Customers
--Results (Partial)--
CompanyName                              Country
---------------------------------------- ---------------

Alfreds Futterkiste                      Germany
Ana Trujillo Emparedados y helados       Mexico
Antonio Moreno Taquería                  Mexico
...
Wolski  Zajazd                           Poland


(91 row(s) affected)
```

Note that only 91 rows are returned. Each table contains 91 rows so you might
have expected 182 rows to be returned. The default behavior of UNION is such
that duplicate rows are removed from the resultset.

If you want to return all rows, including duplicates, use the optional ALL argument as follows:

```
USE Northwind
go
SELECT CompanyName, Country
FROM Customers_NameAndCountry
UNION ALL
SELECT CompanyName, Country
FROM Customers
--Results (Partial)--
CompanyName                              Country
---------------------------------------- ---------------

Alfreds Futterkiste                      Germany
```

```
Ana Trujillo Emparedados y helados        Mexico
Antonio Moreno Taquería                   Mexico
...
Wolski  Zajazd                            Poland

(182 row(s) affected)
```

These examples were presented for demonstration purposes only and are not reflective of real-world uses of the UNION clause. Presenting a real-world use of UNION with the data available in either **pubs** or **Northwind** is impossible, so next you will create two tables and populate them with sample data for a more realistic example.

Assume you have a data warehousing-type application in which you use aggregate tables to hold quarterly sales information. (Please note this type of design should not be used with transactional applications: it is only used for situations in which the number of rows is so large that querying a single table is prohibitively slow.) The tables for the first two quarters of 2000 are named **Q1_2000** and **Q2_2000** respectively, and they have the structures shown by the following statements.

```
CREATE TABLE Q1_2000
(
 Region varchar(5) NOT NULL,
 CustomerID varchar(10) NOT NULL,
 SalesAmount money NOT NULL,
 SalesDate smalldatetime NOT NULL
)
CREATE TABLE Q2_2000
(
 Region varchar(5) NOT NULL,
 CustomerID varchar(10) NOT NULL,
 SalesAmount money NOT NULL,
 SalesDate smalldatetime NOT NULL
)
```

When data analysis is performed on multiple quarters, UNION is used to combine the data into a single resultset. The following shows how this is accomplished.

```
SELECT Region,
       CustomerID,
       SalesAmount,
       SalesDate,
       'Q12000'
FROM Q1_2000
```

```
UNION
SELECT Region,
       CustomerID,
       SalesAmount,
       SalesDate,
       'Q22000'
FROM Q2_2000
```

Each select contains a constraint (e.g., 'Q12000') so that individual quarters can be discerned in the combined resultset.

As more quarters are added, you simply add additional code segments as shown.

```
SELECT Region,
       CustomerID,
       SalesAmount,
       SalesDate,
       'Q12000'
FROM Q1_2000
UNION
SELECT Region,
       CustomerID,
       SalesAmount,
       SalesDate,
       'Q22000'
FROM Q2_2000
UNION
SELECT Region,
       CustomerID,
       SalesAmount,
       SalesDate,
       'Q32000'
FROM Q3_2000
```

I have found the UNION operator especially useful when creating reports that require different *types* of data to be displayed on the same report. The one requirement you have to be careful of is that the column list for each SELECT must have compatible data types. The following SELECT generates an error because **CompanyName** (nvarchar) and **Freight** (money) are not compatible data types.

```
USE Northwind
go
SELECT CompanyName
FROM Customers
```

```
UNION
SELECT Freight
FROM Orders
--Results--
Server: Msg 257, Level 16, State 3, Line 1
Implicit conversion from data type nvarchar to money is not allowed. Use the CON-
VERT function to run this query.
```

When you want to create a UNION with data of different types you need to add *column fillers* to the column list. The following statement uses column fillers to facilitate the disparate data types.

```
USE Northwind
go
SELECT CompanyName, 99999 AS Freight
FROM Customers
UNION
SELECT 'ColumnFiller', Freight
FROM Orders
ORDER BY Freight
--Results (Partial)--
```

CompanyName	Freight
ColumnFiller	.0200
ColumnFiller	.1200
ColumnFiller	.1400
...	
ColumnFiller	1007.6400
Alfreds Futterkiste	99999.0000
Ana Trujillo Emparedados y helados	99999.0000
...	

Note that an ORDER BY clause could only be applied to the final SELECT statement in the UNION.

Logical Operators

A logical operator is used to test for truth in a condition. The examples covered so far have limited the use of this type of operator to AND. The more popular logical operators supported by T-SQL are described here.

AND

```
boolean_expression AND boolean_expression
```

Tests for true in both `boolean_expressions`.

OR

```
boolean_expression OR boolean_expression
```

Tests for true in either `boolean_expression`.

NOT

```
[ NOT ] boolean_expression
```

Negates a `boolean_expression`.

IN

```
test_expression [ NOT ] IN
    (
        subquery
        | expression [ ,...n ]
    )
```

Tests for existence of the `test_expression` in the `subquery` or `expression list`.

LIKE

```
match_expression [ NOT ] LIKE pattern [ ESCAPE escape_character ]
```

Tests whether `match_expression` matches the supplied character pattern. Wildcard characters are used to create varying patterns. The available wildcard characters are shown in Table 4-1.

Table 4-1. Wildcard Characters

CHARACTER	DESCRIPTION
%	A string of zero or more characters.
_	A single character.

Table 4-1. Wildcard Characters (Continued)

CHARACTER	DESCRIPTION
[ ]	A character in the specified range. The range can be specified as series of characters (e.g., [lmnopqr]) or with a hyphen between the first and last characters (e.g., [l-r]).
[^]	A character not in the specified range. The opposite of the behavior with [ ].

BETWEEN

```
test_expression [ NOT ] BETWEEN begin_expression AND end_expression
```

Tests for the existence of test_expression in the range of values.

EXISTS

```
EXISTS subquery
```

Tests for the existence of rows in the subquery.

Logical Operator Examples

Examples of how to use all the logical operators, except EXISTS, are covered here. EXISTS will be covered later in the section "Correlated Subqueries."

AND and OR   The following example shows how AND and OR are used to filter the resultset.

```
USE Northwind
go
SELECT CompanyName,
       City,
       Country
FROM Customers
WHERE City = 'London' AND
            Country = 'UK' OR
       City = 'Madrid'
--Results--
CompanyName                               City              Country
---------------------------------------   ---------------   ---------------
Around the Horn                           London            UK
Bólido Comidas preparadas                 Madrid            Spain
```

B's Beverages	London	UK
Consolidated Holdings	London	UK
Eastern Connection	London	UK
FISSA Fabrica Inter. Salchichas S.A.	Madrid	Spain
North/South	London	UK
Romero y tomillo	Madrid	Spain
Seven Seas Imports	London	UK

IN The following shows how IN is used to return the companies located in the list of cities.

```
USE Northwind
go
SELECT CompanyName,
       City
FROM Customers
WHERE City IN ('London','Madrid','Seattle')
--Results--
CompanyName                                City
------------------------------------------ ---------------
Around the Horn                            London
B's Beverages                              London
Consolidated Holdings                      London
Eastern Connection                         London
North/South                                London
Seven Seas Imports                         London
Bólido Comidas preparadas                  Madrid
FISSA Fabrica Inter. Salchichas S.A.       Madrid
Romero y tomillo                           Madrid
White Clover Markets                       Seattle
```

NOT The NOT operator can be used to negate the evaluation of the expression. The following example couples NOT with IN to return all the rows where the **City** value is not in the supplied list.

```
USE Northwind
go
SELECT CompanyName,
       City
FROM Customers
WHERE City NOT IN ('London','Madrid','Seattle')
--Results (Partial)--
```

CompanyName	City
Drachenblut Delikatessen	Aachen
Rattlesnake Canyon Grocery	Albuquerque
Old World Delicatessen	Anchorage
Vaffeljernet	Århus
...	

LIKE   LIKE is the most flexible of the logical operators. The wildcard characters allow you to create search expressions to find any character pattern. The following shows how to use LIKE to find all the company names that start with "Ch."

```
USE Northwind
go
SELECT CompanyName
FROM Customers
WHERE CompanyName LIKE 'Ch%'
--Results--
CompanyName
---------------------------------------
Chop-suey Chinese
```

The next example shows how to find all customers that have "eno" in their names.

```
USE Northwind
go
SELECT CompanyName
FROM Customers
WHERE CompanyName LIKE '%eno%'
--Results--
CompanyName
---------------------------------------
Antonio Moreno Taquería
```

The last example shows how to find the customer names that start with "A," have any character as the second letter and whose third character is in the range of "m" to "z."

```
USE Northwind
go
SELECT CompanyName
FROM Customers
WHERE CompanyName LIKE 'A_[m-z]%'
```

```
--Results--
CompanyName
----------------------------------------
Antonio Moreno Taquería
Around the Horn
```

BETWEEN   In the "WHERE" section presented earlier in the chapter, an example was covered that used `WHERE OrderDate > '1/1/97' AND OrderDate < '1/31/97'` to filter the orders in the supplied date range. A slight variation of this example can be rewritten using the BETWEEN logical operator. Be aware that it is not exactly the same as the previous example because BETWEEN includes the comparison values in the criteria. The following shows how BETWEEN is used to filter the resultset.

```
USE Northwind
go
SELECT COUNT(*)
FROM Orders
WHERE OrderDate BETWEEN '1/1/97' AND '1/31/97'
--Results--
-----------
33
```

The earlier example returned a count of 30, because it excluded orders entered on 1/1/97 and 1/31/97.

Table and Column Aliasing

Table aliasing allows you to abbreviate references to a table in a SQL statement. In order to alias a table name you simply follow the table name with `AS alias`. The following shows how to alias the **Orders** table to the letter "a."

```
USE Northwind
go
SELECT a.CompanyName
FROM Customers AS a
WHERE a.CompanyName LIKE 'M%'
--Results--
CompanyName
----------------------------------------
Magazzini Alimentari Riuniti
Maison Dewey
Mère Paillarde
Morgenstern Gesundkost
```

The alias value can be used to reference the columns that belong to the table. Table aliasing does not make much sense when only one table is involved, but as you start using JOINs and more tables are added to the mix, they can help make code easier to read.

The naming convention you use for aliases is completely arbitrary, and the only requirement is that they adhere to the rules for naming identifiers. I use the letters of the alphabet, so the first table referenced in a statement is aliased to "a," the second to "b," and so on. Many developers use the first letter of the table name, so in the previous example the alias would be "c." As you work through the examples in the next section, the benefits of table aliasing should become more evident.

The AS portion of the alias syntax is optional and will be omitted in most of the examples in the book. The following produces the same result as the previous example.

```
USE Northwind
go
SELECT a.CompanyName
FROM Customers a
WHERE a.CompanyName LIKE 'M%'
--Results--
CompanyName
----------------------------------------
Magazzini Alimentari Riuniti
Maison Dewey
Mère Paillarde
Morgenstern Gesundkost
```

Column aliasing is similar to table aliasing in that you *substitute* a new value for a column's name. In practice, the only time I use column aliasing is when a derived column is referenced in the SELECT statement. Several of the examples covered earlier used derived columns and none of them had a column name in the resultset. The following uses a previous example to demonstrate how column aliasing can add more meaning to the resultset.

```
USE Northwind
go
SELECT TOP 10 CustomerID,
              COUNT(CustomerID) AS OrderCount
FROM Orders
GROUP BY CustomerID
ORDER BY COUNT(CustomerID) DESC
--Results (Partial)--
```

```
CustomerID OrderCount
---------- -----------
SAVEA      31
ERNSH      30
...
```

Instead of having no column name over the count, `OrderCount` is designated so the results can be more easily understood. Even though AS is optional, I always include it for column aliases because it makes the code easier to read.

Analyzing the Northwind Database

The tables in the **Northwind** database are used frequently in the examples presented in Parts One and Two of the book. Most of the examples reference only one or two tables in the database so limited knowledge of the schema is sufficient. In the next section, however, there are a few examples that reference three or more tables and an understanding of how the tables are related will be helpful.

The most efficient way to learn about Northwind is to create a database diagram via Enterprise Manager. The following steps show how this is done.

1. Expand the target server, and then expand the Databases folder.

2. Right-click **Northwind**, highlight New, and select Database Diagram.

3. Click Next to get past the wizard's initial dialog.

4. In the Available table list box, select the table whose name does not begin with "sys."

5. Click Next, and then click Finish to create the diagram.

Once the diagram is displayed use the magnifying glass icon on the toolbar to increase the size of the graphics. Take a few minutes to study the relationships between the tables before continuing with the next section.

JOINs

The JOIN allows you to *combine* two or more tables to produce a resultset. It is fundamental to producing meaningful data in relational databases because in a well-normalized database the data held in individual tables is not that useful until it is related to data from the other database tables. The FROM portion of the SELECT statement is:

```
FROM Table1 INNER | {{LEFT | RIGHT | FULL [OUTER]}} | CROSS JOIN Table2
```

As you can see, only three types of JOINS are used in T-SQL:

- INNER JOIN

- OUTER JOIN

- CROSS JOINs

INNER JOIN

The INNER JOIN allows you to use comparison operators to compare the values in columns from two or more tables and join the results accordingly. Note that the INNER JOIN is the default join, so when no qualifier is provided an INNER JOIN is constructed. The simplest, most-used form of the INNER JOIN is an equi-join, where the join is contingent on columns from two or more tables being equal. There is also the not-equal join where not equal comparison operators are used to filter data. Books Online makes reference to another form of the equi-join called a natural join. A natural join simply does an equi-join on the columns with the same name from each table without specifying the column names in the ON portion of the JOIN. T-SQL, however, does not support the natural join syntax so the Books Online reference promotes confusion.

OUTER JOIN

The OUTER JOIN is more forgiving than the INNER JOIN. When an INNER JOIN is used to produce a resultset, there must be an exact match on the comparison operator in order for a row to be returned. For example, if you use an INNER JOIN to relate the **Customers** and **Orders** on **CustomerID**, only those **Customers** with a corresponding row in **Orders** will be returned.

An OUTER JOIN will return all the rows in the *base* table (**Customers**) regardless of whether there is a matching row in the join table (**Orders**). Since there are no values to return from the join table, the join table columns referenced in the select_list will contain a NULL value.

There are three versions of the OUTER JOIN: LEFT, RIGHT, and FULL. The join qualifier (e.g., LEFT) indicates which table will have all their rows returned. When LEFT is specified, the base table is on the left side of the JOIN. When RIGHT is used, the base table is on the right side of the join. The FULL option retrieves all rows from both tables, placing NULLS in the columns where there is no match with the other table. OUTER JOINs can be a little confusing, but be assured there are good reasons for having them and there use will become clearer in the OUTER JOIN Examples section later in the chapter.

Please note that the use of the word OUTER in an OUTER JOIN is optional. For example, the following two partial SELECT statements are equivalent.

```
...FROM Customers LEFT JOIN Orders ON...
...FROM Customers LEFT OUTER JOIN Orders ON...
```

I will not use OUTER in an effort to produce more compact, readable code. There is a non-ANSI version of the OUTER JOIN that has been torturing beginner SQL programmers for years. This version specifies the join type in the WHERE clause and can produce errant results. The syntax used to place the OUTER JOIN in the WHERE clause looks like the following:

```
WHERE Table1.FieldName *= Table2.FieldName
```

This syntax creates a LEFT OUTER JOIN because the asterisk is on the left side of the equal sign. To create a RIGHT OUTER JOIN you simply move the asterisk to the right side of the equal sign.

I do not want to spend any time covering why this approach produces errant results: I just want you to be aware of the syntax if you encounter it in any applications that you happen to inherit. If you do encounter a statement that uses this syntax, you need to replace it with ANSI syntax. Microsoft has been promising to remove support for the *= syntax for the last three versions of SQL Server, so you can be sure that it will eventually happen.

CROSS JOIN

A CROSS JOIN produces a resultset composed of each row in **Table1** combined with all the rows in **Table2**. I don't really know of any practical examples using the CROSS JOIN, but you definitely need to be aware of them. If you use the WHERE clause approach to specifying join conditions and forget to specify a condition, you must be able to determine why such a large resultset is produced.

INNER JOIN Examples

This section contains quite a few examples that not only show you how to join two or more tables together, but also show you how to use the SELECT clauses we covered earlier in the chapter to produce more meaningful resultsets.

Two Table Joins

The following example shows how to reference two tables in one SELECT.

```
USE Northwind
go
SELECT CompanyName, ShipName
FROM Customers, Orders
--Results (Partial)--
CompanyName                              ShipName
---------------------------------------- ----------------------------------------
Alfreds Futterkiste                      Vins et alcools Chevalier
Ana Trujillo Emparedados y helados       Vins et alcools Chevalier
...
Wolski  Zajazd                           Rattlesnake Canyon Grocery

(75530 row(s) affected)
```

This statement has an error in it and causes a useless resultset to be returned. I omitted the JOIN portion of the statement and that resulted in a CROSS JOIN (a.k.a. Cartesian product). Did you notice that 75,330 rows were returned? The **Customers** table contains 91 rows, the **Orders** table contains 830 rows, and the product of 91*830 is 75,330. Every row in **Customers** is joined to every row in **Orders**.

Let's add a JOIN so the data will be meaningful and an ORDER BY so it is easier to analyze.

```
USE Northwind
go
SELECT Customers.CompanyName,
       Orders.ShipName
FROM Customers
INNER JOIN Orders ON Customers.CustomerID = Orders.CustomerID
ORDER BY Customers.CompanyName
--Results (Partial)--
CompanyName                              ShipName
---------------------------------------- ----------------------------------------
Alfreds Futterkiste                      Alfreds Futterkiste
Alfreds Futterkiste                      Alfred's Futterkiste
...
Wolski  Zajazd                           Wolski Zajazd
Wolski  Zajazd                           Wolski Zajazd

(830 row(s) affected)
```

Notice that the column names in the select_list and the JOIN are qualified with the table names in which they are located. Qualifying column names in the select_list or JOIN is required when columns with identical names are referenced in the same statement. This allows the Query Processor to differentiate between the **CustomerID** column in **Customers** and the one in **Orders**. In this example the only identical column name is **CustomerID**: the other columns were qualified so it is easy to tell to which table they belong. The INNER JOIN on the **CustomerID** column was added and now the query returns 830 rows. If you review the resultset you will see a lot of repeating values. The following shows how the DISTINCT clause can be used to eliminate the repeating values.

```
USE Northwind
go
SELECT DISTINCT Customers.CompanyName,
                Orders.ShipName
FROM Customers
INNER JOIN Orders ON Customers.CustomerID = Orders.CustomerID
ORDER BY Customers.CompanyName
--Results (Partial)--
```

CompanyName	ShipName
Alfreds Futterkiste	Alfreds Futterkiste
Alfreds Futterkiste	Alfred's Futterkiste
...	
Wolski Zajazd	Wolski Zajazd

```
(90 row(s) affected)
```

Notice that only 90 rows are returned. The only interesting information that could be gained from analyzing this resultset is which customers use a **ShipName** that is different from their **CompanyName**. We can determine this very easily by adding a WHERE clause to the query.

```
USE Northwind
go
SELECT DISTINCT Customers.CompanyName,
                Orders.ShipName
FROM Customers
INNER JOIN Orders ON Customers.CustomerID = Orders.CustomerID
WHERE Customers.CompanyName <> Orders.ShipName
ORDER BY Customers.CompanyName
```

```
--Results--
CompanyName                              ShipName
----------------------------------       ----------------------------------------
Alfreds Futterkiste                      Alfred's Futterkiste
Blondesddsl père et fils                 Blondel père et fils
Galería del gastrónomo                   Galería del gastrónómo
Tradição Hipermercados                   Tradiçao Hipermercados
Wolski  Zajazd                           Wolski Zajazd
```

Only five rows are returned when this query is executed. If you look closely at the data, you will see that the difference between the names for each of the first four rows is a spelling error between the **CompanyName** and the **ShipName**.

The examples presented so far in this chapter use the ANSI syntax for producing an INNER JOIN. With the ANSI syntax you specify the JOIN condition in the FROM clause of the SELECT statement. You can also use the WHERE clause of the SELECT to specify a join condition. This approach is used quite heavily in the real world and sporadically in the Books Online. We can rewrite the previous example using the following syntax. Note that table aliasing is used to make the code more legible.

```
USE Northwind
go
SELECT DISTINCT a.CompanyName,
               b.ShipName
FROM Customers a, Orders b
WHERE a.CustomerID = b.CustomerID AND
      a.CompanyName <> b.ShipName
ORDER BY a.CompanyName
--Results--
CompanyName                              ShipName
----------------------------------       ----------------------------------------
Alfreds Futterkiste                      Alfred's Futterkiste
Blondesddsl père et fils                 Blondel père et fils
Galería del gastrónomo                   Galería del gastrónómo
Tradição Hipermercados                   Tradiçao Hipermercados
Wolski  Zajazd                           Wolski Zajazd
```

Both this and the ANSI syntax produce the same results, so it is simply a matter of preference as to which approach you use. As you will see in the next section, however, the location of the join criteria does affect OUTER JOINS, and the ANSI syntax must be used to produce the desired results. I am fairly rigid when it comes to producing consistent code so I will use the ANSI syntax exclusively for all further JOIN operations in this book.

The following example shows the **CompanyName** and **OrderDate** values for all customers who have placed an order.

```
USE Northwind
go
SELECT a.CompanyName, b.OrderDate
FROM Customers a
INNER JOIN Orders b ON a.CustomerID = b.CustomerID
ORDER BY a.CompanyName, b.OrderDate
--Results (Partial)--
CompanyName                          OrderDate
------------------------------------ ---------------------------

Alfreds Futterkiste                  1997-08-25 00:00:00.000
Alfreds Futterkiste                  1997-10-03 00:00:00.000
Alfreds Futterkiste                  1997-10-13 00:00:00.000
...
```

The GROUP BY and HAVING clauses were covered earlier in the chapter, so we can use them now to produce a more meaningful resultset. The following shows only those customers who have placed one order.

```
USE Northwind
go
SELECT a.CompanyName
FROM Customers a
INNER JOIN Orders b ON a.CustomerID = b.CustomerID
GROUP BY a.CompanyName
HAVING COUNT(a.CompanyName) = 1
ORDER BY a.CompanyName
--Results--
CompanyName
----------------------------------------

Centro comercial Moctezuma
```

This type of data analysis is good because it can help you identify which accounts need attention. A more realistic request, however, might be to produce a report that shows the total number of orders placed by each company sorted in descending order—from most to least number of orders. This can be done with the following:

```
USE Northwind
go
SELECT a.CompanyName,
       COUNT(a.CompanyName) AS OrderCount
```

```
FROM Customers a
INNER JOIN Orders b ON a.CustomerID = b.CustomerID
GROUP BY a.CompanyName
ORDER BY COUNT(a.CompanyName) DESC
--Results--
CompanyName                              OrderCount
---------------------------------------- -----------
Save-a-lot Markets                       31
Ernst Handel                             30
QUICK-Stop                               28
Hungry Owl All-Night Grocers             19
...
```

You might also want to look at the orders on a per-year basis and this can be accomplished with the following:

```
USE Northwind
go
SELECT a.CompanyName,
       COUNT(a.CompanyName) AS OrderCount
FROM Customers a
INNER JOIN Orders b ON a.CustomerID = b.CustomerID
WHERE b.OrderDate BETWEEN '1/1/98' AND '12/31/98'
GROUP BY a.CompanyName
ORDER BY COUNT(a.CompanyName) DESC
--Results (Partial)--
CompanyName                              OrderCount
---------------------------------------- -----------
Save-a-lot Markets                       11
Ernst Handel                             9
Folk och fä HB                           9
...
```

Note that the BETWEEN predicate is a filter on dates. Chapter 11 will demonstrate how to encapsulate this type of data analysis in a stored procedure that accepts the date range values as parameters. The stored procedure approach is much more flexible as you can pass in any date values to produce results by day, week, month, quarter, or year.

Three or More Table Joins

To add a third table to the SELECT you simply add another JOIN that references the new table. The following example shows how to retrieve the last name of the employee who is responsible for an order. It also sorts the resultset, so you can easily see which employees have helped a given customer.

```
USE Northwind
go
SELECT a.CompanyName,
       b.OrderDate,
       c.LastName
FROM Customers a
INNER JOIN Orders b ON a.CustomerID = b.CustomerID
INNER JOIN Employees c ON b.EmployeeID = c.EmployeeID
ORDER BY a.CompanyName, c.LastName
--Results (Partial)--
CompanyName                         OrderDate                  LastName
----------------------------------- -------------------------- -------------

Alfreds Futterkiste                 1998-01-15 00:00:00.000    Davolio
Alfreds Futterkiste                 1998-03-16 00:00:00.000    Davolio
Alfreds Futterkiste                 1998-04-09 00:00:00.000    Leverling
...
```

A more meaningful resultset can be produced by counting the number of orders an employee has produced for each company with the following:

```
USE Northwind
go
SELECT a.CompanyName,
       c.LastName,
       COUNT(c.LastName) AS OrderCount
FROM Customers AS a
INNER JOIN Orders b ON a.CustomerID = b.CustomerID
INNER JOIN Employees c ON b.EmployeeID = c.EmployeeID
GROUP BY a.CompanyName, c.LastName
--Results (Partial)--
CompanyName                            LastName               OrderCount
-------------------------------------- ---------------------- -----------

Berglunds snabbköp                     Buchanan               2
Blondesddsl père et fils               Buchanan               1
Bon app'                               Buchanan               1
...
```

With the same approach you can add another table to the query. This time look at the products that are associated with each order placed by a customer.

```
USE Northwind
go
SELECT a.CompanyName,
       b.OrderDate,
       d.ProductName
FROM Customers a
INNER JOIN Orders b ON a.CustomerID = b.CustomerID
INNER JOIN [Order Details] c ON b.OrderID = c.OrderID
INNER JOIN Products d ON c.ProductID = d.ProductID
GROUP BY a.CompanyName, b.OrderDate, d.ProductName
--Results (Partial)--
```

CompanyName	OrderDate	ProductName
Alfreds Futterkiste	1997-08-25 00:00:00.000	Chartreuse verte
Alfreds Futterkiste	1997-08-25 00:00:00.000	Rössle Sauerkraut
Alfreds Futterkiste	1997-08-25 00:00:00.000	Spegesild

...

Multi-table joins are simple to develop once you understand that each successive table is added with another JOIN clause.

SELF Joins

The SELF JOIN is just another form of the INNER JOIN in which a single table is joined to itself. The **Employees** table in **Northwind** has a column called **ReportsTo** that contains the employee ID of each employee's supervisor. The following example shows how to retrieve the **LastName** for both the individual employee and their supervisor.

```
USE Northwind
go
SELECT a.LastName AS Employee,
       b.LastName AS Supervisor
FROM Employees a
INNER JOIN Employees b
ON a.ReportsTo = b.EmployeeID
--Results (Partial)--
```

```
Employee            Supervisor
------------------- -------------------
Davolio             Fuller
Leverling           Fuller
Peacock             Fuller
...
```

OUTER JOIN Examples

The OUTER JOIN examples are slightly more complicated than the INNER JOIN examples, so they will be covered in a little more detail. The first shows how to return a resultset of all customers and the numbers of orders they have placed.

```
USE Northwind
go
SELECT a.CompanyName,
       COUNT(b.OrderDate) AS OrderCount
FROM Customers a
LEFT JOIN Orders b ON a.CustomerID = b.CustomerID
GROUP BY a.CompanyName
--Results (Partial)---
CompanyName                              OrderCount
---------------------------------------- -----------
Bon app'                                 17
France restauration                      3
...
FISSA Fabrica Inter. Salchichas S.A.     0
...
Franchi S.p.A.                           6
Königlich Essen                          14
Paris spécialités                        0
```

Notice that the **OrderCount** value for both FISSA Fabrica Inter. Salchichas S.A. and Paris spécialités is zero. That means no rows for these companies were in the **Orders** table. Had an INNER JOIN been used, these two companies would not have been included in the resultset because they would fail the comparison operation.

Earlier in the chapter I mentioned that the LEFT or RIGHT referred to whether the table is on the left or right side of the JOIN. I personally never use a RIGHT JOIN because I always place the *base* table on which the statement is being performed after FROM, which means it is always on the left. We can switch the order of the tables, change the LEFT to RIGHT, and produce the same results as in the previous example.

```
USE Northwind
go
SELECT b.CompanyName,
       COUNT(a.OrderDate) AS OrderCount
FROM  Orders a
RIGHT JOIN Customers b ON a.CustomerID = b.CustomerID
GROUP BY b.CompanyName
--Results (Partial)--
CompanyName                               OrderCount
---------------------------------------   -----------
Bon app'                                  17
France restauration                       3
..
FISSA Fabrica Inter. Salchichas S.A.      0
...
Franchi S.p.A.                            6
Königlich Essen                           14
Paris spécialités                         0
```

In the next example we use two LEFT JOINs in the same SELECT to ensure that no order has ever been created that does not have at least one associated **OrderDetail** record.

```
USE Northwind
go
SELECT a.CompanyName, b.OrderDate, c.OrderID
FROM Customers a
LEFT JOIN Orders b ON a.CustomerID = b.CustomerID
LEFT JOIN [Order Details] c ON b.OrderID = c.OrderID
WHERE b.OrderDate IS NOT NULL AND
      c.OrderID IS NULL
--Results--
CompanyName                               OrderDate                   OrderID
---------------------------------------   -------------------------   -----------

(0 row(s) affected)
```

As you can see, we want records where the **OrderDate** is NOT NULL (indicating an **Orders** record exists) and the **OrderID** is NULL (indicating an **OrderDetails** record does not exist).

When you execute this query, you will see that no rows are returned. This is good because having an order with no associated **OrderDetail** record would indicate a programming error in the order creation process. The proper way to ensure that records are created in both tables when a new order is entered is to wrap the INSERT statements for both tables in a TRANSACTION. Transactions are discussed at the beginning of Chapter 5.

The next example uses both an INNER and an OUTER JOIN in the same statement. Unfortunately, the **Northwind** database does not provide sufficient data to illustrate this type of statement, so we will have to add our own. If you look at the database diagram for **Northwind** (created earlier in the chapter), you will notice two tables are used to associate a customer's demographic information. **CustomerDemographics** is used to hold the actual demographic descriptor and **CustomerCustomerDemo** serves as the junction table (aka associative table) that relates one or more **CustomerDemographic** rows to a customer.

If this was a production database (used by a real company) and the customer demographic information was populated, one of the things that would be interesting to determine is what are the demographics associated with the customers who have never placed an order. You identified those customers earlier, so now add a demographic row for one of them in order to demonstrate the statement combining an INNER and OUTER JOIN.

The first thing you need to do is add a row to **CustomerDemographics** with the following INSERT statement.

```
USE Northwind
go
INSERT CustomerDemographics (CustomerTypeID,CustomerDesc)
VALUES ('A1','Annual revenue less than $100,000')
--Results--
(1 row(s) affected)
```

Next INSERT two rows in **CustomerCustomerDemo** that contain the **CustomerID**s for Paris spécialités and FISSA Fabrica Inter. Salchichas S.A. and the **CustomerTypeID** for the row we just created in **CustomerDemographics**. The **CustomerID** values for Paris spécialités and FISSA Fabrica Inter. Salchichas S.A. are "PARIS" and "FISSA," so the following INSERTs will create the needed rows.

```
USE Northwind
go
INSERT CustomerCustomerDemo (CustomerID, CustomerTypeID) VALUES ('PARIS','A1')
INSERT CustomerCustomerDemo (CustomerID, CustomerTypeID) VALUES ('FISSA','A1')
--Results--
(1 row(s) affected)
(1 row(s) affected)
```

Now that the data has been *fixed*, the following statement is executed to show the demographic information associated with each customer who has never placed an order.

```
USE Northwind
go
SELECT a.CompanyName, d.CustomerDesc
FROM Customers a
LEFT JOIN Orders b ON a.CustomerID = b.CustomerID
INNER JOIN CustomerCustomerDemo c ON a.CustomerID = c.CustomerID
INNER JOIN CustomerDemographics d ON c.CustomerTypeID = d.CustomerTypeID
WHERE b.OrderDate IS NULL
--Results--
CompanyName                              CustomerDesc
---------------------------------------  ----------------------------------
FISSA Fabrica Inter. Salchichas S.A.     Annual revenue less than $100,000
Paris spécialités                        Annual revenue less than $100,000
```

As you can see from the INNER JOIN on **CustomerCustomerDemo**, this query assumes the tracking demographic information was required. Obviously this was not the case, but for the sake of this example we needed to assume this was true.

Subqueries

A subquery is a SELECT statement that returns a fixed resultset and is nested in a SELECT, INSERT, UPDATE, or DELETE statement or another subquery. A subquery is often referred to as an inner query because it is located within another SELECT statement. When a subquery is used with a SELECT statement, the *first* SELECT is referred to as an outer query. This may seem confusing, but we can clear this up by taking a look at a few examples.

The following SELECT returns the product name for every product whose unit price is greater than the average unit price of all products. The aggregate function AVG simply calculates the average of all the values in the **UnitPrice** column.

```
USE Northwind
go
SELECT ProductName, CategoryID
FROM Products
WHERE UnitPrice > (SELECT AVG(UnitPrice)
                   FROM Products)
```

```
--Results (Partial)--
ProductName                              CategoryID
---------------------------------------- -----------
Uncle Bob's Organic Dried Pears          7
Northwoods Cranberry Sauce               2
Mishi Kobe Niku                          6
...
```

`SELECT ProductName…` is the outer query and `SELECT AVG(UnitPrice)…` is the inner query.

The subquery definition states that it must return a fixed resultset—one value. If the AVG function was omitted in the previous example, all the **UnitPrice** values would have been returned and the following error message would have been generated.

```
Server: Msg 512, Level 16, State 1, Line 1
Subquery returned more than 1 value. This is not permitted when the subquery fol-
lows =, !=, <, <= , >, >= or when the subquery is used as an expression.
```

This requirement is pretty easy to understand because the comparison operators referenced in the error message require a single value in order to be evaluated. The definition does, however, get a little confusing when a subquery is used to check for existence (IN or NOT IN). For example, the following returns the **CompanyName** of the customers who have never placed an order.

```
USE Northwind
go
SELECT CompanyName
FROM Customers
WHERE CustomerID NOT IN (SELECT CustomerID
                         FROM Orders)

--Results--
CompanyName
-----------------------------------------
FISSA Fabrica Inter. Salchichas S.A.
Paris spécialités
```

The inner query obviously returns more than one value. (As a matter of fact it returns 830.) The inner query is processed first (once) and its resultset is used to test existence for the outer query. This is analogous to using the IN with a list of values—e.g., IN ('London', 'Madrid', 'Seattle').

The last example uses a subquery in an expression. The next statement calculates the difference in an individual product's price from the lowest, average and maximum prices of all products and then sorts the resultset on the minimum difference (the same as sorting on **UnitPrice**).

```
USE Northwind
go
SELECT UnitPrice,
       (SELECT MIN(UnitPrice) FROM Products) AS MinPrice,_
       UnitPrice - (SELECT MIN(UnitPrice) FROM Products) AS MinDifference,
       (SELECT AVG(UnitPrice) FROM Products) AS AvgPrice,_
       UnitPrice - (SELECT AVG(UnitPrice) FROM Products) AS AvgDifference,
       (SELECT MAX(UnitPrice) FROM Products) AS MaxPrice,_
       UnitPrice - (SELECT MAX(UnitPrice) FROM Products) AS MaxDifference
FROM Products
ORDER BY MinDifference
--Results (Partial)--
UnitPrice MinPrice MinDifference AvgPrice AvgDifference MaxPrice MaxDifference
--------- -------- ------------- -------- ------------- -------- ------------
18.0000   2.5000   15.5000       29.0455  -11.0455      263.5000 -245.5000
19.0000   2.5000   16.5000       29.0455  -10.0455      263.5000 -244.5000
10.0000   2.5000   7.5000        29.0455  -19.0455      263.5000 -253.5000
...
```

TIP   Re-Creating Northwind

Some of the examples in this chapter make changes to the data in the ***Northwind*** *database. If you want to restore* ***Northwind*** *to its original state you can use the instnwnd.sql file that is copied to you hard drive when SQL Server is installed. The file is located in the* ***MSSQL\install*** *subdirectory and contains the statements to drop and recreate the database—restoring it to its original state. If you installed SQL Server 2000 as an upgrade to an existing version, the MSSQL subdirectory will be located off the root of the C drive (default installation). If you performed a "clean" install (no existing versions of SQL Server) the subdirectory will be located under the Program Files\Microsoft SQL Server subdirectory.*

Correlated Subqueries

A correlated subquery is one where the inner query references columns in the outer query. This type of subquery is used as a pseudo looping operation because the inner query is executed for each row processed by the outer query. Note that an important factor in discerning a subquery (discussed in the previous section) from a correlated subquery is that a subquery can be executed on its own. The inner query (in bold) in the example shown below can be executed on its own and the average unit price of all products will be returned.

```
SELECT ProductName
FROM Products
WHERE UnitPrice > (SELECT AVG(UnitPrice)
                   FROM Products)
```

A correlated subquery is dependent on the outer query and cannot be executed on its own.

Let's look at an example to see how the correlated subquery is processed. The following shows the most recent order date for each customer who has placed an order.

```
USE Northwind
go
SELECT CompanyName,
       (SELECT MAX(OrderDate)
        FROM Orders
        WHERE Customers.CustomerID = Orders.CustomerID) AS LastOrder
FROM Customers
ORDER BY CompanyName
--Results--
CompanyName                          LastOrder
------------------------------------ ---------------------------

Alfreds Futterkiste                  1998-04-09 00:00:00.000
Ana Trujillo Emparedados y helados   1998-03-04 00:00:00.000
Antonio Moreno Taquería              1998-01-28 00:00:00.000
...
```

The inner query uses the current **CustomerID** value from the outer query to determine the most recent **OrderDate** using the MAX function. This type of query can be a little confusing until you picture the process in your mind. Picture the **Customers** table being processed one row at a time, and for each row the inner query is executed with the current value of the **CustomerID** column.

Most beginning SQL programmers would have implemented the previous example with a looping operation. They probably would have (depending on their experience) either created an ADO recordset or a SQL cursor and looked up the last **OrderDate** value for each record as it was being processed by the looping operation. As I stated earlier in the chapter, this is not an efficient way to perform the operation because you are not taking advantage of the inherent processing power of the database engine.

A more experienced SQL programmer would have used the GROUP BY clause and the MAX function to solve the problem. The following returns the same result-set as the previous statement in a much more efficient manner because no inner query is executed for each row in **Customers** table.

```
USE Northwind
go
SELECT CompanyName,
       MAX(OrderDate) AS LastOrder
FROM Customers
INNER JOIN Orders ON Customers.CustomerID = Orders.CustomerID
GROUP BY CompanyName
ORDER BY CompanyName
--Results (Partial)--
```

CompanyName	LastOrder
Alfreds Futterkiste	1998-04-09 00:00:00.000
Ana Trujillo Emparedados y helados	1998-03-04 00:00:00.000
Antonio Moreno Taquería	1998-01-28 00:00:00.000
...	

Earlier in the chapter I mentioned the EXISTS logical operator and it can be used as an alternative approach to using the IN operator. The EXISTS operator tests for the existence of rows by performing intersection and differences on two sets of data. The following shows how it is used with a correlated subquery to determine which customers have never placed an order.

```
USE Northwind
go
SELECT a.CompanyName
FROM Customers a
WHERE NOT EXISTS (SELECT CompanyName
                  FROM Orders b
                  WHERE a.CustomerID = b.CustomerID)
--Results--
```

```
CompanyName
-----------------------------------------
Paris spécialités
FISSA Fabrica Inter. Salchichas S.A.
```

Derived Tables

A derived table (a.k.a. materialized table) is one that is constructed with a SELECT statement and then referenced by another SELECT. This is a slightly complicated concept, but one that can be easily explained with an example. The following shows how to return all the rows in a derived table.

```
USE Northwind
go
SELECT *
FROM (SELECT CustomerID,
             CompanyName
      FROM Customers) AS DerivedTable
--Results (Partial)--
CustomerID CompanyName
---------- ----------------------------------------
ALFKI      Alfreds Futterkiste
ANATR      Ana Trujillo Emparedados y helados
ANTON      Antonio Moreno Taquería
...
```

This example has no practical value and is only used to illustrate the concept. You will realize the practical value of derived tables when you start performing summary operations. For example, the following shows how to determine the top five order-producing customers.

```
USE Northwind
go
SELECT TOP 5 WITH TIES *
FROM (SELECT CompanyName,
             COUNT(CompanyName) AS OrderCount
      FROM Customers
      INNER JOIN Orders ON Customers.CustomerID = Orders.CustomerID
      GROUP BY CompanyName) AS DerivedTable
ORDER BY OrderCount DESC
```

```
--Results--
CompanyName                              OrderCount
---------------------------------------- -----------
Save-a-lot Markets                       31
Ernst Handel                             30
QUICK-Stop                               28
Folk och fä HB                           19
Hungry Owl All-Night Grocers             19
```

The inner SELECT is used to derive an order summary table and the outer SELECT is used to get the TOP N order producers from the derived table.

Cross-Database Queries

Creating a query that retrieves data from two different databases is as easy as qualifying the tables involved in the query with the DatabaseNames in which the tables are located. The fully qualified name of a database object has the following parts.

```
ServerName.DatabaseName.Owner.ObjectName
```

In order to create a cross-database query with the examples you have been working with, you need to create one of tables in another database. The following SELECT uses the INTO clause to create the **Orders** table in the **pubs** database.

```
USE Northwind
go
SELECT *
INTO pubs..Orders
FROM Northwind..Orders
--Results--
(830 row(s) affected)
```

Now that you have another copy of **Orders** in **pubs**, you can modify one of the earlier examples to work with the new table.

```
USE Northwind
go
SELECT DISTINCT a.CompanyName, b.ShipName
FROM Customers a
INNER JOIN pubs..Orders b ON a.CustomerID = b.CustomerID
WHERE a.CompanyName <> b.ShipName
```

```
--Results--
CompanyName                              ShipName
---------------------------------------  ---------------------------------------
Alfreds Futterkiste                      Alfred's Futterkiste
Blondesddsl père et fils                 Blondel père et fils
Galería del gastrónomo                   Galería del gastronómo
Tradição Hipermercados                   Tradiçao Hipermercados
Wolski  Zajazd                           Wolski Zajazd
```

Notice no object owner was specified in these examples. You are not required to specify the owner when the object you are referencing is owned by the dbo (database owner). The biggest "gotcha" when performing cross-database queries is permissions: your login must be a user in both databases and have SELECT permission on both tables.

Cross-Server Queries

Creating a cross-server query involves some upfront work, because the server on which the query is executed (called the local server) must be made *aware* of the server where the remote data is located. In order to make a local server aware of a remote server, you must register the remote server with the local one using either the system stored procedure **sp_addlinkedserver** or the Linked Servers option via the Security folder in Enterprise Manager. For more information on how to create a linked server please see the Books Online topic: **sp_addlinkedserver.**

Assume you have two servers: Ace and Eagle, and the **Orders** table referenced in the previous example is located in the **pubs** database on Eagle. If Ace registers Eagle as a linked server, you can use the following query to retrieve data from tables.

```
SELECT DISTINCT a.CompanyName, b.ShipName
FROM Customers a
INNER JOIN Eagle.pubs.dbo.Orders b ON a.CustomerID = b.CustomerID
WHERE a.CompanyName <> b.ShipName
```

The reference to the remote table requires a four-part identifier: Server.Database.Owner.Table.

Control-of-Flow Statements

When you have two or more statements in a code segment they are, by default, executed sequentially. The following statements use a temporary table to illustrate this default behavior.

```
USE tempdb
go
CREATE TABLE #Flow
(
 Flo_UniqueID int IDENTITY,
 Flo_Name varchar(10)
)
go
INSERT #Flow (Flo_Name) VALUES ('While')

SELECT * FROM #Flow
--Results--
(1 row(s) affected)

Flo_UniqueID Flo_Name
------------ ----------
1            While
```

The temporary table **#Flow** is created, a row is inserted into **#Flow** and then the new row is retrieved with a SELECT.

The control-of-flow statements available in T-SQL allow you to alter the default behavior using conditional logic so you can control the order of execution. The following modifies the previous example so the SELECT is only executed when the **Flo_UniqueID** value is greater than five. The *current* value of **Flo_UniqueID** is determined with the @@IDENTITY function. @@IDENTITY returns the last value inserted into a column defined with the IDENTITY property.

```
USE tempdb
go
INSERT Flow (Flo_Name) VALUES ('While')
IF @@IDENTITY > 5
 BEGIN
  SELECT *
  FROM Flow
 END
--Results--

(1 row(s) affected)
```

A resultset will not be returned until the code is executed 4 more times—when the sixth row is added.

Control-of-Flow Keywords

The control-of-flow portion of T-SQL is made up of the following keywords.

BEGIN…END

The combination BEGIN…END is used to group statements for execution. The default behavior of the conditional operations discussed below is to execute a single statement if they evaluate to true; however, you can process many statements by using BEGIN…END. The following shows how to extend the previous example to execute multiple statements when the conditional operation evaluates to true.

```
USE tempdb
go
INSERT #Flow (Flo_Name) VALUES ('While')
IF @@IDENTITY > 5
 BEGIN
  SELECT *
  FROM #Flow

  SELECT COUNT(*) AS RecordCount
  FROM #Flow
 END
--Results--
(1 row(s) affected)
```

IF […ELSE]

The IF […ELSE] combination is used to control statement execution based on a Boolean expression. The complete syntax is:

```
IF Boolean_expression { sql_statement | statement_block }
[
    ELSE
    { sql_statement | statement_block } ]
```

We covered the simplest use of the statement in the previous example. The following extends the previous example to include the ELSE portion of the statement.

```
USE tempdb
go
INSERT #Flow (Flo_Name) VALUES ('While')
IF @@IDENTITY < 5
 BEGIN
  SELECT *
  FROM #Flow

  SELECT COUNT(*) AS RecordCount
  FROM #Flow
 END
ELSE
 BEGIN
  SELECT GETDATE()
 END
--Results--
(1 row(s) affected)

Flo_UniqueID Flo_Name
------------ ----------
1            While
2            While
3            While
4            While

(4 row(s) affected)

RecordCount
-----------
4
```

You should notice that the comparison operator on @@IDENTITY was changed to less than, which is why the resultset is produced.

The syntax for IF indicates a sql_statement or statement_block can be used to form the expression. The following shows how to use a sql_statement as the expression.

```
USE tempdb
go
INSERT #Flow (Flo_Name) VALUES ('While')
IF (SELECT COUNT(*) FROM #Flow) > 5
  SELECT *
  FROM #Flow
--Results--
(1 row(s) affected)
```

I did not use BEGIN...END after the IF, because only one statement was executed after the expression evaluates to true. In practice, I include BEGIN...END even if only one statement is executed. This makes the code more legible and can help eliminate programming bugs if you happen to add multiple statements after the IF, but forget to *wrap* them in BEGIN...END. The following example demonstrates what happens when multiple statements are *intended* for execution, but BEGIN...END is omitted.

```
USE tempdb
go
INSERT #Flow (Flo_Name) VALUES ('While')
IF (SELECT COUNT(*) AS RecordCount FROM #Flow) < 5
  SELECT *
  FROM #Flow

  SELECT GETDATE()
--Results--

(1 row(s) affected)


---------------------------
2000-08-16 16:12:37.123
```

The intention is to execute the two SELECT statements only when the **Record-Count** value is less than five. The second SELECT, however, is executed every time the code segment is executed because I forgot to wrap it in BEGIN...END.

WHILE

The WHILE keyword is used to create looping operations. More specifically, it is used to execute one or more statements, as long as the expression it is testing evaluates to true. The complete syntax is shown here.

```
WHILE Boolean_expression
    { sql_statement | statement_block }
    [ BREAK ]
    { sql_statement | statement_block }
    [ CONTINUE ]
```

The following shows how to use WHILE to print values to the screen as long as the expression is true.

```
DECLARE @Counter smallint
SET @Counter = 1
WHILE @Counter < 5
 BEGIN
  PRINT @Counter
  SET @Counter = @Counter + 1
 END
PRINT 'Loop Complete'
--Results--
1
2
3
4
Loop Complete
```

Once the expression evaluates to false, the looping operation is halted and the next statement that appears after END is executed.

The BREAK and CONTINUE keywords can be used to control execution within the WHILE loop. BREAK terminates execution of the WHILE loop, which causes the statement that appears after the END to execute. CONTINUE causes the WHILE loop to immediately start over. The following example shows how they are used to control flow within the looping operation.

```
USE tempdb
go
CREATE TABLE #Counter (Cou_Value tinyint)
go

DECLARE @Counter smallint
SET @Counter = 1

WHILE @Counter < 10
 BEGIN
   IF @Counter = 5
    BEGIN
     INSERT #Counter (Cou_Value) VALUES (@Counter)
     BREAK
    END
   ELSE
    BEGIN
     SET @Counter = @Counter + 1
```

```
      CONTINUE
    END
  END

SELECT Cou_Value FROM #Counter
--Results--
(1 row(s) affected)

Cou_Value
---------
5
```

The WHILE loop processes until **@Counter** reaches five, then a row is inserted into **Counter** and the loop is terminated.

WHILE loops can be nested to create a loop within a loop. The following example shows how this is implemented.

```
DECLARE @OuterCounter smallint,
        @InnerCounter smallint
SET @OuterCounter = 0
SET @InnerCounter = 1

WHILE @OuterCounter < 2
 BEGIN
  PRINT '** Outer Loop **'

   WHILE @InnerCounter < 5
    BEGIN
     PRINT 'Inner Loop'
     SET @InnerCounter = @InnerCounter + 1
    END

   SET @InnerCounter = 1
   SET @OuterCounter = @OuterCounter + 1
 END
--Results--
** Outer Loop **
Inner Loop
Inner Loop
Inner Loop
Inner Loop
** Outer Loop **
Inner Loop
Inner Loop
```

```
Inner Loop
Inner Loop
```

The inner WHILE is executed four times for every one execution of the outer WHILE.

RETURN

The RETURN keyword is used to terminate a code segment. RETURN is primarily used in stored procedures to indicate whether they were successfully executed. The following example shows how RETURN can be used in a stored procedure to return the @@ERROR value to the calling application. The @@ERROR function stores the error value for the most recently executed SQL statement. When the SQL statement executes successfully, @@ERROR is equal to zero.

```
USE tempdb
go
CREATE PROCEDURE ps_Orders_SELECT
AS
DECLARE @ErrorValue smallint

SELECT COUNT(*)
FROM Northwind..Orders

SET @ErrorValue = @@Error

RETURN @ErrorValue
go

DECLARE @ReturnValue smallint
EXEC @ReturnValue = ps_Orders_SELECT
PRINT 'Return Value = ' + CAST(@ReturnValue AS varchar(5))
--Results--
-----------
830

(1 row(s) affected)

Return Value = 0
```

WAITFOR

The WAITFOR keyword is used to delay the execution of one or more statements to the specified time. The syntax of WAITFOR follows.

```
WAITFOR { DELAY 'time' | TIME 'time' }
```

The *time* parameter must be specified in the format HH:MM:SS.

The following example shows how to create a ten-second delay between the executions of the SELECT statements.

```
WAITFOR DELAY '00:00:10'
SELECT GETDATE()
--Results--
---------------------------
2000-08-16 16:25:33.270
```

When TIME is used, you simply specify the time at which the statements that follow WAITFOR will be executed. The SELECT shown in this example will not execute until one second before midnight.

```
WAITFOR DELAY '23:59:59'
SELECT GETDATE()
```

GOTO

The GOTO keyword is used to move statement execution to an area in a batch defined as a label. The following shows how GOTO moves to a label when a test condition evaluates to true. I will use GOTO to implement error-handling code in both Chapters 11 and 14.

```
DECLARE @Counter smallint
SET @Counter = 1
WHILE @Counter < 5
 BEGIN
  IF @Counter = 3
   BEGIN
    GOTO EndOfCode
   END
  SET @Counter = @Counter+1
 END

PRINT 'Loop Complete'
```

```
EndOfCode:
PRINT 'Skipped PRINT statement'
--Results--
Skipped PRINT statement
```

CURSORS

Cursors are used to process a resultset one row at a time. If you are a beginning SQL programmer they will probably look pretty appealing to you, but I encourage you to use them as a last resort only. As I mentioned at the beginning of the chapter, SQL is a set-oriented programming language; so any approach that processes rows one at a time, as opposed to the entire set, is going to be inefficient.

The basic syntax for creating a cursor is as follows:

```
DECLARE cursor_name [ INSENSITIVE ] [ SCROLL ] CURSOR
FOR select_statement
```

You simply specify a `cursor_name` and provide the `select_statement` that populates the cursor. The INSENSITIVE argument affects how the cursor is created and whether or not data modifications made to the tables on which the `select_statement` is based are reflected in the cursor. More specifically, when INSENSITIVE is used, the cursor is created in **tempdb** and data modifications are not reflected in the cursorafter it has been created.

The SCROLL argument dictates how a cursor is navigated. If SCROLL is not used the cursor can only be processed sequentially. When SCROLL is used the cursor supports forward, backward and relative navigation.

Once a cursor is created you have to explicitly open it with the OPEN statement. The basic syntax for OPEN is shown here.

```
OPEN cursor_name
```

In order to release any locks held on the tables listed in the `select_statement`, you must CLOSE it. Closing a cursor does not remove it from memory, but FETCH statements cannot be executed against it until the cursor is reopened. The basic syntax for CLOSE follows.

```
CLOSE cursor_name
```

Creating and opening a cursor gives you a recordset to work with, but the important part is navigation. Cursor navigation is done with the FETCH statement. The basic syntax of FETCH is shown here.

```
FETCH   [ NEXT | PRIOR | FIRST | LAST ]
FROM  cursor_name
INTO @variable_name [ ,...n ]
```

The NEXT, PRIOR, FIRST, or LAST option dictates which cursor's row will be used to populate @variable_name..

While traversing a cursor, you should keep track of your location relative to its beginning and end. There is no end-of or beginning-of cursor functionality, but there is a function that indicates whether or not your last FETCH was successful. The function is @@FETCH_STATUS and it contains one of three values after a FETCH is completed. It contains 0 if the FETCH was successful, -1 if the FETCH was beyond (beginning or end) the resultset, or a –2 if the row is no longer in the cursor. The first two values are self-explanatory, but the last one may need elaboration.

The INSENSITIVE argument discussed earlier dictates whether or not a cursor is automatically updated when the tables referenced in select_statement are modified. When the cursor is automatically updated, there is a chance that a row originally included in the resultset would be removed aif it is deleted from the table referenced in select_statement. The –2 value allows you to trap for this scenario and act accordingly.

When a cursor is created, memory is allocated to hold its contents. Once you are through with a cursor, you remove it from memory using DEALLOCATE. The basic syntax of DEALLOCATE follows.

```
DEALLOCATE @cursor_variable_name
```

Now that you have covered the major components of the CURSOR let's look at an example of how they are implemented. The following example shows how to create a cursor that contains all of the user-defined tables in a database and use dynamic SQL to determine how many rows are in each table.

```
USE Northwind
go
DECLARE crs_TableCount INSENSITIVE CURSOR
FOR SELECT name
    FROM sysobjects
    WHERE xtype = 'U'

OPEN crs_TableCount

DECLARE @TableName varchar(40)
DECLARE @TableCount smallint
```

```
WHILE @@FETCH_STATUS <> -1
 BEGIN
  FETCH NEXT FROM crs_TableCount INTO @TableName
  PRINT @TableName
  EXEC('SELECT COUNT(*) FROM '+ @TableName)
 END

CLOSE crs_TableCount
DEALLOCATE crs_TableCount
--Results (Partial)--
Employees


-----------
9


Categories


-----------
8


Customers


-----------
91
...
```

We used all the cursor components previously discussed and a WHILE to modify the **@TableName** variable for each row in the cursor.

If you are not familiar with the **sysobjects** table the previous example may not make sense. The **sysobjects** table is used to hold information about all the objects in a database. The **xtype** column stores an indicator of the type of object held in each row. The value for a user-defined table is "u," so filtering for this criteria produces the desired resultset.

Another example that uses a cursor with dynamic SQL is presented in Chapter 13. In that example a stored procedure is created that allows object permissions (e.g., EXECUTE) to be dynamically applied to the specified users and objects. It's an interesting use of a cursor, but you need to have an understanding of how stored procedures work before you attempt it.

Before You Go

We covered quite a bit of material in this chapter, but if you worked through all the examples you should be pretty comfortable with the data retrieving aspect of DML. The SELECT statement and the various JOINs were covered in detail and a number of examples were presented that demonstrated how to retrieve and manipulate data stored in one or more tables. The T-SQL control-of-flow statements were used to add conditional logic to statement processing. In the last section, I presented a brief coverage of cursors.

In the next chapter you will see the data modification aspect of DML. The INSERT, UPDATE and DELETE statements will be covered and numerous examples will be presented to demonstrate how they are used to perform data modification operations.

DML: Inserting, Updating, and Deleting Data

DML (DATA MANIPULATION LANGUAGE) is the subset of T-SQL that allows you to manipulate data stored in objects created by DDL (Data Definition Language) statements. Chapter 4 covered the data retrieval aspect of DML and this chapter explores the data modification portion of DML. Data modification is fundamental to using a database, and fortunately the statements used to this are fairly straightforward. The examples presented in this chapter will demonstrate how easy it is to add, update, and delete data from a table.

> **NOTE Sample Code**
>
> *The sample code for this chapter can be downloaded at either* http://www.apress.com *or* http://www.SQLBook.com. *Download CodeCentric.zip and extract and access the Ch05.sql file.*

Before You Get Started

Before you start in on the data modification statements, I want to cover transactions. A basic understanding of how transaction logs work will help you better understand the material presented here, so if you are not familiar with them please see the Books Online topic: Transaction Log Architecture.

A transaction is the fundamental component used to ensure that two or more data modification statements that are dependent on each other are completed as a whole or not at all. The classic example illustrating the importance of a transaction is the transfer of money between two bank accounts.

Let's say you want to transfer $1,000 from your checking account to your savings account, the following statements will make the required changes; but what happens if there is a system failure after the first UPDATE is executed?

```
UPDATE Checking
SET Che_Balance = Che_Balance - 1000
WHERE Che_AcctNumber = @Che_AcctNumber

UPDATE Saving
SET Sav_Balance = Sav_Balance + 1000
WHERE Sav_AcctNumber = @Sav_AcctNumber
```

If there is a system failure after the first UPDATE statement and there is no mechanism in place to capture the fact that the second UPDATE was not executed, the Sav_Balance value is off by $1,000.

SQL Server allows you to avoid this scenario by using the BEGIN TRANS-ACTION and COMMIT TRANSACTION statements. The following shows how they *fix* the previous example.

```
BEGIN TRANSACTION
 UPDATE Checking
 SET Che_Balance = Che_Balance - 1000
 WHERE Che_AcctNumber = @Che_AcctNumber

 UPDATE Saving
 SET Sav_Balance = Sav_Balance + 1000
 WHERE Sav_AcctNumber = @Sav_AcctNumber
 COMMIT TRANSACTION
```

When the BEGIN TRANSACTION statement is executed, a *marker* is placed in the transaction log indicating the statements that follow are a part of a transaction. When the COMMIT TRANSACTION statement is executed, another marker is placed in the transaction log indicating all statements were processed and the data modifications are then committed to the database. If there is a system failure during the middle of the transaction, the close marker would not be placed in the transaction log and when the system is re-started the recovery process detects and rolls back any uncompleted transactions. In the above scenario, if a system failure occurred after the first UPDATE the statement would be rolled back when the system was restarted and the two accounts would still be in balance.

You can also explicitly *undo* data modification statements inside a transaction by using the ROLLBACK TRANSACTION statement. Once ROLLBACK TRANS-ACTION is issued, all data modification statements that have been executed since BEGIN TRANSACTION are erased and no change is made to the database.

This statement is often used in conjunction with the @@ERROR system func-tion. @@ERROR is used to determine if a SQL statement executes successfully. When a statement executes successfully, @@ERROR is equal to 0: when it fails, @@ERROR contains the ID of the error message generated. The text of the error messages generated by SQL Server is stored in the **sysmessages** table in the master database, and the message ID is contained in the **error** column. When @@ERROR is used inside a transaction, a ROLLBACK is issued when a statement does not execute successfully. The following shows how this technique is used in the previous example.

```
BEGIN TRANSACTION
 UPDATE Checking
 SET Che_Balance = Che_Balance - 1000
 WHERE Che_AcctNumber = @Che_AcctNumber
IF @@ERROR <> 0
 BEGIN
  ROLLBACK TRANSACTION
  RETURN
END

 UPDATE Saving
 SET Sav_Balance = Sav_Balance + 1000
WHERE Sav_AcctNumber = @Sav_AcctNumber
IF @@ERROR <> 0
 BEGIN
  ROLLBACK TRANSACTION
  RETURN
END
 COMMIT TRANSACTION
```

INSERT

The INSERT statement is used to insert data into a table or view. The basic syntax of the statement is shown here.

```
INSERT table_name | view_name  [( column1, column2… )] VALUES (value1, value2...)
```

You specify the table_name or view_name on which the INSERT statement operates, the columns that will be populated, and the values to be inserted into the columns. Specifying column names is optional except when the INSERT acts on a VIEW that is based on two or more tables.

Statement Permissions

Permission to execute INSERT defaults to the fixed-server role **sysadmin** and to the fixed-database roles **db_owner** and **db_datawriter**. The ability to grant INSERT permission on a table or view defaults to the members of **sysadmin**, **db_owner**, **db_ddladmin** and the object's owner and is not transferable.

Inserting Data

Let's create a table and insert some data so we can cover the various uses of the INSERT statement. The following table uses the IDENTITY property on the **Pro_UniqueID** column to generate a unique ID for each new row and includes a DEFAULT constraint on **Pro_Type** to make sure a valid property type is always assigned.

```
USE tempdb
go
CREATE TABLE Property
(
 Pro_UniqueID smallint IDENTITY PRIMARY KEY,
 Pro_Name varchar(30) NOT NULL,
 Pro_Type varchar(15) DEFAULT 'Strip Center'
)
--Results--
The command(s) completed successfully.
```

The following INSERT statement adds a row by explicitly listing the values for the columns.

```
USE tempdb
go
INSERT Property (Pro_Name, Pro_Type) VALUES ('Braes Heights','Office Building')
--Results--
(1 row(s) affected)
```

Notice that the column names of the table are included even though they are optional parameters of the statement. In my opinion, including column names in INSERT statements makes them much easier to read and maintain, so I always include them; however, you could have written the statement as follows and achieved the same results.

```
USE tempdb
go
INSERT Property VALUES ('Braes Heights','Office Building')
```

Including a reference to or a value for **Pro_UniqueID** is unnecessary because SQL Server automatically generates a value each time a row is inserted. As a matter of fact, if you try to explicitly enter a value into the column, the following error message is generated.

```
Server: Msg 8101, Level 16, State 1, Line 1
An explicit value for the identity column in table 'Property' can only be specified
when a column list is used and IDENTITY_INSERT is ON.
```

The IDENTITY_INSERT setting referenced in the error message is the table-level property that allows values to be inserted into a column defined with the IDENTITY property. The following code will set the needed table-level property, insert a row by specifying values for all three columns, and then turn off the table-level property.

```
USE tempdb
go
SET IDENTITY_INSERT Property ON
INSERT Property (Pro_UniqueID, Pro_Name, Pro_Type) _
    VALUES (2,'Sharpstown','Office Building')
SET IDENTITY_INSERT Property OFF
--Results--
(1 row(s) affected)
```

The default constraint on **Pro_Type** (defined in the CREATE TABLE statement) is the only other interesting property of the table. It allows you to avoid specifying both a column name and an associated value when the constant associated with the DEFAULT constraint is the desired value for the column. The following code will insert a new record and automatically assign the value "Strip Center" to the **Pro_Type** column.

```
USE tempdb
go
INSERT Property (Pro_Name) VALUES ('Braes Heights')
--Results--
(1 row(s) affected)
```

You can also specify the column name and still use the constant associated with the DEFAULT constraint with the following syntax.

```
USE tempdb
go
INSERT Property (Pro_Name,Pro_Type) VALUES ('Braes Heights',DEFAULT)
```

```
--Results--
(1 row(s) affected)
```

The keyword DEFAULT in the value list indicates the constant associated with the constraint should be used.

INSERT with SELECT

Using the SELECT statement with INSERT is a very efficient way to populate a table. We'll use a quick table-creation technique to see how this is accomplished. The following code uses the INTO clause of SELECT to quickly create a copy of the **Property** table. Note that the WHERE clause of the SELECT references a non-existent property name, so the comparison operation evaluates to false. When the WHERE clause evaluates to false the new table is still created, but no data is inserted. When the statements are executed, we end up with an empty table that has the same structure as the one referenced in the FROM clause.

```
USE tempdb
go
--*Create table
SELECT *
INTO Property2
FROM Property
WHERE Pro_Name = '99'
```

Now that **Property2** exists, we can populate it with the data in **Property** using the following:

```
USE tempdb
go
INSERT Property2 (Pro_Name, Pro_Type)
SELECT Pro_Name, Pro_Type
FROM Property

SELECT *
FROM Property2
--Results--

(3 row(s) affected)
```

```
Pro_UniqueID Pro_Name                         Pro_Type
------------ ---------------------------- ---------------
1            Braes Heights                    Office Building
2            Sharpstown                       Office Building
3            Braes Heights                    Strip Center
```

This approach can be used with any form of the SELECT statement, so populating tables with values from two or more tables is really easy. The following statements create a new table and then populate it with data from the **Customers**, **Orders**, and **Employees** tables in the **Northwind** database.

```
USE tempdb
go
CREATE TABLE CustomerOrderEmployee
(
 Customer nvarchar(40),
 OrderID int,
 Employee nvarchar(20)
)

INSERT CustomerOrderEmployee (Customer, OrderID, Employee)
SELECT a.CompanyName, b.OrderID, c.LastName
FROM Northwind..Customers a
INNER JOIN Northwind..Orders b ON a.CustomerID = b.CustomerID
INNER JOIN Northwind..Employees c ON b.EmployeeID = c.EmployeeID

SELECT *
FROM CustomerOrderEmployee
--Results (Partial)--
(830 row(s) affected)


Customer                                OrderID     Employee
--------------------------------------- ----------- --------------------
Vins et alcools Chevalier               10248       Buchanan
Toms Spezialitäten                      10249       Suyama
Hanari Carnes                           10250       Peacock
...
```

> **TIP Select into/bulk copy Setting No Longer Used**
>
> *In pre-2000 versions of SQL Server, you had to have the Select into/bulk copy setting set to true before SELECT…INTO could be executed in the target database. This is no longer true in SQL Server 2000, but be aware that executing SELECT…INTO can affect your ability to recover a database. Please see the Books Online topic: Selecting a Recovery Model for more information on how this statement affects the different recovery models.*

INSERT with EXEC

Inserting data into a table with the results returned by an EXEC statement is just an extension of the previous two examples. This approach can be used to insert the data returned by a stored procedure into a table as long as the stored procedure executes a SELECT or READTEXT statement. Since stored procedures have not been covered, I will keep the example simple. The following stored procedure creates a resultset that contains all the values in the **CompanyName** column of the **Customers** table.

```
USE tempdb
go
CREATE PROCEDURE ps_Customers_SELECT
AS
SELECT CompanyName
FROM Northwind..Customers
go
--Results--
The command(s) completed successfully.
```

Once it is created, you call it with the EXEC statement as shown here.

```
USE tempdb
go
EXEC ps_Customers_SELECT
--Results (Partial)--
CompanyName
----------------------------------------
Alfreds Futterkiste
Ana Trujillo Emparedados y helados
Antonio Moreno Taquería

...
```

The following code creates an empty table and then populates it with the results returned by **ps_Customers_SELECT**.

```
USE tempdb
go
CREATE TABLE CompanyNames (CompanyName nvarchar(40))
go

INSERT CompanyNames
EXEC ps_Customers_SELECT

SELECT *
FROM CompanyNames
--Results (Partial)--

(91 row(s) affected)

CompanyName
----------------------------------------
Alfreds Futterkiste
Ana Trujillo Emparedados y helados
Antonio Moreno Taquería
...
```

INSERT and VIEWs

Using INSERT to populate the tables on which a view is based is very similar to using a *real* table. The only restrictions to inserting data into a view are that it must be updateable, and that when it is based on two or more tables, only one table can be populated at a time. This topic will be covered in detail in Chapter 8.

UPDATE

The UPDATE statement allows you to modify existing data in a table or view. The basic syntax of the statement is shown here.

```
UPDATE table_name | view_name
SET column_name =  value1, value2…
[ FROM { < table_source > } [ ,...n ] ]
[WHERE < search_condition > ]
```

It allows you to specify the table or view, list individual columns within the target table, optionally reference source tables and optionally specify a search criteria.

> **TIP   Inserting Data Stored in Data Files**
>
> *One of three methods can be used when you need to insert data stored in a data file into a view or table. The three methods are Data Transformation Services (DTS) Import Wizard, the BULK INSERT statement, and the bcp command-line utility. The DTS Import Wizard is the easiest to use when working with data stored in text file format, but be aware it does not support native SQL Server format. The BULK INSERT and bcp command line utilities can be used to insert data stored in text, native and Unicode formats. A native data file is produced when the bcp command line utility is used to export data from SQL Server. The example "Calling DTS Packages via a Stored Procedure" in Chapter 13 demonstrates how to use the Import Wizard to load a text file into a table. For more information on these methods please see the appropriate Books Online topic: DTS Import/Export Wizard, BULK INSERT, or bcp utility.*

Statement Permissions

Permission to execute UPDATE defaults to the fixed-server role **sysadmin** and to the fixed-database roles **db_owner** and **db_datawriter**. The ability to grant UPDATE permission on a table or view defaults to the members of **sysadmin**, **db_owner**, **db_ddladmin** and the object's owner and is not transferable.

Updating Data

Use the **Property** table created in the previous section to experiment with the UPDATE statement. The following example shows how to change all the values in the **Pro_Type** column to "Land."

```
USE tempdb
go
UPDATE Property
SET Pro_Type = 'Land'
--Results--
(3 row(s) affected)
```

Use the statement shown here to set the values equal to the constant associated with the column's DEFAULT constraint ("Strip Center").

```
USE tempdb
go
UPDATE Property
SET Pro_Type = DEFAULT
--Results--
(3 row(s) affected)
```

It is rare that you update the values in a column for an entire table, so a more realistic example would be to use the WHERE clause to restrict which rows are updated. The following statement uses the property's name to restrict the update to one row.

```
USE tempdb
go
UPDATE Property
SET Pro_Type = 'Office Building'
WHERE Pro_Name = 'Sharpstown'
--Results--
(1 row(s) affected)
```

To update multiple columns in one statement you simply add all the desired columns and their associated values. The following shows how to update both **Pro_Name** and **Pro_Type** with one statement.

```
USE tempdb
go
UPDATE Property
SET Pro_Name = 'Sharpstown II',
    Pro_Type = 'Office Building'
WHERE Pro_Name = 'Sharpstown'
--Results--
(1 row(s) affected)
```

UPDATE and Correlated Subquery

The UPDATE statement can be used with a correlated subquery to produce useful results. Assume you have an **OrdersSummary** table that is updated with data from the **Orders** table at the end of each month. The following statements show the process for creating **OrdersSummary**, populating it with key values and then updating it with the data in **Orders**. Correlated subqueries were covered in Chapter 4.

```
USE tempdb
go
CREATE TABLE OrdersSummary
(
```

```
    CustomerID nchar(5),
    OrderCount int
)
go
--Populate OrdersSummary with IDs
INSERT OrdersSummary
SELECT CustomerID, 0
FROM Northwind..Customers
go
--*Update each ID with summary sales data
UPDATE OrdersSummary
SET OrderCount = OrderCount + (SELECT COUNT(OrderID)
                                FROM Northwind..Orders  a
                                WHERE OrdersSummary.CustomerID = a.CustomerID AND
                                    OrderDate BETWEEN '7/1/96' AND '7/31/96')


SELECT *
FROM OrdersSummary
ORDER BY OrderCount DESC,
        CustomerID
--Results (Partial)--
(91 row(s) affected)


(91 row(s) affected)

CustomerID OrderCount
---------- -----------
ERNSH      2
HANAR      2
BLONP      1
...
```

The UPDATE sets **OrderCount** equal to its current value plus the value returned by the SELECT. Simply adjust the date ranges to add additional months to the summary table. The following adds August of 1996 to the summary table.

```
UPDATE OrdersSummary
SET OrderCount = OrderCount + (SELECT COUNT(OrderID)
                                FROM Northwind..Orders AS a
                                WHERE OrdersSummary.CustomerID = a.CustomerID AND
                                    OrderDate BETWEEN '8/1/96' AND '8/31/96')
```

```
SELECT *
FROM OrdersSummary
ORDER BY OrderCount DESC,
         CustomerID
--Results (Partial)--

(91 row(s) affected)

CustomerID OrderCount
---------- -----------
QUICK      3
RATTC      3
BERGS      2
...
```

UPDATE and VIEWs

Using UPDATE to populate the tables on which a view is based in very similar to using a *real* table. The only restrictions to inserting data into a view is that it must be updateable and that when it is based on two or more tables only one table can be populated at a time. Examples of updating a view will be covered in Chapter 8.

DELETE

The DELETE statement is used to delete rows from a table or view. The basic syntax of the statement is shown here.

```
DELETE table_name | view_name
[ FROM table_source ]
[ WHERE search_condition ]
```

You specify the table or view on which the DELETE will be performed, optionally specify tables_source to restrict the rows deleted, and optionally specify search_condition to filter the rows deleted.

Statement Permissions

Permission to execute DELETE defaults to the fixed-server role **sysadmin** and to the fixed-database roles **db_owner** and **db_datawriter**. The ability to grant DELETE permission on a table or view defaults to the members of **sysadmin**, **db_owner**, **db_ddladmin** and the object's owner and is not transferable.

Deleting Data

The following example shows how to delete a single row of the **OrdersSummary** table created in the previous section.

```
USE tempdb
go
DELETE OrdersSummary
WHERE CustomerID = 'ALFKI'
--Results--
(1 row(s) affected)
```

The WHERE clause on the DELETE can be as complicated as needed. The following shows how to delete the rows in which both the **OrderCount** value is equal to two and the first character of the **CustomerID** value is 'T.'

```
USE tempdb
go
DELETE OrdersSummary
WHERE  OrderCount = 2 AND
       SUBSTRING(CustomerID,1,1) = 'T'
--Results--
(1 row(s) affected)
```

If you want to delete all the rows in the table, omit the WHERE clause as shown here.

```
USE tempdb
go
DELETE OrdersSummary
--Results--
(89 row(s) affected)
```

DELETE and FROM

You can use the FROM clause of DELETE to remove rows based on contents of one or more tables. For example, the following removes all the **Products** rows associated with the given SupplierID.

```
USE Northwind
go
DELETE Products
FROM Products a
INNER JOIN Suppliers b ON a.SupplierID = b.SupplierID AND
                          b.CompanyName = 'Pavlova, Ltd.'
```

The previous statement is valid, but if you try to execute it the following error message is generated.

```
Server: Msg 547, Level 16, State 1, Line 1
DELETE statement conflicted with COLUMN REFERENCE constraint
'FK_Order_Details_Products'. The conflict occurred in database 'Northwind', table
'Order Details', column 'ProductID'.
The statement has been terminated.
```

This tells me the designers of the **Northwind** database knew what they were doing because they implemented a FOREIGN KEY constraint that prohibits orphaned rows. Had the statement executed successfully, the **Products** data associated with the previously entered **Orders** (actually **OrderDetails**) would have been deleted. If this happens you *lose* the products for all orders that referenced the deleted products. When the parent row of a parent-child relationship is deleted, the remaining child row is referred to as *orphaned* and is of no value to the database. In other words, when the parent row is deleted the child becomes useless because it points to a non-existent row in the parent table.

TIP   TRUNCATE TABLE versus DELETE

The TRUNCATE TABLE statement can be used to remove all the rows from a table and is much more efficient than using the DELETE statement to perform the same operation. The reason for this is that DELETE is a fully logged operation, which means the DELETE for each row is stored in the transaction log. The TRUNCATE TABLE statement, on the other hand, only logs the extents (defined in the "Space-Used Calculation" sidebar in Chapter 2) used by the table, so the amount of time spent logging the process is significantly reduced. The TRUNCATE TABLE statement, unlike DELETE, does not cause the triggers attached to a table to fire.

Before You Go

This chapter covered the DML statements that allow you to insert, update, and delete data in a table or view. It also demonstrated how transactions can be used to ensure that all statements in a multi-statement batch are successfully executed before the changes are committed to the database.

In the next chapter you are going to cover some of the more useful functions that come with SQL Server 2000. For example, you will learn how to use the SUB-STRING function to manipulate character strings and the CONVERT function to display datetime values in varying formats. Using T-SQL built-in functions is key to advancing your skills as a SQL programmer, so I encourage you to read the chapter thoroughly.

CHAPTER 6

Built-In Functions

THERE ARE TWO TYPES OF FUNCTIONS AVAILABLE in SQL Server 2000: built-in and user-defined. *Built-in functions* are a part of T-SQL, and they are similar in nature to functions you have used in other programming languages. For example, Visual Basic uses the NOW function to return the current system time while T-SQL uses the GETDATE() function to return the same information. *User-defined functions*, which are new to SQL 2000, are functions you create using the CREATE FUNC-TION statement. User-defined functions are covered in detail in Chapter 7.

SQL Server 2000 comes with more than 140 built-in functions. They are broken into ten categories, but we are only going to cover five of them in this chapter. As a matter of fact, we are not even going to cover all the functions in each of the five categories, just the ones you are most likely to use in your programming endeavors. *All* the functions used in the examples throughout the book are covered here, so if while working through the examples you run across one you are not familiar with, you can find a detailed explanation in this chapter. For complete coverage of all the built-in functions see the Books Online topic: Functions.

> **NOTE Sample Code**
>
> *The sample code for this chapter can be downloaded at either* http://www.apress.com *or* http://www.SQLBook.com. *Download CodeCentric.zip and extract and access the Ch06.sql file.*

Before You Get Started

Before we dive into the functions, let's cover three topics that will help you understand when functions can be used, how a server configuration setting can affect their behavior, and an easy way to help remember their syntax.

Deterministic versus Nondeterministic Functions

Functions are classified as either *deterministic* or *nondeterministic*. Deterministic functions are those that return the same value every time they are executed with the same parameters. A good example of a deterministic function is LEN, which returns the number of characters that make up a character string (e.g., LEN('ABC') = 3). Every time you execute LEN with the same parameter, the exact same integer value is returned. Nondeterministic functions may not return the same value when executed with the same parameters. GETDATE() is a perfect example of a nondeterministic function.

This categorization of functions is new to SQL Server 2000 and has an effect on computed columns and views. An index cannot be created on a computed column based on a nondeterministic function. In like manner, a clustered index cannot be created on a view that contains a nondeterministic function.

Database Compatibility Levels

The database compatibility level configuration, introduced in SQL Server 7, lets you control the functionality a database supports. It was added for two main reasons:

- SQL Server 7 introduced changes that altered the expected behavior of pre-7 functionality.

- A tremendous number of applications written around pre-7 behavior would *break* when they were upgraded to SQL Server 7.

The compatibility setting allowed developers to ease into SQL Server 7. They were able to upgrade and gain the performance benefits and administrative enhancements that were added, but still maintain the expected behavior of the pre-7 versions.

In order to check and set a database's compatibility setting, you use the system stored procedure sp_dbcmptlevel. The complete syntax for sp_dbcmptlevel follows:

```
sp_dbcmptlevel [ [ @dbname = ] name ]    [ , [ @new_cmptlevel = ] version ]
```

To determine the compatibility level of **Northwind** execute the following in Query Analyzer.

```
USE Northwind
go
sp_dbcmptlevel 'Northwind'
--Results--
The current compatibility level is 80.
```

To change **Northwind**'s compatibility setting to 65 (and then back to 80), use the following:

```
USE Northwind
go
sp_dbcmptlevel 'Northwind','65'
go
sp_dbcmptlevel 'Northwind'
go
sp_dbcmptlevel 'Northwind','80'
go
sp_dbcmptlevel 'Northwind'
--Results--
DBCC execution completed. If DBCC printed error messages, contact your system
administrator.
The current compatibility level is 65.
DBCC execution completed. If DBCC printed error messages, contact your system
administrator.
The current compatibility level is 80.
```

The domain of version is 80, 70, 65, and 60 and these values are displayed when **sp_dbcmptlevel** is executed without parameters.

When a database's compatibility setting is less than 80, it will not support functionality introduced in SQL Server 2000. If a database's compatibility setting is 65 or less, it will not support functionality introduced in either SQL Server 7 or SQL Server 2000. This setting has caused problems for more than a handful of developers. They read a Books Online topic and implement code per the descriptions and examples provided, only to encounter errors. If this happens to you, check the compatibility setting of the database to make sure it is set to the proper value for the functionality you are trying to implement.

Object Browser and Function Syntax

The built-in functions provided with SQL Server 2000 are in some cases very similar to those provided with other programming languages. When you use two or more programming languages that possess similar syntax for the same function, it is easy to mix up the two *versions*, which results in having to look up the function's syntax in a language resource. SQL Server 2000 eliminates the lookup process for T-SQL functions by including their syntax in Object Browser.

Object Browser is a component within Query Analyzer that provides information on the tables, views, stored procedures, and functions within a database. If you need help remembering the exact syntax of a function (or simply want to save some typing), you can use this new functionality to quickly copy-n-paste it into Query Analyzer.

For example, to use the new feature to copy-n-paste the syntax for the SUBSTRING function, follow these steps.

1. If the Object Browser is not activated in Query Analyzer, press F8.

2. Expand the String Functions folder (a sub-folder in Common Objects).

3. Right-click SUBSTRING, highlight Script Object to Clipboard As, and select Execute.

4. Place the cursor in the Editor Pane, right-click, and select Paste.

The syntax for each and every built-in function is only a few clicks away.

String Functions

The string functions that come with SQL Server 2000 manipulate character data and are very similar to many that you will find in other programming languages. String functions are used quite often in database applications, so we will cover a number of examples here.

ASCII

```
ASCII ( character_expression )
```

The ASCII function returns the ASCII value associated with a character. The following shows how to return the ASCII value associated with the upper and lowercase 'W.'

```
SELECT ASCII('W'), ASCII('w')
--Results--
----------- -----------
87          119
```

ASCII can help implement pseudo-case-sensitive searches. Assume you have a column called **Descriptor,** it contains values that have identical character patterns, but the first letter for each identical pattern is either upper- or lowercase. Furthermore, you want to implement search criteria that filters on the proper case. The following shows how to do this with the ASCII function. Note that a temporary table is used in this example. Temporary tables are declared with the # sign and exist until the connection in which they were created is closed. For more information on temporary tables please see the "Temporary Tables" tip in Chapter 3.

```
USE tempdb
go
CREATE TABLE #CaseSensitive (Descriptor varchar(10))
go
INSERT #CaseSensitive VALUES ('sosa')
INSERT #CaseSensitive VALUES ('Sosa')
go
DECLARE @Descriptor varchar(10)
SET @Descriptor = 'Sosa'

SELECT Descriptor
FROM #CaseSensitive
WHERE Descriptor = @Descriptor AND
      ASCII(Descriptor) = ASCII(@Descriptor)
--Results--
Descriptor
----------
Sosa
```

The first comparison operator in the WHERE clause restricts the resultset to the sosa rows, and the second gets the matching ASCII value for the first character in the **@Descriptor** variable. By default, the ASCII function returns the leftmost character in the string so there was no need to specify which character was used for the comparison. You can extend this example to test the ASCII values of all the characters in a string, but you have to use a looping operation (described in Chapter 4) and the SUBSTRING function, which is described later in this section.

The previous example was presented for illustrative purposes only. If you need to implement a case-sensitive search on a database that is not configured as case-sensitive, use the CAST function to convert both sides of the comparison operation to the varbinary data type. The following shows how CAST is used with the previous example to implement this technique.

```
DECLARE @Descriptor varchar(10)
SET @Descriptor = 'Sosa'

SELECT Descriptor
FROM #CaseSensitive
WHERE CAST(Descriptor AS varbinary) = CAST(@Descriptor AS varbinary)
--Results--
Descriptor
----------
Sosa
```

CAST is discussed in the "System Functions" section later in this chapter.

CHAR

```
CHAR ( integer_expression )
```

The CHAR function returns the ASCII character associated with the supplied integer. The following shows how to use the WHILE construct to display the printable range of ASCII characters.

```
DECLARE @Value smallint
SET @Value = 33
WHILE @Value <= 126
 BEGIN
  PRINT CHAR(@Value)
  SET @Value = @Value + 1
 END
--Results (Partial)--
!
"
#
$
%
...
z
{
|
}
~
...
```

CHARINDEX

```
CHARINDEX ( expression1 , expression2 [ , start_location ] )
```

The CHARINDEX function finds the starting location of one or more characters within a character string. The following shows how you find the first comma in a comma-separated string.

```
DECLARE @String varchar(25)
SET @String = '1,2,3,4'
SELECT CHARINDEX(',',@String)
--Results--
-----------
2
```

The string you are looking for is expression1, and expression2 is the string to be searched. You can use the optional start_location parameter to specify the start position of the search. The following shows how to find the location of the first comma after the third character (2) in the string.

```
DECLARE @String varchar(25)
SET @String = '1,2,3,4'
SELECT CHARINDEX(',',@String,3)
--Results--
-----------
4
```

The value returned is "4," which means CHARINDEX always returns the location relative to the beginning of the string, and not the start_location.

You can also use CHARINDEX to find the starting position of a character pattern (more than one character) within a character string. The following shows how to find the start position of the double-dashes.

```
DECLARE @String varchar(25)
SET @String = 'A329--Big Bertha 9'
SELECT CHARINDEX('--',@String)
--Results--
-----------
5
```

When expression1 is not found within expression2, a zero is returned.

CHARINDEX is one of the functions whose behavior changes depending on a database's compatibility setting. More specifically, when the setting is 65, the function returns NULL if both `expression1` and `expression2` are NULL. When set to 70 or higher, the function returns NULL if either expression is NULL.

LEFT

```
LEFT ( character_expression , integer_expression )
```

The LEFT function returns the specified number of characters starting from the leftmost character of the column. The following shows how to return the four left-most characters in the string.

```
DECLARE @String varchar(25)
SET @String = '1,2,3,4'
SELECT LEFT(@String,4)
--Results--
----
1,2,
```

LEN

```
LEN ( string_expression )
```

The LEN function determines the number of characters that make up a character string. The following shows how to determine the number of characters in the **@String** variable used in the previous example.

```
DECLARE @String varchar(25)
SET @String = '1,2,3,4'
SELECT LEN(@String)
--Results--
-----------
7
```

LOWER

```
LOWER ( character_expression )
```

You convert a character string to all lowercase characters with the LOWER function. The following shows how to use LOWER to convert the value in **@String** to lowercase letters.

```
DECLARE @String varchar(10)
SET @String = 'GRIFFEY'
SELECT LOWER(@String)
--Results--
--------------------
griffey
```

LTRIM

```
LTRIM ( character_expression )
```

The LTRIM function removes blank spaces that precede a character string. The following shows how LTRIM is used.

```
USE tempdb
go
CREATE TABLE #LTRIM_Example (Descriptor varchar(10))
go
INSERT #LTRIM_Example VALUES ('  Sosa')
SELECT Descriptor FROM #LTRIM_Example
SELECT LTRIM(Descriptor) FROM #LTRIM_Example
--Results--
Descriptor
----------
  Sosa


----------
Sosa
```

The first SELECT retrieves the value with the leading blanks, while the second removes them.

I have only used LTRIM a few times in practice and each time was a result of an existing programming error. More specifically, code had been implemented that did not check for and reject leading blanks, and this caused queries to produce undesired results when the column was referenced in a WHERE clause. In our last example, the following SELECT would not return any rows because the blanks would cause the comparison to evaluate to false.

```
SELECT Descriptor
FROM #LTRIM_Example
WHERE Descriptor = 'Sosa'
--Results--
Descriptor
----------
```

If you encounter a situation where a column's values have one or more leading blanks, you can use the following approach to remove them.

```
UPDATE #LTRIM_Example
SET Descriptor = SUBSTRING(Descriptor,2,LEN(Descriptor))
WHERE SUBSTRING(Descriptor,1,1) = ' '
--Results--
The command(s) completed successfully.
```

When more than one leading blank is present, you simply execute the statement for each blank. You can, of course, implement a looping operation that will loop until there are no more leading blanks, but the approach used here is good enough if you are only going to use it occasionally.

NCHAR

```
NCHAR ( integer_expression )
```

The NCHAR function displays the Unicode character associated with a given integer. If you are not familiar with Unicode, please see "Character Data Type (Unicode)" in Chapter 2. The following shows how to display the character associated with the value "202."

```
SELECT NCHAR(202)
--Results--
----
Ê
```

PATINDEX

```
PATINDEX ( '%pattern%' , expression )
```

The PATINDEX function finds the starting location of a character pattern within a character string. The % characters indicate the ability to use wildcard characters in the search. The PATINDEX function, unlike CHARINDEX, can be used on columns defined with the text data type. The following shows how it works.

```
USE tempdb
go
CREATE TABLE #PATINDEX_Example (Descriptor varchar(100))
Go
INSERT #PATINDEX_Example VALUES ('Baseball is as American as apple pie')
go
SELECT PATINDEX('%merica%',Descriptor) FROM #PATINDEX_Example
--Results--
-----------
17
```

The result is "17," which is the character position of the 'm' in "American."

The function returns a zero when the pattern is not found, so PATINDEX can be used in a WHERE clause to filter on the provided character pattern. The following inserts two more rows into #**PATINDEX_Example** and shows how to use PATINDEX in a WHERE clause.

```
INSERT #PATINDEX_Example VALUES ('The Dallas Cowboys are America''s team')
INSERT #PATINDEX_Example VALUES ('Tiger Woods is the world''s greatest golfer')
go
SELECT Descriptor
FROM #PATINDEX_Example
WHERE PATINDEX('%America%',Descriptor) > 0
--Results--
Descriptor
--------------------------------------------------------------------------------
The Dallas Cowboys are America's team
```

If you examine the INSERT statements you will notice that double single-quotes are used to insert an apostrophe in the column. If they are not used an error is generated because the database engine would try to execute the statement using only the part up to the second single quote, and that results in an invalid statement. When you embed either a single or double-quote within a character string, double-up on the quote character so it will not *break apart* the statement.

REPLACE

```
REPLACE ( 'string_expression1' , 'string_expression2' , 'string_expression3' )
```

The REPLACE function replaces string_expression2 with string_expression3 in the parent string, string_expression1. The following shows how REPLACE works.

```
DECLARE @ParentString varchar(50)
SET @ParentString = 'Tiger Woods is the world''s greatest golfer'
SELECT REPLACE (@ParentString, 'o' , 'x' )
--Results--
------------------------------------------------------------
Tiger Wxxds is the wxrld's greatest gxlfer
```

REVERSE

```
REVERSE ( character_expression )
```

The REVERSE function is used to reverse the order of a character string. The following demonstrates how the function is used to alter the order of a character string.

```
SELECT REVERSE ('Tiger Woods is the world''s greatest golfer')
--Results--
-----------------------------------------
reflog tsetaerg s'dlrow eht si sdooW regiT
```

REVERSE can also be used to find the last occurrence of a character in a string The following shows how to find the last comma in the string.

```
DECLARE @String varchar(25)
SET @String = '1,2,3,4'
SELECT CHARINDEX(',',REVERSE(@String))
--Results--
-----------
2
```

RIGHT

```
RIGHT ( character_expression , integer_expression )
```

The RIGHT function returns the given number of characters starting at the right-most position of the column. The following, using the **#PATINDEX_Example** table created in a previous example, shows how RIGHT is implemented.

```
SELECT RIGHT(Descriptor,10) FROM #PATINDEX_Example
--Results--
----------
ica's game
ica's team
est golfer
```

The only thing you need to keep in mind when working with RIGHT is that it will return blank values for columns defined with char or nchar if the specified column positions are not populated. The following example demonstrates this behavior. (Notice that **Descriptor** is defined using char, not varchar.)

```
CREATE TABLE #RIGHT_Example (Descriptor char(10))
go
INSERT #RIGHT_Example VALUES ('1234567890')
INSERT #RIGHT_Example VALUES ('12345')
go
SELECT RIGHT(Descriptor,5)

FROM #RIGHT_Example
--Results--
-----
67890
```

Two rows are returned when you execute the statements, but you will only see one value "67890." The second row returns blank spaces for the last five column positions.

RTRIM

```
RTRIM ( character_expression )
```

The RTRIM function removes all blank spaces to the right of the last character in a column. It can be used with the **#Right_Example** temporary table created in the last example to remove the blanks to the right of the character strings.

```
SELECT RIGHT(RTRIM(Descriptor),5) FROM #RIGHT_Example
--Results--
-----
67890
12345
```

The RTRIM function trims all the blank spaces that occur after the last character of all columns, so as long as the column is populated a value will be displayed.

STR

```
STR ( float_expression [ , length [ , decimal ] ] )
```

The STR function converts approximate numeric data to a character expression. The following shows how STR works:

```
DECLARE @Value float
SET @Value = 4534.876

SELECT STR(@Value)
SELECT STR(@Value,6,1)
SELECT STR(@Value,8,3)
--Results--
----------
      4535


------
4534.9


--------
4534.876
```

Note that only part of the value in **@Value** is returned until the third SELECT is executed. The other STR function calls do not specify proper length and decimal values, so only the portion that *fits* is returned.

SUBSTRING

```
SUBSTRING ( expression , start , length )
```

The SUBSTRING function retrieves the specified number of characters when character data is supplied and the specified number of bytes when image or text data is supplied. The basic use with character data is shown here.

```
DECLARE @Value varchar(25)
SET @Value = 'A342-Titlest 975D'

SELECT SUBSTRING(@Value,6,25)
```

```
--Results--
------------------------
Titlest 975D
```

The function returns all characters past the fifth one (the '-').

On many occasions, I have encountered a column whose values were a con-catenation of a product code and a descriptor. The previous example is similar to what I have seen, but most of the time the code portion varied in length. Imple-menting a basic SUBSTRING does not work because you do not know what value to specify for the start argument. The CHARINDEX function can be used in these situations because it returns the starting position of the code-descriptor separator, and we can use that value to retrieve the desired portion of the string. The follow-ing example shows how this is implemented.

```
CREATE TABLE #SUBSTR_Example (Descriptor varchar(35))
go
INSERT #SUBSTR_Example VALUES ('A432-Titlest 975D')
INSERT #SUBSTR_Example VALUES ('B1432-Scotty Cameron Putter')
INSERT #SUBSTR_Example VALUES ('C14-Golden Bear Irons')

SELECT SUBSTRING(Descriptor, CHARINDEX('-',Descriptor)+1,25) AS ProductDescription
FROM #SUBSTR_Example
--Results--
ProductDescription
------------------------
Titlest 975D
Scotty Cameron Putter
Golden Bear Irons
```

The data encoding shown in this example is not good database design because it results in multi-value columns, which violates a fundamental rule of normaliza-tion. The proper way to store these values is in their own columns. I only covered the *decoding* technique because you are bound to run into it if you work with databases for very long.

UNICODE

```
UNICODE ( 'ncharacter_expression' )
```

The UNICODE function works in the same manner as CHAR, except that it returns the Unicode integer mapping for the first character in the supplied expession. The follow-ing example shows how it determines the Unicode value for the Arabic letter 'Ê.'

```
SELECT UNICODE('ÊÓÜÜÇáÜÜí')
--Results--
-----------
202
```

UPPER

```
UPPER ( character_expression )
```

The UPPER function simply converts all characters in a string to their uppercase equivalents. This is the reverse of the LOWER function. The following shows how it is used.

```
DECLARE @String varchar(10)
SET @String = 'griffey'
SELECT UPPER(@String)
--Results--
--------------------
GRIFFEY
```

Date and Time Functions

Over the last two years of participating in the SQL Server newsgroups, I have seen countless requests that ask how to manipulate datetime data. The examples shown in this section should cover the possible scenarios you will encounter on your projects. Before we get started on these functions I want to cover what might be a point of confusion to those readers who are new to SQL Server: there is no data type that only stores date values. The datetime data type, as the name suggests, stores both a date and a time value. If you do not include the time portion when inserting data in a column or variable defined as datetime, the time portion defaults to midnight. If only the time value is specified, the date portion defaults to 1/1/1900. The following demonstrates the default properties.

```
--*Specify date portion only
DECLARE @DateValue datetime
SET @DateValue = '1/1/2000'
SELECT @DateValue
--Results--
--------------------------
2000-01-01 00:00:00.000
--*Specify time portion only
DECLARE @DateValue datetime
```

```
SET @DateValue = '11:00:00.000'
SELECT @DateValue
--Results--
--------------------------
1900-01-01 11:00:00.000
```

There is another nuance to working with datetime data that confuses developers and it concerns the century portion of the data. When only the year is specified, any value equal to or greater than 50 will default to 1900 (e.g., 1950) while any value less than 50 will default to 2000 (e.g., 2049). The following examples demonstrate this default behavior.

```
--*Example 1
DECLARE @DateValue datetime
SET @DateValue = '1/1/50'
SELECT @DateValue
--Results--
-------------------------------------------------------
1950-01-01 00:00:00.000
```

```
--*Example 2
DECLARE @DateValue datetime
SET @DateValue = '1/1/49'
SELECT @DateValue
--Results--
-------------------------------------------------------
2049-01-01 00:00:00.000
```

DATEADD

```
DATEADD ( datepart , number, date )
```

The DATEADD function performs date math. You supply a date, the part of the date you want to add or subtract, and the number of units to add or substract. The most-used values for datepart are year, quarter, month, week, day, hour, and minute. For additional values supported, please see the Books Online topic "DATEADD." The following shows how DATEADD is used:

```
DECLARE @DateValue smalldatetime
SET @DateValue = '10/22/99'
SELECT DATEADD(year,1,@DateValue)
SELECT DATEADD(quarter,1,@DateValue)
SELECT DATEADD(month,1,@DateValue)
```

```
SELECT DATEADD(week,1,@DateValue)
SELECT DATEADD(day,1,@DateValue)
SELECT DATEADD(hour,1,@DateValue
--Results--
--------------------------
2000-10-22 00:00:00


 --------------------------
2000-01-22 00:00:00


 --------------------------
1999-11-22 00:00:00


--------------------------
1999-10-29 00:00:00


--------------------------
1999-10-23 00:00:00


--------------------------
1999-10-22 01:00:00
```

The DATEADD function can be especially useful if you want to create a *rolling* period filter criteria. Say you want to give end users the ability to query order information with a start date range, but the length of range is specified in units. For example, how many orders were placed within ten days of 4/1/98? The following shows how this query is constructed using the BETWEEN function.

```
USE Northwind
go
DECLARE @DateStart smalldatetime,
        @RangeValue smallint
SET @DateStart = '4/1/98'
SET @RangeValue = 10
SELECT COUNT(OrderDate)
FROM Orders
WHERE OrderDate BETWEEN @DateStart AND DATEADD(day,@RangeValue,@DateStart)
--Results--
-----------
27
```

DATEDIFF

```
DATEDIFF ( datepart , startdate , enddate )
```

You determine the specified difference between two date values with the DATED-IFF function. Like with DATEADD, you specify datepart to get a particular *piece* of the calculation. The following shows how to use DATEDIFF to find some common differences between two dates.

```
DECLARE @StartDate smalldatetime, @EndDate smalldatetime
SET @StartDate = '2/1/00'
SET @EndDate = '6/24/00'

SELECT DATEDIFF(month,@StartDate,@EndDate)
SELECT DATEDIFF(week,@StartDate,@EndDate)
SELECT DATEDIFF(day,@StartDate,@EndDate)
SELECT DATEDIFF(hour,@StartDate,@EndDate)
--Results--
-----------
4

-----------
20

-----------
144

-----------
3456
```

The DATEDIFF function can also create exception reports that show *open* items. For example, the following uses the GETDATE() function to find all rows that have been open for more than ten days.

```
USE tempdb
go
CREATE TABLE #DATEDIFF_Example (OrderDate smalldatetime, ShipDate smalldatetime)
go
INSERT #DATEDIFF_Example VALUES ('6/1/00','6/7/00')
INSERT #DATEDIFF_Example VALUES ('6/1/00','6/10/00')
INSERT #DATEDIFF_Example VALUES ('6/1/00',NULL)
SELECT OrderDate,ShipDate
FROM #DATEDIFF_Example
WHERE ShipDate IS NULL AND
```

```
        DATEDIFF(day,OrderDate,GETDATE()) > 10
--Results--
OrderDate                    ShipDate
-------------------------    -------------------------
2000-06-01 00:00:00          NULL
```

DATENAME

```
DATENAME ( datepart , date )
```

The DATENAME function returns the character description associated with the specified datepart of a date value. The following uses the WHILE construct to display the day for each date in the range.

```
DECLARE @StartDate smalldatetime, @EndDate smalldatetime
SET @StartDate = '6/1/00'
SET @EndDate = '6/30/00'

WHILE @StartDate < @EndDate
 BEGIN
  PRINT DATENAME(weekday,@StartDate)
  SET @StartDate = DATEADD(day,1,@StartDate)
 END
--Results--
Thursday
Friday
Saturday
...
Tuesday
Wednesday
Thursday
```

DATEPART

```
DATEPART ( datepart , date )
```

The DATEPART function returns an integer value associated with the specified datepart of a date. The following shows how to get the integer value for the specified datepart values.

```
SELECT GETDATE() AS 'Date'
SELECT DATEPART(year,GETDATE()) AS 'year'
```

```
SELECT DATEPART(month,GETDATE()) AS 'month'
SELECT DATEPART(day,GETDATE()) AS 'day'
SELECT DATEPART(weekday,GETDATE()) AS 'weekday'
SELECT DATEPART(hour,GETDATE()) AS 'hour'
SELECT DATEPART(minute,GETDATE()) AS 'minute'
--Results--
 Date
--------------------------
2000-07-03 17:15:05.570

year
-----------
2000

month
-----------
7

day
-----------
3

weekday
-----------
2

hour
-----------
17

minute
-----------
15
```

You can use the DATEPART function to determine the number of business days in a given date range. The following uses a WHILE construct and the BETWEEN function to show how this is accomplished. Keep in mind that Sunday = Day 1 and Saturday = Day 7, so Monday through Friday is the range 2–6.

```
DECLARE @StartDate smalldatetime, @EndDate smalldatetime, @Counter tinyint
SET @StartDate = '6/1/00'
SET @EndDate = '6/30/00'
SET @Counter= 0
```

```
WHILE @StartDate <= @EndDate
 BEGIN
  IF DATEPART(weekday,@StartDate) BETWEEN 2 AND 6
   BEGIN
    SET @Counter = @Counter + 1
   END

  SET @StartDate = DATEADD(day,1,@StartDate)
 END
PRINT @Counter
--Results--
22
```

DAY

```
DAY ( date )
```

The DAY function returns the integer value of the day associated with a given date. The following shows how it returns the day associated with the supplied date. In this example, GETDATE() returned a date that fell on a Monday—Sunday = 1, Monday = 2...Friday = 6, and Saturday = 7.

```
SELECT DAY(GETDATE())
--Results--
-----------
2
```

GETDATE()

```
GETDATE ( )
```

The GETDATE() function returns the current system date and time for the system on which SQL Server is installed. We have used GETDATE in several examples presented so far in this chapter, but the most basic way to use the function is shown here.

```
SELECT GETDATE()
--Results--
-------------------------
2000-07-02 17:57:01.127
```

GETUTCDATE()

The GETUTCDATE() function, new to SQL Server 2000, returns the current UTC (Universal Time Coordinate). The UTC is synonymous with Greenwich Mean Time and is calculated using local time and the time zone setting for the server on which SQL Server is installed. The following shows how GETUTCDATE is used.

```
SELECT GETDATE()
--Results--
---------------------------
2000-07-02 22:57:52.340
```

MONTH

```
MONTH ( date )
```

The MONTH function returns the integer value associated with the month for a supplied date. We use GETDATE again to demonstrate the results for a July 2, 2000 run date.

```
SELECT MONTH(GETDATE())
--Results--
-----------
7
```

YEAR

```
YEAR ( date )
```

The YEAR function returns the integer value associated with the year of the supplied date. The following shows how to determine the year for the date value returned by GETDATE().

```
SELECT YEAR(GETDATE())
--Results--
-----------
2000
```

Mathematical Functions

The mathematical functions in SQL Server 2000 are straightforward. This section provides a brief explanation of each function and an example of how they are implemented.

CEILING

```
CEILING ( numeric_expression )
```

The CEILING function returns the smallest integer value that is greater than or equal to numeric_expression. The following example shows how it is used.

```
DECLARE @Val1 numeric(5,2),@Val2 float
SET @Val1 = 54.09
SET @Val2 = -122.09343342

SELECT CEILING(@Val1)
SELECT CEILING(@Val2)
--Results--
-------
55


-------------------------------------------------------
-122.0
```

EXP

```
EXP ( float_expression )
```

The EXP function returns the exponential value of float_expression. The following example shows how to use EXP.

```
DECLARE @Val float
SET @Val = -122.09343342

SELECT EXP(@Val)
--Results--
-------------------------------------------------------
9.4513879305465039E-54
```

FLOOR

```
FLOOR ( numeric_expression )
```

The FLOOR function returns the largest integer value less than or equal to
numeric_expression. The following example shows how it used.

```
DECLARE @Val1 numeric(5,2),@Val2 float
SET @Val1 = 54.09
SET @Val2 = -122.09343342

SELECT FLOOR(@Val1)
SELECT FLOOR(@Val2)
--Results--
-------
54


------------------------------------------------------
-123.0
```

POWER

```
POWER ( numeric_expression , y )
```

The POWER function returns the value produced when numeric_expression is
raised to the y power. The following example shows how to use the POWER
function.

```
DECLARE @Val1 int,@Val2 tinyint
SET @Val1 = 22
SET @Val2 = 3

SELECT POWER(@Val1,@Val2)
--Results--
-----------
10648
```

RAND

```
RAND ( [ seed ] )
```

The RAND function returns a random float value whose range is 0 to 1. The optional seed value allows you to specify a start value for the function. The following shows how it is used.

```
SET NOCOUNT ON
DECLARE @Val int
SET @Val = 3435493

SELECT RAND(@Val)
--Results--
-------------------------------------------------------
0.7270164757753963
```

ROUND

```
ROUND ( numeric_expression , length [ , function ] )
```

The ROUND function allows you to round numeric_expression to the specified length or degree of precision. When a positive length argument is supplied, the rounding occurs on the right side of the decimal. When a negative number is used, the rounding occurs on the left side of the decimal. The function argument allows you to negate any rounding and simply truncate numeric_expression to the supplied length. The default value for function is zero, and when any other value is supplied the value is truncated.

The following example shows how to round a decimal expression to varying degrees of precision.

```
DECLARE @Val decimal(9,4)
SET @Val = 6983.3639

SELECT ROUND(@Val,0)
SELECT ROUND(@Val,1)
SELECT ROUND(@Val,2)
SELECT ROUND(@Val,3)
SELECT ROUND(@Val,4)
--Results--
-----------
6983.0000


-----------
6983.4000


-----------
```

6983.3600

6983.3640

6983.3639

This example uses a negative value for length to show the results of rounding on the left side of the decimal.

```
DECLARE @Val decimal(9,4)
SET @Val = 6983.3639

SELECT ROUND(@Val,0)
SELECT ROUND(@Val,-1)
SELECT ROUND(@Val,-2)
SELECT ROUND(@Val,-3)
SELECT ROUND(@Val,-4)
--Results--
-----------
6983.0000

-----------
6980.0000

-----------
7000.0000

-----------
7000.0000

-----------
10000.0000
```

The last example shows that the value is truncated when a nonzero value for function is used.

```
DECLARE @Val decimal(9,4)
SET @Val = 6983.3639

SELECT ROUND(@Val,0,1)
SELECT ROUND(@Val,1,1)
SELECT ROUND(@Val,2,1)
```

```
SELECT ROUND(@Val,3,1)
--Results--
-----------
6983.0000


-----------
6983.3000


-----------
6983.3600


-----------
6983.3630
```

Aggregate Functions

The aggregate functions in SQL Server 2000 enable you to perform calculations on a set of values to return a single value. Aggregate functions are frequently used with the GROUP BY clause of the SELECT statement because the purpose of the GROUP BY is to reduce two or more rows with like-grouping columns to a single value.

AVG

```
AVG ( [ ALL | DISTINCT ] expression )
```

The AVG function allows you to calculate the average value of the supplied expression. The optional DISTINCT argument specifies that the calucation will only be performed on unique instances of a value within the expression. The following example shows how AVG is implemented.

```
CREATE TABLE #AVG_Example (Value decimal(4,2))
go
INSERT #AVG_Example VALUES (5)
INSERT #AVG_Example VALUES (NULL)
INSERT #AVG_Example VALUES (10)

SELECT AVG(Value) FROM #AVG_Example
--Results--
-----------------------------------------
7.500000
```

Warning: Null value eliminated by aggregate or other set operation.

Note the warning message displayed when the example is executed. Since NULL is an undetermined value it cannot participate in the calculation.

The next example extends the previous one to show how the DISTINCT argument works.

```
INSERT #AVG_Example VALUES (5)

SELECT AVG(Value) FROM #AVG_Example
SELECT AVG(DISTINCT Value) FROM #AVG_Example
--Results--
-----------------------------------------
6.666666

Warning: Null value eliminated by aggregate or other set operation.


-----------------------------------------
7.500000

Warning: Null value eliminated by aggregate or other set operation.
```

You will note that the second SELECT returns the same value as the previous example because the DISTINCT argument causes the *second* five to be omitted from the calculation.

COUNT

```
COUNT ( { [ ALL | DISTINCT ] expression ] | * } )
```

The COUNT function allows you to count the number of values in the expression. The optional DISTINCT argument allows you to omit duplicate values in the calculation. When the * is used instead of expression, the function simply returns a count of all the rows in a table. The DISTINCT argument cannot be used when * is specified. The following example shows how COUNT is used.

```
CREATE TABLE #COUNT_Example (Value decimal(4,2))
go
INSERT #COUNT_Example VALUES (5)
INSERT #COUNT_Example VALUES (NULL)
INSERT #COUNT_Example VALUES (10)
INSERT #COUNT_Example VALUES (5)

SELECT COUNT(Value) FROM #COUNT_Example
SELECT COUNT(DISTINCT Value) FROM #COUNT_Example
```

```
SELECT COUNT(*) FROM #COUNT_Example
--Results--
-----------
3
```

```
Warning: Null value eliminated by aggregate or other set operation.
```

```
-----------
2
```

```
Warning: Null value eliminated by aggregate or other set operation.
```

```
-----------
4
```

Note that the NULL value is omitted in the calculation when Value is specified but included when * is used.

MAX

```
MAX ( [ ALL | DISTINCT ] expression )
```

The MAX function returns the maximum value in the expression. The DISTINCT argument does not affect the calculation and is only included for SQL-92 compatibility. The following example shows how MAX is implemented.

```
CREATE TABLE #MAX_Example (Value decimal(4,2))
go
INSERT #MAX_Example VALUES (5)
INSERT #MAX_Example VALUES (NULL)
INSERT #MAX_Example VALUES (10)
INSERT #MAX_Example VALUES (10.01)
```

```
SELECT MAX(Value) FROM #MAX_Example
--Results--
------
10.01
```

```
Warning: Null value eliminated by aggregate or other set operation.
```

MIN

```
MIN ( [ ALL | DISTINCT ] expression )
```

The MIN function returns the minimum value in the expression. As with MAX, the optional DISTINCT argument is included for SQL-92 compatibilty only. The following shows how MIN is used.

```
CREATE TABLE #MIN_Example (Value decimal(4,2))
go
INSERT #MIN_Example VALUES (5)
INSERT #MIN_Example VALUES (NULL)
INSERT #MIN_Example VALUES (10)
INSERT #MIN_Example VALUES (5)

SELECT MIN(Value) FROM #MIN_Example
--Results--
----
5

Warning: Null value eliminated by aggregate or other set operation.
```

SUM

```
SUM ( [ ALL | DISTINCT ] expression )
```

The SUM function calculates the sum of the values in the supplied expression. The optional DISTINCT argument specifies that duplicate values will not be included in the calculation. The following example shows how SUM is used.

```
CREATE TABLE #SUM_Example (Value tinyint)
go
INSERT #SUM_Example VALUES (5)
INSERT #SUM_Example VALUES (NULL)
INSERT #SUM_Example VALUES (10)
INSERT #SUM_Example VALUES (5)

SELECT SUM(Value) FROM #SUM_Example
SELECT SUM(DISTINCT Value) FROM #SUM_Example
--Results--
-----------
20
```

```
Warning: Null value eliminated by aggregate or other set operation.


-----------

15


Warning: Null value eliminated by aggregate or other set operation.
```

> **TIP   Global Variables Have Been Renamed**
>
> *If you have experience working with pre-7 versions of SQL Server but never got around to upgrading to SQL Server 7, you should know that the concept of global variables (as it relates to system-supplied, system-wide variables that are prefaced with @@) no longer exists. These are now called functions. The term global variable now refers to functionality in DTS (Data Transformation Services). More specifically, a global variable allows values to be shared among two or more ActiveX scripts.*

System Functions

The system functions in SQL Server 2000 evaluate expressions and return information about database objects and server level settings. A few of the functions covered in this section (e.g., CAST) are used quite frequently by SQL programmers, so make sure you read about each one before moving on to another part of the book.

CASE

The CASE function comes in two flavors—simple and searched—and the syntax for each follows.

Simple CASE

```
CASE input_expression
    WHEN when_expression THEN result_expression
        [ ...n ]
    [
        ELSE else_result_expression
```

```
        ]
END
```

Searched CASE

```
CASE
    WHEN boolean_expression THEN result_expression
        [ ...n ]
    [
        ELSE else_result_expression
    ]
END
```

CASE returns an expression based on two or more evaluated expressions. One of the more frequently asked questions in the newsgroups concerns T-SQL's support of an IIF function. T-SQL does not have an IIF function, but CASE can implement similar functionality. The following example shows how to use a simple CASE to implement IIF functionality.

```
SELECT Greeting = CASE DATEPART(hour, GETDATE())
                WHEN 12 THEN 'Noon'
                ELSE 'Not Noon'
                END
--Results--
Greeting
--------
Noon
```

The following example shows how to use a searched CASE to determine an appropriate greeting. The statement was executed at 4:45 PM (16:45), so the third WHEN evaluated to true.

```
SELECT Greeting = CASE
        WHEN DATEPART(hour,GETDATE()) BETWEEN 0 AND 6 THEN 'Early Morning'
        WHEN DATEPART(hour,GETDATE()) BETWEEN 7 AND 11 THEN 'Morning'
        WHEN DATEPART(hour,GETDATE()) BETWEEN 12 AND 17 THEN 'Afternoon'
        ELSE 'EVENING'
        END
--Results--
Greeting
-------------
Afternoon
```

CAST

```
CAST ( expression AS data_type )
```

The CAST function converts the supplied expression to the specified data_type. Only system data types can be used for the data_type argument, so user-defined data types are not allowed. The following shows how CAST allows a mathematical operation to be performed on a variable defined with the sql_variant data type.

```
DECLARE @Val sql_variant
SET @Val = 7
SELECT CAST(@Val AS int)+65
--Results--
-----------
72
```

Had the CAST function been omitted, the following error message would have been produced.

```
Server: Msg 403, Level 16, State 1, Line 3
Invalid operator for data type. Operator equals add, type equals sql_variant.
```

You cannot perform mathematical operations on a variable or column defined as sql_variant until is has been CAST (or CONVERTed) to the appropriate data type.

CAST is only required when SQL Server cannot implicitly convert data from one type to another. To learn what data types can be implicitly converted, see Figure 2-2, "Implicit Conversion Chart," provided under the section "Implicit Conversion" in Chapter 2. The following example shows the error message generated when a data type cannot be implicitly converted.

```
DECLARE @Val money
SET @Val = 34.84
PRINT @Val
--Result--
Server: Msg 257, Level 16, State 3, Line 3
Implicit conversion from data type money to nvarchar is not allowed. Use the CON-
VERT function to run this query.
```

The following shows how CAST produces a valid statement.

```
DECLARE @Val money
SET @Val = 34.84
PRINT CAST(@Val AS varchar(10))
```

```
--Results--
34.84
```

The CAST function provides functionality that is similar to the CONVERT function, which is covered next.

CONVERT

```
CONVERT ( data_type [ ( length ) ] , expression [ , style ] )
```

The CONVERT function converts the expression to the specified data_type in a manner similar to which the CAST function does so; but it provides a style argument that allows you to control the format of date values. The following shows how CONVERT performs the same operation as CAST.

```
DECLARE @Val sql_variant
SET @Val = 7
SELECT CONVERT(int,@Val)+65
--Result--
-----------
72
```

The next example shows how you use the style argument of CONVERT to control the format of date values. For a complete listing of the different styles that can be applied to a date value, please see the Books Online topic: Cast and Convert.

```
SELECT GETDATE()
SELECT CONVERT(varchar(24),GETDATE())
SELECT CONVERT(varchar(24),GETDATE(),01)
SELECT CONVERT(varchar(24),GETDATE(),101)
SELECT CONVERT(varchar(24),GETDATE(),14)
--Result--
--------------------------
2000-07-03 12:51:46.210


------------------------
Jul  3 2000 12:51PM


------------------------
07/03/00


------------------------
```

```
07/03/2000

------------------------
12:51:46:210
```

COALESCE

```
COALESCE ( expression [ ,...n ] )
```

The COALESCE function returns the first non-NULL value in the provided `expression`. The following shows how it returns the first non-NULL value from three variables.

```
DECLARE @Val1 int,@Val2 int, @Val3 int
SET @Val1 = NULL
SET @Val2 = 3
SET @Val3 = NULL

SELECT COALESCE(@Val1,@Val2,@Val3)
--Result--
-----------
3
```

CURRENT_TIMESTAMP

```
CURRENT_TIMESTAMP
```

The CURRENT_TIMESTAMP returns the current system date and time on which SQL Server is running. It produces the same results as the GETDATE() function. The following shows how it retrieved the current date and time at this writing.

```
SELECT CURRENT_TIMESTAMP
--Result--
 -------------------------
2000-07-01 18:05:18.433
```

CURRENT_USER

CURRENT_USER

The CURRENT_USER function returns the login associated with the current user of the database. This function is used with triggers (see Chapter 14) to implement audit trail functionality that tracks the last user who modified a row. The following shows how it returns the current user, Sammy.

```
SELECT CURRENT_USER
--Result--
-------------------------------------------------------------------------------
Sammy
```

Please note that when you are logged in with a login that is a member of the fixed-server role **sysadmin**, **dbo** is returned instead of the name associated with the login. Because I am a member of the this role on my computer, the following is displayed when I execute CURRENT_USER.

```
SELECT CURRENT_USER
--Result--
-------------------------------------------------------------------------------
dbo
```

DATALENGTH

DATALENGTH (*expression*)

The DATALENGTH function returns the actual number of bytes used by a variable or column. The following shows how it determines the actual number of characters that are in a column defined with the varchar data type. Note that nvarchar requires two bytes for every character, while varchar requires one.

```
CREATE TABLE #DATALENGTH_EXAMPLE (Descriptor varchar(30))
go
INSERT #DATALENGTH_EXAMPLE VALUES ('Sammy')
INSERT #DATALENGTH_EXAMPLE VALUES ('Mark')
INSERT #DATALENGTH_EXAMPLE VALUES ('Bo')

SELECT DATALENGTH(Descriptor), Descriptor
FROM #DATALENGTH_EXAMPLE
```

```
--Results--
          Descriptor
---------- ------------------------------
5         Sammy
4         Mark
2         Bo
```

@@ERROR

@@ERROR

The @@Error function traps for errors in SQL statements. When a SQL Statement is executed successfully, the value of @@Error is zero. When a SQL Statement generates an error, @@Error contains the error number associated with the error message. Please note that as soon a the next statement is executed successfully, @@Error is set to zero. All the system messages (approximately 3700) used by SQL Server are stored in the **sysmessages** table in the **master** database. In order to view them (sorted by severity) execute the following statement in Query Analyzer.

```
SELECT * FROM master..sysmessages ORDER BY severity
```

The following example shows how @@Error prints a custom message to the screen when an error is generated. This example is overly simple and is only included to show the basics of @@ERROR. More realistic error-handling techniques are presented in the "Error Handling" section of Chapter 11.

```
USE Northwind
go
DELETE Customers

IF @@ERROR <> 0
   PRINT 'An Error Message was Generated'
Server: Msg 547, Level 16, State 1, Line 1
--Results--
[DELETE statement conflicted with COLUMN REFERENCE constraint
'FK_Orders_Customers'. The conflict occurred in database 'Northwind', table
'Orders', column 'CustomerID'.
The statement has been terminated.
An Error Message was Generated
```

When you try to delete all the rows in **Customers,** the FOREIGN KEY constraint is violated because of the related rows in the **Orders** table.

@@IDENTITY

@@IDENTITY

The @@IDENTITY function returns the last value inserted into a column defined using the IDENTITY property. The following demonstrates how it used to find the last value inserted into the **Value** column.

```
CREATE TABLE #IDENTITY_Example (Value smallint IDENTITY, Descriptor varchar(20))
go
INSERT #IDENTITY_Example VALUES ('Piazza')
SELECT @@IDENTITY
--Results--
----------------------------------------
1
```

IDENTITY

IDENTITY (data_type [, seed , increment]) AS column_name

The IDENTITY function adds an IDENTITY column to a table created with a SELECT …INTO newTable.… The optional seed and increment arguments work in the same manner as in the IDENTITY property described in Chapter 2. The following example shows how it is used to add an IDENTITY column to a new version of the **Customers** table.

```
USE Northwind
go
SELECT IDENTITY(int) AS Customers_UniqueID,*
INTO #Customers
FROM Customers

SELECT Customers_UniqueID,
       CustomerID
FROM #Customers
--Results (Partial)--
Customers_UniqueID CustomerID
------------------ ----------
1                  ALFKI
2                  ANATR
3                  ANTON
...
```

ISDATE

```
ISDATE ( expression )
```

The ISDATE function evaluates the expression to determine if it is a valid date. It returns a one when the expression is a valid date and a zero when the expression is not a valid date. The following example shows how ISDATE determines whether the value of **@Val** is a valid date.

```
--*Invalid Date
DECLARE @Val char(8)
SET @Val = '99/00/00'
SELECT ISDATE(@Val)
--Results--
-----------
0


--*Valid Date
DECLARE @Val char(8)
SET @Val = '01/01/00'
SELECT ISDATE(@Val)
--Results--
-----------
1
```

The ISDATE function accepts any parameter that can be implicitly converted to a date, so the following examples work as well

```
--*Example 1
DECLARE @Val char(8)
SET @Val = '5/1/2000'
SELECT ISDATE(@Val)
--Results--
-----------
1


--*Example 2
DECLARE @Val char(8)
SET @Val = 'May 1 2000'
SELECT ISDATE(@Val)
--Results--
-----------
1
```

ISNULL

```
ISNULL ( check_expression , replacement_value )
```

The ISNULL function replaces a check_expression that evaluates to NULL with the replacement_value. The following shows how ISNULL returns the average of a column that contains NULL values.

```
CREATE TABLE #ISNULL_Example (Price smallmoney)
go
INSERT #ISNULL_Example VALUES (5.00)
INSERT #ISNULL_Example VALUES (NULL)
INSERT #ISNULL_Example VALUES (5.00)
INSERT #ISNULL_Example VALUES (NULL)

SELECT ISNULL(Price, 0)
FROM #ISNULL_Example

SELECT AVG(Price)
FROM #ISNULL_Example

SELECT AVG(ISNULL(Price, 0))
FROM #ISNULL_Example
--Results--
------------
5.0000
.0000
5.0000
.0000


---------------------
5.0000

Warning: Null value eliminated by aggregate or other set operation.

---------------------
2.5000
```

The second SELECT actually calculates the *true* average, because a NULL value is undefined and should not be included in a mathematical operation.

ISNUMERIC

```
ISNUMERIC ( expression )
```

The ISNUMERIC function determines if the supplied expression is a valid numeric value. You can use ISNUMERIC to avoid errors by testing whether a value is numeric before attempting to use it to perform a mathematical operation.

```
--*Invalid Value
DECLARE @Val varchar(10)
SET @Val = 'tt'
SELECT ISNUMERIC(@Val)
--Results--
-----------
0


--*Valid Value
DECLARE @Val varchar(10)
SET @Val = 100
SELECT ISNUMERIC(@Val)
--Results--
-----------
1
```

NEWID()

```
NEWID ( )
```

The NEWID function returns a globally unique identifier. It is most often used to generate values for columns defined with the uniqueidentifier data type. The uniqueidentifier data type should be avoided unless you are planning on implementing merge replication. The following shows how to use NEWID()to populate a column defined with the uniqueidentifier data type.

```
CREATE TABLE #NEWID_Example (Value uniqueidentifier)
go
INSERT #NEWID_Example SELECT NEWID()
SELECT Value FROM #NEWID_Example
--Results--
Value
-------------------------------------
1B5B0ED4-4F7D-11D4-922F-0080C8DE6E2A
```

@@ROWCOUNT

@@ROWCOUNT

The @@ROWCOUNT function returns the number of rows affected by a SQL statement. The following shows how it determines the number of rows deleted from the table.

```
CREATE TABLE #ROWCOUNT_Example (Value smallint)
go
INSERT #ROWCOUNT_Example VALUES (5)
INSERT #ROWCOUNT_Example VALUES (10)
INSERT #ROWCOUNT_Example VALUES (15)

DELETE #ROWCOUNT_Example WHERE Value <= 10
SELECT @@ROWCOUNT
--Results--
-----------
2
```

Before You Go

I presented quite a few built-in functions in this chapter, so you should have learned about more than a couple that you can use in your programming endeavors. Remember, though, that we did not cover all the built-in functions that are available in SQL Server 2000. Before you move on, I recommend you take a look at the Books Online topic: Functions to make sure you have an idea of the functions that are available.

The next chapter covers user-defined functions. SQL Server developers have been asking for user-defined functions with the last few releases of the product, so now you can discover how the much-anticipated objects work.

User-Defined Functions

SQL SERVER 2000 PROVIDES TWO TYPES OF FUNCTIONS: built-in and user-defined. Chapter 6 covered some of the commonly used built-in functions, and this chapter focuses on the user-defined type. The ability to create user-defined functions has been on developers's wish lists for several releases of SQL Server. Now that the functionality exists, let's see if we can learn how it can be used to write more efficient T-SQL statements.

> **NOTE Sample Code**
>
> *The sample code for this chapter can be downloaded at either* http://www.apress.com *or* http://www.SQLBook.com. *Download CodeCentric.zip and extract and access the Ch07.sql file.*

Before You Get Started

The goal of this chapter is to cover all of the hows, whats, and whys of creating and implementing user-defined functions. This should not present much of a challenge if you have created functions in other SQL dialects (e.g., PL/SQL). For T-SQL programmers, however, it will take some time to learn how they can be used to streamline current programming practices.

After we learn how user-defined functions are created and implemented, we need to review our existing code to see where a user-defined function would have been a more efficient way to implement the same functionality. I am not suggesting that you rewrite production code that already works as desired, but the fastest way to learn how this new functionality will help you in the future is to see how it could have helped you in the past.

Please make sure you have read "Deterministic versus Nondeterministic Functions" in Chapter 6 before continuing. Understanding the differences between the two types of built-in functions will allow you to better understand how user-defined functions can be implemented.

For some background information on the origin of user-defined functions, see "The History of Stored Procedures" in Chapter 11. As you will see, the standard that dictates how stored procedures are implemented also applies to user-defined functions.

User-Defined Functions

A user-defined function is a database object that encapsulates one or more Transact-SQL statements for reuse. This definition is similar to the one for stored procedures presented in Chapter 11, but there are many important differences between user-defined functions and stored procedures—the most pronounced being what types of data they can return. Before we cover all the nuances of user-defined functions and how they differ from stored procedures, let's create one so you can see how easy they are to create and reference.

The following statement shows how to create a function that accepts two input parameters, sums them together and then returns the sum to the calling statement.

```
CREATE FUNCTION fx_SumTwoValues
(
 @Val1 int,
 @Val2 int
)
RETURNS int
AS
BEGIN
    RETURN (@Val1+@Val2)
END
```

The structure of the CREATE FUNCTION statement is fairly straightforward. You provide an object name (**fx_SumTwoValues**), input parameters (**@Val1** and **@Val2**), the type of data the function will return (int) and the statement(s) the function executes are located between the BEGIN…END block. The following SELECT statement calls the function. Note that the two-part name (owner.object_name) is required when calling this function.

```
SELECT dbo.fx_SumTwoValues(1,2) AS SumOfTwoValues
--Results--
SumOfTwoValues

--------------
3
```

When the SELECT is executed, the input parameters 1 and 2 are added together and the sum 3 is returned. You can use any values that either are, or can be, implicitly converted to an int data type for the input parameters. Keep in mind, though, that only an int can be returned, so the following statement will not produce the desired results.

```
SELECT dbo.fx_SumTwoValues(1.98,2.78) AS SumOfTwoValues
--Result--
SumOfTwoValues
--------------
3
```

The function returns a 3, which indicates the decimal portion of the parameters are truncated before the calculation occurs.

SQL Server's ability to implicitly convert data (discussed in Chapter 2) allows the following to execute successfully.

```
SELECT dbo.fx_SumTwoValues('7','7') AS SumOfTwoValues
--Results--
SumOfTwoValues
--------------
14
```

When values that cannot be converted to an int are passed to the function, the following error message is generated.

```
SELECT dbo.fx_SumTwoValues('Y','7') AS SumOfTwoValues
--Results--
Server: Msg 245, Level 16, State 1, Line 1
Syntax error converting the varchar value 'Y' to a column of data type int.
```

Three Types of User-Defined Functions

Now that you have seen how easy it is to create and implement a simple function, let's cover the three different types of user-defined functions and some of the nuances of how they are implemented.

Scalar Functions

A scalar function returns a single value of the data type referenced in the RETURNS clause of the CREATE FUNCTION statement. The returned data can be of any type except text, ntext, image, cursor, or timestamp.

The example we covered in the previous section is a scalar function. Although the previous example only contained one statement in the BEGIN...END block, a scalar function can contain an unlimited number of statements as long as only one value is returned. The following example uses a WHILE construct to demonstrate this.

```
CREATE FUNCTION fx_SumTwoValues2
(
 @Val1 int,
 @Val2 int
)
RETURNS int
AS
BEGIN
 WHILE @Val1 < 100
  BEGIN
   SET @Val1 = @Val1 + 1
  END
  RETURN (@Val1+@Val2)
END
go
SELECT dbo.fx_SumTwoValues2(1,7) AS SumOfTwoValues
--Results--
SumOfTwoValues
--------------
107
```

The **@Val1** input parameter is set to 1 when the function is called, but the WHILE increments the parameter to 100 before the RETURN statement is executed. Note that the two-part name (owner.object_name) is used to call the function. Scalar functions require that their two-part names be used when they are called. As you will see in the next two sections, this is not the case with the other two types of functions.

Inline Table-Valued Functions

An inline table-valued function returns a variable of data type table whose value is derived from a single SELECT statement. Since the return value is derived from the SELECT statement, there is no BEGIN/END block needed in the CREATE FUNCTION statement. There is also no need to specify the table variable name (or column definitions for the table variable) because the structure of the returned value is generated from the columns that compose the SELECT statement.

Because the results are a function of the columns referenced in the SELECT, no duplicate column names are allowed and all derived columns must have an associated alias.

The following uses the **Customer** table in the **Northwind** database to show how an inline table-valued function is implemented.

```
USE Northwind
go
CREATE FUNCTION fx_Customers_ByCity
(
 @City nvarchar(15)
)
RETURNS table
AS
RETURN (
        SELECT CompanyName
        FROM Customers
        WHERE City = @City
        )
go
SELECT * FROM fx_Customers_ByCity('London')
--Results (Partial)--
CompanyName

-----------------------------------------
Around the Horn

....

Seven Seas Imports
```

Multi-Statement Table-Valued Functions

The multi-statement table-valued function is slightly more complicated than the other two types of functions because it uses multiple statements to *build* the table that is returned to the calling statement. Unlike the inline table-valued function, a table variable must be explicitly declared and defined.

The following example shows how to implement a multi-statement table-valued function that populates and returns a table variable.

```
USE Northwind
go
CREATE FUNCTION fx_OrdersByDateRangeAndCount
(
 @OrderDateStart smalldatetime,
 @OrderDateEnd smalldatetime,
```

```
 @OrderCount smallint
)
RETURNS @OrdersByDateRange TABLE
(
 CustomerID nchar(5),
 CompanyName nvarchar(40),
 OrderCount smallint,
 Ranking char(1)
 )
AS
BEGIN
 --Statement 1
 INSERT @OrdersByDateRange
 SELECT a.CustomerID,
        a.CompanyName,
        COUNT(a.CustomerID) AS OrderCount,
        'B'
 FROM Customers a
 JOIN Orders b ON a.CustomerID = b.CustomerID
 WHERE OrderDate BETWEEN @OrderDateStart AND @OrderDateEnd
 GROUP BY a.CustomerID, a.CompanyName
 HAVING COUNT(a.CustomerID) > @OrderCount

 --Statement 2
 UPDATE @OrdersByDateRange
 SET Ranking = 'A'
 WHERE CustomerID IN (SELECT TOP 5 WITH TIES CustomerID
                       FROM (SELECT a.CustomerID,
                                    COUNT(a.CustomerID) AS OrderTotal
                             FROM  Customers a
                             JOIN Orders b ON a.CustomerID = b.CustomerID
                             GROUP BY a.CustomerID) AS DerivedTable
                       ORDER BY OrderTotal DESC)

 RETURN
END
```

The main difference between this example and the one in the previous section is that we were required to specify the structure of the **@OrdersByDateRange** table variable used to hold the resultset and list **@OrdersByDateRange** in the RETURNS clause. As you can see from the input parameter list, the function accepts a start date, an end date and an order count value to filter the resultset.

The first statement (--Statement 1) uses the input parameters to populate the table variable with customers who meet the specified criteria. The second statement

(`--Statement 2`) updates the rows in table variable to identify the top five *overall* order placers. The IN portion of the UPDATE may seem a little confusing at first glance, but all its doing is using a derived table to select the **CustomerID** values of the top five order producers. Derived tables are discussed in Chapter 4.

You can use the following to find the companies who have submitted more than two orders between 1/1/96 and 1/1/97.

```
SELECT *
FROM fx_OrdersByDateRangeAndCount ('1/1/96','1/1/97',2)
ORDER By Ranking
--Results (Partial)--
CustomerID CompanyName                               OrderCount Ranking
---------- ----------------------------------------- ---------- -------
ERNSH      Ernst Handel                              6          A
FOLKO      Folk och fä HB                            3          A
HUNGO      Hungry Owl All-Night Grocers              5          A
QUICK      QUICK-Stop                                6          A
SAVEA      Save-a-lot Markets                        3          A
SEVES      Seven Seas Imports                        3          B
SPLIR      Split Rail Beer & Ale                     5          B
...
```

The rows ranking values of 'A' indicate the top five order placers of all companies. The function allows you to perform two operations with one object. Retrieve the companies who have placed more than two orders between 1/1/96 and 1/1/97 and let me know if any of these companies are my top five order producers.

One of the advantages of using this type of function over a view is that the body of the function can contain multiple SQL statements to populate the table variable, whereas a view is composed of only one statement. The advantage of using multi-statement table-valued function versus a stored procedure is that the function can be referenced in the FROM clause of a SELECT statement while a stored procedure cannot. Had a stored procedure been used to return the same data, the resultset could only be accessed with the EXECUTE command.

CREATE FUNCTION

Now that we have covered the three types of user-defined functions and why they should be used instead of their object counterparts, let's take a look at the full syntax of the CREATE FUNCTION statement.

Scalar Functions

The full syntax of CREATE FUNCTION for a scalar function is shown here.

```
CREATE  FUNCTION [ owner_name. ] function_name
    ( [ { @parameter_name scalar_parameter_data_type [ = default ] } [ ,...n ] ] )

RETURNS scalar_return_data_type

[ WITH < function_option> [,...n] ]

[ AS ]

BEGIN
    function_body
    RETURN scalar_expression
END
---
< function_option> :: [{ENCRYPTION}] | {{SCHEMABINDING}]
```

In short, you supply a function_name (and optionally the owner_name), any input @parameter_name and its associated scalar_parameter_data_type, the scalar_return_data_type of the return value, any WITH arguments, the function_body, and the scalar_expression that is the result of the function_body statement. When you compare the full syntax to the example created earlier, you will see that the only clause not used is WITH. As you can see from the domain of < function_option >, ENCRYPTION and/or SCHEMABINDING are valid arguments for the WITH clause. Since our example demonstrated all but the WITH clause, we will only cover its arguments next.

WITH ENCRYPTION

The ENCRYPTION argument allows you to *hide* the code used to create the function. Use this option when you feel your statements are proprietary and should not be shared with users. A little background information is needed before you can fully understand the ramifications of using this argument. When you create a function or a stored procedure, the text used to create the object is stored in a system table called **syscomments**. You can see the text of the last function created by executing the following. (Note that this is not a scalar function.)

```
USE Northwind
go
SELECT b.text
FROM sysobjects a
```

```
INNER JOIN syscomments b ON a.id = b.id
WHERE a.name = 'fx_OrdersByDateRangeAndCount'
--Results--
CREATE FUNCTION fx_OrdersByDateRangeAndCount
…·

 OrderCount smallint
 )
```

The **text** column in **syscomments** is defined as nvarchar(4000), but only the first 256 characters of the character string are displayed. The 256 limit is a default setting in Query Analyzer that can easily be changed. If you would like to ensure that the full text of the function is stored in **syscomments,** simply adjust the maximum number of characters displayed per column by completing the following:

1. Click Tools on the main menu in Query Analyzer and select Options.

2. Click the Results tab and change the value in Maximum characters per column to 400.

3. Click OK and then re-execute the query.

Querying the system table directly is not the preferred method for accessing the text used to create a function or stored procedure. Querying or accessing the data in the system tables directly is generally frowned upon because the system tables can change from release-to-release, and any programs that access them directly would no longer work as expected. Having said this, however, I will periodically use examples that access the system tables directly in an effort to familiarize you with their layout. Understanding the layout of the tables that hold the system information of SQL Server can give you an advantage when troubleshooting programming or administration issues.

There are two other preferred methods of viewing the text associated with a function. The first is to use the SELECT shown here to query an Information Schema View. Information Schema Views are discussed in detail in Chapter 8.

```
SELECT ROUTINE_DEFINITION
FROM INFORMATION_SCHEMA.ROUTINES
WHERE ROUTINE_NAME = 'fx_OrdersByDateRangeAndCount'
--Results--
ROUTINE_DEFINITION
---------------------------------------------------------------------------
CREATE FUNCTION fx_OrdersByDateRangeAndCount
(
 @OrderDateStart smalldatetime,
 @OrderDateEnd smalldatetime,
```

```
@OrderCount smallint
)
RETURNS @OrdersByDateRange TABLE
(
 CustomerID nchar(5),
 CompanyName nvarchar(40),
 OrderCount smallint,
 Ra
```

The second is to use the system stored procedure **sp_helptext**. The advantage of using **sp_helptext** is that it will return the full text in **syscomments** regardless of the maximum characters per column setting in Query Analyzer. The following shows how it is used to display the text of **fx_OrdersByDateRangeAndCount.**

```
sp_helptext 'fx_OrdersByDateRangeAndCount'
--Results (Partial)--
Text
---------------
CREATE FUNCTION fx_OrdersByDateRangeAndCount
(
....
 RETURN
END
```

The following statements DROP and CREATE **fx_OrdersByDateRangeAndCount** with the WITH ENCRYPTION argument and show the resultset returned when the text of the procedure is accessed with an Information Schema View.

```
DROP FUNCTION fx_OrdersByDateRangeAndCount
go
CREATE FUNCTION fx_OrdersByDateRangeAndCount
(
 @OrderDateStart smalldatetime,
 @OrderDateEnd smalldatetime,
 @OrderCount smallint
)
RETURNS @OrdersByDateRange TABLE
(
 CustomerID nchar(5),
 CompanyName nvarchar(40),
 OrderCount smallint,
 Ranking char(1)
 )
WITH ENCRYPTION
```

```
AS
BEGIN
 --Statement 1
 INSERT @OrdersByDateRange
 SELECT a.CustomerID,
        a.CompanyName,
        COUNT(a.CustomerID) AS OrderCount,
        'B'
 FROM Customers a
 JOIN Orders b ON a.CustomerID = b.CustomerID
 WHERE OrderDate BETWEEN @OrderDateStart AND @OrderDateEnd
 GROUP BY a.CustomerID, a.CompanyName
 HAVING COUNT(a.CustomerID) > @OrderCount

 --Statement 2
 UPDATE @OrdersByDateRange
 SET Ranking = 'A'
 WHERE CustomerID IN (SELECT TOP 5 WITH TIES CustomerID
                        FROM (SELECT a.CustomerID,
                                     COUNT(a.CustomerID) AS OrderTotal
                              FROM  Customers a
                              JOIN Orders b ON a.CustomerID = b.CustomerID
                              GROUP BY a.CustomerID) AS DerivedTable
                      ORDER BY OrderTotal DESC)

 RETURN
END
go
SELECT ROUTINE_DEFINITION
FROM INFORMATION_SCHEMA.ROUTINES
WHERE ROUTINE_NAME = 'fx_OrdersByDateRangeAndCount'
--Results--
ROUTINE_DEFINITION
------------------
NULL
```

As you can see, the **Text** column of **syscomments** (as seen through the schema view) is NULL. There are potential pitfalls of encrypting a function, so use this option with caution. Once encrypted, the contents of the function are not available via the schema views or Query Analyzer, so you need to make sure a copy is archived for later use.

You probably noticed that I used a multi-statement table-valued function to demonstrate the ENCRYPTION argument even though this section discusses scalar functions. The text of the scalar function created earlier is less than 256 characters, so using it would not allow me to demonstrate Query Analyzer's default display setting of 256 characters per column. The ENCRYPTION argument works the same regardless of the type of function you are dealing with, so it will not be addressed when discussing the syntax of the other two function types.

WITH SCHEMABINDING

The SCHEMABINDING argument is fairly straightforward. When used, it restricts the database objects that are referenced by the function from being modified with the DROP or ALTER statements. I will demonstrate this by changing the example used in the inline table-valued function section.

The following statements DROP and CREATE **fx_Customers_ByCity** using the WITH SCHEMABINDING argument and then attempt to ALTER the **CompanyName** column referenced in the function. Please note that a two-part name (e.g., **dbo.Customers**) must be used for the database objects referenced by the function when the WITH SCHEMABINDING clause is used.

```
DROP FUNCTION fx_Customers_ByCity
go
CREATE FUNCTION fx_Customers_ByCity
(
 @City nvarchar(15)
)
RETURNS table
WITH SCHEMABINDING
AS
RETURN (
        SELECT CompanyName
        FROM dbo.Customers
        WHERE City = @City
        )
go
ALTER TABLE Customers ALTER COLUMN CompanyName nvarchar(50)
--Results--
Server: Msg 5074, Level 16, State 3, Line 1
The object 'fx_Customers_ByCity' is dependent on column 'CompanyName'.
Server: Msg 4922, Level 16, State 1, Line 1
ALTER TABLE ALTER COLUMN CompanyName failed because one or more objects access this
column.
```

As expected, the ALTER TABLE statement failed because **fx_Customers_ByCity** is bound to the **CompanyName** column. This is a very valuable feature and I recommend its use on all the functions you create. Using WITH SCHEMABINDING will help to ensure that your functions always work as expected. In other words, it will protect the function from rogue developers who modify objects without under-standing the ramifications of their actions.

Advanced Scalar Function Example

The **fx_SumTwoValues** example covered earlier was very simple and was only included to show the general layout of the CREATE FUNCTION statement. In the real world, you are most likely going to be using CREATE FUNCTION to imple-ment more-complicated functionality. With this in mind, let's create a function that allows us to determine the number of workdays (M-F) in a given date range. The following shows how this is accomplished.

```
CREATE FUNCTION fx_WorkDaysInDateRange
(
 @DateStart smalldatetime,
 @DateEnd smalldatetime
)
RETURNS smallint
AS
BEGIN
 DECLARE @WorkDays smallint
 SET @WorkDays = 0
 WHILE @DateStart <= @DateEnd
  BEGIN
   IF DATEPART(weekday,@DateStart) BETWEEN 2 AND 5
    BEGIN
     SET @WorkDays = @WorkDays + 1
    END
   SET @DateStart = DATEADD(day,1,@DateStart)
  END
  RETURN @WorkDays
END
go
SELECT dbo.fx_WorkDaysInDateRange('7/1/00','7/30/00') AS WorkDays
--Results--
WorkDays
--------
16
```

The function uses a WHILE construct, two built-in date functions and the BETWEEN predicate to facilitate the calculation. The DATEPART function (dis-cussed in Chapter 6) returns an integer value associated with the day of week

(Sunday = 1, Monday = 2, …, Saturday = 7), and the DATEADD function adds one day to **@DateStart** as the WHILE is processed. If the current value in **@DateStart** is BETWEEN 2 AND 5 (Monday–Friday), the **@WorkDays** variable is incremented by one.

How to Find Functions in sysobjects

Each object in a database occupies one row in the **sysobjects** system table. Many of you may be accustomed to looking up database object names using **sysobjects**. For example, I have often looked up all the stored procedures in a database by executing the following statement.

```
USE Northwind
    go
    SELECT name
    FROM sysobjects
    WHERE type = 'P'
    --Results--
    name

    -------

    CustOrderHist

    ….

    Ten Most Expensive Products
```

Because user-defined functions are new to SQL Server 2000, you probably do not know what value occupies their type column. After creating the examples in the previous sections, I executed the statement shown here to determine the values used to designate user-defined functions.

```
SELECT RTRIM(name)+'-->'+type  AS ObjectAndType
    FROM sysobjects
    WHERE name LIKE 'fx%'
    --Results--
    ObjectAndType

    ----------------

    fx_Customers_ByCity-->IF
    fx_OrdersByDateRangeAndCount-->TF
    fx_SumTwoValues-->FN
```

It turns out that each category of function has its own type value. More specifically, FN designates a scalar function, IF designates an inline table-valued function, and TF designates a multi-statement table-valued function. In general, Information Schema Views should be used rather than querying the system tables directly, but old habits are hard to break.

Inline Table-Valued Function

The full syntax of CREATE FUNCTION for an inline table-valued function is shown here.

```
CREATE FUNCTION [ owner_name. ] function_name
( [ { @parameter_name scalar_parameter_data_type [ = default ] } [ ,...n ] ] )

RETURNS TABLE

[ WITH < function_option > [ ,...n ] ]

[ AS ]

RETURN [ ( ] select-stmt [ ) ]
---
< function_option > ::=
    { ENCRYPTION | SCHEMABINDING }
```

Note that in our earlier example from the "Inline Table-Valued Functions" section, we used all aspects of the syntax except the WITH clause. Since we covered the WITH clause in detail in the previous section and the same guidelines apply here, no further coverage is necessary.

The inline table-valued example covered earlier is fairly indicative of how you might use one in the real world. Let's create a more advanced example that demonstrates how the resultset returned by a function can be manipulated just like a table. The following shows how to create a function that returns all customers and the number of orders they have placed. The SELECT that references the function demonstrates that you can manipulate the resultset it returns as if it were a *real* table.

```
CREATE FUNCTION fx_Customers_ByOrderCount ()
RETURNS table
AS
RETURN (
        SELECT CompanyName, COUNT(a.CompanyName) AS OrderCount
        FROM Customers a
        LEFT JOIN Orders b ON a.CustomerID = b.CustomerID
        GROUP BY a.CompanyName
        )
go
SELECT TOP 5 *
FROM fx_Customers_ByOrderCount ()
ORDER BY OrderCount DESC
--Results--
```

CompanyName	OrderCount
Save-a-lot Markets	31
Ernst Handel	30
QUICK-Stop	28
Folk och fä HB	19
Hungry Owl All-Night Grocers	19

Multi-Statement Table-Valued Functions

The full syntax for CREATE FUNCTION when a multi-statement table-valued function is desired is shown here.

```
CREATE FUNCTION [ owner_name. ] function_name
    ( [ { @parameter_name scalar_parameter_data_type [ = default ] } [ ,...n ] ] )

RETURNS @return_variable TABLE < table_type_definition >

[ WITH < function_option > [ ,...n ] ]

[ AS ]

BEGIN
    function_body
    RETURN
END
---
< function_option > ::=
    { ENCRYPTION | SCHEMABINDING }

< table_type_definition > :: =
    ( { column_definition | table_constraint } [ ,...n ] )
```

All aspects of the syntax were covered in the example presented in the "Multi-Statement Table-Valued Functions" section earlier in the chapter. The example presented earlier demonstrated advanced use of this type of function so no further coverage is provided.

ALTER FUNCTION

The syntax for the ALTER FUNCTION statement is similar to the CREATE FUNCTION syntax discussed previously. Just remember that when you use the ALTER

User-Defined Functions

FUNCTION statement to modify a function, the permissions that have been applied to the function remain in place.

In the two examples I presented earlier, the DROP FUNCTION statement was executed before re-creating the function with the WITH clause. When you DROP a function, or any other database object for that matter, any permissions that have been applied to the object are also dropped. Once a function has been created and permissions applied, you should always use ALTER FUNCTION to make any changes.

Scalar Functions

```
ALTER FUNCTION [ owner_name. ] function_name
  ( [ { @parameter_name scalar_parameter_data_type [ = default ] } [ ,...n ] ] )
RETURNS scalar_return_data_type
[ WITH < function_option > [,...n] ]
[ AS ]
BEGIN
    function_body
    RETURN scalar_expression
END
```

Inline Table-Valued Functions

```
ALTER FUNCTION [ owner_name. ] function_name
    ( [ { @parameter_name scalar_parameter_data_type [ = default ] } [ ,...n ] ] )
RETURNS TABLE
[ WITH < function_option > [ ,...n ] ]
[ AS ]
RETURN [ ( ] select-stmt [ ) ]
```

Multi-Statement Table-Valued Functions

```
ALTER FUNCTION [ owner_name. ] function_name
    ( [ { @parameter_name scalar_parameter_data_type [ = default ] } [ ,...n ] ] )
RETURNS @return_variable TABLE < table_type_definition >
[ WITH < function_option > [ ,...n ] ]
[ AS ]
BEGIN
    function_body
    RETURN
END
```

209

```
< function_option > ::=
    { ENCRYPTION | SCHEMABINDING }
< table_type_definition > :: =
    ( { column_definition | table_constraint } [ ,...n ] )
```

DROP FUNCTION

```
DROP FUNCTION { [ owner_name. ] function_name } [ ,...n ]
```

The DROP FUNCTION statement is straightforward. You supply the function_name and, optionally, the owner_name if the function does not belong to your user ID. Several examples using DROP FUNCTION were presented earlier in the chapter.

Function Considerations

The following sections cover nonsyntax topics that are applicable to the three types of functions.

Statement Permissions

The statement and object permissions applicable to user-defined functions are described in this section.

CREATE

Permission to execute CREATE FUNCTION defaults to the members of the fixed server role **sysadmin** and the database roles **db_owner** and **db_ddladmin.** Members of **sysadmin** or **db_owner** can GRANT permission to execute this statement to other users.

EXECUTE

Permission to execute a user-defined function defaults to its owner and members of **sysadmin** and **db_owner.** In order for other users to reference a user-defined function, they must have been granted EXECUTE permission on the object.

DROP

Permission to DROP a function is only provided to the function's owner and to the members of either **sysadmin** or **db_owner**.

Nondeterministic Built-In Functions

A nondeterministic function (covered in Chapter 6) is one that may not always return the same value even when it is called with the same input parameters. For a full listing of nondeterministic functions please see the Books Online topic: Deterministic and Nondeterministic Functions.

Nondeterministic functions are not allowed in a user-defined function. The following example shows the error message generated when you try to create a function that contains a nondeterministic function.

```
CREATE FUNCTION fx_CurrentTime
AS
RETURNS datetime
AS
SELECT GETDATE()
--Results--
Server: Msg 156, Level 15, State 1, Procedure fx_CurrentTime, Line 2
Incorrect syntax near the keyword 'AS'.
Server: Msg 443, Level 16, State 1, Procedure fx_CurrentTime, Line 5
Illegal use of 'getdate' within a FUNCTION.
```

TEXT IN ROW

The TEXT IN ROW setting affects both inline table-valued functions and multi-statement table-valued functions. In short, it restricts the number of characters returned by either type of function to 256. So, regardless of the number of characters in the column referenced by these types of functions, only the first 256 characters are returned.

Before You Go

This chapter covered the three types of user-defined functions available in SQL Server 2000. User-defined functions can simplify SQL programming and reduce the effort required to implement functionality that is used on a recurring basis. Now that this functionality exists, you should be cognizant of when it should be used to implement a solution as a function. It may take a little longer to stop what you are accustomed to doing and create a function, but in the long run the extra effort should be worth it.

The next chapter covers both user-defined and information schema views. User-defined views are used to minimize the skill-level needed to retrieve data from a database and implement security by restricting access to one or more table. Information schema views are used to retrieve metadata information about the about the objects in an instance of SQL Server.

CHAPTER 8

Views

TWO TYPES OF VIEWS ARE AVAILABLE IN **SQL SERVER 2000:** user-defined and information schema. Developers create user-defined views with the CREATE VIEW
statement. Information schema views (which have been around since version 7)
come with SQL Server 2000 and were created by members of the SQL Server development team. Both types of views are discussed in this chapter.

> **NOTE Sample Code**
>
> *The sample code for this chapter can be downloaded at either*
> http://www.apress.com *or* http://www.SQLBook.com. *Download*
> *CodeCentric.zip and extract and access the Ch08.sql file.*

Before You Get Started

As you will see in more detail later in the chapter, two of the main benefits of using
views are that you can *hide* the logic required to produce a resultset and restrict
access to specific columns within a table. The first use works nicely when you have
developers or users who want access to data but do not have the necessary
knowledge of relational database theory and/or T-SQL to construct the required
statements. If you work in an environment where less-experienced users need
access to data at the table-level, I suggest using views so you can avoid the training
costs required to teach them the necessary skills. Using views to implement security is a technique used to restrict access to certain columns within a table. For
example, you would use this approach to make sure developers could not directly
access a table that contains salary information.

If you do not work in an environment where either one of the scenarios
applies, I suggest you use stored procedures for all data access. Using a single
approach to accessing data makes system maintenance easier—especially when
an intuitive naming convention is used. Many developers overlook the long-term
benefits of creating applications that are easy to maintain, but this should be high
priority when designing a system. Because I am a consultant who does work for
many different companies, I must design and implement systems that can be

easily maintained by my clients' in-house staff. Accomplishing this aim eliminates the maintenance-related phone calls that take lots of time but produce very little revenue. Teaching a client's staff about data access via a single method, stored procedures, flattens the learning curve and enables them to more easily manage *their* applications.

Views

A view is a database object that is composed of a SELECT statement that references one or more tables or views. A view is often called a virtual table because it *appears* to be a *real* table when referenced in a SELECT statement. A real table is one that is created with the CREATE TABLE statement discussed in Chapter 3.

Views are often used to implement security by providing limited access to the columns in a table. For example, let's say you have a table called **Employees** that holds employee information, and one of the columns in the table holds employees' salary amounts. The only members of the development team that are allowed to access the **Salary** column are in management and belong to the Developer-Management group. The rest of the development team, members of the Developer group, needs access to the other columns in the table. To implement the needed security you make two changes: First, restrict SELECT permission on **Employees** to only those developers in the DeveloperManagement group. Second, create a view that references all columns except **Salary** and grant SELECT permission on the view to the Developer group. This type of issue could also be resolved by granting column-level permissions on the table. For more information on this solution see the Books Online topic: Granting Permissions.

Views are commonly used to make data more accessible to less-experienced developers and users. In some environments, personnel who do not possess programming skills are given the ability to access (read-only, of course) tables directly using tools like Query Analyzer. This gives the users more power, but places a burden on developers because many users do not have the skills required to retrieve the data they need to perform their job. When a complex database design is used, multi-table inner and outer joins are often required to produce meaningful result-sets, and many users do not possess the skill to construct these types of statements.

When a user encounters a situation they cannot solve on their own, they ask for assistance from a developer. A smart developer will try to assess the data the users wants to access ahead of time and create a view that reduces the complex operation to a simple SELECT. For example, let's say you have a group of users who have an ongoing need to analyze the sales data produced by a SELECT that references seven tables—five inner and two outer joins. Instead of trying to teach the users how to create the SELECT, you create a view called **SalesSummary,** and they simply execute `SELECT * FROM SalesSummary` to produce the desired resultset.

CREATE VIEW

A user-defined view is one that is created with the CREATE VIEW statement. The complete syntax of CREATE VIEW is shown here.

```
CREATE [ < owner > ] VIEW view_name [ ( column [ ,...n ] ) ]
[ WITH ENCRYPTION | SCHEMABINDING | VIEW_METADATA ]
AS
select_statement
[ WITH CHECK OPTION ]
```

CREATE VIEW Arguments

[< owner >]

Optional argument that specifies the view's owner.

view_name

Name of the view.

[(column [,...n])]

Column names that reference the columns retrieved in the view. Specifying a column name is required when columns that have the same name are referenced in select_statement or a calculated column is created by select_statement. You can also alias a column referenced in select_statement by providing a new column name with this option.

[WITH ENCRYPTION | SCHEMABINDING | VIEW_METADATA]

Optional arguments that specify behavior of the view. The ENCRYPTION argument specifies the text of the view is encrypted in the **syscomments** table. SCHEMA-BINDING prohibits any table or user-defined function referenced in the view from being dropped or altered as long as the binding is in place. This prohibits the view from becoming nonfunctional when a developer inadvertently tries to change an object referenced by the view. The VIEW_METADATA argument specifies that SQL Server will return the view's metadata, not the tables referenced in the view, when metadata is browsed using either DBLIB or OLE DB APIs. You can combine these arguments by separating them with a comma (e.g., WITH ENCRYPTION, SCHEMABINDING).

The ramifications of using the ENCRYPTION and SCHEMABINDING arguments are discussed in Chapter 7, under the section entitled "CREATE FUNCTION."

select_statement

Retrieves the actual and calculated columns referenced in the view. Both tables and other views can be referenced in select_statement.

[WITH CHECK OPTION]

Optional argument that ensures all rows visible by the view remain visible after a data modification statement is executed via the view. This sounds complex but can be easily explained with an example. Assume you have a table called **Orders,** and it has a column named **Status**. Further, suppose that a view (**vw_HotOrders**) is created that retrieves only those orders whose **Status** value is greater than eight (e.g., WHERE Status > 8). If you try to update the **Status** column of a row via the view with a value that is less than eight, the statement will fail because the update would cause the row to *fall* out of the view's selection criteria.

View Limitations

There are several restrictions to creating a view. The SELECT statement that creates a view cannot use or reference any of the following:

- COMPUTE or COMPUTE BY clause

- ORDER BY clause unless TOP is used

- INTO

- A temporary table

A view's SELECT cannot reference more than 1024 columns or be combined with other T-SQL statements in a single batch.

Indexed Views

The ability to index a view is new to SQL Server 2000. The resultset produced by a nonindexed view is generated at execution time and is not stored in the database. The resultset of a view that is created with a unique clustered index is stored in the database in a similar manner to a table with a unique clustered index. Indexed views provide a significant performance benefit over nonindexed views when the view is accessed frequently and is based on a complex SELECT statement that produces a large number of rows. Like other indexes, however, system overhead is required to maintain the index, so make sure you only use this new functionality in the proper situations.

To create an index on a view, the following requirements must be met.

- The ANSI_NULLS and QUOTED_IDENTIFIER options must have been set to ON when the view was created.

- The ANSI_NULLS option must have been ON when the tables that are referenced by the view were created.

- The view cannot reference another view.

- The tables referenced by the view must be in the same database and have the same owner.

- The view must have been created with the SCHEMABINDING option.

- Any user-defined functions referenced by the view must have been created with the SCHEMABINDING option.

- Tables and user-defined functions referenced in the view must be referenced with two-part names (Owner.ObjectName).

- All functions referenced in the view must be deterministic.

- Column names must be explicitly referenced in the SELECT statement—SELECT* references are not allowed.

- A column used in a simple expression cannot be referenced more than once.

For a view to be indexed it cannot contain any of the following:

- A derived table.

- A rowset function.

- The UNION clause.

- A subquery.

- OUTER or self-joins.

- The TOP argument.

- An ORDER BY clause.

- The DISTINCT argument.

- The COUNT(*) function. (However, COUNT_BIG(*) can be.)

- The aggregate functions AVG, MAX, MIN, STDEV, STDEVP, VAR and VARP.

- SUM that is base on a nullable expression.

- The CONTAINS or FREETEXT functions.

- GROUP BY without COUNT_BIG(*). Further, the HAVING, CUBE or ROLLUP arguments cannot be used.

- SELECT statement that references columns defined with the `text`, `ntext`, or `image` data types.

- Columns defined with the float data type or expressions that evaluate to a float data type.

Note that you must create a clustered index on a view before any non-clustered indexes can be added. When you execute the CREATE INDEX statement on a view, the following restrictions apply.

- Only the view's owner can create the index.

- The settings ANSI_NULLS, ANSI_PADDING, ANSI_WARNING, ARITHBORT, CONCAT_NULL_YIELDS_NULL, and QUOTED_IDENTIFIERS are set to on and NUMERIC_ROUNDABORT is set to off.

- When you include a GROUP BY in the SELECT statement, you can only base the clustered index on the columns referenced by GROUP BY.

We will cover a couple of examples later in the chapter that show how to create an index on a view.

Updateable Views

Updateable views are not new to SQL Server 2000, but the ability to update them has been increased substantially with the introduction of the INSTEAD OF trigger.

To execute an INSERT or UPDATE statement on a view that does not have an INSTEAD OF trigger the following restrictions apply.

- The view cannot use any aggregate functions (e.g., AVG, SUM) or GROUP BY, DISTINCT, UNION, or TOP clauses.

- Derived columns cannot be updated through a view.

- If the view references more than one table, only columns from one table at a time can be modified.

- The same rules (e.g., nullability, DEFAULT, and FOREIGN KEY constraints) that apply to a regular table also apply to views.

To fully understand how an INSTEAD OF trigger increases the ability to update a view, you must have a general understanding of how triggers work. (Triggers are covered in more detail in Chapter 12, but a general explanation is provided here so you can more easily understand this topic.) A trigger is a database object that contains one or more SQL Statements that are attached to a table and executed when a predefined action (e.g., INSERT statement) is executed on the table. For example, let's say you want to send an email to the Order Processing Manager every time a *hot* order (one that needs immediate attention) is input into the system. You could create an INSERT trigger on the **Orders** table and when an order was entered that met the *hot* criteria, the trigger would fire and the statements inside the trigger would send the email.

There are two types of triggers: AFTER and INSTEAD OF. An AFTER trigger is the type described in the example scenario in the last paragraph. The statements inside the trigger are executed after the action (in this case, after the new row is inserted) is completed. The INSTEAD OF trigger prohibits the action from being carried out, but does execute the statements inside the trigger. If the **Orders** table had an associated INSTEAD OF trigger, instead of a new row being inserted into the table, the statements inside the trigger are executed—the trigger code replaces the INSERT action. The trick here is that a special table called **inserted** is populated with the values contained in the INSERT statement, and the statements in the trigger can reference **inserted**. Think of **inserted** as a temporary table that can be referenced with the same column names as the table to which the trigger is attached. If you require further explanation of this type of trigger, please see Chapter 12.

Now that INSTEAD OF triggers have been covered, you can understand how they circumvent some of the update restrictions put on views that do not have this type of trigger. The values referenced in an INSERT or UPDATE statement can be accessed from the statements in the trigger, and the modification can be made directly on the tables referenced in the view. I present an example later in the chapter, but only include it for completeness. I encourage you to avoid this convoluted way of performing data modifications and use more direct means like explicit INSERT or UPDATE statements encapsulated in stored procedures

Statement Permissions

The ability to create a view defaults to members of the fixed-server role **sysadmin** and the fixed-database roles **db_owner** and **db_ddladmin**. Members of **sysadmin** and **db_owner** can grant CREATE VIEW permission to other users. The user creating the view must have SELECT permission on all tables or views referenced in the view, and EXECUTE permission on any user-defined functions referenced in the view. In order to use the WITH SCHEMABINDING argument, the user must have REFERENCES permission on all objects referenced in the view.

Creating Views

You can create a view using both Query Analyzer and Enterprise Manager, and both methods are described in this section. Please note that the settings for both SET QUOTED_IDENTIFIER and SET ANSI_NULLS are encapsulated with the view at create-time. In other words, regardless of the values of these settings when the view is referenced in a statement, the settings revert to the values at the time the view was created.

Query Analyzer

To create a view in Query Analyzer, type the text of the CREATE VIEW statement in Editor Pane and execute the statement. The following example shows how to create a simple view based on the **Orders** table in the **Northwind** database.

```
USE tempdb
go
CREATE VIEW vw_Customers
AS
SELECT CompanyName,
       City,
       Country
FROM Northwind..Customers
go
--Results--
The command(s) completed successfully.
```

You can reference the view just like a table with the following statement.

```
USE tempdb
go
SELECT *
FROM vw_Customers
--Results (Partial)--
CompanyName                          City             Country
------------------------------------ ---------------- --------
Alfreds Futterkiste                  Berlin           Germany
Ana Trujillo Emparedados y helados   México D.F.      Mexico
Antonio Moreno Taquería              México D.F.      Mexico
...
```

You can also apply WHERE and ORDER BY clauses as shown.

```
USE tempdb
go
SELECT *
FROM vw_Customers
WHERE City = 'London'
ORDER BY CompanyName
--Results (Partial)--
CompanyName                          City             Country
------------------------------------ ---------------- ---------------
Around the Horn                      London           UK
B's Beverages                        London           UK
Consolidated Holdings                London           UK
...
```

TIP CREATE VIEW Templates

You can use the new template feature of SQL Server 2000 to make this process more efficient by selecting a predefined template that contains the required portion of the statement. Click the Template tab in the lower left of the Object Browser window, expand the Create View folder, and then drag-n-drop the template name to the Editor Pane. You can also add new templates via the Edit > Insert Template option on the main menu of Query Analyzer.

Enterprise Manager

Enterprise Manager provides two methods for creating views: New View/Query Designer and the Create View Wizard. Both methods are described here.

New View/Query Designer   This approach allows you to construct and test a SELECT statement, and then save it as a view. To create a view with this approach, complete the following.

1. Expand a Server and then expand the Databases folder.

2. Expand the Database in which the view is to be created, right-click Views, and select New View.

3. Click the right-most icon (yellow plus sign) and select the table, view, or function from the Table Add dialog. Note that you can use the CRTL key to make multiple selections at once.

4. Drag and drop the desired columns into the Grid Pane and apply any filter criteria.

5. Click the Run icon (exclamation point) on the toolbar to ensure the proper resultset is returned.

6. Once you are sure the proper SELECT statement has been created, click the diskette icon on the toolbar, specify the view's name, and click OK.

Figure 8-1 shows the Query Designer dialog with two tables in the Diagram Pane.

Create View Wizard   To create a view with the Create View Wizard, complete the following:

1. Click Tools on the main menu and select Wizards.

2. Expand the Databases option, select Create View Wizard, and click OK.

3. Select the database, table(s) and columns, supply any required WHERE clauses, provide a name for the view, and press Finish to create the view.

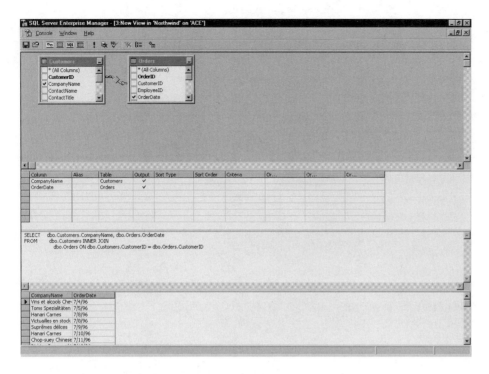

Figure 8-1. Query Designer Dialog

Working with Views

The following examples show how to create and update views with varying levels of complexity.

Single-table View

The first example demonstrates the ease with which you can restrict access to certain columns within a table. If the **Customers** table contained columns that held sensitive information, you would deny SELECT permission on the table and limit access with views like the one shown here.

```
USE tempdb
go
CREATE VIEW vw_Customers_ContactName
AS
SELECT CompanyName,
       ContactName,
       Phone,
       Fax
```

```
FROM Northwind..Customers
go


SELECT *
FROM vw_Customers_ContactName
ORDER BY ContactName
--Results (Partial)--
```

CompanyName	ContactName	Phone	Fax
Romero y tomillo	Alejandra Camino	(91) 745 6200	(91) 745 6210
Morgenstern Gesundkost	Alexander Feuer	0342-023176	NULL
Ana Trujillo Emparedados y helado	Ana Trujillo	(5) 555-4729	(5) 555-3745

...

Multi-table View

The example shown here creates a view based on a SELECT that includes a four-table join.

```
USE tempdb
go
CREATE VIEW vw_Customers_OrderDetail
AS
SELECT a.CompanyName,
       b.OrderID,
       d.ProductName
FROM Northwind..Customers a
JOIN Northwind..Orders b ON a.CustomerID = b.CustomerID
JOIN Northwind..[Order Details] c ON b.OrderID = c.OrderID
JOIN Northwind..Products d ON c.ProductID = d.ProductID
--Results--
The command(s) completed successfully.
```

The complex part of joining these tables together is now *hidden* in the view, so a less experienced user can now easily perform queries like showing which customer(s) ordered a particular product as follows:

```
USE tempdb
go
SELECT DISTINCT CompanyName
FROM vw_Customers_OrderDetail
WHERE ProductName = 'Geitost'
```

```
--Results (Partial)--
CompanyName
----------------------------------------
Antonio Moreno Taquería
Bottom-Dollar Markets
B's Beverages
...
```

A View in a View

This example demonstrates how to reference a view within another view's definition.

```
USE tempdb
go
CREATE VIEW vw_Customers_OrderByEmployee
AS
SELECT DISTINCT a.CompanyName,
       a.OrderID,
       b.FirstName+b.LastName AS EmployeeName
FROM vw_Customers_OrderDetail a
JOIN Northwind..Employees b ON a.EmployeeID = b.EmployeeID
go
SELECT *
FROM vw_Customers_OrderByEmployee
--Results (Partial)--
CompanyName                             OrderID     EmployeeName
--------------------------------------- ----------- -----------------------------
-
Alfreds Futterkiste                     10643       MichaelSuyama
Alfreds Futterkiste                     10692       MargaretPeacock
Alfreds Futterkiste                     10702       MargaretPeacock
...
```

Creating a Unique Clustered Index on a View

Please note that the examples shown here are for demonstration purposes only. These views do not fit the criteria for creating an index on a view, which is a large resultset accessed on a frequent basis. The first example attempts to create an index on **vw_Customers**.

```
USE tempdb
go
```

```
CREATE UNIQUE CLUSTERED INDEX ndx_CompanyName
ON vw_Customers (CompanyName)
--Results--
Server: Msg 1939, Level 16, State 1, Line 1
Cannot create index on view 'vw_Customers'. It is not schema bound.
```

This example actually violates several of the conditions required to index a view and is fundamentally incorrect when it comes to creating a unique clustered index. The conditions violated are listed as follows:

- The view must be created with the SCHEMABINDING argument.

- The view must reference tables in the same database.

- To create a UNIQUE CLUSTERED index, the value in the column referenced by the index must contain unique values.

The following statement creates the view in **Northwind** and adds SCHEMABINDING.

```
USE Northwind
go
CREATE VIEW vw_Customers
WITH SCHEMABINDING
AS
SELECT CustomerID,
       CompanyName,
       City,
       Country
FROM dbo.Customers
go

CREATE UNIQUE CLUSTERED INDEX ndx_CompanyName
ON vw_Customers (CustomerID)
```

Creating a Non-clustered Index on a View

Now that the view has a UNIQUE CLUSTERED index, non-clustered indexes can be applied. The following shows how to add another index to the view.

```
USE Northwind
go
CREATE INDEX ndx_City
ON vw_Customers (City)
```

Update via a View

The following example shows how to update the **CompanyName** in **Customers** via **vw_Customers**.

```
USE Northwind
go
UPDATE vw_Customers
SET CompanyName = CompanyName + '2'
WHERE CustomerID = 'ALFKI'

SELECT CompanyName
FROM customers
WHERE CustomerID = 'ALFKI'
--Results --

CompanyName
----------------------------------------
Alfreds Futterkiste2
```

The next example creates a new view that references columns from two tables, and then demonstrates what happens when you try to update a column from each table.

```
USE Northwind
go
CREATE VIEW vw_Customers_OrderDetail_2
AS
SELECT a.CustomerID,
       a.CompanyName,
       b.OrderID,
       b.ShipName,
       b.EmployeeID,
       d.ProductName
FROM Customers a
JOIN Orders b ON a.CustomerID = b.CustomerID
JOIN [Order Details] c ON b.OrderID = c.OrderID
JOIN Products d ON c.ProductID = d.ProductID
go
UPDATE vw_Customers_OrderDetail_2
SET CompanyName = CompanyName + '2',
    ShipName = ShipName + '2'
WHERE CustomerID = 'ALFKI' AND
      OrderID = 10643
```

```
--Results--
Server: Msg 4405, Level 16, State 2, Line 1
View or function 'vw_Customers_OrderDetail_2' is not updatable because the _
   modification affects multiple base_ tables referenced.
```

The following shows how to break this task into two statements.

```
USE Northwind
go
UPDATE vw_Customers_OrderDetail_2
SET CompanyName = CompanyName + '2'
WHERE CustomerID = 'ALFKI'

UPDATE vw_Customers_OrderDetail_2
SET ShipName = ShipName + '2'
WHERE OrderID = 10643

SELECT CompanyName
FROM Customers
WHERE CustomerID = 'ALFKI'

SELECT ShipName
FROM Orders
WHERE OrderID = 10643
--Results--


(1 row(s) affected)

CompanyName
----------------------------------------
Alfreds Futterkiste22

(1 row(s) affected)

ShipName
----------------------------------------
Alfreds Futterkiste2
```

To perform an INSERT on a table referenced in a view, all the NOT NULL col-umns without a DEFAULT constraint must by referenced in the INSERT statement. The following statement creates a view on the **Employees** table that references one NULL and three NOT NULL columns.

```
USE Northwind
go
CREATE VIEW vw_Employees
AS
SELECT EmployeeID,
       LastName,
       FirstName,
       Title
FROM Employees

SELECT *
FROM vw_Employees
--Results (Partial)--
EmployeeID  LastName             FirstName  Title
----------- -------------------- ---------- ------------------------------

1           Davolio              Nancy      Sales Representative
2           Fuller               Andrew     Vice President, Sales
3           Leverling            Janet      Sales Representative
...
```

The statements shown next demonstrate what happens when the INSERT statement does not reference all NOT NULL columns.

```
USE Northwind
go
INSERT vw_Employees
(
 LastName,
 Title
)
VALUES
(
 'Woods',
 'Vice President, Manufacturing'
)
--Results--
Server: Msg 515, Level 16, State 2, Line 1
Cannot insert the value NULL into column 'FirstName', table _
    'Northwind.dbo.Employees'; column does not allow nulls. INSERT fails.
The statement has been terminated.
```

This is expected behavior because you cannot insert a row into a table unless all the NOT NULL columns that do not have a DEFAULT constraint have a supplied value. This applies to explicit INSERTs on tables as well. This statement creates a new row in **Employees**.

```
USE Northwind
go
INSERT vw_Employees
(
 LastName,
 FirstName,
 Title
)
VALUES
(
 'Woods',
 'Natalie',
 'Vice President, Manufacturing'
)

SELECT  LastName,
        FirstName,
        Title
FROM Employees
WHERE EmployeeID = @@IDENTITY
--Results--
(1 row(s) affected)

LastName              FirstName  Title
-------------------- ---------- -------------------------------
Woods                 Natalie    Vice President, Manufacturing
```

You should note that the @@IDENTITY function retrieves the latest IDENTITY value inserted into **Employees**. The primary key of **Employees** (**EmployeeID**) is defined with the IDENTITY property, and @@IDENTITY contains the latest value for this column when a row is inserted into the table.

ALTER VIEW

The complete syntax of the ALTER VIEW statement is shown here.

```
ALTER VIEW view_name [ ( column [ ,...n ] ) ]
[ WITH ENCRYPTION | SCHEMABINDING | VIEW_METADATA ]
AS
    select_statement
[ WITH CHECK OPTION ]
```

The same arguments are used for CREATE VIEW, so the descriptions covered earlier apply here. Please note that when you use ALTER VIEW, any permissions applied to the view are maintained. If you DROP/CREATE the view to make changes, you lose all permissions when the DROP VIEW statement is executed.

Statement Permissions

The ability to alter a view defaults to members of the fixed-server role **sysadmin** and the fixed-database roles **db_owner** and **db_ddladmin** and is not transferable. The user creating the view must have SELECT permission on all tables or views referenced in the view and EXECUTE permission on any user-defined functions referenced in the view. To use the WITH SCHEMABINDING argument, the user must have REFERENCES permission on all objects referenced in the view.

Altering Views

A view can be altered in both Query Analyzer and Enterprise Manager. Both methods are described here.

Query Analyzer

Altering a view in Query Analyzer is very straightforward. Complete the following to get the text of **vw_Employees** in the Editor Pane.

1. Expand the **Northwind** database, and then expand the Views folder.

2. Right-click **vw_Employees** and select Edit. This places the text of the view in the Editor Pane prefaced by the ALTER VIEW statement.

3. Modify the view, and then execute the ALTER VIEW statement by clicking the Run icon (green arrow) on the toolbar.

The following example shows how to alter the text of **vw_Employees** to include order production information for each employee.

```
USE Northwind
go
ALTER VIEW vw_Employees
AS
SELECT a.FirstName+' '+a.LastName AS EmployeeName,
       COUNT(b.OrderID) AS OrderCount
```

```
FROM Employees a
LEFT JOIN Orders b ON a.EmployeeID = b.EmployeeID
GROUP BY a.FirstName+' '+a.LastName
--Results--
The command(s) completed successfully.
```

Now that the view has been altered to include order production information, the name **vw_Employees** is no longer indicative of the information it returns. The following statements show how to use the system stored procedure **sp_rename** to give the view a name that more accurately describes the resultset it returns.

```
USE Northwind
go
sp_rename 'vw_Employees', 'vw_Employees_OrderCount'
--Results--
Caution: Changing any part of an object name could break scripts and stored
procedures.
The object was renamed to 'vw_Employees_OrderCount'.
```

The following shows the resultset produced by **vw_Employees_OrderCount**.

```
USE Northwind
go
SELECT *
FROM vw_Employees_OrderCount
ORDER BY OrderCount DESC
--Results (Partial)--
EmployeeName                      OrderCount
------------------------------    -----------
Margaret Peacock                  156
Janet Leverling                   127
Nancy Davolio                     123
...
```

TIP LEFT JOINs and Views

*Do not reference a column from the unpreserved table in a LEFT JOIN oper-
ation, as the results are not predictable. The unpreserved table is the one
that appears after LEFT JOIN (**Orders** in the previous example).*

Enterprise Manager

Complete the following to edit a view in Enterprise Manager.

1. Expand a Server and then expand the Databases folder.

2. Expand the database in which the view is located and select the Views option.

3. Right-click the view in the Detail Pane and select Design View.

4. Once the Query Designer is active, make the desired changes, click the Run icon (exclamation point) to verify the desired resultset is produced, and then click the Diskette icon to save the view.

Figure 8-2 shows the contents of Query Designer when **vw_Employees_OrderCount** is opened in this manner.

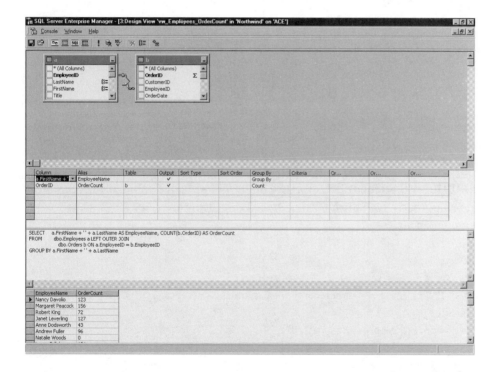

Figure 8-2. Query Designer Dialog

DROP VIEW

The complete syntax of the DROP VIEW statement is shown here.

```
DROP VIEW { view } [ ,...n ]
```

This statement is very straightforward. Simply specify the name of one or more views and execute the statement.

Statement Permissions

The ability to drop a view defaults to members of the fixed-server role **sysadmin** and the fixed-database roles **db_owner** and **db_ddladmin**. Members of **sysadmin** and **db_owner** can grant CREATE VIEW permission to other users.

Dropping Views

You can drop a view in both Query Analyzer and Enterprise Manager. Both methods are described here.

Query Analyzer

There are two tools used to drop a view in Query Analyzer: DROP VIEW statement and Object Browser.

DROP VIEW Statement   To drop two of the views created earlier using the statement approach, type the following in the Editor Pane and click the Execute Query icon (green arrow).

```
USE Northwind
go
DROP VIEW vw_Employees_OrderCount, vw_Customers_OrderDetail_2
--Results--
The command(s) completed successfully.
```

Object Browser   Complete the following in Object Browser to drop a view.

1. Expand the database in which the view is located and then expand the Views folder.

2. Right-click the view, select Delete, and then confirm the deletion by clicking OK.

Enterprise Manager

Complete the following steps to drop a view in Enterprise Manager.

1. Expand a Server and then expand the Databases folder.

2. Expand the Database in which the view is located and select the Views option.

3. Right-click the view in the Detail Pane and select Delete.

4. Confirm the deletion by clicking the Drop All button.

Information Schema Views

The information schema views that come with SQL Server 2000 access the metadata of various database objects. These views conform to the SQL-92 standard and are the preferred way for accessing metadata. The views reference the system tables that are commonly referred to as the database catalog. I recommended that you do not reference the system tables directly in applications. Their structure can change from version to version, and any statements that do reference them directly may not work when new versions of the product are released. The information schema views are shown in Table 8-1.

Table 8-1. Information Schema Views

VIEW	DESCRIPTION
CHECK_CONSTRAINTS	Displays the CHECK constraints in the database.
COLUMN_DOMAIN_USAGE	Displays the columns in the database that were defined with a user-defined data type.
COLUMN_PRIVILEGES	Displays the column permissions granted to or by the current user.
COLUMNS	Displays the columns in the database.
CONSTRAINT_COLUMN_USAGE	Displays the columns that have an associated CONSTRAINT.
CONSTRAINT_TABLE_USAGE	Displays the table that has associated CONSTRAINTS.

Table 8-1. Information Schema Views (Continued)

VIEW	DESCRIPTION
DOMAIN_CONSTRAINTS	Displays the columns defined with user-defined data types that have an associated RULE.
DOMAINS	Displays the user-defined data types.
KEY_COLUMN_USAGE	Displays the columns that have been defined as keys.
PARAMETERS	Displays the parameters used by the user-defined functions and stored procedures in the database.
REFERENTIAL_CONSTRAINTS	Displays the FOREIGN KEY constraints in the database.
ROUTINES	Displays the user-defined functions and stored procedures in the database.
ROUTINE_COLUMNS	Displays the columns returned by the table-valued functions in the database.
SCHEMATA	Displays the databases the current user can access.
TABLE_CONSTRAINTS	Displays the table constraints in the database.
TABLE_PRIVILEGES	Displays the table privileges granted to or by the current user.
TABLES	Displays the tables in the current database.
VIEW_COLUMN_USAGE	Displays the columns referenced by the views in the database.
VIEW_TABLE_USAGE	Displays the tables referenced by the views in the database.
VIEWS	Displays the views in the database.

Please note that schema views are executed in the context of the current database, so all information displayed is per that database. For a detailed description of the columns returned by each schema view please see the Books Online topic per the view's name, e.g., "CHECK_CONSTRAINTS."

Statement Permissions

The information schema views can be accessed by all users, but they will only return information on objects for which the user has appropriate permissions.

Accessing Information Schema Views

The following examples demonstrate how the information schema views can be used to retrieve the metadata of the objects in a database. The first example shows how to create a resultset that displays all the tables in the **Northwind** database.

```
USE Northwind
go
SELECT *
FROM INFORMATION_SCHEMA.TABLES
--Results (Partial)--
TABLE_CATALOG  TABLE_SCHEMA  TABLE_NAME                      TABLE_TYPE
-------------  ------------  ------------------------------  ----------
Northwind      dbo           Alphabetical list of products     VIEW
Northwind      dbo           Categories                      BASE TABLE
Northwind      dbo           Category Sales for 1997           VIEW
...
```

The next example shows the ordinal position and parameter type (IN or OUT) of the parameters defined in the **Employee Sales by Country** stored procedure.

```
USE Northwind
go
SELECT PARAMETER_NAME,
       ORDINAL_POSITION,
       PARAMETER_MODE
FROM INFORMATION_SCHEMA.PARAMETERS
WHERE SPECIFIC_NAME = 'Employee Sales by Country'
--Results--
PARAMETER_NAME    ORDINAL_POSITION    PARAMETER_MODE
--------------    ----------------    --------------
@Beginning_Date          1                 IN
@Ending_Date             2                 IN
```

Using Schema Views to Learn SQL Server Architecture

You can use the information schema views listed in Table 8.1 to gain insight into the architecture of SQL Server 2000. More specifically, you can examine their contents to see the relationships between the tables that make up the database catalog. The views are located in the **master** database, and you can use any of the ALTER methods described in the CREATE VIEW section to examine their contents. The following is the contents of the **COLUMN_DOMAIN_USAGE** view.

```
--Identifies columns that have a user defined datatype where the
--current user has some permissions on table
ALTER  view INFORMATION_SCHEMA.COLUMN_DOMAIN_USAGE
 as
select
                db_name()                 as DOMAIN_CATALOG
                ,user_name(typ.uid)       as DOMAIN_SCHEMA
                ,typ.name                 as DOMAIN_NAME
                ,db_name()                as TABLE_CATALOG
                ,user_name(obj.uid)       as TABLE_SCHEMA
                ,obj.name                 as TABLE_NAME
                ,col.name                 as COLUMN_NAME
FROM
                sysobjects obj
                ,syscolumns col
                ,systypes typ
WHERE
                permissions(obj.id) != 0
                AND obj.id = col.id
                AND col.xusertype = typ.xusertype
                AND typ.xusertype > 256          -- UDF Type
```

Before You Go

This chapter covered how to create, alter, and access user-defined views. It also provided some insight as to when they should be used to implement required functionality. In addition to user-defined views, the information schema views that come with SQL Server 2000 were also discussed.

The next chapter details many of the system stored procedures available in SQL Server 2000. System stored procedures perform administrative functions and provide information about server configuration settings and the database objects that reside on a server.

Part II

Procedures and Triggers

CHAPTER 9

System Stored Procedures

THERE ARE THREE TYPES OF STORED PROCEDURES available in SQL Server 2000: system, extended, and user-defined. This chapter concentrates on system stored procedures. Extended stored procedures are covered in Chapter 10, and the basics of user-defined stored procedures are covered in Chapter 11. The book concludes with Chapters 13 and 14, which tie all these topics together via extensive examples.

If you are a SQL programmer who does not perform any SQL Server administrative duties, you may not need to read this chapter in detail. In general, system stored procedures are used to perform administrative functions and are of little use to a programmer. Even if you fall into this category, I encourage you to at least browse the chapter and read some of the background information for the various categories of system stored procedures. The information may pique your interest in a topic (e.g., SQL Server Agent) and entice you to research it further to expand your SQL Server skills.

> **NOTE   Sample Code**
>
> *The sample code for this chapter can be downloaded at either* `http://www.apress.com` *or* `http://www.SQLBook.com.` *Download CodeCentric.zip and extract and access the Ch09.sql file.*

Before You Get Started

The system stored procedures that come with SQL Server 2000 allow you, in general, to interact with the system tables that are used to store information about the server, the databases on the server, and all the objects within each database. Understanding the design of the system tables should help you better understand how system stored procedures work and aid you in unravelling some of the mysteries of SQL Server—which should better prepare you to troubleshoot problems you encounter while working with the product. A brief overview of system databases and tables follows.

System Databases

Four system databases are created when you install SQL Server. A brief description of each database and its primary function is given in this section.

master

The **master** database is the main component of an instance of SQL Server. It stores all the server-level information such as server settings, logins, and startup parameters. It also stores all the information about each database created within the particular instance of SQL Server.

Since the **master** database stores all the key information about an instance of SQL Server, it is imperative that it be included in your backup and recovery strategy. More specifically, **master** should be backed up immediately after a server-wide change (e.g., creating a database) is implemented. If you do not back up **master** after a server-wide change is implemented and you are forced to restore the database from an outdated backup, all changes made after the backup was created are lost.

model

The **model** database acts as a template for all user-created databases. When a new database is created, its default size and contents are exactly the same as **model**. For this reason you can use **model** to hold objects that you want in all your databases. A good example of the type of object you might add to **model** is a user-defined data type. User-defined data types (discussed in Chapter 2) allow you to create a user-friendly name (e.g., ZipCode) and alias it to a column definition like varchar(15) NOT NULL. If you have a lot of user-defined types (perhaps part of a corporate-wide data dictionary), you can create them all in **model** and be assured they will be available in all the databases created on the instance of SQL Server.

msdb

The **msdb** database holds information about jobs, alerts, and operators. A *job* is a defined task that is scheduled to be executed on a period basis, an *alert* is a defined response to an event that occurs within SQL Server, and an *operator* is a user who is notified when a job fails or an alert is triggered. A more detailed description of the components used by SQL Server Agent is provided later in this chapter under the "SQL Server Agent Tables" heading.

tempdb

SQL Server uses the **tempdb** database for temporary storage of work tables and other non-persistent database objects. The **tempdb** database is recreated every time SQL Server is started, so you never want to create objects within the database that you intend to use on a regular basis. Because of this automatic cleanup, however, it serves as a nice *scratch pad* when you are experimenting with DDL or DML statements.

System Tables

System tables hold information about a particular installation of SQL Server. For example, there is a table called **sysdatabases** in **master** that holds information about each database on an instance of SQL Server. A table called **sysobjects** exists in each database to hold information about all the objects created in the database. A few tables exist only in **master**, and they are generally referred to as the System Catalog. Several tables exist in each database, and they are referred to as the Database Catalog. Other system tables are created in a database when it is configured for a particular activity like replication.

The following sections list the tables that reside in **master**, **msdb**, and the user-defined databases. The system tables created when replication is implemented on a server/database are not covered here. If you would like to review the tables used by replication, please see the Books Online topic: System Tables. I encourage you to execute a SELECT * on each table referenced so you can examine their contents. If you need help understanding a table's structure, please check the Books Online topic: <tablename> (in which the user substitutes the name of the table they want to lookup).

Note that some of the tables that follow are actually views. SQL Server 7 implemented a new database design for the system tables and some of the pre-7 tables were not included in the new design. There were, however, numerous applications that had been built around the old design, and this presented a problem because the new design would *break* these applications. Microsoft needed to ensure that any functionality built around the pre-7 design worked as expected, so they built views to simulate the tables that were not included in the redesign. Be aware that some of the system tables are not *real* tables or views, but virtual tables created on the fly when referenced in a statement. A virtual table is built from information stored internally by SQL Server and is presented in a table format so it can be read more easily.

> **TIP Do Not Alter System Tables**
>
> *Do not alter the system tables in any way. Altering a system table may cause irreparable damage or render certain functionality useless. As a matter of fact, you should only reference a system table directly if no other means (e.g., Informational Schema Views) exist.*

System Tables in the master Database

TABLE	DESCRIPTION
sysaltfiles	Contains the files that compose a database.
syscacheobjects	Contains information about how SQL Server's cache is being utilized.
syscharsets	Contains one row for each character set and sort order that is available for use in the instance of SQL Server. The default character set and sort order for the instance is specified in the **sysconfigures** table.
sysconfigures	Contains one row of each configuration option set on the server.
syscurconfigs	A view (not a table) that provides current information on configuration settings.
sysdatabases	Contains a row for each database that resides in an instance of SQL Server.
sysdevices	Contains a row for each disk or tape backup and database file on the server.
syslanguages	Contains one row for each language that is available for use on the instance of SQL Server.
syslockinfo	Contains information on all lock requests with the server.
syslogins	Contains one row for each login created on the server.
sysmessages	Contains one row for the text of each warning or error message used by SQL Server.
sysoledbusers	Contains one row for the users associated with a linked server.
sysperfinfo	A representation of the performance counters used by Performance Monitor (an NT tool that allows you to monitor SQL Server).
sysprocesses	Contains a row for each client and/or server process.

(Continued)

TABLE	DESCRIPTION
sysremotelogins	Contains one row for each remote login that can execute stored procedures on the server.
sysservers	Contains one row for each remote SQL Server server that can be accessed as an OLE DB source.

System Tables in Every Database

TABLE	DESCRIPTION
syscolumns	Contains a row for each column in all tables and views, and for each parameter referenced in a stored procedure.
syscomments	Contains one or more rows that hold the text of the CREATE statements used to produce each stored procedure, user-defined function, trigger, view, default, or check constraint in the database.
sysconstraints	A view that displays the relationship between a constraint and the objects it references.
sysdepends	Contains relationship information for the objects that reside in a database. For example, when a stored procedure is created, a row is added to **sysdepends** for each database object the stored procedure references.
sysfilegroups	Contains a row for each filegroup used by the database. There is at least one entry for the primary file group associated with each database.
sysfiles	Contains one row for each file used by the database.
sysforeignkeys	Contains one row for each foreign key constraint in the database.
sysfulltextcatalogs	Contains one row for each full-text catalog created off the database.
sysindexes	Contains one row for each index and table in the database.
sysindexkeys	Contains a row for each column that is used to define an index.
sysmembers	Contains a row for each member of a fixed-database role.
sysobjects	Contains one row for each object created in the database.
syspermissions	Contains a row for each permission that has been set in the database.

(Continued)

TABLE	DESCRIPTION
sysprotects	Contains a row for each statement permission (GRANT and DENY) that has been set in the database.
sysreferences	Contains a row for each foreign key created in the database.
systypes	Contains one row for each system and user-defined type in the database.
sysusers	Contains one row for each user, group, or system role in the database.

System Tables in the msdb Database

The system tables in **msdb** are divided into two categories: those that hold information about SQL Server Agent and those that hold information about database backup and restore activity. We'll cover both categories in this section.

SQL Server Agent Tables

Before I discuss the agent tables, let's cover some background information in case you don't have much administrative experience with SQL Server. SQL Server Agent allows you to more easily and proactively manage SQL Server by giving you the ability to configure tasks that run on a period basis or respond to events that occur on the server (e.g., transaction log exceeding a capacity limit).

For example, let's say you have aggregate tables (e.g., denormalized consolidation tables) that need to be updated from the transactional system two times a day. You can create a *job* that executes the statement used to aggregate the data and assign a *schedule* that executes the job at the specified times.

A good example of proactive server management is creating an *alert* that notifies an *operator* when a defined event occurs. For example, you could set an alert that notifies (via email or pager) the DBA when a database's transaction log file becomes more than 80 percent full.

The following provides a general description of the components used by the SQL Server Agent. This is by no means complete coverage of the topic, so if you want to learn more, please see the Books Online topic: Automating Administrative Tasks.

SQLServerAgent Service   The SQLServerAgent service is a Windows service (just like the MSSQLServer service) that is responsible for executing jobs, monitoring SQL Server, and firing event-based alerts.

Job   A job is a defined set of tasks to be executed on a period basis.

Alert An alert is a defined event/response that is executed when the event occurs.

Operator An operator is a user who is notified when an alert is fired.

You can configure SQL Server Agent to run on an individual server or, if you have multiple servers that require similar management, you can create a *master* Agent Server that distributes jobs to the dependent or target servers. This configuration reduces maintenance efforts because you are not required to create the same job/alert/operator on all the servers.

TABLE	DESCRIPTION
sysalerts	Contains a row for each defined alert.
syscategories	Contains a row for each category that is used to group alerts, jobs, and operators.
sysdownloadlist	Contains a row for each download instruction to be executed by the target servers.
sysjobhistory	Contains one row for each executed job.
sysjobs	Contains a row for each defined job.
sysjobschedules	Contains one row for each defined schedule used to execute a job.
sysjobservers	Contains one row for each relationship defined between a master and target server.
sysjobsteps	Contains one row for each step defined in a job.
sysnotifications	Contains one row for each notification method used to contact an operator when an alert is fired.
sysoperators	Contains one row for each defined operator.
systargetservergroupmembers	Contains one row for each target server who is a member of a multi-server configuration.
systargetservergroups	Contains one row for each target server group that is a member of a multi-server configuration.
systargetservers	Contains one row for each target server in the multi-server operation domain.
systaskids	Contains one row for each task ID that was upgraded from a pre-7 version of SQL Server. This provides a mapping of old-to-new IDs.

Database Backup and Restore Tables

The tables used to record information about backup and recovery operations are fairly straightforward. Should you need a primer on the backup and restore operations in SQL Server 2000, please see the Books Online topic: Types of Backup and Restore Processes.

TABLE	DESCRIPTION
backupfile	Contains one row for each data or log file that has been backed up.
backupmediafamily	Contains one row for each member of a defined media family.
backupmediaset	Contains one row for each defined backup mediaset.
backupset	Contains a row for each backup set.
restorefile	Contains one row for each file that has been restored.
restorefilegroup	Contains one row for filegroup that has been restored.
restorehistory	Contains one row for each restore operation.

What Are System Stored Procedures?

System stored procedures are database objects that allow you to either obtain information about the objects within an instance of SQL Server or perform an administrative function on the server. In general, every system stored procedure has a GUI counterpart that performs the same functionality. Exceptions exist, and in some cases the procedure approach provides you with more information than the GUI method. As SQL Server has evolved, the tools that come with the product (e.g., Enterprise Manager) have become much more robust and the reliance on system stored procedures has decreased.

System stored procedures are created in the same manner as user-defined stored procedures, but their names begin with the prefix "sp_" and are located in the **master** database. Be aware that not all stored procedures that start with the "sp_" prefix are system stored procedures. Some of the stored procedures that start with "sp_" are actually extended stored procedures, but were created using the "sp_" prefix because of the way in which SQL Server processes a procedure that begins with the prefix. We'll cover extended stored procedures in detail in the next chapter, but for now you should know that extended stored procedures are created using a programming language like C++ and are *attached* to an instance of SQL Server so they can be called like a user-defined or system stored procedure. In general, extended stored procedures have an "xp_" prefix in their names.

Why are some extended stored procedures created using the "sp_" prefix? When a stored procedure whose name begins with "sp_" is called, SQL Server looks for the object in the **master** database. If it does not find it in **master**, it looks for the procedure in the active database. This behavior allows you to create a general purpose stored procedure that can be accessed from within any database on the server without having to specify the call with the three-part name `database.owner.name`.

Viewing a System Stored Procedure

A system stored procedure is created using T-SQL, so you can view the statements of which it is composed in the same manner as a user-defined stored procedure. The following shows the text of **sp_databases**.

```
create proc sp_databases
as
set nocount on
declare @name sysname
declare @SQL  nvarchar(600)

/* Use temporary table to sum up database size w/o using group by */
create table #databases
(
 DATABASE_NAME sysname NOT NULL,
 size int NOT NULL
)

declare c1 cursor for
 select name
 from master.dbo.sysdatabases
 where has_dbaccess(name) = 1 -- Only look at databases to which we have access

open c1
fetch c1 into @name

while @@fetch_status >= 0
 begin
  select @SQL = 'insert into #databases select N'''+ @name + ''', sum(size) from '_
                               + QuoteName(@name) + '.dbo.sysfiles'
 /* Insert row for each database */
 execute (@SQL)
 fetch c1 into @name
end
deallocate c1
```

```
select DATABASE_NAME,
      DATABASE_SIZE = size*8,/* Convert from 8192 byte pages to K */
      REMARKS = convert(varchar(254),null)        /* Remarks are NULL */
from #databases
order by 1
```

As you can see, the system stored procedure is created using the same Transact-SQL statements available to you or me. The procedure uses a cursor to loop through the database names held in **sysdatabases** and the contents in **sysfiles** to determine the size of each database. The output generated by **sp_databases** is shown here.

```
USE master
go
sp_databases
--Results--
DATABASE_NAME  DATABASE_SIZE  REMARKS
-------------- -------------- ----------
master         15296          NULL
model          1920           NULL
msdb           10496          NULL
Northwind      6272           NULL
pubs           3264           NULL
tempdb         8704           NULL
```

Reviewing system stored procedures is a great way to increase your programming skills and learn more about the internal workings of SQL Server. Some of the functionality implemented in the procedures is complicated, so don't get frustrated if it takes you a few minutes to understand how it works.

You can view the text of a system stored procedure in one of three ways. The first uses the system stored procedure **sp_helptext** to retrieve the text of the target procedure. This approach is shown here.

```
USE master
go
EXEC sp_helptext 'sp_databases'
--Results (Partial)--
Text
-----------------------------------------------------------------------------
/*             Procedure for 8.0 server */
create proc sp_databases
as
              set nocount on
              declare @name sysname
              declare @SQL  nvarchar(600)
...
```

The second approach uses Object Browser to place the text of the procedure in the Editor Pane. Complete the following in Query Analyzer to do this with **sp_databases**.

1. Expand the **master** database, and then expand the Stored Procedure folder.

2. Scroll down until you see **sp_databases**, right-click the procedure, high-light Select Script Object to New Window As, and select Create.

The third approach uses the Stored Procedure Properties Dialog in Enterprise Manager. Complete the following to access this dialog.

1. Expand a server and then expand the Databases folder.

2. Expand the **master** database and select the Stored Procedures option.

3. Scroll down until you see **sp_helptext** and then double-click the procedure.

Categories of System Stored Procedures

The system stored procedures that come with SQL Server 2000 are broken into the nine categories shown here.

CATEGORY	PURPOSE
Catalog	Provides ODBC schema information about the objects within an instance of SQL Server.
Cursor	Provides cursor variable functionality.
Distributed Queries	Provides the ability to create and manage distributed queries.
SQL Server Agent	Used by SQL Server Agent to manage scheduled jobs and alert-based activities.
Replication	Replication management.
Security	Security management.
System	General SQL Server maintenance.
XML	Process calls to OPENXML.
Web Assistant	Implements Web Assistant functionality.

We'll cover some of the more popular procedures in each category except replication and cursor. As mentioned in the Preface, replication will not be covered in this book, so we will not address any replication procedures. The cursor category is not covered because for all but advanced cursor operations, you do not need to know the information provided by these procedures. To get an idea of how many system stored procedures there are, execute the following SELECT in Query Analyzer.

```
USE master
go
SELECT COUNT(*) AS spCount
FROM sysobjects
WHERE name like 'sp%'
--Results--
spCount
-----------
973
```

> **TIP Examine System Stored Procedures**
>
> *As you work through the following sections, use the Object Browser to review the text of the procedures. Because the system tables they reference were covered previously, you should be better prepared to understand exactly how they work or why a particular operation is carried out.*

Catalog

The procedures in this category are used to return metadata (properties of the data) information about the objects in SQL Server. They were created so the same information would be returned regardless of the changes that occur to the underlying system table over time. A set of views called *information schema views* also returns much of the data returned by catalog procedures. Information schema views are covered in Chapter 8.

The term "catalog" is industry-accepted terminology used to describe the tables that hold the metadata of an RDBMS. The procedures listed here also obtain information about non-SQL Server databases that are ODBC-compliant, so in some cases you will see *extra* data being returned that correlates to a more general ODBC term rather than the specific term used by SQL Server.

Please note that permission to execute any one of these procedures defaults to the **public** role so any valid user can access and run them. In general, any user can execute any system stored procedure that does not allow server configuration or data modification changes.

sp_databases

```
sp_databases
```

This procedure returns the database names for all databases that reside in the particular instance of SQL Server. As you can see in the syntax, there are no input parameters for this procedure. The data returned by **sp_databases** is shown here.

```
EXEC sp_databases
--Results--
DATABASE_NAME   DATABASE_SIZE   REMARKS
--------------  --------------  ----------

master          15296           NULL
model            1920           NULL
msdb            10496           NULL
Northwind        6272           NULL
pubs             3264           NULL
tempdb           8704           NULL
```

sp_tables

```
sp_tables [ [ @table_name = ] 'name' ]
    [ , [ @table_owner = ] 'owner' ]
    [ , [ @table_qualifier = ] 'qualifier' ]
    [ , [ @table_type = ] "type" ]
```

This procedure returns a list of all the objects (e.g., tables and views) that can appear in the FROM clause of a statement. The results returned by **sp_tables** are shown here.

```
USE Northwind
go
EXEC sp_tables
--Results--
```

TABLE_QUALIFIER	TABLE_OWNER	TABLE_NAME	TABLE_TYPE	REMARKS
Northwind	dbo	syscolumns	SYSTEM TABLE	NULL
...				
Northwind	dbo	Categories	TABLE	NULL
...				
Northwind	dbo	Invoices	VIEW	NULL

You can limit the resultset by supplying one of the optional parameters. For example, if you want to return only those objects that are views, use the following code.

```
USE Northwind
go
EXEC sp_tables @table_type = 'view'
--Results--
TABLE_QUALIFIER  TABLE_OWNER  TABLE_NAME  TABLE_TYPE  REMARKS
---------------  -----------  ----------  ----------  -----------

...
Northwind        dbo          Invoices    VIEW        NULL
...
```

The TABLE_QUALIFIER value will always be the database name when this procedure is executed against SQL Server. It is included because some DBMSs that support a three-part naming convention (`qualifier.owner.name`) do not use the database name as the `qualifier`. The **Remarks** columns will always be NULL for SQL Server, but there are other DBMSs that will return a value.

Be aware that the procedure does not work per the syntax shown in Books Online, which omits the `table_` portion of the parameter names. Using the syntax shown in Books Online, you would expect the following to return view information, but instead an error message is produced.

```
EXEC sp_tables @type = "'VIEW'"
--Results--
Server: Msg 8145, Level 16, State 2, Procedure sp_tables, Line 0
@type is not a parameter for procedure sp_tables.
```

When you view the procedure's parameters in Object Browser (as shown in Figure 9-1), you can you can quickly determine their proper names.

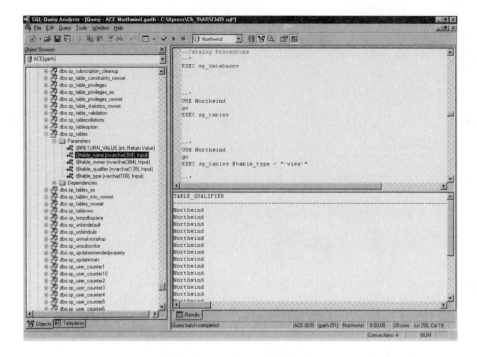

Figure 9-1. Viewing the parameters in Object Browser

sp_table_privileges

```
sp_table_privileges [ @table_name_pattern = ] 'table_name_pattern'
    [ , [ @table_owner_pattern = ] 'table_owner_pattern' ]
    [ , [ @table_qualifier = ] 'table_qualifier' ]
```

This procedure returns the permissions associated with a table. The following shows the output when only the table name is supplied.

```
USE Northwind
go
EXEC sp_table_privileges 'Orders'
--Results--
TABLE_QUALIFIER   TABLE_OWNER   TABLE_NAME   ...   GRANTEE   PRIVILEGE    IS_GRANTABLE
----------------  ------------  -----------  ----  --------  ----------   -------------

Northwind         dbo           Orders       dbo   dbo       DELETE       YES
Northwind         dbo           Orders       dbo   dbo       INSERT       YES
Northwind         dbo           Orders       dbo   dbo       REFERENCES   YES
Northwind         dbo           Orders       dbo   dbo       SELECT       YES
Northwind         dbo           Orders       dbo   dbo       UPDATE       YES
```

All columns should be self-explanatory except for **IS_GRANTABLE**. This column indicates whether the user ID in the **GRANTEE** column has permission to grant the permission listed in **PRIVILEGE** to other users. Note that the procedure does not return permissions about server roles. For example, the **public** role has access to the tables, but this is not shown in the resultset returned by the procedure.

sp_columns

```
sp_columns [ @table_name = ] object
    [ , [ @table_owner = ] owner ]
    [ , [ @table_qualifier = ] qualifier ]
    [ , [ @column_name = ] column ]
    [ , [ @ODBCVer = ] ODBCVer ]
```

This procedure returns the column names for the supplied table or view. The output is too wide to show here, so I will list the columns returned instead.

COLUMN	DESCRIPTION
TABLE_QUALIFIER	Database name.
TABLE_OWNER	Object owner.
TABLE_NAME	Object name.
COLUMN_NAME	Column name.
DATA_TYPE	Integer code for ODBC data type.
TYPE_NAME	Descriptor the DBMS uses to represent the integer data type value in DATA_TYPE.
PRECISION	Number of significant digits.
LENGTH	Transfer size of the data.
SCALE	Number of digits to the right of the decimal.
RADIX	Base for numeric data types.
NULLABLE	Nullability. 0 = NOT NULL, 1 = NULL.
REMARKS	Always returns NULL for SQL Server.
COLUMN_DEF	Default value for the column.
SQL_DATA_TYPE	Value of the type field used in the descriptor. Is the same as the value in DATA_TYPE except when datetime or the SQL-92 interval data type is used.

(Continued)

COLUMN	DESCRIPTION
SQL_DATETIME_SUB	Subtype code for the datetime and SQL-92 interval data types.
CHAR_OCTET_LENGTH	Maximum number of bytes allowed in a numeric or character column.
ORDINAL_POSITION	Ordinal position of the column within the table.
IS_NULLABLE	Used to indicate ISO compliance with respect to nullability. Yes = NULL, No = NOT NULL. ISO dictates that a column defined as NOT NULL cannot return an empty string.
SS_DATA_TYPE	SQL Server data type. Corresponds to the **type** column in the system table **systypes**.

sp_column_privileges

```
sp_column_privileges [ @table_name = ] 'table_name'
    [ , [ @table_owner = ] 'table_owner' ]
    [ , [ @table_qualifier = ] 'table_qualifier' ]
    [ , [ @column_name = ] 'column' ]
```

This procedure returns the column-level permissions for the supplied table. The output is shown here.

```
USE Northwind
go
EXEC sp_column_privileges 'Orders'
--Results--
TABLE_QUALIFIER TABLE_OWNER TABLE_NAME COLUMN_NAME ... GRANTEE PRIVILEGE IS_GRANTABLE
--------------- ----------- ---------- ----------- --- ------- --------- -----------
Northwind       dbo         Orders     CustomerID  dbo dbo     INSERT    YES
...
Northwind       dbo         Orders     ShipVia     dbo dbo     UPDATE    YES
```

As with **sp_table_privileges**, the value in **IS_GRANTABLE** indicates whether the **GRANTEE** can grant the **PRIVILEGE** to another user.

sp_pkeys

```
sp_pkeys [ @table_name = ] 'name'
    [ , [ @table_owner = ] 'owner' ]
    [ , [ @table_qualifier = ] 'qualifier' ]
```

This procedure lists the column(s) that comprise the primary key on the supplied table. The output is shown here.

```
USE Northwind
go
sp_pkeys 'Orders'
--Results--
TABLE_QUALIFIER  TABLE_OWNER  TABLE_NAME  COLUMN_NAME  KEY_SEQ  PK_NAME
---------------- ------------ ----------- ------------ -------- --------
Northwind        dbo          Orders      OrderID      1        PK_Orders
```

sp_fkeys

```
sp_fkeys [ @pktable_name = ] 'pktable_name'
    [ , [ @pktable_owner = ] 'pktable_owner' ]
    [ , [ @pktable_qualifier = ] 'pktable_qualifier' ]
    { , [ @fktable_name = ] 'fktable_name' }
    [ , [ @fktable_owner = ] 'fktable_owner' ]
    [ , [ @fktable_qualifier = ] 'fktable_qualifier' ]
```

This procedure, new to SQL Server 2000, returns the foreign key information on the supplied table. The results are too wide to list here, so I will list the column definitions instead.

COLUMN	DESCRIPTION
PKTABLE_QUALIFIER	Database name.
PKTABLE_OWNER	Table owner of parent table (i.e., table with primary key).
PKTABLE_NAME	Table name of parent table.
PKCOLUMN_NAME	Name of the column(s) comprising the primary key.
FKTABLE_QUALIFIER	Database name.
FKTABLE_OWNER	Table owner of child table (i.e., table with foreign key).
FKTABLE_NAME	Table name of child table.
FKCOLUMN_NAME	Name of the foreign key column(s).
KEY_SEQ	Sequence number of the columns when a multi-column primary key is used.
UPDATE_RULE	Indicates whether an UPDATE is cascaded to the child table. 0 = Cascade, 1 = No Cascade, 2 = Set Foreign Key to NULL.

(Continued)

COLUMN	DESCRIPTION
DELETE_RULE	Indicates whether a DELETE is cascaded to the child table. 0 = Cascade, 1 = No Cascade, 2 = Set Foreign Key to NULL.
FK_NAME	Descriptor of the foreign key.
PK_NAME	Descriptor of the primary key.
DEFERRABILITY	Reserved for future use. Currently returns 7 for all tables.

sp_stored_procedures

```
sp_stored_procedures [[@sp_name =] 'name']
    [,[@sp_owner =] 'owner']
    [,[@sp_qualifier =] 'qualifier']
```

This procedure returns all the stored procedures in the active database. The results are too wide to list here, so I'll list the column definitions instead.

COLUMN	DESCRIPTION
PROCEDURE_QUALIFIER	Database name.
PROCEDURE_OWNER	Procedure owner.
PROCEDURE_NAME	Procedure name.
NUM_INPUT_PARAMS	Reserved for future use.
NUM_OUTPUT_PARAMS	Reserved for future use.
NUM_RESULT_SETS	Reserved for future use.
REMARKS	Procedure description. Not used in SQL Server.
PROCEDURE_TYPE	Returns 2 for SQL Server.

sp_sproc_columns

```
sp_sproc_columns [[@procedure_name =] 'name']
    [,[@procedure_owner =] 'owner']
    [,[@procedure_qualifier =] 'qualifier']
    [,[@column_name =] 'column_name']
    [,[@ODBCVer =] 'ODBCVer']
```

This procedure returns information about the input and output parameters used with a stored procedure. The resultset returned is too wide to show here, so I will list the columns returned instead.

COLUMN	DESCRIPTION
PROCEDURE_QUALIFIER	Database name.
PROCEDURE_OWNER	Procedure owner.
PROCEDURE_NAME	Procedure name.
COLUMN_NAME	Parameter name.
COLUMN_TYPE	Parameter type (e.g., input or output).
DATA_TYPE	ODBC data type indicator.
TYPE_NAME	Description of ODBC data type.
PRECISION	Number of significant digits.
LENGTH	Transfer size of the data.
SCALE	Number of digits to the right of the decimal
RADIX	Base for numeric data types.
NULLABLE	Nullability. 0 = NOT NULL, 1 = NULL.
REMARKS	Always returns NULL for SQL Server.
COLUMN_DEF	Default value for the column.
SQL_DATA_TYPE	Value of the type field used in the descriptor. Is the same as the value in DATA_TYPE except when datetime or the SQL-92 interval data type is used.
SQL_DATETIME_SUB	Subtype code for the datetime and SQL-92 interval data types.
CHAR_OCTET_LENGTH	Maximum number of bytes allowed in a binary or character column.
ORDINAL_POSITION	The ordinal position of the column within the table
IS_NULLABLE	Used to indicate ISO compliance with respect to nullability. Yes = NULL, No = NOT NULL. ISO dictates that a column defined as NOT NULL cannot return an empty string.
SS_DATA_TYPE	SQL Server data type. Corresponds to the **type** column in the system table **systypes**.

sp_statistics

```
sp_statistics [@table_name =] 'table_name'
    [,[@table_owner =] 'owner']
    [,[@table_qualifier =] 'qualifier']
    [,[@index_name =] 'index_name']
    [,[@is_unique =] 'is_unique']
    [,[@accuracy =] 'accuracy']
```

This procedure returns index and statistic information for the supplied table or indexed view. The resultset returned is too wide to wide to show here, so I will list the columns returned instead.

COLUMN	DESCRIPTION
TABLE_QUALIFIER	Database name.
TABLE_OWNER	Object owner.
TABLE_NAME	Object name.
NON_UNIQUE	Indicate whether the index requires unique values. 0 = Unique, 1 = Non-Unique.
INDEX_QUALIFIER	In SQL Server, object name of table or view to which the index belongs.
INDEX_NAME	Name of the index.
TYPE	The type of information contained in the row. 0 = statistics, 1 = Clustered, 2 = Hashed, or 3 = Other.
SEQ_IN_INDEX	Position of the columns within an index.
COLUMN_NAME	Columns name of each column that makes up the index.
COLLATION	In SQL Server, this value is always "A" for "ascending."
CARDINALITY	Number of rows in the table or unique values in the index.
PAGES	Number of pages used to store the index or table.
FILTER_CONDITION	No value is returned for SQL Server.

Using Catalog Procedures

As you have probably surmised, it is unlikely you will be using the catalog procedures extensively in the applications you deploy for general use. Usually you will use these procedures in isolation to provide information about a particular object you are working with. Trying to use these procedures in an application is cumbersome because in order to work with the resultset, you must create a temporary table to hold the values returned and then query the temporary table. Should you wish to create an application that works with metadata, I suggest you use the information schema views that are covered in Chapter 8.

Distributed Queries

You can use the system stored procedures presented in this section to create *connections* to other SQL Server servers and non-SQL Server OLE DB data sources. Once you have made the connection, you can implement distributed queries that act on two more disparate data sources. A simple example of a distributed query is one that retrieves data stored in both Access and SQL Server. For more information on distributed queries, please see the Books Online topic: Distributed Queries.

Permission to execute the procedures discussed here default to the **sysadmin** and **setupadmin** fixed-server roles.

sp_addlinkedserver

```
sp_addlinkedserver [ @server = ] 'server'
    [ , [ @srvproduct = ] 'product_name' ]
    [ , [ @provider = ] 'provider_name' ]
    [ , [ @datasrc = ] 'data_source' ]
    [ , [ @location = ] 'location' ]
    [ , [ @provstr = ] 'provider_string' ]
    [ , [ @catalog = ] 'catalog' ]
```

This procedure allows you to create a connection parameter to an OLE DB data source. The following example shows how to connect to the **Northwind** database in Access.

```
sp_addlinkedserver @server = 'AccessOnAce',
                   @srvproduct = 'OLE DB Provider for Jet',
                   @provider = 'Microsoft.Jet.OLEDB.4.0',
                   @datasrc = 'C:\Program Files\Microsoft_
    Office\Office\Samples\Northwind.mdb'
--Results--
(1 row(s) affected)

(1 row(s) affected)
```

If you review the text of the procedure you will see that the results indicate one row was added to the **sysservers** system table and another was added to **sysxlogins**. Even though the procedure executed successfully, you cannot query the new data source until the appropriate login information is added.

sp_addlinkedsrvlogin

```
sp_addlinkedsrvlogin [ @rmtsrvname = ] 'rmtsrvname'

    [ , [ @useself = ] 'useself' ]

    [ , [ @locallogin = ] 'locallogin' ]

    [ , [ @rmtuser = ] 'rmtuser' ]

    [ , [ @rmtpassword = ] 'rmtpassword' ]
```

This procedure allows you to add a login to a remote server. The following specifies that the local credentials will not be verified on the remoter server.

```
EXEC sp_addlinkedsrvlogin @rmtsrvname  = 'AccessOnAce',
                          @useself = 'false',
                          @locallogin = NULL,
                          @rmtuser = NULL,
                          @rmtpassword =  NULL
--Results--

(0 row(s) affected)

(0 row(s) affected)

(0 row(s) affected)

(1 row(s) affected)
```

Now that the connection and login information has been set, query the remote datasource with the following.

```
SELECT CompanyName
FROM AccessOnAce...Customers
--Results--
CompanyName
```

```
----------------------------------------
Alfreds Futterkiste
Ana Trujillo Emparedados y helados
...
Wolski  Zajazd
```

Please note that the four-part name is used to reference the remote datasource. The four-part name consists of `linked_server_name.catalog.schema.object_name`, but only `linked_server` and `object_name` are required to connect to an Access database.

sp_droplinkedsrvlogin

```
sp_droplinkedsrvlogin [ @rmtsrvname = ] 'rmtsrvname' ,

    [ @locallogin = ] 'locallogin'
```

This procedure drops a remote login. In the previous example, I used NULL for the `locallogin`, so the same must be done here to drop the entry in the system table. The following shows how to delete the previously created login record.

```
EXEC sp_droplinkedsrvlogin @rmtsrvname =  'AccessOnAce' ,
                            @locallogin = NULL
--Results--

(0 row(s) affected)


(1 row(s) affected)
```

sp_linkedservers

```
sp_linkedservers
```

This procedure reviews the configuration parameters of all linked servers. The resultset is too wide to show here, so I will list the columns returned instead.

COLUMN	DESCRIPTION
SRV_NAME	Name of the linked server.
SRV_PROVIDERNAME	Name of the OLE DB Provider used to access the remote source.

(Continued)

COLUMN	DESCRIPTION
SRV_PRODUCT	Product name of the remote source.
SRV_DATASOURCE	OLE DB data source property.
SRV_PROVIDERSTRING	OLE DB provider string.
SRV_LOCATION	OLE DB location property.
SRV_CAT	OLE DB catalog property.

SQL Server Agent

The SQL Server Agent system stored procedures are used to create and manage jobs, alerts, and operators. For a brief discussion of the functionality provided by SQL Server Agent, see "System Tables" earlier in this chapter. Implementing and managing Agent functionality is much easier using Enterprise Manager and is the preferred method for managing jobs, alerts, and operators. This section will give you an idea of the functionality that can be implemented using alerts.

Permission to execute these procedures defaults to the **sysadmin** fixed-server role and is not transferable.

Please note that all procedures must be executed in the **msdb** database.

sp_add_operator

```
sp_add_operator [ @name = ] 'name'
    [ , [ @enabled = ] enabled ]
    [ , [ @email_address = ] 'email_address' ]
    [ , [ @pager_address = ] 'pager_address' ]
    [ , [ @weekday_pager_start_time = ] weekday_pager_start_time ]
    [ , [ @weekday_pager_end_time = ] weekday_pager_end_time ]
    [ , [ @saturday_pager_start_time = ] saturday_pager_start_time ]
    [ , [ @saturday_pager_end_time = ] saturday_pager_end_time ]
    [ , [ @sunday_pager_start_time = ] sunday_pager_start_time ]
    [ , [ @sunday_pager_end_time = ] sunday_pager_end_time ]
    [ , [ @pager_days = ] pager_days ]
    [ , [ @netsend_address = ] 'netsend_address' ]
    [ , [ @category_name = ] 'category' ]
```

This procedure allows you to add an operator and set their notification parameters. The start_time, end_time, and pager_days parameters allow you to restrict the times an operator can be notified.

sp_add_ job

```
sp_add_job [ @job_name = ] 'job_name'
    [ , [ @enabled = ] enabled ]
    [ , [ @description = ] 'description' ]
    [ , [ @start_step_id = ] step_id ]
    [ , [ @category_name = ] 'category' ]
    [ , [ @category_id = ] category_id ]
    [ , [ @owner_login_name = ] 'login' ]
    [ , [ @notify_level_eventlog = ] eventlog_level ]
    [ , [ @notify_level_email = ] email_level ]
    [ , [ @notify_level_netsend = ] netsend_level ]
    [ , [ @notify_level_page = ] page_level ]
    [ , [ @notify_email_operator_name = ] 'email_name' ]
    [ , [ @notify_netsend_operator_name = ] 'netsend_name' ]
    [ , [ @notify_page_operator_name = ] 'page_name' ]
    [ , [ @delete_level = ] delete_level ]
    [ , [ @job_id = ] job_id OUTPUT ]
```

This procedure allows you to create a job. You can configure several notification parameters to let an operator know the job has been executed.

sp_add_alert

```
sp_add_alert [ @name = ] 'name'
    [ , [ @message_id = ] message_id ]
    [ , [ @severity = ] severity ]
    [ , [ @enabled = ] enabled ]
    [ , [ @delay_between_responses = ] delay_between_responses ]
    [ , [ @notification_message = ] 'notification_message' ]
    [ , [ @include_event_description_in = ] include_event_description_in ]
    [ , [ @database_name = ] 'database' ]
    [ , [ @event_description_keyword = ] 'event_description_keyword_pattern' ]
    [ , { [ @job_id = ] job_id | [ @job_name = ] 'job_name' } ]
    [ , [ @raise_snmp_trap = ] raise_snmp_trap ]
    [ , [ @performance_condition = ] 'performance_condition' ]
    [ , [ @category_name = ] 'category' ]
```

This procedure allows you to create an alert. You can either specify a specific error message ID (**message_id**) or a message severity level (**severity**) that triggers the alert. Recall that all error messages used by SQL Server are stored in the **sysmessages** table and have an associated severity level. An alert can only be defined on an error message that is written to the NT Application Log. By default, only those error messages with a severity level of 19 or above (you can query **sysmessages** to review these) are written to the log, but you can use the **sp_altermessage** system stored procedure to alter this behavior so that any message is written to the log. **sp_altermessage** is covered in the System section later in this chapter.

You should also note that the syntax allows you to specify either a job_id or job_name. When a job is specified, it is executed when the alert is fired. This type of functionality will allow you to do things like dump a transaction log when it becomes full or exceeds a certain capacity limit.

An alert can be associated to a specific database. When the database parameter is specified, the alert will only fire if the event occurs within that database.

sp_add_jobschedule

```
sp_add_jobschedule [ @job_id = ] job_id, | [ @job_name = ] 'job_name',
    [ @name = ] 'name'
    [ , [ @enabled = ] enabled ]
    [ , [ @freq_type = ] freq_type ]
    [ , [ @freq_interval = ] freq_interval ]
    [ , [ @freq_subday_type = ] freq_subday_type ]
    [ , [ @freq_subday_interval = ] freq_subday_interval ]
    [ , [ @freq_relative_interval = ] freq_relative_interval ]
    [ , [ @freq_recurrence_factor = ] freq_recurrence_factor ]
    [ , [ @active_start_date = ] active_start_date ]
    [ , [ @active_end_date = ] active_end_date ]
    [ , [ @active_start_time = ] active_start_time ]
    [ , [ @active_end_time = ] active_end_time ]
```

This procedure allows you to create a schedule that determines when a job is executed. You simply supply a name and the associated job and specify the frequency at which it should be executed.

sp_add_notification

```
sp_add_notification [ @alert_name = ] 'alert' ,
    [ @operator_name = ] 'operator' ,
    [ @notification_method = ] notification_method
```

This procedure allows you to create a notification, which is simply the relation of an alert to the operators to be notified when it is fired.

Other Agent Procedures

This group of system stored procedures includes many more that allow you to update, delete, or find information about a particular job, alert, or operator. Should you want to review these procedures, please see the Books Online topic: System Stored Procedures. Keep in mind, though, that the Enterprise Manager approach to implementing the Agent functionality is the preferred method, and using it will make this process much easier.

Security

This group of system stored procedures allows you to manage certain aspects of security within an instance of SQL Server. In order to understand how these procedures are used, you must have general knowledge of SQL Server's security model. With this in mind, a general explanation of how security is implemented in SQL Server is provided For more exhaustive coverage SQL Server Security, please see the section of the Books Online that starts with the topic: Managing Security.

Unlike other categories, permission to execute the procedures in this category varies and will be addressed on a procedure basis.

SQL Server Security

To access an instance of SQL Server, you must have a login. The login can either be explicitly created *inside* SQL Server, or an NT account can be granted permission to access the server. Creating the login is only the first of a two-part process. To access a particular database, the login must be a user in that database. Once the login is added as a user to a database, either user permissions can be applied individually, or the user can be added to a fixed-server, fixed-database, or user-defined role.

SQL Server allows for three types of security roles: fixed-server, fixed-database, and user-defined. As the names suggest, the *fixed* roles have scope that is bound by either the server or a database. Using these roles is a very efficient way to manage security because you avoid managing permissions on an individual user basis. The user-defined roles are similar to the groups you might be accustomed to working with in NT. You simply create the role, apply security at the role-level, and add users.

Another type of user-defined role is the *application* role. In an application role, the application that attaches to SQL Server handles security. This type of role allows the authentication process to occur at the application level. The users can be required to type in the application role's password, or it can be hard-coded into the application. When a user logs in via the application, all permissions are governed by what has been assigned to the application role.

Let's look at two more security issues that sometimes confuse those new to SQL Server. The first concerns the **sa** login. The **sa** login does not work within SQL Server's security model. When a developer or administrator uses the **sa** login they are not bound by any security constraints and can perform any operation within the server. The **sa** login should not be used in the general operation of the server. Instead, each user who needs server-wide privileges should have their own login that belongs to the fixed-server role **sysadmin**.

The second issue concerns the fixed-database role **public** and the **guest** user account. Every user added to a database is automatically added to the **public** role. Therefore, any permissions granted to **public** are automatically granted to the new user. In general, the best approach is to remove all permissions from **public** so new users cannot accidentally get access to database objects. The **guest** user can also weaken a security strategy. Earlier I mentioned that creating a login and granting access to a database is a two-part process. When a database contains the **guest** user, any login that is not explicitly made a user of the database can gain access via the **guest** account. The **guest** account is only required to be present in the **master** and **tempdb** databases and in general should not be used in other databases. Both **Northwind** and **pubs** include the **guest** account, and this allows access to these databases for a login even if it is not explicitly made a user of either database.

sp_addlogin

```
sp_addlogin [ @loginame = ] 'login'
    [ , [ @passwd = ] 'password' ]
    [ , [ @defdb = ] 'database' ]
    [ , [ @deflanguage = ] 'language' ]
    [ , [ @sid = ] sid ]
    [ , [ @encryptopt = ] 'encryption_option' ]
```

This procedure allows you to create a login in SQL Server. The following shows how to create a login with the name **Sara**.

```
EXEC sp_addlogin @loginame = 'Sara'
--Results--
New login created.
```

The problem with this login is that it has not been assigned access to any databases. When the login attempts to access any database that does not contain the **guest** user account, the following error message is generated.

```
Server: Msg 916, Level 14, State 1, Line 1
Server user 'sara' is not a valid user in database 'DatabaseName'.
```

Because both **Northwind** and **pubs** contain the **guest** user, the login will have access to those databases and any object to which **guest** has been granted permission.

The proper way to create a login is to assign both a password and a default database at the time it is created. The following shows how to create a login with a password and default database.

```
EXEC sp_addlogin @loginame =  'Sara2',
          @passwd = 'blue',
          @defdb =  'Northwind'
--Results--
 New login created.
```

Specifying a default database will cause Enterprise Manager and Query Analyzer to make the specified database active when the user logs in to SQL Server. If the database you specify does not contain a **guest** user, the login will not be able to gain access until it is added as a user.

Permission to execute this procedure defaults to the **sysadmin** and **securityadmin** fixed-server roles and cannot be transferred.

sp_grantdbaccess

```
sp_grantdbaccess [@loginame =] 'login'
    [,[@name_in_db =] 'name_in_db' [OUTPUT]]
```

This procedure allows you to grant a login access to the specified database. The following shows how to grant the **Sara2** login access to the **Northwind** database.

```
USE Northwind
go
EXEC sp_grantdbaccess @loginame = 'Sara2'
--Results--
Granted database access to 'Sara2'.
```

Be aware that you must be in the target database before executing the procedure.

Permission to execute this procedure defaults to the fixed-server role **sysadmin** and the fixed-database roles **db_accessadmin** and **db_owner**, and it is not transferable.

sp_grantlogin

```
sp_grantlogin [@loginame =] 'login'
```

This procedure allows you to grant access to an NT login or group. The following shows how you would grant access to an NT login, **Randy**.

```
EXEC sp_grantlogin @loginame = 'Domain\Randy'
--Results--
Granted login access to 'Domain\Randy'.
```

Notice that the domain name has to be specified when adding an NT user or group.

Permission to execute this procedure defaults to the **sysadmin** and **securityadmin** fixed-server roles and is not transferable.

sp_helplogins

```
sp_helplogins
```

This procedure returns a resultset that contains all the logins and their associated users on the server. The results are too wide to show here, so the columns returned will be covered instead. Please note that the procedure returns two sets of data.

SET I

COLUMN	DESCRIPTION
LoginName	Login name.
SID	Security identifier.
DefDBName	Default database.
DefLangName	Default language name.
Auser	Indicates whether the login has an associated user name in a database—Yes/No.
ARemote	Indicates whether the login has an associated remote login—Yes/No.

SET II

COLUMN	DESCRIPTION
LoginName	Login name.
DBName	Default database.
UserName	User name in database.
UserOrAlias	Indicates whether the user is a user or has been added as a member to a fixed-database role.

Permission to execute this procedure defaults to the **sysadmin** and **securityadmin** fixed-server roles and is not transferable.

sp_helpuser

```
sp_helpuser [ [ @name_in_db = ] 'security_account' ]
```

This procedure displays the users and the roles to which they belong in the specified database. The following example shows the resultset returned.

```
EXEC sp_helpuser
--Results--
UserName GroupName    LoginName   DefDBName UserID SID
-------- ----------   ----------  --------- ------ --------------------------------
dbo      db_owner     NULL        NULL      1      0x0105000000000005150000000C050F702
Sara2    public       Sara2       CCI       5      0x7AEC2AA1AF5CD41192440080C8DE6E2A
```

Permission to execute this procedure defaults to the **public** role.

sp_password

```
sp_password [ [ @old = ] 'old_password' , ]
    { [ @new =] 'new_password' }
    [ , [ @loginame = ] 'login' ]
```

This procedure changes the password for the specified login. The following shows how to change the password for the **Sara2** login created earlier.

```
EXEC sp_password @old = 'blue',
            @new = 'green',
            @loginame =  'Sara2'
--Results--
Password changed.
```

Permission to execute this procedure defaults to the **public** role for users who are changing their own password; otherwise, only a member of the fixed-server role **sysadmin** can change for another user.

sp_validatelogins

```
sp_validatelogins
```
This procedure allows you to determine when the login information associated with an NT user and group has been orphaned—in other words, when the SQL Server login information has had the user or group entries deleted in NT. The following shows the results returned after I deleted the NT user **Randy** used earlier.

```
EXEC sp_validatelogins
--Results--
SID                                                           NT Login
------------------------------------------------------------  ---------
0x010500000000000515000000C050F70298266E5C69055777F0030000   Domain\Randy
```

Permission to execute this procedure defaults to the **sysadmin** and **securityadmin** fixed-server roles and is not transferable.

sp_denylogin

```
sp_denylogin [ @loginame = ] 'login'
```

This procedure prevents an NT user or group from connecting to an instance of SQL Server. The following shows how to prohibit the NT user **Tipper** from accessing SQL Server.

```
EXEC sp_revokelogin @loginame = 'Domain\Tipper'
--Results--
Revoked login access from 'Domain\Tipper'.
```

sp_revokelogin

```
sp_revokelogin [ @loginame = ] 'login'
```

This procedure allows you to remove the entries in the system tables for NT user and groups created with the system stored procedures **sp_grantlogin** or **sp_denylogin**. The following shows how it is used to delete the **Randy** user created earlier.

```
EXEC sp_revokelogin @loginame = 'Domain\Randy'
--Results--
Revoked login access from 'Domain\Randy'.
```

Permission to execute this procedure defaults to the **sysadmin** and **securityadmin** fixed-server roles and is not transferable.

sp_revokedbaccess

```
sp_revokedbaccess [ @name_in_db = ] 'name'
```

This procedure allows you to remove a user from the current database. The following shows how to remove the **Sara2** user added earlier.

```
USE Northwind
go
EXEC sp_revokedbaccess @name_in_db =  'Sara2'
--Results--
User has been dropped from current database.
```

Permission to execute this procedure defaults to the **sysadmin** fixed-server role and the fixed-database roles **db_owner** and **db_accessadmin**, and it is not transferable.

sp_changeobjectowner

```
sp_changeobjectowner [ @objname = ] 'object' , [ @newowner = ] 'owner'
```

This procedure allows you to change the owner of an object located in the current database. It can be most helpful when you accidentally create an object with a user that is not aliased to **dbo** and the object needs to be referenced without a two-part name. The following shows how you to add the **Sara** login created earlier to **North-wind** and then change the owner of the **Orders** table—to **Sara**, then back to **dbo**.

```
USE Northwind
go
EXEC sp_grantdbaccess @loginame = 'Sara'
go
EXEC sp_changeobjectowner @objname =  'Orders',
                          @newowner = 'Sara'
go
EXEC sp_changeobjectowner @objname =  'Sara.Orders',
                          @newowner = 'dbo'
--Results--
Granted database access to 'Sara'.
Caution: Changing any part of an object name could break scripts and stored_
procedures.
Caution: Changing any part of an object name could break scripts and stored_
procedures.
```

Permission to execute this procedure defaults to the **sysadmin** fixed-server role and the fixed-database roles **db_owner, db_ddldmin**, and **db_securityadmin** and is not transferable.

sp_addrole

```
sp_addrole [ @rolename = ] 'role'
    [ , [ @ownername = ] 'owner' ]
```

This procedure allows you to create a new role in the current database. The following shows how to create a new role in **Northwind**.

```
USE Northwind
go
EXEC sp_addrole @rolename =  'Auditors'
--Results--
New role added.
```

Permission to execute this procedure defaults to the **sysadmin** fixed-server role and the fixed-database roles **db_owner** and **db_securityadmin** and is not transferable.

sp_addrolemember

```
sp_addrolemember [ @rolename = ] 'role' ,
    [ @membername = ] 'security_account'
```

This procedure allows you to add a user to the specified role. The following adds the user Sara to the **Auditors** role created in the previous example.

```
USE Northwind
go
EXEC sp_addrolemember @rolename = 'Auditors' ,
                      @membername =  'Sara'
--Results--
'Sara' added to role 'Auditors'.
```

Permission to execute this procedure defaults to the **sysadmin** fixed-server role and the fixed-database roles **db_owner** and **db_securityadmin**. Any role owner, specified with the owner parameter when the role was created, can add members to *their* role.

sp_addapprole

```
sp_addapprole [ @rolename = ] 'role'
    , [ @password = ] 'password'
```

This procedure allows you to add an application role to the current database. The following shows how to add an application role to **Northwind**.

```
EXEC sp_addapprole @rolename =   'AcctApp',
                   @password =   'MoneyFunnel'
--Results--
New application role added.
```

Be aware there is no procedure that allows you to add a member to an application role because the application is *the* login. The application enforces security (who can use the app.), and the database permissions are applied to the application role.

Permission to execute this procedure defaults to the **sysadmin** fixed-server role and the fixed-database roles **db_owner** and **db_securityadmin**.

sp_srvrolepermission

```
sp_srvrolepermission [[@srvrolename =] 'role']
```

This procedure allows you to view the permissions that have been given to a fixed-server role. The following displays the permissions assigned to the fixed-server role **securityadmin**.

```
EXEC sp_srvrolepermission @srvrolename = 'securityadmin'
--Results--
ServerRole                         Permission
---------------------------------- ------------------------------------
securityadmin                      Add member to securityadmin
securityadmin                      Grant/deny/revoke CREATE DATABASE
securityadmin                      Read the error log
securityadmin                      sp_addlinkedsrvlogin
securityadmin                      sp_addlogin
securityadmin                      sp_defaultdb
securityadmin                      sp_defaultlanguage
securityadmin                      sp_denylogin
securityadmin                      sp_droplinkedsrvlogin
securityadmin                      sp_droplogin
securityadmin                      sp_dropremotelogin
securityadmin                      sp_grantlogin
securityadmin                      sp_helplogins
securityadmin                      sp_remoteoption (update)
securityadmin                      sp_remoteoption update part
securityadmin                      sp_revokelogin
```

Permission to execute this procedure defaults to the **public** role.

Other Security Procedures

Numerous other security-related system stored procedures are available. To review them, please see the Books Online topic: System Stored Procedures.

System

The system stored procedures in this category are used to perform general system maintenance. These procedures are fairly straightforward, so you won't need a primer to understand how they are used.

sp_executesql

```
sp_executesql [@stmt =] stmt
[
    {, [@params =] N'@parameter_name  data_type [,...n]' }
    {, [@param1 =] 'value1' [,...n] }
]
```

This procedure allows you to compile a SQL Statement for execution. The main benefit of using sp_executesql is that the execution plan is stored in memory and can be re-used on subsequent execution of the statement with different parameters. The following shows how to use the procedure to create a dynamic query on the **Orders** table.

```
USE Northwind
go
--Create variables
DECLARE @StartDate datetime
DECLARE @SQLString nvarchar(200)
DECLARE @ParmDefinition nvarchar(100)

--Populate variables
SET @SQLString = N'SELECT OrderID, CustomerID FROM Orders WHERE OrderDate > = _
@FilterDate'
SET @ParmDefinition = N'@FilterDate datetime'
SET @StartDate = '05/05/98'
--Execut First Query
EXECUTE sp_executesql @SQLString,
                      @ParmDefinition,
                      @FilterDate = @StartDate

--Change the filter date
SET @StartDate = '05/06/98'

--Execute second query
EXECUTE sp_executesql @SQLString,
                      @ParmDefinition,
                      @FilterDate = @StartDate
--Results--
OrderID     CustomerID
----------- ----------

11070       LEHMS
11071       LILAS
11072       ERNSH
11073       PERIC
11074       SIMOB
11075       RICSU
11076       BONAP
11077       RATTC
```

```
OrderID      CustomerID
-----------  ----------
11074        SIMOB
11075        RICSU
11076        BONAP
11077        RATTC
```

The second query will execute more efficiently than the first because the execution plan used to process the request is already in cache.

Permission to execute this procedure defaults to the **public** role.

sp_addtype

```
sp_addtype [ @typename = ] type,
    [ @phystype = ] system_data_type
    [ , [ @nulltype = ] 'null_type' ]
    [ , [ @owner = ] 'owner_name' ]
```

This procedure allows you to create a user-defined type. Chapter 2 covered user-defined types, so if you are not familiar with them, please review the "User-Defined Types" section in that Chapter. The following shows how to create a user-defined type that is used to define a column that holds state abbreviations and cannot contain NULLs.

```
USE Northwind
go
EXEC sp_addtype @typename = State,
                @phystype = 'char(2)',
                @nulltype = 'Not Null'

--Results--
(1 row(s) affected)

Type added.
```

Permission to execute this procedure defaults to the **public** role.

sp_droptype

This procedure allows you to delete a user-defined type. The following shows how to delete the data type created in the previous example.

```
USE Northwind
go
EXEC sp_droptype @typename = State
--Results--

(1 row(s) affected)

(0 row(s) affected)

Type has been dropped.
```

Permission to execute this procedure defaults to the **sysadmin** fixed-server role, the **db_ddladmin** and **db_owner** fixed-database roles, and the owner of the user-defined type.

sp_configure

```
sp_configure [ [ @configname = ] 'name' ]
    [ , [ @configvalue = ] 'value' ]
```

This procedure allows you to display and change server configuration settings. The following shows all the settings that can be changed with the procedure.

```
EXEC sp_configure
--Results--
```

name	minimum	maximum	config_value	run_value
allow updates	0	1	0	0
default language	0	9999	0	0
max text repl size (B)	0	2147483647	65536	65536
nested triggers	0	1	1	1
remote access	0	1	1	1
remote login timeout (s)	0	2147483647	5	5
remote proc trans	0	1	0	0
remote query timeout (s)	0	2147483647	0	0
show advanced options	0	1	0	0
user options	0	16383	0	0

You will see an option called "show advanced options," which allows display of advanced configuration options. They are not displayed by default, but we can use the following to change the default behavior.

```
EXEC sp_configure @configname =  'show advanced options',
            @configvalue = '1'
RECONFIGURE WITH OVERRIDE
--Results--
DBCC execution completed. If DBCC printed error messages, contact your
system administrator. Configuration option 'show advanced options' changed
from 1 to 0. Run the RECONFIGURE statement to install.
```

The RECONFIGURE WITH OVERRIDE statement makes the setting take place immediately, so that the next time you execute sp_configure the 36 rows shown here are
returned.

name	minimum	maximum	config_value	run_value
affinity mask	0	2147483647	0	0
allow updates	0	1	0	0
awe enabled	0	1	0	0
c2 audit mode	0	1	0	0
cost threshold for parallelism	0	32767	5	5
cursor threshold	-1	2147483647	-1	-1
default full-text language	0	2147483647	1033	1033
default language	0	9999	0	0
fill factor (%)	0	100	0	0
index create memory (KB)	704	2147483647	0	0
lightweight pooling	0	1	0	0
locks	5000	2147483647	0	0
max degree of parallelism	0	32	0	0
max server memory (MB)	4	2147483647	2147483647	2147483647
max text repl size (B)	0	2147483647	65536	65536
max worker threads	10	32767	255	255
media retention	0	365	0	0
min memory per query (KB)	512	2147483647	1024	1024
min server memory (MB)	0	2147483647	0	0
nested triggers	0	1	1	1
network packet size (B)	512	65536	4096	4096
open objects	0	2147483647	0	0
priority boost	0	1	0	0
query governor cost limit	0	2147483647	0	0
query wait (s)	-1	2147483647	-1	-1
recovery interval (min)	0	32767	0	0
remote access	0	1	1	1
remote login timeout (s)	0	2147483647	5	5
remote proc trans	0	1	0	0
remote query timeout (s)	0	2147483647	0	0

scan for startup procs	0	1	0	0
set working set size	0	1	0	0
show advanced options	0	1	1	1
two digit year cutoff	1753	9999	2049	2049
user connections	0	32767	0	0
user options	0	16383	0	0

When RECONFIGURE is not executed, the setting change does not take affect until SQL Server is restarted. Please note there are several settings (e.g., max worker threads) that require SQL Server to be restarted before they take affect. Advanced options should only be changed by those who fully understand the ramifications of the change. For more information on server configuration settings, please see the Books Online topic: Setting Configuration Options.

sp_dbcmptlevel

```
sp_dbcmptlevel [ [ @dbname = ] name ]
    [ , [ @new_cmptlevel = ] version ]
```

This procedure allows you to review or change a database's compatibility setting. This setting was added so that applications written around functionality in pre-7 and 2000 versions could execute as desired in 7 or 2000 without being rewritten. To see the available settings, execute the statement as shown here.

```
EXEC sp_dbcmptlevel
--Results--
Valid values of database compatibility level are 60, 65, 70, or 80.
```

Note that there is no 2000 compatibility level value. This level is designated by the "80" value. The following example shows how to check the existing setting, change it to 6.5 compatibility, and then change it back to 2000 compatibility.

```
--Check existing setting
EXEC sp_dbcmptlevel @dbname = 'Northwind'

--Change to 6.5 compatibility
EXEC sp_dbcmptlevel @dbname = 'Northwind',
                    @new_cmptlevel = '65'

--Verify change
EXEC sp_dbcmptlevel @dbname = 'Northwind'

--Change back to 2000 compatibility
```

```
EXEC sp_dbcmptlevel @dbname = 'Northwind',
                    @new_cmptlevel = '80'
--Results--
The current compatibility level is 80.

DBCC execution completed. If DBCC printed error messages, contact your system
administrator.

The current compatibility level is 65.

DBCC execution completed. If DBCC printed error messages, contact your system_
administrator.
```

To find out what functionality/behavior changed among versions, please see the Books Online topic: SQL Server Backward Compatibility Details.

Permission to execute this procedure defaults to the **sysadmin** fixed-server role and the **db_owner** fixed-database role of the target database.

sp_datatype_info

```
sp_datatype_info [ [ @data_type = ] data_type ]
                 [ , [ @ODBCVer = ] odbc_version ]
```

This procedure allows you to display the data types available in SQL Server 2000. The resultset of the procedure is too wide to display here, so I will list the columns returned instead.

COLUMN	DESCRIPTION
TYPE_NAME	Data type name.
DATA_TYPE	ODBC data type value.
PRECISION	Maximum precision of the data type.
LITERAL_PREFIX	Character(s) used before a constant (e.g., N' for Unicode and 0x for binary)
LITERAL_SUFFIX	Character used to terminate a constant (e.g., to terminate a character string)
CREATE_PARAMS	Description of the parameters used to define the data type.
NULLABLE	Indicates whether the data type can contain NULLs (0=NOT NULL, 1=NULL).

(Continued)

COLUMN	DESCRIPTION
CASE_SENSITIVE	Indicates whether the data type is case-sensitive (0=All columns, 1=All columns per collation).
SEARCHABLE	Indicates whether the column can be used in a WHERE clause (0=No, 1=Yes).
UNSIGNED_ATTRIBUTE	Indicates the sign of the data type (0=signed, 1=unsigned).
MONEY	Indicates the money data type (0=Not a money data type, 1=money data type).
AUTO_INCREMENT	Specifies auto-incrementing (0=Not auto-incrementing, 1=auto-incrementing, NULL=non applicable).
LOCAL_TYPE_NAME	Localized version of the data type name.
MINIMUM_SCALE	Minimum scale of the data type.
MAXIMUM_SCALE	Maximum scale of the data type.
SQL_DATA_TYPE	SQL data type indicator.
SQL_DATETIME_SUB	Datetime or ANSI interval sub-type value.
NUM_PREC_RADIX	Number of bits or digits used for calculating the maximum number a data type can hold.
INTERVAL_PRECISION	Value of interval leading precision.
USERTYPE	Value used in the **usertype** column in the **systypes** system table.

Permission to execute this procedure defaults to the **public** role.

sp_procoption

```
sp_procoption [ @ProcName = ] 'procedure'
    , [ @OptionName = ] 'option'
    , [ @OptionValue = ] 'value'
```

This procedure allows you to configure a stored procedure so that it automatically executes when SQL Server is started. This setting can come in handy when you are working with an application that accesses a number of tables on a frequent basis. You can create a stored procedure that executes a SELECT on each table, which causes them to be loaded into RAM. The first time a user performs an action that references the table(s), processing time is reduced because the target tables are already in RAM.

The following shows how to configure a stored procedure to execute when SQL Server is started.

```
USE master
go
CREATE PROCEDURE dbo.StartupExample
AS
SELECT GETDATE()
go
sp_procoption @ProcName = 'StartupExample',
              @OptionName = 'startup',
              @OptionValue = 'true'
--Results--
The command(s) completed successfully.
```

Notice that the procedure was created in the **master** database and its name was prefaced with **dbo**. Only procedures owned by **dbo** that are located in the **master** database can be set to auto-start.

Permission to execute this procedure defaults to the **sysadmin** fixed-server role.

sp_rename

```
sp_rename [ @objname = ] 'object_name' ,
          [ @newname = ] 'new_name'
          [ , [ @objtype = ] 'object_type' ]
```

This procedure allows you to rename a database or database object. When **sp_rename** is used to rename a database, the obj_type parameter value "Database" must be specified. For database objects, the parameter is optional. When views or stored procedures are renamed, it is often better to drop and re-created them because this will ensure any old execution plan for either one has been removed from the procedure cache.

The following shows how to rename the user-defined type **State** created in earlier in this section.

```
USE Northwind
go
EXEC sp_rename @objname = 'State' ,
               @newname = 'State_New'
--Results--
Caution: Changing any part of an object name could break scripts and stored
procedures.
The userdatatype was renamed to 'State_New'.
```

Notice the warning message displayed when the procedure is executed. Any process that references the old name will now fail because the procedure has been renamed.

Permission to execute this procedure defaults to the fixed-server role **sysadmin**, the fixed-database roles **db_owner** and **db_ddladmin**, and the owner of the target object.

sp_depends

```
sp_depends [ @objname = ] 'object'
```

This procedure allows you to determine what objects are dependent on the specified object. Be aware that it only reports on dependencies within the database it is located; any references to objects in other databases will not be reported. The following shows the dependencies on the **Orders** table.

```
USE Northwind
go
EXEC sp_depends @objname = 'Orders'
--Results--
In the current database, the specified object is referenced by the following:
name                                             type
----------------------------------------------   ----------------
dbo.CustOrderHist                                stored procedure
dbo.CustOrdersOrders                             stored procedure
dbo.Employee Sales by Country                    stored procedure
dbo.fx_Customers_ByOrderCount                    inline function
dbo.fx_OrdersByDateRangeAndCount                 table function
dbo.Invoices                                     view
dbo.LargeOrderShippers                           table function
dbo.Orders Qry                                   view
dbo.Product Sales for 1997                       view
etc.
```

Permission to execute the procedure defaults to the **public** role.

sp_help

```
sp_help [ [ @objname = ] name ]
```

This procedure allows you to view information about all the objects in a database or only the specified object. The resultset returned varies depending on the object type, so the most efficient way to see the values returned is to execute the following statements.

```
--All objects in database
EXEC sp_help

--Table
EXEC sp_help @objname = 'Orders'

--Stored Procedure
EXEC sp_help @objname = 'CustOrdersDetail'

--View
EXEC sp_help @objname = 'Invoices'

--Date type
EXEC sp_help 'int'
```

Permission to execute this procedure defaults to the **public** role.

sp_altermessage

```
sp_altermessage [ @message_id = ] message_number ,
    [ @parameter = ] 'write_to_log' ,
    [ @parameter_value = ] 'value'
```

This procedure allows you to specify that an entry is written to the NT Log when the supplied error message is generated. By default, only error messages with a severity level of 19 or higher are written to the NT Log. The valid parameter is 'WITH_LOG,' and the two parameter values are "true" and "false." The following shows how to change the "Incorrect syntax near '%.*ls'." error message to write to the NT Log. The example also changes it back to the default setting because there is no reason to write this error to the NT Log.

```
sp_altermessage 102, 'WITH_LOG', 'true'
go
sp_altermessage 102, 'WITH_LOG', 'false'
```

You can review the error messages used by SQL Server by querying the **sysmessages** table in the **master** database.

Other System Procedures

There are more than 60 procedures in this category, so I encourage you to take a quick look at their names in Books Online before continuing. To review these procedures, see the Books Online topic: System Stored Procedures.

Web Assistant

The Web Assistant procedures allow you to configure and manage a task that creates HTML pages from data stored in SQL Server. A basic understanding of HTML will help you understand some parameters, so if you are not familiar with HTML, please read Appendix A before continuing.

sp_makewebtask

```
sp_makewebtask [@outputfile =] 'outputfile', [@query =] 'query'
    [, [@fixedfont =] fixedfont]
    [, [@bold =] bold]
    [, [@italic =] italic]
    [, [@colheaders =] colheaders]
    [, [@lastupdated =] lastupdated]
    [, [@HTMLHeader =] HTMLHeader]
    [, [@username =] username]
    [, [@dbname =] dbname]
    [, [@templatefile =] 'templatefile']
    [, [@webpagetitle =] 'webpagetitle']
    [, [@resultstitle =] 'resultstitle']
    [
        [, [@URL =] 'URL', [@reftext =] 'reftext']
        | [, [@table_urls =] table_urls, [@url_query =] 'url_query']
    ]
    [, [@whentype =] whentype]
    [, [@targetdate =] targetdate]
    [, [@targettime =] targettime]
    [, [@dayflags =] dayflags]
    [, [@numunits =] numunits]
    [, [@unittype =] unittype]
    [, [@procname =] procname ]
    [, [@maketask =] maketask]
    [, [@rowcnt =] rowcnt]
    [, [@tabborder =] tabborder]
    [, [@singlerow =] singlerow]
```

```
[, [@blobfmt =] blobfmt]
[, [@nrowsperpage =] n]
[, [@datachg =] table_column_list]
[, [@charset =] characterset]
[, [@codepage =] codepage]
```

This procedure allows you to create a Web task. The number of parameters accepted by **sp_makewebtask** may make the procedure seem complex, but it is actually quite easy to use. When the procedure is executed, a user-defined stored procedure is created and executed to produce the output file. Depending on the value of @whentype, the procedure is either deleted immediately after execution or maintained for later use. When no value is specified, the default behavior is to delete the procedure immediately after execution.

The following shows how to create a simple HTML page that contains the customer names held in the **Customers** table.

```
USE Northwind
go
EXEC sp_makewebtask @outputfile = 'C:\MSSQL7\Binn\Customers.html',
                    @query =  'SELECT CompanyName FROM Customers',
                    @bold = 1,
                    @colheaders = 1,
                    @webpagetitle = 'Web Task Example',
                    @procname =  'CustomerNames'
--Results--
The command(s) completed successfully.
```

The @bold and @colheaders parameters specify (1 = True). The results will be displayed in bold text with the column name as the column heading and the @webpagetitle set as the <title> tag in the document. Once you execute the procedure you can double-click on Customers.html (using Windows Explorer) and the document will be displayed in Internet Explorer as shown in Figure 9-2. Be aware that because the default for @whentype was used, the procedure that created the page was deleted immediately after execution so you will not find it on the server.

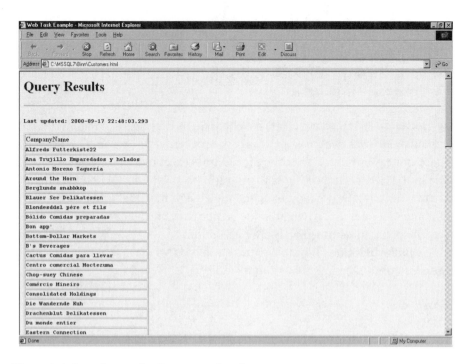

Figure 9-2. Page layout for Customers.html

You can configure the task (with the @whentype parameter) to run at a specified time(s) or on demand. The following example uses the parameter to specify that the task is executed on demand using **sp_runwebtask**.

```
USE Northwind
go
EXEC sp_makewebtask @outputfile = 'C:\MSSQL7\Binn\Customers.html',
                    @query =  'SELECT CompanyName FROM Customers',
                    @bold = 1,
                    @colheaders = 1,
                    @webpagetitle = 'Web Task Example',
                    @procname =  'CustomerNames',
                    @whentype = 5
--Results--
The command(s) completed successfully.
```

Once **sp_makewebtask** has executed, you can use Object Browser to view the procedure the statement created. The following shows the text of the procedure created by the previous example.

```
SET QUOTED_IDENTIFIER ON
GO
SET ANSI_NULLS ON
GO

 CREATE PROCEDURE [CustomerNames]  AS SELECT CompanyName FROM Customers
GO
SET QUOTED_IDENTIFIER OFF
GO
SET ANSI_NULLS ON
GO
```

As you can see, the procedure contains the SELECT statement provided in the @query parameter.

Permission to execute the procedure is provided to those users who have SELECT permission on the objects referenced in @query, the statement permission to create stored procedures and access to the file location referenced in @outputfile.

sp_runwebtask

```
sp_runwebtask [ [ @procname = ] 'procname' ]
    [ , [ @outputfile = ] 'outputfile'
```

This procedure allows you to execute a task created with sp_makewebtask. The following shows how to execute the task created in the previous example.

```
EXEC sp_runwebtask @procname =  'CustomerNames'
--Results--
The command(s) completed successfully.
```

Once the procedure is executed, you can review the file to make sure it contains the desired resultset.

Permission to execute this procedure defaults to those users who have SELECT permission referenced by the objects in the @query parameter.

sp_dropwebtask

```
sp_dropwebtask { [ @procname = ] 'procname' | [ , @outputfile = ] 'outputfile' }
```

This procedure allows you to delete a Web task. The following shows how to delete the Web task used in the previous example.

```
sp_dropwebtask @procname =  'CustomerNames'
--Results--
The command(s) completed successfully.
```

Once the procedure is executed, you can use Object Browser to verify that the CustomerNames stored procedure has been deleted.

Permission to execute the procedure defaults to the owner of the Web task and is not transferable.

Before You Go

We covered a tremendous amount of information in this chapter. If you read it all you should have learned a few things about SQL Server's architecture and security model, SQL Server Agent, and the how to create HTML documents whose content is derived from a SELECT statement. Many of the procedures covered may not be of immediate use to SQL Programmers, but be assured that understanding the system tables and procedures in SQL Server will provide you with a better understanding of the product, which will only help you perform your job in a more effective manner.

In the next chapter we cover the extended stored procedures that come with SQL server 2000. Extended stored procedures allow you to extend the functionality of SQL Server by creating external programs that can be referenced like a stored procedure.

CHAPTER 10

Extended Stored
Procedures

EXTENDED STORED PROCEDURES ALLOW YOU to extend the inherent functionality of
SQL Server 2000 by referencing programs written in languages like C++ as if they
were either a system or user-defined stored procedure. As long as the programs are
compiled as dynamic-link libraries (DLLs) and contain extended stored procedure
API functionality, they can be *attached* to SQL Server and referenced like the other
procedures presented in the book. This chapter will cover several of the system-
supplied extended stored procedures that come with SQL Server 2000 and the
steps involved in creating a custom extended stored procedure.

> **NOTE Sample Code**
>
> *The sample code for this chapter can be downloaded at either*
> http://www.apress.com *or* http://www.SQLBook.com. *Download
> CodeCentric.zip and extract and access Ch10.zip. The file
> contains the .sql and .dll files referenced in the chapter.*

Before You Get Started

One of the more useful extended stored procedures is **xp_sendmail**. I will cover it
in detail later in the chapter, but for now just be aware that you can use it to send
email to one or more recipients. To use **xp_sendmail**, a SQLMail session must be
started. Configuring SQLMail is an administrative-type function, but since there
are a few examples that use **xp_sendmail** in Chapters 13 and 14 limited coverage
of the topic is provided here.

SQL Mail

SQL Mail is the component of the MSSQLServer Service that allows SQL Server to process email messages. This is the mail service that will be discussed in this chapter. There is another mail component that is associated with the SQLServerAgent Service that allows mail to be sent as a result of an Alert being fired. It is fairly easy to confuse the functionality provided by each service, but the bottom line is the first component is the one that you will use when implementing programming functionality like sending email in a stored procedure. You will use the second when you want to send mail as a result of an administration issue like a transaction log becoming 90 percent full.

Regardless of the component you desire to use, a SQL Mail session must be running before mail can be processed. Before you can start a SQL Mail session, a mail profile must be configured and associated with the login that is assigned to the MSSQLServer Service. If you do not have a lot of experience working with mail servers this whole process can be confusing.

There are a couple of things you need to realize before this process starts to make sense:

- For you (leave SQL Server out of this for a minute) to process (read/send) email from a computer, it must have mail client software (e.g., Outlook) installed.

- Even if the computer you are using does have mail client software installed, you cannot access the local mail server until a mailbox has been created on the server and connection information has been defined at the client computer. Defining the connection information at the client is the profile creation process, which defines how you access the mailbox. Once your mailbox and profile have been created, you can start the mail client, log on to the mail server (you can configure the mail client to do this automatically), and process mail. This same process applies to SQL Server, but instead of creating the mail profile for your login, you create one for the login that is associated with the MSSQLServer Service.

Use the following two-part process to set up SQL Mail.

Creating a Mail Profile

1. Create a mailbox on the mail server for the login associated with the MSSQLServer Service. You can use the Services icon in Control Panel to check the account associated with the Service. Once the Services dialog is open, select MSSQLServer and click Startup. Please note that the local system account cannot be used as the login for the MSSQLServer Service when configuring SQLMail.

2. If it is not already present, install mail client software on the SQL Server server.

3. Log on to the SQL Server server using the account associated with the MSSQLServer Service.

4. Create a mail profile by clicking the Mail icon in Control Panel and specify the connection information for your mailbox.

5. Activate your mail client software and test the profile by sending and receiving an email. Once you have confirmed that you can send and receive email, move on to the next set of steps.

Configuring SQL Mail

1. In Enterprise Manager, expand a server and then expand Support Services.

2. Right click SQL Mail and select Profile.

3. Click the down arrow next to the Profile Name field and select the profile created previously.

4. Click Test to verify SQL Mail can successfully start and stop.

5. If you want SQL Mail to start automatically when SQL Server is started, click the Autostart SQL Mail when... checkbox.

That's all there is to configuring SQL Mail. If you have any problems see the Books Online topic: Help with SQL Mail, or if you have access to an NT Administrator ask for assistance. The first time I set up SQL Mail I elected for the second option. I had no experience configuring mailboxes and profiles and found an NT Administrator who was willing to explain the process.

Now that the SQL Mail is configured, it can be used in the **xp_sendmail** examples later in the chapter.

> **CAUTION NT Mail Client**
>
> *I have tried to use the mail client that comes with NT to implement SQL Mail on more than one occasion and each time the mail processes did not work as desired. I do not know why this mail client causes problems, but I have read in the newsgroups that other developers have experienced similar problems. On each occasion the problems went away when either Outlook or Outlook Express was installed on the server. Because of these experiences, I recommend that you do not use the NT mail client to implement SQL Mail.*

Extended Stored Procedures

A number of extended stored procedures come with SQL Server 2000, but only the ones you are most likely to use in your programming endeavors are covered here. In addition to the ones that come with the product, you have the ability to create a custom extended stored procedure and link it to an instance of SQL Server.

System-Supplied Extended Stored Procedures

System-supplied extended stored procedures were developed by members of the SQL Server Development Team and are loaded on your server when SQL Server is installed. Most of the extended procedures that come with SQL Server are named using an "xp_" prefix (e.g., **xp_sendmail**). This prefix differentiates these procedures from other database objects but adds no special functionality. When you call a procedure whose name begins with "xp_" from a database other than **master**, you must specify its location with the three-part name master.. xp_procedurename. Other extended stored procedures are named with the "sp_" prefix. This same prefix is used to name system stored procedures. Any stored procedure located in the **master** database that starts with the "sp_" prefix can be called from any user-defined database without specifying the database location. In other words, you call a procedure that is located in **master** and starts with "sp_" as if it is in the current database, because SQL Server's default behavior is to look for procedures that start with this prefix in **master** first and then in the current database.

I describe some of the more useful system-supplied extended stored procedures in this section. They are separated into two categories: general use and OLE Automation. Microsoft now refers to "OLE Automation" as "Automation", but the Books Online still uses the old terminology. I will use "OLE Automation" in this book to eliminate in confusion that might arise from being different than the Books Online.

General Programming Use

The two extended procedures described in this section are for general programming use and are not specific to a particular technology. I provided the categorization so that the extended procedures presented in the next section are more easily discernable from the extended procedures that come with SQL Server.

xp_cmdshell

This procedure executes an operating system command. The complete syntax is shown here.

```
xp_cmdshell {'command_string'} [, no_output]
```

Parameters

```
{'command_string'}
```

The operating system command that is executed. The command_string can be up to 256 characters.

```
[, no_output]
```

Optional parameter that specifies the output generated by the command is not returned to the client application that called the extended procedure. The following example shows how to display the contents of a subdirectory.

```
USE master
go
EXEC xp_cmdshell 'dir c:'
--Results (Partial)--
output
-------------------------------
 Volume in drive C has no label.
 Volume Serial Number is 2876-AD19
NULL
 Directory of C:\WINNT\system32
NULL
08/17/00  04:29p       <DIR>          .
08/17/00  04:29p       <DIR>          ..
01/23/99  06:43a               615 $winnt$.inf
...
```

The next example shows how to copy a file from one subdirectory to another.

```
USE master
go
EXEC xp_cmdshell 'copy c:\config.sys c:\temp'
--Results--
output
---------------------------------
        1 file(s) copied.
NULL
```

If you were executing this statement within a stored procedure, the output information would not be needed and you could suppress it with the following.

```
USE master
go
EXEC xp_cmdshell 'copy c:\config.sys c:\temp', NO_OUTPUT
--Results--
The command(s) completed successfully.
```

Permissions   I have seen quite a few posts in the newsgroups concerning problems developers were having with **xp_cmdshell**, and most were the result of their misunderstanding of how permissions work for this procedure. When the user executing the procedure is a member of the fixed-server role **sysadmin**, the command is executed within the security context of the NT login associated with the MSSQLServer Service. When the user who executes the command is not a member of **sysadmin**, the command is executed in the security context of the auto-created NT login SQLAgentCmdExec.

This may sound a little confusing, but it is simply a matter of rights. Leave SQL Server out of the picture for a minute and concentrate on the NT logins. If you logon to a computer with the login associated with the MSSQLServer Service and can execute the command via Command Prompt, members of **sysadmin** have the appropriate rights for the command. If you can do the same with the SQLAgentCmdExec login, then users who are not members of **sysadmin** have the rights to execute the command.

Let's look at an example just to make sure there is no confusion. Assume the login associated with the MSSQLServer Service is named SQLLogin, and you want to create a SQL Server process that copies files from another server that hosts the company's mission-critical accounting package. Due to the importance of the files on the accounting server, only certain logins (not SQLLogin) have access to its D: drive—where the target files are stored. When you try to execute **xp_cmdshell** to perform the copy, the process will fail because SQLLogin does not have rights to access the D: drive on the accounting server. The problem is difficult to troubleshoot because you do not see the error generated by the command. The proper way to troubleshoot this issue is to logon to the SQL Server server with SQLLogin and try to execute the copy command via Command Prompt. When you do, an error message will be generated and you can troubleshoot accordingly (e.g., give SQLLogin read permission on \\AcctServer\D$).

xp_sendmail

This procedure sends email to one or more recipients. The contents of the email can be generated in three ways:

- Hard-coded

- Built from variables

- Returned as the results of a query

Please note that **xp_sendmail** cannot be successfully executed until SQLMail is running. The steps to setup SQLMail were covered in the "Before You Get Started" section earlier in this chapter. The partial syntax of the procedure is shown here.

```
xp_sendmail {[@recipients =] 'recipients [;...n]'}
    [,[@message =] 'message']
    [,[@query =] 'query']
    [,[@copy_recipients =] 'copy_recipients [;...n]'
    [,[@blind_copy_recipients =] 'blind_copy_recipients [;...n]'
    [,[@subject =] 'subject']
    [,[@attach_results =] 'attach_value']
```

Parameters

```
{[@recipients =] 'recipients [;...n]'}
```

The individual(s) to whom the email is sent. When more than one recipient is listed, the email addresses are separated by a semi-colon.

```
[,[@message =] 'message']
```

Optional parameter that specifies the message body for the email. The maximum length of the message is 7,990 characters.

```
[,[@query =] 'query']
```

Optional parameter that creates the resultset shown in the message body of the email.

```
[,[@copy_recipients =] 'copy_recipients [;...n]'
```

Optional parameter that specifies the individuals to whom the email is copied. When more than one recipient is listed the email addresses are separated by a semi-colon.

```
[,[@blind_copy_recipients =] 'blind_copy_recipients [;...n]'
```

Optional parameter that specifies the individuals to whom the email is blind copied. When more than one recipient is listed, the email addresses are separated by a semi-colon.

```
[,[@subject =] 'subject']
```

Optional parameter that specifies the subject line of the email

```
[@attach_results =] 'attach_value'
```

Optional parameter specifying whether the resultset generated by **@query** should be sent as an attachment. The default when the parameter is not specified is false, which means the resultset is included in the body of the message. When the value is true, a .txt file is created that contains the resultset and is attached to the email.

Note that the parameter names (e.g., @recipients=) are optional. I suggest you include the parameter names in your procedures as it makes them much easier to maintain and troubleshoot. The following example shows how to send an email to my company email address.

```
USE master
go
EXEC xp_sendmail @recipients = 'garth@DataDrivenWebSites.com',
                 @subject = 'Contact Added',
                 @Message = 'A new contact has been added to the prospects database.'
```

More complex examples of how this procedure is used to implement notification functionality are covered in Chapter 12.

Object Permissions   Permission to execute **xp_sendmail** defaults to members of the fixed-server role **sysadmin**. Members of **sysadmin** can grant execute permission to any user.

OLE Automation Procedures

I use the following extended stored procedures to instantiate and work with automation objects. Programmers use these procedures with T-SQL to invoke the
functionality of other applications. Many programs (e.g., Word, Visio, SQL Server)
expose automation objects via an API; so once you learn the basic technique of
creating and calling one, it is just a matter of learning the objects, methods and
properties of the particular client software whose functionality you want to access.

One of the main components of SQL Server's architecture is SQL-DMO (Distributed Management Objects). SQL-DMO is an API that encapsulates all the
database and replication functionality of SQL Server. It can be used by any application that supports COM or Automation Objects. I chose to use SQL-DMO for the
examples in this chapter because you have easy access to the application's documentation. For a general introduction to SQL-DMO, please see the Books Online
topic: Developing SQL-DMO Applications. For an explanation of a particular
object, property or method, please see the Books Online topic: SQL-DMO
Reference.

Object Permissions

Only a member of the fixed-server role **sysadmin** can execute the **sp_OA** series of
procedures.

sp_OACreate

This procedure creates an instance of the automation object. The object is loaded
in the same address space as SQL Server and thus runs as an extension of SQL
Server.

```
sp_OACreate progid, | clsid,
    objecttoken OUTPUT
    [ , context ]
```

Parameters

```
progid, | clsid,
```

The program or class identifier that uniquely identifies the automation object. The
progid parameter is of the form "OLEComponent.Object" and the clsid is of the
form "{nnnnnnnn-nnnn-nnnn-nnnn-nnnnnnnnnnnn}." The documentation for
the software whose objects you are trying to access will indicate the descriptor or
ID that should be used.

```
objecttoken OUTPUT
```

The object token that references the object in subsequent procedure calls.

```
[ , context ]
```

Specifies the context in which the object is executed. The valid values are 1 for an in-process server, 4 for a local server and 5 (default value) for both in-process and local. In-process servers are implemented as .dll's and they run in the same memory space as SQL Server. A local server is implemented as an .exe, and it has its own memory space.

Example   The following shows how to access the SQL-DMO API to create a SQL Server automation object and display the associated object reference (token).

```
DECLARE @object int

-- Create a Server object.
--The SQLServer object contains the objects and collections that
--are used to perform administrative tasks via SQL-DMO.
EXEC sp_OACreate 'SQLDMO.SQLServer', @object OUT
PRINT @object
--Results--
16711422
```

sp_OAMethod

This procedure calls a method of an automation object.

```
sp_OAMethod objecttoken,
    methodname
    [ , returnvalue OUTPUT ]
    [ , [ @parametername = ] parameter [ OUTPUT ]
    [ ...n ] ]
```

Parameters

```
objecttoken,
```

The object reference generated by **sp_OACreate**.

methodname

The object's method that is being called.

[, *returnvalue* **OUTPUT**]

Return value generated by the method. When the method returns a value and returnvalue is not specified, a single-row single-column resultset is created on the application that called the method. The returnvalue variable must be of a compatible type with that returned by the method.

[, [*@parametername* =] *parameter* [**OUTPUT**]

One or more parameters of the method. The method's parameters must be specified after methodname and returnvalue and must be of a compatible type with those in the automation object.

Example   The following example extends the previous one by adding two method calls—one to connect to the server and one to verify the connection was successful. Please note the DMO syntax for the methods are shown as comments above the calls. See the Books Online topics: Connect Method and VerifyConnection Method for a full description of each method. To execute this example you need to modify the ServerName/Login/Password per your environment.

```
DECLARE @object int,
@ReturnValue varchar(30)

-- Create a Server object
--The SQLServer object contains the objects and collections that
--are used to perform administrative tasks via SQL-DMO.
EXEC sp_OACreate 'SQLDMO.SQLServer', @object OUT

-- Call the Connect method
--object.Connect( [ ServerName ] , [ Login ] , [ Password ] )
EXEC sp_OAMethod @object, 'Connect', NULL, 'ServerName','Login','Password'

-- Call the VerifyConnection method
--object.VerifyConnection( [ ReconnectIfDead ] ) as Boolean
EXEC sp_OAMethod @object, 'VerifyConnection', @ReturnValue OUT
PRINT @ReturnValue
--Results--
True
```

sp_OAGetProperty

This procedure gets the property value of an Automation Object.

```
sp_OAGetProperty objecttoken,
    propertyname
    [ , propertyvalue OUTPUT ]
    [ , index...]
```

Parameters

`objecttoken,`

The object identifier generated by **sp_OACreate.**

`propertyname`

The property's name.

[, *propertyvalue* **OUTPUT**]

The value associated with the property. If the return value is an automation object, the propertyvalue variable must be an int data type.

[, *index...*]

Any index parameters associated with the property.

Example   The following example shows how to get the value of the reference the Databases collection.

```
DECLARE @object int,
@ErrorValue int

-- Create a Server object
--The SQLServer object contains the objects and collections that
--are used to perform administrative tasks via SQL-DMO.
EXEC sp_OACreate 'SQLDMO.SQLServer', @object OUT

-- Call the Connect method
--object.Connect( [ ServerName ] , [ Login ] , [ Password ] )
EXEC sp_OAMethod @object, 'Connect', NULL, 'ServerName','Login','Password'
```

```
-- Get a reference to the Databases collection.
--The Databases collection contains the Database objects of an
--instance of SQL Server
EXEC sp_OAGetProperty @object, 'Databases', @object OUT
PRINT @object
--Results--
33488638
```

Please note how I reused the **@object** variable to get the reference to the Databases collection. For this particular example I did not need to keep track of the reference to the Server object, so the variable was reused. Had a reference to both objects been required, another variable (e.g., @dbobject int) would have been created.

sp_OASetProperty

This procedure sets the value of a method's property.

```
sp_OASetProperty objecttoken,
    propertyname,
    newvalue
    [ , index... ]
```

Parameters

```
objecttoken,
```

The object identifier generated by **sp_OACreate.**

```
propertyname,
```

The name of the property whose value is to be set.

```
newvalue
```

The new value for the property.

```
[ , index... ]
```

Any index parameters associated with the property.

Example   The following example shows how to modify the Querytimeout property of the Server object. Once the new value is set, **sp_OAGetProperty** verifies the new value. The default value for Querytimeout is –1 (negative one), which means there is no timeout.

```
DECLARE @object int,
 @ReturnValue int

-- Create a Server object
--The SQLServer object contains the objects and collections that
--are used to perform administrative tasks via SQL-DMO.
EXEC sp_OACreate 'SQLDMO.SQLServer', @object OUT

-- Set the QueryTimeout property
--object.QueryTimeout [= value]
EXEC sp_OASetProperty @object, 'QueryTimeout', 60

-- Get the current value of QueryTimeout
EXEC sp_OAGetProperty @object, 'QueryTimeout', @ReturnValue OUT
PRINT @ReturnValue
--Results--
60
```

sp_OADestroy

This procedure explicitly destroys an automation object. If **sp_OADestroy** is not called, the object is automatically destroyed when the batch that created it terminates.

```
sp_OADestroy objecttoken
```

Parameters

```
Objecttoken
```

The object identifier generated by **sp_OACreate**.

Example   The following example shows how to explicitly destroy an automation object.

```
DECLARE @object int

-- Create a Server object.
--The SQLServer object contains the objects and collections that
--are used to perform administrative tasks via SQL-DMO.
EXEC sp_OACreate 'SQLDMO.SQLServer', @object OUT
```

```
-- Destroy Server object.
--The SQLServer object contains the objects and collections that
--are used to perform administrative tasks via SQL-DMO.
EXEC sp_OADestroy @object
--Results--
The command(s) completed successfully.
```

sp_OAGetErrorInfo

This procedure allows you to see the errors generated by the **sp_OA** series of extended procedures.

```
sp_OAGetErrorInfo [ objecttoken ]
    [ , source OUTPUT ]
    [ , description OUTPUT ]
    [ , helpfile OUTPUT ]
    [ , helpid OUTPUT ]
```

Arguments

`[ objecttoken ]`

Optional argument of the object identifier generated by **sp_OACreate.** When the object identifier is specified, only the error information for the associated object is displayed. When the argument is NULL, the error information for the batch is displayed.

`[ , source OUTPUT ]`

Holds the source of the error. Variable must be defined with char, varchar, nchar or nvarchar data type.

`[ , description OUTPUT ]`

Holds the descriptions of the error. Variable must be defined with char, varchar, nchar or nvarchar data type.

`[ , helpfile OUTPUT ]`

Holds the Help file for the object. Variable must be defined with char, varchar, nchar or nvarchar data type.

`[ , helpid OUTPUT ]`

Holds the Help file context ID.

Example None of the examples covered so far trapped for errors. I deliberately did this so the code would be easier to read and understand, but you should always trap for errors in production code. The following example shows how to use **sp_OAGetErrorInfo** to trap for a logon error. The **ServerName** argument for the Connect method is not correct ("Xace" should be "ace").

```
DECLARE @object int,
@ErrorValue int,
@ErrorMessage nvarchar(255)

-- Create a Server object.
--The SQLServer object contains the objects and collections that
--are used to perform administrative tasks via SQL-DMO.
EXEC @ErrorValue =  sp_OACreate 'SQLDMO.SQLServer', @object OUT
IF @ErrorValue <> 0
BEGIN
   EXEC sp_OAGetErrorInfo @object, NULL, @ErrorMessage OUT
   SELECT @ErrorMessage AS ErrorMessage
   RETURN
END

-- Call the Connect method
--object.Connect( [ ServerName ] , [ Login ] , [ Password ] )
EXEC @ErrorValue = sp_OAMethod @object, 'Connect', NULL, 'Xace','garth','password'
IF @ErrorValue <> 0
BEGIN
   EXEC sp_OAGetErrorInfo @object, NULL, @ErrorMessage OUT
   SELECT @ErrorMessage AS ErrorMessage
   RETURN
END
--Results--
ErrorMessage
-----------------------------------------------------------------------------
[Microsoft][ODBC SQL Server Driver][DBNETLIB]Specified SQL server not found.
[Microsoft][ODBC SQL Server Driver][DBNETLIB]ConnectionOpen (Connect()).
```

I used the **@ErrorMessage** variable to hold the text of the error message. If I had not specified this variable, the output for all four arguments (source, description, help file, help ID) would have been displayed. When the output for the four arguments is displayed it is very difficult to read.

Pulling it all Together

I outlined the previous **sp_OA** examples for demonstration purposes only and have
not shown how these extended procedures can implement practical functionality
with SQL-DMO. In this final example, the extended procedures show how you can
programmatically generate the DDL used to create a table. The following shows how
to obtain the DDL of the **Customers** table in the **Northwind** database using the
Script method. The database and table names are set in variables at the beginning
of the batch, so you can easily create the DDL for any table on the server.

```
DECLARE @object int,
@ErrorValue int,
@ErrorMessage varchar(255),
@DDL varchar(8000),
@DatabaseName sysname,
        @TableName sysname

--Set database and table name
SET @DatabaseName = 'Northwind'
SET @TableName = 'customers'

-- Create a Server object
--The SQLServer object contains the objects and collections that
--are used to perform administrative tasks via SQL-DMO.
EXEC @ErrorValue = sp_OACreate 'SQLDMO.SQLServer', @object OUT
IF @ErrorValue <> 0
BEGIN
   EXEC sp_OAGetErrorInfo @object, NULL, @ErrorMessage OUT
   SELECT @ErrorMessage AS ErrorMessage
   RETURN
END



-- Call the Connect method
--object.Connect( [ ServerName ] , [ Login ] , [ Password ] )
EXEC @ErrorValue = sp_OAMethod @object, 'Connect', NULL, 'ServerName', _
                  'Login','Password'
IF @ErrorValue <> 0
BEGIN
   EXEC sp_OAGetErrorInfo @object, NULL, @ErrorMessage OUT
   SELECT @ErrorMessage AS ErrorMessage
   RETURN
END
```

```
-- Get a reference to the Databases collection.
EXEC @ErrorValue = sp_OAGetProperty @object, 'Databases', @object OUT
IF @ErrorValue <> 0
BEGIN
   EXEC sp_OAGetErrorInfo @object, NULL, @ErrorMessage OUT
   SELECT @ErrorMessage AS ErrorMessage
   RETURN
END


-- Get a reference to Northwind from the Databases collection
--object.Item( Name | Position ) as Object
EXEC @ErrorValue = sp_OAMethod @object, 'Item', @object OUT, @DatabaseName
IF @ErrorValue <> 0
BEGIN
   EXEC sp_OAGetErrorInfo @object, NULL, @ErrorMessage OUT
   SELECT @ErrorMessage AS ErrorMessage
   RETURN
END


-- Get a reference to Customers from Tables collection
--object.Tables( Name ) as Object
EXEC @ErrorValue = sp_OAMethod @object, 'Tables', @object OUT, @TableName
IF @ErrorValue <> 0
BEGIN
   EXEC sp_OAGetErrorInfo @object, NULL, @ErrorMessage OUT
   SELECT @ErrorMessage AS ErrorMessage
   RETURN
END

-- Call the Script method.
--object.Script( [ ScriptType ] [, ScriptFilePath ] [, Script2Type ] ) as String
EXEC @ErrorValue = sp_OAMethod @object, 'Script', @DDL OUT
IF @ErrorValue <> 0
BEGIN
   EXEC sp_OAGetErrorInfo @object, NULL, @ErrorMessage OUT
   SELECT @ErrorMessage AS ErrorMessage
   RETURN
END

PRINT @DDL
```

```
--Results (partial)--
CREATE TABLE [Customers] (
    [CustomerID] [nchar]

    ...
    )  ON [PRIMARY]
) ON [PRIMARY]
GO
```

The key to this batch is the Script method. Once a reference to the **Customers** tables is retrieved from the Tables collection, the Script method is called and the **@DDL** variable is populated with the DDL for the table.

The real challenge when working with the **sp_OA** series of procedures is understanding the objects, methods and properties exposed by an application's API. Fortunately for developers who want to use the functionality in SQL-DMO, the documentation is pretty good. If you want access to the functionality of another application you will have to review its documentation to verify that it supports automation objects and that their methods and properties are adequately described.

Viewing Procedure Properties

Not all systems-supplied extended stored procedures are implemented as .dll's. There are quite a few that actually reference internal SQL Server functionality—part of the .exe files that compose SQL Server. You can identify these procedures by reviewing the Extended Stored Procedure Properties dialog in Enterprise Manager. Complete the following steps to view the properties of an extended procedure.

1. Expand a Server and then expand the **master** database.

2. Select Extended Stored Procedures and view the procedures in the Detail Pane.

3. Right click any procedure and select Properties.

When the path input box contains the name of a .dll, the procedure is implemented via a .dll. When the input box contains "(server internal)," the procedure is internal to SQL Server. Figures 10-1 and 10-2 show the Properties dialog for **sp_OACreate** and **sp_Cursor**.

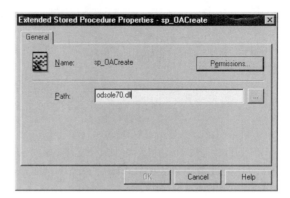

*Figure 10-1. Properties of **sp_OACreate***

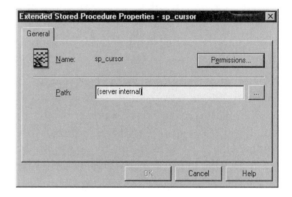

*Figure 10-2. Properties of **sp_Cursor***

If you would like to review all the extended stored procedures please see the Books Online topic: System Stored Procedures, and then scroll to the "General Extended Procedures" section.

Custom Extended Stored Procedures

Fortunately for most SQL Programmers, the extended stored procedures listed in the previous section can be used without requiring the programmer to have any knowledge of the language that was used to create them. All these procedures were created with either C or C++, so intermediate to advanced knowledge of these languages is required in order to create custom extended stored procedures that provide similar functionality. Two reasons C and C++ are the best languages for creating extended procedures follow.

- They can create a 32-bit .dll.

- The Extended Stored Procedure API was written in C and can be included as a header file in C and C++ programs.

The Extended Stored Procedure API is the set of APIs that allows the database engine to communicate with the server Net libraries. It replaces the ODS (Open Data Services) API that was used in pre-2000 versions of SQL Server. The actual extended procedure functions in the API have not changed, but all non-procedure functions were removed so the new name is more reflective of the functionality it provides.

Any language that can create a .dll can be used to create an extended procedure, but the functionality provided by the Extended Stored Procedure API would have to be re-created in the language in order for the .dll to work as expected.

> **WARNING Test Extended Procedures with Care**
>
> *Special care should be given to testing extended procedures. They run in the same memory space as SQL Server, so any access violations or other errors caused by the extended procedure could affect SQL Server.*

Object Permissions

Only members of the fixed-server role **sysadmin** can attach an extended procedure to an instance of SQL Server.

Creating Extended Stored Procedures

The example shown in this section is based on sample code that comes with SQL Server 2000. The sample code can be found in the .zip file in the Devtools\Samples\ods subdirectory on the SQL Server 2000 CD. When you extract the .zip file it will create a subdirectory called xp_hello. If you are familiar with C or C++ you can use the files in the xp_hello subdirectory to create the xp_hello.dll used in this example. Since the bulk of the readers of the book will not be C or C++ programmers, I included the xp_hello.dll in the example file for this chapter. Please download, extract, and find the file before continuing.

The process for attaching an extended procedure is the same regardless of the complexity of the code in the .dll. Once you learn how to attach the simple example shown here, you will have the ability to attach a .dll of any level of complexity.

Once you find the xp_hello.dll included in the example file for this chapter, copy it to the C:\MSSQL7\Binn before continuing. Note that if you did not upgrade an existing version of SQL Server to SQL Server 2000, the directory in which the file should be placed is C:\Program Files\Microsoft SQL Server\Mssql\Binn.

Attaching and Deleting Extended Stored Procedures

Once you have created and tested the .dll in its host environment, you can attach it to and delete it from an instance of SQL Server using either Query Analyzer or Enterprise Manager. (For those of you who decide to use the provided .dll, note that the creating and testing parts of this process are already complete.) Both the SQL Server and Query Analyzer approaches are described here.

Query Analyzer

To add an extended stored procedure in Query Analyzer use the system stored procedure **sp_addextendedproc**. The following shows how to attach xp_hello.dll.

```
sp_addextendedproc 'xp_hello', 'xp_hello.dll'
```

Once the procedure has been added, you can execute it with the following:

```
DECLARE @ReturnValue varchar(20)
EXEC xp_hello @ReturnValue OUTPUT
PRINT  @ReturnValue
--Results--
Hello World!
```

To remove an extended stored procedure in Query Analyzer use the system stored procedure **sp_dropextendedproc**. The following shows how to remove xp_hello.dll.

```
sp_dropextendedproc 'xp_hello'
```

Enterprise Manager

Complete the following to add an extended procedure in Enterprise Manager.

1. Expand a Server and then expand the Databases folder.

2. Expand the **master** database, right click Extended Stored Procedures and select New Extended Stored Procedure.

3. Populate the Name and Path fields with valid values and click OK.

In order to remove an extended procedure in Enterprise Manager, simply select the Extended Stored Procedure option, right click the procedure name in the Detail Pane and select Delete.

Before You Go

This chapter covered system-supplied and custom extended stored procedures. Admittedly, certain aspects of these objects can be confusing. Some are named with "xp_" and others with "sp_"; some are implemented with .dlls and others are calls to the SQL Server internals. Although they can be a little puzzling, they are very useful when it comes to implementing certain functionality not readily available in either T-SQL or the tools (e.g., Enterprise Manager) that come with the product.

The next chapter covers user-defined stored procedures, which is the main topic of this book. Understanding user-defined stored procedures is key to improving your skills as a SQL Programmer, so be prepared to be challenged by the material presented in Chapter 11.

CHAPTER 11

User-Defined Stored Procedures

USER-DEFINED STORED PROCEDURES ARE USED EXTENSIVELY by SQL programmers. Understanding how to create, manage, and the various ways to use them will put you on the right track to becoming a senior-level SQL programmer. After you complete this chapter and the extensive examples presented in Chapters 13 and 14, you should be prepared to tackle most any SQL programming task you encounter.

NOTE Sample Code

The sample code for this chapter is available for download at either `http://www.apress.com` *or* `http://www.SQLBook.com`. *Download CodeCentric.zip, extract the contents, and look for the file named Ch11.sql.*

Before You Get Started

This chapter assumes you have a good understanding of T-SQL (Transact-SQL) basics. If you are relatively new to T-SQL, please consider reading through Part I of this book before continuing. Although it is not required, you might find it beneficial to read through the "Before You Get Started" section in Chapter 9, which discusses the **syscomments** system table. User-defined stored procedures are stored in the **syscomments** system table, so understanding how the table relates to a database as a whole might provide more insight into how they are implemented.

User-Defined Stored Procedures

A *stored procedure* is a database object that allows you to encapsulate one or more T-SQL statements in an execution plan. Instead of sending individual statements to the server for execution, a stored procedure allows you to group statements and make a single call to the server. This can prove very efficient when you write code that encapsulates complex business rules. The next four sections discuss the main benefits of using stored procedures.

Managing Permissions

A simple example will help to demonstrate how stored procedures can be used to reduce the effort required to manage object permissions. Let's say you have a database that stores customer and invoice information and you would like to "clean up" invoices that are more than one year old and delete customers who have not done business with you (caused you to create an invoice) in more than three years. Assume that you have a fairly normalized database design like the one shown in Figure 11-1.

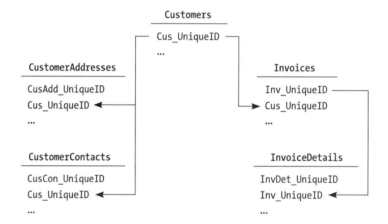

Figure 11-1. A partial table schema

If you coded this business process without using a stored procedure, you would be required to send five DELETE statements to the server:

1. Delete the InvoiceDetails records.

2. Delete the Invoices records.

3. Delete the CustomerAddresses records.

4. Delete the CustomerContacts records.

5. Delete the Customers records.

This approach is inefficient because the required client-side code is cumbersome to create and maintain, and you have to maintain table-level permissions (e.g., DELETE permission) on all the tables referenced by the statements.

The stored procedure approach is more efficient because all of the statements are contained in a single database object that can be called from the client application. This makes the client-side code more readable (maintainable), but the real benefit is with managing permissions. Instead of having to grant DELETE permission on the five tables to all the end users who will be executing the process, you simply give them EXECUTE permission on the stored procedure.

Manipulating Data

Let's think about another scenario that would make using stored procedures a more efficient development approach. Assume you are an expert Visual Basic programmer and you are just handed a specification for an application that will use SQL Server as the back end. After reviewing the specification you determine the application could probably be incorporated into the intranet your company is planning on implementing. You know enough about ASP (Active Server Pages) to fulfill the specification with a browser-based application, but you must develop and deliver it before the intranet will be ready.

If you used SQL passthrough (a.k.a. ad hoc or dynamic SQL) and embedded all the data manipulation statements in client-side code, converting the VB application to an ASP, browser-based application would be painful. SQL passthrough, for those of you not familiar with the term, is a technique whereby individual SQL statements are constructed as strings within the client application and then passed through to the database server for execution. Using the passthrough approach, you would have to cut-n-copy all the SQL statements embedded in the VB app into the ASP pages—a cumbersome and error-prone endeavor. If you used stored procedures to perform all the data manipulation, all you would have to do is convert the GUI portion of the VB application to ASP.

This scenario, of course, applies to all programming languages. As long as the programming language you use can *talk* to stored procedures and all the data manipulation the application performs is completed via stored procedures, converting an application from one development language to another is much easier.

Grouping Like Code

Another important benefit many developers overlook when assessing whether to use stored procedures is the ability to group like code. By that I mean the ability to logically group all the data manipulation code that is used in an application. Let's review a real-world scenario to understand why this point is so important. Have you ever developed an application per specification only to have it change once the end users got their hands on it? If you have, then you may have come to accept this as a reality of the development process: end users help create specifications, but end users usually alter the specification once they see what they asked for. Instead of fighting the inevitable, it may be more useful to create ways that will allow these types of changes (and subsequent maintenance of the application) to be made more easily.

One way I do this is with a naming convention that allows me to quickly determine which procedures act on a specific table. The naming convention is discussed in detail later, but the point I want to cover here is that the main table on which a stored procedure operates is always included in the name. That way, if the specification changes call for adding fields to four different tables, there is no guessing which stored procedures need to be modified. If you use SQL passthrough, all the modules in which the code might exist need to be searched to determine where modifications need to be made.

Using Execution Plans

Before moving on, I want to discuss execution plans, which are the most *important* reason to use stored procedures. An execution plan is the way in which the statement(s) contained in the stored procedure is processed by the database engine. Before you can fully understand how an execution plan is used you must understand what happens when you execute a stored procedure. I will cover this in detail a little later in this chapter, but for now keep these two points in mind:

- An execution plan is loaded into memory when a stored procedure is executed.

- It can be used for more than one call to the stored procedure.

Assume you have an application that is used by five hundred end users. Three hundred of those users use the same functionality (e.g., looking up customer information) throughout the workday. If SQL passthrough were used, each time the lookup function was called SQL Server would have to go through the steps required to process the SELECT statement. Using the stored procedure approach, the execution plan is loaded into memory once, and each subsequent call would use the same plan. This reduces the number of steps and the amount of memory required to complete the operation. There are certain situations that prohibit the use of an existing plan, but in general, this is how it works.

The History of Stored Procedures

The first database applications were implemented on mainframe computers using programming languages like COBOL. As you are probably aware, the mainframe architecture was such that one or more large computers (the mainframe) provided data storage and computer processing, and many dumb terminals interacted with the mainframe. The terminals provided no local storage or processing and only served as input/output devices for the mainframe. This type of architecture certainly had its limitations, but the one thing it did not require is high-bandwidth networks because all the processing was completed on the mainframe.

Over time database systems evolved, and a milestone was reached with the introduction of the client/server architecture in the late 80s. The client computers were no longer dumb and could both store and process data locally. Around this same time, the first SQL standard, SQL-86, was introduced. SQL-86 contained minimal functionality and provided no mechanisms for processing complex code on the database server. As a result, when the first SQL-based applications were implemented, network traffic increased dramatically because large amounts of data were being sent to client computers for processing.

Database vendors quickly realized (via complaints from their customers) the limitations of SQL-86 and researched ways to extend the base functionality so both performance and functionality could be increased. They concluded that the best way to solve the problems was to write their own extensions to SQL-86. These vendor-specific extensions allowed a client computer to request that the database server perform complex operations and only send the resultset back to the client. Of course, the problem with the extensions was that each vendor created its own without regard for how the other vendors were implementing similar functionality. For example, Sybase and Microsoft, who once held a joint interest in SQL Server, implemented their extensions via Transact-SQL, while Oracle did theirs with PL/SQL.

In 1991, ISO/IEC Standards members recognized the value of server-side processing and the problems caused by the vendor-specific extensions and thus started the process of creating a new standard to address the issue. In 1996, ISO/IEC 9075-4:1996 was finally introduced as Part 4 of the SQL-92. The working title of the standard is: "Information Tech—Database Languages—SQL-Part 4: Persistent Stored Modules." The "Persistent Stored Modules" portion of the title indicates that the functionality will be implemented in a modular form and that it will persist (unless explicitly deleted) as stored objects in the database. The standard not only details the language used to create and manage procedures, but other features like user-defined functions, control-of-flow statements, and error-handling.

Technically speaking, SQL Server does not implement modules as detailed in the standard. A module is defined as a collection of procedures. The main benefit of storing two or more procedures in a module is that each can share common database objects like cursors. SQL Server does not provide the functionality to group procedures in a module, but instead stores them as individual database objects. According to a senior Microsoft employee, there has been only one request for module functionality in the last five years, so it does not seem like the lack of support has caused much concern from their customers.

> **TIP Stored Procedure Abbreviations**
>
> *If you read the SQL Server newsgroups, you will undoubtedly see the name "stored procedure" abbreviated in a couple different ways. The most commonly used abbreviation I have seen is "stored proc," but some folks only use "proc." And just so you know, when someone uses either one of these abbreviations they are referring to user-defined stored procedures. The other two types of stored procedures (system and extended) are always referred to with full names, so no misunderstanding occurs. I will not use any abbreviations in this book, but you should know about them so there is no confusion when you see them in print.*

Creation and Execution Process

When you execute a CREATE PROCEDURE statement (limited, generic syntax shown here), it is parsed and as long as it contains no syntax errors, the text of the procedure is stored in the **syscomments** system table.

```
CREATE PROCEDURE procedure_name
[ { @parameter data_type }] [ ,...n ]
AS
sql_statement [ ...n ]
```

When you execute the stored procedure, the Query Processor examines the text of the procedure to verify that all the objects it references exist. In addition, it verifies that all variables created within the procedure have compatible data types for the operations in which they are used. After these two requirements have been met, the Query Optimizer examines the statements in the procedure to create an execution plan, which is used by the database engine to process the statements. The analysis of the statements and subsequent execution plan creation are referred to as the *compilation* process.

Once the execution plan is created, it is placed in memory in an area called the *procedure cache*. Exactly how an execution plan is created cannot be predetermined (this is a function of how the Query Optimizer was built and is proprietary information), but the following are some of the factors that affect the outcome.

- The size of the tables referenced in the statements

- Indexes and the distribution of data within an index

- Comparison operations used in the WHERE clause

- The type of joins used in the SELECT statements

- The use of UNION, GROUP BY, or ORDER BY clauses

An execution plan is actually composed of two data structures. The first is called the *query plan*, and it does not contain any user-specific (e.g., parameter values) information about the statements. There are never more than two (one for parallel processing and one for sequential processing) in cache. The second is called the *execution context*, and it contains user-specific information for the call to the procedure. There can be as many plans as there are open calls, but if one already exists and is not in use, it will be re-used by the database engine.

Deferred Name Resolution

Did you notice that only the syntax of statement is verified when a stored procedure is created? When you created a stored procedure in pre-7 versions of SQL Server, all the objects it referenced had to exist at create-time or an error message was generated. This is no longer the case in SQL Server 2000, and the process that facilitates this is called *deferred name resolution*.

Procedure Cache and Plan Re-Use

The procedure cache is used to hold execution plans. Once a procedure's execution plan has been placed in memory, it is used repeatedly when the stored procedure is called. In other words, the execution plan for a procedure is only created the first time it is invoked, and subsequent calls to the procedure are more efficient because the compilation process is avoided. In certain cases the Query Optimizer will decide to mark an existing plan as invalid and recompile it the next time the procedure is called. The following are examples of when an execution plan might be marked invalid.

- The structure of a table referenced by the procedure is altered.

- An index used by the plan has been dropped.

- An index's statistics are updated after the plan was created.

- A large number of INSERT or DELETE statements are executed that affect the distribution of values in the column(s) that compose the primary key

You can explicitly force a plan to be recompiled by using the system stored procedure **sp_recompile** or by using the WITH RECOMPILE argument (discussed later in this chapter).

Once an execution plan is placed in procedure cache, it stays there until either SQL Server is restarted or the space occupied by the plan is required for other processes. The database engine uses a method referred to as LRU (least recently used) to determine which procedure should be removed to make room for the pending process. In short, an age value is calculated for each procedure, and this value decrements by one with each cycle of a server process called the lazywriter. The age value assigned is a function of the cost factor (how much resources are required for compilation) and the number of times it has been used, so *expensive* procedures are less likely to removed from memory. Once the age value of a procedure is decremented to zero and the space it occupies is need for another process, the lazywriter process removes it from memory.

Stored Procedure versus Non-Procedure Processing

The Query Processor is the component of SQL Server that is responsible for processing all requests sent to an instance of SQL Server. It can process statements in two ways: single statement or batch. In either case, a single execution plan fulfills the request.

In pre-7 versions of SQL Server, tremendous performance gains could be realized by using stored procedures over individual SQL statement processing. The execution plan for a stored procedure was created and stored at create-time, so when one was executed, all the database engine needed to do was retrieve the plan and execute accordingly. When an individual statement was processed, it had to be checked for syntax errors and then have an execution plan built and placed in memory. The stored procedure approach of creating and storing the execution plan had certain limitations (mostly surrounding changing data structures and updated index statistic values), so it was replaced with the approach described in the previous section.

The individual statement processing approach was also changed in SQL Server 7. A feature was added so that you could prepare a statement for processing and then place its execution plan in memory. Subsequent calls using the same statement would re-use the existing plan and thus be processed much more efficiently. In order to prepare a statement for processing, the system stored procedure **sp_executesql** is used. This system stored procedure was covered in the "Systems" section of Chapter 9.

Earlier in the chapter I said one advantage of using stored procedures was the performance benefits compared to the non-procedure approach. After reading the preceding two paragraphs, you might be wondering if there really are any performance advantages in using stored procedures. Although the advantages have decreased significantly in the past two versions of SQL Server, there is still a slight performance advantage to using stored procedures. More specifically, because the statements contained in a procedure are always the same, the Query Optimizer will always find an existing execution plan, assuming one exists, in cache. It does not mean it will always use it, but it will find it. When a non-procedure approach is used, even the slightest change in the statement will cause Query Optimizer to build a new execution plan.

CREATE PROCEDURE Syntax

Now that you understand the processes completed when a stored procedure is created and executed, let's take a look at the complete syntax for the CREATE PROCEDURE statement. The full syntax of the statement is shown here.

```
CREATE PROC [ EDURE ] procedure_name [ ; number ]
    [ { @parameter data_type }
        [ VARYING ] [ = default ] [ OUTPUT ]
    ] [ ,...n ]

[ WITH
    { RECOMPILE | ENCRYPTION | RECOMPILE , ENCRYPTION } ]

[ FOR REPLICATION ]

AS sql_statement [ ...n ]
```

Component Descriptions

The components of CREATE PROCEDURE are described here.

CREATE PROC [EDURE]

This is required syntax and, as you can see, you do not have to include the full name "procedure." Earlier I mentioned abbreviations used to reference stored procedures; now you know why "proc" is widely used. I always use the full name, just by habit, but the following two examples are both valid.

```
CREATE PROCEDURE ps_UTIL_CurrentSystemTime1
AS
SELECT GETDATE()
go


CREATE PROC ps_UTIL_CurrentSystemTime2
AS
SELECT GETDATE()
```

procedure_name [; number]

This argument allows you to specify the identifier used to reference the procedure. As with any other database object, the identifier is limited to 128 characters. I have to say, though, that even using my verbose naming convention I have never even come close to reaching this limit.

A new feature in SQL Server 2000 is the ability to create temporary stored procedures. To create a temporary procedure, preface the identifier with # for locally scoped procedures or ## for global procedures.

You will notice that you can optionally append a number to a procedure's identifier. I never use this argument (I like my identifiers to be very descriptive), but the logic behind it is that you group like procedures and drop them all at the same time. The following shows how this works.

```
USE tempdb
go
CREATE PROCEDURE ps_UTIL_SELECT_CurrentSystemTime;1
AS
SELECT GETDATE()

go
```

```
CREATE PROCEDURE ps_UTIL_SELECT_CurrentSystemTime;2
AS
SELECT GETDATE()
go
DROP PROCEDURE ps_UTIL_SELECT_CurrentSystemTime
go
EXEC ps_UTIL_SELECT_CurrentSystemTime;1
EXEC ps_UTIL_SELECT_CurrentSystemTime;2
--Results--
Server: Msg 2812, Level 16, State 62, Line 1
Could not find stored procedure 'ps_UTIL_SELECT_CurrentSystemTime'.
Server: Msg 2812, Level 16, State 62, Line 2
Could not find stored procedure 'ps_UTIL_SELECT_CurrentSystemTime'.
```

Both procedures are created individually but deleted with a single DROP statement.

[{ @parameter data_type } [VARYING] [= default] [OUTPUT]] [,...n]

These optional arguments allow you to specify the parameters used in the stored procedure. When a parameter is declared you are only required to specify the parameter identifier (@parameter) and its associated data type (data_type). VARYING is used with cursor parameters to indicate the results can vary by execution. The = default option allows you to assign a value to the parameter when no value is supplied in the call to the procedure. The OUTPUT argument indicates the parameter is used to return a value to the calling application. The , . . . n indicates that you can use multiple parameters (maximum of 1,024). The examples shown later in this chapter demonstrate how to implement each argument.

[WITH { RECOMPILE | ENCRYPTION | RECOMPILE , ENCRYPTION }]

The RECOMPILE argument prohibits the procedure's execution plan from being cached. You use this argument only after you determine that there is no benefit in having the plan cached. For example, if the Query Optimizer creates a new execution plan every time the procedure is called, there is no reason to have its execution plan persist in memory. Stored procedures that are based on dynamic SQL is an example of a procedure that will not produce a re-usable plan. An example of this type of procedure is provided later in this chapter.

The ENCRYPTION argument is used to encrypt the text of the procedure. The ramifications of using the WITH ENCRYPTION option were discussed in the "CREATE FUNCTION" section of Chapter 7.

[FOR REPLICATION]

This argument specifies that the procedure is only executed during replication. Replication is not covered in this book, so we will not be using this argument in any examples.

AS sql_statement [...n]

This argument forms the body of the procedure by specifying the one or more (...n) statements the procedure executes when it is called.

General Notes on Stored Procedures

The following list describes some of the limits and restrictions of using stored procedures.

- The maximum size of a stored procedure is 128MB, so be confident that you will never create a procedure that exceeds this limit.

- You can specify the owner of the procedure by including the user's identifier in the procedure's identifier. (Object ownership was discussed in the "Before You Get Started" section of Chapter 3.)

- Stored procedures can only be created in the current database. They can, however, reference multiple databases (and servers, for that matter) in the statements they execute.

- Stored procedures cannot be referenced in a SELECT statement. You can use a user-defined function to implement this type of functionality.

- A stored procedure can call another stored procedure. This is called *nesting*, and the maximum nesting level is 32. Keep in mind, though, that the nesting level (maintained in the system function @@NESTINGLEVEL) only exceeds one when the nested procedure calls another procedure. In other words, one stored procedure can call numerous other procedures, but as long as the called procedure does not call another procedure, the value in @@NESTINGLEVEL is one. This is shown in Figure 11-2.

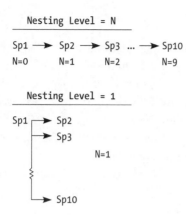

Figure 11-2. Stored procedure nesting levels

Permissions

Two types of permissions apply to stored procedures: the ability to create them (statement permissions) and the ability to execute them (object permissions). Both types are discussed here.

Statement Permissions

The ability to create a stored procedure defaults to the **sysadmin** fixed-server role and the **db_owner** and **db_ddladmin** fixed-database roles. A member of either **sysadmin** or **db_owner** can grant this permission to any valid user.

Object Permissions

The ability to execute a stored procedure defaults to the object's owner and members of **sysadmin** and **db_owner**. The owner of a procedure and members of both **sysadmin** and **db_owner** can grant EXECUTE permission on the object to any valid user.

Creating Stored Procedures

You can create a stored procedure in multiple ways using both Query Analyzer and Enterprise Manager. The following sections discuss the various ways to create a stored procedure using both tools.

Query Analyzer

To create a stored procedure in Query Analyzer, type the text of the procedure in the Editor Pane and execute the statement. You can create and execute the procedures in this chapter very easily (avoiding any typing) by using the example code file (Ch11.sql) for this chapter. The instructions for obtaining Ch11.sql are located at the beginning of this chapter. Simply open the file in Query Analyzer, highlight the appropriate code snippet, and press CTRL+E (you can also click the Run button, but I prefer using the shortcut key-combo).

The first example creates a procedure that uses SELECT to get the current system time.

```
USE tempdb
go
CREATE PROCEDURE ps_UTIL_SELECT_CurrentSystemTime
AS
SELECT GETDATE() AS CurrentSystemTime
```

Once the procedure is created, you can execute it using the following.

```
EXEC ps_UTIL_SELECT_CurrentSystemTime
--Results--
CurrentSystemTime
---------------------------
2000-08-01 17:04:24.983
```

In order to execute a stored procedure, you must have EXECUTE permission on the object. This permission is applied by default to the object's owner, the fixed-server role **sysadmin**, and the fixed-database role **db_owner**.

Let's create another login so we can see what happens when a login that is not the object's owner or a member of the fixed roles tries to execute a procedure. The code shown here uses system stored procedure **sp_addlogin** (discussed in Chapter 9) to create a login whose identifier is **tiger**, password is "eagle," and default database is **tempdb**. After the login is created, **sp_adduser** adds it as a user to **tempdb**. Please note that you can use Enterprise Manager to add the new login/user, but for the sake of brevity I used the system stored procedure approach.

```
sp_addlogin 'tiger','eagle','tempdb'
go
USE tempdb
go
sp_adduser 'tiger'
--Results--
```

```
New login created.
Granted database access to 'tiger'.
```

Now that you have completed this, make another connection to the server using File>Connect on the main menu of Query Analyzer using the new **tiger** login. Execute the following via the new connection and note the error message generated.

```
USE tempdb
go
EXEC ps_UTIL_CurrentSystemTime
--Results--
Server: Msg 229, Level 14, State 5, Procedure ps_UTIL_SELECT_CurrentSystemTime,_
    Line 1
EXECUTE permission denied on object 'ps_UTIL_SELECT_CurrentSystemTime', database_
    'tempdb',_ owner 'dbo'.
```

Use the following statement to give **tiger** EXECUTE permission on the procedure. Please note that you will have to use the initial connection (e.g., the one used to create the procedure) to apply the permission.

```
USE tempdb
go
GRANT EXECUTE ON ps_UTIL_SELECT_CurrentDateTime TO tiger
```

Now you can use the second connection to the server to successfully execute the procedure.

Since we have the new login, let's go ahead and take a look at what happens when **tiger** tries to create a procedure. Execute the following using the **tiger** connection.

```
USE tempdb
go
CREATE PROCEDURE ps_UTIL_SELECT_CurrentSystemTime
AS
SELECT GETDATE() AS CurrentSystemTime
go
--Results--
Server: Msg 262, Level 14, State 1, Procedure ps_UTIL_SELECT_CurrentSystemTime,
Line 3
CREATE PROCEDURE permission denied, database 'tempdb', owner 'dbo'.
```

The login has not been granted the statement permission CREATE PROCE-DURE, so the error is generated. Use the following to grant the appropriate permission (be sure to use the correct connection).

```
GRANT CREATE PROCEDURE TO tiger
--Results--
The command(s) completed successfully.
```

Now that **tiger** has been granted permission to create stored procedures, re-execute the CREATE PROCEDURE statement. After it completes, execute the following SELECT.

```
SELECT ROUTINE_NAME,
       SPECIFIC_SCHEMA
FROM INFORMATION_SCHEMA.Routines
--Results--
ROUTINE_NAME                        SPECIFIC_SCHEMA
----------------------------------- -----------------
ps_UTIL_SELECT_CurrentSystemTime    dbo
ps_UTIL_SELECT_CurrentSystemTime    tiger
```

This example uses an INFORMATION_SCHEMA view (discussed in Chapter 8) to obtain metadata information about the procedures. Notice that we were allowed to use the same procedure name because each object has a different owner. Which procedure does the following statement execute?

```
USE tempdb
go
EXEC ps_UTIL_CurrentSystemTime
```

The procedure owned by **dbo** executes when no owner is specified. If you want to execute the **tiger** version of the procedure, you have to use the following.

```
USE tempdb
go
EXEC tiger.ps_UTIL_CurrentSystemTime
```

Both versions of the procedure produce the same results, but they are two completely different objects because they have different owners.

Stored Procedure Naming Convention

The name you give to a stored procedure is only required to adhere to the rules for all object identifiers. The procedures created earlier could just as easily have been named "x" or "y," but I like to use a naming convention that helps me determine the function performed by each procedure. My stored procedure names consists of four segments (two required and two optional) as shown in Table 11-1.

Table 11-1. Stored Procedure Naming Convention

PART	DESCRIPTION
ps_	I use this to indicate that the database object is a stored procedure. This helps differentiate *my* stored procedures from the system stored procedures that come with SQL Server (they start with sp_). There is no hidden meaning in "ps"—it is simply the reverse of "sp."
TableName_	This is the main table on which the stored procedure operates. If your stored procedure operates on more than one table, simply pick the one it should be associated with most. If the procedure does not operate on a table, I use "UTIL" (short for "utility") in place of a table name.
Verb	The domain values for this segment are SELECT, INSERT, UPDATE, or DELETE, because these are the main actions you can perform on your data. When a "UTIL" procedure is created, this part is optional; otherwise it is required.
_Comment	This segment is optional and can help you remember what action(s) the stored procedure(s) perform(s). A sample comment might be "_ByUniqueID." When used in this context "ps_Customers_SELECT_ByUniqueID," it indicates the stored procedure returns a single row based on a filter criterion of the table's primary key.

Admittedly this naming convention is a tad verbose, but I do have my reasons for using it. First, I like to have all the stored procedures that act on a particular table grouped together. This allows me to more quickly identify which ones need to be modified if the structure of a table changes. Second, knowing the number of procedures associated with a table and the actions they perform helps assess how much the table is used. (For example, if the procedures associated with a table contain the four verbs SELECT, INSERT, UPDATE, and DELETE, I can quickly assess that it is probably used more than a table that simply has one SELECT-type procedure.) And last, the comment portion helps to further define the function each stored procedure performs.

The procedure names used so far in this chapter serve as good examples of the value of this type of naming convention. You can look at any one of them and know exactly what it does without looking at the body of the procedure. Regardless of whether you adopt my convention, use another's, or create your own, I strongly encourage you to adopt and stick with a naming convention for all your database objects.

CAUTION Avoid Naming Stored Procedures with "sp_"

Do not begin stored procedures names with the "sp_" prefix. When a stored procedure that begins with "sp_" is executed, the compiler looks for the stored procedure in the master *database first, then uses object qualifiers and owner information to find the stored procedure. This is obviously less efficient than having the compiler look in the current database, which is the behavior when a stored procedure name does not begin with "sp_."*

Stored Procedure Templates

There is a new feature in SQL Server 2000 that allows you to access templates that can be used to more efficiently create procedures. A template simply provides the base statements you want to use when creating a procedure.

In order to access the default templates that come with the product, complete the following.

1. Open a blank Editor Pane in Query Analyzer by clicking File on the main menu and selecting New.

2. Click Edit on the main menu and select Insert Template…

3. Double-click the Create Procedure folder and review the three templates.

4. Select the Create Procedure Basic Template and click Open.

Figure 11-3 shows the basic template.

The format for the default templates does not conform to my naming convention or formatting preferences, but this type of issue is not a problem because you can easily add your own templates. The templates are simply text files, and as long as they are placed in the proper subdirectory, they will be available for selection. To add a template for selection, simply use a .tql file extension for the file name and place it in the Program Files\Microsoft SQL Server\80\Tools\Templates\SQL Query Analyzer\Create Procedure folder.

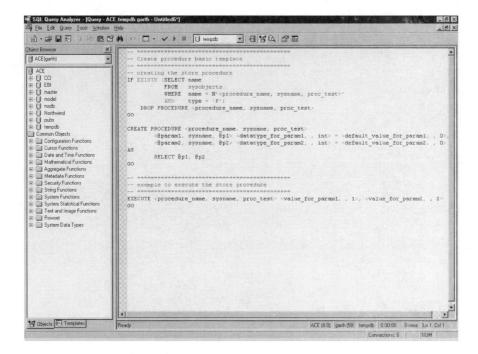

Figure 11-3. Stored procedure templates

TIP Quick Access to Templates

A number of object templates are available in SQL Server 2000. To see all the template categories and make a quick selection of an individual template, click the down arrow next to the New Query icon on the toolbar in Query Analyzer. The New Query icon is the left-most icon on the toolbar, and it looks like a page of paper with its upper-right corner folded over.

Enterprise Manager

Enterprise Manager has a Stored Procedures Properties dialog that allows you to create and alter a procedure and manage its associated permissions. To access the dialog to create a procedure, complete the following.

1. Expand a database off the server tree.

2. Right-click Stored Procedures and select New Stored Procedure.

Figure 11-4 shows how to do this using **Northwind** as the target database.

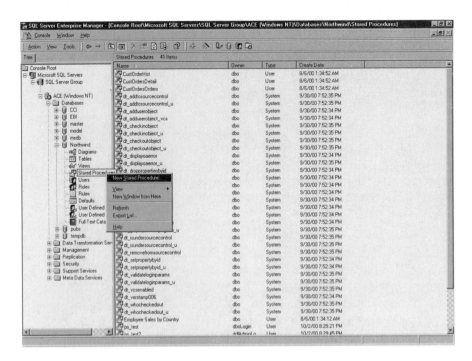

Figure 11-4. Opening Stored Procedure Properties dialog

Once the dialog is open, simply type the text of procedure and use the Check Syntax option to verify the statements are valid. Figure 11-5 shows a dialog populated with a valid CREATE PROCEDURE statement.

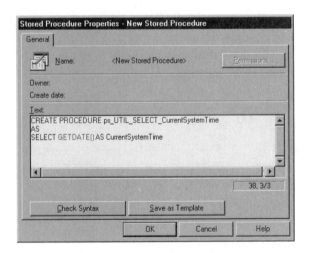

Figure 11-5. Stored Procedure Properties dialog

Notice that the Permissions button is grayed out. This makes sense because the procedure has yet to be created—you cannot assign permissions until after you create an object. Once you click the OK button, the procedure is created. The next time you access it with the Stored Procedure Properties dialog, the Permissions button will be available for selection.

Stored Procedure Wizard

You can also create stored procedures using the Stored Procedure Wizard included with Enterprise Manager. To access the wizard, complete the following.

1. Open Enterprise Manager and connect to the target server.

2. Click the Tools option off the main menu and select Wizards…

3. Expand the Database category, select Create Stored Procedure Wizard, and click OK.

The wizard walks you through the process of selecting a target database and table(s) and the type of procedure (INSERT, UPDATE, and DELETE) you want for each table. It is extremely easy to use, so give it a try and see if you like the code it generates. If you do, you can certainly use it to reduce typing time if you have a lot of basic procedures to create. I do not care for the extensive use of brackets or the parameter naming convention, so if I use it I have to spend time editing the auto-generated code.

ALTER PROCEDURE Syntax

Similar to any other programming endeavor, you will be changing stored procedures as new requirements are added to your project. The most efficient way to change a stored procedure is to use the ALTER PROCEDURE statement. The reason ALTER PROCEDURE is more efficient than dropping and re-creating is because you only need one statement and permissions are maintained. The permissions granted on a procedure are dropped when a procedure is dropped, so any permissions that existed will have to be explicitly granted after the procedure is re-created. When you use ALTER PROCEDURE, permissions are not affected.

The full syntax of the statement is shown here.

```
ALTER PROC [ EDURE ] procedure_name [ ; number ]
    [ { @parameter data_type }
        [ VARYING ] [ = default ] [ OUTPUT ]
    ] [ ,...n ]
[ WITH
    { RECOMPILE | ENCRYPTION
        | RECOMPILE , ENCRYPTION
    }
]
[ FOR REPLICATION ]
AS
    sql_statement [ ...n ]
```

The exact same arguments are available to ALTER PROCEDURE as CREATE PROCEDURE, so no further coverage is needed.

Statement Permissions

The ability to alter a stored procedure defaults to the **sysadmin** fixed-server role and the **db_owner** and **db_ddladmin** fixed-database roles. A member of either **sysadmin** or **db_owner** can grant this permission to any valid user.

> ### TIP Quoted Identifiers
>
> *The default settings of Query Analyzer do not allow use of double quotes to enclose character strings in a stored procedure (or any batch, for that matter). To use double quotes, you must alter the default behavior with* SET QUOTED_IDENTIFIER ON.

Altering Stored Procedures

The following approaches are used to modify a stored procedure.

Query Analyzer

In pre-2000 versions of SQL Server, if you wanted to get the contents of an existing stored procedure in Query Analyzer you had to either use the system stored procedure **sp_helptext** or cut-n-copy the text from the Stored Procedure Editor in Enterprise Manager. The Object Browser included with SQL Server 2000 makes this process much easier.

You can automatically *wrap* the text of a procedure in an ALTER statement using the following steps.

1. Expand a database in the Object Browser, and then expand the Stored Procedures folder.

2. Right-click the target procedure and select Edit.

Figure 11-6 shows the results of this process.

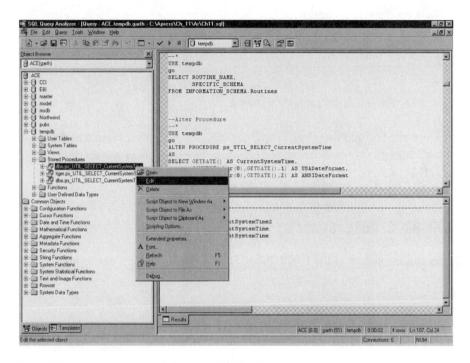

Figure 11-6. Altering a procedure via Object Browser

Once the text of the procedure is placed in Query Analyzer, modify it accordingly and execute the ALTER statement. The following shows how to modify the **ps_UTIL_SELECT_CurrentSystemTime** procedure created previously.

```
USE tempdb
go
ALTER PROCEDURE ps_UTIL_SELECT_CurrentSystemTime
AS
SELECT GETDATE() AS CurrentSystemTime,
       CONVERT(char(8),GETDATE(),1) AS USADateFormat,
       CONVERT(char(8),GETDATE(),2) AS ANSIDateFormat
```

```
go
EXEC ps_UTIL_SELECT_CurrentSystemTime
--Results--
CurrentSystemTime          USADateFormat ANSIDateFormat
-------------------------- ------------- --------------
2000-08-01 19:58:11.543    08/01/00      00.08.01
```

Enterprise Manager

To modify a stored procedure in Enterprise Manager, complete the following.

1. Expand the database in which the procedure is located and select Stored Procedures.

2. Double-click the target procedure.

Once the Stored Procedure Properties dialog is activated, simply make the desired changes, use the Check Syntax button to ensure there are no typos, and then click OK.

DROP PROCEDURE Syntax

The complete syntax of the DROP PROCEDURE statement is shown here.

```
DROP PROCEDURE { procedure } [ ,...n ]
```

To delete one or more procedures, simply provide the stored procedure name. As with all other database objects, once they are dropped they are permanently deleted from the database. If you mistakenly drop a procedure, you must re-create it from a saved script file or recover it from a database backup. The first option is much quicker than the second, so I always keep a scripted file of my databases on hand.

Statement Permissions

The ability to drop a stored procedure defaults to the procedure's owner, **sysadmin** fixed-server role and **db_owner** and **db_ddladmin** fixed-database roles and is not transferable.

Dropping Stored Procedures

Use the following approaches to drop a stored procedure.

Query Analyzer

There are two ways to drop a procedure in Query Analyzer. The first way is to use the DROP PROCEDURE statement discussed in the previous section and the second involves using Object Browser. The first approach is shown here.

```
USE tempdb
go
DROP PROCEDURE ps_UTIL_SELECT_CurrentSystemTime
--Results--
The command(s) completed successfully.
```

In Object Browser, you simply right-click the target procedure and select Delete.

Enterprise Manager

Use the following steps in Enterprise Manager to delete a procedure.

1. Expand the database in which the procedure is located and select Stored Procedures.

2. Highlight the target procedure, right-click, and select Delete.

Managing Permissions

As mentioned earlier, one of the main benefits of using stored procedures concerns permission management. When you do not use stored procedures, you must have explicit rights to perform an action on each database object a statement references. When you use stored procedures, you only need permission to execute the procedure.

As you can imagine, managing permissions on a system with numerous users and many tables and views could be very time consuming if each user or group needs explicit permission for each object they access. You should take great care assessing and planning a security strategy before implementing a security model on a complex database system that will have numerous users.

Creating roles (analogous to Windows NT groups) that allow you to efficiently manage permissions is key to ensuring that security is maintained with the least amount of effort.

Use the following methods to manage permissions on a stored procedure.

Query Analyzer

The GRANT, REVOKE, and DENY statements are used to manage permissions. I used the GRANT statement earlier and the other two are used in a similar manner.

Enterprise Manager

In Enterprise Manager, open the Stored Procedure Properties dialog for the target procedure and click the Permissions button.

Debugging Stored Procedures

Before SQL Server 2000, the only way to debug a stored procedure was with the development tools that came with C++, VB, and Visual Interdev. SQL Server 2000 comes with a stored procedure debugger accessed via Object Browser. Use the following steps to invoke the stored procedure debugger.

1. Activate Object Browser in Query Analyzer.

2. Expand the database in which the target procedure is located.

3. Expand the Stored Procedures folder, right-click the target stored procedure, and select Debug.

Please note the debugger will not work if the SQL Server Service (MSSQLServer) is configured to log on as a local system account. You can use Control Panel/Services to see how the Service is configured.

If you try to use the debugger when it is configured to log on with a local system account, a warning message is displayed that says it "might" not work properly and to check the Event Viewer for messages. When I tried to run the debugger under the incompatible configuration, the options (e.g., toggle points) were not available and the following message was inserted into the Event Viewer Application Log.

```
SQL Server when started as service must not log on as System Account. Reset to
logon as user account using Control Panel.
```

Once I configured the Service to log on a domain account, the debugger worked as expected.

In general, the debugger will only be of use when you have a stored procedure that contains looping operations. The following overly simplified procedure shows you how the debugger works.

```
USE tempdb
go
CREATE PROCEDURE ps_LoopingExample
@MaxValue smallint = 10
AS
DECLARE @Counter smallint
SET @Counter = 1

WHILE @Counter < @MaxValue
 BEGIN
  PRINT CAST(@Counter AS varchar(5))
  SET @Counter = @Counter + 1
 END
go
EXEC ps_LoopingExample 11
--Results--
1
2
3
4
5
6
7
8
9
10
```

This procedure optionally accepts a parameter and then prints the current value of **@Counter** until the **@MaxValue** is reached. Right-click the procedure in Object Browser (don't forget to refresh the Stored Procedure folder after you create the procedure), select Debug, type the number 11 in the Value Input box, and click Execute. Once the debugger window activates, use the F11 key to step through the procedure. As you step through the procedure, the values in the Local Variables window display the current value of **@Counter** and **@MaxValue**. Figure 11-7 shows the final results.

> **TIP Reboot Server after Changing from Local to NT Account**
>
> *If you change the MSSQLServer service to log on using an NT account, you should re-boot your computer before attempting to use the debugger.*

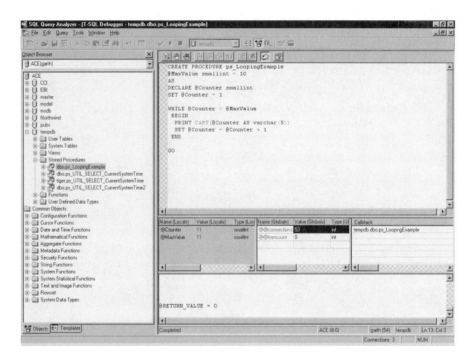

Figure 11-7. Stored Procedure Debugger

Managing Stored Procedures

The following sections discuss two approaches that allow you to more effectively manage your stored procedures.

Adding/Editing/Listing Object Descriptions

One of the more formidable challenges when working in a group development environment is to ensure that each developer is aware of the existing code for a particular project. Using an intuitive naming convention is certainly a great way to start, but what you really need is a way for the developers to easily review a description of all the objects in a database. In pre-2000 versions of SQL Server, if you wanted to maintain such a list you had to either create and populate your own tables within SQL Server or use the data dictionary functionality of a CASE tool like ERWin. SQL Server 2000 adds this capability through a set of extended properties that can be attached to certain database objects. These extended properties can be used to add descriptions to stored procedures.

You can use two methods to manage an extended property on a stored procedure. The first method involves using Object Browser, and the second uses system stored procedures.

Object Browser

In Object Browser, use the following steps to add an extended property.

1. Expand the database in which the procedure is located and then expand the Stored Procedures folder.

2. Right-click the target procedure and select Extended Properties.

3. Input a name for the extended property and a description as shown in Figure 11-8.

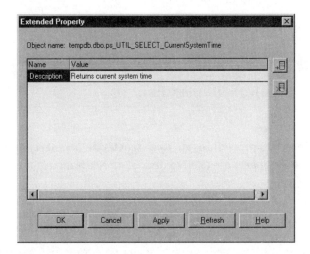

Figure 11-8. Adding Extended properties

When you want to edit or delete an extended property, access it in the same manner, and then edit or delete accordingly.

Using System Stored Procedures

To add a description using system stored procedures, use **sp_addextendedproperty**. The following shows how to add the same extended property (with a different name) shown in Figure 11-8 using the system stored procedure.

```
USE tempdb
go
sp_addextendedproperty @name = 'Description_2',
                       @value = 'Returns current system time',
                       @level0type = 'user',
                       @level0name =  'dbo',
                       @level1type = 'procedure',
                       @level1name = 'ps_UTIL_SELECT_CurrentSystemTime'
--Results--
(1 row(s) affected)
```

The parameters used are described here.

PARAMETER	DESCRIPTION
@name	The name of the column used to hold the description.
@value	The actual description for the object.
@level0type	The user-defined type (USER, TYPE, or NULL).
@level0name	The name of @level0type.
@level1type	The type of object (TABLE, VIEW, PROCEDURE, FUNCTION, DEFAULT, RULE, and NULL).

The system stored procedures **sp_updateextendedproperty** and **sp_dropextendedproperty** are used to update or delete an extended property.

Listing Descriptions

Once the descriptions have been added for all procedures, use the following to give developers access to the descriptions for all procedures in a database.

```
SELECT   * FROM ::fn_listextendedproperty (NULL, 'user', 'dbo', 'procedure', _
    'NULL, NULL, NULL)
--Results--
```

```
objtype    objname                         name          value
---------  ------------------------------- ------------  --------------------------
PROCEDURE  ps_UTIL_SELECT_CurrentSystemTime Description   Returns current system time
PROCEDURE  ps_UTIL_SELECT_CurrentSystemTime Description_2 Returns current system time
```

A realistic scenario for getting this information to the developers would be to create a browser-based interface that allows them to specify the objects whose descriptions they would like to review. In Chapter 13, I will give an example for this scenario.

Comments

Comments not only enhance the readability of code but can decrease the effort required to maintain it, as well. I do think there is such a thing as comment over-kill, but at a minimum each procedure you create should contain the following information:

- The name of the person who created/last modified the procedure.

- The date the procedure was created.

- The date the procedure was last changed.

- Any special knowledge required to understand how the procedure works.

In addition to general create/modification information, you should also comment any complex or unusual code segments within the procedure. Keep in mind that you will not always be the person maintaining the code; any helpful comments you add will be appreciated by those who are.

For the sake of brevity I will not include the header comment information in the examples presented in this book. I will, however, comment portions of code where the purpose or operations performed are not obvious.

Stored Procedure Examples

The best way to learn how to use stored procedures is through examples. The examples previously shown were overly simple (some might say useless) in an effort to make the material easier to understand. The following sections contain more real-world examples, which should help you better understand how to use procedures in your programming endeavors.

Retrieving Data

The examples in this section show how to use stored procedures to retrieve data from one or more tables.

Example 1: Simple SELECT

The following example shows how to create and execute a procedure that retrieves all the values in the **CompanyName** column from the **Customers** table in the **Northwind** database.

```
USE Northwind
go
CREATE PROCEDURE ps_Customers_SELECT_CompanyName
AS
SELECT CompanyName
FROM Customers
go
EXEC ps_Customers_SELECT_CompanyName
--Results (Partial)--
CompanyName
----------------------------------------
Alfreds Futterkiste
Ana Trujillo Emparedados y helados
Antonio Moreno Taquería
....
```

Example 2: Filtering Resultset with One Parameter

You can extend the functionality of the previous procedure by adding a parameter that accepts a character string for use with the LIKE comparison operator. This procedure could be used with an interface that allows the user to input a value that restricts the resultset to only those companies whose name starts with the provided character string.

```
USE Northwind
go
CREATE PROCEDURE ps_Customers_SELECT_CompanyNamePartial
@CompanyName nvarchar(40)
AS
SELECT CompanyName
FROM Customers
```

```
WHERE CompanyName LIKE @CompanyName+'%'
go
EXEC ps_Customers_SELECT_CompanyNamePartial 'A'
--Results--
CompanyName
----------------------------------------
Alfreds Futterkiste
Ana Trujillo Emparedados y helados
Antonio Moreno Taquería
Around the Horn
```

The parameter will accept up to 40 characters, so you can restrict the resultset by passing more characters to the procedure.

```
USE Northwind
go
EXEC ps_Customers_SELECT_CompanyNamePartial 'Al'
--Results--
CompanyName
----------------------------------------
Alfreds Futterkiste
```

Example 3: Filtering Resultset with Multiple Parameters

The next example shows you how to pass multiple parameters that are used to restrict the resultset.

```
USE Northwind
go
CREATE PROCEDURE ps_Customers_SELECT_CompanyOrdersByDateRange
@CustomerID nchar(5),
@OrderDateStart datetime,
@OrderDateEnd datetime
AS
SELECT CompanyName,
       OrderDate
FROM Customers a
JOIN Orders b ON a.CustomerID = b.CustomerID
WHERE a.CustomerID = @CustomerID AND
      b.OrderDate BETWEEN @OrderDateStart AND @OrderDateEnd
go
EXEC ps_Customers_SELECT_CompanyOrdersByDateRange 'ALFKI','1/1/97','1/1/98'
--Results--
```

```
CompanyName                             OrderDate
--------------------------------------- ---------------------------
Alfreds Futterkiste                     1997-08-25 00:00:00.000
Alfreds Futterkiste                     1997-10-03 00:00:00.000
Alfreds Futterkiste                     1997-10-13 00:00:00.000
```

The unique identifier for a customer is supplied along with a start and end date to restrict the rows returned. Note that I did not specify the parameter names in the procedure call. This is fine as long as you order the parameter values in the same order as they are listed in the procedure, but if they are not ordered correctly, it will cause an error. You can avoid this issue by always using the parameter names. The following shows that parameters can be listed in any order when their names are specified.

```
USE Northwind
go
EXEC ps_Customers_SELECT_CompanyOrdersByDateRange @OrderDateEnd = '1/1/98', _
    @CustomerID = 'ALFKI',@OrderDateStart = '1/1/97'
--Results--
CompanyName                             OrderDate
--------------------------------------- ---------------------------
Alfreds Futterkiste                     1997-08-25 00:00:00.000
Alfreds Futterkiste                     1997-10-03 00:00:00.000
Alfreds Futterkiste                     1997-10-13 00:00:00.000
```

This procedure is limiting because it forces you to supply a customer ID on every call. Trying to execute it without this parameter generates the following error.

```
USE Northwind
go
EXEC ps_Customers_SELECT_CompanyOrdersByDateRange @OrderDateEnd = '1/1/98', _
    @OrderDateStart = '1/1/97'
--Results--
Server: Msg 201, Level 16, State 3, Procedure
ps_Customers_SELECT_CompanyOrdersByDateRange, Line 0
Procedure 'ps_Customers_SELECT_CompanyOrdersByDateRange' expects parameter _
    '@CustomerID', which was not supplied.
```

You can modify this procedure so that, when no customer ID parameter is required, all the customers who have placed an order in the given date range are returned. The following example uses the ALTER PROCEDURE statement to make the change.

```
USE Northwind
go
ALTER PROCEDURE ps_Customers_SELECT_CompanyOrdersByDateRange
@CustomerID nchar(5) = NULL ,
@OrderDateStart datetime,
@OrderDateEnd datetime
AS
SELECT CompanyName,
       OrderDate
FROM Customers a
JOIN Orders b ON a.CustomerID = b.CustomerID
WHERE (@CustomerID IS NULL OR a.CustomerID = @CustomerID) AND
      b.OrderDate BETWEEN @OrderDateStart AND @OrderDateEnd
ORDER BY a.CompanyName
go
EXEC ps_Customers_SELECT_CompanyOrdersByDateRange @OrderDateEnd = '1/1/98',_
     @OrderDateStart = '1/1/97'
--Results (Partial)--
CompanyName                          OrderDate
------------------------------------ ---------------------------

Alfreds Futterkiste                  1997-08-25 00:00:00.000
Alfreds Futterkiste                  1997-10-03 00:00:00.000
Alfreds Futterkiste                  1997-10-13 00:00:00.000
Ana Trujillo Emparedados y helados   1997-11-28 00:00:00.000
Ana Trujillo Emparedados y helados   1997-08-08 00:00:00.000
....
```

Notice that I added a default value of NULL to @CustomerID, I added an additional WHERE clause, and I included an ORDER BY to sort the resultset. The additional WHERE clause criteria is the key to making the procedure retrieve all rows when no **CustomerID** is supplied. When no value is supplied, the condition evaluates to true for all records, so the only restriction is on **OrderDate**. In other words, if a **CustomerID** value is not supplied, @CustomerID is equal to NULL and @CustomerID IS NULL evaluates true for every record accessed by the SELECT statement.

Example 4: Ordering a Resultset by a Parameter

The following example shows how to dynamically order a resultset based on a parameter passed to the procedure.

```
USE Northwind
go
CREATE PROCEDURE ps_Customers_SELECT_OrderByParameter
```

```
@SortColumn varchar(10)
AS
SELECT CompanyName,
       ContactName,
       CASE @SortColumn WHEN 'Company' THEN CompanyName
                        WHEN 'Contact' THEN ContactName
       END AS SortColumn
FROM Customers
ORDER BY SortColumn
--Results--
The command(s) completed successfully.
```

The key here is using the CASE function to determine what column to sort on. The alias for the expression returned by the CASE is referenced in the ORDER BY, not the actual column name. For example, when @SortColumn is equal to 'Company,' the alias for the CASE statement (SortColumn) is equal to 'CompanyName,' and this value is used in the ORDER BY clause. The following shows the call used to sort the resultset by **CompanyName**.

```
USE Northwind
go
ps_Customers_SELECT_OrderByParameter 'Company'
-- Results (Partial) --
CustomerID SortColumn
---------- ----------------------------------------
ALFKI      Alfreds Futterkiste
ANATR      Ana Trujillo Emparedados y helados
ANTON      Antonio Moreno Taquería
....
```

Modifying Data

The examples in this section show how you use stored procedures to modify data. For the sake of simplicity, you will create a table with a limited number of columns for the examples. The following statement creates the table used in the examples.

```
USE tempdb
go
CREATE TABLE Contacts
(
 Con_UniqueID smallint IDENTITY PRIMARY KEY,
 Con_FName varchar(30) NOT NULL,
 Con_LName varchar(30) NOT NULL,
```

```
 Con_Email varchar(40) NULL,
)
--Results--
The command(s) completed successfully.
```

Example 1: Inserting Data

The stored procedure shown here inserts a row into the **Contacts** table.

```
USE tempdb
go
CREATE PROCEDURE ps_Contacts_INSERT
@Con_FName varchar(30),
@Con_LName varchar(30),
@Con_Email varchar(40) = NULL
AS
INSERT Contacts
(
 Con_FName,
 Con_LName,
 Con_Email
)
VALUES
(
 @Con_FName,
 @Con_LName,
 @Con_Email
)
--Results--
The command(s) completed successfully.
```

Only two parameters are required because the **Con_UniqueID** column is defined with the IDENTITY property, and @Con_Email has a default value assigned. The following shows multiple examples of how it is used to create a new row in **Contacts**.

```
USE tempdb
go
EXEC ps_Contacts_INSERT 'Roger','Clemens','Roger@Rocket.com'

EXEC ps_Contacts_INSERT 'Pedro','Martinez'

EXEC ps_Contacts_INSERT @Con_Email = 'Nolan@5NoHitters.com',
```

```
                                @Con_LName = 'Ryan',
                                @Con_FName = 'Nolan'


SELECT Con_UniqueID,
        RTRIM(Con_FName)+' '+Con_LName AS ContactName,
        Con_Email
FROM Contacts
ORDER BY Con_LName
--Results--


(1 row(s) affected)


(1 row(s) affected)


(1 row(s) affected)


Con_UniqueID ContactName                                 Con_Email
------------ ---------------------------------------     ------------------------

1            Roger Clemens                               Roger@Rocket.com
2            Pedro Martinez                              NULL
3            Nolan Ryan                                  Nolan@5NoHitters.com
```

Example 2: Updating Data

The following shows the stored procedure used to update a row in the **Contacts** table.

```
USE tempdb
go
CREATE PROCEDURE ps_Contacts_UPDATE
@Con_UniqueID smallint,
@Con_FName varchar(30),
@Con_LName varchar(30),
@Con_Email varchar(40)
AS
UPDATE Contacts
SET Con_FName = @Con_FName,
    Con_LName = @Con_LName,
    Con_Email = @Con_Email
WHERE Con_UniqueID = @Con_UniqueID
--Results--
The command(s) completed successfully.
```

Notice that I added the primary key to the parameter list, and I used a WHERE clause with the UPDATE statement to update only the desired record.

The following examples show the different ways to update the data in **Contacts**.

```
USE tempdb
go
EXEC ps_Contacts_UPDATE 1,'The Rocket','Clemens','Roger@Rocket.com'

EXEC ps_Contacts_UPDATE 2,'Pedro','Martinez','Pedro@BoSox.com'

EXEC ps_Contacts_UPDATE @Con_UniqueID = 3,
                        @Con_Email = 'Nolan@HallOfFame.com',
                        @Con_LName = 'Ryan',
                        @Con_FName = 'Nolan'


SELECT Con_UniqueID,
       RTRIM(Con_FName)+' '+Con_LName AS ContactName,
       Con_Email
FROM Contacts
ORDER BY Con_Lname

--Results--

(1 row(s) affected)

(1 row(s) affected)

(1 row(s) affected)

Con_UniqueID ContactName                   Con_Email
------------ ----------------------------- ----------------------------------------
1            The Rocket Clemens            Roger@Rocket.com
2            Pedro Martinez                Pedro@BoSox.com
3            Nolan Ryan                    Nolan@HallOfFame.com
```

Example 3: Populating a Table with Results of a Stored Procedure

The previous two examples were fairly straightforward because the values inserted were explicitly listed in the modification statements. This example gets slightly more complex because the resultset returned by a procedure is used to populate a table. This is very similar to using a SELECT statement to populate a table, but it seems more complex because you cannot *see* where the data is coming from. To demonstrate this, I will create a table (**Contacts_Target**) with the same structure as **Contacts**.

```
CREATE TABLE Contacts_Target
(
 Con_UniqueID smallint IDENTITY PRIMARY KEY,
 Con_FName varchar(30) NOT NULL,
 Con_LName varchar(30) NOT NULL,
 Con_Email varchar(40) NULL,
)
--Results--
The command(s) completed successfully.
```

Now that the target table exists, you need a procedure that returns all the columns in the source table. The following procedure returns all the rows in **Contacts**.

```
USE tempdb
go
CREATE PROCEDURE ps_Contacts_SELECT
AS
SELECT Con_UniqueID,
       Con_FName,
       Con_LName,
       Con_Email
FROM Contacts
--Results--
The command(s) completed successfully.
```

You should note that both the source and target tables use the IDENTITY property to define the primary key column. By default, you cannot insert values into an IDENTITY column because its purpose to save you the trouble of finding the next valid value. You can, however, override the default behavior with the IDENTITY_INSERT setting. The following example uses this setting along with **ps_Contacts_SELECT** to populate **Contacts_Target** with all the data in **Contacts**.

```
SET IDENTITY_INSERT Contacts_Target ON
GO
INSERT Contacts_Target (Con_UniqueID,Con_FName,Con_LName,Con_Email)
EXEC ps_Contacts_SELECT

SELECT * FROM Contacts_Target

--Results--
```

```
(3 row(s) affected)

Con_UniqueID Con_FName   Con_LName             Con_Email
------------ ----------- --------------------- --------------------------
1            The Rocket  Clemens               Roger@Rocket.com
2            Pedro       Martinez              Pedro@BoSox.com
3            Nolan       Ryan                  Nolan@HallOfFame.com
```

When you override the default behavior and insert values into an IDENTITY column, you must list the column names in the target table. The following shows the error message generated when this requirement is not met.

```
USE tempdb
go
SET IDENTITY_INSERT Contacts_Target ON
GO
INSERT Contacts_Target
EXEC ps_Contacts_SELECT
--Results--

Server: Msg 545, Level 16, State 1, Line 1
Explicit value must be specified for identity column in table 'Contacts_Target'_
when IDENTITY_INSERT is set to ON.
```

Using an OUTPUT Parameter

The examples covered so far have only used INPUT parameters, but there is another type called an OUTPUT parameter that can be very useful. An OUTPUT parameter returns values to the calling application. In general, you use an OUTPUT parameter to avoid the overhead associated with creating a resultset. The following example shows how to use an OUTPUT parameter to return a foreign key value to the calling application.

Using OUTPUT to Determine Foreign Key Value

I will create a child table for **Contacts** to complete this example. Let's assume that each contact can have one or more associated addresses. The following statement creates the table and constraint that enforces the relationship.

```
CREATE TABLE ContactsAddress
(
 ConAdd_UniqueID smallint IDENTITY PRIMARY KEY,
 Con_UniqueID smallint FOREIGN KEY REFERENCES Contacts (Con_UniqueID) NOT NULL,
 ConAdd_Address varchar(20) NOT NULL,
 ConAdd_City varchar(20) NOT NULL,
 ConAdd_State char(2) NOT NULL
)
--Results--
The command(s) completed successfully.
```

This example is based on a multi-part form scenario typically used to implement Web site registration functionality. Assume that the general contact information is gathered on one page and the user has to submit this data in order to get to the page that will allow one or more addresses to be added. To associate the address information with the proper parent record, the primary key for the contact record must be returned to the client application. The following modifies **ps_Contacts_INSERT** so the primary key is returned.

```
ALTER PROCEDURE ps_Contacts_INSERT
@Con_FName varchar(30),
@Con_LName varchar(30),
@Con_Email varchar(40) = NULL,
@Con_UniqueID int OUTPUT
AS
INSERT Contacts
(
 Con_FName,
 Con_LName,
 Con_Email
)
VALUES
(
 @Con_FName,
 @Con_LName,
 @Con_Email
)

SET @Con_UniqueID = @@IDENTITY
--Results--
The command(s) completed successfully.
```

The @Con_UniqueID OUTPUT parameter serves as *placeholder* in memory for the data assigned by the SET statement. The @@IDENTITY function holds the latest value inserted into an IDENTITY column. The following shows how to call the procedure and display the value returned.

```
DECLARE @Con_UniqueID int

EXEC ps_Contacts_INSERT 'Jeff',
                        'Bagwell',
                        'jeff@Astros.com',
                        @Con_UniqueID OUTPUT

PRINT CAST(@Con_UniqueID AS varchar(10))
--Results--
(1 row(s) affected)

4
```

You must declare a variable (@Con_UniqueID) and pass it to the procedure as an OUTPUT parameter. Please note the variable *outside* the procedure does not have to have the same name as the one on the inside. The following illustrates this point.

```
DECLARE @ID int

EXEC ps_Contacts_INSERT 'Jeff',
                        'Bagwell',
                        'jeff@Astros.com',
                        @ID OUTPUT

PRINT CAST(@ID AS varchar(10))
--Return--
(1 row(s) affected)

5
```

Now that you know how to get the primary key for the **Contacts** row, let's complete the example by creating a child record in **Contacts_Address**. In order to do this we need a procedure that inserts a record into **Contracts_Address**. The procedure used to do this is shown here.

```
CREATE PROCEDURE ps_ContactsAddress_INSERT
@Con_UniqueID int,
@ConAdd_Address varchar(20),
@ConAdd_City varchar(20),
@ConAdd_State char(2)
AS
INSERT ContactsAddress
(
 Con_UniqueID,
```

```
 ConAdd_Address,
 ConAdd_City,
 ConAdd_State
)
VALUES
(
 @Con_UniqueID,
 @ConAdd_Address,
 @ConAdd_City,
 @ConAdd_State
)
```

With all the required objects now in place, the following statements will create a row in both tables.

```
DECLARE @Con_UniqueID int

--*Create Parent Record in Contacts
EXEC ps_Contacts_INSERT 'Jeff',
                        'Bagwell',
                        'jeff@Astros.com',
                        @Con_UniqueID OUTPUT

--*Create Child Record in ContactsAddress
EXEC ps_ContactsAddress_INSERT @Con_UniqueID,
                               'EnronField',
                               'Houston',
                               'TX'

--*Join Tables to Ensure Inserts Worked as Expected
SELECT a.Con_FName,
       b.ConAdd_Address
FROM Contacts a
JOIN ContactsAddress b ON a.Con_UniqueID = b.Con_UniqueID
--Results--
Con_FName                     ConAdd_Address
----------------------------- --------------------
Jeff                          EnronField
```

As you can see, I inserted the appropriate foreign key into **ContactsAddress**. Appendix B contains an example that shows how to use ADO (ActiveX Data Objects) to get the OUTPUT parameter value returned by a stored procedure.

Dynamic SQL

Dynamic SQL allows you to build statements on the fly using parameters or variables. The *final* statement is dependent on the values supplied, which makes the this type of solution very flexible. Dynamic SQL does, however, have its drawbacks. More specifically, it is impossible for the Query Optimizer to recognize existing execution plans for a dynamic SQL query, so a new plan is built and cached on each execution.

You must use the EXECUTE (EXEC) statement to implement dynamic SQL solutions. The statement takes both character strings and variables as parameters. In addition, multiple variables can be concatenated together to produce a single statement. The following three code snippets produce the same results.

```
--Code Snippet 1
EXEC('SELECT * FROM Customers')

--Code Snippet 2
DECLARE @sqlString varchar(100)
SET @sqlString = 'SELECT * FROM Customers'
EXEC (@sqlString)

--Code Snippet 3
DECLARE @sqlString1 varchar(100),
        @sqlString2 varchar(100)


SET @sqlString1 = 'SELECT * '
SET @sqlString2 = ' FROM Customers'
EXEC (@sqlString1+@sqlString2)
```

The examples that follow show two real-world uses of dynamic SQL.

Example 1: Selecting TOP N Rows Dynamically

This procedure demonstrates how to use a parameter to specify the number of rows returned by a SELECT statement.

```
USE Northwind
go
CREATE PROCEDURE ps_Customers_SELECT_TopN
@TopValue smallint
AS


EXEC('SELECT TOP '+ @TopValue + ' * FROM Customers ORDER BY CompanyName')
```

The following shows how to return the top five rows in the **Customers** table.

```
USE Northwind
go
EXEC ps_Customers_SELECT_TopN 5
--Results--
CompanyName
----------------------------------------
Alfreds Futterkiste
Ana Trujillo Emparedados y helados
Antonio Moreno Taquería
Around the Horn
Berglunds snabbköp
```

*Example 2: Selecting * Dynamically*

This example demonstrates how to create a SELECT statement that uses the supplied parameter as the table name. More specifically, it shows how to create a procedure that will return all columns for the table referenced in the parameter.

```
USE Northwind
go
CREATE PROCEDURE ps_UTIL_SELECT_FromProvidedName
@TableName nvarchar(128)
AS
EXEC('SELECT * FROM '+ @TableName)
```

Similar to the previous example, the statement is concatenated with parameter and then executed with EXEC. The following shows how to return all the columns in the **Region** table.

```
USE Northwind
go
EXEC ps_UTIL_SELECT_FromProvidedName 'Region'
--Results--
RegionID    RegionDescription
----------- --------------------------------------------------
1           Eastern
2           Western
3           Northern
4           Southern
```

Configure Hot-Key Combo in Query Analyzer

You can use the procedure in the previous example with a new feature in Query Analyzer to facilitate development. More specifically, you can use the new customization feature to configure a hot-key combo so that the stored procedure is called when the key combo is pressed. You can use this to examine the contents of a table without having to execute a SELECT *—simply highlight the table's name and press the key combo.

In Query Analyzer, click Tools on the main menu and select Customize. Type the name of the procedure (ps_UTIL_SELECT_FromProvidedName) in the Stored Procedure column for the CTRL+3 combo (assuming you are not already using this combo) as shown in Figure 11-9.

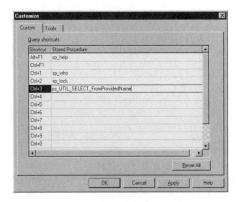

Figure 11-9. Customize dialog

Click OK to save the setting and close the dialog. Highlight a table name in the Editor Pane of Query Analyzer and press CTRL+3.

You should know that if you create the procedure in a user database, it will only be available in that database. You can, however, make the procedure available in all databases by changing its name so that it starts with "sp_" and creating it in the master database. Recall from Chapter 9 that the reason system stored procedures (and some extended stored procedures, too) use the "sp_" prefix is because it makes them available to all databases.

Calling Stored Procedures from Applications

Writing solid stored procedures that manipulate data is only part of the development process. In order to complete the process you access them via client applications available to end-users. The following examples demonstrate how to call a stored procedure using ADO. I will describe two methods, so even if your particular development environment does not support ADO, you might gain enough insight here to adopt the examples to your needs. Please note that the examples shown here are based on ASP technology. If you are not familiar with ASP, you can get a brief overview in Appendix B.

The following code snippet shows how to call a stored procedure using the Execute()method. The basis for the example is that you have an interface that allows the user to supply a character string, and all rows whose customer name begins with the string are returned.

```
REM Create ADO objects and establish database connection
Set SQLConn = server.CreateObject("ADODB.Connection")
Set rs = server.CreateObject("ADODB.RecordSet")
SQLConn.Open "Driver={SQL Server};Server=SQL1;Database=DB; Uid=ID;Pwd=pass"
SQLConn.Open
REM Build Procedue Call in variable
sSQL = "EXEC ps_Customers_SELECT_ByPartialName "
sSQL = sSQL & request.form("CusNamePartial") & "'"
REM Execute Procedure Call
SET rs = SQLConn.Execute(sSQL)
SQLConn.Close
….
```

As you can see, two ADO objects are created, a connection is made to the database, a string is built that contains a valid SQL statement, and the string is executed. The key to using this approach is to make sure that you pass a valid statement to the server via the Execute() method. When I encounter problems with this approach, I use response.write to write the contents of the string (sSQL) to the screen and troubleshoot accordingly. If the string can be copy-n-pasted into Query Analyzer and successfully executed, you can eliminate any server-side issues and concentrate on the client-side code.

You can modify the previous example so the call includes the parameter name. This can be helpful for debugging purposes if the procedure contains a large number of parameters. The following example shows how to add the parameter name.

```
REM Establish database connection
Set SQLConn = server.CreateObject("ADODB.Connection")
Set rs = server.CreateObject("ADODB.RecordSet")
SQLConn.Open "Driver={SQL Server};Server=SQL1;Database=DB; Uid=ID;Pwd=pass"
SQLConn.Open
REM Build Procedue Call in variable
```

```
sSQL = "EXEC ps_Customers_SELECT_ByPartialName "
sSQL = sSQL & "@CustomerName = '" & request.form("CusNamePartial") & "'"
REM Execute Procedure Call
SET rs = SQLConn.Execute(sSQL)
SQLConn.Close
….
```

The next example uses the ADO command object to call the procedure used in the previous examples. At first glance, it may seem complex, but rest assured it is simply a matter of understanding the syntax used to call this type of Command object. Appendix B explains this type of call in detail.

```
Set SQLConn = server.CreateObject("ADODB.Connection")
Set rs = server.CreateObject("ADODB.RecordSet")
Set cmd1 = server.CreateObject("ADODB.Command")
SQLConn.Open "Driver={SQL Server};Server=SQL1;Database=DB; Uid=ID;Pwd=pass"
SQLConn.Open
cmd1.ActiveConnection = SQLConn
cmd1.CommandType = adCmdStoredProc
cmd1.CommandText = " ps_Customers_SELECT_ByPartialName"
cmd1.Parameters.Append_
cmd1.CreateParameter("@CustomerName",adVarChar,adParamInput,30, _
    CustomerNamePartial)
Set rs = cmd1.Execute
SQLConn.close
….
```

Error Handling

The error handling functionality available in T-SQL is very limited. When an error is encountered within a stored procedure, the best you can do (assuming it's a non-fatal error) is halt the sequential processing of the code and either branch to another code segment in the procedure or return processing to the calling application. Notice that the previous sentence is specific to non-fatal errors. There are two type of errors in SQL Server 2000: fatal and non-fatal. Fatal errors cause a procedure to abort processing and terminate the connection with the client application. Non-fatal errors do not abort processing a procedure or affect the connection with the client application. When a non-fatal error occurs within a procedure, processing continues on the line of code that follows the one that caused the error.

The following example demonstrates how a fatal error affects a procedure.

```
USE tempdb
go
CREATE PROCEDURE ps_FatalError_SELECT
AS
SELECT * FROM NonExistentTable
PRINT 'Fatal Error'
go
EXEC ps_ FatalError _SELECT
--Results--
Server: Msg 208, Level 16, State 1, Procedure ps_ FatalError_SELECT, Line 3
Invalid object name 'NonExistentTable'.
```

The SELECT in the procedure references a table that does not exist, which produces a fatal error. The procedure aborts processing immediately after the error and the PRINT statement is not executed.

To demonstrate how a non-fatal error is processed, I need to create the following table.

```
USE tempdb
go
CREATE TABLE NonFatal
(
 Column1 int IDENTITY,
 Column2 int NOT NULL
)
--Results--

The command(s) completed successfully.
```

This example uses a procedure to INSERT a row into **NonFatal**, but does not include a value for **Column2** (defined as NOT NULL).

```
USE tempdb
go
CREATE PROCEDURE ps_NonFatal_INSERT
@Column2 int = NULL
AS
INSERT NonFatal VALUES (@Column2)
PRINT 'NonFatal'
go
EXEC ps_NonFatal_INSERT
--Results--
```

```
Server: Msg 515, Level 16, State 2, Procedure ps_NonFatal_INSERT, Line 4
Cannot insert the value NULL into column 'Column2', table 'tempdb.dbo.NonFatal';_
    column does not_ allow nulls. INSERT fails.
The statement has been terminated.
```
NonFatal

The last line of the results (shown in bold) demonstrates that the error did not affect the processing of the procedure—the PRINT statement executed as desired.

You might be wondering what actions cause fatal errors. Unfortunately, the actions that cause a fatal error are not well documented. Each error has an associated severity level that is a value between 0–25. The errors with a severity level of 20 or above are all fatal, but once you get below this value there is no well-defined rule as to which errors are fatal. In truth, though, worrying about which errors are fatal is a bit useless because there is no code you can implement that will allow you to handle them gracefully. The best you can do is trap for non-fatal errors.

We need to cover one more very important issue about non-fatal errors and transactions before moving on to the next topic. It is a common misconception among novice developers that wrapping two or more statements in a BEGIN TRANSACTION…COMMIT TRANSACTION construct will produce an "all or nothing" result. Assume you have two INSERT statements wrapped in a transaction as shown here.

```
BEGIN TRANSACTION
  INSERT TableOne VALUES …
  INSERT TableTwo VALUES …
COMMIT TRANSACTION
```

Many developers believe that if the second INSERT fails, the first INSERT will not be committed to the database. If the second INSERT fails as a result of a fatal error, the first INSERT is not committed to the database because the procedure aborts processing and COMMIT TRANSACTION is not executed. However, if the second INSERT fails as a result of a non-fatal error, the first INSERT *is* committed to the database. Any statements that are successfully executed between BEGIN TRANSACTION…COMMIT TRANSACTION are saved to the database when the COMMIT is executed. The next section will demonstrate how error handling code can be used to avoid *partial* changes to the database.

The remainder of this section discusses the @@ERROR system function, the RAISERROR statement, and how to handle error message information returned to a client application.

@@ERROR

The @@ERROR system function is used to implement error handling code. It contains the error ID produced by the last SQL statement executed during a client's connection. When a statement executes successfully, @@ERROR contains 0. To determine if a statement executes successfully, an IF statement is used to check the value of the function immediately after the target statement executes. It is imperative that @@ERROR be checked immediately after the target statement, because its value is reset when the next statement executes successfully.

Let's alter **ps_NonFatal_INSERT** to use @@ERROR with the following.

```
USE tempdb
go
ALTER PROCEDURE ps_NonFatal_INSERT
@Column2 int = NULL
AS
INSERT NonFatal VALUES (@Column2)
IF @@ERROR <> 0
 BEGIN
  PRINT 'Error Occured'
 END
--Results—
The command(s) completed successfully.
```

When an error occurs, the PRINT statement produces the "Error Occurred" message. The following code shows the results of a valid call to **ps_NonFatal_INSERT**.

```
USE tempdb
go
EXEC ps_NonFatal_INSERT 111
--Results--
(1 row(s) affected)
```

The next example shows the results of a call that produces the "does not allow nulls" error.

```
USE tempdb
go
EXEC ps_NonFatal_INSERT
--Results--
Server: Msg 515, Level 16, State 2, Procedure ps_NonFatal_INSERT, Line 4
Cannot insert the value NULL into column 'Column2', table 'tempdb.dbo.NonFatal';_
```

```
column does not_ allow nulls. INSERT fails.
The statement has been terminated.
```
Error Occured

The last line of the results (in bold) indicates the PRINT statement executed as expected.

Let's take a look at what happens when @@ERROR is not referenced immediately after the target statement. The following alters **ps_NonFatal_INSERT** to print the value of @@ERROR.

```
USE tempdb
go
ALTER PROCEDURE ps_NonFatal_INSERT
@Column2 int = NULL
AS
INSERT NonFatal VALUES (@Column2)
IF @@ERROR <> 0
 BEGIN
  PRINT @@Error
 END
```

Now we can re-execute the invalid call to see the value of @@ERROR.
```
USE tempdb
go
EXEC ps_NonFatal_INSERT
--Results--
Server: Msg 515, Level 16, State 2, Procedure ps_NonFatal_INSERT, Line 4
Cannot insert the value NULL into column 'Column2', table 'tempdb.dbo.NonFatal';_
   column does not_ allow nulls. INSERT fails.
The statement has been terminated.
0
```

Even though the INSERT produced an error, the value of @@ERROR is 0 because it is referenced after the IF statement. The IF statement executed successfully, so @@ERROR was reset to 0. If you need the error code in another part of the procedure use a variable to store the value. The following statement alters the example procedure to produce the desired result.

```
USE tempdb
go
ALTER PROCEDURE ps_NonFatal_INSERT
@Column2 int = NULL
AS
DECLARE @ErrorMsgID int
```

```
INSERT NonFatal VALUES (@Column2)
SET @ErrorMsgID = @@ERROR
IF @ErrorMsgID <> 0
 BEGIN
  PRINT @ErrorMsgID
 END
```

Let's re-execute the procedure to verify the error handling code works as expected.

```
USE tempdb
go
EXEC ps_NonFatal_INSERT
--Results--
Server: Msg 515, Level 16, State 2, Procedure ps_NonFatal_INSERT, Line 6
Cannot insert the value NULL into column 'Column2', table 'tempdb.dbo.NonFatal';_
   column does not_ allow nulls. INSERT fails.
The statement has been terminated.
515
```

The code works as expected because "515" is shown on the last line of the results. The system error message displayed ("Server: Msg 515, Level 16…Cannot insert…The statement has been terminated.") in the Results Pane is produced by Query Analyzer and is not a function of *our* error handling code. Query Analyzer was written in C++, which has error handling functionality to get both the error ID and error message from SQL Server. Accessing error information from a client application is discussed later in the chapter in the "Handling Errors in the Client Application" section.

Now that you understand the basics of how to use @@ERROR, let's take a look at how it should be used in production-quality code. In production code you should check the value of @@ERROR after each statement in a procedure and respond accordingly. In general, when an error is encountered control is returned to the calling application. The following shows how this approach is implemented. Note that the code is not complete and is used for illustrative purposes only.

```
CREATE PROCEDURE ps_ErrorHandling_Example
AS
DECLARE @ErrorMsgID int

INSERT Table1 VALUES…
SET @ErrorMsgID = @@ERROR
IF @ErrorMsgID <> 0
 BEGIN
  RETURN @ErrorMsgID
 END
```

```
SELECT * FROM …
SET @ErrorMsgID = @@ERROR
IF @ErrorMsgID <> 0
 BEGIN
  RETURN @ErrorMsgID
 END


UPDATE Table2 SET…
SET @ErrorMsgID = @@ERROR
IF @ErrorMsgID <> 0
 BEGIN
  RETURN @ErrorMsgID
 END
```

When an error is encountered, the procedure halts execution and returns the error ID to the calling application. Returning the error ID is handy when working within Query Analyzer, but when any standard database API (ADO or OLE DB) is used you can use its error handling functionality to obtain both the error ID and the message.

Let's revisit our earlier example that discussed the partial update that occurred as a result of a misunderstanding of how BEGIN TRANSACTION…COMMIT TRANSACTION works. Assume you have multiple INSERT statements within a procedure and all need to execute successfully in order to produce the desired results. The proper way to ensure the desired results is to check @@ERROR after each INSERT. If an error is encountered ROLLBACK any successful INSERTs so they are not omitted to the database. The following example shows how this is implemented.

```
CREATE PROCEDURE ps_ErrorHandling_Example
AS
DECLARE @ErrorMsgID int
BEGIN TRANSACTION
 INSERT Table1 VALUES…
     SET @ErrorMsgID = @@ERROR
     IF @ErrorMsgID <> 0
     BEGIN
       ROLLBACK TRANSACTION
       RETURN @ErrorMsgID
     END


INSERT Table2 VALUES…
     SET @ErrorMsgID = @@ERROR
     IF @ErrorMsgID <> 0
     BEGIN
```

```
    IF @@TRANCOUNT > 0
      ROLLBACK TRANSACTION
      RETURN @ErrorMsgID
    END


COMMIT TRANSACTION
```

When either INSERT produces an error, a ROLLBACK is executed, the execution of the procedure is halted and control is returned to the calling application. The system function @@TRANCOUNT keeps track of the number of open transactions. By default, no open transactions, its value is 0. When a BEGIN TRANSACTION is issued, its value increments by 1. When a COMMIT TRANSACTION is issued, its value decrements by 1. If both INSERT statements succeed and the COMMIT is issued, @@TRANCOUNT's value is 0 when the ROLLBACK is encountered. This produces an error because you cannot issue a ROLLBACK when there are no open transactions. The IF protects this error from happening.

The GOTO statement can be used to reduce the amount of code needed to implement the type of error handling demonstrated in the previous example. GOTO simply transfers the execution of the procedure to a line defined with a label. The following shows how to use GOTO to modify the previous example.

```
CREATE PROCEDURE ps_ErrorHandling_Example
AS
DECLARE @ErrorMsgID int
BEGIN TRANSACTION
 INSERT Table1 VALUES...
 SET @ErrorMsgID = @@ERROR
  IF @ErrorMsgID <> 0
    GOTO ErrorHandler

 INSERT Table2 VALUES...
 SET @ErrorMsgID = @@ERROR
 IF @ErrorMsgID <> 0
   GOTO ErrorHandler

COMMIT TRANSACTION

ErrorHandler:
 ROLLBACK TRANSACTION
 RETURN @ErrorMsgID
```

When an error is encountered, processing is transferred to the ErrorHandler: label, a ROLLBACK is executed and control is returned to the calling application.

RAISERROR

The RAISERROR statement is used to produce an ad hoc error message or to retrieve a custom message that is stored in the **sysmessages** table. You can use this statement with the error handling code presented in the previous section to implement custom error messages in your applications. The syntax of the statement is shown here.

```
RAISERROR ( { msg_id | msg_str } { , severity , state }
    [ , argument [ ,...n ] ] )
    [ WITH option [ ,...n ] ]
```

A description of the components of the statement follows.

msg_id

The ID for an error message, which is stored in the **error** column in **sysmessages**. The domain of the **error** column for custom messages are values greater than 50,000.

msg_str

A custom message that is not contained in **sysmessages**. The maximum length of the message is 400 characters. Variable substitution can be used to create a more meaningful message.

severity

The severity level associated with the error. The valid values are 0–25. Severity levels 0–18 can be used by any user, but 19–25 are only available to members of the fixed-server role **sysadmin**. When levels 19–25 are used, the WITH LOG option is required.

state

A value that indicates the invocation state of the error. The valid values are 0–127. This value is not used by SQL Server.

Argument, ...

One or more variables that are used to customize the message. For example, you could pass the current process ID (@@SPID) so it could be displayed in the message.

WITH option, ...

The three values that can be used with this optional argument are described here.

OPTION	DESCRIPTION
LOG	Forces the error to logged in the SQL Server error log and the NT application log.
NOWAIT	Sends the message immediately to the client.
SETERROR	Sets @@ERROR to the unique ID for the message or 50,000.

The number of options available for the statement make it seem complicated, but it is actually easy to use. The following shows how to create an ad hoc message with a severity of 10 and a state of 1.

```
RAISERROR ('An error occured updating the NonFatal table',10,1)
--Results--
An error occured updating the NonFatal table
```

The statement does not have to be used in conjunction with any other code, but for our purposes it will be used with the error handling code presented earlier. The following alters the **ps_NonFatal_INSERT** procedure to use RAISERROR.

```
USE tempdb
go
ALTER PROCEDURE ps_NonFatal_INSERT
@Column2 int = NULL
AS
DECLARE @ErrorMsgID int

INSERT NonFatal VALUES (@Column2)
SET @ErrorMsgID = @@ERROR
IF @ErrorMsgID <> 0
 BEGIN
  RAISERROR ('An error occured updating the NonFatal table',10,1)
 END
```

When an error-producing call is made to the procedure, the custom message is passed to the client. The following shows the output generated by Query Analyzer.

```
USE tempdb
go
EXEC ps_NonFatal_INSERT
--Results--
Server: Msg 515, Level 16, State 2, Procedure ps_NonFatal_INSERT, Line 6
Cannot insert the value NULL into column 'Column2', table 'tempdb.dbo.NonFatal';_
   column does not_ allow nulls. INSERT fails.
The statement has been terminated.
An error occured updating the NonFatal table
```

The output may seem confusing because we still see the same error message displayed before we started using RAISERROR. The custom error (in bold) is also displayed. The output is a function of Query Analyzer and we cannot control its behavior. When you develop client applications you will have control over what is displayed to the end user so the output will be less confusing.

We can use variable substitution to add the actual error number to the message. This will allow us to send the end user a message that doesn't confuse them and provide the technical person with the information needed to troubleshoot the problem. The following statement alters the example procedure so that the error ID is displayed.

```
USE tempdb
go
ALTER PROCEDURE ps_NonFatal_INSERT
@Column2 int = NULL
AS
DECLARE @ErrorMsgID int

INSERT NonFatal VALUES (@Column2)
SET @ErrorMsgID = @@ERROR
IF @ErrorMsgID <> 0
 BEGIN
  RAISERROR ('An error occured updating the NonFatal table (%d)',10,1,@ErrorMsgID )
 END
```

The % and @ErrorMsgID are the key to adding the error ID to the message. The % is used as a placeholder for the variable and d indicates the data type of the variable. All the codes for the data types supported are listed in the BOL topic: RAISERROR, but the two most used codes are *d* and *s*. The d code is used when the variable is an integer and s is used when the variable is a character string. The @ErrorMsgID variable is simply listed in the argument portion of the call. When more than one argument is used list them in the order in which they occur in the message. The following shows the output with the error ID added.

```
USE tempdb
go
EXEC ps_NonFatal_INSERT
--Results--
Server: Msg 515, Level 16, State 2, Procedure ps_NonFatal_INSERT, Line 6
Cannot insert the value NULL into column 'Column2', table 'tempdb.dbo.NonFatal';_
   column does not_ allow nulls. INSERT fails.
The statement has been terminated.
An error occured updating the NonFatal table (515)
```

Let's add a character string variable to the message to demonstrate how a multi-variable statement works. The following alters our example procedure to add the user name to the message.

```
USE tempdb
go
ALTER PROCEDURE ps_NonFatal_INSERT
@Column2 int = NULL
AS
DECLARE @ErrorMsgID int,
        @UserName sysname
SET @UserName = USER_NAME()

INSERT NonFatal VALUES (@Column2)
SET @ErrorMsgID = @@ERROR
IF @ErrorMsgID <> 0
 BEGIN
  RAISERROR ('An error occured updating the NonFatal table _
(%d),(%s)',10,1,@ErrorMsgID,@UserName)
 END
```

The additional parameter holder is added with the specified variable type and the variable is added to the argument list. The following shows the new form of the error message.

```
USE tempdb
go
EXEC ps_NonFatal_INSERT
--Results--
Server: Msg 515, Level 16, State 2, Procedure ps_NonFatal_INSERT, Line 8
Cannot insert the value NULL into column 'Column2', table 'tempdb.dbo.NonFatal'; _
   column does not allow nulls. INSERT fails.
The statement has been terminated.
An error occured updating the NonFatal table (515),(garth)
```

Adding a Permanent Custom Message

If you have a message that is going to be used frequently, it is more efficient to add it to the **sysmessages** table and reference it by its unique ID. The system stored procedure **sp_addmessages** adds an error message to **sysmessages**. The following shows how to add a new error message.

```
sp_addmessage @msgnum = 50001,
              @severity = 10,
              @msgtext = 'An error occured updating the NonFatal table'
--Results--
(1 row(s) affected)
```

Note that the ID for a custom message must be greater than 50,000. The new message can be accessed with RAISERROR using the following.

```
RAISERROR (50001,10,1)
--Results--
An error occured updating the NonFatal table
```

Creating International Messages

RAISERROR gives you the ability to reference error messages in a user's native language. The **sysmessages** table has a column called **msglangid** that holds the language associated with the message. You can create the same message (use the same error value) in different languages using the **mslandid** column to differentiate versions. Your code calls the message as usual and the correct version of the message is chosen based on the language that was specified when the client connection was established. For more information on this, see the Books Online topics: SET LANGUAGE and sp_helplanguage.

Handling Errors in the Client Application

There are two approaches to handling SQL Server errors in a client application. The first approach involves using the error handling functionality of the client and the second sends an explicit return value to the client so it can respond accordingly. Both method are described in this section.

Client Error Handling Functionality

Three of the Most popular development languages/technologies are: VB, C++, and ASP. All three support ADO, so the example presented here will demonstrate how to use the ADO errors collection to access the errors returned by SQL Server. Before a custom error message can be sent to a client application that uses OLE-DB to connect to SQL Server, the stored procedure needs to be modified with the SET NOCOUNT ON statement. This statement prohibits intermediary results from being sent to the client, which in this case causes OLE-DB to terminate processing before the custom error message is sent to the application. The following code shows how to alter the procedure.

```
USE tempdb
go
ALTER PROCEDURE ps_NonFatal_INSERT
@Column2 int = NULL
AS
SET NOCOUNT ON
DECLARE @ErrorMsgID int,
        @UserName sysname
SET @UserName = USER_NAME()

INSERT NonFatal VALUES (@Column2)
SET @ErrorMsgID = @@ERROR
IF @ErrorMsgID <> 0
 BEGIN
  RAISERROR (50001,17,1)
END
```

The SET NOCOUNT ON setting is not needed to send custom messages to applications that connect to SQL Server with ODBC.

The following example is based on ASP. If you are not familiar with ASP you need to read Appendix B before continuing.

```
<!--#include file="adovbs.inc"-->
<%
 On Error Resume Next

 Set objConn = server.CreateObject("ADODB.Connection")
 REM DSN-Less OLE-DB
 ObjConn.Open _
"Provider=SQLOLEDB;Server=Ace;Database=tempdb; _
Uid=garth;Pwd=password"

 Set cmd1 = server.CreateObject("ADODB.Command")
```

```
cmd1.ActiveConnection = objConn
cmd1.CommandType = adCmdStoredProc
cmd1.CommandText = "ps_NonFatal_INSERT"
cmd1.Parameters.Append
cmd1.CreateParameter("Column2",adInteger,adParamInput,,NULL)
cmd1.Execute


i = 0
For Each error_item in objConn.Errors
 response.write objConn.Errors(i).Description & "<br>"
 response.write objConn.Errors(i).NativeError & "<br>"
 i = i + 1
Next
%>
```

The errors collection of the Connection object is used to capture the errors returned by the server. When the page is executed the following output is generated.

```
[Microsoft][ODBC SQL Server Driver][SQL Server]Cannot insert the value NULL into_
   column 'Column2', table 'tempdb.dbo.NonFatal'; column does not allow nulls._
   INSERT fails.
515
[Microsoft][ODBC SQL Server Driver][SQL Server]The statement has been terminated.
3621
[Microsoft][ODBC SQL Server Driver][SQL Server]An error occured updating the _
   NonFatal table
50001
```

The system generated messages are returned along with the custom message returned by RAISERROR. You can use programming logic to discern system from custom error messages because the latter will have a **NativeError** value greater than 50,000. In addition, string manipulation code can be used to strip away the part of the message that might confuse the end user. The following shows how this done (partial code).

```
...
i = 0
For Each error_item in objConn.Errors
 If objConn.Errors(i).NativeError > 50000 Then
  response.write
Mid(objConn.Errors(i).Description,InStrRev(objConn.Errors(i).Description,"]")+1)
End If
 i = i + 1
Next
%>
```

This output generated by the revised code is shown here.

```
An error occured updating the NonFatal table
```

Returning an Explicit Value to the Client

The previous example relied on the error capabilities of the client application to catch the error generated by SQL Server. The approach described in this section is less elegant but easier to understand if you are not aware of the error handling capabilities of the client. More specifically, an OUTPUT parameter is used to send an error value to the client so it can respond accordingly.

The following shows how to alter the example procedure per this approach.

```
USE tempdb
go
ALTER PROCEDURE ps_NonFatal_INSERT
@Column2 int = NULL,
@ErrorCode tinyint OUTPUT
AS
DECLARE @ErrorMsgID int,
        @UserName sysname
SET @UserName = USER_NAME()

INSERT NonFatal VALUES (@Column2)
IF @@ERROR <> 0
 SET @ErrorCode =  99
ELSE
 SET @ErrorCode =  0
```

In this case, 99 is returned when the INSERT statement generates an error, and 0 is returned when it executes successfully. The code shown here will display a generic error message when 99 is returned.

```
<!--#include file="adovbs.inc"-->
<%
 On Error Resume Next

 Set objConn = server.CreateObject("ADODB.Connection")
 REM DSN-Less OLE-DB
ObjConn.Open _
"Provider=SQLOLEDB;Server=Ace;Database=tempdb; _
Uid=garth;Pwd=password"
 Set cmd1 = server.CreateObject("ADODB.Command")
 cmd1.ActiveConnection = objConn
```

```
cmd1.CommandType = adCmdStoredProc
cmd1.CommandText = "ps_NonFatal_INSERT"
cmd1.Parameters.Append
cmd1.CreateParameter("Column2",adInteger,adParamInput,,NULL)
cmd1.Parameters.Append cmd1.CreateParameter("ErrorCode",adTinyint,adParamOutput)
cmd1.Execute

If cmd1.Parameters("ReturnCode") = 99 Then
  response.write "Error Occured"
End If
%>
```

If you had a procedure that contained multiple statements and wanted to display a statement-specific error message, you would associate a unique value with each RETURN. The client code would look for a particular value and display the appropriate message.

Preventing Errors from Getting to the Database

It's important that you understand the error handling capabilities of SQL Server 2000, but is more important that you understand how to use good programming practices to eliminate errors from getting to the database. For example, let's say your client application allows a user to populate a form whose content is used to insert data into one or more tables in a database. If an input box on the form is the source for a column that is defined as NOT NULL, do not allow the user to submit the data to database until the required field is populated. In ASP, client-side JScript is used to make sure a required field is populated. You can see an example of this approach in Appendix A.

Another good programming practice that can prevent errors is the use of dynamically populated drop-down and list boxes. Assume you have an application that allows you to enter employee data into an Employees table. One of the columns in Employees is populated with the department ID in which the employee works. The department data is stored in a lookup table (Departments) that consists of a primary key and a department name and there is a foreign key relationship defined between Employees and Departments.

The error-prone approach to implementing this type of functionality is to hard-code the primary key and name for each department in the client application. This approach can cause two types of errors. The first is a typo in one of the primary key values on the client. If an invalid value is passed to the database, a foreign key violation will be generated. The second type of error concerns out-of-sync data. Assume an extraneous department is eliminated from Departments, but not from the hard-coded values in the client application. If the non-existent department is passed to the database, a foreign key violation will be generated.

Before You Go

In this chapter I discussed the benefits of using stored procedures and demonstrated the basics of how they are created, modified, and deleted. I also showed how to more effectively manage them using the new extended property functionality introduced in SQL Server 2000. I used a number of examples to demonstrate how to use stored procedures to encapsulate common data manipulation actions. In addition, I covered two ASP methods of calling a stored procedure from a client application, as well as some common techniques for working with SQL Server error messages.

If you completed all the examples presented in this chapter, you should be pretty comfortable working with stored procedures. The basics of creating and managing stored procedures are fairly straightforward. The challenging part of implementing good procedures is understanding T-SQL well enough to know how to efficiently construct the statements that compose the body of the object. Chapter 13 and 14 will demonstrate how stored procedures are used in the real world to implement solutions. Once you complete that material you will be ready to tackle most any SQL programming task using stored procedures.

The next chapter covers triggers—the most misunderstood database object in SQL Server. Triggers can be used to solve a variety of programming tasks, so be sure to read on and learn how they can help you create more effective solutions.

CHAPTER 12

Triggers

THIS CHAPTER IS RELATIVELY SHORT BECAUSE TRIGGERS are very much like stored procedures. They are created in a similar manner and processed in the exact same way, but the method in which they called is different. When you read about triggers, you will often hear them referred to as a way to enforce business rules. This is certainly true, but referring to them in this way may makes them seem more complex than they really are. Triggers are simply a way to make something happen when something else happens—it's that simple.

> **NOTE Sample Code**
>
> *The sample code for this chapter is available for download at either* `http://www.apress.com` *or* `http://www.SQLBook.com`. *Download CodeCentric.zip, extract the contents, and look for the file named Ch12.sql.*

Before You Get Started

It is imperative that you understand user-defined stored procedures before reading this chapter. If you have not read Chapter 11, please do so before continuing. It may also help you to understand how the extended stored procedure **xp_sendmail** works. If you are not familiar with this procedure, please read about it in Chapter 10.

Trigger Fundamentals

A trigger is a stored procedure that has been *attached* to a table or view. More specifically, they are one or more SQL statements that are stored for server-side execution but are only executed when a certain action is performed on the table (or view) to which they are attached. They are not explicitly executed by users but as a result of an action performed on a table. The actions that cause a trigger to be executed are INSERT, UPDATE, and DELETE statements. For example, when a table has an associated INSERT trigger, the statements in the trigger are executed when a row is inserted into the table.

A trigger is processed in the same manner as a stored procedure, so all the compilation and execution plan coverage in the "Using Execution Plans" section of Chapter 11 also applies to triggers.

Inserted and Deleted Tables

Other than the fact that a trigger *cannot* be explicitly executed by an end-user, the main difference between a trigger and a stored procedure is that triggers have access to two special virtual tables called **inserted** and **deleted**. These virtual tables are based on the contents of the transaction log and reference the values affected by the INSERT, UPDATE, or DELETE statements performed against the table to which the trigger is attached. They are not real tables, but a handy way to reference the contents of the transaction log. The structure of both **inserted** and **deleted** is identical to the base table, so the columns in each table have the same identifier.

The **inserted** table contains copies of the new or updated rows when an INSERT or UPDATE is executed. The **deleted** table contains the deleted rows when a DELETE is executed or the *old* values when an UPDATE an executed. You can use these virtual tables to test for certain conditions that require an action to be performed. Figure 12.1 shows the tables created by each type of trigger.

> **TIP Non-logged Operations Do Not Fire Triggers**
>
> *A non-logged operation does not insert data into the transaction log. The contents of both **inserted** and **deleted** are based on the transaction log. Therefore, a non-logged operation cannot cause a trigger to fire, because there is no data for the trigger to reference—both **inserted** and **deleted** would be empty.*

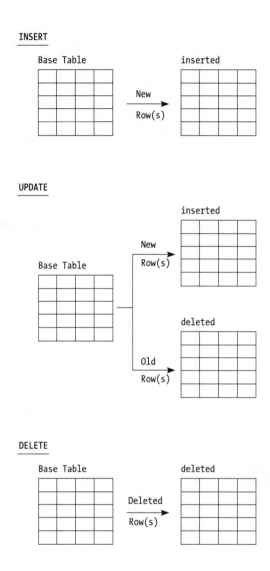

Figure 12-1. Trigger processing for INSERT, UPDATE, and DELETE

When to Use Triggers

The following overview of a real-world example of using triggers will help you better understand when they can be used to implement required functionality. One of my clients is a commercial real estate company who does business with companies like IBM that have multiple divisions (e.g., IBM North, IBM South) across the country. The client has different operational regions (e.g., Northeast, Southwest) and each one is responsible for their own geographical territory. The different regions operate autonomously and do not communicate potential business with one another.

385

A typical problem that arose was that the client had three or four business proposals submitted to one company, IBM, but each originated in a different region. Because the different regions did not communicate, it was impossible for the client to know how much potential *overall* business they had from IBM. This put the client at a competitive disadvantage to their competition who could recognize *all* potential business across regions. The competition could offer incentives based on all potential business, but the client could not. In other words, poor communication between the regional operations was causing the client to lose business because they did not offer price breaks or incentives based on all potential business.

An intranet application was created to address this issue, and each region head was required to enter new business initiatives within their region. An initiative is simply the start of communications with a company for potential business. The limited table structure shown in Figure 12-2 was used to define the relationships between a parent company, its divisions, and its associated engagements.

Figure 12-2. ParentCompanies/Companies/Engagements table structures

An INSERT trigger was created on the **Engagements** table that *watched* for new engagements. When a row was inserted, the values in the **inserted** table were used to construct a SELECT that allowed the associated value in **ParentCompany.Ini_EmailNotfication** to be determined. When this value was "Y," an email was sent to the Business Development Manager so he could make sure the larger, multi-region customers received the attention they deserved.

The examples covered later in the chapter will show the details of creating a trigger, but I thought it might help to know how one can be used before continuing.

Two Types of Triggers

There are two types of triggers available in SQL Server 2000: AFTER and INSTEAD OF. The AFTER designation for a trigger is new to SQL Server 2000, but the functionality it supports has been around for several versions of the product. In pre-2000 version of SQL Server, AFTER triggers were known as FOR triggers. The FOR syntax is still supported for backward compatibility, but you should make every effort to use the new syntax. INSTEAD OF triggers are new to SQL Server 2000. I will describe both types here.

AFTER Triggers

An AFTER trigger executes SQL statements after the action to which they are attached has completed. The previous example is an AFTER trigger. The email was sent after a row was inserted into the **Engagement** table. In like manner, you can use DELETE and UPDATE triggers to fire events after DELETE and UPDATE statements are completed. AFTER triggers can be created on tables, but cannot be used with views.

INSTEAD OF Triggers

The INSTEAD OF trigger is new to SQL Server 2000 and was primarily introduced to help with updateable views. More specifically, they allow views that would not normally be updateable to support updates. If you are not familiar with the concept of updateable views, please see "Updateable Views" in Chapter 8. Even though the INSTEAD OF trigger was primarily added for views, it can also be used on a table.

   The SQL statements contained in an INSTEAD OF trigger are executed, but the action associated with the trigger is not. For example, let's say you create an INSERT, INSTEAD OF trigger on a table. When an INSERT statement is executed on the table, the INSERT action is ignored but the statements in the INSTEAD OF trigger are executed. This behavior allows the virtual **inserted** and **deleted** tables to be populated and referenced by the SQL statements in the trigger.

CREATE TRIGGER Syntax

There are two versions of the CREATE TRIGGER statement. The first is for detecting table-level changes, and the second is for detecting changes at the column-level. I will cover both versions here.

Table-Level Changes Syntax

The syntax of the CREATE TRIGGER statement used when you want to catch changes at the table level is shown here.

```
CREATE TRIGGER trigger_name
ON { table | view }
[ WITH ENCRYPTION ]
{
    { { FOR | AFTER | INSTEAD OF }
```

```
      { [ DELETE ] [ , ] [ INSERT ] [ , ] [ UPDATE ] }
      [ WITH APPEND ]
      [ NOT FOR REPLICATION ]
      AS
      sql_statement [ ...n ]
}
```

A description of the components of the statement follows.

CREATE TRIGGER trigger_name ON { table | view }

Specifies the trigger's identifier and the table or view to which it is attached.

[WITH ENCRYPTION]

Optional argument that allows you to specify that the statements that comprise the trigger are encrypted in the **syscomments** table.

{ FOR | AFTER | INSTEAD OF } { [DELETE] [,] [INSERT] [,] [UPDATE]

Allows you to determine when the trigger is executed.

[WITH APPEND]

Optional argument that is included for backward compatibility. You must use this argument when the following conditions are met.

- The database compatibility level is set to 65 or lower.

- You create a trigger on a table that already has a trigger of the same type. For example, when you are adding (appending) a second or third INSERT trigger to a table.

[NOT FOR REPLICATION]

Optional argument that indicates the trigger will not fire when the action that fires the trigger is generated by replication.

sql_statement [...n]

SQL statements executed when the trigger is fired.

Column-Level Changes Syntax

The full syntax for CREATE TRIGGER where the actions performed are dependent on changes at the column level is shown here.

```
CREATE TRIGGER trigger_name
ON { table | view }
[ WITH ENCRYPTION ]
   { ( FOR | AFTER | INSTEAD OF )
       { [ INSERT ] [ , ] [ UPDATE ] }
       [ WITH APPEND ]
       [ NOT FOR REPLICATION ]
       AS
       { IF UPDATE ( column )
          [ { AND | OR } UPDATE ( column ) ]
             [ ...n ]
       | IF ( COLUMNS_UPDATED ( ) { bitwise_operator } updated_bitmask )
             { comparison_operator } column_bitmask [ ...n ]
       }
       sql_statement [ ...n ]
}
```

Note that only the code shown in bold will be covered here. The previous section provided coverage of the other parts of the statement.

{ [INSERT] [,] [UPDATE] }

These options indicate what actions can be used to define when a column-level trigger is fired. Please note that unlike the table-level trigger, a column-level trigger cannot be fired as a result of a DELETE.

```
{ IF UPDATE ( column )
...
     { comparison_operator } column_bitmask [ ...n ]
}
```

Statements that allow you to configure the trigger so that it fires when the specified columns are changed. The first option allows you to specify one or more columns using UPDATE(), so that a Boolean true is returned if the column is updated. The second option uses bitwise operations to determine which columns within the table were inserted or updated.

General Comments

The following general comments apply to triggers.

- Triggers cannot be created on system tables.

- DELETE triggers are not fired when TRUNCATE TABLE is executed on a table. The TRUNCATE statement does not cause the data rows affected to be written to the transaction log, so there is nothing to populate **inserted** or **deleted**.

- You cannot execute any database creation or modification statements (e.g., ALTER DATABASE) or perform any backup or restore operations within a trigger.

- You should not use triggers to return data to users using the SELECT statement or to set variable values using SET. Should you need to perform either one of the statements in a trigger, make sure you start the sql_statement portion of the trigger with SET NOCOUNT ON.

- When cascading deletes are used, the triggers on the parent or child table do not fire until the final cascading delete has completed.

Statement Permissions

CREATE TRIGGER permission defaults to the fixed-server role **sysadmin**, the fixed-database roles **db_owner** and **db_ddladmin** and the table owner and are not transferable.

Object Permissions

To execute an AFTER TRIGGER, the user only needs permission to execute the action statement on the table. In other words, if you can perform an INSERT, UPDATE, or DELETE on the table, the associated AFTER TRIGGER will fire. When using an INSTEAD OF trigger on a view, the user must have INSERT, UPDATE, and DELETE permission on all the tables referenced by the view regardless of whether the trigger performs any of these actions.

Creating Triggers

The following sections discuss the two ways to create triggers using Query Analyzer and Enterprise Manager.

Before you create the triggers, use the following statements to create the tables referenced in the examples.

```
USE tempdb
go
CREATE TABLE Orders
(
 Ord_UniqueID smallint IDENTITY PRIMARY KEY,
 Ord_Name varchar(30) NOT NULL,
 Ord_Priority tinyint NOT NULL,
 Ord_Date smalldatetime DEFAULT GETDATE()
)
go
CREATE TABLE HotOrders
(
 HotOrd_UniqueID smallint IDENTITY NOT NULL,
 Ord_UniqueID smallint FOREIGN KEY REFERENCES Orders(Ord_UniqueID) NOT NULL
)
--Results--
The command(s) completed successfully.
```

The **Orders** table holds general information about an order, and the **Hot-Orders** table holds information about orders whose **Ord_Priority** value is greater than 6. In the real world you would not insert hot orders into another table, but rather send an email to the persons responsible for order processing. To send an email in a trigger, you need to make a call to the extended stored procedure **xp_sendmail**. As you will recall from Chapter 10, using **xp_sendmail** requires SQL Mail to be configured.

In case you don't have SQL Mail configured I am going to demonstrate how INSERT and UPDATE triggers work by inserting the data that meets the criteria into **HotOrders**. I included the code needed to implement the email functionality for those who do have SQL Mail configured. If you fall into this category, simply remove the comment marks (/*...*/) and modify the email address referenced in the code.

Query Analyzer

To create a trigger in Query Analyzer, type the text of the trigger in the Editor Pane and execute the statement. You can do this very easily (avoiding any typing) by using the sample code file (Ch12.sql) for this chapter. Directions for obtaining the sample file are provided at the beginning of the chapter. Simply open the file in Query Analyzer, highlight the code snippet shown here, and press CRTL+E (you can also press the Run button, but I prefer using the shortcut key combo).

Creating an INSERT Trigger

The following shows how to create an INSERT trigger that *catches* the orders whose priority is greater than 6.

```
USE tempdb
go
CREATE TRIGGER tr_Orders_INSERT_HotOrders
ON Orders
AFTER INSERT
AS
--Determine if hot orders have been entered
IF EXISTS (SELECT * FROM inserted WHERE Ord_Priority > 6)
 BEGIN
  --HotOrders code
  INSERT HotOrders (Ord_UniqueID)
  SELECT Ord_UniqueID FROM inserted
  WHERE Ord_Priority > 6

  /*
  --Email code
  DECLARE  @Count smallint,
           @EmailMessage varchar(100)
  --Determine number of "hot" orders
  SELECT @Count = COUNT(Ord_UniqueID)
```

```
FROM inserted
WHERE Ord_Priority > 6
--Build message
SELECT @EmailMessage = CAST(@COUNT AS varchar(3))+ 'Hot Order(s) Entered'
--Send email
EXEC master..xp_sendmail @recipients = 'garth@SQLBook.com',
                          @message = @EmailMessage,
                          @subject = 'Hot Orders Entered'
 */
END
--Results--
The command(s) completed successfully.
```

The IF statement checks **inserted** to determine whether the orders entered have a priority greater than 6. When the IF evaluates to true, rows are inserted into **HotOrders** to capture the unique ID of the hot orders.

The email portion of the code (commented out with /*...*/) does three things. First, it determines the number of hot orders entered. Second, it concatenates this value with a string to build the message portion of the email. The CAST function converts the smallint value to varchar. And third, it uses **xp_sendmail** to send the email.

The following statements show that the trigger works as expected.

```
USE tempdb
go
INSERT Orders (Ord_Name, Ord_Priority) VALUES ('First Order',6)
INSERT Orders (Ord_Name, Ord_Priority) VALUES ('Second Order',9)
INSERT Orders (Ord_Name, Ord_Priority) VALUES ('Third Order',10)

SELECT a.Ord_Name, b.*
FROM Orders a
JOIN HotOrders b ON a.Ord_UniqueID = b.Ord_UniqueID
--Results--
```

Ord_Name	HotOrd_UniqueID	Ord_UniqueID
Second Order	1	2
Third Order	2	3

Notice that only the orders with a priority of 9 and 10 were inserted into the **HotOrders** table.

Two rows in the **Orders** table have a priority greater than 6. We can use these rows to demonstrate that the trigger can handle multi-row insert statements. The

following example uses the existing data to insert two more hot orders into the
Orders table within the same statement.

```
INSERT Orders (Ord_Name, Ord_Priority)
SELECT Ord_Name, Ord_Priority
FROM Orders
WHERE Ord_Priority > 6

SELECT a.Ord_Name, b.*
FROM Orders a
JOIN HotOrders b ON a.Ord_UniqueID = b.Ord_UniqueID
--Results--
```

Ord_Name	HotOrd_UniqueID	Ord_UniqueID
Second Order	1	2
Third Order	2	3
Second Order	3	4
Third Order	4	5

Two rows were also added to **HotOrders** indicating that the trigger works as
expected.

As demonstrated, **tr_Orders_ INSERT_HotOrders** was written to handle multi-
row insert statements. In general, only one order (single-row insert) would be
entered at a time, but it is important that you design for multi-row insert statements
because of the way triggers work. More specifically, a trigger is only fired once per
statement. If the trigger would have been written to handle only a single-row insert,
unexpected results would occur. The following statements drop the existing trigger
and create a new one that was written to only hand single-row inserts.

```
USE tempdb
go
DROP TRIGGER tr_Orders_ INSERT_HotOrders
go
CREATE TRIGGER tr_Orders_ INSERT_HotOrdersSingleRow
ON Orders
AFTER INSERT
AS
--Determine if hot order has been entered
IF (SELECT COUNT(*) FROM inserted WHERE Ord_Priority > 6) = 1
 BEGIN
  --HotOrders code
  INSERT HotOrders (Ord_UniqueID)
  SELECT Ord_UniqueID FROM inserted
```

```
/*
--Email code
--Build message
SELECT @EmailMessage = CAST(@COUNT AS varchar(3))+ ' Hot Order(s) Entered'
--Send email
EXEC master..xp_sendmail @recipients = 'garth@SQLBook.com',
                         @subject = 'Hot Order Entered'
*/
END
```

The IF Statement has been modified so it only checks to see if *one* row was entered whose order priority is greater than 6. If more than more row is entered with a priority greater than 6 the trigger will not work as expected because data will not be inserted into the **HotOrders** table. There are now four rows in the **Orders** table whose priority is greater than 6. The following INSERT statement references this data to show that the new trigger will miss hot orders when more than one is added within a single statement.

```
USE tempdb
go
INSERT Orders (Ord_Name, Ord_Priority)
SELECT Ord_Name, Ord_Priority
FROM Orders
WHERE Ord_Priority > 6

SELECT a.Ord_Name, b.*
FROM Orders a
JOIN HotOrders b ON a.Ord_UniqueID =  b.Ord_UniqueID
--Results--
```

Ord_Name	HotOrd_UniqueID	Ord_UniqueID
Second Order	1	2
Third Order	2	3
Second Order	3	4
Third Order	4	5

There are still only four rows in the **HotOrders** table. The trigger fired once per statement, not per row inserted, so the additional "hot" rows in the **inserted** table cause the trigger to fail because there was more than one with a **Ord_Priority** greater than 6.

Before moving on, drop **tr_Orders_ INSERT_HotOrdersSingleRow** and replace it with **tr_Orders_ INSERT_HotOrders** using the following.

```
USE tempdb
go
DROP TRIGGER tr_Orders_ INSERT_HotOrdersSingleRow
go
CREATE TRIGGER tr_Orders_ INSERT_HotOrders
ON Orders
AFTER INSERT
AS
--Determine if hot orders have been entered
IF EXISTS (SELECT * FROM inserted WHERE Ord_Priority > 6)
 BEGIN
  --HotOrders code
  INSERT HotOrders (Ord_UniqueID)
  SELECT Ord_UniqueID FROM inserted
  WHERE Ord_Priority > 6

  /*
  --Email code
  DECLARE  @Count smallint,
           @EmailMessage varchar(100)
  --Determine number of "hot" orders
  SELECT @Count = COUNT(Ord_UniqueID)
  FROM inserted
  WHERE Ord_Priority > 6
  --Build message
  SELECT @EmailMessage = CAST(@COUNT AS varchar(3))+ ' Hot Order(s) Entered'
  --Send email
  EXEC master..xp_sendmail @recipients = 'garth@SQLBook.com',
                           @message = @EmailMessage,
                           @subject = 'Hot Orders Entered'
  */
 END
```

Creating an UPDATE Trigger

The previous example only accounted for rows inserted into the table. Realistically the priority of an order could change post-entry, and you want to catch this type of change too. The following example creates an UPDATE trigger whose statements execute when an order's priority changes to a value greater than 6.

```
USE tempdb
go
CREATE TRIGGER tr_Orders_UPDATE_HotOrders
ON Orders
AFTER UPDATE
AS

--Make sure priority was changed
IF NOT UPDATE(Ord_Priority)
 BEGIN
  RETURN
 END

--Determine if priority was changed to greater than 6
IF EXISTS (SELECT *
          FROM inserted a
          JOIN deleted b ON a.Ord_UniqueID = b.Ord_UniqueID
          WHERE b.Ord_Priority <= 6 AND
                a.Ord_Priority > 6)
 BEGIN

  --HotOrders code
  INSERT HotOrders (Ord_UniqueID)
  SELECT a.Ord_UniqueID
  FROM inserted a
  JOIN deleted b ON a.Ord_UniqueID = b.Ord_UniqueID
  WHERE b.Ord_Priority <= 6 AND
        a.Ord_Priority > 6
  /*
  --Email code
  DECLARE  @Count smallint,
           @EmailMessage varchar(100)
  --Determine number of "hot" orders
  SELECT @Count = COUNT(a.Ord_UniqueID)
  FROM inserted a
  JOIN deleted b ON a.Ord_UniqueID = b.Ord_UniqueID
  WHERE b.Ord_Priority <= 6 AND
        a.Ord_Priority > 6
  --Build message
  SELECT @EmailMessage = CAST(@COUNT AS varchar(3))+ ' Order(s) was Updated to Hot_
  Status'
  --Send email
  EXEC master..xp_sendmail @recipients = 'garth@SQLBook.com',
                           @message = @EmailMessage,
```

```
                            @subject = 'Order Updated to Hot Status'
   */
   END
```

The trigger's first action is to use the IF UPDATE option to make sure **Ord_Priority** was modified. If an order's priority hasn't changed, there is no need to execute the remaining statements, so RETURN is executed to return operation to the calling procedure.

The next code block checks to see if an order's priority has changed from a value less than or equal to 6 to a value greater than 6. For example, if an order's priority changed from 3 to 6, no action should be performed. This is important because you only want to track "hot" changes. Both the **inserted** and **deleted** tables are used to perform the check. The **inserted** table holds the new values and **deleted** holds the old values.

Before you test the new trigger, check the current contents of **HotOrders** with the following.

```
USE tempdb
go
SELECT a.Ord_Name, b.*
FROM Orders a
JOIN HotOrders b ON a.Ord_UniqueID =  b.Ord_UniqueID
--Results--
```

Ord_Name	HotOrd_UniqueID	Ord_UniqueID
Second Order	1	2
Third Order	2	3
Second Order	3	4
Third Order	4	5

As you can see, the only original order not considered hot is "first order." The order priority for "first order" is 6. The following statements change the **Ord_Priority** value from 6 to 9 and verify that the update trigger works as expected.

```
USE tempdb
go
UPDATE Orders
SET Ord_Priority = 9
WHERE Ord_UniqueID = 1

SELECT a.Ord_Name, b.*
FROM Orders a
JOIN HotOrders b ON a.Ord_UniqueID = b.Ord_UniqueID
--Results--
```

Ord_Name	HotOrd_UniqueID	Ord_UniqueID
Second Order	1	2
Third Order	2	3
Second Order	3	4
Third Order	4	5
First Order	5	1

Enterprise Manager

Enterprise Manager's Trigger Properties dialog allows you to create and modify the triggers attached to a table. To access the Trigger Properties dialog, complete the following.

1. Expand a database, and then select Tables.

2. Right-click the target table, highlight All Tasks, and select Manage Triggers.

Figure 12-3 shows the Trigger Properties dialog.

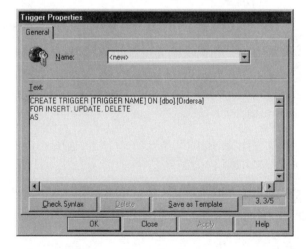

Figure 12-3. Trigger Properties dialog

To create a trigger, modify the text per your specifications, click Check Syntax to verify there are no typos, and click Apply.

Did you notice the Save as Template button on the dialog? If you do not care for the default CREATE TRIGGER statement that displays when you access the dialog, make the changes you desire and click Save as Template.

ALTER TRIGGER Syntax

The ALTER TRIGGER statement is used to make modifications to an existing trigger. The complete syntax of ALTER TRIGGER for both types of triggers (table and column-level) is shown here.

Table-Level

```
ALTER TRIGGER trigger_name
ON ( table | view )
[ WITH ENCRYPTION ]
{
    { ( FOR | AFTER | INSTEAD OF ) { [ DELETE ] [ , ] [ INSERT ] [ , ] [ UPDATE ] }
        [ NOT FOR REPLICATION ]
        AS
        sql_statement [ ...n ]
    }
```

Column-Level

```
ALTER TRIGGER trigger_name
ON ( table | view )
[ WITH ENCRYPTION ]

    { ( FOR | AFTER | INSTEAD OF ) { [ INSERT ] [ , ] [ UPDATE ] }
        [ NOT FOR REPLICATION ]
        AS
        { IF UPDATE ( column )
        [ { AND | OR } UPDATE ( column ) ]
        [ ...n ]
        | IF ( COLUMNS_UPDATED ( ) { bitwise_operator } updated_bitmask )
        { comparison_operator } column_bitmask [ ...n ]
        }
        sql_statement [ ...n ]
    }
}
```

I covered all the available options in the CREATE TRIGGER statement section, so I have not provided descriptions here.

Statement Permissions

ALTER TRIGGER permission defaults to the fixed-server role **sysadmin**, the fixed-database roles **db_owner** and **db_ddladmin** and the table owner and are not transferable.

Object Permissions

To execute an AFTER TRIGGER, the user only needs permission to execute the action statement on the table. In other words, if you can perform an INSERT, UPDATE, or DELETE on the table, the associated AFTER TRIGGER will fire. When you use an INSTEAD OF trigger on a view, you must have INSERT, UPDATE, and DELETE permission on all the tables referenced by the view, regardless of whether the trigger performs any of these actions.

Altering Triggers

You can use Query Analyzer and Enterprise Manager to alter a trigger. I will describe both methods in this section.

Query Analyzer

You can use two methods to get the text of an existing trigger in the Editor Pane of Query Analyzer. The first method uses the system stored procedure **sp_helptext**, and the second uses the Edit option in Object Browser. To use the first method, execute the following in Query Analyzer, cut-n-copy the text shown in the Detail Pane into the Editor pane, and then change CREATE to ALTER.

```
USE tempdb
go
sp_helptext 'tr_Orders_INSERT_HotOrders'
--Results--

Text
-------------------------------------------------------------------------------
CREATE TRIGGER tr_Orders_INSERT_HotOrders
```

```
ON Orders
AFTER INSERT
AS
--Determine if hot orders have been entered
IF EXISTS (SELECT * FROM inserted WHERE Ord_Priority > 6)
 BEGIN
  --HotOrders code
  INSERT HotOrders (Ord_UniqueID)
  SELECT Ord_UniqueID FROM inserted
  WHERE Ord_Priority > 6

  /*
  --Email code
  DECLARE  @Count smallint,
           @EmailMessage varchar(100)
  --Determine number of "hot" orders
  SELECT @Count = COUNT(Ord_UniqueID)
  FROM inserted
  WHERE Ord_Priority > 6
  --Build message
  SELECT @EmailMessage = CAST(@COUNT AS varchar(3))+ ' Hot Order(s) Entered'
  --Send email
  EXEC master..xp_sendmail @recipients = 'garth@SQLBook.com',
                           @message = @EmailMessage,
                           @subject = 'Hot Orders Entered'
  */
END
```

The second method uses Object Browser (new to SQL Server 2000). Use the following steps to place the text of the trigger in Editor Pane.

1. If Object Browser is not already active, press the F8 key to activate the pane.

2. Expand **tempdb** and expand the User Tables folder.

3. Expand the **Orders** table, and then expand the Triggers folder.

4. Right-click the **tr_Orders_HotOrders** and select Edit.

The text of the trigger is copied in a new window of Editor Pane, and ALTER TRIGGER is automatically added before the body of the trigger.

The following shows how to modify the INSERT trigger so that the requirement for a hot order is greater than or equal to 8.

```
USE tempdb
go
ALTER TRIGGER tr_Orders_INSERT_HotOrders
ON Orders
AFTER INSERT
AS
--Determine if hot orders have been entered
IF EXISTS (SELECT * FROM inserted WHERE Ord_Priority >= 8)
 BEGIN

  --HotOrders code
  INSERT HotOrders (Ord_UniqueID)
  SELECT Ord_UniqueID FROM inserted
  WHERE Ord_Priority >= 8

  /*
  --Email code
  DECLARE  @Count smallint,
           @EmailMessage varchar(100)
  --Determine number of "hot" orders
  SELECT @Count = COUNT(Ord_UniqueID)
  FROM inserted
  WHERE Ord_Priority >= 8
  --Build message
  SELECT @EmailMessage = CAST(@COUNT AS varchar(3))+ ' Hot Order(s) Entered'
  --Send email
  EXEC master..xp_sendmail @recipients = 'garth@SQLBook.com',
                           @message = @EmailMessage,
                           @subject = 'Hot Orders Entered'
  */
 END
```

Use the same approach to modify the UPDATE trigger.

Enterprise Manager

Enterprise Manager's Trigger Properties dialog allows you to create and modify the triggers attached to a table. To modify a trigger with the Trigger Properties dialog, complete the following.

1. Expand a database, and then select Tables.

2. Right-click the target table, highlight All Tasks, and select Manage Triggers.

3. Click the down arrow next to the Name field and select the target trigger.

4. Make the desired modifications, click the Check Syntax button to ensure there are no typos, and then click Apply.

DROP TRIGGER Syntax

The complete syntax of the DROP TRIGGER statement is shown here.

```
DROP TRIGGER { trigger } [ ,...n ]
```

You simply supply the names of the triggers you want to delete.

Statement Permissions

DROP TRIGGER permission defaults to the fixed-server role **sysadmin**, the fixed-database roles **db_owner** and **db_ddladmin**, and the table owner and are not transferable.

Dropping Triggers

The following sections cover the methods used to drop a trigger.

Query Analyzer

You can use two methods to drop a trigger in Query Analyzer. The first involves executing the DROP TRIGGER statement, and the second involves using Object Browser. In order to drop the trigger created earlier using the first approach, simply execute the following statements.

```
USE tempdb
go
DROP TRIGGER tr_Orders_HotOrders
--Results--
The command(s) completed successfully.
```

To use Object Browser to drop a trigger, complete the following.

1. Expand the database in which the trigger is located, and then expand the User Tables folder.

2. Expand the table to which the trigger is attached, and then expand the Triggers folder.

3. Right-click the target trigger, select Delete, and then confirm the deletion by clicking OK.

Enterprise Manager

Enterprise Manager's Trigger Properties dialog allows you to create and modify the triggers attached to a table. To delete a trigger with the Trigger Properties dialog, complete the following.

1. Expand a database and then select Tables.

2. Right-click the target table, highlight All Tasks, and select Manage Triggers.

3. Click the down arrow next to the Name field and select the target trigger.

4. Click the Delete button, and then confirm the deletion by clicking Yes.

TIP Implementing Audit Trail Functionality

The browser-based database application created in Chapter 14 uses triggers to implement audit trail functionality that tracks which user made a change in a particular table. Implementing an audit trail is interesting, so make sure you read this chapter to see another example of how triggers are used in the real-world.

Before You Go

This chapter presented the basics of creating, altering, and deleting triggers. I also discussed **inserted** and **deleted** virtual tables and implemented two examples to demonstrate how they are used to test the data modifications made to a table.

Chapters 13 and 14 present more real-world examples of how triggers implement required functionality. Be sure to read both chapters if you plan to use triggers on your projects.

This chapter concludes Part II of the book. Part III builds on all the material presented in Parts I and Part II by demonstrating real-world examples that I have used on my projects. I am quite sure you will find at least a few you can use to make your development efforts more successful.

Part III

Putting SQL to Work

CHAPTER 13

Procedures and Triggers by Example

CHAPTER 13 CONTAINS DETAILED EXAMPLES THAT DEMONSTRATE how to apply the material covered in the previous chapters. Each example is based on a real-world scenario, so you should be able to find at least a few that you can use in your programming endeavors.

Be aware that the examples are presented with the assumption that the you have sufficient knowledge of the material presented in Chapters 1–12. If you are not familiar with a certain programming concept or functionality, you can read the relevant chapter(s) as you work through the example.

> NOTE Sample Code
>
> *The sample code for this chapter can be downloaded at either* http://www.apress.com *or* http://www.SQLBook.com. *Download and extract CodeCentric.zip and then extract Ch13.zip. The SQL statements used in the examples are located in Ch13.sql. The .asp files create GUIs, and the .rpt files are Crystal Reports.*

Before You Get Started

A few of the examples included in this chapter use ASP (Active Server Pages) technology to show a complete example. By complete, I mean add a front-end that interfaces with the database objects created in the example. You are not required to know ASP in order to learn from the examples, but to fully implement some of them an understanding of this technology is needed.

In an effort to provide a basic understanding of ASP, I have included two appendixes in this book. Appendix A contains an HTML Primer, and Appendix B contains an ASP Primer. They cover the basics of both topics but are not intended to be a complete resource for learning either HTML or ASP. In the appendixes I have listed books and Web sites that offer more in depth coverage of these topics.

A sample database called **CodeCentric** is used throughout this chapter. The following lists the SQL Statements used to create the database.

```
USE master
GO
CREATE DATABASE CodeCentric
ON
(
 NAME = 'CodeCentric_data',
 FILENAME = 'c:\mssql7\data\CodeCentric.mdf',
 SIZE = 5MB,
 MAXSIZE = 20MB,
 FILEGROWTH = 2MB
)
LOG ON
(
 NAME = 'CodeCentric_log',
 FILENAME = 'c:\mssql7\data\CodeCentric.ldf',
 SIZE = 5MB,
 MAXSIZE = 15MB,
 FILEGROWTH = 2MB
)
go
```

Verify the FILENAME parameters per your computer's configuration before executing the statement.

The Examples

The examples presented in this chapter demonstrate how stored procedures and triggers are used to implement solutions in the real world. Each example is organized in the following manner:

- Overview—A general description of the example covered.

- Technical Details—A brief description of the technology or object used in the example.

- Solution—The code used to implement the solution. In some of the examples I will include a sub-section titled "Adding the Interface" to demonstrate how to create an ASP front-end to interact with the procedures.

Now that you understand how the examples are laid out, let's get started.

Example 1: Multi-Parameter Search Screen

Many of my clients ask for search screens that allow users to query data by supplying one or more search parameters. For example, a commercial real estate company wanted the ability to search for vacant spaces in strip centers based on square footage, city location, and space location within the center. Implementing this functionality with a stored procedure is fairly simple once you learn how to use the COALESCE function. The example presented here shows how to search a table that contains baseball player statistics (e.g., batting average, home runs, etc.). After mastering the concepts presented here you will be able to adopt the solution to situations you encounter on your projects.

Technical Details

The following statements create the table and sample data used in this example.

```
USE CodeCentric
go
CREATE TABLE Players
(
  Pla_UniqueID int IDENTITY PRIMARY KEY,
  Pla_FName varchar(30) NOT NULL,
  Pla_LName varchar(30) NOT NULL,
  Pla_BattingAverage smallint NOT NULL,
  Pla_HomeRuns smallint NOT NULL,
  Pla_RBIs smallint NOT NULL,
  Pla_StolenBases smallint NOT NULL
)
INSERT Players VALUES ('Hank','Aaron',305,755,2297,240)
INSERT Players VALUES ('Jeff','Bagwell',304,263,961,158)
INSERT Players VALUES ('Barry','Bonds',288,445,1299,460)
INSERT Players VALUES ('George','Brett',305,317,1595,201)
INSERT Players VALUES ('Ernie','Banks',274,512,1636,50)
INSERT Players VALUES ('Tony','Gwynn',339,133,1104,318)
INSERT Players VALUES ('Paul','O''neil',290,242,1099,105)
INSERT Players VALUES ('Cal','Ripken Jr.',278,402,1571,36)
INSERT Players VALUES ('Mo','Vaughn',301,263,860,28)
INSERT Players VALUES ('Ted','Williams',344,521,1839,24)

SELECT Pla_FName+' '+Pla_LName AS Name,
       Pla_BattingAverage,
       Pla_HomeRuns,
       Pla_RBIs,
```

```
        Pla_StolenBases
FROM Players
ORDER BY Pla_LName
--Results--
```

Name	Pla_BattingAverage	Pla_HomeRuns	Pla_RBIs	Pla_StolenBases
Hank Aaron	305	755	2297	240
Jeff Bagwell	304	263	961	158
Ernie Banks	274	512	1636	50
Barry Bonds	288	445	1299	460
George Brett	305	317	1595	201
Tony Gwynn	339	133	1104	318
Paul O'neil	290	242	1099	105
Cal Ripken Jr.	278	402	1571	36
Mo Vaughn	301	263	860	28
Ted Williams	344	521	1839	24

The goal is to create a procedure that allows the user to specify zero, one, or more search parameters to filter the data and a sort parameter that orders the data. In addition to this, an OUTPUT parameter needs to be used to return the number of rows in the resultset to the calling statement. The parameters needed to implement the procedure are listed in Table 13-1.

Table 13-1. Search Parameters

PARAMETER	DESCRIPTION
@OrderBy	Indicates what column the data should be sorted on.
@ Pla_BattingAverage	Minimum batting average.
@Pla_HomeRuns	Minimum home runs.
@Pla_RBIs	Minimum RBIs.
@Pla_StolenBases	Minimum stolen bases.

Solution

The stored procedure used to accomplish the goal is shown here.

```
USE CodeCentric
go
CREATE PROCEDURE ps_Player_SELECT_ByStats
@OrderBy tinyint = 1,
```

```
@Pla_BattingAverage smallint = NULL,
@Pla_HomeRuns smallint = NULL,
@Pla_RBIs smallint = NULL,
@Pla_StolenBases smallint = NULL,
@RowsReturned smallint = NULL OUTPUT
AS
SET NOCOUNT ON

SELECT substring(Pla_FName+' '+Pla_LName,1,20) AS Name,
       Pla_BattingAverage,
       Pla_HomeRuns,
       Pla_RBIs,
       Pla_StolenBases
FROM Players
WHERE Pla_BattingAverage >= COALESCE(@Pla_BattingAverage,0) AND
      Pla_HomeRuns >= COALESCE(@Pla_HomeRuns,0) AND
      Pla_RBIs >= COALESCE(@Pla_RBIs,0) AND
      Pla_StolenBases >= COALESCE(@Pla_StolenBases,0)
ORDER BY CASE WHEN @OrderBY = 1 THEN Pla_BattingAverage
              WHEN @OrderBY = 2 THEN Pla_HomeRuns
              WHEN @OrderBY = 3 THEN Pla_RBIs
              WHEN @OrderBY = 4 THEN Pla_StolenBases
              END DESC

SET @RowsReturned = @@ROWCOUNT
```

The complex segments of the procedure are shown in bold. The first uses the COALESCE statement to determine what value to use for the comparison operation. The COALESCE statement returns the first NON NULL data in its list of values. When a parameter value is not supplied, the parameter is set equal to NULL and COALESCE returns a 0 for the particular comparison operation. A value in the stat columns is always greater than 0, so when 0 is used the comparison evaluates to true.

The second piece of complex code is the CASE statement used to determine the sort for the resultset. The default value associated with the **@OrderBy** parameter is 1, so when no value is specified the resultset is sorted on the batting average.

The following examples demonstrate how the procedure is used to query the data. The first example returns all players sorted by batting average.

```
USE CodeCentric
go
EXEC ps_Player_SELECT_ByStats
--Results--
```

Name	Pla_BattingAverage	Pla_HomeRuns	Pla_RBIs	Pla_StolenBases
Ted Williams	344	521	1839	24
Tony Gwynn	339	133	1104	318
Hank Aaron	305	755	2297	240
George Brett	305	317	1595	201
Jeff Bagwell	304	263	961	158
Mo Vaughn	301	263	860	28
Paul O'neil	290	242	1099	105
Barry Bonds	288	445	1299	460
Cal Ripken Jr.	278	402	1571	36
Ernie Banks	274	512	1636	50

No parameters are supplied, so 0 is used for all comparison operations and 1 is used to determine sort criteria.

The next example shows how to return only those players whose batting average is greater than 300, sorted on batting average.

```
USE CodeCentric
go
EXEC ps_Player_SELECT_ByStats @Pla_BattingAverage=300
--Results--
```

Name	Pla_BattingAverage	Pla_HomeRuns	Pla_RBIs	Pla_StolenBases
Ted Williams	344	521	1839	24
Tony Gwynn	339	133	1104	318
George Brett	305	317	1595	201
Hank Aaron	305	755	2297	240
Jeff Bagwell	304	263	961	158
Mo Vaughn	301	263	860	28

The following demonstrates the real power of this solution by allowing us to specify multiple search criteria and order the results on the stolen bases.

```
USE CodeCentric
go
EXEC ps_Player_SELECT_ByStats @OrderBy=4,
                        @Pla_BattingAverage=300,
                        @Pla_HomeRuns=300,
                        @Pla_RBIs=1000,
                        @Pla_StolenBases=200
--Results--
```

Name	Pla_BattingAverage	Pla_HomeRuns	Pla_RBIs	Pla_StolenBases
Hank Aaron	305	755	2297	240
George Brett	305	317	1595	201

To this point we have not used the OUTPUT parameter to determine how many rows are returned by the SELECT. The following shows how this is done.

```
DECLARE @RowsReturned smallint
EXEC ps_Player_SELECT_ByStats 2,300,400,NULL,NULL,@RowsReturned OUTPUT
PRINT 'Rows Returned = ' + CAST(@RowsReturned AS varchar(3))
--Results--
```

Name	Pla_BattingAverage	Pla_HomeRuns	Pla_RBIs	Pla_StolenBases
Hank Aaron	305	755	2297	240
Ted Williams	344	521	1839	24

```
Rows Returned = 2
```

A variable must be declared to hold the value of the OUTPUT parameter referenced in the stored procedure. The variable does not need to have the same name as the OUPUT parameter because it is simply a placeholder in memory where the OUTPUT value is stored.

In the previous examples the **@ParamName=Value** syntax (e.g., @Pla_HomeRuns=300) was used to call the procedure. This syntax produces an error when using an OUTPUT parameter, so only the parameter values are passed to the procedure. When parameter names are skipped, a NULL must be used as a placeholder if no value is supplied.

Adding the Interface

The interface for this solution is produced by SearchScreen.asp in the chapter's sample files. The layout for the page is shown in Figure 13-1.

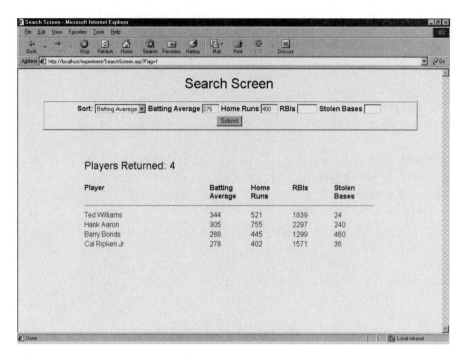

Figure 13-1. Search Screen interface

You input zero, one, or more parameters, click Submit, and the row count and desired results are displayed. The code used to produce the screen is shown here.

```
<% Option Explicit %>
<!--#include file="adovbs.inc"-->
<HTML>

 <HEAD>
   <title>Search Screen</title>
 </HEAD>

 <%
 On Error Resume Next
 Dim objConn, cmd1, rs, RowsReturned
 Dim Pla_BattingAverage, Pla_HomeRuns, Pla_RBIs, Pla_StolenBases

 Set objConn = server.CreateObject("ADODB.Connection")
 REM DSN-Less OLE-DB
 objConn.Open"Provider=SQLOLEDB;ServerName;Database=CodeCentric; _
        Uid=UserID;Pwd=Password"
 %>
```

```
<BODY bgcolor="beige" width="80%">
<center>
<font face="arial" size=6>Search Screen</font>
<FORM name="LoginAdd" method="post" action="SearchScreen.asp?Flag=1">
<TABLE border=2 width="90%">
 <tr>
  <td>
   <TABLE align="center">
    <tr>
      <td align="left"><font face="arial"><b>Sort:</b></font></td>
      <td>
        <select name="OrderBy">
        <option value="1" <%If request.form("OrderBy")=1 Then response.write _
              "SELECTED" End If%>>Batting Average
        <option value="2" <%If request.form("OrderBy")=2 Then response.write _
              "SELECTED" End If%>>Home Runs
        <option value="3" <%If request.form("OrderBy")=3 Then response.write _
              "SELECTED" End If%>>RBIs
        <option value="4" <%If request.form("OrderBy")=4 Then response.write _
              "SELECTED" End If%>>Stolen Bases
      </select>
      </td>
      <td align="left"><font face="arial"><b>Batting Average</b></font></td>
      <td align="center"><input type="text" name="Pla_BattingAverage" _
              value="<%=request.form("Pla_BattingAverage")%>" size=4 max_
              length=3></td>
      <td align="left"><font face="arial"><b>Home Runs</b></font></td>
      <td align="center"><input type="text" name="Pla_HomeRuns" _
              value="<%=request.form("Pla_HomeRuns")%>" size=4 maxlength=3></td>
       <td align="left"><font face="arial"><b>RBIs</b></font></td>
       <td align="center"><input type="text" name="Pla_RBIs" _
               value="<%=request.form("Pla_RBIs")%>" size=5 maxlength=4></td>
       <td align="left"><font face="arial"><b>Stolen Bases</b></font></td>
       <td align="center"><input type="text" name="Pla_StolenBases" _
               value="<%=request.form("Pla_StolenBases")%>" size=4 max_
               length=3></td>
    </tr>
    <tr>
      <td align="center" colspan=10><input type="submit" value="Submit"></td>
    </tr>
    </TABLE>
   </td>
```

```
    </tr>
    </TABLE>
    </FORM>

    <%
    If request.querystring("Flag") = "1" Then

     If request.form("Pla_BattingAverage") = "" Then
      Pla_BattingAverage = 0
     Else
      Pla_BattingAverage = request.form("Pla_BattingAverage")
     End If

     If request.form("Pla_HomeRuns") = "" Then
      Pla_HomeRuns = 0
     Else
      Pla_HomeRuns = request.form("Pla_HomeRuns")
     End If

     If request.form("Pla_RBIs") = "" Then
      Pla_RBIs = 0
     Else
      Pla_RBIs = request.form("Pla_RBIs")
     End If

     If request.form("Pla_StolenBases") = "" Then
      Pla_StolenBases = 0
     Else
      Pla_StolenBases = request.form("Pla_StolenBases")
     End If

     Set cmd1 = server.CreateObject("ADODB.Command")
     cmd1.ActiveConnection = objConn
     cmd1.CommandType = adCmdStoredProc
     cmd1.CommandText = "ps_Player_SELECT_ByStats"
     cmd1.Parameters.Append cmd1.CreateParameter("OrderBy",adTinyInt, _
               adParamInput,,request.form("OrderBy"))
     cmd1.Parameters.Append cmd1.CreateParameter("Pla_BattingAverage",adSmallint, _
               adParamInput,,Pla_BattingAverage)
     cmd1.Parameters.Append cmd1.CreateParameter("Pla_HomeRuns",adSmallint, _
               adParamInput,,Pla_HomeRuns)
     cmd1.Parameters.Append cmd1.CreateParameter("Pla_RBIs",adSmallint, _
               adParamInput,,Pla_RBIs)
```

```
cmd1.Parameters.Append cmd1.CreateParameter("Pla_StolenBases",adSmallint, _
            adParamInput,,Pla_StolenBases)
cmd1.Parameters.Append cmd1.CreateParameter("RowsReturned",adSmallInt, _
            adParamOutput)
cmd1.Execute
RowsReturned = cmd1.Parameters("RowsReturned")
SET rs= cmd1.Execute

%>
  <TABLE align="center" width="70%">
   <tr>
     <td> </td>
   </tr>
   <tr>
     <td> </td>
   </tr>
   <tr>
     <td colspan=5><font face="arial" size=5>Players Returned: _
        <%=RowsReturned%></font></td>
   </tr>
   <tr>


   <td> </td>
   </tr>
   <tr>
   <td width="30%" valign="top"><font face="arial"><b>Player</b></td>
   <td width="10%" valign="top"><font face="arial"><b>Batting Average</b></td>
   <td width="10%" valign="top"><font face="arial"><b>Home<br> Runs</b></td>
   <td width="10%" valign="top"><font face="arial"><b>RBIs</b></td>
   <td width="10%" valign="top"><font face="arial"><b>Stolen Bases</b></td>
   </tr>
   <tr>
   <td colspan=5><hr></td>
   </tr>
<%
 Do Until rs.Eof
%>
   <tr>
   <td><font face="Arial"><%=rs("Name")%></font></td>
   <td><font face="Arial"><%=rs("Pla_BattingAverage")%></font></td>
   <td><font face="Arial"><%=rs("Pla_HomeRuns")%></font></td>
   <td><font face="Arial"><%=rs("Pla_RBIs")%></font></td>
   <td><font face="Arial"><%=rs("Pla_StolenBases")%></font></td>
   </tr>
<%
```

419

```
        rs.MoveNext
        Loop
        rs.Close
      %>
      </TABLE>
      <%
      End If
      %>

    </center>
   </BODY>
</HTML>
```

It's simple ASP, but there is one piece of code that might cause some confusion. The code shown in bold sets the parameter values to 0 when no value is specified. This is necessary because when no value is placed in input box, the value associated with the box is ''. Passing this value to the procedure produces an error, because '' cannot be converted to the smallint data type.

If you do not have the ability to implement this page and test it on your own, go to http://www.SQLBook.com and click the Examples link. Experiment with different stat values and sort orders to verify the procedure works as expected.

Example2: Parsing a Comma Separated List

I do a lot of intranet development using ASP, and I often create data input pages that use a multi-select list box. The multi-select list boxes are generally used to display lookup values like an attribute that is associated with a parent table. A quick example scenario should make this a little easier to understand.

Let's say you have a Web site that lists retailers (e.g., WalMart), and you need to create an add screen that allows users to input information about each retailer that wants to be listed on the site. Since a retailer can sell more than one category of products, the add screen needs to support the ability to select more than one category from a multi-select list box. Figure 13-2 shows the interface for this example.

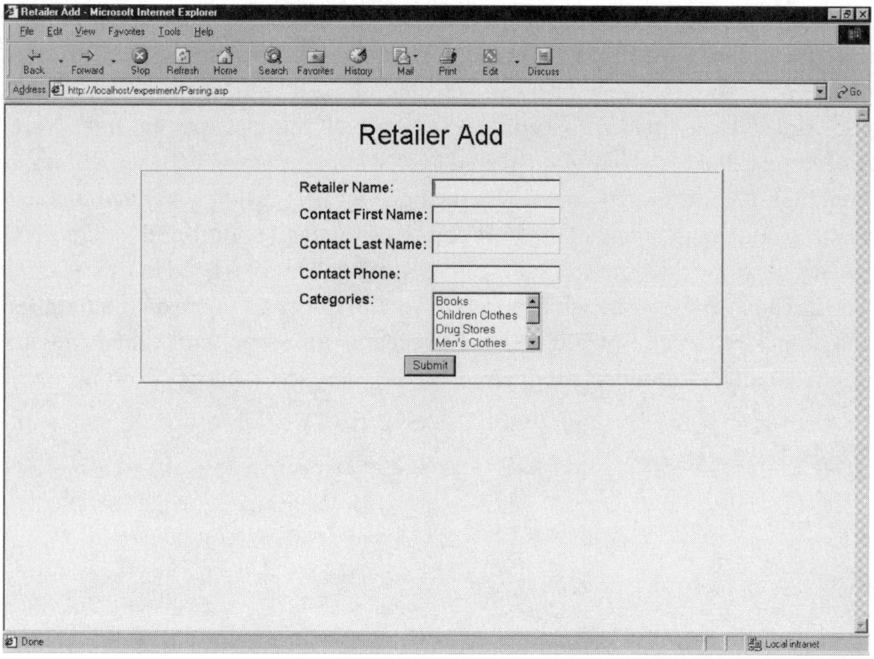

Figure 13-2. ASP interface

In ASP, when a multi-select list box is used the values selected are captured as a comma-separated list (e.g., Value1,Value2,Value3…).

This example shows how to use control-flow-statements to populate a junction table with values contained in a comma-separated list. The term *junction table* (a.k.a., associative table) refers to a table that contains values used to resolve a one-to-one or one-to-many relationship. The primary key of the parent table is stored with the primary key of the child table in the junction table for each relation between the two tables.

Technical Details

A version of the code used to create the multi-select list box used in this example is shown here.

```
<select name="CategoryList" multiple>
<option value=1>Shoes
<option value=2>Men's Clothes
<option value=3>Women's Clothes
</select>
```

The actual code is more complicated than this because it dynamically creates the option tag values with the data in the lookup table, but this will do for our purposes. When more than one option is selected, the individual values from each option are concatenated with a comma separator. If options one and three were chosen, the value of CategoryList would be 1,3. If all three were chosen, the value would be 1,2,3. After the user submits the page for processing, you need to parse the string and create a row in the junction table for each parent-child relationship.

The following statements create and populate the tables used in this example. If you already worked through Example 7, you do not need to create the **Retailers** and **Categories** tables, but you do need to execute the statements that create the sample data. The **RetailersCategories** table is a junction table as described earlier

```
USE CodeCentric
go
CREATE TABLE Retailers
(
 Ret_UniqueID int IDENTITY PRIMARY KEY,
 Ret_Name varchar(30) NOT NULL,
 Ret_ContactFName varchar(30) NOT NULL,
 Ret_ContactLName varchar(30) NOT NULL,
 Ret_ContactPhone varchar(15) NOT NULL
)

CREATE TABLE Categories
(
 Cat_UniqueID smallint IDENTITY PRIMARY KEY,
 Cat_Description varchar(30) NOT NULL
)
go
INSERT Categories VALUES ('Shoes')
INSERT Categories VALUES ('Men''s Clothes')
INSERT Categories VALUES ('Women''s Clothes')
INSERT Categories VALUES ('Children Clothes')
INSERT Categories VALUES ('Drug Stores')
INSERT Categories VALUES ('Books')
INSERT Categories VALUES ('Sporting Goods')

CREATE TABLE RetailersCategories
(
 Ret_UniqueID int REFERENCES Retailers(Ret_UniqueID),
 Cat_UniqueID smallint REFERENCES Categories(Cat_UniqueID),
 CONSTRAINT PK_RetailersCategories PRIMARY KEY ( Ret_UniqueID,Cat_UniqueID)
)
```

Solution

There are two stored procedures used in this example. The first procedure populates the multi-select list box shown in Figure 13-2. It performs a simple SELECT on the **Categories** table.

```
USE CodeCentric
go
CREATE PROCEDURE ps_Categories_SELECT
AS
SELECT  Cat_UniqueID,
        Cat_Description
FROM Categories
ORDER BY Cat_Description
```

The second procedure creates the **Retailers** and **RetailersCategories** rows when the Submit button is clicked on the interface.

```
CREATE PROCEDURE ps_Retailer_INSERT
@Ret_Name varchar(30),
@Ret_ContactFName varchar(30),
@Ret_ContactLName varchar(30),
@Ret_ContactPhone varchar(15),
@CategoryList varchar(200)
AS

--Step 1: Create variables
DECLARE @UniqueID int,
        @CurVal smallint


--Step 2: Wrap INSERTs in a transaction
BEGIN TRANSACTION

  --Step 3: Create the parent row in Retailers
  INSERT Retailers
  (
   Ret_Name,
   Ret_ContactFName,
   Ret_ContactLName,
   Ret_ContactPhone
  )
  VALUES
  (
```

```
      @Ret_Name,
      @Ret_ContactFName,
      @Ret_ContactLName,
      @Ret_ContactPhone
      )
    IF @@ERROR <> 0
     GOTO ErrorRoutine


    --Step 4: Get the primary key of the row inserted into Retailers
    SELECT @UniqueID = @@IDENTITY


    --Step 5: Append a comma to the end of @CategoryList to ease
    --the processing of the string
    SELECT @CategoryList = @CategoryList+','


    --Step 6: Start the looping operation
    WHILE CHARINDEX(',',@CategoryList) > 0
     BEGIN
      SELECT @CurVal = CONVERT(smallint,SUBSTRING(@CategoryList _
                    ,1,CHARINDEX(',',@CategoryList)-1))
       --Step 7: Add current row to RetailerCategories
       INSERT RetailersCategories VALUES (@UniqueID,CONVERT(smallint,@CurVal))
       IF @@ERROR <> 0
        GOTO ErrorRoutine
       --Step 8: Remove current value from string
       SELECT @CategoryList = SUBSTRING(@CategoryList, _
                    CHARINDEX(',',@CategoryList)+1,DATALENGTH(@CategoryList))
     END

COMMIT TRANSACTION

ErrorRoutine:
ROLLBACK TRANSACTION
RETURN
```

After the row is inserted into **Retailers** (Step 3), the @@IDENTITY function is used to populate **@UniqueID** with the primary key for the retailer (Step 4). Starting in Step 6, the **@CategoryList** variable is processed one value at a time by using the SUBSTRING and CHARINDEX functions to determine when a value begins and ends. Once an individual value is found, it is inserted into the **@CurVal** variable. The **@CurVal** and **@UniqueID** variables are used to create a row in **RetailersCategories** (Step 7). The **@CategoryList** variable is updated with a new value that does not include the one just inserted into **RetailCategory** (Step 8). Control is returned to the WHILE statement and **@CategoryList** is checked to determine if there are any more values to be processed.

Both INSERTs are wrapped in a TRANSACTION (started at Step 2) and error handling code is used to prohibit a partial update. A partial update would occur if the **Retailer** row was created but a an error caused the **RetailCategories** INSERT to fail.

Steps 7 and 8 are the most difficult to understand. The easiest way to explain how they work is to think about how you would go about manually parsing a comma-delimited string that looks like this: "1,2,3,4,5," The first thing you have to do is figure out where the first value ends. This is the first occurrence of a comma, minus one character position. The CHARINDEX function is used in conjunction with SUBSTRING to determine each unique value. The SUBSTRING function starts in position 1 of the string, and then CHARINDEX—1 is used to determine the last character *before* the first comma.

Step 8 removes the value that was just inserted into **RetailersCategories** by determining the first character after the first comma and then placing it and the remaining characters in the **@CategoryList** variable.

The first time I used these techniques I had to go slowly and print the value after each operation. The following code snippet shows how this is done. The CONVERT function was removed to make the code easier to understand.

```
DECLARE @CategoryList varchar(200),
        @CurVal varchar(10)

SET @CategoryList = '1,2,3,4,5,6,'

WHILE CHARINDEX(',',@CategoryList) > 0
 BEGIN
  SELECT @CurVal = SUBSTRING(@CategoryList,1,CHARINDEX(',',@CategoryList)-1)
  PRINT 'CurVal = ' + @CurVal
  SELECT @CategoryList = SUBSTRING(@CategoryList, _
              CHARINDEX(',',@CategoryList)+1,DATALENGTH(@CategoryList))
  PRINT 'CategoryList = ' + @CategoryList
 END
--Results--
CurVal = 1
CategoryList = 2,3,4,5,6,
CurVal = 2
CategoryList = 3,4,5,6,
CurVal = 3
CategoryList = 4,5,6,
```

```
CurVal = 4
CategoryList = 5,6,
CurVal = 5
CategoryList = 6,
CurVal = 6
CategoryList =
```

The results show that the statements simply find the first value in the list and then remove it until all the items are processed.

TIP The VB/VBScript Solution

*A VB/VBScript solution can be used to achieve the same results as the previous example. This solution requires you to create the **Retailers** row in one step, return the unique ID to the client, and then loop through an array that has each unique ID for the category selected. This solution is facilitated by the Split function, which causes each item in the list to placed in an element of an array.*

I prefer the approach shown in the example because it requires only one call to the database. The alternative will require [1 + the number of elements selected] calls to the database. I can certainly understand, though, that the VB/VBScript solution might be a little easier to understand.

Adding the Interface

The ASP used to create the user interface is held in Parsing.asp and is shown here.

```
<% Option Explicit %>
<!--#include file="adovbs.inc"-->
<HTML>

 <HEAD>
  <script>
   function checkData ()
   {
    if (document.RetailerAdd.Ret_Name.value == "")
    {
     alert("You must enter a retailer name. Please correct this and _
             Submit! again")
     document.RetailerAdd.Ret_Name.focus()
```

```
   return false
   }
   if (document.RetailerAdd.Ret_ContactFName.value == "")
   {
    alert("You must enter the contact's first name. Please correct this and _
            Submit! again")
    document.RetailerAdd.Ret_ContactFName.focus()
    return false
   }
   if (document.RetailerAdd.Ret_ContactLName.value == "")
   {
    alert("You must enter the contact's last name. Please correct this and _
            Submit! again")
    document.RetailerAdd.Ret_ContactLName.focus()
    return false
   }
   if (document.RetailerAdd.Ret_ContactPhone.value == "")
   {
    alert("You must enter the contact's phone number. Please correct this _
            and Submit! again")
    document.RetailerAdd.Ret_ContactPhone.focus()
    return false
   }
   if (document.RetailerAdd.CategoryList.value == "")
   {
    alert("You must select at least one category. Please correct this and _
            Submit! again")
    document.RetailerAdd.CategoryList.focus()
    return false
   }
   }
 </script>
  <title>Retailer Add</title>
</HEAD>

<%
 On Error Resume Next
 Dim objConn, cmd1, cmd2, rs, ErrorMessage

 Set objConn = server.CreateObject("ADODB.Connection")
 REM DSN-Less OLE-DB
 objConn.Open "Provider=SQLOLEDB;Server=ServerName; _
                      Database=CodeCentric;Uid=UserID;Pwd=Password"
```

```
         If request.form("Ret_Name") <> "" Then

     Set cmd2 = server.CreateObject("ADODB.Command")
     cmd2.ActiveConnection = objConn
     cmd2.CommandType = adCmdStoredProc
     cmd2.CommandText = "ps_Retailer_INSERT"
     cmd2.Parameters.Append cmd2.CreateParameter("Ret_Name",adVarChar, _
               adParamInput,30,request.form("Ret_Name"))
     cmd2.Parameters.Append cmd2.CreateParameter("Ret_ContactFName",adVarChar, _
               adParamInput,30,request.form("Ret_ContactFName"))
     cmd2.Parameters.Append cmd2.CreateParameter("Ret_ContactLName",adVarChar, _
               adParamInput,30,request.form("Ret_ContactLName"))
     cmd2.Parameters.Append cmd2.CreateParameter("Ret_ContactPhone",adVarChar, _
               adParamInput,30,request.form("Ret_ContactPhone"))
     cmd2.Parameters.Append cmd2.CreateParameter("CategoryList",adVarChar, _
               adParamInput,128,request.form("CategoryList"))

     cmd2.Execute
     ErrorMessage = Err.description

    End If
   %>

   <BODY bgcolor="beige">
    <center>
    <font face="arial" size=6>Retailer Add</font>

    <FORM name="RetailerAdd" method="post" action="Parsing.asp" _
          onsubmit="return checkData()">
    <TABLE border=2 width="70%">
     <tr>
      <td align="center" valign="top">
       <TABLE>
        <tr>
         <td align="left"><font face="arial"><b>Retailer Name:</b></font></td>
         <td><input type="text" name="Ret_Name" size=20 maxlength=30</td>
        </tr>
        <tr>
         <td align="left"><font face="arial"> _
               <b>Contact First Name:</b></font></td>
         <td><input type="text" name="Ret_ContactFName" size=20 maxlength=30</td>
        </tr>
        <tr>
         <td align="left"><font face="arial"><b>Contact Last Name:</b></font></td>
```

```
      <td><input type="text" name="Ret_ContactLName" size=20 maxlength=30</td>
    </tr>
    <tr>
     <td align="left"><font face="arial"><b>Contact Phone:</b></font></td>
     <td><input type="text" name="Ret_ContactPhone" size=20 maxlength=15</td>
    </tr>
    <tr>
      <td align="left" valign="top"><font_ face="arial"> _
           <b>Categories:</b></font></td>
     <td>
     <select name="CategoryList" multiple>
      <%
       Set cmd1 = server.CreateObject("ADODB.Command")
       cmd1.ActiveConnection = objConn
       cmd1.CommandType = adCmdStoredProc
       cmd1.CommandText = "ps_Categories_SELECT"
       Set rs = cmd1.Execute
       Do Until rs.Eof
        %>
        <option value='<%=rs("Cat_UniqueID")%>'><%=rs("Cat_Description")%>
        <%
         rs.MoveNext
        Loop
        rs.Close
        Set rs = Nothing
        %>
      </select>
     </td>
    </tr>
    <tr>
       <td align="center" colspan=2><input type="submit"_ value="Submit"></td>
    </tr>
   </TABLE>
  </td>
 </tr>
</TABLE>

</FORM>
</center>
</BODY>
</HTML>
```

This is simple ASP code and is very similar to the examples covered in Appendix B, so I will not describe the code. If you implement this code on your computer, make sure you modify the database connection information listed on the line after `REM DSN-Less OLE-DB`.

Example 3: Dynamically Applying Object Permissions

This example demonstrates how to use a cursor and dynamic SQL to grant access to database objects to a group of users. You may remember what I have a said a few times in the book that cursors should only be used when a set-based operation is not possible. This example is one of those rare occasions when there is no set-based solution to accomplish the same results.

The last time I had to use this solution was for a client who was implementing a corporate accounting package that had an add-on, third-party budgeting module. The core application used stored procedures to perform all data manipulation operations so access to tables and views were granted through the procedures. The budgeting module, however, used SQL passthrough so all the users who were going to use it needed explicit permissions on a large number (more than 100) of tables. Instead of having to apply the permissions on a table-by-table basis via Enterprise Manager, I used the technique shown here to quickly grant the appropriate permissions to the proper users.

Technical Details

The GRANT statement is used to grant varying levels of access to database objects. It is also used give a user the ability to perform various tasks (e.g., backing up a database) in a database or on a server. When a user needs read-only access to a table or view, you grant them SELECT permission on the object. In like manner, when a user needs to modify the data held in a table, you grant them INSERT, UPDATE, or DELETE permission, depending on the type of modification(s) they need to make. When a user needs to use a stored procedure, grant EXECUTE permission on the object. That's all you need to know about permissions to understand this example. If you need further explanation on how permissions are implemented in SQL Server, please see the "Permissions" section in Chapter 3.

The valid users in a database are stored in the **name** column of the **sysusers** system table. This example uses **sysusers** to verify the user or group passed to the procedure is valid. In general, it is considered a poor programming practice to access the system tables directly. If their structure changes as different versions of the product are released, the code that references the antiquated structure will be rendered useless. There are times, however, when accessing a system table directly is the most efficient way to implement a solution.

There is a set of system-supplied database objects called Information Schema Views that return meta data about the objects in a database. Several of these views are used to populate a cursor with the names of the target objects. If you are not familiar with these views, please see "Information Schema Views" section in Chapter 8.

Solution

The procedure used in this example accepts the four parameters described in Table 13-2.

Table 13-2. Procedure Parameters

PARAMETER	DESCRIPTION
@UserGroup	The user or group to whom the permissions are applied.
@ObjectType	The type of objects to which the permission will be applied. The valid values are: Tables, Views and Procedures. When you want to apply permissions to all the tables in the database use Tables as the value for this parameter.
@Permission	The permission to be applied. The valid values for Tables and Views are: SELECT, INSERT, UPDATE, and DELETE. The valid value for Procedures is EXECUTE.
@ReturnValue	OUTPUT parameter that indicates success or failure.

The text of the procedure is shown here. Read the descriptions associated with each step.

```
USE Northwind
go
CREATE PROCEDURE ps_UTIL_SetPermissions
@UserGroup sysname,
@ObjectType sysname,
@Permission varchar(20),
@ReturnValue varchar(12) OUTPUT
AS
SET NOCOUNT ON

--Step 1: Check to see if @UserGroup is a user in @Database
IF NOT EXISTS (SELECT name
            FROM sysusers
```

```
                      WHERE name = @UserGroup)
 BEGIN
  SET @ReturnValue = 'InvalidUser'
  RETURN
 END


--Step 2: Determine object type and build SELECT using the
--appropriate information schema view
DECLARE @SQL varchar(1000)

IF @ObjectType = 'Tables'
 BEGIN
  SET @SQL = 'SELECT Table_Name FROM Information_Schema.Tables'
 END

IF @ObjectType = 'Views'
 BEGIN
  SET @SQL = 'SELECT Table_Name FROM Information_Schema.Views'
 END

IF @ObjectType = 'Procedures'
 BEGIN
  SET @SQL = 'SELECT Specific_Name FROM Information_Schema.Routines'
 END


--Step 3: Create cursor that holds all the names of the objects
--returned by the SELECT
EXEC ('DECLARE PermissionsCursor CURSOR FOR '+ @SQL)
IF @@Error <> 0
 BEGIN
  SET @ReturnValue = 'CursorFailed'
  RETURN
 END


--Step 4: Open cursor and place first record in the @ObjectName
--variable
OPEN PermissionsCursor

DECLARE @ObjectName sysname
```

```
FETCH NEXT FROM PermissionsCursor
INTO @ObjectName


--Step 5: Loop through cursor applying @Permission on @ObjectName
--to @UserGroup. The brackets around @ObjectName account of names
--with embedded spaces.
WHILE @@FETCH_STATUS = 0
 BEGIN
  EXEC ('GRANT '+ @Permission +' ON [' + @ObjectName + '] TO ' + @UserGroup)
  FETCH NEXT FROM PermissionsCursor INTO @ObjectName
END


--Step 6: Clear cursor from memory and send success to calling
--application
CLOSE PermissionsCursor
DEALLOCATE PermissionsCursor
SET @ReturnValue = 'Success'
GO
```

This procedure uses conditional logic to determine whether the target database objects are tables, views, or procedures (Step 2) and then populates the cursor accordingly (Step 3). Once the cursor is populated, it is traversed and the GRANT statements are dynamically built based on the current value of **@ObjectName** and the **@Permission** parameter. Notice the brackets in the line that begins EXEC ('GRANT ' +... (in Step 5). They are required because a reference to an object with a space embedded in its name must be surrounded by brackets (e.g., [Order Details]).

When you execute the procedure with valid parameters, "success" is returned via the OUTPUT parameter. The following statement shows how to grant EXECUTE permission on all the stored procedures in a database to the user "garth." Make sure you modify the statement to reference a valid user if you execute it on your server.

```
USE Northwind
go
DECLARE @ReturnValue varchar(12)
EXEC ps_UTIL_SetPermissions 'garth','procedures','execute',@ReturnValue OUTPUT
PRINT @ReturnValue
--Results--
Success
```

If an invalid user is specified, the error checking code in Step 1 sets the return value to "InvalidUser" and returns control to Query Analzyer.

```
DECLARE @ReturnValue varchar(12)
EXEC ps_UTIL_SetPermissions 'Xgarth','procedure','execute',@ReturnValue OUTPUT
PRINT @ReturnValue
--Results--
InvalidUser
```

Example 4: Email Notification System

One of the projects I recently completed was a data-driven Web site whose source data was generated from a legacy accounting package and employee maintenance. The bulk of the site's data came from the accounting package, but there was also some important data input by several employees. (The process used to import the legacy data will be discussed in Example 9, but for now we will concentrate on the data the employees maintained.) Because the site was new, a few of the employees were having trouble remembering to complete and/or verify the weekly updates they were responsible for making. It was important that all the updates be completed in order for the data displayed on the Web site to be complete and accurate, so I created an customizable email notification system that sent them a friendly reminder each week.

Technical Details

In order to fully understand this solution you need to be familiar with SQL Server Jobs. I will cover the steps required to create a job, but you will need a general understanding of what they are and how they work if you plan to implement this type of solution in a production environment. Brief coverage of this topic was presented in the "SQL Server Agent Table" section of Chapter 9; you can also find it in the Books Online topic: Scheduling Jobs.

SQL Mail needs to be configured and running on the server before this solution can be implemented. The steps involved in setting up SQL Mail were covered in the "Before You Get Started" section of Chapter 10.

Solution

The following table tracks information about each weekly notification.

```
USE CodeCentric
go
CREATE TABLE EmailNotifications
(
EmaNot_UniqueID tinyint IDENTITY (1, 1) NOT NULL ,
EmaNot_Recipient varchar (50) NOT NULL ,
EmaNot_EmailAddress varchar (50) NOT NULL ,
EmaNot_EmailAddressCC varchar (50) NULL ,
EmaNot_Message varchar (300) NOT NULL
)
```

Each row holds a recipient's name and email address, the message body, and optionally an address to which the email should be CCed. The following INSERT creates a sample row using my contact information. Please modify the data per your contact information before you execute the example.

```
USE CodeCentric
go
INSERT EmailNotifications
(
 EmaNot_Recipient,
 EmaNot_EmailAddress,
 EmaNot_EmailAddressCC,
 EmaNot_Message
)
VALUES
(
 'Garth Wells',
 'garth@DataDrivenWebSites.com',
 'garth@SQLBook.com',
 'Write weekly newsletter'
)
```

The stored procedure that sends the notifications is shown here. Note that SET QUOTED_IDENTIFIER OFF is executed before the CREATE PROCEDURE because double-quotes are used within the procedure to *build* the **xp_sendmail** statement. A procedure will run under the settings that were in place when it was created regardless of the actual settings at execution time.

```
USE CodeCentric
go
SET QUOTED_IDENTIFIER OFF
go
CREATE PROCEDURE sp_EmailNotifications
AS
DECLARE  @EmaNot_Recipient varchar(50),
         @EmaNot_EmailAddress varchar(50),
         @EmaNot_EmailAddressCC varchar(50),
         @EmaNot_Subject varchar(30),
         @EmaNot_Message varchar(300),
         @SQL varchar(1000)

--Create cursor to hold notification data
DECLARE Email_cursor CURSOR FORWARD_ONLY FOR
SELECT EmaNot_Recipient,
       EmaNot_EmailAddress,
       EmaNot_EmailAddressCC,
       EmaNot_Message
FROM EmailNotifications

OPEN Email_cursor

--Place first row in variables
FETCH NEXT FROM Email_cursor
INTO @EmaNot_Recipient,
     @EmaNot_EmailAddress,
     @EmaNot_EmailAddressCC,
     @EmaNot_Message

--Start looping operation
WHILE @@FETCH_STATUS = 0
 BEGIN
  --Build valid sp_sendmail statement using variables
  SET @SQL =          "master..xp_sendmail "
  SET @SQL = @SQL + "@recipients='"+@EmaNot_EmailAddress +"',"
  IF @EmaNot_EmailAddressCC <> ''
   BEGIN
    SET @SQL = @SQL + "@copy_recipients='"+@EmaNot_EmailAddressCC +"',"
   END
  SET @SQL = @SQL + "@subject='Web Site Database Updates'"+","
  SET @SQL = @SQL + "@message='"+@EmaNot_Message+"'"
  EXEC (@SQL)
  --PRINT @SQL
```

```
--Get next row from cursor
FETCH NEXT FROM Email_cursor
INTO @EmaNot_Recipient,
     @EmaNot_EmailAddress,
     @EmaNot_EmailAddressCC,
     @EmaNot_Message

END

--Remove cursor from memory
CLOSE Email_cursor
DEALLOCATE Email_cursor
go
SET QUOTED_IDENTIFIER ON
```

This procedure simply loads the contents of **EmailNotifications** into a cursor, loops through it building valid **xp_sendmail** statements for each row in the cursor, and then executes the statement with EXEC.

If you do not have SQL Mail configured but still want to experiment with the code, comment out the EXEC (@SQL) line and remove the comment characters from the PRINT @SQL line. Once you have done this, you can execute the procedure as shown here.

```
USE CodeCentric
go
EXEC sp_EmailNotifications
--Results (Formatted)--
master..xp_sendmail @recipients='garth@DataDrivenWebSites.com',
                    @copy_recipients='garth@SQLBook.com',
                    @subject='Web Site Database Updates',
                    @message='Write weekly newsletter'
```

The result shows the procedure produced a valid **xp_sendmail** statement, so the process should work as expected when SQL Mail is configured and tested.

Scheduling the Process

Now that the procedure is working as desired, I will create and schedule a Job to run the procedure on a period basis. The following steps create the Job in Enterprise Manager.

1.   Expand a Server and then expand the Management folder.

2. Verify SQL Server Agent is running. If a green arrow shows next to the SQL Server Agent option, it is running. If it is not running (shown with a red dot), right-click SQL Server Agent and select Start.

3. Expand the SQL Server Agent option, right-click Jobs, and select New Job.

4. Supply a Job Name and Description as shown in Figure 13-3.

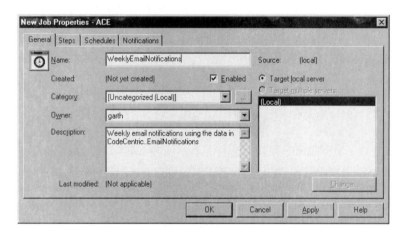

Figure 13-3. New Job Properties dialog

5. Click the Steps tab and then click the New button.

6. Supply the Step name and the command to be executed as shown in Figure 13-4. Click the Parse button to make sure there are no typos and then click OK.

7. Click the Schedules tab and then click New Schedule.

8. Input a Schedule name as shown in Figure 13-5. Click OK to accept the default schedule of Sunday at Midnight.

9. Click OK on the New Job Dialog and the job is created.

As long as SQL Server Agent is running at midnight on each Sunday, the procedure will be executed and the notifications sent to the recipients. If you want to execute the job immediately, right-click it in the Detail Pane and select Start Job. If you decide to run the job on a different interval you can change the schedule by right-clicking on the job, selecting Properties, clicking the Schedules tab and then clicking the Edit button.

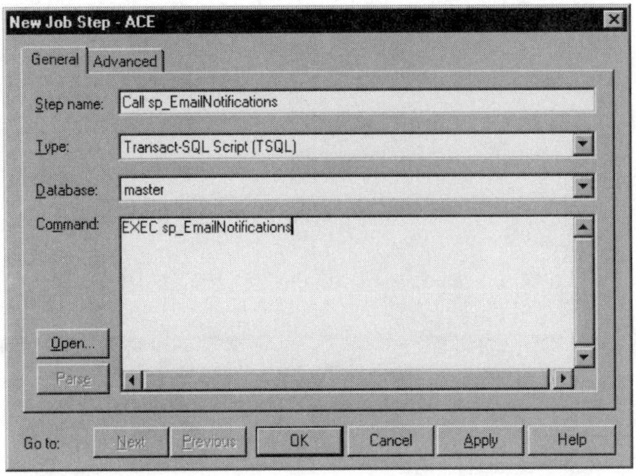

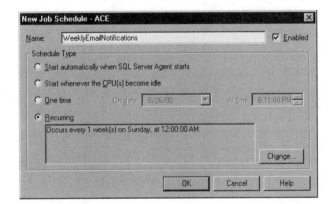

Figure 13-4. New Job Step dialog

Figure 13-5. New Job Schedule Dialog

Another Level of Complexity

Assume you had some users who needed to be notified daily, but others who only needed monthly notifications. To add this functionality simply add another column (**EmaNot_Interval**) to **EmailNotifications** that indicates the period of notification (e.g., D—Daily, W—Weekly, and M—Monthly). Add a parameter to **sp_EmailNotifications** that accepts the period interval value and populates the cursor based on the specified parameter (WHERE EmaNot_Interval = @EmaNot_Interval). The last step is to create a job for each interval and, in the procedure call associated with the job, specify the proper period interval value. I will leave this process to you to complete on your own.

Example 5: Counting Views and Clicks on www.Fine-Art.com

One of my most interesting clients is a company called Internet for the Fine Arts. The President and CEO is Troy Getz and he has been providing artists and art owners the ability to list their art on the Internet since 1996. One of his site's most used areas is the search screen that allows users to search for specific types of art. The search screen is shown in Figure 13-6 and can be accessed at http://www.fine-art.com (Once the site is activated, click Art Listing Service on the main menu).

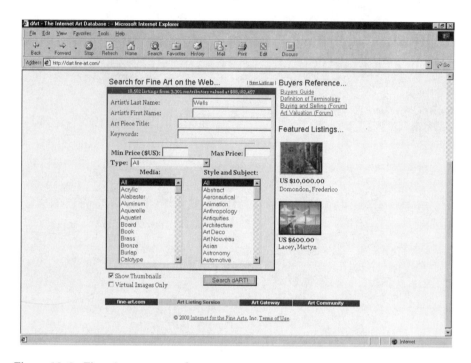

Figure 13-6. Fine-Art.com search screen

A user specifies the desired search criteria, clicks the Search dART! button, and the listings that match the criteria are displayed. Figure 13-7 shows the results screen of a search for Artists whose last name is "Wells."

If a user sees a listing that interests them, they can click on its graphic or title to get more detailed information. Figure 13-8 shows the results (partial screen shot) of a click-through to a listing's details.

Troy is always trying to improve his customer's (the people who list art work on his site) ability to use Fine-Art.com to effectively sell their art via his site. With this in mind, he thought it would be beneficial to provide them with statistics that showed how many *views* and *click-throughs* their pieces received. A view occurs any time a listing is displayed on the site (Figure 13-7) and a click-through occurs when a user clicks it to see its details (Figure 13-8).

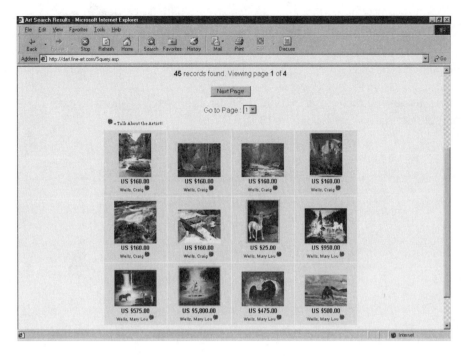

Figure 13-7. Search results

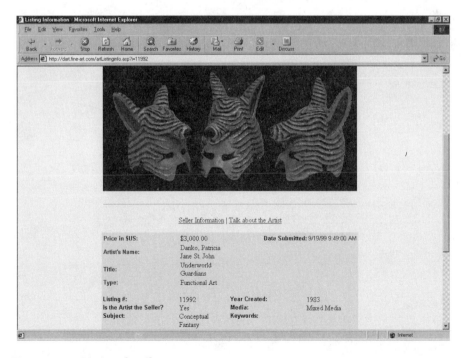

Figure 13-8. Listing details

This example shows how this process was implemented on Fine-Art.com.

Technical Details

There are several tables used to hold the Customer, Art, and Statistics data. A partial schema is shown in Figure 13-9.

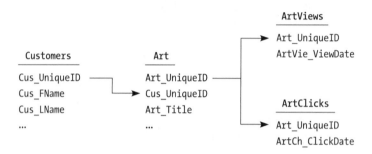

Figure 13-9. Partial schema

The statements I used to create the tables detailed in Figure 13-9 are shown here.

```
CREATE TABLE Customers
(
Cus_UniqueID int IDENTITY PRIMARY KEY,
Cus_Fname varchar(30) NOT NULL,
Cus_LName varchar(30) NOT NULL
)

CREATE TABLE Art
(
Art_UniqueID int IDENTITY PRIMARY KEY,
Cus_UniqueID int FOREIGN KEY REFERENCES Customers (Cus_UniqueID),
Art_Title varchar(30) NOT NULL,
Art_ArtistFName varchar(30) NOT NULL
)

CREATE TABLE ArtViews
(
Art_UniqueID int NOT NULL REFERENCES Art (Art_UniqueID),
ArtVie_ViewDate datetime NOT NULL
```

```
PRIMARY KEY (Art_UniqueID,ArtVie_ViewDate)
)

CREATE TABLE ArtClicks
(
 Art_UniqueID int NOT NULL REFERENCES Art (Art_UniqueID),
 ArtCli_ClickDate datetime NOT NULL
 PRIMARY KEY (Art_UniqueID,ArtCli_ClickDate)
)
```

The **ArtViews** table records views and the **ArtClicks** table records click-throughs. The click and view dates are recorded so reporting can be done on a period basis. For example, when a customer logs on to the site and accesses their personal management page they can see how many total views or click-throughs their pieces have received in total and how many occurred in the last seven days. Allowing the customer to see the last seven day stats helps them to determine if the piece has been gaining or losing interest. Note that the datetime data type was used versus smalldatetime to record the date information because it provides greater accuracy. The smalldatetime is only accurate to one minute, so if a piece is viewed or clicked more than once in the same minute a PRIMARY KEY violation would be generated. I overlooked this when I initially implemented the solution and learned the hard way!

Solution

Data is added to **ArtViews** when the pieces are initially shown on the site (Fig 13-7). Data is added to **ArtClicks** when the pieces are clicked while they are being viewed (Fig 13-8). I cannot show the ASP code that is used to display the pieces on the site because it is proprietary. You do not, however, have to see the exact code to understand how the process works. When a search is performed, the data for the pieces that meet the search criteria are loaded into a recordset. The recordset is then traversed with a Do Loop and its contents sent to the requesting browser. As each new record is read from the recordset, a call to the stored procedure shown here is made to create a row in **ArtViews.**

```
CREATE PROCEDURE ps_ArtViews_INSERT
@Art_UniqueID int
AS
INSERT ArtViews
(
 Art_UniqueID,
 ArtVie_ViewDate
)
```

```
VALUES
(
 @Art_UniqueID,
 GETDATE()
)
```

The recordset contains the primary key (**Art_UniqueID**), so as each row is processed it is *dropped* into the procedure and the data is captured.

When a user clicks a listing, an ASP page is called with the listing's unique identifier so its details can be retrieved from the database and sent to the browser. The first thing the page does is make a call to the procedure shown here to create a row in **ArtClicks**.

```
CREATE PROCEDURE ps_ArtClicks_INSERT
@Art_UniqueID int
AS
INSERT ArtClicks
(
 Art_UniqueID,
 ArtCli_ClickDate
)
VALUES
(
 @Art_UniqueID,
 GETDATE()
)
```

Viewing the Results

The most interesting part of this solution is the SELECT that produces the stats the customer sees when they access their management page. The purpose of the management page is to allow a customer to add/remove pieces and review the activity for their pieces on the site. The following procedure creates the summary statistics that are displayed when a customer accesses the page.

```
USE CodeCentric
go
CREATE PROCEDURE ps_Art_WeeklyActivity
@Cus_UniqueID int
AS
SELECT Cus_FName+' '+Cus_LName AS Name,
       (SELECT COUNT(b.Art_UniqueID)
        FROM Art b
```

```
         WHERE a.Cus_UniqueID = b.Cus_UniqueID) AS TotalCnt,
      (SELECT COUNT(e.Art_UniqueID)
       FROM ArtViews e
       INNER JOIN Art f ON e.Art_UniqueID = f.Art_UniqueID AND
                           f.Cus_UniqueID = a.Cus_UniqueID) AS TotalViewCnt,
      (SELECT COUNT(g.Art_UniqueID)
       FROM ArtClicks g
       INNER JOIN Art h ON g.Art_UniqueID = h.Art_UniqueID AND
                           h.Cus_UniqueID = a.Cus_UniqueID) AS TotalClickCnt,
      (SELECT COUNT(i.Art_UniqueID)
       FROM ArtViews i
       INNER JOIN Art j ON i.Art_UniqueID = j.Art_UniqueID AND
                           j.Cus_UniqueID = a.Cus_UniqueID AND
             DATEDIFF(day,i.ArtVie_ViewDate,GETDATE()) <= 7) _
                AS WeeklyViewCnt,
      (SELECT COUNT(k.Art_UniqueID)
       FROM ArtClicks k
       INNER JOIN Art l ON k.Art_UniqueID = l.Art_UniqueID AND
                           l.Cus_UniqueID = a.Cus_UniqueID AND
             DATEDIFF(day,k.ArtCli_ClickDate,GETDATE()) <= 7) _
                AS WeeklyClickCnt
FROM Customers a
WHERE Cus_UniqueID = @Cus_UniqueID
```

The SELECT used in the procedure may look a little complicated, but all it is doing is using multiple table aliases on **Art** to calculate the following.

TotalCount—Total number of pieces submitted.

TotalViewCount—Total number of views.

TotalClickCount—Total number of click-throughs.

WeeklyViewCount—Views in last 7 days.

WeeklyClickCount—Clicks in last 7 days.

When you read the statement concentrate on each segment that starts with (SELECT... and ends with the ...AS AliasName. These segments are individual queries that are part of a correlated subquery. A correlated subquery consists of an inner and an outer query. The inner query is executed for each row in the outer query. There are five inner queries used in this statement and each one is executed for the outer query SELECT Cus_FName+' '+Cus_LName AS CustomerName, ...FROM Customers a. The inner queries all reference a.Cus_UniqueID, which is how the correlation to the outer query is made.

You should note that the statement could have been written so that **@Cus_UniqueID** was hard-coded into each inner query, but that would have restricted its use to one customer at a time. With the approach used, any number of customers could have the statistics calculated at one time. For example, if the WHERE clause is omitted the stats for all customers are returned.

The chapter's sample code file contains INSERT statements that allow you to generate some views and clicks data. The first set of INSERTs create rows in **Art** and the next two sets create rows **ArtViews** and **ArtClicks**. The statements are constructed so the date columns (e.g., **ArtCli_ClickDate**) are populated relative to the current date. After you execute the statements execute the procedure as shown here to see the same results.

```
EXEC ps_Art_WeeklyActivity @Cus_UniqueID = 1
--Results--
Name           TotalCnt TotalViewCnt TotalClickCnt WeeklyViewCnt WeeklyClickCnt
-------------- -------- ------------ ------------- ------------- --------------
Steve Francis  2        7            4             5             3
```

This shows the stat data for Steve Francis—the customer associated with the **Cus_UniqueID** value of 1. The output from the procedure is not very aesthetically appealing when viewed in Query Analyzer. When a customer accesses their management page on Fine-Art.com, they see a screen that looks like Figure 13-10 (partial).

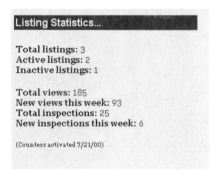

Figure 13-10. Activity stats

I encourage you to alter **ps_Art_WeeklyActivity** so that the stats for all customers are returned.

Deleting Views and Clicks Data

Over time, the items listed on the fine-art.com web site are sold and the customers delete the listings from the database. When this occurs, the data for the listings in **ArtViews** and **ArtClicks** needs to be deleted. The most efficient way to accomplish this is with a DELETE trigger attached to the **Art** table. The trigger used to delete the views and click-through data is shown here.

```
USE CodeCentric
go
CREATE TRIGGER tr_Art_DELETE_ClickViewCount
ON Art FOR DELETE AS
--Step 1: Remove views data
DELETE ArtViews
WHERE Art_UniqueID = (SELECT Art_UniqueID FROM deleted)

--Step 2: Remove clicks data
DELETE ArtClicks
WHERE Art_UniqueID = (SELECT Art_UniqueID FROM deleted)
```

The trigger is fairly straightforward. Step 1 references the **Art_UniqueID** value in the **deleted** table to remove the **ArtViews** data, and Step 2 uses the same approach to remove the listings data in **ArtClicks**.

Example 6: Custom Web Stat Counter

If you have been working with or reading about Web sites, you will know that one of the most important measures of a site's success is the traffic it generates. Overall success is measured in page views and unique visitors, but you also want to know the frequency at which the different areas on the site are being visited. There are quite a few software packages on the market that allow you to do extensive traffic analysis, but if you only want basic stats, you can create your own tool for producing a Site Traffic Summary Report using the inherent functionality of IIS (Internet Information Server) and the procedures shown in this example.

Technical Details

Internet Information Server has two methods for logging Web site activity. The first is to log the data to a system file and the second is to log the data to an ODBC data source. Configuring IIS to log a site's activity to an ODBC data source is fairly easy. You simply create the **InetLog** table shown here, create an ODBC System DSN that points to the database in which the table was created and use the Web Site Property Sheet to configure ODBC logging to the DSN. This process is explained in detail in the IIS Documentation under the title: Preparing for ODBC Logging.

```
USE CodeCentric
go
CREATE TABLE InetLog
(
 ClientHost varchar(255),
 UserName varchar(255),
 LogTime datetime,
 Service varchar(255),
 Machine varchar( 255),
 Serverip varchar( 50),
 ProcessingTime int,
 BytesRecvd int,
 BytesSent int,
 ServiceStatus int,
 Win32Status int,
 Operation varchar(255),
 Target varchar(255),
 Parameters varchar(255)
)
```

Once ODBC logging is configured, you can use Query Analyzer to view the table and see the number of rows added. Even if your site generates minimal traffic, the numbers add up very quickly. The large number of rows in **InetLog** require that a summary table solution be used to produce the Site Traffic Summary Report in a timely manner. In other words, creating a summary report from the data in **InetLog** will take too long to process because of it size, so the data will be summarized into another table to expedite report processing.

The following SELECT shows the data from **InetLog** used to generated the stats. Please note the IP Address was altered to protect the innocent.

```
SELECT ClientHost,
       LogTime,
       Target
FROM InetLog
--Results --
ClientHost      LogTime                    Target
--------------  -------------------------  ----------------
999.999.227.69  2000-09-04 21:35:29.000    /Default.asp
999.999.227.69  2000-09-04 21:35:31.000    /logo.gif
```

```
999.999.227.69    2000-09-04 21:35:30.000    /Credentials.asp
999.999.227.69    2000-09-04 21:35:31.000    /Products.asp
...
```

The **ClientHost** column holds the IP of the visitor, the **LogTime** holds the time of the visit, and the **Target** holds the page the visitor accessed. The second entry indicates that rows are created when graphics are loaded, but we want to exclude these types of entries from our stats.

If you are not familiar with how Web stats are calculated, it will help you to know that there two main categories: unique visits and page views. A unique visit is one IP per day (multiple returns in the same day do not count), but the page views stat is all pages accessed by the user, regardless of how many times they visit the site in one day.

Solution

To produce the Site Traffic Summary Report in a timely manner, I created a summary table and placed INSERT triggers on **InetLog**. Every time a record is added to **InetLog**, the trigger is fired and logic is processed to determine if the summary table needs updating. The structure of the summary table is shown here.

```
USE CodeCentric
go
CREATE TABLE LogSummary
(
 LogSum_UniqueID int IDENTITY PRIMARY KEY,
 LogSum_Category varchar(30) NOT NULL,
 LogSum_VisitCount int NOT NULL
)
```

The **LogSum_Category** column holds a descriptor for the individual stat that is being tracked. My client only wanted to track unique visits, total page visits, and the number of times each major area of the site was accessed. The first two items are fairly easy to understand, but the "major area" might be confusing. If you go to my company's Web site (http://www.DataDrivenWebSites.com) and take a look at the main navigation bar, you will see Services, Clients, Credentials.... Each of these correlate to a major area of the site. If a user clicks the Services option, that click would count as a page visit to the Services area. I am not sure how many companies actually track site traffic in this manner, but that's what my client wanted.

My client also wanted to track visits by employee access and total access. If the user was on the corporate network, two categories (Visit—Company and Visit—Total) would get updated when an employee visited the site. If the visitor came from outside the corporate network only one category (VisitTotal) would get updated. This was not too difficult to implement because the range of IP addresses for the corporate network was known, so logic was built that filtered on this criteria. Trapping for a particular page view is fairly straightforward. As long as you know the name of the page that is associated with Major Area, you simply filter accordingly.

Let's assume we are configuring this custom counter for my company's Web site and that the major areas are defined by these pages: Sevices.asp, Clients.asp, Credentials.asp, Products.asp, Opportunities.asp, and Contact.asp. Assume further that I want to break out the stats by company versus non-company access and that all client computers on my company's network have IP addresses that start with 10.10.10. The following statements create the required rows in **LogSummary.**

```
USE CodeCentric
go
INSERT LogSummary VALUES ('Overall Visits - DD',0)
INSERT LogSummary VALUES ('Overall Visits - All',0)
INSERT LogSummary VALUES ('Total Page Count - DD',0)
INSERT LogSummary VALUES ('Total Page Count - All',0)
INSERT LogSummary VALUES ('Services - DD',0)
INSERT LogSummary VALUES ('Services - All',0)
INSERT LogSummary VALUES ('Clients - DD',0)
INSERT LogSummary VALUES ('Clients - All',0)
INSERT LogSummary VALUES ('Credentials - DD',0)
INSERT LogSummary VALUES ('Credentials - All',0)
INSERT LogSummary VALUES ('Products - DD',0)
INSERT LogSummary VALUES ('Products - All',0)
INSERT LogSummary VALUES ('Opportunities - DD',0)
INSERT LogSummary VALUES ('Opportunities - All',0)
INSERT LogSummary VALUES ('Contacts - DD',0)
INSERT LogSummary VALUES ('Contacts - All',0)

SELECT *
FROM LogSummary
ORDER BY LogSum_UniqueID
--Results--
LogSum_UniqueID LogSum_Category                 LogSum_VisitCount
--------------- ------------------------------- -----------------
1               Overall Visits - DD             0
2               Overall Visits - All            0
3               Total Page Count - DD           0
4               Total Page Count - All          0
5               Services - DD                   0
6               Services - All                  0
```

7	Clients - DD	0
8	Clients - All	0
9	Credentials - DD	0
10	Credentials - All	0
11	Products - DD	0
12	Products - All	0
13	Opportunities - DD	0
14	Opportunities - All	0
15	Contacts - DD	0
16	Contacts - All	0

There are two rows for each category—one containing "DD" and one containing "All." The DD stands for DataDriven, and that will track stats on visits from inside my network. The All rows will track overall traffic.

The INSERT trigger used to populate **LogSummary** is shown here.

```
CREATE TRIGGER tr_InetLog_INSERT
ON InetLog
FOR INSERT
AS

SET NOCOUNT ON

--Step 1: Retreive current value from inserted
DECLARE @Page varchar(255),
        @IP varchar(255),
        @IPComplete varchar(255)

SELECT @Page = RTRIM(Target),
              @IP = SUBSTRING(ClientHost,1,8),
              @IPComplete = RTRIM(ClientHost)
FROM inserted



--Step 2: Determine which, if any, rows in LogSummary
--should be updated

--Segment 1: Overall Visit
--Code Block 1: DD
IF (@Page = '/Default.asp' AND @IP = '10.10.10')
 BEGIN
   --Make sure visit is unique per day
   IF (SELECT COUNT(InetLog.ClientHost)
      FROM InetLog, inserted
```

```
            WHERE Inetlog.ClientHost = inserted.ClientHost AND
            CONVERT(varchar(8),InetLog.LogTime,101) = _
                CONVERT(varchar(8),GETDATE(),1)) = 1


    UPDATE LogSummary
    SET LogSum_VisitCount = LogSum_VisitCount + 1
    WHERE LogSum_Category = 'Overall Visits - DD'
    END


  --Code Block 2:All
  IF (@Page = '/Default.asp')
   BEGIN
    --Make sure visit is unique per day
    IF (SELECT COUNT(InetLog.ClientHost)
        FROM InetLog, inserted
        WHERE Inetlog.ClientHost = inserted.ClientHost AND
        CONVERT(varchar(8),InetLog.LogTime,101) = _
                CONVERT(varchar(8),GETDATE(),1)) = 1


      UPDATE  LogSummary
      SET LogSum_VisitCount = LogSum_VisitCount + 1
      WHERE LogSum_Category = 'Overall Visits - All'
    END


  -- Segment 2: Total Page Count (exclude graphics and stylesheets)
  --Code Block 1: DD
  IF (
      RIGHT(@Page,3) <> 'jpg' AND
      RIGHT(@Page,3) <> 'gif' AND
      RIGHT(@Page,3) <> 'css' AND
      @IP = '10.10.10'
      )
   UPDATE  LogSummary
   SET LogSum_VisitCount = LogSum_VisitCount + 1
   WHERE LogSum_Category = 'Total Page Count - DD'


  --Code Block 2: All
  IF (
      RIGHT(@Page,3) <> 'jpg' AND
      RIGHT(@Page,3) <> 'gif' AND
      RIGHT(@Page,3) <> 'css'
      )
   UPDATE LogSummary
   SET LogSum_VisitCount = LogSum_VisitCount + 1
```

```
 WHERE LogSum_Category = 'Total Page Count - All'



-- Segment 3: Services
--Code Block 1: DD
IF (@Page = '/Services.asp' AND @IP = '10.10.10')
 UPDATE   LogSummary
 SET LogSum_VisitCount = LogSum_VisitCount + 1
 WHERE LogSum_Category = 'Services - DD'

--Code Block 2: All
IF (@Page = '/Services.asp')
 UPDATE   LogSummary
 SET LogSum_VisitCount = LogSum_VisitCount + 1
 WHERE LogSum_Category = 'Services - All'



-- Segment 4: Clients
--Code Block 1: DD
IF (@Page = '/Clients.asp' AND @IP = '10.10.10')
 UPDATE   LogSummary
 SET LogSum_VisitCount = LogSum_VisitCount + 1
 WHERE LogSum_Category = 'Clients - DD'

--Code Block 2: All
IF (@Page = '/Clients.asp')
 UPDATE   LogSummary
 SET LogSum_VisitCount = LogSum_VisitCount + 1
 WHERE LogSum_Category = 'Clients - All'



-- Segment 5: Credentials
--Code Block 1: DD
IF (@Page = '/Credentials.asp' AND @IP = '10.10.10')
 UPDATE   LogSummary
 SET LogSum_VisitCount = LogSum_VisitCount + 1
 WHERE LogSum_Category = 'Credentials - DD'

--Code Block 2: All
IF (@Page = '/Credentials.asp')
 UPDATE   LogSummary
 SET LogSum_VisitCount = LogSum_VisitCount + 1
 WHERE LogSum_Category = 'Credentials - All'
```

```
-- Segment 6: Products
--Code Block 1: DD
IF (@Page = '/Products.asp' AND @IP = '10.10.10')
 UPDATE  LogSum_LogSummary
 SET LogSum_VisitCount = LogSum_VisitCount + 1
 WHERE LogSum_Category = 'Products.asp - DD'

--Code Block 2: All
IF (@Page = '/Products.asp')
 UPDATE  LogSummary
 SET LogSum_VisitCount = LogSum_VisitCount + 1
 WHERE LogSum_Category = 'Products - All'


-- Segment 7: Opportunities
--Code Block 1: DD
IF (@Page = '/Opportunities.asp' AND @IP = '10.10.10')
 UPDATE  LogSum_LogSummary
 SET LogSum_VisitCount = LogSum_VisitCount + 1
 WHERE LogSum_Category = 'Opportunities - DD'

--Code Block 2: All
IF (@Page = '/Opportunities.asp')
 UPDATE  LogSummary
 SET LogSum_VisitCount = LogSum_VisitCount + 1
 WHERE LogSum_Category = 'Opportunities - All'


-- Segment 8: Contact
--Code Block 1: DD
IF (@Page = '/Contact.asp' AND @IP = '10.10.10')
 UPDATE  LogSum_LogSummary
 SET LogSum_VisitCount = LogSum_VisitCount + 1
 WHERE LogSum_Category = 'Contact - DD'

--Code Block 2: All
IF (@Page = '/Contact.asp')
 UPDATE  LogSummary
 SET LogSum_VisitCount = LogSum_VisitCount + 1
 WHERE LogSum_Category = 'Contact - All'
```

The trigger is pretty long, but it has a lot of similar code so it's fairly easy to understand once you see how it is organized. In Step 1, the current values of

inserted are placed into variables for processing in Step 2. Note that only the first three segments of the IP are placed in **@IP**. Step 2 is broken into eight segments. The first two segments calculate visits and page views and the rest calculate visits to a major area of the site.

Each segment has two code blocks. The first code block in each segment uses the **@Page** variable to determine the appropriate category to update and the **@IP** variable to determine if the visitor came from within the company's network. When both criteria are met, the associated DD category is updated. In Code Block 2, **@Page** is checked and, when the criteria is met, the associated All category is updated.

The only complicated code used in the trigger is contained in Segment 1 of Step 2 and is prefaced with `--Make sure visit is unique per day`. To verify a unique visit, the **inserted** table joins with **InetLog** to determine if there is only one matching row per the date. When there is only one matching row, this is a unique visit and **LogSummary** is updated. When the user returns after an initial visit on a given day, there will be more than one matching row in **InetLog** and **LogSummary** is not updated. Notice that the date values were converted to the MM/DD/YY format in the WHERE clause to eliminate the time portion of the value.

You will also notice some unusual code in Segment 2. The following snippet eliminates the loading of graphics and stylesheets from the page view count.

```
...
RIGHT(@Page,3) <> 'jpg' AND
RIGHT(@Page,3) <> 'gif' AND
RIGHT(@Page,3) <> 'css' AND

...
```

When a Web page contains references to other files or graphics, a row is created in **InetLog** when the referenced item is sent to the users browsers. If a single Web page contains references to five different graphics, six rows are created in **InetLog** when the page is accessed. If you do not account for this behavior, the overall page views will not be indicative of actual traffic.

This solution makes analyzing site traffic quick and easy. The **LogSummary** table never contains more than 16 rows, so the resultset is returned almost instantaneously. The only aspect of this solution we did not address is archiving. My client wanted the data archived on a monthly basis, so I created a process that loads the *current* data into an archiving table (**LogSummaryArchive**). When the Site Traffic Summary Report is run the first resultset is gathered from **LogSummary** and the remainder is gathered from LogSummaryArchive. This allows an infinite number of months to be tracked and analyzed as the data is simply shown one month after another in most-recent to oldest order.

There are a number of INSERT statements included in the sample code file that will allow you to test the trigger. Execute each statement individually and then examine the contents of both **InetLog** and **LogSummary**. Experiment with the trigger until you are comfortable with the concept of how a trigger can update a summary table. You may never implement this type of solution to track Web site traffic, but this approach can solve a number of other problems.

Example 7: Browser-Based Data Dictionary

When you develop a database application that uses more than a handful of tables, it is very handy to have a listing of all the tables and columns in the database. In addition to having the base information like column name and data type, it is also beneficial to have a short descriptor for both the tables and columns. Unless you implemented a custom solution, adding a descriptor to either type of object *inside* of SQL Server was not possible before SQL Server 2000.

SQL Server 2000 gives you the ability to add descriptors with the **sp_addextendedproperty** system stored procedure. This example not only shows how to use this procedure to add descriptors to tables and columns, it also shows how to create a browser-based interface for viewing this information on a table-by-table basis.

Technical Details

The **sp_addextendedproperty** system stored procedure adds extended properties to database objects. For example, you can use this procedure to add a descriptor to one or more columns in a table. Once extended properties have been added to an object, the system function **::fn_listextendedproperty** retrieves the information.

There is a set of system-supplied database objects called Information Schema Views that return meta data about the objects in a database. If you are not familiar with these views, please see the "Information Schema Views" section in Chapter 8.

The statements that create the tables and add the extended properties referenced in this example are shown here. If you completed Example 2, you do not need to create the tables, but you do need to execute the **sp_addextendedproperty** statements.

```
USE CodeCentric
go
CREATE TABLE Retailers
(
Ret_UniqueID int IDENTITY PRIMARY KEY,
Ret_Name varchar(30) NOT NULL,
Ret_ContactFName varchar(30) NOT NULL,
Ret_ContactLName varchar(30) NOT NULL,
Ret_ContactPhone varchar(15) NOT NULL
```

```
)
--Step 1 Add table-level description
EXEC sp_addextendedproperty  @name = 'TableDescription',
                             @value = 'Retail Companies ',
                             @level0type = 'user',
                             @level0name = dbo,
                             @level1type = 'table',
                             @level1name = 'Retailers'


--Step 2 Add column-level descriptions
EXEC sp_addextendedproperty  @name = 'ColumnDescription',
                             @value = 'Unique ID per Retailer',
                             @level0type = 'user',
                             @level0name = dbo,
                             @level1type = 'table',
                             @level1name = 'Retailers',
                             @level2type = 'column',
                             @level2name = Ret_UniqueID


EXEC sp_addextendedproperty  @name = 'ColumnDescription',
                             @value = 'Retailer Name',
                             @level0type = 'user',
                             @level0name = dbo,
                             @level1type = 'table',
                             @level1name = 'Retailers',
                             @level2type = 'column',
                             @level2name = Ret_Name


EXEC sp_addextendedproperty  @name = 'ColumnDescription',
                             @value = 'Contact First Name',
                             @level0type = 'user',
                             @level0name = dbo,
                             @level1type = 'table',
                             @level1name = 'Retailers',
                             @level2type = 'column',
                             @level2name = Ret_ContactFName


EXEC sp_addextendedproperty  @name = 'ColumnDescription',
                             @value = 'Contact Last Name',
                             @level0type = 'user',
                             @level0name = dbo,
                             @level1type = 'table',
                             @level1name = 'Retailers',
                             @level2type = 'column',
```

```
                                  @level2name = Ret_ContactLName


        EXEC sp_addextendedproperty  @name = 'ColumnDescription',
                                  @value = 'Contact Phone',
                                  @level0type = 'user',
                                  @level0name = dbo,
                                  @level1type = 'table',
                                  @level1name = 'Retailers',
                                  @level2type = 'column',
                                  @level2name = Ret_ContactPhone


CREATE TABLE Categories
(
 Cat_UniqueID smallint IDENTITY PRIMARY KEY,
 Cat_Description varchar(30) NOT NULL
)
--Step 1 Add table-level description
EXEC sp_addextendedproperty  @name = 'TableDescription',
                                  @value = 'Retail Categories',
                                  @level0type = 'user',
                                  @level0name = dbo,
                                  @level1type = 'table',
                                  @level1name = 'Categories'


--Step 2 Add column-level description
EXEC sp_addextendedproperty  @name = 'ColumnDescription',
                                  @value = 'Category Unique ID',
                                  @level0type = 'user',
                                  @level0name = dbo,
                                  @level1type = 'table',
                                  @level1name = 'Categories',
                                  @level2type = 'column',
                                  @level2name = Cat_UniqueID


        EXEC sp_addextendedproperty  @name = 'ColumnDescription',
                                  @value = 'Category Description',
                                  @level0type = 'user',
                                  @level0name = dbo,
                                  @level1type = 'table',
                                  @level1name = 'Categories',
                                  @level2type = 'column',
                                  @level2name = Cat_Description
```

The **sp_addextendedproperty** procedure can seem quite confusing the first time you see it used, but not too bad once you understand how the type (e.g., @level0type) and name (e.g., @level0name) parameters are used. Let's look at the procedure used to add a table-level description to **Retailers**.

```
EXEC sp_addextendedproperty  @name = 'TableDescription',
                             @value = 'Retail Companies ',
                             @level0type = 'user',
                             @level0name = dbo,
                             @level1type = 'table',
                             @level1name = 'Retailers'
```

The first two parameters add the custom descriptor. The name of the extended property is called 'TableDescription' and the value associated with property is 'Retail Companies.' The other parameters specify to which object the property is associated. The @level0type = 'user' indicates the object to which the property is associated is user-defined. The @level0name = 'dbo' means the user-defined object is owned by **dbo**. The @level1type = 'table' indicates the object is a table. The @level1name = 'Retailers' is the name of the table. Translating the procedure call into English would look like this: "Create a new property called 'TableDesciption' with a value of 'Retail Companies' on the **Retailers** table that is owned by **dbo**."

The call that adds a property at the column-level is similar to the table-level approach. The following shows how to add a descriptor to the **Ret_UniqueID** column.

```
EXEC sp_addextendedproperty  @name = 'ColumnDescription',
                             @value = 'Unique ID per Retailer',
                             @level0type = 'user',
                             @level0name = dbo,
                             @level1type = 'table',
                             @level1name = 'Retailers',
                             @level2type = 'column',
                             @level2name = Ret_UniqueID
```

The values for the first two parameters have changed and another set of type and name parameters has been added. The new property name is called 'Column-Description' and its value is 'Unique ID per Retailer.' The additional type and name parameters specify to which column the property belongs.

After the extended properties are created, the **::fn_listextendedproperty** system function retrieves the values. The function is used with a SELECT statement and its parameters are listed below. Notice how the functions parameters correspond to the parameters used with **sp_addextendedproperty**.

```
::fn_listextendedproperty (
    { default | [ @name = ] 'property_name' | NULL }
    , { default | [ @level0type = ] 'level0_object_type' | NULL }
    , { default | [ @level0name = ] 'level0_object_name' | NULL }
    , { default | [ @level1type = ] 'level1_object_type' | NULL }
    , { default | [ @level1name = ] 'level1_object_name' | NULL }
    , { default | [ @level2type = ] 'level2_object_type' | NULL }
    , { default | [ @level2name = ] 'level2_object_name' | NULL }
    )
```

The following SELECT demonstrates how to use the function to retrieve the column names and descriptors associated with **Retailers**.

```
SELECT   ObjName, Value
FROM    ::fn_listextendedproperty (NULL, 'user', 'dbo', 'table', _
           'Retailers', 'column', NULL)
--Results--

ObjName                    Value
----------------    --------------------------
Ret_ContactFName      Contact First Name
Ret_ContactLName      Contact Last Name
Ret_ContactPhone      Contact Phone
Ret_Name              Retailer Name
Ret_UniqueID          Unique ID per Retailer
```

In the next section this type of SELECT is wrapped in a user-defined function to make the solution more flexible.

Solution

The following statements show the user-defined functions used to retrieve the table and column descriptors created in the previous section. Both use a parameter value with **::fn_listextendedproperty** to retrieve the descriptor on an object-by-object basis.

```
--Function retrieves table description
CREATE FUNCTION TableDesc (@TableName sysname)
RETURNS varchar(100)
AS
BEGIN
 DECLARE @TableDesc varchar(100)
```

```
SELECT @TableDesc = CAST(value AS varchar(128))
FROM   ::fn_listextendedproperty (NULL, 'user', 'dbo', 'table', _
             @TableName, NULL, default)
RETURN @TableDesc
END
go



--Function retrieves column description
CREATE FUNCTION ColDesc (@TableName sysname, @ColumnName sysname)
RETURNS varchar(100)
AS
BEGIN
 DECLARE @ColDesc varchar(100)

 SELECT @ColDesc = CAST(value AS varchar(128))
 FROM   ::fn_listextendedproperty (NULL, 'user', 'dbo', 'table', _
             @TableName, 'column', default)
 WHERE objname = @ColumnName
 RETURN @ColDesc
END
Go
```

Data Dictionary Procedure

The procedure that retrieves table and column information is shown here. (Please note that line numbers were added so code could be easily referenced.)

```
1    CREATE PROCEDURE ps_UTIL_DataDictionary
2    @TableName sysname
3    AS
4
5    --Retrieve data dictionary
6    SELECT @TableName AS TableName,
7           Column_Name,
8           Data_Type+' '+CASE WHEN Character_Maximum_Length IS NOT NULL THEN _
9                        '('+ CAST(Character_Maximum_Length AS varchar(20))+')'
10                          ELSE ''
11                        END AS DataType,
12          CASE WHEN Is_Nullable = 'Yes' THEN 'NULL'
13               ELSE 'NOT NULL'
14          END AS Nullabillity,
```

```
15          dbo.ColDesc(@TableName,Column_Name) AS ColDescription,
16          dbo.TableDesc(@TableName) AS TableDescription
17   FROM Information_Schema.Columns where Table_Name = @TableName
18   ORDER BY Ordinal_Position
```

The procedure accepts the table name for which the meta data is desired and uses both information schema views and the **ColDesc** and **TableDesc** functions (created in the previous section) to retrieve base and extended information. The base information is pulled from the **Information_Schema** and the extended information is returned using the functions.

The SELECT statement looks complex, but if you look at in segments you can understand how it works. Lines 1–7 are very straightforward and should not cause any confusion. Lines 8–11 determine whether the data type associated with a column has a length attribute and displays a descriptor accordingly. If the data type does have a length attribute (NOT NULL), the value is surrounded by parenthesis to format the output. This will be clearer when you look at the output from a call. Lines 12–14 use another CASE to add formatting to the output. If the **Is_Nullable** column contains a 'Yes,' NULL shows in the output; otherwise, NOT NULL displays. Lines 15–18 are similar to many SELECT statements you have worked with and require no explanation.

Let's execute the procedure to see if the resultset it produces will help you better understand how it works. The following shows the results produced for the **Categories** table.

```
EXEC ps_UTIL_DataDictionary @TableName = 'Categories'
--Results--
TableName   Column_Name      DataType      Nullabillity ColDescription        TableDescription
----------  ---------------  ------------  ------------ --------------------  ------------------
Categories  Cat_UniqueID     smallint      NOT NULL     Category Unique ID    Retail Categories
Categories  Cat_Description  varchar (30)  NOT NULL     Category Description  Retail Categories
```

Note that the **DataType** value for **Cat_Description** contains "(30)", whereas the **Cat_UniqueID** column has no length shown. A varchar has a length attribute, but a smallint does not. This output is a result of the CASE listed on Lines 8–11.

Table List Procedure

We use one more procedure in this example, and it returns all the tables in a database. It is used to produce the contents of a drop-down list for the interface and is shown here.

```
USE tempdb
go
CREATE PROCEDURE ps_UTIL_SELECT_Tables
AS
SELECT Table_Name FROM Information_Schema.tables
WHERE Table_Type = 'BASE TABLE'
ORDER BY Table_Name
```

Adding the Interface

The interface allows a user to specify the table whose structure they wish to view.
The ASP file (DataDictionary.asp) used to generate the page is shown here.

```
<!--#include file="adovbs.inc"-->
<HTML>

<HEAD>
  <title>Data Dictionary</title>
</HEAD>
<%
 On Error Resume Next
 Set objConn = server.CreateObject("ADODB.Connection")
 REM DSN-Less OLE-DB
 objConn.Open"Provider=SQLOLEDB;Server=Servername;Database=CodeCentric; _
        Uid=UserID;Pwd=Password"
%>

<BODY bgcolor="beige">
 <center>
 <font face="arial" size=6>Data Dictionary</font>

 <FORM name="LoginAdd" method="post" action="DataDictionary.asp?Flag=1">
 <TABLE border=2 width="70%">
  <tr>
   <td align="center" valign="top">
    <TABLE>
     <tr>
        <td align="left"><font face="arial"><b>Table:</b></font></td>
      <td>
      <select name="TableName">
       <%
       Set cmd1 = server.CreateObject("ADODB.Command")
       cmd1.ActiveConnection = objConn
       cmd1.CommandType = adCmdStoredProc
```

```
            cmd1.CommandText = "ps_UTIL_SELECT_Tables"
            Set rs = cmd1.Execute
            Do Until rs.Eof
            %>
             <option value='<%=rs("Table_Name")%>'><%=rs("Table_Name")%>
             <%
               rs.MoveNext
             Loop
             rs.Close
             Set rs = Nothing
             %>
           </select>
         </td>
       </tr>
         <tr><td align="center" colspan=2> _
               <input type="submit"_ value="Submit"></td></tr>
     </TABLE>
    </td>
  </tr>
</TABLE>

<%
  If request.querystring("Flag") <> "" Then

    Set cmd2 = server.CreateObject("ADODB.Command")
    cmd2.ActiveConnection = objConn
    cmd2.CommandType = adCmdStoredProc
    cmd2.CommandText = "ps_UTIL_DataDictionary"
    cmd2.Parameters.Append cmd2.CreateParameter("loginame",adVarChar, _
                adParamInput,128,request.form("TableName"))

    SET rs = cmd2.Execute
%>
  <TABLE align="center" width="90%">
   <tr>
    <td> </td>
   </tr>
   <tr>
    <td> </td>
   </tr>
   <tr>
    <td colspan=4><font face="arial" size=5> _
        Table Name: <%=rs("TableName")%></font></td>
   </tr>
```

```
     <tr>
      <td colspan=4><font face="arial"> _
          Table Description: <%=rs("TableDescription")%></font></td>
     </tr>
     <tr>
      <td> </td>
     </tr>
     <tr>
      <td width="20%"><font face="arial"><b>Column Name</b></td>
      <td width="15%"><font face="arial"><b>Data Type</b></td>
      <td width="15%"><font face="arial"><b>Nullability</b></td>
      < td><font face="arial"><b>Description</b></td>
     </tr>
     <tr>
      <td colspan=4><hr></td>
     </tr>
     <%
     Do Until rs.Eof
     %>
      <tr>
      <td><font face="Arial"><%=rs("COLUMN_NAME")%></font></td>
      <td><font face="Arial"><%=rs("DataType")%></font></td>
      <td><font face="Arial"><%=rs("Nullabillity")%></font></td>
      <td><font face="Arial"><%=rs("ColDescription")%></font></td>
     </tr>
     <%
     rs.MoveNext
     Loop
     rs.Close
     %>
</TABLE>
   <%
End If
   %>

 </FORM>
 </center>
 </BODY>
</HTML>
```

Upon initially being called, the TableName dropdown is populated with all the tables in the **CodeCentric** database. When the Submit button is clicked, the page calls itself, executes the **ps_UTIL_DataDictionary** stored procedure, and displays the resultset. The output for the **Retailers** table is shown in Figure 13-11.

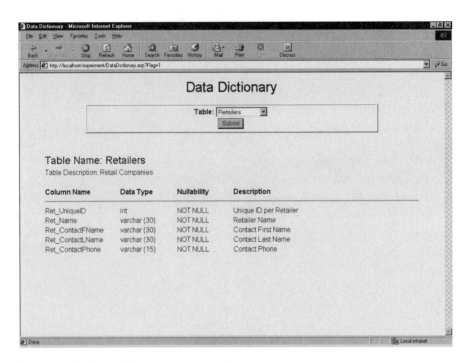

Figure 13-11. Data Dictionary screen

Example 8: Crystal Reports and Stored Procedures

Crystal Reports is the most widely used report writer on the market today. I started working with the product about five years ago, and my first experiences (explained in the next section) with it will help you to understand why I included this example in the book.

A copy of Crystal Reports version 7 and a working knowledge of how to create a simple report is required to complete this example. If you have Crystal Reports version 8, you need to visit Seagate's Web site (http://www.Seagate.com) to get the vendor-supplied ASP files. To run the ASP included with this example, you need to the Crystal Reports ActiveX Report Viewer configured per your Web site. You can find configuration details for the ActiveX Viewer on Seagate's Web site.

Although installation of the component is not covered here, I will let you know from personal experience that you should install the complete Web Reports Server even if you're just going to use the Viewer. Trying to load the Viewer alone is too complicated because you cannot determine exactly what files need to be loaded and what configuration changes need to be made. Installing the Web Reports Server will install more than you actually need, but it will load all the necessary Viewer files and make the necessary configuration changes.

TIP Crystal ActiveX Viewer

If your company does a lot of browser-based development where reports are used on a frequent basis, I strongly encourage you to check out Crystal's ActiveX Viewer. It allows you to run normal (.rpt) Crystal Reports from a browser and provides some nice navigational features. The documentation is pretty poor, but Seagate's Web site does give some good examples of how to use it, and a quick call to their Technical Support should allow you to work through any problems you encounter during the installation process.

Technical Details

When I first started working with Crystal Reports, I used it in the traditional way that is described in the documentation. I added the tables on which a report was based to the Design Window, modified the default joins accordingly, and then selected the columns for the report. Figure 13-12 shows how this process is started today (version X) with Standard Report Expert.

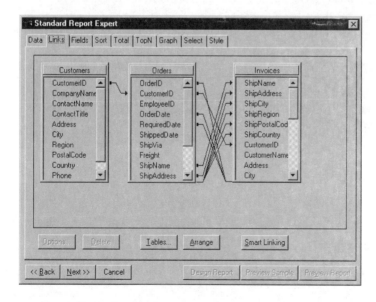

Figure 13-12. Crystal Standard Report Expert

This standard report creation approach allows Crystal to create the SQL statements necessary to retrieve the desired data. The problem with the standard approach, however, is that is uses client-side processing to manipulate the data. I won't go into all the gory details of how the client-side processing works, but in a nutshell it pulls all the data from each table referenced in SELECT to the client, makes the necessary joins, and the filters the data per any WHERE clause conditions. If the SELECT references five tables, *all* the data in each will be pulled to the client to execute the report. This is not only extremely inefficient, but requires the client running the report have substantial memory and hard drive space when a report is references large tables.

In my particular situation the reports I developed ran fine at first, but the time it took to process them became longer (and unacceptable) in a very short time. I was working on a new install of a credit processing system and at first there was relatively no data in the database. Because the company processed a lot of credit applications, the data grew at a quick rate. As the data grew, so to did the resources required to process the reports.

After struggling with the issue for a day or so, I placed a call to the credit application processing system's designers and was then told about using stored procedures as the data source for Crystal Reports. They explained that this approach forced all data manipulation to occur on the server (in this case the most powerful box on the network) and that only the results were sent to the client. I quickly got up to speed on how to create stored procedures and changed the reports as quickly as possible. Once the reports were changed, the processing time decreased significantly and my users were happy with the system.

The ability to support server-side processing was added to Crystal Reports in version 7 of the product. If you are forced to create reports based on tables, you may want to consider using this option to save resources and increase the speed at which the reports are executed. The Knowledgebase Article: c2002101 on Seagate's Web site explains how server-side processing is configured.

The following files are used in this example and are included in the example files for this chapter. The last three files are the vendor-supplied ASP files referenced in the previous section. If you use Crystal Reports 8, these are the files you need to download from Seagate's Web site.

- CrystalReports.rpt

- CrystalReports.asp

- CrystalReportsRespond.asp

- AlwaysRequiredSteps.asp

- MoreRequiredSteps.asp

- SmartViewerActiveX.asp

Solution

The following stored procedure produces a filtered resultset that shows the company name, order date and salesperson for each order placed in the supplied date range.

```
USE Northwind
go
CREATE PROCEDURE ps_Customers_OrdersSalesperson
@OrderDateStart varchar(8),
@OrderDateEnd varchar(8)
AS
SELECT a.CompanyName,
       b.OrderDate,
       c.FirstName+' '+c.LastName AS Salesperson
FROM Customers a
INNER JOIN Orders b ON a.CustomerID = b.CustomerID
INNER JOIN Employees c ON b.EmployeeID = c.EmployeeID
WHERE b.OrderDate BETWEEN @OrderDateStart AND @OrderDateEnd
ORDER BY a.CompanyName, c.LastName
go

EXEC ps_Customers_OrdersSalesperson '1/1/97','1/31/97'
--Results (Partial)--
CompanyName                        OrderDate                   Salesperson
---------------------------------- --------------------------- ----------------
Bottom-Dollar Markets              1997-01-10 00:00:00.000     Anne Dodsworth
Bottom-Dollar Markets              1997-01-10 00:00:00.000     Janet Leverling
Bottom-Dollar Markets              1997-01-30 00:00:00.000     Margaret Peacock
Eastern Connection                 1997-01-01 00:00:00.000     Nancy Davolio
Ernst Handel                       1997-01-02 00:00:00.000     Laura Callahan
```

Note that the datatypes used for the procedure's parameters are defined as varchar(8) even though the **OrderDate** field is defined as datetime. The reason for this is that Crystal Reports has a bug that prohibits using datetime parameters in stored procedures. The workaround is to define the parameters using the char or varchar data types. SQL Server implicitly converts the values when they are referenced in the BETWEEN function, so no conversion is necessary.

Once the procedure is created, complete the following in order to configure Crystal to *look* for the stored procedures in the target database.

1.   Start Crystal Reports.

2.   If the Welcome Dialog appears, click Cancel to close the dialog.

3. Click File on the main menu and select Options.

4. Click the SQL tab and make sure the Stored Procedures option is checked in the Allow reporting on section of the dialog. Figure 13-13 show what this looks like.

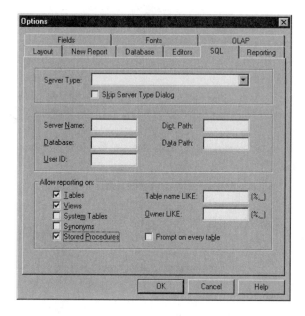

Figure 13-13. Configuring Crystal to report on stored procedures

Now complete the following to create the report.

1. Click File on the main menu and select New.

2. Click the Standard icon on the Report Gallery dialog.

3. Click SQL/ODBC on the Standard Report Expert dialog.

4. Scroll down the options in the Server Type list box and select Microsoft SQL Server.

5. Supply the required login information, specify **Northwind** in the Database field, and click OK.

6. Scroll down the SQL Tables list, select northwind.dbo.Proc(ps_Customers_OrdersSalesperson), and click the Add button.

7. Populate the variable fields with 1/1/97 and 1/31/97 and click OK.

After applying some minor formatting (e.g., suppressing the group header and footer), the report looks like the one shown in Figure 13-14.

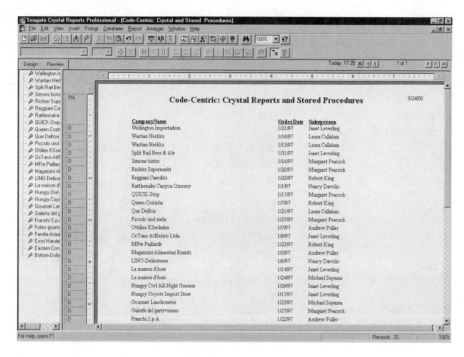

Figure 13-14. Sample Crystal Report

Adding the Interface

Now that the report has been created and tested, a user interface can be created in ASP that allows the user to specify the date range and then execute the report. The code for implementing this functionality has been placed in two files so it will be easier to understand. The ASP that produces the user interface is shown next. The screen it produces is shown in Figure 13-15.

```
<HTML>
 <HEAD>
  <script type="text/javascript">
  function checkData ()
   {
   if (document.Reports.StartDate.value == "")
    {
     alert("You must enter a start date. Please correct this and Submit! again")
     document.Reports.StartDate.focus()
     return false
    }

    if (document.Reports.EndDate.value == "")
     {
      alert("You must enter an end date. Please correct this and Submit! again")
      document.Reports.EndDate.focus()
      return false
     }
    }
  </script>

  <title>Customer Orders by Salesperson</title>
 </HEAD>

<BODY bgcolor="beige">
 <center>
  <font face="Arial" size="4"><b>Customer Orders by Salesperson</a></b></font>

  <TABLE width="70%" align="center" border=2>
   <tr>
    <td>
     <FORM name="Reports" method="post" _
           action="CrystalReportsRespond.asp" onsubmit="return checkData()">
     <TABLE width="50%" cellspacing="0" align="center">
      <tr><td> </td></tr>
      <tr><td> </td></tr>
      <tr><td> </td></tr>
      <tr>
        <td align="right"><b>Start Date:</b></td>
        <td align="left"><input type="text" name="StartDate" size=8></td>
        <td align="right"><b>End Date:</b></td>
        <td align="left"><input type="text" name="EndDate" size=8></td>
      </tr>
       <tr><td> </td></tr>
```

```
      <tr><td> </td></tr>
    <tr>
    <td align="center" colspan=5><input type="submit" value="Submit"></td>
    </tr>
    </TABLE>
    </FORM>
  </td>
 </tr>
</TABLE>

</center>
</BODY>

</HTML>
```

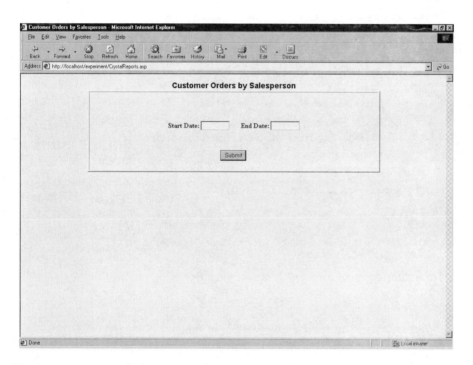

Figure 13-15. Crystal Reports interface

The respond page used in this example contains all the code and includes files needed by the ActiveX Viewer. All of the include files are supplied by Seagate, so I will let you explore them on your own if you wish. The respond page is shown next. (Please note line numbers were added so the code could be easily referenced.)

```
1     <%
2      response.expires = 0
3      response.expiresabsolute = Now() - 1
4      response.addHeader "pragma","no-cache"
5      response.addHeader "cache-control","private"
6      response.CacheControl = "no-cache"
7     %>
8
9
10    <title>Customer Orders by Salesperson</title>
11
12    <%
13     ReportName = "CrystalReports.rpt"
14    %>
15
16    <!-- #include file="AlwaysRequiredSteps.asp" -->
17
18    <%
19     Set crtable = session("oRpt").Database.Tables.Item(1)
20     Set session("StoredProcParamCollection") = _
                  session("oRpt").ParameterFields
21     Set ThisParam = session("StoredProcParamCollection").item(1)
22     Set ThisParam2 = session("StoredProcParamCollection").item(2)
23
24     NewParamValue = request.form("StartDate")
25     NewParamValue2 = request.form("EndDate")
26
27     Call ThisParam.SetCurrentValue (cstr(NewParamValue), 12)
28     Call ThisParam2.SetCurrentValue (cstr(NewParamValue2), 12)
29
30     crtable.SetLogonInfo "Ace", "Northwind", "garth", "password"
31    %>

<!-- #include file="MoreRequiredSteps.asp" -->
<!-- #include file="SmartViewerActiveX.asp" -->
```

The name of the report (CrystalReports.rpt) is placed in a variable on Line 13 and the required Application (session ("oApp")) and Report (session("oRpt")) objects are created and placed in session variables in AlwaysRequiredSteps.asp. On Line 19 the database object on which the report is based is retrieved and placed in a variable. Line 20 creates a session variable for the parameters collection of the report and Lines 21 and 22 set each parameter equal to a local variable. Lines 24 and 25 get the date range values input by the user, and Lines 27 and 28 set the values for the parameters. Line 30 sets the login information for the report, and the rest is all code provided by Seagate. You may have to examine the code shown in the .asp files a couple of times before it all makes sense. One last thing about the code in CrystalReportsRespond.asp: Lines 2–6 prohibit the report from being cached. It is extremely important that you make sure a report does not get cached by IIS. When a report is cached, subsequent calls to it within the same browser session will retrieve the same data regardless of any modifications that might have been performed on the underlying data. In other words, no data changes are reflected on the report because the first *copy* of the report is cached and re-used until it is flushed from memory.

When the ActiveX Viewer is activated it looks like Figure 13-16.

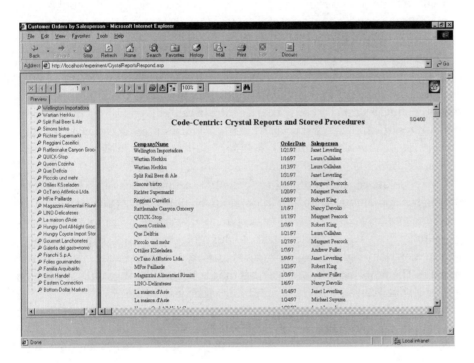

Figure 13-16. ActiveX Viewer interface

Notice the component is activated within my browser (Internet Explorer) and the same report shown earlier is loaded. The Viewer allows you to zoom, export, print, and search the contents of the report.

Example 9: Calling DTS Packages with a Stored Procedure

DTS (Data Transformation Services) was added in SQL Server 7 and in my opinion is the most useful data-transfer software I have ever worked with. DTS allows you to take data in one format (e.g., Access) and convert it to another (e.g., SQL Server). It works with a myriad data formats that include dBase, text files, Excel, FoxPro, and any ODBC or OLE DB compliant products. Fully covering DTS is a book unto itself, so I provide only limited coverage here. I will show how to create a DTS Package using the DTS Import Wizard and then execute the package via a stored procedure that is called from an ASP page. You can use this type of solution on your projects to empower non-technical users to transfer and load data that they otherwise could not access.

One of my biggest clients is a REIT (Real Estate Investment Trust), and they own more than 100 retail strip centers across the southern United States. About two years ago I started a project that would allow them to get their property information online. A property consists of a center; a center is composed of one or more suites (the individual spaces in a center); and a suite is occupied by a tenant. Most of their centers have quite a few suites, so in aggregate there are more than 2000 suites/tenants.

Maintaining general information on the 100+ centers is easy and could be done manually. Maintaining occupancy information on more than 2,000 suites is not an easy task, and because of the volume of changes it would be cost-prohibitive to try to maintain this data manually. The key to this project was that the suite/tenant information was *already* being maintained in the property management accounting package. The problem, however, was that the accounting package did not store the data in an open format and could only be accessed via text files.

To make a long story short, I was able to create DTS packages that loaded the accounting data into a SQL Server database and then create ASP pages that accessed the data via the Internet. The real beauty of this type of solution is that the data used on the Web site was already being maintained for operational purposes in the normal course of business.

Once the initial data load processes are created, the only extra effort required to get useful data on the Web is periodic loads from the source data. Depending on the state of the source data, this can be either very complex or trivial. In this case it was extremely complex; multiple levels of loading and scrubbing needed to be applied to the data before it was *approved* to be shown on the Web site. The multiple levels required that the users have a GUI that allowed them to transfer the data to intermediary tables, review the results of the scrubbing process and then load the data into the live tables. This was accomplished using some of the techniques described in this example.

Technical Details

To complete this example I need to create a DTS Package using the DTS Import Wizard. A file called Customers_DTS.txt is included in this chapter's sample files. The file was created using the DTS Export Wizard and contains the data held in the **Customers** table in **Northwind** database. Make sure you have this file on a local hard drive before continuing.

Complete the following steps in Enterprise Manager to create a DTS Package that loads the data in Customers.txt into the **Customers_DTS** table in the **CodeCentric** database. The **Customers_DTS** table will be created by the import process, so no DDL statements need to be explicitly executed.

1. Click Tools on the main menu, highlight Data Transformation Services, and select Import Data.

2. Click Next to get past the initial screen displayed by the wizard.

3. Select Text File from the Source dropdown and then click the ellipsis button to locate Customers.txt on your local hard drive.

4. Once you have selected the file, click the Next button.

5. The screen should look like Figure 13-17. Notice that each column is delimited with a comma and the other options are fairly standard. Accept the defaults presented on the dialog by clicking Next.

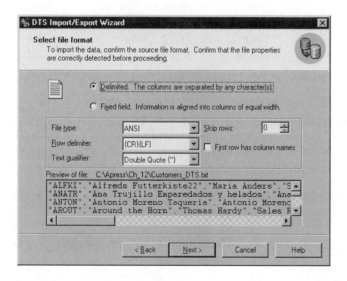

Figure 13-17. Select File Format dialog

6. We verified the column delimiter in the previous step, so click Next to accept the default of Comma.

7. Select your Server from the Server dropdown, supply the appropriate login information, and click the Database dropdown to select the **CodeCentric** database. The results of these actions are shown in Figure 13-18. Click Next to continue.

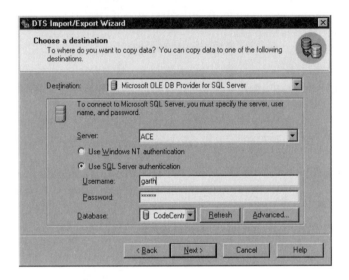

Figure 13-18. Choose a Destination dialog

8. Click the ellipsis button in the Transform column and note the information shown in the dialog. Figure 13-19 shows my screen. Notice that no useful column names are provided because there were none in the source data. Also notice that varchar(255) is used for the data type of all the columns. When the source data is in a string format, the Wizard uses varchar(255) as the default data type. You can change column names and data types if you wish, but I am going to accept the default values. Check the Drop and recreate destination table box and then click OK. Click Next to continue.

9. Check the Save DTS Package option on the Save, Schedule and Replicate package dialog, and click Next.

10. Supply a Name (**Customers_DTS**) and Description data as shown in Figure 13-20.

11. Click the Next button and then click Finish.

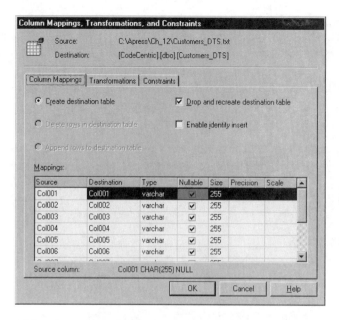

Figure 13-19. Mappings, Transformations, and Constraints dialog

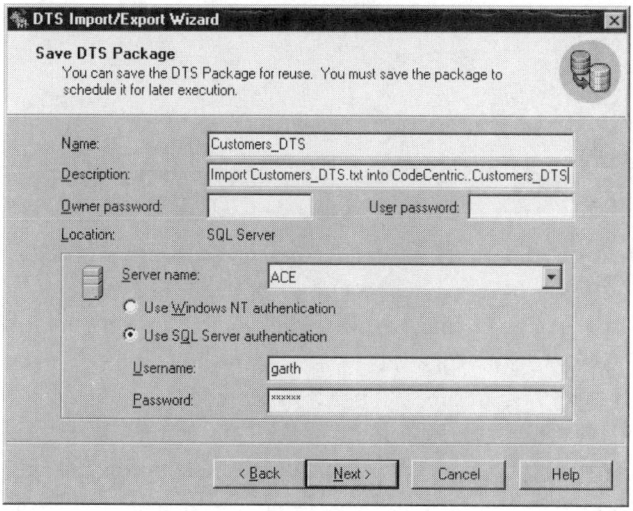

Figure 13-20. Naming the package

Once the wizard has completed, you can access the **Customers_DTS** table in the **CodeCentric** database and examine the DTS Package created by the process. Complete the following to review the package.

1. Expand the Data Transformation Services option and select Local Packages. If the package you created is not shown, press F5 to refresh the screen.

2. Right-click the package in the Detail Pane and select Design Package. Figure 13-21 shows the results of this process.

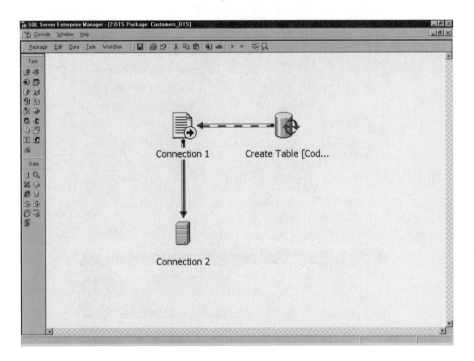

Figure 13-21. DTS Package Designer

You can execute the package again by right-clicking and selecting Execute. Because of the way the package was created, you can drop the **Customers_DTS** and it will be created when the package is executed.

Exploring the rest of the functionality available in DTS is up to you. There is a tremendous amount you can do with the tool, so if you import/export data on a frequent basis I encourage you to spend some time researching its features. For this example all we needed was a quick lesson in how to create and execute a simple package. The remainder of this example will demonstrate how to execute the package via a stored procedure that is called from an ASP page.

Solution

The following procedure executes the **Customers_DTS** package.

```
USE CodeCentric
go
CREATE PROCEDURE ps_UTIL_ExecuteDTSPackage
@ServerName sysname,
@ServerUserName sysname,
@ServerPassword sysname,
@PackageName sysname
AS
DECLARE @ErrorValue int,
        @Object int,
        @ErrorDescription varchar(255)


--Create a package Object
EXEC @ErrorValue = sp_OACreate 'DTS.Package', @Object OUTPUT
IF @ErrorValue <> 0
BEGIN
   EXEC sp_OAGetErrorInfo @Object, NULL, @ErrorDescription OUT
   SELECT @ErrorDescription AS ErrorDescription
   RETURN
END


--Load method with required parameters
EXEC @ErrorValue = sp_OAMethod @Object,
                               'LoadFromSqlServer',
                               NULL,
                               @ServerName=@ServerName,
                               @ServerUserName=@ServerUserName,
                               @PackageName=@PackageName,
                               @Flags=0,
                               @PackagePassword = '',
                               @ServerPassword = @ServerPassword

IF @ErrorValue <> 0
 BEGIN
  EXEC sp_OAGetErrorInfo @Object, NULL, @ErrorDescription OUT
  SELECT @ErrorDescription AS ErrorDescription
  RETURN
 END



--Execute method
EXEC @ErrorValue = sp_OAMethod @Object, 'Execute'
IF @ErrorValue <> 0
 BEGIN
  EXEC sp_OAGetErrorInfo @Object, NULL, @ErrorDescription OUT
```

```
  SELECT @ErrorDescription AS ErrorDescription
  RETURN
 END


--Unitialize package
EXEC @ErrorValue = sp_OAMethod @Object, 'UnInitialize'

--Destroy package Object
EXEC @ErrorValue = sp_OADestroy @Object
```

The code probably looks like hieroglyphics unless you have experience working with the **sp_OA** series of extended stored procedures. If you have not worked with them before and want to understand exactly what's going on, please see the "OLE Automation Procedures" section in Chapter 10. The key part of the procedure is the call to **LoadFromSQLServer** shown in bold. Otherwise it simply calls the proper objects and methods.

The following statements show how to verify the procedure successfully executes the package. Make sure you change the ServerName, UserID, and Password values per your setup.

```
USE CodeCentric
go
SET NOCOUNT ON

--Empty table
TRUNCATE TABLE Customers_DTS

--Count rows in table
SELECT COUNT(*) FROM Customers_DTS

--Execute procedure
EXEC ps_UTIL_ExecuteDTSPackage 'ServerName','UserID','Password','Customers_DTS'

--Count rows in table
SELECT COUNT(*) FROM Customers_DTS
--Results--
-----------
0


-----------
91
```

The first SELECT COUNT(*)... shows the table is empty, but the one executed after **ps_UTIL_ExecuteDTSPackage** is executed returns 91 rows.

Adding the Interface

The ASP needed to execute this package is contained in DTS.asp and is shown here.

```
<% Option Explicit %>
<!--#include file="adovbs.inc"-->
<HTML>

 <HEAD>
   <title>DTS Data Loader</title>
 </HEAD>

 <%
 On Error Resume Next
 Dim objConn, cmd1, ErrorMessage

 Set objConn = server.CreateObject("ADODB.Connection")
 REM DSN-Less OLE-DB
 objConn.Open "Provider=SQLOLEDB;Server=SeverName; _
        Database=CodeCentric;Uid=UserID;Pwd=Password"

 If request.querystring("Flag") <> "" Then

   Set cmd1 = server.CreateObject("ADODB.Command")
   cmd1.ActiveConnection = objConn
   cmd1.CommandType = adCmdStoredProc
   cmd1.CommandText = "ps_UTIL_ExecuteDTSPackage"
   cmd1.Parameters.Append cmd1.CreateParameter("ServerName",adVarChar, _
              adParamInput,128,"ServerName")
   cmd1.Parameters.Append cmd1.CreateParameter("ServerUserName",adVarChar, _
              adParamInput,128,"UserID")
   cmd1.Parameters.Append cmd1.CreateParameter("ServerPassword",adVarChar, _
          adParamInput,128,"password")
   cmd1.Parameters.Append cmd1.CreateParameter("PackageName",adVarChar, _
              adParamInput,128,"Customers_DTS")
   cmd1.Parameters.Append cmd1.CreateParameter("ReturnMessage",adVarChar, _
              adParamOutput,255)
```

```
    cmd1.Execute
    ErrorMessage = cmd1.Parameters("ReturnMessage")

  End If
%>

<BODY bgcolor="beige" width="50%">
 <center>
  <font face="arial" size=6>DTS Data Loader</font>
  <p> 
  <p> 
  <font face="arial"><a href="dts.asp?Flag=1">Load Customer_DTS</a></font>
  <%
   If ErrorMessage = "Success" Then
  %>
    <p> 
    <font face="arial">The package was successfully executed</font>
  <%
   Else
  %>
    <p> 
    <font face="arial">The package execution failed</font>
    <font face="arial"><%=ErrorMessage%></font>
  <%
   End If
  %>
 </center>
 </BODY>
</HTML>
```

This is a simple interface that calls itself with `Flag=1` when the hyperlink is clicked. This causes the procedure to execute which in turn executes the DTS Package. The interface is shown in Figure 13-22.

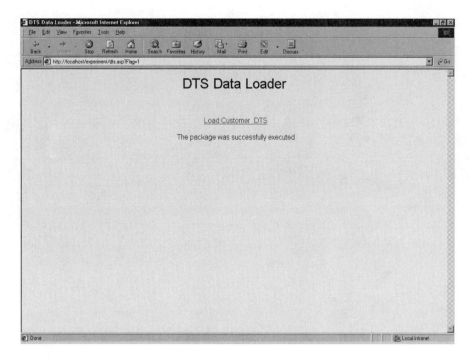

Figure 13-22. ASP page

Before You Go

The examples I presented in this chapter showed how stored procedures and triggers are used in the real world to implement database solutions. In addition, I used ASP technology to complete some of the examples so you could see how the front- and back-ends work together. Some of the examples were fairly specific to a type of industry, but the concepts presented should be adaptable to most types of businesses. After all, data is data. People want to accumulate and report on data regardless of the industry.

The material I will present in the next chapter shows how to create a simple browser-based application. If you are contemplating creating a corporate intranet or any simple database application with SQL Server 2000, you will definitely want to spend some time reviewing how the application is created.

CHAPTER 14

Building an Application

THE MAIN PURPOSE OF THIS CHAPTER IS TO SHOW the SQL statements and ASP pages required to create a browser-based database application. I will create a real-world scenario by providing specifications to which the application must adhere. Then I will list the SQL statements that create the database and database objects that support the application. In the final section I will list the .asp files that create the application's front-end. The application consists of nine tables, twenty-one stored procedures, four triggers, and twenty-nine .asp files, so there is plenty of sample code that shows exactly how the application is built.

NOTE Sample Code

The sample code for this chapter is available for download at either:
`http://www.apress.com` *or* `http://www.SQLBook.com.` *Download CodeCentric.zip, extract the contents and look for the file named Ch14.zip. It contains Ch14.sql and the .asp files used to create the application front-end.*

Before You Get Started

This chapter is divided into two main sections: Specifications and Database Code. The first section describes the functionality the application needs to support, and the second details the SQL statements used to create the database objects used by the application. All the SQL statements used in the example are presented in this chapter, but the front-end ASP code is not. The ASP files are located in the chapter's sample file and are extremely easy to install if you have experience working with ASP.

You can get a general understanding of how the SQL statements are used to implement the back-end functionality without working with the application front-end. I do not, however, think you can fully appreciate how some of the procedures are used until you experiment with the application and determine which action calls a specific procedure. Even if you do not have experience developing browser-based applications with ASP, you can still see how the application works by visiting the book's supporting web site at http://www.SQLBook.com and entering the examples area.

Business Scenario

The example presented in this chapter is based on the needs of a nationwide commercial real estate company whose main product is leasable space in the buildings they own or manage. The company has a 50-member sales force and each salesperson (real estate broker) reports to one of three regional managers. The regional managers report to the Vice President of Leasing who, in turn, reports to the company's CEO.

The VP of Leasing wants to better understand the efforts that result in a successful lease negotiation. With this goal in mind, he asked the IS (Information Systems) Group to analyze the situation and determine if there is a software-solution that could help them more effectively manage the group's efforts. After conducting interviews with some of the individual brokers and regional managers, the IS group concluded that a database application that allowed the brokers to track all sales calls would help management better understand the efforts required to close a lease negotiation. The VP agreed and the IS group began the development process by creating an application specification that was used to define the functionality the application is to support.

Do not be concerned if you are not familiar with the commercial real estate industry. Simply think of leasable space as any product with a large price tag. Products that have a large price tag often require the sales force to call on the customer multiple times throughout the *sales cycle* in order to successfully close the deal. Sales cycle defines the start and finish of the sales process—from the first customer contact to the customer buying or rejecting the product.

Specifications

The following specification format is similar to one I have used on some of my projects to define the functionality an application will support. This process can also be thought of as a formal definition of the scope of work that is to be performed for the client. More detailed or rigorous formats exist, but for the size of my projects (less than $25,000) this is sufficient. Note that there is a Definitions section in the specification. This section is included for my benefit more than the customer's. I often work in an industry (or area of an industry) where I have no previous work experience; defining the key terms on which the application is based ensures that I fully understand what the customer is talking about when a particular term is used.

Using some variation of this specification before you start programming can protect you from *scope creep*—one of the biggest problems I face as an independent developer. Scope creep is the expanding of the functionality an application is supposed to support after an initial agreement has been made. This has happened on almost all the projects I have worked on and can be especially detrimental to an independent developer because we often use lump sum or not-to-exceed type estimates where the amount of profit is contingent on our estimates being correct. Having a specification that defines the scope of work will help to identify scope creep so additional fees can be negotiated. If the client asks for functionality not originally in the estimate, you simply inform them that it is *new* and that additional development time and costs need to be negotiated.

Sales Efforts Management (SEM) Specification

Purpose

The purpose of the Sales Efforts Management (SEM) software is to allow the sales engagements and sales calls of the sales force to be tracked in an efficient manner so the results of the sales efforts can be analyzed.

Application Owner

The Leasing Department is the owner of the application. All changes or additional functionality must be approved by John Smith, Vice President of Leasing.

Definitions

The following definitions are used in this specification:

- Broker—An employee whose main job is to lease space to customers (prospective tenants).

- Sales Engagement—The formal definition of a sales effort. A way of *labeling* an attempt to lease space to a customer. A sales engagement always has a lead salesperson, is made up of one or more sales calls with a status of either: "Open," "Closed—Success," or "Closed—Failed."

- Sales Call—A broker interaction with a customer where the purpose is to get the customer to commit to leasing space. A sales call is conducted with one or more salespersons and is always associated with a Sales Engagement.

- Sales Cycle—Defines the start and finish of the sales process, from first customer contact to either the customer buying or rejecting the product.

Logical Model

The logical relationship of the entities involved in the sales process is shown in Figure 14-1.

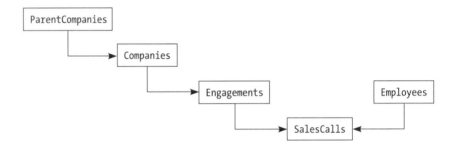

Figure 14-1. Logical model

General Functional Description

- Each company pursued is associated with a parent company. When a company is its own parent, a *dummy* parent is created.

- Contact information is tracked at both the parent and subsidiary company level.

- A company can be designated as a VIC (very important client), which means that the Vice President of Leasing is sent a system-generated email every time a sales engagement is created for that company.

- When a member of the sales force starts a new sales effort with a company, an engagement record must be created. The engagement information must include a general description, a start and end date, and a status that indicates the state of the engagement. An engagement always has an associated lead salesperson who is responsible for the effort. An engagement always has an associated status. The valid status values are: "Open," "Closed—Success," and "Closed—Failed."

- When one or more members of the sales force interacts with a potential customer, a sales call record is created. A sales call must contain a description, its costs, and a rating to indicate the success of the call. The valid ratings are "Excellent," "Good," "Fair" and "Poor."

- The application will have audit trail functionality that tracks database changes by employee.

- A user must be able to retrieve all engagements and sales calls by parent company and company name.

Database Diagram

The database diagram that presents the tables and their relationships is shown in Figure 14-2.

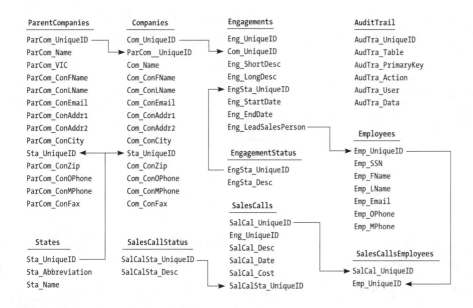

Figure 14-2. SEM Database diagram

Table and Column Descriptions

ParentCompanies—Holds information about a parent company. A parent company can be associated with one or more companies.

COLUMN	DATA TYPE	NULLS	DESCRIPTION
ParCom_UniqueID	smallint	No	Unique identifier (IDENTITY)
ParCom_Name	varchar(30)	No	Parent company name
ParCom_VIC	char(1)	No	Very important client (Y/N)
ParCom_ConFName	varchar(30)	No	Contact's first name
ParCom_ConLName	varchar(30)	No	Contact's last name
ParCom_ConEmail	varchar(30)	No	Contact's email address
ParCom_ConAddr1	varchar(30)	No	Address (line 1)
ParCom_ConAddr2	varchar(30)	Yes	Address (line 2)
ParCom_ConCity	varchar(30)	No	City
Sta_UniqueID	tinyint	Yes	State ID (FK with States)
ParCom_ConZip	varchar(15)	No	Zip code
ParCom_ConOPhone	char(10)	No	Contact's office phone number
ParCom_ConMPhone	char(10)	Yes	Contact's mobile phone number
ParCom_ConFax	char(10)	Yes	Contact's fax number

Companies—Holds information about a company. A company is associated with a parent company and has one or more associated sales engagements.

COLUMN	DATA TYPE	NULLS	DESCRIPTION
Com_UniqueID	smallint	No	Unique identifier (IDENTITY)
ParCom_UniqueID	smallint	No	Parent company ID (FK with ParentCompanies)
Com_Name	varchar(30)	No	Company name
Com_ConFName	varchar(30)	No	Contact's first name
Com_ConLName	varchar(30)	No	Contact's last name

COLUMN	DATA TYPE	NULLS	DESCRIPTION
Com_ConEmail	varchar(30)	No	Contact's email address
Com_ConAddr1	varchar(30)	No	Address (line 1)
Com_ConAddr2	varchar(30)	Yes	Address (line 2)
Com_ConCity	varchar(30)	No	City
Sta_UniqueID	tinyint	Yes	State ID (FK with States)
Com_ConZip	varchar(15)	No	Zip code
Com_ConOPhone	char(10)	No	Contact's office phone number
Com_ConMPhone	char(10)	Yes	Contact's mobile phone number
Com_ConFax	char(10)	Yes	Contact's fax number

Employees—Holds information about employees. An employee can be associated with one or more sales engagements as a lead salesperson. An employee can be associated with one or more sales calls as a participant. A limited number of fields are provided for this table.

COLUMN	DATA TYPE	NULLS	DESCRIPTION
Emp_UniqueID	smallint	No	Unique identifier (IDENTITY)
Emp_SSN	char(9)	No	Social Security number
Emp_FName	varchar(30)	No	Employee's first name
Emp_LName	varchar(30)	No	Employee's last name
Emp_Email	varchar(30)	No	Employee's email
Emp_OPhone	char(10)	No	Employee's office phone number
Emp_MPhone	char(10)	Yes	Employee's mobile phone number

Engagements—Holds information about a sales engagement, which relates a company to a sales effort. There is one or more engagements per company.

COLUMN	DATA TYPE	NULLS	DESCRIPTION
Eng_UniqueID	smallint	No	Unique identifier (IDENTITY)
Com_UniqueID	smallint	No	Company ID (FK with Companies)

COLUMN	DATA TYPE	NULLS	DESCRIPTION
Eng_ShortDesc	varchar(50)	No	Short description of engagement
Eng_LongDesc	varchar(500)	No	Long description of engagement
EngSta_UniqueID	tinyint	No	Engagement status ID (FK with EngagementStatus)
Eng_StartDate	smalldatetime	No	Engagement start date
Eng_EndDate	smalldatetime	Yes	Engagement end date

SalesCalls—Holds information about a sales call. There is one or more sales calls per engagement.

COLUMN	DATA TYPE	NULLS	DESCRIPTION
SalCal_UniqueID	int	No	Unique identifier (IDENTITY)
Eng_UniqueID	smalling	No	Engagement ID (FK with Engagements)
SalCal_Desc	varchar(100)	No	Sales call description
SalCal_Date	smalldatetime	No	Sales call date
SalCal_Cost	smallmoney	No	Sales cal cost
SalCalSta_UniqueID	tinyint	No	Sales call status ID (FK with SalesCallStatus)

SalesCallsEmployees—Relates a sales call with the employee(s) who participated in the call. There is one or more employees that participate in a sales call.

COLUMN	DATA TYPE	NULLS	DESCRIPTION
SalCal_UniqueID	int	No	Sales call ID (FK with SalesCall)
Emp_UniqueID	smallint	No	Employee ID

EngagementStatus—Holds the domain of engagement status values. The valid values are: Open, Closed—Success, and Closed—Failed.

COLUMN	DATA TYPE	NULLS	DESCRIPTION
EngSta_UniqueID	tinyint	No	Unique identifier (IDENTITY)
EngSta_Desc	varchar(30)	No	Status description

SalesCallStatus—Holds the domain of sales calls status values. The valid values are: Excellent, Good, Fair, and Poor.

COLUMN	DATA TYPE	NULLS	DESCRIPTION
SalCalSta_UniqueID	tinyint	No	Unique identifier (IDENTITY)
SalCalSta_Desc	varchar(30)	No	Status description

States—Holds the domain of states in parent companies and companies reside.

COLUMN	DATA TYPE	NULLS	DESCRIPTION
Sta_UniqueID	tinyint	No	Unique identifier (IDENTITY)
Sta_Abbreviation	char(2)	No	State's abbreviation
Sta_Name	varchar(20)	No	State's name

AuditTrail—Holds audit trail information about changes made to tables.

COLUMN	DATA TYPE	NULLS	DESCRIPTION
AudTra_UniqueID	int	No	Unique identifier (IDENTITY)
AudTra_Table	sysname	No	Table to which change was made
AudTra_UniqueID	smallint	No	Primary key of record to which change was made
AudTra_Action	varchar(10)	No	Type of change (e.g., INSERT, UPDATE)
AudTra_User	sysname	No	User who made change
AudTra_Date	smalldatetime	No	Date change was made

Schedule

The SEM application will be developed within one week of the signing of this specification.

Costs

The cost to develop SEM will be $1,500.

Changes to Original Scope of Work

All changes to this functional specification will be implemented as appendices to this document and must be signed by John Smith, Vice President of Leasing.

Signed: _____   **Signed:** _____

Date: _____   **Date:** _____

Garth Wells, *President,*   John Smith, *Vice President of Leasing,*
DataDrivenWebSites.com, Inc.   ClientCompany, Inc.

Database Code

In this section we will look at the SQL statements that create the database and database objects for the application. Because of the naming convention used, the purpose of most the objects will be intuitively obvious. For each non-lookup table shown in Figure 14-2 there is an associated set of stored procedures that a facilitate INSERT, UPDATE, DELETE, and SELECT actions. The lookup tables only require a SELECT procedure because they are populated at create-time and will not be changed with a frequency that justifies maintenance screens. There are also two SELECT procedures per non-lookup table. One returns all the rows in a table and the other returns a row based on unique ID. When applicable, a reference to where the procedure is called by the application is provided.

I have made no attempt to explain each and every line of code of the procedures and triggers used in SEM. Doing so would quadruple the length of the chapter and make it very long and tedious reading. Instead of spending all your time reading, I wrote this so you get a general understanding of the application and can spend the rest of the time working with the code.

To understand how the application works, you need to do three things:

- Have a fundamental understanding of the database design. Make sure you understand how each table is used and how it relates to the other tables in the database.

- Examine the stored procedures and make sure you can determine what each does based their names. For example, if the name of a procedure is **ps_Employees_INSERT**, the procedure creates new rows in the **Employees** table. If the name of a procedure is **ps_ParentCompanies_SELECT_ByUniqueID**, it retrieves a row from **ParentCompanies** based on the table's unique ID.

- Understand the naming convention of the .asp files and how that can be used to determine what procedures are used in a given page. For example, if the name of the file is SEM_EmpAdd.asp, it adds a row to the **Employees** table and uses **ps_Employees_INSERT** to complete the process. The file names and purpose of each .asp file is listed at the end of the chapter. Detailed explanation of the code in the .asp files is not provided. The code is very simple, and if you have worked through Appendices A and B you should be able to read them and quickly determine how they work.

Database

Use the following statements to create the database for the application. If you already have a database called **SEM** or use different drives to hold database files, please modify accordingly.

```
USE master
GO
CREATE DATABASE SEM
ON
(
 NAME = 'SEM_Data',
 FILENAME = ' c:\Program Files\Microsoft SQL Server\Mssql\Data\SEM.mdf',
 SIZE = 5MB,
 MAXSIZE = 20MB,
 FILEGROWTH = 2MB
)
LOG ON
(
 NAME = 'SEM_Log',
 FILENAME = ' c:\Program Files\Microsoft SQL Server\Mssql\DataSEM.ldf',
```

```
  SIZE = 5MB,
  MAXSIZE = 15MB,
  FILEGROWTH = 2MB
)
go

EXEC sp_dboption 'SEM', 'trunc. log on chkpt.', 'TRUE'
go
```

The database option configuration change is not required, but I usually set it to true during the development stage of a project. When truncate log on checkpoint is set to true, data modification statements are not permanently logged in the transaction log, which reduces server management duties.

Tables

In this section I have listed the statements that create the tables used to support the application. This design uses cascading deletes. Please see the **ParCom_UniqueID** column in **Companies** to see how they are implemented. The tables are listed in the same order as they appear in the Ch14.sql file. This order is necessary because FOREIGN KEY constraints are used. For example, the **States** table must be created before **ParentCompanies** because the unique ID of **States** is referenced in the CREATE TABLE statement for **ParentCompanies**. All tables are created in the **SEM** database.

States

```
CREATE TABLE States
(
 Sta_UniqueID tinyint IDENTITY PRIMARY KEY,
 Sta_Abbreviaton char(2) NOT NULL,
 Sta_Name varchar(15) NOT NULL
)
go
INSERT States VALUES ('CA','California')
INSERT States VALUES ('NY','New York')
INSERT States VALUES ('TX','Texas')
```

ParentCompanies

```
CREATE TABLE ParentCompanies
(
 ParCom_UniqueID  smallint IDENTITY PRIMARY KEY,
 ParCom_Name varchar(30) NOT NULL,
 ParCom_Vic char(1) NOT NULL CHECK (ParCom_Vic IN ('Y','N')),
 ParCom_ConFName varchar(30) NOT NULL,
 ParCom_ConLName varchar(30) NOT NULL,
 ParCom_ConEmail varchar(30) NOT NULL,
 ParCom_ConAddr1 varchar(30) NOT NULL,
 ParCom_ConAddr2 varchar(30) NULL,
 ParCom_ConCity varchar(30) NOT NULL,
 Sta_UniqueID tinyint NOT NULL FOREIGN KEY REFERENCES States(Sta_UniqueID),
 ParCom_ConZip varchar(15) NOT NULL,
 ParCom_ConOPhone char(10) NOT NULL,
 ParCom_ConMPhone char(10) NULL,
 ParCom_Fax char(10) NULL
)
```

Companies

```
CREATE TABLE Companies
(
 Com_UniqueID  smallint IDENTITY PRIMARY KEY,
 ParCom_UniqueID  smallint FOREIGN KEY REFERENCES ParentCompanies(ParCom_UniqueID)
ON DELETE CASCADE,
 Com_Name varchar(30) NOT NULL,
 Com_ConFName varchar(30) NOT NULL,
 Com_ConLName varchar(30) NOT NULL,
 Com_ConEmail varchar(30) NOT NULL,
 Com_ConAddr1 varchar(30) NOT NULL,
 Com_ConAddr2 varchar(30) NULL,
 Com_ConCity varchar(30) NOT NULL,
 Sta_UniqueID tinyint NOT NULL FOREIGN KEY REFERENCES States(Sta_UniqueID),
 Com_ConZip varchar(15) NOT NULL,
 Com_ConOPhone char(10) NOT NULL,
 Com_ConMPhone char(10) NULL,
 Com_Fax char(10) NULL
)
```

Employees

```
CREATE TABLE Employees
(
 Emp_UniqueID smallint IDENTITY PRIMARY KEY,
 Emp_SSN char(9) NOT NULL UNIQUE,
 Emp_FName varchar(30) NOT NULL,
 Emp_LName varchar(30) NOT NULL,
 Emp_Email varchar(30) NOT NULL,
 Emp_OPhone char(10) NOT NULL,
 Emp_MPhone char(10) NULL,
)
```

EngagementStatus

```
CREATE TABLE EngagementStatus
(
 EngSta_UniqueID tinyint IDENTITY PRIMARY KEY,
 EngSta_Desc varchar(30) NOT NULL
)
go
INSERT EngagementStatus VALUES ('Open')
INSERT EngagementStatus VALUES ('Closed - Success')
INSERT EngagementStatus VALUES ('Closde - Failure')
```

Engagements

```
CREATE TABLE Engagements
(
 Eng_UniqueID smallint IDENTITY PRIMARY KEY,
 Com_UniqueID smallint NOT NULL FOREIGN KEY REFERENCES Companies(Com_UniqueID) ON_
      DELETE CASCADE,
 Eng_ShortDesc varchar(50) NOT NULL,
 Eng_LongDesc varchar(500) NOT NULL,
 EngSta_UniqueID tinyint NOT NULL FOREIGN KEY REFERENCES_
EngagementStatus(EngSta_UniqueID),
 Eng_StartDate smalldatetime NOT NULL,
 Eng_EndDate smalldatetime NULL,
 Eng_LeadSalesPerson smallint NOT NULL FOREIGN KEY REFERENCES
Employees(Emp_UniqueID),
)
```

SalesCallStatus

```
CREATE TABLE SalesCallStatus
(
 SalCalSta_UniqueID tinyint IDENTITY PRIMARY KEY,
 SalCalSta_Desc varchar(30) NOT NULL
)
go
INSERT SalesCallStatus VALUES ('Excellent')
INSERT SalesCallStatus VALUES ('Good')
INSERT SalesCallStatus VALUES ('Fair')
INSERT SalesCallStatus VALUES ('Poor')
```

SalesCalls

```
CREATE TABLE SalesCalls
(
 SalCal_UniqueID smallint IDENTITY PRIMARY KEY,
 Eng_UniqueID smallint NOT NULL FOREIGN KEY REFERENCES Engagements (Eng_UniqueID)_
     ON DELETE CASCADE,
 SalCal_Desc varchar(100) NOT NULL,
 SalCal_Date smalldatetime NOT NULL,
 SalCal_Cost smallmoney NOT NULL,
 SalCalSta_UniqueID tinyint NOT NULL FOREIGN KEY REFERENCES
SalesCallStatus(SalCalSta_UniqueID),
)
```

SalesCallsEmployees

```
CREATE TABLE SalesCallsEmployees
(
 SalCal_UniqueID smallint NOT NULL FOREIGN KEY REFERENCES SalesCalls
(SalCal_UniqueID) ON DELETE CASCADE,
 Emp_UnqiueID smallint NOT NULL FOREIGN KEY REFERENCES Employees (Emp_UniqueID),
)
```

Stored Procedures

As expected, the stored procedures make up the bulk of the server-side code for the application. The procedures are categorized per table and comments are only provided where a particular procedure's purpose is not obvious. Comments are also provided when a procedure contains a complex code segment that requires explanation.

Before I start on the procedures let's look at how I implement edit functionality in a browser-based application. This will help you better understand why I used a particular type of procedure. When you invoke the application you will see options for adding and listing data, but none for editing. The ability to edit a record is provided after a list is displayed. For example, when a user lists the data for parent companies, only the columns that are required to uniquely identify a parent company are displayed. If the user wants to edit the data associated with a particular parent company, they click the left-most field, which activates an edit screen. The procedures that conform to the naming convention **ps_TableName_SELECT** display the lists. If this is not clear, please work with the application on http://www.SQLBook.com before continuing.

States

Name: ps_States_SELECT

Purpose: Retrieves all rows from **States**. Procedure is called from SEM_ParComAdd.asp and SEM_ComAdd.asp to populate the State list box.

```
CREATE PROCEDURE ps_States_SELECT
AS
SELECT Sta_UniqueID,
       Sta_Abbreviaton+' - '+Sta_Name AS State
FROM States
ORDER BY Sta_Abbreviaton
```

EngagementStatus

Name: ps_EngagementStatus_SELECT

Purpose: Retreives all rows from **EngagementStatus**. Procedure is called from SEM_EngAdd.asp and SEM_EngEdit.asp to populate Status list box.

```
CREATE PROCEDURE ps_EngagementStatus_SELECT
AS
SELECT EngSta_UniqueID,
       EngSta_Desc
FROM EngagementStatus
ORDER BY EngSta_Desc
```

SalesCallStatus

Name: ps_SalesCallStatus_SELECT

Purpose: Retrieves all rows from **SalesCallStatus**. Procedure is called from SEM_SalCalAdd.asp and SEM_SalCalEdit.asp to populate Status list box.

```
CREATE PROCEDURE ps_SalesCallStatus_SELECT
AS
SELECT SalCalSta_UniqueID,
       SalCalSta_Desc
FROM SalesCallStatus
ORDER BY SalCalSta_Desc
```

ParentCompanies

Name: ps_ParentCompanies_INSERT

Purpose: Creates a row in **ParentCompanies**. Procedure is called from SEM_ParComAddRespond.asp.

```
CREATE PROCEDURE ps_ParentCompanies_INSERT
@ParCom_Name varchar(30),
@ParCom_VIC char(1),
@ParCom_ConFName varchar(30),
@ParCom_ConLName varchar(30),
@ParCom_ConEmail varchar(30),
@ParCom_ConAddr1 varchar(30),
@ParCom_ConAddr2 varchar(30),
@ParCom_ConCity varchar(30),
@Sta_UniqueID tinyint,
@ParCom_ConZip varchar(15),
@ParCom_ConOPhone char(10),
@ParCom_ConMPhone char(10),
@ParCom_Fax char(10)
AS
INSERT ParentCompanies
(
 ParCom_Name,
 ParCom_VIC,
 ParCom_ConFName,
 ParCom_ConLName,
 ParCom_ConEmail,
```

```
ParCom_ConAddr1,
ParCom_ConAddr2,
ParCom_ConCity,
Sta_UniqueID,
ParCom_ConZip,
ParCom_ConOPhone,
ParCom_ConMPhone,
ParCom_Fax
)
VALUES
(
@ParCom_Name,
@ParCom_VIC,
@ParCom_ConFName,
@ParCom_ConLName,
@ParCom_ConEmail,
@ParCom_ConAddr1,
@ParCom_ConAddr2,
@ParCom_ConCity,
@Sta_UniqueID,
@ParCom_ConZip,
@ParCom_ConOPhone,
@ParCom_ConMPhone,
@ParCom_Fax
)
```

Name: ps_ParentCompanies_UPDATE

Purpose: Updates a row in **ParentCompanies**. Procedure is called from SEM_ParComEditRespond.asp.

```
CREATE PROCEDURE ps_ParentCompanies_UPDATE
@ParCom_UniqueID  smallint,
@ParCom_Name varchar(30),
@ParCom_VIC char(1),
@ParCom_ConFName varchar(30),
@ParCom_ConLName varchar(30),
@ParCom_ConEmail varchar(30),
@ParCom_ConAddr1 varchar(30),
@ParCom_ConAddr2 varchar(30),
@ParCom_ConCity varchar(30),
@Sta_UniqueID char(2),
@ParCom_ConZip varchar(15),
@ParCom_ConOPhone char(10),
```

```
@ParCom_ConMPhone char(10),
@ParCom_Fax char(10)
AS
UPDATE ParentCompanies
SET ParCom_Name = @ParCom_Name,
    ParCom_VIC = @ParCom_VIC,
    ParCom_ConFName = @ParCom_ConFName,
    ParCom_ConLName = @ParCom_ConLName,
    ParCom_ConEmail = @ParCom_ConEmail,
    ParCom_ConAddr1 = @ParCom_ConAddr1,
    ParCom_ConAddr2 = @ParCom_ConAddr2,
    ParCom_ConCity = @ParCom_ConCity,
    Sta_UniqueID = @Sta_UniqueID,
    ParCom_ConZip = @ParCom_ConZip,
    ParCom_ConOPhone = @ParCom_ConOPhone,
    ParCom_ConMPhone = @ParCom_ConMPhone,
    ParCom_Fax = @ParCom_Fax
WHERE ParCom_UniqueID = @ParCom_UniqueID
```

Name: ps_ParentCompanies_DELETE

Purpose: Deletes a row in **ParentCompanies**. Procedure is called from SEM_ParComEditRespond.asp.

```
CREATE PROCEDURE ps_DELETE_ParentCompanies
@ParCom_UniqueID  smallint
AS
DELETE ParentCompanies
WHERE ParCom_UniqueID = @ParCom_UniqueID
```

Name: ps_ParentCompanies_SELECT

Purpose: Retrieves all rows from **ParentCompanies**. Procedure is called from SEM_ParComList.asp.

```
CREATE PROCEDURE ps_ParentCompanies_SELECT
AS
SELECT ParCom_UniqueID
       ParCom_Name,
       ParCom_ConFName+' '+ParCom_ConLName AS ContactName,
       ParCom_ConEmail
FROM ParentCompanies
ORDER BY ParCom_Name
```

Name: ps_ParentCompanies_SELECT_ByUniqueID

Purpose: Retrieves a single row from **ParentCompanies**. Procedure is called from SEM_ParComEditRespond.asp.

```
CREATE PROCEDURE ps_ParentCompanies_SELECT_ByUniqueID
@ParCom_UniqueID smallint
AS
SELECT ParCom_UniqueID,
       ParCom_Name,
       ParCom_VIC,
       ParCom_ConFName,
       ParCom_ConLName,
       ParCom_ConEmail,
       ParCom_ConAddr1,
       ParCom_ConAddr2,
       ParCom_ConCity,
       Sta_UniqueID,
       ParCom_ConZip,
       ParCom_ConOPhone,
       ParCom_ConMPhone,
       ParCom_Fax
FROM ParentCompanies
WHERE ParCom_UniqueID = @ParCom_UniqueID
```

Companies

Name: ps_Companies_INSERT

Purpose: Create a row in **Companies**. Procedure is called from SEM_ComAddRespond.asp.

```
CREATE PROCEDURE ps_Companies_INSERT
@ParCom_UniqueID smallint,
@Com_Name varchar(30),
@Com_ConFName varchar(30),
@Com_ConLName varchar(30),
@Com_ConEmail varchar(30),
@Com_ConAddr1 varchar(30),
@Com_ConAddr2 varchar(30),
@Com_ConCity varchar(30),
@Sta_UniqueID char(2),
@Com_ConZip varchar(15),
```

```
@Com_ConOPhone char(10),
@Com_ConMPhone char(10),
@Com_Fax char(10)
AS
INSERT Companies
(
 ParCom_UniqueID,
 Com_Name,
 Com_ConFName,
 Com_ConLName,
 Com_ConEmail,
 Com_ConAddr1,
 Com_ConAddr2,
 Com_ConCity,
 Sta_UniqueID,
 Com_ConZip,
 Com_ConOPhone,
 Com_ConMPhone,
 Com_Fax
)
VALUES
(
 @ParCom_UniqueID,
 @Com_Name,
 @Com_ConFName,
 @Com_ConLName,
 @Com_ConEmail,
 @Com_ConAddr1,
 @Com_ConAddr2,
 @Com_ConCity,
 @Sta_UniqueID,
 @Com_ConZip,
 @Com_ConOPhone,
 @Com_ConMPhone,
 @Com_Fax
)
```

Name: ps_Companies_ UPDATE

Purpose: Updates a row in **Companies**. Procedure is called from SEM_ComEditRespond.asp.

```
CREATE PROCEDURE ps_Companies_UPDATE
@Com_UniqueID  smallint,
```

507

```
@ParCom_UniqueID smallint,
@Com_Name varchar(30),
@Com_ConFName varchar(30),
@Com_ConLName varchar(30),
@Com_ConEmail varchar(30),
@Com_ConAddr1 varchar(30),
@Com_ConAddr2 varchar(30),
@Com_ConCity varchar(30),
@Sta_UniqueID char(2),
@Com_ConZip varchar(15),
@Com_ConOPhone char(10),
@Com_ConMPhone char(10),
@Com_Fax char(10)
AS
UPDATE Companies
SET ParCom_UniqueID = @ParCom_UniqueID,
    Com_Name = @Com_Name,
    Com_ConFName = @Com_ConFName,
    Com_ConLName = @Com_ConLName,
    Com_ConEmail = @Com_ConEmail,
    Com_ConAddr1 = @Com_ConAddr1,
    Com_ConAddr2 = @Com_ConAddr2,
    Com_ConCity = @Com_ConCity,
    Sta_UniqueID = @Sta_UniqueID,
    Com_ConZip = @Com_ConZip,
    Com_ConOPhone = @Com_ConOPhone,
    Com_ConMPhone = @Com_ConMPhone,
    Com_Fax = @Com_Fax
WHERE Com_UniqueID = @Com_UniqueID
```

Name: ps_Companies_DELETE

Purpose: Deletes a row from **Companies**. Procedure is called from SEM_ComEditRespond.asp.

```
CREATE PROCEDURE ps_Companies_DELETE
@Com_UniqueID  smallint
AS
DELETE Companies
WHERE Com_UniqueID = @Com_UniqueID
```

Name: ps_Companies_SELECT

Purpose: Retrieves all rows from **Companies**. Procedure is called from SEM_ComList.asp.

```
CREATE PROCEDURE ps_Companies_SELECT
AS
SELECT b.ParCom_Name,
       a.Com_UniqueID,
       a.Com_Name,
       a.Com_ConFName+' '+a.Com_ConLName AS ContactName,
       a.Com_ConEmail
FROM Companies a
JOIN ParentCompanies b ON a.ParCom_UniqueID = b.ParCom_UniqueID
ORDER BY b.ParCom_Name, a.Com_Name
go
```

Name: ps_Companies_SELECT_ByUniqueID

Purpose: Retrieves a single row from **Companies**. Procedure is called from SEM_ComEditRespond.asp.

```
CREATE PROCEDURE ps_Companies_SELECT_ByUniqueID
@Com_UniqueID smallint
AS
SELECT Com_UniqueID,
       ParCom_UniqueID,
       Com_Name,
       Com_ConFName,
       Com_ConLName,
       Com_ConEmail,
       Com_ConAddr1,
       Com_ConAddr2,
       Com_ConCity,
       Sta_UniqueID,
       Com_ConZip,
       Com_ConOPhone,
       Com_ConMPhone,
       Com_Fax
FROM Companies
WHERE Com_UniqueID = @Com_UniqueID
```

Employees

Name: ps_Employees_INSERT

Purpose: Creates a row in **Employees**. Procedure is called from SEM_EmpAddRespond.asp.

```
CREATE PROCEDURE ps_Employees_INSERT
@Emp_SSN char(9),
@Emp_FName varchar(30),
@Emp_LName varchar(50),
@Emp_Email varchar(30),
@Emp_OPhone char(10),
@Emp_MPhone char(10)
AS
INSERT Employees
(
 Emp_SSN,
 Emp_FName,
 Emp_LName,
 Emp_Email,
 Emp_OPhone,
 Emp_MPhone
)
VALUES
(
 @Emp_SSN,
 @Emp_FName,
 @Emp_LName,
 @Emp_Email,
 @Emp_OPhone,
 @Emp_MPhone
)
```

Name: ps_Employees_UPDATE

Purpose: Updates a row in **Employees**. Procedure is called from SEM_EmpEditRespond.asp.

```
CREATE PROCEDURE ps_Employees_UPDATE
@Emp_UniqueID smallint,
@Emp_SSN char(9),
@Emp_FName varchar(30),
@Emp_LName varchar(50),
```

```
@Emp_Email varchar(30),
@Emp_OPhone char(10),
@Emp_MPhone char(10)
AS
UPDATE Employees
SET Emp_SSN = @Emp_SSN,
    Emp_FName = @Emp_FName,
    Emp_LName = @Emp_LName,
    Emp_Email = @Emp_Email,
    Emp_OPhone = @Emp_OPhone,
    Emp_MPhone = @Emp_MPhone
WHERE Emp_UniqueID = @Emp_UniqueID
```

Name: ps_Employees_DELETE

Purpose: Deletes a row in **Employees**. Procedure is called from SEM_EmpEditRespond.asp.

```
CREATE PROCEDURE ps_Employees_DELETE
@Emp_UniqueID smallint
AS
DELETE Employees
WHERE Emp_UniqueID = @Emp_UniqueID
```

Name: ps_Employees_SELECT

Purpose: Retrieves all rows from **Employees**. Procedure is called from SEM_EmpList.asp.

```
CREATE PROCEDURE ps_Employees_SELECT
AS
SELECT Emp_UniqueID,
       Emp_SSN,
       Emp_FName+' '+Emp_LName AS EmpName,
       Emp_Email,
       Emp_OPhone,
       Emp_MPhone
FROM Employees
ORDER BY Emp_LName
```

Name: ps_Employees_ SELECT_ByUniqueID

Purpose: Retrieves a single row from **Employees**. Procedure is called from SEM_EmpEditRespond.asp.

```
CREATE PROCEDURE ps_Employees_SELECT_ByUniqueID
@Emp_UniqueID smallint
AS
SELECT Emp_UniqueID,
        Emp_SSN,
        Emp_FName+' '+Emp_LName AS EmpName,
        Emp_Email,
        Emp_OPhone,
        Emp_MPhone
FROM Employees
WHERE Emp_UniqueID = @Emp_UniqueID
```

Engagements

Name: ps_Engagements_INSERT

Purpose: Creates a row in **Engagements**. Procedure is called from SEM_EngAddRespond.asp.

```
CREATE PROCEDURE ps_Engagements_INSERT
@Com_UniqueID smallint,
@Eng_ShortDesc varchar(50),
@Eng_LongDesc varchar(500),
@EngSta_UniqueID tinyint,
@Eng_StartDate smalldatetime,
@Eng_EndDate smalldatetime,
@Eng_LeadSalesPerson smallint
AS
INSERT Engagements
(
 Com_UniqueID,
 Eng_ShortDesc,
 Eng_LongDesc,
 EngSta_UniqueID,
 Eng_StartDate,
 Eng_EndDate,
 Eng_LeadSalesPerson
)
```

```
VALUES
(
 @Com_UniqueID,
 @Eng_ShortDesc,
 @Eng_LongDesc,
 @EngSta_UniqueID,
 @Eng_StartDate,
 @Eng_EndDate,
 @Eng_LeadSalesPerson
)
```

Name: ps_Engagements_UPDATE

Purpose: Updates a row in **Engagements**. Procedure is called from
SEM_EngEditRespond.asp.

```
CREATE PROCEDURE ps_Engagements_UPDATE
@Eng_UniqueID smallint,
@Com_UniqueID smallint,
@Eng_ShortDesc varchar(50),
@Eng_LongDesc varchar(500),
@EngSta_UniqueID tinyint,
@Eng_StartDate smalldatetime,
@Eng_EndDate smalldatetime,
@Eng_LeadSalesPerson int
AS
UPDATE Engagements
SET Com_UniqueID = @Com_UniqueID,
    Eng_ShortDesc = @Eng_ShortDesc,
    Eng_LongDesc = @Eng_LongDesc,
    EngSta_UniqueID = @EngSta_UniqueID,
    Eng_StartDate = @Eng_StartDate,
    Eng_EndDate = @Eng_EndDate,
    Eng_LeadSalesPerson = @Eng_LeadSalesPerson
WHERE Eng_UniqueID = @Eng_UniqueID
```

Name: ps_Engagements_DELETE

Purpose: Deletes a row from **Engagements**. Procedure is called from
SEM_EngEditRespond.asp.

```
CREATE PROCEDURE ps_Engagements_DELETE
@Eng_UniqueID smallint
AS
```

```
DELETE Engagements
WHERE Eng_UniqueID = @Eng_UniqueID
```

Name: ps_Engagements_SELECT

Purpose: Retrieves all rows from **Engagements**. Procedure is called from SEM_EngList.asp.

```
CREATE PROCEDURE ps_Engagements_SELECT
AS
SELECT a.Eng_UniqueID,
       b.Com_Name,
       a.Eng_ShortDesc,
       a.Eng_LongDesc,
       a.EngSta_UniqueID,
       a.Eng_StartDate,
       a.Eng_EndDate,
       a.Eng_LeadSalesPerson
FROM Engagements a
JOIN Companies b ON a.Com_UniqueID = b.Com_UniqueID
ORDER BY b.Com_Name,
         a.Eng_ShortDesc
```

Name: ps_Engagements_SELECT_ByUniqueID

Purpose: Retrieves a single row from **Engagements**. Procedure is called from SEM_EngEditRespond.asp.

```
CREATE PROCEDURE ps_Engagements_SELECT_ByUniqueID
@Eng_UniqueID smallint
AS
SELECT Eng_UniqueID,
       Com_UniqueID,
       Eng_ShortDesc,
       Eng_LongDesc,
       EngSta_UniqueID,
       Eng_StartDate,
       Eng_EndDate,
       Eng_LeadSalesPerson
FROM Engagements
WHERE Eng_UniqueID = @Eng_UniqueID
```

SalesCalls

Name: ps_SalesCalls_INSERT

Purpose: Creates a row in **SalesCalls** and one or more rows in
SalesCallsEmployees. Procedure is called from SEM_SalCalAddRespond.asp.

```
CREATE PROCEDURE ps_SalesCalls_INSERT
@Eng_UniqueID smallint,
@SalCal_Desc varchar(100),
@SalCal_Date smalldatetime,
@SalCal_Cost smallmoney,
@SalCalSta_UniqueID tinyint,
@EmployeeList varchar(100)
AS

--Wrap INSERTs in TRANSACTION
BEGIN TRANSACTION

 --Part I
 INSERT SalesCalls
 (
  Eng_UniqueID,
  SalCal_Desc,
  SalCal_Date,
  SalCal_Cost,
  SalCalSta_UniqueID
 )
 VALUES
 (
  @Eng_UniqueID,
  @SalCal_Desc,
  @SalCal_Date,
  @SalCal_Cost,
  @SalCalSta_UniqueID
 )
IF @@ERROR <> 0
 GOTO ErrorHandler

 --Part II
 DECLARE @UniqueID smallint,
         @CurVal smallint

 --Get the primary key of the row inserted into SalesCalls
```

```
SET @UniqueID = @@IDENTITY

--Append a comma to the end of @EmployeeList to ease
--processing of the string
SET @EmployeeList = @EmployeeList+','

--Start the looping operation
WHILE CHARINDEX(',',@EmployeeList) > 0
 BEGIN
  SET @CurVal =_
CONVERT(smallint,SUBSTRING(@EmployeeList,1,CHARINDEX(',',@EmployeeList)-1))
   --Add current row to SalesCallsEmployees
   INSERT SalesCallsEmployees VALUES (@UniqueID,@CurVal)
   IF @@ERROR <> 0
    GOTO ErrorHandler

   SET @EmployeeList =_
SUBSTRING(@EmployeeList,CHARINDEX(',',@EmployeeList)+1,DATALENGTH(@EmployeeList))
  END

COMMIT TRANSACTION

ErrorHandler:
IF @@TRANCOUNT > 0
 ROLLBACK TRAN
RETURN
```

This is the first complicated procedure listed in this section. It populates both the **SalesCalls** and **SalesCallsEmployees** tables and uses the parsing technique introduced in Chapter 13, "Example 2: Parsing a Comma Separated List." If you did not study that example, please do so before continuing.

Part I of the procedure takes the base sales call information and creates a row in **SalesCalls**. Part II takes the comma-delimited string that holds the unique identifiers for the employees who participated in the sales call and parses and inserts them into **SalesCallsEmployees**. The comma-delimited string is generated by the multi-select list box used on the Sales Call Data Entry screens.

Note that both Part I and II are *wrapped* in a TRANSACTION to avoid a partial update. After the first INSERT completes, @@ERROR is checked to make sure no errors occur. The second INSERT is checked for every trip through the WHILE loop. If an error occurs after an INSERT, processing is transferred to ErrorHandler:, a ROLLBACK is issued, and control is returned to the calling application. This ensures that all pieces of the transaction are completed successfully or not at all.

Name: ps_SalesCalls_UPDATE

Purpose: Updates a row in **SalesCalls** and inserts one or more rows in
SalesCallsEmployees. Procedure is called from SEM_SalCalEditRespond.asp

```
CREATE PROCEDURE ps_SalesCalls_UPDATE
@SalCal_UniqueID smallint,
@Eng_UniqueID smallint,
@SalCal_Desc varchar(100),
@SalCal_Date smalldatetime,
@SalCal_Cost smallmoney,
@SalCalSta_UniqueID tinyint,
@EmployeeList varchar(100)
AS


--Wrap INSERTs in TRANSACTION
BEGIN TRANSACTION

 --Part I
 UPDATE SalesCalls
 SET Eng_UniqueID = @Eng_UniqueID,
     SalCal_Desc = @SalCal_Desc,
     SalCal_Date = @SalCal_Date,
     SalCal_Cost = @SalCal_Cost,
     SalCalSta_UniqueID = @SalCalSta_UniqueID
 WHERE SalCal_UniqueID = @SalCal_UniqueID
 IF @@ERROR <> 0
  GOTO ErrorHandler

 --Part II
 DECLARE @UniqueID int,
         @CurVal smallint

 --Get the primary key of the row inserted into SalesCallsEmployees
 SELECT @UniqueID = @SalCal_UniqueID

 --Remove existing records (easier to process with this approach)
 DELETE SalesCallsEmployees
 WHERE SalCal_UniqueID = @SalCal_UniqueID
 IF @@ERROR <> 0
  GOTO ErrorHandler

 --Append a comma to the end of @EmployeeList to ease
 --the processing of the string
```

```
SET @EmployeeList = @EmployeeList+','

--Start the looping operation
WHILE CHARINDEX(',',@EmployeeList) > 0
 BEGIN
  SET @CurVal =_
CONVERT(smallint,SUBSTRING(@EmployeeList,1,CHARINDEX(',',@EmployeeList)-1))
   --Add current row to SalesCallsEmployees
   INSERT SalesCallsEmployees VALUES (@UniqueID,@CurVal)
    IF @@ERROR <> 0
     GOTO ErrorHandler

  SET @EmployeeList =_
SUBSTRING(@EmployeeList,CHARINDEX(',',@EmployeeList)+1,DATALENGTH(@EmployeeList))
  END
COMMIT TRANSACTION

ErrorHandler:
IF @@TRANCOUNT > 0
 ROLLBACK TRAN
RETURN
```

This procedure is very similar to the previous one, but notice that a new section in Part II deletes the existing entries in **SalesCallsEmployees** for the specified sales call. Deleting the existing entries and re-adding the current employees is much easier than trying to determine which ones were de-selected or newly selected. If you are having a hard time picturing how this works, access the Sales Call Edit screen and look at the Employees multi-select box. If the DELETE/INSERT approach is not used, you are required to determine which employee(s) were added to the sales call and which employee(s) were removed.

Name: ps_SalesCalls_DELETE

Purpose: Deletes a row from **SalesCalls** and one or more rows from **SalesCallsEmployees**. Procedure is called from SEM_SalCalEditRespond.asp.

```
CREATE PROCEDURE ps_SalesCalls_DELETE
@SalCal_UniqueID smallint
AS
DELETE SalesCalls
WHERE SalCal_UniqueID = @SalCal_UniqueID
```

Please note that DELETE only needs to be executed on **SalesCalls** because a cascading delete was implemented on the FOREIGN KEY constraint from

SalesCallsEmployees. All associated rows in **SalesCallsEmployees** are automatically deleted when their parent row in **SalesCalls** is deleted.

Name: ps_SalesCalls_SELECT

Purpose: Retrieves all rows from **SalesCalls**. Procedure is called from SEM_SalCalList.asp.

```
CREATE PROCEDURE ps_SalesCalls_SELECT
AS
SELECT c.Com_Name,
       a.SalCal_Desc,
       a.SalCal_UniqueID
FROM SalesCalls a
JOIN Engagements b ON a.Eng_UniqueID = b.Eng_UniqueID
JOIN Companies c ON b.Com_UniqueID = c.Com_UniqueID
ORDER BY c.Com_Name,
         a.SalCal_Desc
```

Name: ps_SalesCalls_SELECT_ByUniqueID

Purpose: Procedure is called from SEM_.asp.

```
CREATE PROCEDURE ps_SalesCalls_SELECT_ByUniqueID
@SalCal_UniqueID smallint
AS
SELECT SalCal_UniqueID,
       Eng_UniqueID,
       SalCal_Desc,
       SalCal_Date,
       SalCal_Cost,
       SalCalSta_UniqueID
FROM SalesCalls
WHERE SalCal_UniqueID = @SalCal_UniqueID
```

Triggers

Triggers are used to implement two types of features in this application: email notification and audit trail tracking. Both features are described here.

Email Notification

The specification requires that an email be sent to the Vice President of Leasing when a sales engagement is added for a company that has been designated as a VIC (very important client). A parent company whose **ParCom_VIC** column is "Y" is a VIC. The triggers use this column to determine when an email is sent.

Two triggers are needed to implement the email notification functionality. Please note that in these examples the email sending code (e.g., **xp_sendmail**) is commented out and replaced with INSERT statements. This is done because many of you will not have environments that support email (e.g., your personal home computers), and the INSERT statements will allow you to verify the trigger code is working as expected. If your environment does support email, simply remove the comment marks and modify the email address accordingly. Configuring SQL Server to support **xp_sendmail** was covered in the Before You Get Started section in Chapter 10.

The structure of the temporary table used to prove the triggers are working as expected is shown here. It allows us to capture the name of the company, the type of activity (engagement or sales call), and the description for the activity.

```
CREATE TABLE EmailNotification
(
 EmaNot_UniqueID smallint IDENTITY PRIMARY KEY,
 EmaNot_Company  varchar(30),
 EmaNot_Activity varchar(20) NOT NULL,
 EmaNot_Description varchar(100) NOT NULL
)
```

Engagements

The first trigger is added to **SalesEngagements** table and is shown here.

```
SET QUOTED_IDENTIFIER OFF
go
CREATE TRIGGER tr_Engagements_EmailNotification
ON Engagements
FOR INSERT
AS

--Part I: Check ParentCompanies for email notification
IF (SELECT a.ParCom_VIC
    FROM ParentCompanies a
    JOIN Companies b ON a.ParCom_UniqueID = b.Com_UniqueID
    JOIN inserted c ON b.Com_UniqueID = c.Com_UniqueID) = 'Y'
```

```
BEGIN
 --Create variables
 DECLARE @Company varchar(30),
         @Description varchar(100),
         @Message varchar(300),
         @SQL varchar(200)


 --Part II: Get the company name
 SELECT @Company = a.Com_Name
 FROM Companies a
 JOIN inserted b ON  a.Com_UniqueID = b.Com_UniqueID


 --Part III: Get the engagement description
 SELECT @Description = Eng_ShortDesc
 FROM inserted


 --Part IV: Complete the message portion of the email
 --SET @Message = 'A Sales Enagement was just added for '+ @Company + '.' + _
      CHAR(13)
 --SET @Message =  @Message + 'The description of the enagement is as follows: _
      '+@Description


 --Part V: Build valid xp_ call
 --SET @SQL =          "master..xp_sendmail "
 --SET @SQL = @SQL + "@recipients='garth@SQLBook.com',"
 --SET @SQL = @SQL + "@subject='Sales Engagement Added'"+","
 --SET @SQL = @SQL + "@message='"+@Message+"'"
 --EXEC (@SQL)


 --Part VI: Insert row
 INSERT EmailNotification
 (
  EmaNot_Company,
  EmaNot_Activity,
  EmaNot_Description
 )
 VALUES
 (
  @Company,
  'Sales Engagement',
  @Description
 )
END
```

The first thing to notice is that SET QUOTED_IDENTIFIER OFF is required to create the trigger because double-quotes are used to build the valid **xp_sendmail** call in Part IV. It's not really needed for this particular version of the trigger because Part IV is commented out, but when the comment marks are removed for Part IV, it is required.

Part I of the code joins the **ParentCompanies**, **Companies**, and **inserted** tables to determine if the company is marked as a VIC. When the IF evaluates to true, all the code between the BEGIN…END is executed.

Part II of the code uses an INNER JOIN with the **Companies** table to populate **@Company** with the name of the company for whom the engagement is created. Part III populates **@Description** with the engagement's short description held in the **inserted** table. Parts II and III could have been combined, but they were shown separately so the code would be easier to understand.

Part IV, commented out in this example, shows how to build the body of the email message from hard-coded text and the **@Company** and **@Description** variables. Notice that the CHAR() function inserts a carriage return so the body of the message is formatted. You can use any number of CHAR()s to format the message as desired. Part V builds a valid **xp_sendmail** call with hard-code email address and subject and the **@Message** variable. Be sure to modify the email address per your environment when you implement the code.

Part VI inserts a row in **EmailNotification** to demonstrate that the trigger works as expected. After you insert a row into **SalesEnagements**, check the table to make sure a row is created in **EmailNotification**. Make sure the company for whom the engagement was entered is marked for email notification.

SalesCalls

The next trigger is added to the **SalesCalls** table and is shown here.

```
SET QUOTED_IDENTIFIER OFF
go
CREATE TRIGGER tr_SalesCalls_EmailNotification
ON SalesCalls
FOR INSERT
AS

--Part I: Check company for email notification
IF (SELECT a.ParCom_VIC
    FROM ParentCompanies a
    JOIN Companies b ON a.ParCom_UniqueID = b.ParCom_UniqueID
    JOIN Engagements c ON b.Com_UniqueID = c.Com_UniqueID
    JOIN inserted d ON c.Eng_UniqueID = d.Eng_UniqueID) = 'Y'
```

```
BEGIN
  --Create variables
  DECLARE @Company varchar(30),
          @Description varchar(100),
          @Message varchar(300),
          @SQL varchar(200)

  --Part II: Get the company name
  SELECT @Company = a.Com_Name
  FROM Companies a
  JOIN Engagements b ON a.Com_UniqueID = b.Com_UniqueID
  JOIN inserted c ON b.Eng_UniqueID = c.Eng_UniqueID

  --Part III: Get the call's description
  SELECT @Description = SalCal_Desc
  FROM inserted

  --Part IV: Complete the message portion of the email
  --SET @Message = 'A Sales Call was just added for '+ @Company + '.' + CHAR(13)
  --SET @Message =  @Message + 'The description of the call is as follows:
'+@Description

  --Part V: Build valid xp_ call
  --SET @SQL =          "master..xp_sendmail "
  --SET @SQL = @SQL + "@recipients='john@rec.com',"
  --SET @SQL = @SQL + "@subject='Sales Call Added'"+","
  --SET @SQL = @SQL + "@message='"+@Message+"'"
  --EXEC (@SQL)

  --Part VI: Insert row
  INSERT EmailNotification
  (
   EmaNot_Company,
   EmaNot_Activity,
   EmaNot_Description
  )
  VALUES
  (
   @Company,
   'Sales Call',
   @Description
  )
END
```

This trigger is very similar to the one added to **Engagements;** the only major change is that an additional table is added both Parts I and II to get *back* to the **ParentCompanies** table. Insert a row into **SalesCalls** and then check **EmailNotification** to ensure it works as expected.

Audit Trail Tracking

Implementing audit trial capabilities will allow an application's owner to see who is making changes to the data in a database. This section demonstrates how triggers can track the user who changed the data in a particular table. The following example shows how to implement an audit trail tracking on the **Employees** table. The same technique can be used to implement audit trail tracking on any table in the database.

The structure of the table used to hold the audit trail data is shown here.

```
CREATE TABLE AuditTrail
(
AudTra_UniqueID int IDENTITY PRIMARY KEY,
AudTra_Table sysname NOT NULL,
AudTra_PrimaryKey smallint NOT NULL,
AudTra_Action varchar(10) NOT NULL,
AudTra_User sysname NOT NULL,
AudTra_Date smalldatetime NOT NULL DEFAULT GETDATE()
)
```

The **AuditTrail** table holds the table name, the unique ID of the affected row, the action performed (INSERT, UPDATE, or DELETE), the user name of the person who performed the action, and the date/time the action was performed.

INSERT Trigger

The INSERT trigger on **Employees** is shown here.

```
CREATE TRIGGER tr_Employees_InsertAuditTrail
ON Employees
FOR INSERT
AS
INSERT AuditTrail
(
AudTra_Table,
AudTra_ PrimaryKey,
AudTra_Action,
```

```
 AudTra_User
)
VALUES
(
 'Employees',
 @@IDENTITY,
 'INSERT',
 USER
)
```

When a row is inserted into **Employees**, two hard-coded values (the table name and action) are used in conjunction with two functions (@@IDENTITY and USER) to create a row in **AuditTrail**. We have used the @@IDENTITY function throughout this book, but many of you may not be familiar with the USER function. It simply returns the user name associated with the login that is performing the action.

The following statements demonstrate the trigger works as expected.

```
INSERT Employees
(
 Emp_SSN,
 Emp_FName,
 Emp_LName,
 Emp_Email,
 Emp_OPhone
)
VALUES
(
 '452112323',
 'Craig',
 'Biggio',
 'craig@rec.com',
 '5553331210'
)
go
SELECT AudTra_Table,
       AudTra_PrimaryKey,
       AudTra_Action,
       AudTra_User,
       AudTra_Date
FROM AuditTrail
--Results--
```

AudTra_Table	AudTra_PrimaryKey	AudTra_Action	AudTra_User	AudTra_Date
Employees	5	INSERT	dbo	2000-09-04 03:59:00

UPDATE and DELETE Trigger

One trigger can handle both UPDATEs and DELETEs because of the way these actions affect the **deleted** and **inserted** tables. When an UPDATE is performed, the **deleted** table holds the pre-updated version of the row and the **inserted** table holds the *new* values. A column does not actually have to be updated to be placed in the **inserted** table, so be assured it holds all the values for the columns in a row. When a DELETE is performed, the deleted row is placed in the **deleted** table, but no record is created in **inserted**. Knowing this, we can use logic to determine which action was performed.

The following shows the trigger used to capture both UPDATEs and DELETEs.

```
CREATE TRIGGER tr_Employees_UpdateDeleteAuditTrail
ON Employees
FOR UPDATE, DELETE
AS
--Determine of UPDATE or DELETE was executed
DECLARE @Action varchar(20)
IF EXISTS  (SELECT * FROM inserted)
 SET @Action = 'UPDATE'
ELSE
 SET @Action = 'DELETE'


INSERT AuditTrail
(
 AudTra_Table,
 AudTra_PrimaryKey,
 AudTra_Action,
 AudTra_User
)
SELECT 'Employees',
       Emp_UniqueID,
       @Action,
       USER
FROM deleted
```

The trigger is very similar to the previous one except the segment shown in bold determines whether the action performed was an UPDATE or a DELETE. The following examples show the trigger works as expected.

Example 1

```
UPDATE Employees
SET Emp_FName = 'Bill'
WHERE Emp_UniqueID = 5
go
SELECT AudTra_Table,
       AudTra_PrimaryKey,
       AudTra_Action,
       AudTra_User,
       AudTra_Date
FROM AuditTrail
--Results--
```

AudTra_Table	AudTra_PrimaryKey	AudTra_Action	AudTra_User	AudTra_Date
Employees	5	INSERT	dbo	2000-09-04 03:59:00
Employees	5	UPDATE	dbo	2000-09-04 04:05:00

Example 2

```
DELETE Employees
WHERE Emp_UniqueID = 5

SELECT AudTra_Table,
       AudTra_PrimaryKey,
       AudTra_Action,
       AudTra_User,
       AudTra_Date
FROM AuditTrail
--Results--
```

AudTra_Table	AudTra_PrimaryKey	AudTra_Action	AudTra_User	AudTra_Date
Employees	5	INSERT	dbo	2000-09-04 03:59:00
Employees	5	UPDATE	dbo	2000-09-04 04:05:00
Employees	5	DELETE	dbo	2000-09-04 04:06:00

> **TIP Members of sysadmin Are Shown as dbo**
>
> *When a user is a member of the fixed-server role* **sysadmin**, *the USER function returns* **dbo** *for the user's name. This does not get the actual user name associated with the login, but any member of* **sysadmin** *should be trusted to make changes with the database.*

ASP File List

In the final section we will look at the .asp files that create the application front-end. Before I get to the list, though, I want to cover the naming convention I use for .asp files. I like to group all the files used in an application by starting the file names with an application prefix. An application prefix allows me to quickly identify all the files that belong to an application. This can be very handy if you are not allowed to place the application in its own subdirectory. I use "SEM" to abbreviate this application so all the files will begin with a "SEM_" prefix.

The next part of the name is an abbreviation of the table the file acts on. For example, all the files that act on the **Employee** table start with "SEM_Emp." The next segment of the name is the action the file performs (e.g., Add or Edit). The two files used to add a new employee are named SEM_EmpAdd.asp and SEM_EmpAddRespond.asp.

Two files are used to add a row to **Employees** because the form code is separate from the database modification code. The form code gathers the information from the user and the data modification code makes the call to the database. You are not required to separate the code into two files, but I have done it here to increase readability. This approach is also used in Appendix B, so if you need a quick review of how it works, take a look there.

Table 14-1. ASP Files

FILE NAME	DESCRIPTION
SEM_ParComAdd.asp	Gathers initial information on a parent company.
SEM_ParComAddRespond.asp	Inserts parent company data into table.
SEM_ParComEdit.asp	Displays existing parent company data to be changed.
SEM_ParComEditRespond.asp	Updates existing parent company data.
SEM_ParComList.asp	Lists all parent company data.

Table 14-1. ASP Files (Continued)

FILE NAME	DESCRIPTION
SEM_ComAdd.asp	Gathers initial information on a company.
SEM_ComAddRespond.asp	Inserts company data into table.
SEM_ComEdit.asp	Displays existing company data to be changed.
SEM_ComEditRespond.asp	Updates existing company data.
SEM_ComList.asp	Lists all company data.
SEM_EmpAdd.asp	Gathers initial information on an employee.
SEM_EmpAddRespond.asp	Inserts employee data into table.
SEM_EmpEdit.asp	Displays existing employee data to be changed.
SEM_EmpEditRespond.asp	Updates existing employee data.
SEM_EmpList.asp	Lists all employee data.
SEM_EngAdd.asp	Gathers initial information on an engagement.
SEM_EngAddRespond.asp	Inserts engagement data into table.
SEM_EngEdit.asp	Displays existing engagement data to be changed.
SEM_EngEditRespond.asp	Updates existing engagement data.
SEM_EngList.asp	Lists all engagement data.
SEM_SalCalAdd.asp	Gathers initial information on a sales call.
SEM_SalCalAddRespond.asp	Inserts sales call data into table.
SEM_SalCalEdit.asp	Displays existing sales call data to be changed.
SEM_SalCalEditRespond.asp	Updates existing sales call data.
SEM_SalCalList.asp	Lists all sales call data.
SEM_EngByComList.asp	Lists engagements by company.
SEM_AudTraList.asp	Lists all audit trail data.

Before You Go

In this chapter I presented the specifications and SQL statements needed to create a database application to support sales effort management. The application supports simple INSERT, UPDATE, and DELETE functionality as well as event-based email notification and audit trail functionality. The files needed to implement the application's front-end are listed and provided in the chapter's sample file.

APPENDIX A

HTML Primer

THIS PRIMARY PURPOSE OF THIS PRIMER IS TO teach you just enough HTML (Hypertext Markup Language) so you can understand the examples presented in Chapters 13 and 14. The material presented here is by no means an exhaustive coverage of the topic, so make sure you find additional resources if you are going to work with HTML on a regular basis. The basics of file access via the Internet are also covered along with the processes required to manage a remote Web site. The last section covers resources available on the Internet that you can use to further your knowledge of the topics presented in this appendix.

> **TIP Sample Code**
>
> *The sample code for this appendix can be downloaded at either* `http://www.apress.com` *or* `http://www.SQLBook.com`. *Download and extract CodeCentric.zip and then extract App_A.zip, which contains the .html files referenced in this appendix.*

Before You Get Started

There are two topics I want to cover before you start learning the basics of HTML. You do not need to understand either topic in order to use HTML to create a Web page, but they should give you a better idea of how the Internet works. The first topic concerns understanding how Web pages are accessed and rendered across the Internet and the second focuses on maintaining a remote Web site.

Accessing Web Sites

Two topics need to be covered so you can better understand what happens when you access a Web site. The first concerns the steps that are completed to transfer a target page from the Web site to your computer, and the second covers the stateless nature of the Internet.

Site Connection and File Transfer Steps

Most of you have probably been using the Internet for a while now and are adept at finding the information you need to fulfill your job requirements or satisfy your intellectual curiosity (e.g., obtaining stock quotes or the latest score on a sporting event). When you access a Web site with a base URL (e.g., `http://www.SQLBook.com`), several steps are completed before the target page is displayed on your computer.

Before we look at those steps, let's review how a proxy and DNS server faciliate the Internet connectivity. Understanding how they work should make the steps a little easier to follow.

A proxy server is used for two purposes:

- to restrict access to a company's internal network

- to increase Web site access speed by caching Web pages

A proxy server restricts access to a company's internal network because all *outside* requests are made via the proxy server—there is no direct access to an internal network. The proxy server limits what computers the outside world can see, and thus, limits the ability to gain access to a computer that contains confidential information.

A proxy server can also reduce Web site access speed because it caches pages accessed by users. If multiple users access the same pages on a particular site, all users after the first one get the pages that are located in the proxy server's cache, not from the actual Web site. This can save a tremendous amount of time, especially if the target Web site is located across the country and is a high-traffic site.

A DNS (Domain Name Service) server is used to correlate a URL to an IP address (e.g., `http://www.SQLBook.com` = 216.25.61.222). Your ISP (Internet Service Provider) maintains at least two DNS servers to fulfill the lookup process. Regardless of whether you are an individual working from home or an employee of a major corporation in a high-rise building, you use an ISP to connect to the Internet. The DNS servers used by your ISP have records that correlate a URL to the physical IP address that is used to locate the target Web server. When a URL cannot be found on your ISP's DNS servers, the request is forwarded to an authority DNS server, which is maintained by one of the main providers (e.g., AT&T or UUNet) of Internet access. The servers maintained by the main providers are called *root servers* and are updated by InterNIC with all new primary domain names. InterNIC is the entity responsible for administering domain names, and you can learn more about them by visiting `http://rs.internic.net/faq.html`. Once the URL/IP address data is found it is used to access the target Web site.

Now that you have a general understanding of what these two servers do, let's move on to the steps required to access a Web site. In general, the following occurs after you type the URL into the address bar of your browser:

1. The Web browser first checks to see whether or not it connects to the Internet via a proxy server.

2a. When it connects via a proxy server, it checks to see if the proxy server has the target page cached. If the proxy server does not have the desired page, a DNS server is used to find the IP address of the URL.

    OR

2b. If no proxy server is used, a DNS server is contacted to determine the IP address of the URL.

3. When the target Web server is located, it retrieves the site's default file and sends it to the requesting computer. In other words, when the URL does not reference a specific file, the site's default page (a.k.a., home page) is sent. The default page for a Web site is configured on the target Web server and will most likely be one of the following: index.html, default.html, or default.asp.

4. When the requested page contains references to graphics or items located *outside* the actual page, the Web browser parses those out, locates them, and sends them to the client computer.

5. The Web browser takes the data sent by the proxy or Web server, interprets it, and displays it on your monitor.

The Stateless Nature of the Internet

The connection and transfer processes described in the previous section are completed via HTTP (Hypertext Transfer Protocol). This is why the full address of a Web site begins with "http://." The main benefit of HTTP is that you do not have to maintain a continuous connection to the source computer. You can connect to a Web site, walk away from your computer for an extended period of time, and then come back and refresh the page without having to explicitly connect to the site. This type of connectivity is referred to as *stateless*, because the site does not need to know the previous action, if any, that you performed at the site.

Of course, this stateless connectivity can cause problems when the site needs to *remember* the previous actions you performed. This typically occurs when you are purchasing items on a site via a shopping cart type program. If you have purchased items on a Web site, you may have noticed that there is a fixed time period in which you must complete the purchasing process or you have to start over. When a site needs to maintain state, programming techniques like cookies are used to implement this functionality. A *cookie* is simply a way to identify the computers that connect to a site using a unique identifier. In order for the cookie process to work, however, the unique identifier must be maintained in memory on the Web server. The unique identifier is also stored on the client computer. If the Web server attempted to permanently store the unique identifiers for all computers that connected to it, memory resources would be exhausted and performance problems would occur. To avoid this scenario, Web servers are configured to automatically delete the unique identifiers after a specified period of inactivity. The default period of inactivity for IIS (Internet Information Server) is 20 minutes. If you connect to a Web site that is hosted on IIS, start a process that requires a cookie, and then do not perform any activity for more than 20 minutes (assuming default configuration), the site will *forget* the previous action performed on the site, and you will need to log in again to re-initiate the cookie.

If you are going to spend a lot time implementing Web sites, I encourage you to further explore the topics presented in this section. Understanding the underlying processes of how Web sites are accessed and files are transferred will make you a better developer.

Maintaining a Hosted Web Site

Most of you will work for companies that have a Web site hosted on a local computer. By "local" I mean one that is owned and maintained by company staff in a company-owned facility. This type of solution is great for companies that can afford it, but is cost prohibitive for smaller firms and individuals. The alternative to local hosting is remote hosting using a provider's computers and Internet connectivity.

When you host a site on a remote computer, a little more effort is required to maintain the site. For example, if you want to update a static Web page on a remote site, you make the changes locally and then use FTP (File Transfer Protocol) software to transfer the file to the Web site. When a local computer is used, you can edit the file in place; as soon as the change is saved, it is reflected on the site. An alternative to the FTP approach is using remote access software like PCAnywhere to connect to the computer. However, FTP is preferred when working with Web sites because it is more efficient. Plus, if you host a site with a commercial provider, there is very little chance, because of security concerns, that they will let you connect to the remote computer via any method other than FTP.

There are a number of FTP software programs that can be downloaded on the Internet. I have used LeechFTP for a couple of years now, but just recently learned its developer is discontinuing its development and is replacing it with

BitBeamer (http://www.BitBeamer.com). Another popular product is CuteFTP (http://www.CuteFTP.com). FTP software is extremely easy to use, so experiment with a few to find the one that fits your needs.

Most of you will be interested in creating data-driven Web sites. A data-driven Web site differs from a typical static site in that the bulk of the content displayed on the site's pages is stored in a database. Appendix B discusses the technology used to create this type of site, but I want to briefly cover what's required to maintain a remote database (in this case, SQL Server).

When you sign up for a site that supports SQL Server access, the provider will give you a login and password so you can access the remote SQL Server with both Enterprise Manager and Query Analyzer. Remote access to a SQL Server confuses many developers, but as long as the computer on which SQL Server is installed uses a static IP address and is connected to the Internet, you can connect to it as if it were sitting underneath your desk (or anywhere on your local network). There are certain proxy server or firewall scenarios that restrict the ability to connect to a SQL Server, but as long as you are not being blocked from the server, you should be able to connect to it without a problem.

A client computer must be configured to communicate via TCP/IP to connect to a remote SQL Server. The SQL Server Client Network Utility is used to configure a client's protocols. The Client Network Utility is accessed via the Microsoft SQL Server Group (e.g., Start, Programs, Microsoft SQL Server…). Once it has started, you simply specify TCP/IP as an enabled protocol, as shown in Figure A-1.

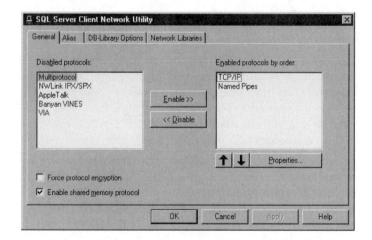

Figure A-1. Configuring TCP/IP via Client Network Utility

> **TIP SQL Server Communicates on Port 1433**
>
> *One of the main problems developers run into when connecting to a remote server has to do with firewall restrictions. When network engineers configure a firewall, their goal is to restrict access to their internal network to all unknown processes. This typically means closing all ports that are not needed to facilitate normal operations. SQL Server communicates on port 1433, which is not a normal port and is usually closed when configuring a firewall. If you are trying to access a SQL Server behind a firewall, mention port 1433 to the network engineers so they can troubleshoot the issue. For more information on this issue you can read Neil Pike's SQL Server FAQ at* `http://www.Windows2000FAQ.com.` *Go to this site and do a search on "How do I connect to SQL Server through a firewall?"*

Free and Fee-Based Hosting Providers

Many of you will want to create a practice Web site so you can build your Web site development skills. If you do not want to share the site with the rest of the world, you can create it on a local computer running IIS. If you do want to share the site, you can choose from two available options. The first option is to use free site hosting provided by many ISPs and a few commercial hosting companies; the second is to pay for the service from a commercial hosting provider.

The ISP option usually requires that you use their services for Internet access. For example, one of my ISPs has a service called FreeWeb that allows you to host a site for free on their computers as long as you have a valid dial-up or DSL account. There is a maximum size restriction of 5MB, and you have to use a virtual domain to access the site (e.g., `freeweb.pdq.net/YourUserName`), but these limitations are OK as long as all you need is a simple site that allows you to hone your skills.

Free commercial hosting is a relatively new service that allows you to maintain a site for free as long as you display banner ads on your site. This might be an attractive alternative if you are short on funds and have a site that can stand the annoying banner ads. Some providers allow you to have access to a SQL Server database so you can implement a data-driven Web site using ASP (Active Server Pages). ASP is discussed in Appendix B.

The alternative to free hosting is a commercial host that charges a monthly fee. Fee-based hosting is by far the most popular hosting arrangement and very easy to set up and maintain. Once you find a provider that meets your site's needs, contact them to provide setup and payment information. They set up a site with the URL you provide and give you login and password information for the site.

If your site is database enabled they will also provide a login and password so you can access and manage your database.

You can find a list of providers (both free and fee-based) here: `http://www.actionjackson.com/hosts/default.asp`. This link is provided for informational purposes only and is not a recommendation for any provider on the list. It is imperative that you do your homework before agreeing to host your site (especially a commercial site) with a provider. There are a number of hosting providers in operation and many run very tight organizations with limited staff. Some have very bad reputations when it comes to providing customer support, which leads to a high degree of frustration for those developers who are just getting started and need a helping hand now and again.

HTML Tags

In their simplest form, Web pages are text files that are composed of HTML tags, textual information, and links to graphics or other Web pages. There are a number of HTML tags that can be used to create Web pages, but in this section we are only going to cover the tags used in the examples presented in Chapters 13 and 14. The following sections describe the fundamentals of using tags and how each is used within a page.

Tag Fundamentals

An HTML tag is declared using the < and > characters. For example, when you create an HTML page, the first tag you place at the top of the page is <HTML>. Most tags require a closing tag. A closing tag is in the same form as the start tag, but contains a / after the <. The closing tag for <HTML> is </HTML>. This format is the same for all tags that require opening and closing tags.

Even though there are tags that *require* a closing tag, some browsers will display data correctly even when they are not included. This tends to confuse many developers who are new to HTML and also leads to unexpected results when a page is accessed by different browsers. IE (Internet Explorer) is the most forgiving browser available, so it will often render pages correctly even though they contain tags that are not properly closed. When you test your page using IE, it works as expected, so you conclude the page is properly constructed . NN (Netscape Navigator) is not as forgiving as IE, so when you access the same page, it *may not* display correctly when a closing tag is omitted. If you are going to build Web sites that support multiple browsers, you need to test the site with each supported browser to ensure it works as expected.

HTML tags are not case-sensitive, but you probably noticed that I capitalized the <HTML> tag. My personal preference is to capitalize major tags and leave all others in lowercase (e.g., `<font>`). The use of the term *major tag* is subjective, so you may not agree with my classifications. The goal for me when deciding which tags are major is to increase readability. Reading an HTML or ASP page that contains a lot of code is not an easy task, so anything you can do to increase readability will help when it comes time to make changes to the page.

An HTML page is separated into two major sections: head and body. The optional head section contains the page's title and can also contain client-side script that is used to validate data entry on a form, among other things. The body section forms the main part of the page and contains the objects and content that you see when the page is displayed in a browser.

Tag Descriptions

The tags used in the Chapters 13 and 14 examples are described here.

`<HTML>...</HTML>`

Designates the start and end of an HTML page.

`<HEAD>...</HEAD>`

Designates the first of two sections of an HTML page. The `<HEAD>` section is optional and is only required when you want to include `<meta>` tags or specify client-side code (designated with the `<script>` tag) that executes before the `<BODY>` section is processed. You will often see the `<title>` tag in this section, but it can also be placed in the `<BODY>` section. The `<meta>` tag is not discussed in this appendix, but in short, it supplies keywords that search engines use to locate your site.

`<BODY>...</BODY>`

Designates the second of two sections of an HTML page. This section is required if you want the page to display any visible content.

`<title>...</title>`

Designates the text that appears in the title bar of your browser.

<script>...</script>

Designates script to be executed on the client. You can use the <script> tag in both sections of an HTML page, but when it appears in the <HEAD> section, the script executes before the contents of the <BODY> section are processed. The type of script you use depends on the browser that is accessing the page. (See the following sidebar to better understand how a particular browser impacts the type of script you can use.)

....

Client-Side Script

Client-side script is code that's embedded between the <script>...</script> tags and is executed on the client computer that accesses the page. Most client-side script is implemented with JScript (a.k.a., JavaScript), because it is supported by all major browsers. IE is the only major browser that supports both VBScript and JScript.

If you are developing intranet applications that will only be accessed by users using IE, or if you only want IE users to access your Web site, then you can use client-side VBScript. Based on my experience, however, using VBScript to implement client-side code is a very bad idea. Even if you are assured by IS Managers or other development personnel that all users use IE, you should still use JScript. Soon after you implement the site or application, you are likely to find that only 95 percent of the users use IE and that for the other 5 percent, the application does not work as expected.

The examples presented in this book use client-side JScript for data validation. JScript is very powerful and allows you to do a lot of interesting things on a Web page, but if you are implementing simple data-driven pages, the odds are you will mainly use it for data validation. For example, if you have an input box that requires an entry, you can use client-side JScript to verify the input box is populated when the user clicks the Submit button. Validating data on the client computer is much more efficient than doing it on the Web server. Client-side validation allows you to avoid a potentially error-generating trip to the server, which may be a great distance from the client.

....

<TABLE>...</TABLE>

The <TABLE> tag is used for formatting purposes. It allows you to define the rows (<tr>) that appear within the table and the data elements (<td>) that appear within a row.

`<tr>...</tr>`

Defines a row within a `<TABLE>` tag.

`<td>`

Defines a data element within a `<tr>` tag.

`<FORM>...</FORM>`

Defines the area of a page in which the user enters information. User information is gathered using the `<input>` and `<select>` tags described next.

`<input>...</input>`

Defines an input box that gathers information from the user.

`<select>...</select> or <select multiple>...</select>`

Defines a drop-down or multi-select list box.

`<option>`

Designates an option of a drop-down or list box created with the `<select>` tag.

`<a>...</a>`

Defines an anchor tag. Anchor tags are used for navigational purposes and allow you to link Web pages. The page referenced in an anchor tag does not have to be on the same server (or even on the same continent) as the source page. In other words, any valid URL will allow you to navigate to a new page on the current site or any other site on the Internet.

`<font>...</font>`

Allows you to specify attributes (e.g., font style and size) for the text located between the tags.

`<center>…</center>`

Designates that the items placed between the tags will be centered on the page. The default is left justification.

`<br>`

Adds a line break within the page.

Tag Attributes

All the tags shown in the previous section except `<center>` and `<br>` have attributes that affect their behavior. It is beyond the scope of this primer to detail the attributes for each tag, so instead, the ones that are used in the examples will be explained as the examples are presented. The use of most attributes are, however, intuitively obvious once you have a general understanding of the purpose of a tag.

Cross-Browser Compatibility

Although this appendix does not directly address this issue, I wanted to give you a heads-up about some problems you might encounter while developing Web sites that support multiple browsers. When developing a Web site, you must decide which browsers it is going to support before the site is created. The reason that you must decide up front is because functionality supported by some browsers is not supported by others. This includes different versions of the same browser, as well. For example, there is a substantial difference between the version 3 and 4 browsers of both IE and NN.

The VBScript issue presented earlier is a good example of a cross-browser development issue that you must decide on before you start creating pages. If you want to support any browser other than IE, you cannot use client-side VBScript. Another example is NN layers. Layers are used to implement some really cool cascading-type functionality in NN, but is not supported by IE.

I don't want to leave you with the impression that you cannot implement browser-specific functionality on a site that is going to support multiple browsers. If you decide to go this route you must, however, trap for browser type and implement code accordingly. This can be a complicated issue, but I wanted to bring it up so you can research any development issues that might affect your first Web site. There is nothing more frustrating than implementing cool functionality on one of your sites only to find that is does not work with a browser the site is supposed to support. A few of the resources listed in the Additional Resources section later in the appendix discuss cross-browser development.

Creating HTML Pages

As you have probably seen in your surfing on the Internet, HTML pages are used by professional developers for commercial sites as well as non-professionals who maintain personal sites. The main reasons for the proliferation of HTML pages are the ease with which they are created and the low cost required to get started. Once you have a basic understanding of the tags required to create a page, all you need is a text editor to start creating pages.

Since all Windows-based computers have Notepad installed, it has became the default *development tool* for many novice developers. Simply open Notepad (or the text editor of your choice), create a new document, add the required tags and text needed to construct the page, and save it using an .html or .htm extension. I present several examples of this process in the next section.

A number of development tools are available to assist in Web site development. One of the more popular tools is Microsoft Front Page, which is used to develop HTML pages and manage Web sites. It allows you to do things like create a site diagram that shows the links between pages and determine which, if any, pages contain invalid links. An *invalid link* is one that points to a non-existent page.

Front Page is limited in its capabilities when it comes to creating Web sites based on ASP technology, so most professional developers use a tool like Microsoft's Visual InterDev (`http://msdn.microsoft.com/vinterdev`) or Allaire's HomeSite (`http://www.allaire.com/products/homesite`) when creating more robust sites. In an effort to keep this appendix simple, the examples presented can be created using a simple text editor. If you are going to create complex Web sites, you should, however, review InterDev and HomeSite to see if they will make your development efforts more efficient.

HTML by Example

Now that you have a basic understanding of the tags used to construct HTML documents, let's take a look at a few examples of how they are used. You are not required to have a Web server installed on your computer to display the pages created by these examples. As long as your computer has a browser installed, you can either double-click the file in Windows Explorer or use File > Open within Internet Explorer to activate the page.

Example 1

The first example demonstrates how to create a basic HTML page. The following code shows how to create example Ex1.html.

```
<HTML>
 <BODY>
  Code Centric: T-SQL Programming with Stored Procedures and Triggers
 </BODY>
</HTML>
```

The `<HTML>…</HTML>` tags designate the document as an HTML page and the `<BODY>…</BODY>` tags specify the main section of the page. The text between `<BODY>…</BODY>` displays when the page is rendered with a browser. The output generated by this page is shown in Figure A-2.

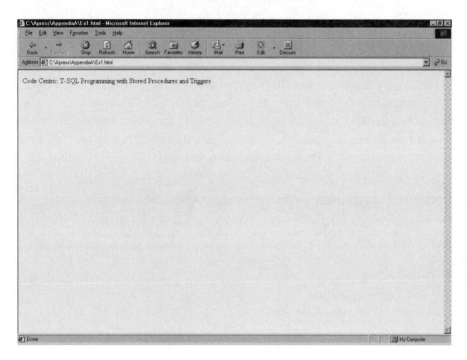

Figure A-2. Output generated by Ex1.html

Look in the title bar of the browser (upper-left on Figure A-2) and note that the address of the page (`C:\Apress\AppendixA\Ex1.html`) is shown as the title. Also notice that the page's content is left-justified, which is the default justification when using HTML.

Example 2

The following changes add a useful title to the browser's title bar and center the page's content.

```
<HTML>
 <HEAD>
  <title>HTML Example 2</title>
 </HEAD>
 <BODY>
  <center>Code Centric: T-SQL Programming with Stored Procedures _
 and Triggers</center>
 </BODY>
</HTML>
```

Note that a new section of the page is added with the <HEAD>…</HEAD> tags. The content of this section is executed before the <BODY>…</BODY> section. It's not required that the <title>…</title> tags be placed in the <HEAD> section, but it has become a programming standard to do so. The modified page is shown in Figure A-3. Notice that the file location title has been replaced with "HTML Example 2."

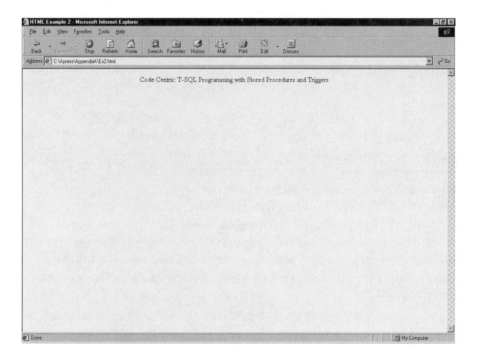

Figure A-3. Output generated by Ex2.html

Example 3

The next example builds on the previous one by using the <TABLE>…</TABLE> tags to build a formatted display area and the <font>…</font> tags to alter the default font characteristics.

```
<HTML>
 <HEAD>
  <title>HTML Example 3</title>
 </HEAD>
 <BODY>
  <center>
   <font face="arial" size=4>Code Centric: T-SQL Programming with _
Stored Procedures and Triggers</font>
   <br>
   <TABLE>
    <tr>
     <td>Chapter 1</td><td>Transact-SQL Overview</td>
    </tr>
    <tr>
     <td>Chapter 2</td><td>Data Types</td>
    </tr>
   </TABLE>
  </center>
 </BODY>
</HTML>
```

The <TABLE>…</TABLE> tags format the rows and columns of a display area on a page. A number of attributes and options can be used with the <TABLE>, <tr>, and <td> tags, so if you are going to develop a lot of Web sites, plan on spending some time learning how to work with these tags. Be aware that the code formatting in this example is used to increase readability and is not required. As a matter of fact, all the content could be placed on a single line and the output would still look the same.

You should know that tools like InterDev and HomeSite eliminate a lot of the mundane formatting work required when building Web pages. Both tools have drag-n-drop capabilities that allow you to place a table on a page and specify the number of rows and data elements. I do, however, like to teach developers to work with tags by hand so they can manually alter auto-generated code when it is not generated as desired. You would be surprised at the number of developers who are at the mercy of their development tool's ability to generate code. I encourage you to spend some time learning the manual process so you are not stuck with the auto-generated code.

The <font> tag is fairly straightforward. In this case it is used to change the font style from the default font to Arial and adjust the size from the default value to default +1. The default font is configured on each browser and the default font size is 3. You can substitute any supported font style name and adjust the size attribute from –7 to 7. The text used in the tables is not affected by the <font> tag, so it is displayed using the browser's default font setting (in this case, Times New Roman). If you are using IE, you can see the default font used by the browser by clicking Tools from the main menu, selecting Internet Options, and clicking the Fonts… button.

The output generated by this code is shown in Figure A-4.

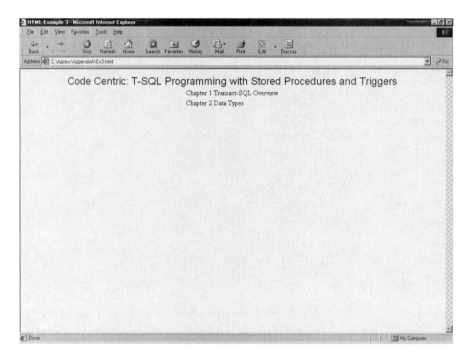

Figure A-4. Output generated by Ex3.html

Example 4

The next example uses the <FORM>, <input>, <select>, and <option> tags to build a data entry screen. In addition, it demonstrates how to use the <a>…</a> tags to create a link to another page. Line numbers were added to ease referencing to specific code segments.

```
1  <HTML>
2  <HEAD>
3   <title>HTML Example 4</title>
4  </HEAD>
5  <BODY>
6   <a href="Ex3.html">Previous Example</a>
7  <center>
8    <font face="arial" size=4>Data Entry Form</font>
9    <br>
10    <FORM name="DataEntry" action="Ex1.html" method="post">
11     <TABLE>
12       <tr>
13       <td>First Name</td><td><input type="text" name="FName" _
         size=15 maxlength=20></td>
14       </tr>
15       <tr>
16         <td>Last Name</td><td><input type="text" name="LName" _
         size=15 maxlength=20></td>
17     </tr>
18     <tr>
19       <td>Occupation</td>
20       <td>
21         <select name="Occupation">
22         <option value=1>Developer
23          <option value=2>DBA
24         <option value=3>Manager
25         </select>
26       </td>
27     </tr>
28     <tr align="center">
29       <td colspan=2><input type="submit" value="Submit"></input></td>
30     </tr>
31   </TABLE>
32   </FORM>
33  </center>
34  </BODY>
35  </HTML>
```

Lines 10–32 make up the form section of the page. The form is defined (see Line 10) with name, action, and method attributes. The form name provides a qualifier for the form's objects and is typically used when more than one form exists on a page. The action attribute defines what happens when the Submit button (Line 29) is clicked. In this case we have configured the page to go to Ex1.html. In real-world scenarios you typically call another page that processes the data input into the form. Appendix B will show how to process the data input into a form using ASP technology. You can process the contents of a form without using ASP, but not when using a database backend. Any non-ASP examples would be useless given the examples presented in the book.

The `method` attribute dictates how the form's values are passed to the page defined in the `action` attribute. When `post` is used the values are hidden from the user and when `get` is used the values are passed in the URL. For example, when the `post` method is used and the first name is populated with "Garth," the last name with "Wells," the occupation with "developer," and Submit is clicked, the URL string is as follows:

```
C:\Apress\AppendixA\Ex1.html
```

When the `get` method is used, the URL string looks like this:

```
file:///C:/Apress/AppendixA/Ex1.html?FName=Garth& LName=Wells&Occupation=1
```

The difference between these two methods will make more sense when we start working with the form's data in Appendix B.

The first and last name input boxes (Lines 13 and 16) are defined with the `<input>…</input>` tags and their attributes are fairly easy to understand. The `type` attribute indicates the values will be text, the `name` assigns a reference for the object, the `size` specifies the size of the box, and `maxlength` indicates that the maximum number of characters that can be typed in the box is 20.

The drop-down box (starting on Line 21) is defined with both the `<select>…</select>` and `<option>` tags. The single `<select>` attribute is the `name` used to reference the input object. The `<option>` tag uses the `value` attribute, but it is not required. Use the `value` attribute when you want to associate a value with the selection that is not the text descriptor. The second URL shown in the get versus post example will help illustrate this point. The value associated with Occupation parameter is 1, which is the value associated with the "Developer" option in the drop-down box. If the `value` attribute would have been omitted, "Developer" would replace 1. The `value` attribute is used when a drop-down is populated with values from a lookup table that contains a primary key and a descriptor. The primary key is assigned to the `value` attribute and the descriptor is used as the text value. I will show you how to dynamically build a drop-down box using the contents of a lookup table in Appendix B.

A link to another page is created on Line 6 using the `<a>…</a>` tags. The `href` attribute specifies the page to go to when the associated text is clicked on the page. The `href` attribute can reference pages on the local computer (Web site) or any valid URL on the Internet.

The page generated by this code is shown in Figure A-5.

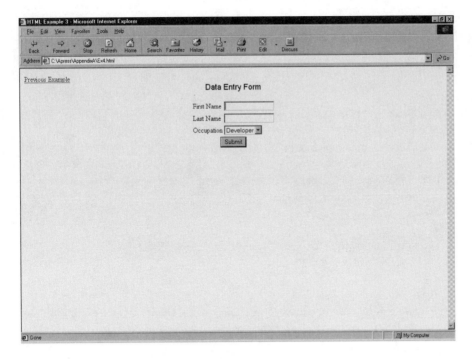

Figure A-5. Output generated by Ex4.html

Example 5

The final example demonstrates how to use client-side code to verify data entry and alters the drop-down created in the previous example to a multi-select list box.

```
<HTML>
<HEAD>
  <title>HTML Example 4</title>
  <script>
   function checkData ()
   {
    if (document.DataEntry.FName.value == "")
    {
     alert("Please fill in First Name.")
     document.DataEntry.FName.focus()
     return false
    }
    if (document.DataEntry.LName.value == "")
    {
     alert("Please fill in Last Name.")
     document.DataEntry.LName.focus()
     return false
```

```
      }
     }
    </script>
  </HEAD>

  <BODY>
   <a href="Ex4.html">Previous Example</a>
   <center>
    <font face="arial" size=4>Data Entry Form</font>
    <br>
    <FORM name="DataEntry" action="Ex1.html" method="post" _
          onsubmit="return_ checkData()"      >
      <TABLE>
       <tr>
        <td>First Name</td><td><input type="text" name="FName" _
            size=15 maxlength=20></td>
       </tr>
       <tr>
        <td>Last Name</td><td><input type="text" name="LName" _
            size=15 maxlength=20></td>
       </tr>
       <tr>
        <td>Occupation</td>
        <td>
         <select name="Occupation" multiple >
          <option value=1>Developer
          <option value=2>DBA
          <option value=3>Manager
         </select>
        </td>
       </tr>
       <tr align="center">
          <td colspan=2><input type="submit" value="Submit"></input></td>
       </tr>
      </TABLE>
    </FORM>
   </center>
  </BODY>
</HTML>
```

The bold code in the <HEAD> section is the JScript that verifies the contents of the two input boxes for first and last name. This code is activated when the Submit button is clicked (see bold code in <FORM> tag) and the content of both input boxes is checked to make sure they are not empty. The first thing you need to learn about JScript is that it is *case-sensitive*. The references to the form (DataEntry) and the input boxes (FName and LName) must match the case used in the "name" attribute. The actual programming code must be proper case as well.

JScript is an object-oriented scripting language, so the dot notation may be new to those of you who have never worked with this type of language. A Web page is referenced using the DOM (Document Object Model), so all items on a page are elements that can be referenced by either their name or array position within a particular object. It's much easier to reference the items by their names, so array referencing will not be covered. JScript uses properties and methods to work with a particular form element. The following line uses the "value" property to determine if the FName input box is populated.

```
document.DataEntry.FName.value == ""
```

The "document" reference simply refers the current page, "DataEntry" is the form, "FName" is the input object, and "==" is the equal operator. When the value in FName is equal to ""(blank), the alert window method notifies the user that it must be populated. Once the user clicks the OK button (see Figure A-7) to clear the dialog, the focus method places the cursor in the FName input box.

The other code added to this example is shown in bold in the <select> tag. When multiple is used the drop-down is turned into a multi-select list box. The CTRL key is used to select multiple options within the list. When multiple options are selected, the value associated with the value attribute for each option selected is placed in a comma-separated list. This may sound like double-talk, but it is easily explained with an example. If you select both DBA and Manager, the value associated with "occupation" is "1,3." If you select all three options, the value associated with "occupation" is "1,2,3." I presented an example in Chapter 13 that demonstrated how to parse a comma-separated string using built-in T-SQL functions. I included the example for the purpose of showing how to manipulate the data selected in a multi-select list box.

The page generated by this code is shown in Figure A-6. The dialog generated when Submit is clicked and there is no value in the FName input box is shown in Figure A-7.

The examples presented in Appendix B will be more interesting because they will show how you take the data entered in a form and insert it into tables in a database. If you are new to HTML and ASP, you might have to read both Appendix A and B a few times to get a full understanding of how these programming technologies work together. If this is the case, don't become discouraged and conclude Web development isn't for you. Creating data-driven Web sites is a complex process because of the multiple technologies involved and the cryptic nomenclature used to describe them. The following sentence illustrates this point:

> "I develop data-driven Web sites that use HTML, client-side JScript, server-side VBScript, and ADO to access data stored in SQL Server."

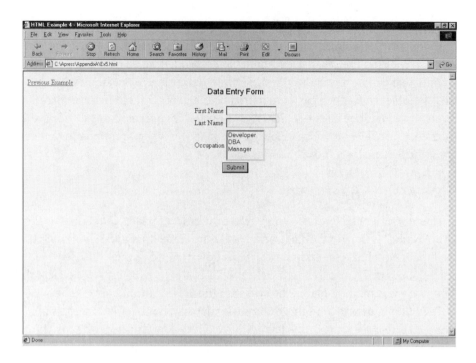

Figure A-6. Output generated by Ex5.html

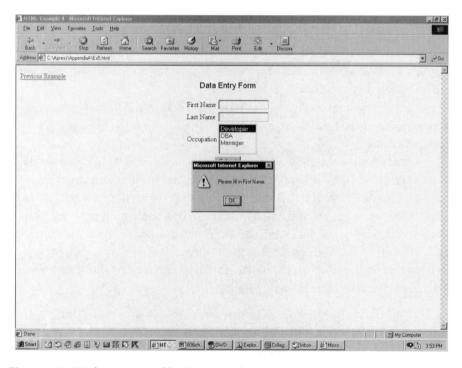

Figure A-7. Dialog generated by JScript code

Additional Resources

The Internet is a great source for learning about the different development technologies being used today. Personally, I try to find all my learning material on the Internet before I research purchasing a book on the topic. When I first started with Web site development a colleague recommended that I check out `http://www.HTMLGoodies.com`. This site contained so many useful tutorials, I did not have to purchase a book on HTML.

Microsoft also maintains a plethora of information on the MSDN section of their Web site. Since Microsoft changes page locations so frequently, I am providing a search topic instead of a direct URL. Simply go to `http://msdn.microsoft.com` and search on the following: "MSDN Online Web Workshop—DHTML, HTML, and CSS Home." Once you find this area of the site, click Show TOC, and you will see a number of topics including Web Content Management and XML.

If you want to learn more about JScript, you can start by going to Microsoft's Web site at `http://msdn.microsoft.com` and doing a search on "scripting." The option that starts off "Microsoft Scripting Technologies…" will take you to a page that has an option for JScript. You should know, though, that if you are going to do anything *interesting* with JScript, you will have to become comfortable with DOM and the basic programming techniques used in JScript. A dependent drop-down box—where the contents of a second drop-down are dependent on the value selected in the first drop-down—is a good example of functionality that will require advanced JScript knowledge. I used a book titled *JavaScript, The Definitive Guide* by David Flanagan (ISBN: 1-56592-392-8) to learn about the DOM and JScript basics.

JScript versus JavaScript

You might have noticed that the title of the book referenced in the previous section uses "JavaScript" and not "JScript." JavaScript is Netscape's implementation of the language and JScript is Microsoft's. The two implementations support different features, and there are subtle differences that need to be understood when programming complex functionality. Flanagan does a good job of specifying the features supported by the two implementations.

Before You Go

In this appendix I covered the basics of HTML and demonstrated how to create simple pages that use a minimal number of HTML tags. I also covered the basics of how a client computer retrieves a page from a Web site, and some of the tasks associated with maintaining a remote Web site. In the final section, I listed resources that you can use to hone your Web site development skills.

Appendix B builds on these topics by showing how ASP technology is used to manipulate data stored in SQL Server.

ASP Primer

THE PURPOSE OF THIS PRIMER IS TO TEACH YOU just enough about ASP (Active Server Pages) to understand the examples presented in Chapters 13 and 14. I will cover how to connect to a SQL Server database using both ODBC and OLE-DB and the various ways to pass SQL statements to the server. In addition, I will demonstrate how to use recordsets to manipulate the data sent to the Web server. The ASP used in the examples in Chapters 13 and 14 is fairly straightforward, so you should not have any problems understanding how it works once you complete this appendix.

> NOTE Sample Code
>
> *The sample code for this appendix can be downloaded at either* http://www.apress.com *or* http://www.SQLBook.com. *Download and extract CodeCentric.zip and then extract App_B.zip, which contains the .sql and .asp files referenced in this appendix.*

Before You Get Started

I want to provide a brief overview of ASP before we start on the examples. Developers new to Web development are often confused about what *makes up* ASP, so this section should help eliminate any confusion you might have. ASP is an application development environment that was created by Microsoft. The technology is used to make Web sites more robust by allowing you to combine HTML, scripting languages, and ActiveX components to produce dynamic content. It provides the ability to dynamically alter the content of a Web page using programming languages before it is sent to the requesting browser.

A comparison between how a HTML page and an ASP page are processed will help explain how this technology adds functionality to a Web site. The examples created in Appendix A are simple HTML pages that are referred to as *static*. When a browser requests a HTML page from a Web server (IIS), it is sent as is and no server-side processing occurs. Client-side code can be used to add functionality to the page, but there is no code that changes the page's content on the server. If the content of a HTML page needs to be changed, it has to be explicitly edited, which is why these pages are called *static*.

An ASP page uses an .asp file extension. When a Web server receives a request for a page with an .asp extension, it is processed by server-side DLLs and then the static and dynamic content is sent to the browser. This server-side processing allows you to change content as a function of conditional logic and add content from data sources that can be accessed with ADO (ActiveX Data Objects). Static content like a page title (e.g., `<title>`) can be combined with dynamic content from a database to produce an *active* page that is always up-to-date.

ASP uses the scripting languages VBScript and JScript and ActiveX components written in programming languages like VB or C++. VBScript and JScript are used to implement server-side scripting. ASP also supports other scripting languages (e.g., PerlScript), but they are not installed by default and will not be covered in this appendix. ASP provides the ability to integrate third-party and custom developed ActiveX components into your Web pages. "Example 8: Crystal Reports and Stored Procedures" in Chapter 13 uses a third-party ActiveX component. If you recall, the Crystal Reports ActiveX Viewer is used to demonstrate how to execute a Crystal Report from a Web page. I will be using Microsoft's ADO extensively in all the examples in Chapters 13 and 14. ADO is general purpose data access methodology that can be used by any programming language that supports ActiveX.

VBScript, JScript and ADO are implemented as server-side DLLs. When the Web server processes an .asp page the appropriate DLL is called as needed. Server-side code is denoted with `<%...%>` marks, so all code in between these symbols is processed on the server. Understanding where code is processed is key to learning ASP. For example, one of the FAQs I see in the ASP newsgroup has to do with trying to use the VBScript MsgBox function in server-side script. When the code is executed on the server, all interaction with the environment is local. Executing MsgBox in server-side script generates an error because a client is not allowed to interact with the server's environment. In like manner, placing HTML in between `<%...%>` will generate an error because HTML is rendered on the client (not the server), so the DLLs do not know how to process this code.

ASP is included with IIS. As long as you have IIS installed you have access to ASP. To learn more about ASP and other Microsoft Web development technologies visit: `http://msdn.microsoft.com/workshop/default.asp`.

Using an Enhanced Text Editor

Developers new to Web development often use Microsoft's Notepad as their primary development tool. As I mentioned in Appendix A, there are two development tools (Visual InterDev and HomeSite) that are geared especially for ASP development. It might, however, be a daunting task to learn a new tool and ASP at the same time. If you do not want to use one of these development tools I suggest you obtain and use a text editor that supports lines numbers (Notepad does not support line numbers). When ASP code contains an error, the line number on which the error occurs is returned to the browser. Using a text editor that displays line numbers will make troubleshooting ASP code easier.

I use the GWD Text Editor. GWD has quite a few nice features and a trial version can be downloaded for free at http://www.gwdsoft.com.

ASP Primer

This primer is broken into two sections: ASP Basics and Working with a Database. In the first section I will cover general information about how server-side code is used to send content to a browser. The second section is fairly detailed because I will cover how to connect to and manipulate data stored in SQL Server.

ASP Basics

As mentioned earlier, ASP supports both VBScript and JScript for implementing server-side code. The examples presented in this book only use VBScript for server-side scripting. VBScript is easier for most developers to learn and provides all the functionality need to work with a database. The documentation for VBScript can be found by going to http://msdn.microsoft.com and executing a search on "VBScript."

The first example converts the Ex1.html sample file used in Appendix A to Ex1.asp. The response object is used to send content to the browser.

```
<HTML>

<BODY>
 Code Centric: T-SQL Programming with Stored Procedures and Triggers
 <%
  Response.write "Ex1.asp"
 %>
</BODY>

</HTML>
```

The output is shown in Figure B-1.

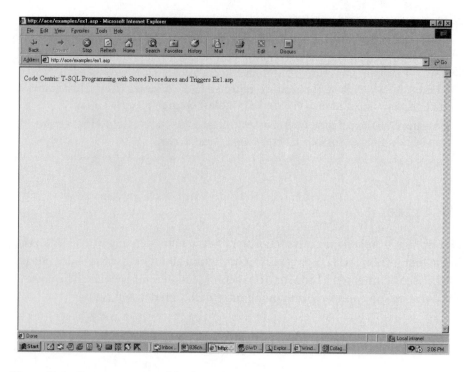

Figure B-1.   Output generated by Ex1.asp

The output generated by the write method of the response object is concatenated with static data on the page. Let's make the output more legible by sending a <br> tag to browser with the following:

```
<HTML>

 <BODY>
  Code Centric: T-SQL Programming with Stored Procedures and Triggers
  <%
   response.write "<br>Ex2.asp"
  %>
 </BODY>

</HTML>
```

The output is shown in Figure B-2.

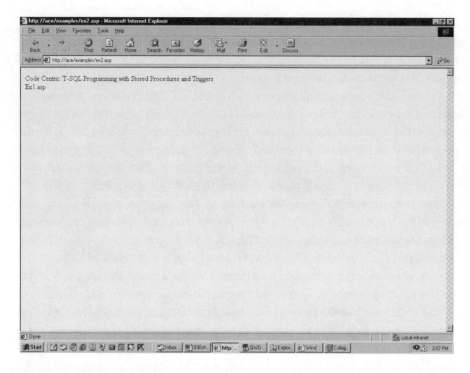

Figure B-2. Output generated by Ex2.asp

Response.write can send both tags and text to a browser. The following example shows how to create two variables that hold string values and send their contents to the browser.

```
<%
 Option Explicit
%>
<HTML>

 <BODY>
  <%
    Dim var1, var2

    var1 = "Code Centric: T-SQL Programming with Stored Procedures and Triggers"
    var2 = "Ex3.asp"
    response.write var1&"<br>"&var2
  %>
 </BODY>

</HTML>
```

The most important code used in this example is `Option Explicit`. When `Option Explicit` is specified, all variables must be explicitly declared with the `Dim` statement. It is a good programming practice to use `Option Explicit`, because it minimizes the chance of referencing invalid variable names. For example, if the `response.write` command references var3 instead of var2, an error is generated that indicates var3 has not been defined. If `Option Explicit` is not included and an invalid variable reference occurs, no error is produced and you are forced to troubleshoot and determine why the results are not as expected. In this particular case it's not that much work to determine where the error lies, but when you start working with .asp files that are a hundred or more lines long it gets a little tedious.

Another interesting thing to note is that no data types are specified in the `Dim` statement. The only data type VBScript supports is variant. A variant can contain both string and numeric data and the context in which the variable is used dictates how its data is processed. For example, when used in math operations the variant behaves as a number; when used as a string it acts like a string. Of course, to participate in a math operation the value of the variant must be convertible to a number.

The different classifications of data a variant can hold are called *subtypes*. For example, Date is a variant subtype. VBScript converts data on-the-fly when it conforms to the rules for a particular subtype. If you are not sure the data held in a variable conforms to the rules for a particular subtype you can use a function to test the data. For example, the IsDate()function is used to test for the Date subtype. You can learn more about subtypes in the VBScript online documentation.

The `response.write` line of the example shows how data is concatenated in VBScript. The "&" character is the concatenation operator, and the two variables and the <br> tag are used to produce the same output as shown in Figure B-2. Notice that the variable initialization and the <br> referenced in the `response.write` line are surrounded by double-quotes. VBScript requires double-quotes when working with string data.

The last example in this section demonstrates how to perform three different looping operations. As you will see when working with the sample application presented in Chapter 14, looping operations are used frequently when working with recordset objects. The following shows how to implement three different looping operations.

```
<%
 Option Explicit
%>
<HTML>

 <BODY>
  <%
   Dim i, A1
```

```
  response.write "Looping Operation 1<br>"
  For i=1 To 5
   response.write i&"<br>"
  Next

  response.write "Looping Operation 2<br>"
  i=1
  Do While i <= 5
   response.write i&"<br>"
   i=i+1
  Loop

  response.write "Looping Operation 3<br>"
  A1 = Array(1,2,3,4,5)
  For Each i In A1
   response.write i&"<br>"
  Next
 %>
</BODY>

</HTML>
```

The first two looping operations are simple Do and For loops which you should find easy to understand. The third operation is a For that is specific to working with arrays and collections. In this example an array is initialized using the Array() statement and is traversed one i at a time. The only confusing part about this construct is the reference to i. This is simply a variable that serves as a placeholder in memory for each element of the array. Once the *current* value is in the variable, it is easier to manipulate in statements that appear between the For…Next construct. This For…Next construct can also be used to work with collections. In the "Error Handling" section of Chapter 13, it is used to navigate the ADO Error collection to produce custom error messages. The output produced by the code is shown in Figure B-3.

Working with Databases

Now that you understand the basics of working with VBScript and sending output to a browser, let's look at some examples that show how to interact with a database. The following statements create two tables that are needed for the examples. The examples will insert data into **Employees** and use **Occupations** as a lookup table.

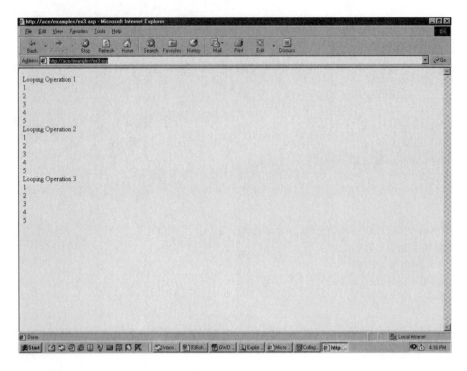

Figure B-3. Output generated by Ex3.asp

```
USE tempdb
go
CREATE TABLE Occupations
(
 Occ_UniqueID tinyint IDENTITY PRIMARY KEY,
 Occ_Desc varchar(30) NOT NULL
)
go
INSERT Occupations VALUES ('Developer')
INSERT Occupations VALUES ('DBA')
INSERT Occupations VALUES ('Manager')

CREATE TABLE Employees
(
 Emp_UniqueID int IDENTITY PRIMARY KEY,
 Emp_FName varchar(30) NOT NULL,
 Emp_LName varchar(30) NOT NULL,
 Occ_UniqueID tinyint NULL REFERENCES Occupations(Occ_UniqueID)
)
go
```

The rest of this appendix will demonstrate how to connect to a database and how to use both SQL Passthrough and stored procedures to interact with the database.

Connecting to a Database

The first thing to do when creating data-driven pages is to establish a connection to the target database. There are two ways to establish a connection to a database with ASP:

- The first involves creating an ODBC DSN via Control Panel. To create an ODBC DSN, click the Data Sources (ODBC) icon in Control Panel, click the System DSN tab, click the Add button, select the SQL Server driver, and specify the connection information. Then use the name of the DSN in the ADO Connection object to establish a connection.

- The second method is called a *DSN-less connection.* With this type of connection you are not required to create an ODBC DSN—hence the name DSN-less. Instead, specify the connection information in a connection string.

When you use a DSN-less connection, you have the option of connecting to the database with two different drivers. You can use either the ODBC driver or the OLE-DB provider. The ODBC driver supports less functionality than the OLE-DB driver, so I use OLE-DB when possible. There are times, however, when you are forced to use ODBC. For example, some ISPs do not allow DSN-less connections, so ODBC is the only option.

I will show the syntax for both connection methods, but I will only use a DSN-less connection in the examples. The DSN-less method is more efficient because one less step is required to obtain the connection information. When a DSN connection is used the connection information must be looked up in the ODBC DSN. When a DSN-less connection is used all the required information is contained in the connection string.

The following (Ex4.asp) shows how to connect to **tempdb** on a SQL Server. The name of the server on which SQL Server resides is "Ace," the user is "garth," and the password is "password." Be sure to modify the connection information per your configuration when you implement the examples. Note that REM is used to create a comment in VBScript. You can also use a single quote, but I save this notation for inline comments.

```
<%
Option Explicit
Dim SQLConn, i, ConnectionProperty

Set SQLConn = server.CreateObject("ADODB.Connection")

REM ODBC DSN
REM  SQLConn.OPEN "DSN=CodeCentric;Uid=garth;Pwd=password"

REM DSN-Less OLE-DB
SQLConn.Open _
"Provider=SQLOLEDB;Server=Ace;Database=tempdb;Uid=garth;Pwd=password"

REM DSN-Less ODBC
REM SQLConn.Open _
"Driver={SQL Server};Server=Ace;Database=tempdb;Uid=garth;Pwd=password"
%>
<HTML>

<BODY>
 <%
  i = 0
  For Each ConnectionProperty in SQLConn.Properties
   response.write_
SQLConn.Properties(i).Name &"-->"& SQLConn.Properties(i).Value & "<br>"
   i = i + 1
  Next

  SQLConn.Close
  Set SQLConn = Nothing
%>
</BODY>

</HTML>
```

The first new command creates an ADO connection object using the SQLConn variable. This must be executed regardless of the connection method you choose.

The next set of statements show the three different ways to connect to the database. The ODBC DSN approach assumes you have a DSN called "CodeCentric." The ODBC and OLE-DB DSN-less methods provide the connection information in the connection string.

The code shown in the <BODY> of the page uses the For...Next construct referenced in the previous section. The ADO connection object has a properties collection that contains numerous attributes that describe the database connection. The name and value properties display the contents of the properties collection.

The fact that the values are displayed proves the connection is successful. To learn more about the ADO connection object see the "Additional Internet Resources" section later in this appendix.

The final two lines of VBScript close the connection object and set the variable equal to Nothing. This frees-up any memory required to maintain these items. This code is not required, but it is considered a good programming practice. The output generated by this page is shown in Figure B-4.

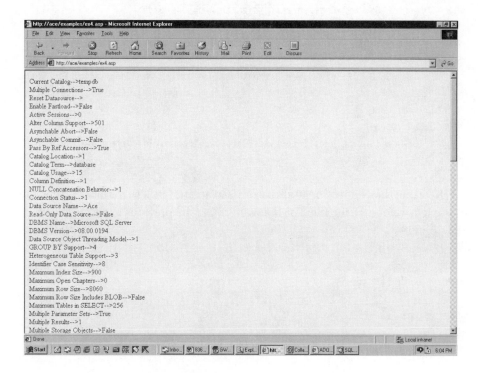

Figure B-4. Output generated by Ex4.asp

Using an Include File to Store Connection Information

An include file streamlines development. When the same code is used in multiple files, it can be placed in a single file and *included* in other files. This approach allows you to make changes to the include file that are automatically reflected in all the files in which it is referenced. There are many uses for include files, but my favorite is to store database connection information. Assume you have both a development and production Web server and a data-driven site that consists of fifty pages that access a database. If the connection information is explicitly listed in all fifty pages, you are required to make fifty changes when the files are moved from development to production. When the fifty files use an include file, you only need to make one change after moving the files into production. The contents of SQLConn.inc are shown here.

```
<%
Dim SQLConn
Set SQLConn = server.CreateObject("ADODB.Connection")

REM ODBC DSN
REM  SQLConn.OPEN "DSN=CodeCentric;Uid=garth;Pwd=password"

REM DSN-Less OLE-DB
SQLConn.Open _
    "Provider=SQLOLEDB;Server=Ace;Database=tempdb;Uid=garth;Pwd=password"

REM DSN-Less ODBC
REM SQLConn.Open _
        "Driver={SQL Server};Server=Ace;Database=tempdb;Uid=garth;Pwd=password"
%>
```

Now that the connection information is in an .inc file, let's modify the previous example to reference the file. The following alters the previous example to use SQLConn.inc.

```
<%
Option Explicit
%>
<!--#include file="SQLConn.inc"-->
<%
Dim i, ConnectionProperty
%>
<HTML>
 <BODY>
  <%
  i = 0
  For Each ConnectionProperty in SQLConn.Properties
   response.write_
SQLConn.Properties(i).Name &"-->"& SQLConn.Properties(i).Value & "<br>"
   i = i + 1
  Next

  SQLConn.Close
  Set SQLConn = Nothing
 %>
</BODY>

</HTML>
```

The #include file="SQLConn.inc" is a directive to load the file before the page is processed on the server. The directive must be surrounded by HTML comment indicators (<!--...-->). The output from Ex5.asp is the same as Ex4.asp.

Interacting with a Database

Now that we can connect to the database, let's look at some examples that show how to access and change its data. There are three ways to interact with a database: SQL Passthrough, ADO recordset object, and ADO command object. Both SQL Passthrough and the ADO command object are covered in this section. The recordset approach to modifying data is not covered because it is the least efficient of three approaches. The recordset object is used in the following examples, but only to hold data returned by the server.

SQL Passthrough

Using SQL Passthrough, you build a valid SQL statement on the client and execute it via the connection object. The results of the statement can be placed in the ADO recordset object for processing. This will no doubt be the easiest way to implement database interaction, but I encourage you to work through the next section before deciding on the approach to use in your applications. The following example (Ex6.asp) demonstrates how to retrieve all the rows in the **Occupations** table. Line numbers are added to the code to help with the explanation.

```
1    <%
2      Option Explicit
3    %>
4    <!--#include file="SQLConn.inc"-->
5    <%
6      Dim SQL, rs
7
8      Set rs = server.CreateObject("ADODB.Recordset")
9    %>
10   <HTML>
11
12   <BODY>
13    <%
14     SQL = "SELECT Occ_UniqueID, Occ_Desc FROM Occupations"
15
16     Set rs = SQLConn.Execute(SQL)
17
18     response.write rs(0)&"-->"&rs(1)
```

```
19
20      rs.close
21      Set rs = Nothing
22      SQLConn.Close
23      Set SQLConn = Nothing
24      %>
25      </BODY>
26
27      </HTML>
```

Notice that no reference to **tempdb** is made in the SELECT. The database in which the statement is executed is specified in the connection string listed in the SQLConn.inc file. On Line 8, the rs variable is declared as an ADO recordset object. This will serve as the container for the results of the SELECT statement. Line 14 initializes the SQL variable with a valid SELECT. Line 16 is the crux of the code because it uses the execute method of the connection object to execute the SELECT. The results are placed in the recordset object. Line 18 sends the contents of the first row of the recordset object to the browser. The rs(0) refers to the ordinal position of the column in the recordset. I do not like this syntax, but I showed it to you because you are bound to see it in other ASP code. I prefer to reference the column names directly as shown on line 19. In my opinion, rs("Occ_UniqueID") is much easier to maintain over time because you do not have to remember the order of the columns returned by the SELECT. It may not seem like that big of an issue in this example, because all you have to do is look up four lines to see the SELECT. When stored procedures are used, however, you cannot see the SELECT, and then the real benefit is noticed. The output of Ex6.asp is shown in Figure B-5.

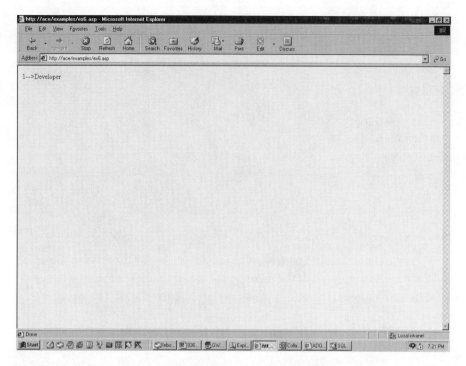

Figure B-5. Output generated by Ex6.asp

The previous example only lists the first row in the recordset. Let's modify the code so all the rows are sent to the browser. The following (Ex7.asp) shows how this is done.

```
<%
 Option Explicit
%>
<!--#include file="SQLConn.inc"-->
<%
 Dim SQL, rs

 Set rs = server.CreateObject("ADODB.Recordset")
%>
<HTML>

<BODY>
  <%
     SQL = "SELECT Occ_UniqueID, Occ_Desc FROM Occupations"

     Set rs = SQLConn.Execute(SQL)
```

```
      Do While NOT rs.eof
        response.write rs("Occ_UniqueID")&"-->"&rs("Occ_Desc")&"<br>"
        rs.MoveNext
      Loop

    rs.Close
    Set rs = Nothing
    SQLConn.Close
    Set SQLConn = Nothing
  %>
 </BODY>

</HTML>
```

The code shown in bold uses a Do...Loop to process all the rows in the record-set. The MoveNext method of the recordset is the key. It moves focus to the next record in the recordset. The output generated by Ex7.asp is shown in Figure B-6

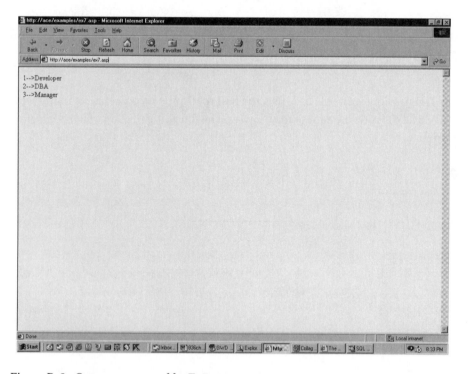

Figure B-6. Output generated by Ex7.asp

The goal in working with the **Occupations** table is to learn how to create a dynamic list box. The previous example demonstrates how to retrieve and loop through all the rows in the table. The next step is to show how to integrate the data with the `<select>` tag. The following (Ex8.asp) code creates a dynamic list box.

```
<%
 Option Explicit
%>
<!--#include file="SQLConn.inc"-->
<%
 Dim SQL, rs

 Set rs = server.CreateObject("ADODB.Recordset")
%>
<HTML>

 <BODY>
  <%
    SQL = "SELECT Occ_UniqueID, Occ_Desc FROM Occupations"

    Set rs = SQLConn.Execute(SQL)

  %>
   <select name="Occ_UniqueID">
    <%
    Do While NOT rs.eof
    %>
     <option value="<%=rs("Occ_UniqueID")%>"><%=rs("Occ_Desc")%>
    <%
     rs.MoveNext
    Loop
    %>
   </select>

  <%
  rs.Close
  Set rs = Nothing
  SQLConn.Close
  Set SQLConn = Nothing
  %>
 </BODY>

</HTML>
```

The code shown in bold is the key to the dynamic list box. The Do...Loop dynamically changes the values used to create the <option> tag portion of the <select>. The value of attribute of <option> is populated with **Occ_UniqueID** and descriptor is created with **Occ_Desc**. The equal sign before each column name reference (e.g., =rs("Occ_UniqueID")) is shorthand for response.write. We could have used response.write to send the contents to the browser, but the code is confusing enough as is. Later in this appendix I will demonstrate how to grab the value selected and use it to create a row in the **Employees** table. The output generated by Ex8.asp is shown in Figure B-7.

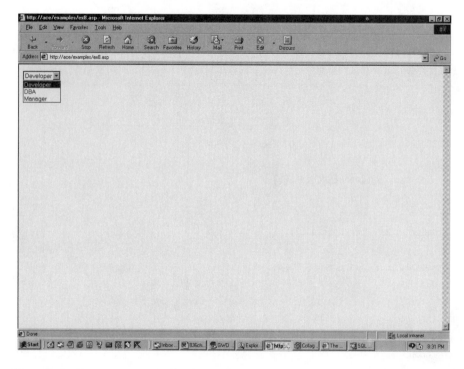

Figure B-7. Output generated by Ex8.asp

All the examples so far have focused on retrieving data from the database. You can, however, execute any valid SQL statement using the Passthrough approach. The following (Ex9.asp) code shows how to create a row in the **Employees** table.

```
<%
 Option Explicit
%>
<!--#include file="SQLConn.inc"-->
```

```
<%
 Dim SQL, Emp_FName, Emp_LName, Occ_UniqueID

 %>
<HTML>

 <BODY>
  <%
   Emp_FName = "Garth"
   Emp_LName = "Wells"
   Occ_UniqueID = 1

   SQL = "INSERT Employees (Emp_FName,Emp_LName,Occ_UniqueID) _
        VALUES ('"&Emp_FName&"','"&Emp_LName&"',"&Occ_UniqueID&")"
   REM response.write SQL

   SQLConn.Execute(SQL)

   SQLConn.Close
   Set SQLConn = Nothing
  %>
 </BODY>

</HTML>
```

The code shown in bold constructs a valid INSERT statement using the variables initialized earlier in the file. When you encounter an error with a statement using the Passthrough approach, you can use `response.write` to troubleshoot the issue. Once the statement is written to the browser, you can cut-n-paste it into Query Analyzer to see if it works. If the statement works in Query Analyzer, you know the problem is with another area of the code. Use the following SELECT to ensure that the INSERT works as expected.

```
USE tempdb
go
SELECT * FROM Employees
--Results--
Emp_UniqueID Emp_FName      Emp_LName                      Occ_UniqueID
------------ -------------- ------------------------------ ------------
1            Garth          Wells                          1
```

I prefer using stored procedures for all data access and modification; the Passthrough approach can be used with these, too. The following creates a stored procedure that inserts a row in **Employees**.

```
USE tempdb
go
CREATE PROCEDURE ps_Employees_INSERT
@Emp_FName varchar(30),
@Emp_LName varchar(30),
@Occ_UniqueID tinyint
AS
INSERT Employees
(
 Emp_FName,
 Emp_LName,
 Occ_UniqueID
)
VALUES
(
 @Emp_FName,
 @Emp_LName,
 @Occ_UniqueID
)
```

To call this procedure from an .asp page, construct a valid EXEC statement that references the procedure and includes the required parameters. If we executed the procedure in Query Analyzer, the call would look like this:

```
EXEC ps_Employees_INSERT @Emp_FName='Sara',@Emp_LName='Wells',@Occ_UniqueID=1
--Results--
(1 row(s) affected)
```

The goal is to construct a string in the .asp page that looks just like this call. The following (Ex10.asp) code shows how this is done.

```
<%
 Option Explicit
%>
<!--#include file="SQLConn.inc"-->
<%
 Dim SQL, Emp_FName, Emp_LName, Occ_UniqueID

%>
<HTML>

 <BODY>
  <%
   Emp_FName = "Shannon"
```

```
    Emp_LName = "Wells"
    Occ_UniqueID = 1

    SQL = "EXEC ps_Employees_INSERT _
          @Emp_FName='"&Emp_FName&"', @Emp_LName='"&Emp_LName&"', _
          @Occ_UniqueID="&Occ_UniqueID
    REM response.write SQL

    SQLConn.Execute(SQL)

    SQLConn.Close
    Set SQLConn = Nothing
    %>
  </BODY>

</HTML>
```

The code shown in bold constructs a valid call to the procedure. There is no output generated, but I can use the following SELECT to show that the code works as expected.

```
SELECT * FROM Employees
--Results--
Emp_UniqueID Emp_FName            Emp_LName                      Occ_UniqueID
------------ -------------------- ------------------------------ ------------
1            Garth                Wells                          1
2            Sara                 Wells                          1
3            Shannon              Wells                          1
```

This method for calling procedures is fairly easy to understand, but it has one important limitation: It is difficult to access stored procedure OUTPUT parameters. The code needed to access an OUTPUT parameter using Passthrough involves accessing multiple recordsets. An example in the next section demonstrates the preferred way of getting an OUTPUT parameter from a procedure.

ADO Command Object

The ADO command object approach to interacting with a database can seem overwhelming if you do not have experience working in a development environment that uses objects, properties, and methods. After working with both the Passthrough and command object for two years, though, I have concluded the extra work required to learn the command approach is well worth the effort. You end up with more rigorous code that not only facilitates working with OUTPUT parameters, but is also easier to maintain.

The first example (Ex11.asp) demonstrates how to call a procedure that retrieves all the rows in the **Occupations** table.

```
<%
 Option Explicit
%>
<!--#include file="SQLConn.inc"-->
<!--#include file="adovbs.inc"-->
<%
 Dim SQL, rs, cmd1, Emp_FName, Emp_LName, Occ_UniqueID

 Set rs = server.CreateObject("ADODB.Recordset")
%>
<HTML>

 <BODY>
  <%
   Set cmd1 = server.CreateObject("ADODB.Command")
   cmd1.ActiveConnection = SQLConn
   cmd1.CommandType = adCmdStoredProc
   cmd1.CommandText = "ps_Occupations_SELECT"

   Set rs = cmd1.Execute

   Do While NOT rs.eof
    response.write rs("Occ_UniqueID")&"-->"&rs("Occ_Desc")&"<br>"
    rs.MoveNext
   Loop

   rs.Close
   Set rs = Nothing
   SQLConn.Close
   Set SQLConn = Nothing
  %>
 </BODY>

</HTML>
```

The first thing you should notice about this code is that another include file was added. The adovbs.inc file comes with IIS and contains user-friendly names for various ADO parameter settings. In this example, adovbs.inc is used to specify a user-friendly name for the CommandType. The actual value used to specify a stored procedure as the CommandType is &H0004. Take a look in adovbs.inc to see the other values it contains.

The code shown in bold is the key to this page. The cmd1 variable is set to an ADO command object and the object's connection, type and text properties are set on the succeeding lines. Once the required properties are set the execute method is used to call the procedure. The results of the call are placed in the rs recordset and it is traversed so the contents are sent to the browser. The output generated by this page is the same as Figure B-6.

In the next example I will demonstrate how to add a row to **Employees** using the **ps_Employees_INSERT** procedure created earlier. This code is slightly more complex because the parameters (and their data types) have to be specified. The following code (Ex12.asp) shows how this is done.

```
<%
 Option Explicit
%>
<!--#include file="SQLConn.inc"-->
<!--#include file="adovbs.inc"-->
<%
 Dim cmd1, SQL, Emp_FName, Emp_LName, Occ_UniqueID
%>
<HTML>

 <BODY>
  <%
   Emp_FName = "Dan"
   Emp_LName = "Wells"
   Occ_UniqueID = 1

   Set cmd1 = server.CreateObject("ADODB.Command")
   cmd1.ActiveConnection = SQLConn
   cmd1.CommandType = adCmdStoredProc
   cmd1.CommandText = "ps_Employees_INSERT"
   cmd1.Parameters.Append cmd1.CreateParameter("Emp_FName", _
                   adVarChar, dParamInput,30,Emp_FName)
   cmd1.Parameters.Append cmd1.CreateParameter("Emp_LName", _
                   adVarChar,adParamInput,30,Emp_LName)
   cmd1.Parameters.Append cmd1.CreateParameter("Occ_UniqueID", _
                   adTinyInt,adParamInput,,Occ_UniqueID)

   cmd1.Execute

   SQLConn.Close
   Set SQLConn = Nothing
  %>
```

```
</BODY>

</HTML>
```

The code shown in bold adds the procedures parameters to the call. The Append method adds an entry to the parameters collection of the command object and the CreateParameter specifies the attributes of the parameter. The attributes of a parameter are: name, data type, INPUT or OUTPUT, and value. The data type attribute must be specified as an ADO constant. Table B-1 shows the SQL Server data type to ADO constant mappings.

Table B-1. Data Type to Constant Mappings

SQL SERVER DATA TYPE	ADO CONSTANT
varchar	adVarChar
datetime	adDate
int	adInteger
smallint	adSmallInt
tinyint	adTinyInt
money	adCurrency
text	adLongVarchar
bit	adBoolean
float	adDouble
real	adSingle

The final example in this section demonstrates how to retrieve an OUTPUT parameter from a stored procedure. The following code modifies the sample procedure to return the primary key of the row created to the calling application.

```
USE tempdb
go
ALTER PROCEDURE ps_Employees_INSERT
@Emp_FName varchar(30),
@Emp_LName varchar(30),
@Occ_UniqueID tinyint,
@PrimaryKey int OUTPUT
AS
```

```
INSERT Employees
(
 Emp_FName,
 Emp_LName,
 Occ_UniqueID
)
VALUES
(
 @Emp_FName,
 @Emp_LName,
 @Occ_UniqueID
)
SET @PrimaryKey = @@IDENTITY
```

Modifying the .asp page to retrieve the primary key is as simple as adding a parameter of the proper type. The following code (Ex13.asp) shows how this is done.

```
<%
 Option Explicit
%>
<!--#include file="SQLConn.inc"-->
<!--#include file="adovbs.inc"-->
<%
 Dim SQLConn, cmd1, SQL, Emp_FName, Emp_LName, Occ_UniqueID
%>
<HTML>
 <BODY>
  <%
   Emp_FName = "Mary Ellen"
   Emp_LName = "Wells"
   Occ_UniqueID = 1

   Set cmd1 = server.CreateObject("ADODB.Command")
   cmd1.ActiveConnection = SQLConn
   cmd1.CommandType = adCmdStoredProc
   cmd1.CommandText = "ps_Employees_INSERT"
   cmd1.Parameters.Append cmd1.CreateParameter("Emp_FName", _
                 adVarChar,adParamInput,30,Emp_FName)
   cmd1.Parameters.Append cmd1.CreateParameter("Emp_LName", _
                 adVarChar,adParamInput,30,Emp_LName)
   cmd1.Parameters.Append cmd1.CreateParameter("Occ_UniqueID", _
                 adTinyInt,adParamInput,,Occ_UniqueID)
   cmd1.Parameters.Append cmd1.CreateParameter("PrimaryKey", _
                 adInteger,adParamOutput)
```

```
        cmd1.Execute

        response.write cmd1.Parameters("PrimaryKey")

        SQLConn.Close
        Set SQLConn = Nothing
      %>
    </BODY>
  </HTML>
```

The line shown in bold adds the OUTPUT parameter to the call. The response.write line sends the PrimaryKey value returned in the parameter to the browser. The output generated by this call is shown in Figure B-8.

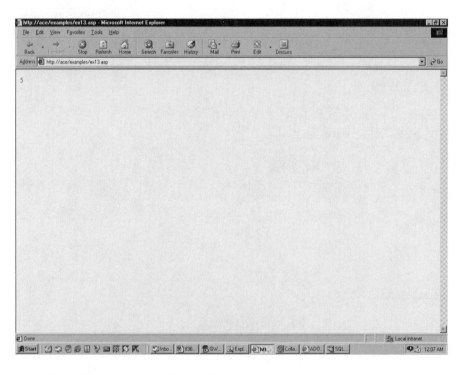

Figure B-8. Output generated by Ex13.asp

Pulling It All Together

In this section I use all the material presented in Appendixes A and B to create a simple database interface. The interface has a menu that allows you to add an employee or list all the employees in the table. The add screen utilizes a dynamic list box so the user can specify the employee's occupation. The list screen combines the data in a recordset with some HTML to produce a formatted output. You can access this interface in the Examples section on the book's supporting Web site (http://www.SQLBook.com).

Before I show you the interface code, the **ps_Employees_INSERT** procedure needs to be altered to remove the OUTPUT parameter. The following modifies the procedure for the examples that follow.

```
USE tempdb
go
ALTER PROCEDURE ps_Employees_INSERT
@Emp_FName varchar(30),
@Emp_LName varchar(30),
@Occ_UniqueID tinyint
AS
INSERT Employees
(
  Emp_FName,
  Emp_LName,
  Occ_UniqueID
)
VALUES
(
  @Emp_FName,
  @Emp_LName,
  @Occ_UniqueID
)
go
```

The following code (AppB_Menu.html) creates the menu screen for the interface.

```
<HTML>

 <HEAD>
  <title>Code Centric -- Appendix B</title>
  </HEAD>
```

```
<BODY bgcolor="beige">
 <center>
  <font face="arial" size=4>Code Centric -- Appendix B</font>
  <p>
  <a href="AppB_EmpAdd.asp"><font face="arial">Add an Employee</font></a>
  <br>
  <a href="AppB_EmpList.asp"><font face="arial">List Employees</font></a>
 </center>
</BODY>

</HTML>
```

This is a simple .html page that contains links to the .asp pages. The output generated by the page is shown in Figure B-9.

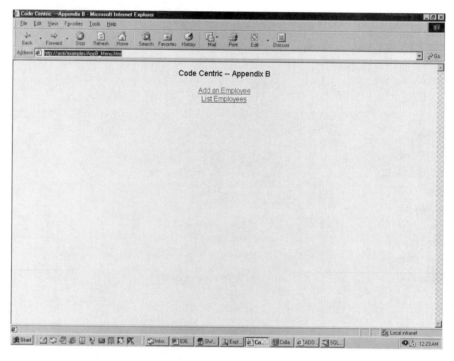

Figure B-9. Output generated by AppB_Menu.html

The AppB_EmpAdd.asp page gathers information from the user and when its Submit button is clicked, calls AppB_EmpAddRespond.asp. The code in AppB_EmpAddRespond.asp can be incorporated into the AppB_EmpAdd.asp, but has been separated to make it easier to understand. The contents of AppB_EmpAdd.asp are shown next.

```
<%
 Option Explicit
%>
<!--#include file="SQLConn.inc"-->
<!--#include file="adovbs.inc"-->
<%
 Dim SQL, cmd1, rs

 Set rs = server.CreateObject("ADODB.Recordset")
%>
<HTML>

 <HEAD>
  <title>Code Centric -- Appendix B</title>

  <script>
   function checkData ()
   {
    if (document.DataEntry.FName.value == "")
    {
     alert("Please fill in First Name.")
     document.DataEntry.FName.focus()
     return false
    }
    if (document.DataEntry.LName.value == "")
    {
     alert("Please fill in Last Name.")
     document.DataEntry.LName.focus()
     return false
    }
   }
  </script>
 </HEAD>

<BODY bgcolor="beige">
 <center>
  <font face="arial" size=4>Employee Add Form</font>
  <br>
  <FORM name="DataEntry" action="AppB_EmpAddRespond.asp" _
        method="post"_ onsubmit="return checkData()">
   <TABLE>
    <tr>
     <td><font face="arial">First Name:</font></td>
      <td><input type="text" name="Emp_FName" size=15 maxlength=20></td>
```

```
          </tr>
          <tr>
           <td><font face="arial">Last Name:</font></td>
           <td><input type="text" name=" Emp_LName" size=15 maxlength=20></td>
          </tr>
          <tr>
           <td><font face="arial">Occupation:</font></td>
           <td>
            <select name="Occ_UniqueID">
            <%
             Set cmd1 = server.CreateObject("ADODB.Command")
             cmd1.ActiveConnection = SQLConn
             cmd1.CommandType = adCmdStoredProc
             cmd1.CommandText = "ps_Occupations_SELECT"
             Set rs = cmd1.Execute

             Do While NOT rs.eof
            %>
            <option value="<%=rs("Occ_UniqueID")%>"><%=rs("Occ_Desc")%>
            <%
              rs.MoveNext
             Loop
            %>
            </select>
           </td>
          </tr>
          <tr align="center">
           <td colspan=2><input type="submit" value="Submit"></input></td>
          </tr>
         </TABLE>
        </FORM>
       </center>
      </BODY>

</HTML>
```

This page simply combines the various elements covered in both appendixes. Client-side JScript is used at the top of the page to ensure the required columns are populated and the ADO command object is used to create a dynamic list box. The output of AppB_EmpAdd.asp is shown in Figure B-10.

Now that the page to gather the employee information is in place, we need one to create a new row in **Employees**. The following code (AppB_EmpAddRespond.asp) shows how this is done.

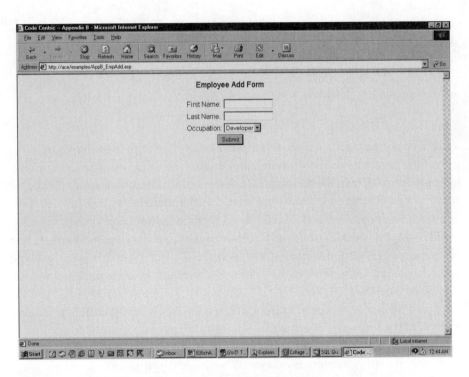

Figure B-10. Output generated by AppB_EmpAdd.asp

```asp
<%
 Option Explicit
%>
<!--#include file="SQLConn.inc"-->
<!--#include file="adovbs.inc"-->
<%
 Dim cmd1
 Set cmd1 = server.CreateObject("ADODB.Command")
 cmd1.ActiveConnection = SQLConn
 cmd1.CommandType = adCmdStoredProc
 cmd1.CommandText = "ps_Employees_INSERT"
 cmd1.Parameters.Append cmd1.CreateParameter("Emp_FName", _
                adVarChar,adParamInput,30, request.form ("Emp_FName")   )
 cmd1.Parameters.Append cmd1.CreateParameter("Emp_LName", _
                adVarChar,adParamInput,30,request.form ("Emp_LName")   )
 cmd1.Parameters.Append cmd1.CreateParameter("Occ_UniqueID", _
                adTinyInt,adParamInput,,,request.form ("Occ_UniqueID")   )

 Cmd1.Execute
```

```
SQLConn.Close
Set SQLConn = Nothing

response.redirect "AppB_Menu.html"
%>
```

This page makes the call to **ps_Employees_INSERT** with the values entered in the calling page. The code shown in bold retrieves the values entered in the <FORM> in AppB_EmpAdd.asp. In the examples presented earlier in this appendix the values used to create a new row were hard-coded into variables. The hard-coded approach is very limited and was only used for demonstration purposes. In real-world examples you will use request.form or request.querystring. Use request.form when the method attribute in the <FORM> tag is set to "post." When it is set to "get," use request.querystring to retrieve the values. All the examples presented in this book use the post method.

The final line on this page calls the menu page, AppB_Menu.html. The redirect method of the response object works as long as the page does not send content to the browser. This page contains no HMTL tags or response.write statements, so it is processed on the server only and sends no data to the browser.

The final page of the interface lists all the rows in the **Employees** table. The stored procedure needed to retrieve the data is shown here.

```
CREATE PROCEDURE ps_Employees_SELECT
AS
SELECT a.Emp_FName+' '+ a.Emp_LName AS EmpName,
        b.Occ_Desc
FROM Employees a
JOIN Occupations b ON a.Occ_UniqueID = b.Occ_UniqueID
ORDER BY a.Emp_LName,a.Emp_FName
```

The following shows the code (AppB_EmpList.asp) used to produce the listing page.

```
<%
 Option Explicit
%>
<!--#include file="SQLConn.inc"-->
<!--#include file="adovbs.inc"-->
<%
 Dim cmd1, rs

 Set rs = server.CreateObject("ADODB.Recordset")
```

```
   Set cmd1 = server.CreateObject("ADODB.Command")
   cmd1.ActiveConnection = SQLConn
   cmd1.CommandType = adCmdStoredProc
   cmd1.CommandText = "ps_Employees_SELECT"
   Set rs = cmd1.Execute

%>
<HTML>
 <HEAD>
  <title>Code Centric -- Appendix B</title>
 </HEAD>

 <BODY bgcolor="beige">
  <center>
   <font face="arial" size=4>Employee List</font>
   <p>
   <TABLE>
    <tr>
     <td><font face="arial">Employee</font></td>
     <td><font face="arial">Occupation</font></td>
    </tr>
    <tr>
     <td colspan=2><hr></td>
    </tr>
    <%
    Do While NOT rs.eof
    %>
    <tr>
     <td><%=rs("EmpName")%></td>
     <td><%=rs("Occ_Desc")%></td>
    </tr>
    <%
    rs.MoveNext
    Loop
    %>
   </TABLE>
  </center>
 </BODY>

</HTML>
```

The page is very straightforward. The command object calls the procedure and then a Do… Loop sends the contents of the recordset to the browser. The output produced by AppB_EmpList.asp is shown in Figure B-11.

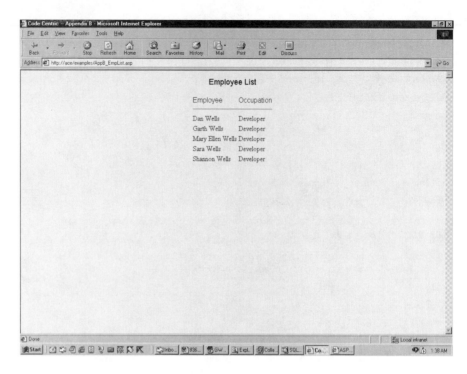

Figure B-11. Output generated by AppB_EmpList.asp

Additional Internet Resources

If you are going to be doing a lot of ASP development, I encourage you to seek out sources on the Internet to help you minimize learning time. My favorite Internet resource is `http://www.4GuysFromRolla.com`. This site has numerous helpful articles that address entry-level, intermediate, and advanced topics. It also has a message board where you can post questions about problems you are having or aspects of technology you do not fully understand.

Another good resource is `http://www.LearnAsp.com`. This is one of the more popular ASP sites on the Internet. It has plenty of tutorials and excellent search capabilities to help you find what you need in a hurry.

If you want to access the best Microsoft resource go to `http://support.microsoft.com` and execute an Article ID search on Q274420. The article's title is "Getting Started with Active Server Pages (ASP)," and it provides a number of links that have useful information on introductory-level topics.

To learn more about the various objects, properties, and methods of ADO check out `http://www.w3schools.com/ado`. It contains quite a bit of concise, well organized information that will help you get up to speed on this powerful programming interface.

There is also a Microsoft hosted newsgroup (microsoft.public.inetserver.asp.db) where you can get help troubleshooting your development issues. I like to read this newsgroup even when I do not need help with a particular issue because it gives me a heads-up on problems other developers have encountered. If you see numerous posts about the same issue, you should take note as you are likely to encounter it in your programming endeavors.

Before You Go

In this appendix I covered the basics of ASP. I also presented general coverage of the components that comprise ASP, along with numerous examples that showed how it is used to connect to and interact with a database. In the final section I listed additional resources to help you further your knowledge of this most interesting technology.

In Appendix C we'll look at ways to use Query Analyzer and Index Tuning Wizard to ensure that a query is performing at an optimal level.

Query Optimization and Application Performance Primer

THE MAIN GOAL OF THIS APPENDIX IS to demonstrate how you can use Query Analyzer and Index Tuning Wizard to ensure that a query is performing at an optimal level. This goal will be accomplished by showing you how to do three things:

- Use the Display Estimated Execution Plan option to determine when a comparison operation can be resolved into a search argument (SARG).

- Use the Display Estimated Execution Plan option to determine the resources required to execute a given query.

- Use the Index Tuning Wizard to analyze and recommend indexes.

We will also cover some design techniques that will ensure an application is performing in an optimal manner.

The material covered in this appendix is very specific to solving the programming aspect of performance problems. Another area that addresses hardware-related issues and can affect an application's performance is performance tuning. *Performance tuning* involves monitoring a server to ensure that its hardware can adequately support the applications that it hosts. For example, you can use the Windows 2000 System Monitor or Windows NT Performance Monitor to make sure that the server has the proper number of CPUs and sufficient memory to adequately handle all its processes. This is a very important topic, but unless you have some experience configuring servers, it might be best to leave this issue for the system or network administrator. If you would like to learn more about how to use System Monitor or Performance Monitor, please see documentation for the applicable operating system.

If you want to gain some general knowledge about how hardware can impact performance, you can read a white paper by SQL Server MVP Neil Pike. The MVP (most valued professional) designation is awarded by Microsoft to professionals who not only demonstrate advanced knowledge of a particular product, but the willingness to share their knowledge with others via the newsgroups. The white paper is available for free download in the FAQ section at `http://www.mssqlserver.com`. Neil also recently published a book that contains his enormously popular SQL Server FAQs. The book is titled *SQL Server: Common Problems, Tested Solutions* (ISBN 1-893115-81-X) and is a must-have for developers and administrators alike. You can learn more about Neil's book by visiting the Catalog section at `http://www.apress.com`.

> **NOTE   Sample Code**
>
> *The sample code for this appendix is available for download at either:* `http://www.apress.com` *or* `http://www.SQLBook.com`. *Download CodeCentric.zip, extract the contents, and look for the file named AppC.sql.*

Before You Get Started

Before you start in on the main topics of this appendix, I want to share two examples with you that will help you better understand how poor design decisions can affect an application's performance. The first example demonstrates the negative ramifications of not understanding how to implement a proper indexing strategy, and the second shows how poorly placed and designed code can affect an application's performance.

Please note that the scenarios that follow are provided for learning purposes only and are not meant to be critical of the developers who experienced the problems. The design errors described here are very common, and reading about them should help you avoid the same mistakes.

Over-Indexing a Database

About six years ago I was responsible for administering a mission-critical credit application processing system that was based on a proprietary database. Very soon after I started this job the software vendor created a new version of their product that was based on client-server architecture and used SQL Server as the back-end database. Since this was a major upgrade to their software, the vendor asked that the lead network administrator and I visit their headquarters so we could learn about the application's new architecture and what we needed to do to prepare for the upgrade.

While on site, the lead designer told us about the trouble they had meeting the delivery deadline because of problems they encountered while developing the application. It seems no one on staff had experience working with SQL Server (or any other major RDBMS), so they were learning as they went along. The most interesting comment the designer made pertained to the indexing strategy they used. He said, "Everything was going fine until we started putting data in the database."

Once they started adding a substantial amount of data to the database and accessing it with multiple clients, the application's performance came to a grinding halt. The design flaw was caused by two issues:

- The designers' misunderstanding of resources required to maintain an index.

- The designers' desire to ensure that all user-created reports ran at an optimal level.

The second reason seems contradictory, but is a good example of what can happen when you do not know the implications of a design decision.

The new version of their product replaced the hard-to-access proprietary database with an open database whose data could be very easily accessed with a reporting tool like Crystal Reports. The ability of users to create their own reports became one of their big marketing points, so it was very important that the custom reports ran at an optimal level. The designers' problem, though, was that they did not know exactly what data the users might want to report on. They knew that adding an index to join or filter columns made data access more efficient and surmised that if they created an index on all possible join or filter columns, they would account for all possible reporting scenarios.

The problem with this strategy is that it does not take into account the overhead required to maintain all the indexes. Each index associated with a table has to be updated when a data modification statement is executed on the table, and this requires a certain amount of resources. The application used more than 100 tables, so there were quite a few extraneous indexes. When the client applications started adding, updating, and deleting data at the same time the other clients were running reports, the application as a whole was completely overloaded because of the resources required to perform the requested actions in addition to the resources required to maintain the indexes.

After struggling with the performance problem for a while and not making any progress, the designers' decided to bring in a consultant. The consultant analyzed their database design and indexing strategy and advised them to remove all the indexes that were not being used on a frequent basis. Once the extraneous indexes were removed, the application began to perform at an acceptable speed, and they were able to move forward with product delivery.

The Ramifications of Client-Side Code

About two and a half years ago I started a new contracting assignment with a company that was having trouble with its main database application. The problem was typical of many of the clients I work with. More specifically, the company had an application that had been working and performing as expected for a year or more, but the execution time of its queries was growing slower and more unacceptable with every passing day. As a matter of fact, at the time I arrived a number of executive-level reports could no longer be run because of the impact they had on the application as a whole. Running one of these reports caused the data entry personnel to complain about application speed.

The application was used to track customer information and utilized a SQL Server database back-end and a Cold Fusion front-end. The individuals who designed the application had very little experience working with SQL Server (or any other RDBMS) and no formal training in relational database theory. Since their background was procedural language programming, they used client-side procedural techniques to create the application. For example, if they needed to create a report that displayed the number of customers who subscribed to a particular product, they would create a recordset on the client and loop through it counting the number of products being used. There were quite a few reports that used this technique and they were the ones that were experiencing the problems.

I did not know much about Cold Fusion, so I visited Allaire's (the developer of Cold Fusion) Web site to learn more about the product. It didn't take long to find out that the version of the product my client was using (4.0 if I recall correctly) had a problem handling client-side data manipulation. Having learned this, coupled with my past experience with the problems caused by client-side code, I suggested we move all the data manipulation code for these reports from the client application to stored procedures.

This technique results in a thin-client design. The goal when implementing a thin-client design is to minimize the work done by the client. In other words, the only tasks the client application performs is allowing users to either input data or display the results generated by statements executed on the server.

In this situation, the thin-client approach worked very well. The previously non-working and poorly performing reports started to perform at acceptable speeds once the code was moved from the client application to stored procedures. This was an especially rewarding project because I not only made another client happy, but I was able to convince two more programmers that the thin-client methodology is the right way to design database applications.

> **WARNING   Bad Database Design Equals Poor Performance**
>
> *A good database design is the key to ensuring that an application performs at an optimal level. You have the best chance of making sure an application performs as expected when the database is designed per the normalization rules described in Relational Database Theory. You should know that even if you master the techniques covered in this appendix, it is unlikely that applying them to a poorly designed database will result in acceptable performance. The design flaws of a database design will be exposed as the database grows and the number of simultaneous users increases. And there are few, if any, patches that you can apply to a poorly designed database that will last for more than a short time.*

Query Optimization

Query optimization is a term that refers to the techniques that are used to ensure that your queries are performing at an optimal level. In SQL Server 2000, the techniques are implemented via Query Analyzer, and they allow you to determine two things:

- The way the Query Optimizer processes a query

- The resources required to process a query

Both techniques will be covered in this appendix, but first we must cover some of the basics of how the Query Optimizer processes SQL statements.

Query Optimizer, Indexes, and Search Arguments (SARGs)

This section discusses the components and concepts that you must understand in order to use the optimization tools available in SQL Server 2000.

Query Optimizer

The Query Optimizer is a component of SQL Server that determines the most efficient way to process a particular SQL statement. The Query Optimizer analyzes a statement and produces an execution plan, which details the order in which the tables referenced by the statement are accessed and how the data will be retrieved from each table. The execution plan is composed of one or more steps that show

how the statement is processed. The Query Optimizer uses a cost-based algorithm to determine how the execution plan should be constructed.

The costs associated with processing a SQL Statement are system resources and time required to fulfill the request. The main statistics used to determine costs are shown in Table C-1.

Table C-1. Main Algorithm Factors

ROW COUNT	NUMBER OF ROWS PROCESSED BY A STEP
I/O Cost	Cost of all I/O operations
CPU Cost	CPU cost for the operation
Query Cost	Query Optimizer costs

The references to "cost" in this section all refer to time, or more specifically, the elapsed time that it takes to perform the individual task. For example, the I/O Cost is the elapsed time in seconds it takes to perform the I/O operations. The Query Cost is the overall time (in seconds) that it takes the Query Processor to process and execute a statement. The goal, of course, is to minimize the cost of each operation in the execution plan, which reduces the overall cost of the query.

Indexes

An index is a database object that reduces the time it takes to retrieve rows from a table. SQL Server's indexes use a B-tree structure to hold the key elements (column values) that compose the index and a pointer to the row to which they belong. If SQL Server did not support indexes, every time a SQL statement was executed on a table the table would have to be scanned sequentially until the desired row(s) was found. The B-tree structure of an index reduces the number of rows that the Query Processor accesses in order to produce the desired resultset. Be mindful, though, that each index you create on a table requires maintenance overhead every time a data modification statement is executed on the table. Indexes are discussed in detail in Chapter 3, so please see that chapter if you need more information on how to create and use them.

Search Argument

One of the most common programming actions used with SELECT, UPDATE, or DELETE statements is applying a WHERE clause to specify which rows are affected by the statement. For example, the following shows how to filter the **Customers** table on the **Country** column.

```
USE Northwind
go
SELECT CompanyName
FROM Customers
WHERE Country = 'Mexico'
--Results--
CompanyName
----------------------------------------
Ana Trujillo Emparedados y helados
Antonio Moreno Taquería
Centro comercial Moctezuma
Pericles Comidas clásicas
Tortuga Restaurante
```

When the Query Optimizer receives this request it analyzes the statement and determines how the data should be accessed (the execution plan). The Query Optimizer can decide to do one of three things to determine which rows have 'Mexico' in the **Country** column. It can do a table scan, which looks at all the rows in the table and examines the contents of **Country**; it can use a clustered index scan; or it can use an index that references **Country**. If the Query Optimizer cannot choose a specific index for an operation, it will always choose to use a clustered index scan if one exists on the target table. When a clustered index is not present, a table scan is used. In order for the Query Optimizer to choose the third option, the column on which the comparison operation is being performed must have an associated index.

The Query Optimizer examines all three options and determines which one costs the least (in terms of system resources) to fulfill the request. This is not as simple a decision as you might think. Intuitively, you would think that the Query Optimizer would choose the index option whenever one exists on the target column, but this is not always the case. The index approach must use fewer resources than a table or clustered index scan, and in some cases, there are so many rows accessed that a table or clustered index scan is more efficient than searching the index.

In order for the Query Optimizer to use an index with a statement the comparison operation must be able to be resolved into a search argument (SARG). To produce a valid SARG, the comparison operation must be of the form shown here.

```
Column ComparisonOperator Constant/Variable
```

The previous SELECT conforms to this requirement, so the Query Optimizer *could* choose to use an index to complete the operation. If either the Column or Constant/Variable is acted on by a function (e.g., SUBSTRING) a valid SARG is not produced. The following example uses the SUBSTRING function on the **Country** column, so a SARG cannot be produced and an index cannot be used.

```
USE Northwind
go
SELECT CompanyName,
       Country
FROM Customers
WHERE SUBSTRING(Country,1,1) = 'A'
--Results--
CompanyName                              Country
---------------------------------------- ----------------
Cactus Comidas para llevar               Argentina
Ernst Handel                             Austria
Océano Atlántico Ltda.                   Argentina
Piccolo und mehr                         Austria
Rancho grande                            Argentina
```

The valid ComparisonOperators are: =, <, >, <=, >=, BETWEEN, and sometimes LIKE. The LIKE operator can only produce a valid SARG when the string pattern used for the operation does not start with a wildcard character. An example of this will be shown in the next section.

TIP   Index Statistics

*The Query Optimizer uses the statistics stored on an index to decide whether it should be used to access data. The data captured indicates the distribution of key values in the index and is held on the **sysindexes** table in each database. Starting with SQL Server 7, an index's statistics are automatically updated as a function of the activity that occurs on the table. If you perform a data modification statement that acts on a large number of rows or execute the TRUNCATE statement on a table consider updating the statistics manually using the UPDATE STATISTICS statement. If the statistics information does not reflect the true values held in the indexed column(s) the Query Optimizer will not be able to make informed decisions about how the data should be accessed.*

Query Optimization Tools in Query Analyzer

SQL Server comes with a number of tools that can help developers in their programming endeavors. Quite a few of the ones available in Query Analyzer were covered in Chapter 1, but here we are going to focus on two that will help you optimize the execution of your queries. The first is the Display Estimated Execution Plan option and the second is the Index Tuning Wizard.

Using the Display Estimated Execution Plan

The Display Estimated Execution Plan option allows you to see the execution plan the Query Optimizer creates to process one or more SQL statements. It is used in this section to demonstrate three things:

- How adding an index to a column used in a comparison operation can reduce query costs

- How to determine if a comparison operation can be resolved as a searchable argument

- How to determine which of two or more queries that produce the same resultset is most efficient

To enable the Display Estimated Execution Plan in Query Analyzer, click Query on the main menu and select the Display Estimated Execution Plan. Note that if you have more than one statement in the Editor Pane but only want to see the estimated plan for an individual statement, you can highlight the desired statement and select the option. This is the approach you want to take when working with AppC.sql.

When you click the Query option on the main menu, you will see another option called Show Execution Plan. This option shows the actual execution plan used by Query Optimizer. The actual plan can be affected by SQL Server's current activity (e.g., number of users or current queries that are being executed), so when you want to perform theoretical comparisons, use the Display Estimated Plan option. Optimizing a query per a server's current activity may not lead to consistent results if the activity under which the tests are performed is not typical. The best approach is to learn how to understand what the execution plan is telling you and then use the option you think is best for your environment.

Adding an Index to Reduce Query Costs

The SELECT statements executed thus far have referenced the **Customers** table in the **Northwind** database. You can use the system stored procedure **sp_helpindex** to see the existing indexes on **Customers**.

```
USE Northwind
go
sp_helpindex 'Customers'
--Results--
index_name     index_description                                  index_keys
-------------  -------------------------------------------------  -------------
City           nonclustered located on PRIMARY                    City
CompanyName    nonclustered located on PRIMARY                    CompanyName
PK_Customers   clustered, unique, primary key located on PRIMARY  CustomerID
PostalCode     nonclustered located on PRIMARY                    PostalCode
Region         nonclustered located on PRIMARY                    Region
```

Use the Display Estimated Execution Plan option with the following SELECT and examine the execution plan produced when a comparison operation references a non-indexed column.

```
SELECT CompanyName
FROM Customers
WHERE Country = 'Mexico'
```

Figure C-1 shows the execution plan and the statistics for the plan's main operation—the Clustered Index Scan.

Before we delve into the details of the estimated execution plan, we will cover the proper way to read the output. Tree-structure terminology describes the elements of the output. The left-most icon is called the *root* and the icons to the right of the root are called *nodes*. The output is read from right-to-left, so the right-most icon represents the first operation that occurs when the query is processed. The nodes are referred to as either logical or physical operators. In this example, the root is the SELECT icon and the node to the right is the Clustered Index Scan operator. To see the statistics associated with a node place the mouse pointer over its icon. The individual statistics are contained at the operator level, but the most important statistic, Estimated Subtree Cost, is summarized in the root. The Estimated Subtree Cost terminology may seem a little confusing, but it simply refers to the cost for that portion of the tree. When only one subtree is in the execution plan, it comprises the total cost of the query.

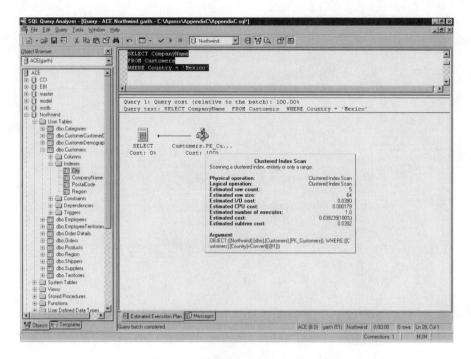

Figure C-1. Estimated execution plan for non-indexed column

Note that the Query Optimizer has opted to use a Clustered Index Scan instead of a Table Scan. A clustered index determines the physical order of the rows within a table. If the column on which the clustered index is based (**CustomerID** in this example) is not used in the comparison operation the Clustered Index Scan has the same effect as a Table Scan. The Query Optimizer will always choose a Clustered Index Scan over a Table Scan when a clustered index exists on the target table.

The Estimated Cost for the Clustered Index Scan is .0392 seconds; this makes up 100 percent of the time required to execute the statement. The 100 percent makes sense because this is the only operator in the execution plan. Notice that the first line of output in Figure C-1 indicates that the Query Cost (relative to the batch) is 100 percent. This also makes sense because there is only one statement in the batch. As you will see in the next section, you can use this output to determine which statement in a multi-statement batch requires the most resources.

Create a non-clustered index on **Country** and then re-examine the estimated execution plan. The following code adds the index, and the new plan is shown in Figure C-2.

```
CREATE NONCLUSTERED INDEX ndx_CustomersCountry
ON Customers (Country)
--Results--
The command(s) completed successfully.
```

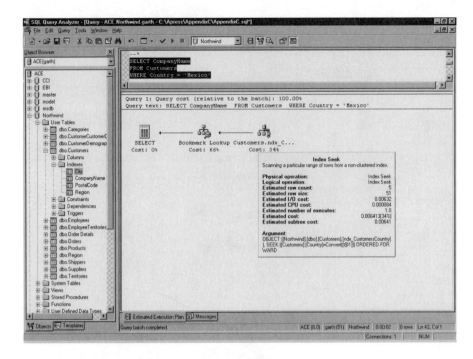

Figure C-2. Estimated execution plan for indexed column

Two operators are used in the new execution plan. The first is Index Seek and the second is Bookmark Lookup. Notice that the cost to perform the Index Seek is 34 percent of the total costs and the Bookmark Lookup is 66 percent of the total costs. When you add the Estimated Cost for each operator (you can't see the value for the Bookmark Lookup) you get .018918. When you place the mouse pointer over the SELECT icon (as shown in Figure C-3), you see that the Estimated Subtree Cost is .0189—the rounded value of the individual operator costs.

When the costs for pre- and post-index queries are compared, you see that the query that used the index realized a 52 percent reduction in costs ([(.0392-.0189)/.0392]*100=51.78). The key points that must be considered, however, are how often will this type of comparison operation be performed and will the cost reduction provided by the index outweigh the increased overhead required to maintain it. If this type of query is performed on a regular basis *and* **Customers** is going to contain a large number of rows, then the index should remain in place. On the other hand, if the query is only executed periodically or **Customers** is not going to contain a larger number of rows, the index should be deleted.

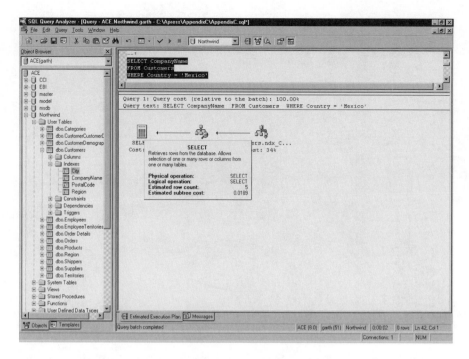

Figure C-3. Estimated subtree cost for execution plan

Creating Valid Search Arguments

The previous section demonstrated that adding an index to a column can significantly reduce the costs associated with producing a resultset. In order for the Query Optimizer to use an existing index, however, the comparison operation must be able to be resolved into a valid SARG. A valid SARG must be of the form

```
Column ComparisonOperator Constant/Variable
```

The following example shows how the execution plan generated by the SELECT presented in the previous section is affected when the SARG requirement is not met. The revised SELECT is shown here, and the execution plan is shown in Figure C-4.

```
SELECT CompanyName
FROM Customers
WHERE SUBSTRING(Country,1,1) = 'A'
```

The SUBSTRING function caused the Query Optimizer to ignore the index and use a Clustered Index Scan. This caused the estimated cost to revert back to .0392, the same estimated cost generated when there was no index on the column.

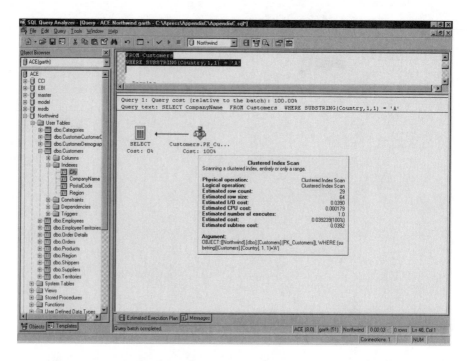

Figure C-4. Estimated execution plan for non-SARG query

The LIKE comparison operator can be used to alter the previous example to produce a valid SARG. The revised query is shown here and the execution plan is shown in Figure C-5.

```
SELECT CompanyName
FROM Customers
WHERE Country LIKE 'A%'
```

The valid SARG allows the Query Optimizer to choose the index and the cost for each operator reverts back to optimal values.

The LIKE comparison operator cannot be used to create a valid SARG in all cases. More specifically, the search string used for the comparison cannot begin with a wildcard character. The following SELECT uses a wildcard as the first character in the search string. This prohibits the Query Optimizer from using the index. The results of this are shown in Figure C-6.

```
SELECT CompanyName
FROM Customers
WHERE Country LIKE '_A%'
```

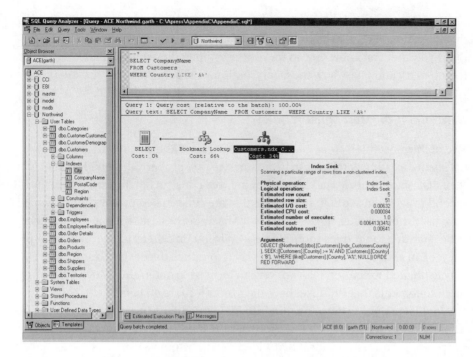

Figure C-5. Estimated execution plan for LIKE query that produces a SARG

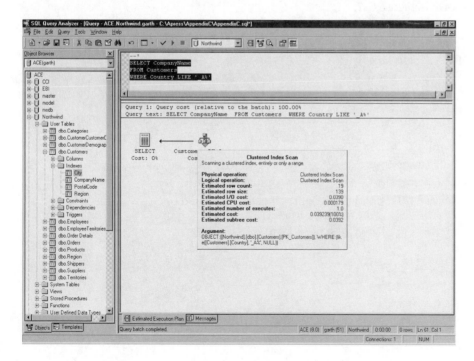

Figure C-6. Estimated execution plan for LIKE query that does not produce a SARG

If you have any questions about whether a given comparison operation produces a valid SARG, use the techniques described here to check the execution plan. Now that you know how to review the estimated execution plan, there is no reason to try and guess how the Query Optimizer is going to execute a query.

Determining the Most Efficient Query

Two of the most interesting functions that I perform as a consultant are to review my clients' existing databases to make sure they are properly designed and analyze their SQL statements to make sure they are well constructed. In performing the second task I often see SQL statements that are constructed in ways I never would have used, but produce the desired resultsets. In some cases the statements need to be rewritten to produce more efficient code, but in others, the developer simply knew of an equally or a more efficient way to produce the desired results. The Display Estimated Execution Plan option can be used to determine which of two or more statements that produce the same results is more efficient.

In this section we examine three SELECT statements that return the same resultset to determine which one produces the most efficient query plan. Each statement produces a resultset that shows those customers who have never placed an order. The first query uses LEFT JOIN with IS NULL, the second NOT EXISTS, and the third NOT IN. The partial execution plans produced by the queries is shown in Figure C-7.

```
--Query 1 -- LEFT JOIN
SELECT CompanyName
FROM Customers a
LEFT JOIN ORDERS b ON a.CustomerID = b.CustomerID
WHERE b.CustomerID IS NULL


--Query 2 -- NOT EXISTS
SELECT CompanyName
FROM Customers a
WHERE NOT EXISTS (SELECT *
                  FROM Orders b
                  WHERE a.CustomerID = b.CustomerID)


--Query 3 -- NOT IN
SELECT CompanyName
FROM Customers
WHERE CustomerID NOT IN (SELECT CustomerID
                         FROM Orders)
```

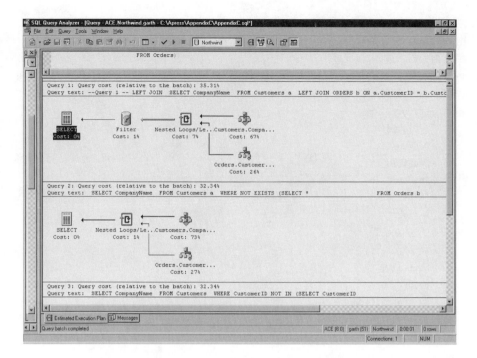

Figure C-7. Estimated execution plans for three SELECT statements

The execution plans for Query 3 are not visible, but you can see the information that will help determine which query is more efficient. The important statistic is "Query cost (relative to batch)." For Query 1 it is 35.31 percent, and for Query 2 and Query 3 it is 32.43 percent. This means that both Query 2 and Query 3 are more efficient than Query 1 and equally efficient as each other.

The "Query cost (relative to batch)." statistic is generated from the Estimated Subtree Cost values for each query. You cannot see the values in Figure C-7, but if you highlight the SELECT icons for each query you will see that the Estimated Subtree Costs for Queries 1–3 are 0.0567, 0.0519, and 0.0519 respectively. The cost relative to the batch is simply the cost for each query divided by the total cost. The calculation to determine the relative to batch cost for Query 1 is [0.0567/(0.0567+0.0519+0.0519)]*100=35.32%.

The relative costs shown in the previous example are misleading. The reason for this is the minimal number of rows in the **Orders** table. The **Orders** table only has 830 rows, so the inefficiencies of one of the queries is not exposed. In order to show how the costs are affected as the number of rows gets larger, I used the statements shown here to create another table called **Orders2** and to populate it with 9,130 rows (executed the INSERT ten times).

```
SELECT *
INTO Orders2
FROM Orders
go
INSERT Orders2
SELECT CustomerID,
       EmployeeID,
       OrderDate,
       RequiredDate,
       ShippedDate,
       ShipVia,
       Freight,
       ShipName,
       ShipAddress,
       ShipCity,
       ShipRegion,
       ShipPostalCode,
       ShipCountry
FROM Orders
```

I then modified the three queries to reference **Orders2** and activated the Display Estimated Execution Plan. The new relative costs are shown in Figure C-8.

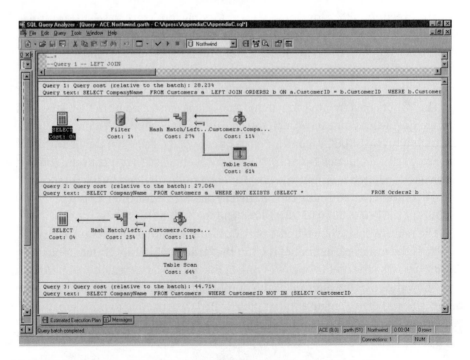

Figure C-8. Estimated execution plans for three SELECT statements

The relative cost for Query 3 increased to over 44 percent. This is a good example of how the size of the database affects a poorly written query.

Determining the Bottleneck

Throughout my career I have often worked on teams on which I was responsible for writing the server-side code (e.g., stored procedures) and one or more other developers were responsible for creating the client application. On numerous occasions we would encounter slow running processes; most of the time the developer of the client code would blame my code for the problem, and I would blame theirs.

The best way I found to determine whose code is at fault is to remove the client-side code from the equation and execute the SQL statements in Query Analyzer. If Query Analyzer executes the statements in a timely manner, the problem is with the client application. Convincing the client-side developer of this is sometimes a problem, but after you demonstrate a few times how quickly the statements are processed by Query Analyzer they usually give in and go review their code.

Let me give you a real-world example so you can better understand how this process works. When I started my first browser-based application project I was responsible for the server-side code and another developer was responsible for the client-side ASP code. The project was moving along at a great pace until we ran into a report that retrieved more than 200 rows from a table and displayed them in a browser. When the report was executed it took more than a minute for the browser to start rendering the HTML, and the developer was convinced that the database code was causing the problem. I knew the problem could not be with the server-side code (a stored procedure) because I had often executed stored procedures that returned a lot more than 200 rows, and they all produced the results in a timely manner. I showed the developer how quickly the procedure ran in Query Analyzer and after a few minutes of explanation he conceded that the problem was on his side of the fence.

It turned out that the problem wasn't with either of our code, but we were simply running into a limitation of the browser. A browser can only render so much HTML at one time, and when you send it such a large amount of text it comes to a grinding halt. If you are a user of Internet search engines like http://www.google.com, you are already familiar with how this limitation is addressed. If you go to google.com and search for "SQL," you will get more than 3 million hits. Of these 3 million hits, the search engine only shows you 10 at a time in order to make the client-side rendering of the HTML more efficient.

Index Tuning Wizard

The ITW (Index Tuning Wizard) makes suggestions about how additional indexes can ensure optimal performance. It can analyze index needs on an entire database or a single query. Both techniques are described in this section.

Before we start using ITW it is necessary to provide some background information on SQL Profiler. SQL Profiler is a tool that captures the activity that occurs within an instance of SQL Server. SQL Profiler captures server events and stores them in either a file or table that is referred to as *trace file*. Once the data is captured it can be used to analyze server performance or troubleshoot issues like finding out what process was running immediately before a server experienced a problem.

SQL Profiler plays an integral role in using ITW. More specifically, a trace file is created that holds DML-specific events so the wizard can analyze the activity that occurs within a database. ITW examines the trace file to determine which objects are being accessed, the type of statements that are executed on the objects, and the execution time of the statements.

SQL Profiler is a very powerful administration and troubleshooting tool, so if you would like to learn more about how it can be used see the Books Online topic: Monitoring with SQL Profiler.

Analyzing a Database

Performing index analysis on a database using ITW is an interesting process. To use ITW you must do the following:

- Use SQL Profiler to capture database activity to a trace file.

- Configure the wizard to read the trace file.

- Examine the results produced by the wizard.

For the wizard to produce useful suggestions, you must capture data that is representative of normal activity within the target database. The example covered here is for illustrative purposes only and does not contain enough data for the wizard to make valid suggestions.

In the "Determining the Most Efficient Query" section earlier in the chapter the **Orders2** table was created and populated with 9,130 rows of data. If you did not create this table on your server, please do so before continuing.

To demonstrate how to use ITW a trace file is created that captures activity performed within the **Northwind** database. Once the trace file is active (capturing events), a series of SQL statements will be executed against **Orders2** to see what type of effect this has on the recommendations made by ITW. Currently there are no indexes on **Orders2**.

Creating a Trace File

To create the trace file, complete the following within Enterprise Manager.

1. Expand a Server Group and select the target server.

2. Click Tools on the main menu and select SQL Profiler.

3. From within SQL Profiler, click File, highlight New, and select Trace.

4. Supply valid login information and click OK. Note that you must be a member of the fixed-server role **sysadmin** to execute SQL Profiler.

5. Populate the Trace name field and click the Save to File checkbox. Specify the location and name of the trace file.

6. Click the Events tab and remove all but the TSQL event classes from the Selected event classes list box as shown in Figure C-9.

Figure C-9. Configuring a trace file

7. Select and expand the TSQL event class in the Available event classes list box.

8. Transfer all the events for this class to the Selected event classes list box as shown in Figure C-10.

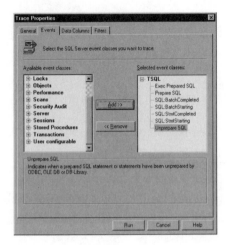

Figure C-10. Add trace events

9. Select the Data Columns tab and browse the columns in the Selected data list box. There are twelve data columns required by ITW, and each one is selected by default.

10. Click the Filters tab and expand the DatabaseName option.

11. Expand the Like option and type in **Northwind** as shown in Figure C-11.

12. Click the Run tab and SQL Profiler is activated.

SQL Profiler will now record all the events specified in the trace definition on the trace file. Let's execute statements in Query Analyzer to see how they affect SQL Profiler. The following statements cause eight events to be recorded in the trace file.

```
USE Northwind
go
SELECT *
FROM Orders2
```

The contents of the trace file after the statements are executed are shown in Figure C-12.

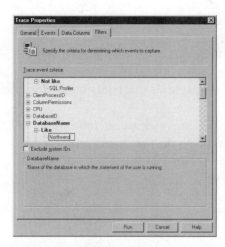

*Figure C-11. Filtering the trace for **Northwind** events*

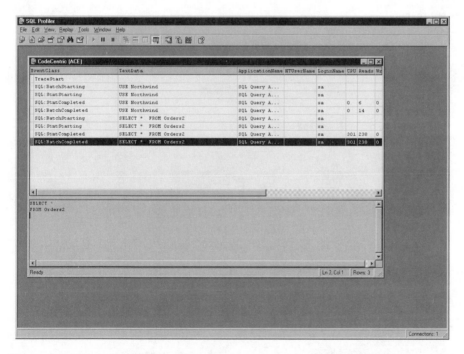

Figure C-12. Trace file contents

Note that each statement caused four events: SQL:BatchStarting,
SQL:StmtStarting, SQL:StmtEnding, and SQL:BatchEnding. Execute the
following SELECT and again view the contents of the trace file.

```
SELECT *
FROM Orders2
WHERE CustomerID = 'CENTC'
```

Four more events are captured that contain the execution statistics for the SELECT.

The next statement we are going to execute is an UPDATE with a WHERE clause. The following changes the **ShipName** value for the specified **CusomerID**.

```
UPDATE Orders2

SET ShipName = 'El Centro Rocket Shop'
WHERE CustomerID = 'VICTE'
```

The last statement is a SELECT that uses **CustomerID** in a comparison operation.

```
SELECT *
FROM Orders2
WHERE CustomerID = 'VICTE'
```

The contents of the trace file after this statement is executed is shown in Figure C-13.

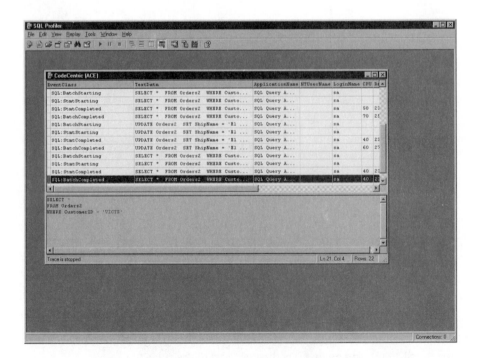

Figure C-13. Trace file contents

> **WARNING** Trace Files Grow Very Quickly
>
> *SQL Profiler trace files grow at an alarming rate when they capture data on a server that generates a lot of activity. Once you create a trace file, make sure you monitor its growth rate for the first few hours so you can ensure that you have plenty of available disk space to hold the contents.*

Running the Trace File in ITW

Now that we have a trace file that contains activity for **Northwind**, let's configure ITW to analyze its contents. In order to invoke ITW from within SQL Profiler, complete the following.

1. Click File on the main menu and select Stop Trace.

2. Click Tools on the main menu and select Index Tuning Wizard.

3. Once ITW is active, click the Next button and supply a valid login.

4. From within the Select Server and Database dialog, select **Northwind** from the Database drop-down box. Accept the other default selections by clicking Next.

5. On the Specify Workload dialog, click the My Workload file and find the .trc file created by SQL Profiler. Figure C-14 shows how this looks on my computer.

6. Click Next to access the Select Tables to Tune dialog, and then click the Select All Tables button.

7. Click the Next button. ITW analyzes the contents of the trace file and then recommends indexes that will improve performance. Figure C-15 shows the recommendations generated by ITW.

8. Click Next to activate the Schedule Index Update Job dialog.

9. Select the Apply Changes check box and accept the default to Execute recommendations now by clicking Next.

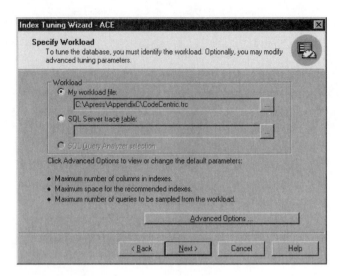

Figure C-14. Accessing the trace file

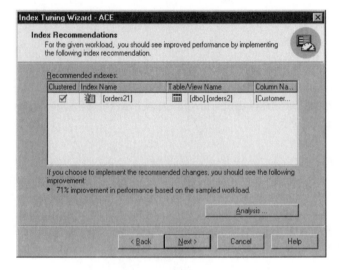

Figure C-15. Index recommendations

10. Click Finish on the final dialog and the new index is created on **Orders2**. The new index is created and given the name **orders21**. Use Object Browser to verify the index exists.

Given the number of statements that used **CustomerID** in comparison operations, it should not surprise you that ITW suggested adding an index to this column. The contents of the trace file are extremely myopic, so you should only think of this example as a way to learn how to use ITW. When you use ITW, make sure the trace files contains data that is representative of normal database activity. Otherwise, its recommendations will be skewed to the specific activity captured by the trace.

I want to caution you not to blindly rely on ITW to determine the indexing strategy you apply to a database. Use it wisely and make sure you examine the recommendations thoroughly before implementing them on a production server.

> **WARNING CREATE INDEX Impacts Performance**
>
> *In the preceding example, I allowed ITW to create the index immediately after it made the recommendations. If you use ITW on a production database, be very cautious about creating indexes during peak usage. Creating an index on a large table will require significant resources and will most likely have a negative impact on performance.*

Analyzing a Query

Using ITW to analyze an individual query is much easier than analyzing an entire database. The reason is that you are not required to use SQL Profiler to create a trace file. Instead, ITW uses the resultset produced by the query as the basis for its recommendations.

The **Orders2** table referenced in the previous section is also going to be used here. If you allowed ITW to create the **orders21** index, please execute the following statement before continuing.

```
DROP INDEX Orders2.Orders21
```

Use ITW via Query Analyzer to analyze the following SELECT.

```
SELECT *
FROM Orders2
WHERE ShipName LIKE 'A%'
ORDER BY ShipName
```

Before you do, though, execute Display Estimated Execution Plan by selecting Query > Display Estimated Execution Plan from the main menu. The results are shown in Figure C-16.

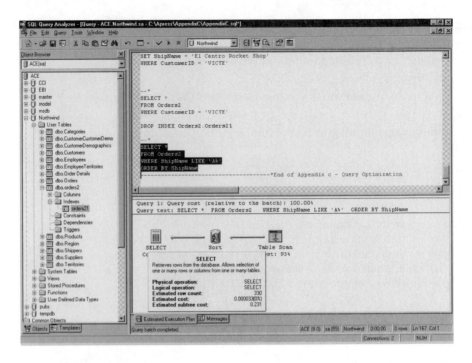

Figure C-16. Estimated execution plan for sample query

Notice that the Estimated Subtree Cost is 0.231. We will run this again after we apply the recommendations given by ITW to determine the usefulness of its suggestions.

To run ITW in Query Analyzer, complete the following.

1. Highlight the target query, click Query on the main menu, and select Index Tuning Wizard.

2. Click Next on the first two dialogs to get to Specify Workload. Notice that SQL Query Analyzer selection radio button is selected as shown in Figure C-17.

3. Click Next and select **Orders2** from the table listing in the Select Tables to Tune dialog.

4. Click Next and ITW generates the recommendation shown in Figure C-18.

5. Click Next and select the Apply Changes check box on the Schedule Index Update dialog.

6. Click Next and then Finish on the final dialog. The new index is created.

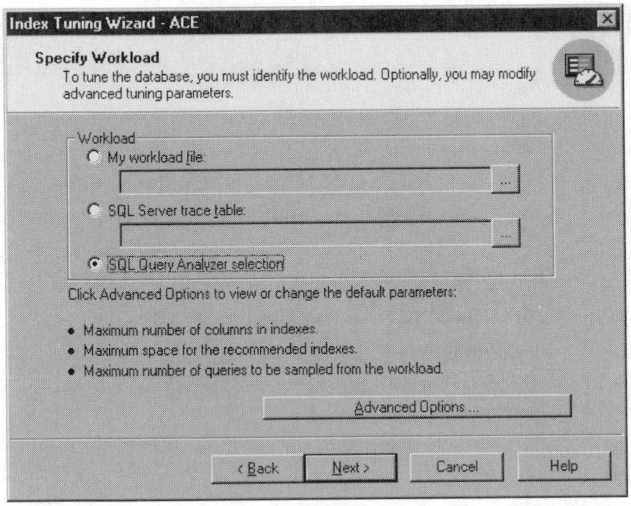

Figure C-17. Specify Workload dialog

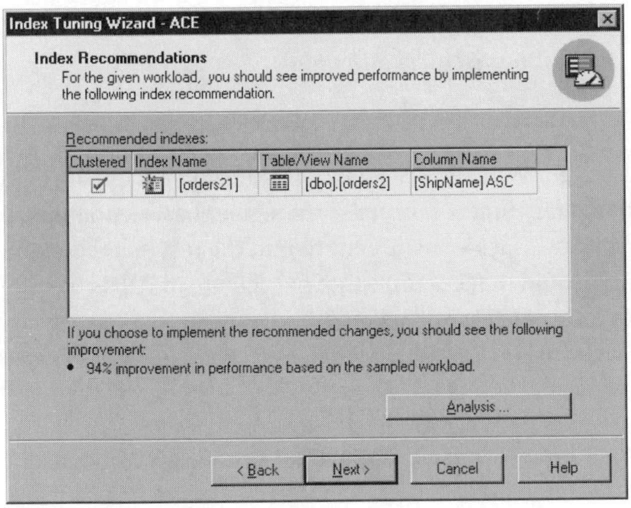

Figure C-18. Index Recommendations dialog

Now that we have accepted ITW's recommendation, let's execute Display Estimated Execution Plan to determine if it had a positive impact on the execution of the query. Figure C-19 shows the results of executing the option.

The Estimated Subtree Query Cost is 0.0127, which is a 94 percent decrease in cost over the 0.231 generated before the index was applied.

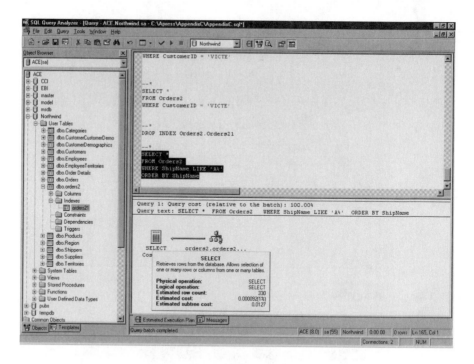

Figure C-19. New estimated execution plan

I suggest using ITW via Query Analyzer when you are having performance problems with a query that is executed on a regular basis. I do think, however, that after you use it a few times you will start to find the results predictable. It's not too difficult to understand that columns that participate in JOINs or comparison operations are the ones ITW will recommend as needing indexes.

SQL Server Loves Memory

Although hardware configuration and performance tuning are not discussed in this appendix, I would be remiss if I did not pass on the following words of wisdom: SQL Server Loves Memory. If there is one area in which you should spend money when buying a new server or upgrading an existing one, it's on memory. SQL Server accesses all data pages via cache, so the more memory on the server, the more data pages that can fit into cache.

If you want to see how this affects query performance, reboot your SQL Server and then execute a query that accesses a large set of data. The first time you execute the query it will be slow because the desired data pages are not cached. The subsequent executions should be much faster because the pages accessed by the query will remain cached until the space they occupy is needed by other pages.

Having too little memory in a server that hosts SQL Server can have a tremendous impact on an application's performance. When a query that accesses a large number of data pages is executed on a server that does not have sufficient memory, the data pages have to be loaded and unloaded from memory until all desired pages are processed. This is very inefficient and can put a tremendous strain on the server when numerous simultaneous users access the server.

Having too much memory is a good thing. If you have a server whose available memory exceeds the size of the databases it hosts, then it is theoretically possible that all the desired data pages are in memory when they are needed.

> **TIP Loading Cache at Startup**
>
> *Chapter 11 discusses auto-start stored procedures. These are procedures that are configured to execute immediately after SQL Server is started. You can use an auto-start procedure to load cache with the most-active tables in your application. For example, you can create an auto-start procedure that performs a* SELECT * *on these tables, and they will be available as soon as they are needed by the application.*

Application Design Issues

A number of application design issues must be considered to ensure an application performs as expected. The major application design issues are discussed here.

Database Design

Database design is the single most important application design issue. A poorly designed database is analogous to a building with a faulty foundation. It doesn't matter how many coats of paint or other features you add above ground, the structure will still fall down when placed under stress.

I recommend that you design your databases to at least third normal form and do not use denormalization techniques unless absolutely necessary. (Denormalization is a good thing, however, when working with data warehousing applications). If you do not understand this concept, I suggest you buy *Relational Database Design Clearly Explained* by Jan Harrington (ISBN 0123264251). It is imperative that you have a good understanding of Relational Database Theory before designing a database application.

If you have a database project that needs immediate attention and cannot wait until you get up to speed on relational concepts, you might consider hiring a consultant to help you design the database. Consultants are expensive, but paying up front is certainly cheaper than paying when the application is no longer meeting user requirements. And as you probably know, it always costs more to fix a mistake than to implement a well-thought-out design. Plus, waiting until an application is not performing as expected also leaves you in a bad bargaining position. You may not have the luxury of waiting until the "right" consultant is available.

Denormalization

Denormalization is a technique that uses a less-than-ideal database design to produce faster data access. Using this technique in data warehousing applications is not only acceptable, but in some cases, the only way to ensure the warehousing application will perform at an optimal speed. It should only be used as a last resort in transactional systems.

Server-Side Processing

Server-side processing refers to placing the data manipulation code used by an application *on* the database server. I recommend you avoid using SQL Passthrough (a.k.a., *ad hoc queries*) and use stored procedures for data manipulation. Client-side data manipulation code not only makes client code harder to read and maintain, but also opens the door for creating less than optimal code. After all, it is much easier to perform a looping operation (bad design) in a procedural language than it is in set-based language like T-SQL.

Indexing Strategy

An indexing strategy refers to the analysis and research that a developer performs to determine the appropriate indexes for a database. The situation I described in the "Over-Indexing a Database" section earlier in this appendix has caused me to take a very cautious approach when it comes to implementing an indexing strategy. In general, I am reactive (instead of proactive) when it comes to creating an index on a non-key column. There are times when it is obvious that the application's performance will benefit by creating a non-key index, but if there is any doubt in my mind that the benefits will not outweigh the overhead associated with maintaining the index, I do not create the index. Instead I monitor the activity on the target table closely and make a decision based on the application's performance after it goes into production.

Test Throughout the Development Cycle

Technically this topic is not so much application design as it is a good programming practice. The main point I want to emphasis here is that you should not wait until pre-production to test the performance of your application. Creating sound performance testing techniques in the early stages of project will make implementing the tests much easier during the development phase. Waiting until the pre-production phase to test performance can not only prove embarrassing, but can cause significant delays in releasing the application if problems are encountered.

Before You Go

The material I presented in this appendix will help you design applications that perform at optimal levels. The Display Estimated Execution Plan option in Query Analyzer was covered in sufficient detail to allow you to determine the following:

- The impact an index has on a query

- Whether a comparison operation can be resolved into a SARG

- The most efficient of one or more queries that produce the same resultset

In addition to these topics, I presented two methods of using ITW to determine when an index is needed to optimize query performance. In the final section I discussed important application design issues that should be considered before the coding phase of a project starts.

XML Primer

THIS APPENDIX WAS INCLUDED WITH TWO GOALS IN MIND. The first is to give you a general introduction to XML (eXtensible Markup Language) technology. If you have read any articles on XML, you probably noticed that quite a few abbreviations are used to describe its components. The proliferation of abbreviations can cause confusion, so I want to explain the major components so you can understand how they work together. The second goal is to demonstrate how to use the functionality of SQL Server to manipulate XML data.

XML is going to play a major role in data transfer technology in the near future. I encourage you to study the material presented in this appendix and seek out other learning material, as well. The sooner you are up-to-speed on XML, the better positioned you will be to take advantage of the opportunities it will create.

NOTE   Sample Code

The sample code for this appendix is available for download at either http://www.apress.com *or* http://www.SQLBook.com. *Download CodeCentric.zip, extract the contents, and look for the file named AppD.zip. This file contains the .sql and .xml files needed to complete the examples.*

Before You Get Started

You must have a general understanding of XML to complete the examples covered in this appendix. I present this primer with this in mind.

The Origin of XML

The purpose of XML is to allow developers to describe data in a simple, easy-to-read format. Developed in 1996, XML is a hybrid of both SGML (Standard Generalized Markup Language) and HTML. SGML, developed in the early 80s, is the first markup language that allowed for describing data, but has cryptic syntax and is not easy to learn. HTML, developed in 1990, is a markup language that provides syntax for data presentation—not data describing.

The creators of XML wanted to take the ease of use of HTML and descriptive properties of SGML and create a new markup language that facilitated data transfer. XML documents are text files, so they can be read across all computer platforms. Once you have a standard for marking up (describing) data and the format of the file in which the descriptions and data are held is cross-platform compatible, you have a very powerful method of transferring data.

EDI (Electronic Data Interchange) Versus XML

EDI is a process that facilitates business-to-business communications by allowing data to be exchanged in standard formats. The data interchange is conducted computer-to-computer in formats defined by ANSI and UN/EDIFACT. The goals of EDI and XML are the same, but the ease with which you can implement one over the other varies greatly. In an EDI scenario, advanced knowledge of the standards are required and custom software is needed to enable it to work over the Internet. With XML, you can get by with basic knowledge of the syntax and it was designed specifically to work over the Internet. Look for XML applications to replace and/or augment EDI as XML technology matures.

XML Basics

The following topics introduce the basics of XML. For more information on any of these topics, please see the "Additional Resources" section at the end of this appendix.

An XML Document

An XML document is generally composed of two parts: a prolog and a document element. The prolog, which is optional, provides general information like the version of the XML specification to which the document adheres. A valid prolog looks like this: `<? xml version="1.0" encoding="UTF-8"?>`. The question marks are prolog indicators and differentiate the tag from a user-defined tag. The version attribute indicates the document adheres to version 1 of the XML specification. The encoding attribute indicates the document is encoded using UTF-8 of the Unicode character set. Unicode is discussed in the "Before You Get Started" section in Chapter 2. The prolog information is supplied so an XML parser knows what kind of document it is working with. An XML parser is a program that reads and interprets XML documents. Microsoft's XML Parser is called MSXML and, at the time this was written, was at version 3.0 (MSMXL 3.0).

The document element portion of an XML document contains data and markup tags that describe the data. The combination of data and a markup tag is called an *element*. Elements are created using tags that describe the data they encompass. Unlike HTML, XML contains no pre-defined tags. An XML tag must adhere to the syntax of the language, but the actual tag itself is created by a developer. The general format of a tag is `<TagName>…</TagName>`. The syntax is very similar to HTML in that it contains a beginning and end tag wrapped around data. The data that appears between the tags is called the element's *value*. A tag that describes a company name takes the form

`<Company>DataDrivenWebSites.com, Inc.</Company>`.

XML tags can also have attributes that help to further define data. A tag with an attribute takes the form

`<TagName attribute="AttributeValue">data</TagName>`.

Note that the attribute value can be surrounded with either single or double-quotes. The `<Company>` tag can be modified to include an attribute as follows:

`<Company BusinessType="Corporation">DataDrivenWebSites.com, Inc.</Company>`.

There is another type of tag used to specify all the data as attributes; no element data is specified. This type of tag is called an *empty-element tag*, and it does not require an end-tag. The following shows how to create the previous tag as an empty-element tag.

`<Company name="DataDrivenWebSites.com, Inc" BusinessType="Corporation"/>`.

The decision to use an element-centric over an attribute-centric design is dictated by the data being accessed. In general, the element-centric approach is used when the data is more complex and contains multiple levels of hierarchy (e.g., multi-table joins). The attribute-centric approach is best used when the data set is small and does not change on a frequent basis. Because most relational databases contain numerous tables that require multi-table joins to produce a meaningful resultset, I use the element-centric approach in this appendix.

If you recall from Appendix A, in some circumstances you can forget to include a closing tag in HTML and the page will still work as expected. This is not the case with XML. If you forget to include a closing tag, the document will generate an error and will not be processed by the parser. HTML tags are not case-sensitive (e.g., `<font>` = `<FONT>`), but XML tags are; `<TagName>data</TagName>` is not equivalent to `<tagname>data</tagname>`. Similar to HTML, XML tags must be properly nested and have no tag overlap. The following code is not correct because the `<City>` tag overlaps the `<Company>` tag.

`<Company>DataDrivenWebSites.com, Inc.<City>Houston</Company></City>`

An XML document that adheres to the requirement previously mentioned is referred to as *well-formed* and will be successfully processed by an XML parser. An example of a well-formed document is shown next. Note that I've added line numbers to facilitate explanation

```
1 <? xml version="1.0" encoding="UTF-8"?>
2 <!-- Doc Version 2.0 Created 12/13/00 -->
3 <CompanyDirectory updated="1/1/01">
4  <Company>
5   <name>DataDrivenWebSites.com, Inc.</name>
6   <businesstype>Corporation</businesstype>
7   <contact title="President">Garth Wells</contact>
8   <phonenumber>713.555.1212</phonenumber>
9  </Company>
10  <Company>
11   <name>Houston Rockets</name>
12   <businesstype>Corporation</businesstype>
13   <contact title="President">Les Alexander</contact>
14   <phonenumber>713.555.3232</phonenumber>
15  </Company>
16 </CompanyDirectory>
```

Line 1 is the prolog that indicates version and encoding information. Line 2 is a comment that indicates the version of the document and the date it was created. Note that XML uses the same comment indicators as HTML. Lines 3 and 16 define the document element (a.k.a. root element) of the document as a Company-Directory. Every document must have only one root element, and the root element contains elements that compose the document. Lines 4–9 and 10–15 describe elements of the CompanyDirectory root. As you can see, a simple XML document is very easy to create and read. Except for the attributes of the prolog, I created all the tags in the document.

The root element/element concept produces XML documents that correspond to a tree structure. Figure D-1 shows the tree structure produced by the sample document.

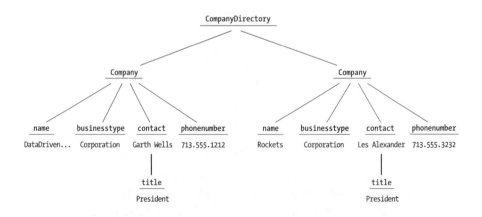

Figure D-1. Tree structure produced by document

The tree structure nature of XML documents is key to ensuring that they are successfully processed by a parser.

You might have noticed there are no tags that indicate how the data should be displayed to an end-user. XML does not concern itself with display issues. Another language, called XSL (eXtensible Stylesheet Language), displays XML data; I will discuss this language later in the appendix.

The Power of XML

When you first read about XML, it's difficult to fully appreciate how powerful it is because it seems so simple. This simplicity, of course, is one of the things that makes it so powerful. Let's review a real-world example so you might better understand why XML is being touted as the data transfer technology of the future.

Suppose you are a manufacturer of computers and you have both corporate and individual customers. Some of your corporate customers have custom purchase order systems that they are required to use to procure equipment. Your individual customers place orders via telephone and your corporate Web site that uses ASP to interact with your database. With traditional systems, you might have two different methods of creating orders in your order management system. If a customer—either corporate or individual—calls in, an employee enters the order into the system. When the Web site is used, the order is entered by the customer.

What if you wanted to streamline the communications with your corporate customers (who make up the bulk of your sales) by allowing their procurement system to communicate directly with your order entry system? The problem with this scenario is that your customers' procurement systems could use multiple formats to store the data.

When XML is used to implement a solution, the format of the source data is irrelevant. As long as your customers can create a text file (and all computer systems can produce a text file) that conforms to a format you specify, they can send the order data across the Internet and automatically be inserted into the target database. The Web site's order entry functionality created with ASP is modified so that it too communicates with the database via XML. This is a much more flexible solution, and the cost of implementing such a system is low relative to an EDI solution.

The real beauty of an XML solution, though, lies in the ease with which new companies can interact with your system. You simply publish a format that the XML documents must conform to and provide a URL to which the documents are sent to create an order. Of course, you could also communicate back to their systems via XML as long as the required format is known.

This type of solution will make more sense as you learn how SQL Server's XML functionality is implemented and complete the examples in the appendix. I did, however, want to provide some context as to how XML is used in the real world.

XML Namespaces

Because an XML tag can be created by any developer, it is highly likely that two or more developers will use the same descriptor to describe different data elements. For example, one developer may use <name> to specify a company name, and another may use it to specify an individual's name. To eliminate the problems this might cause, XML namespaces were introduced.

XML namespaces allow a developer to qualify element names with an alias that refers to a universally unique identifier. The general form of a namespace declaration is <root xmlns="URI">. The root references the root element of the document, xmlns is required syntax that stands for XML namespace, and URI is a globally unique identifier. URI stands for Universal Resource Identifier. Because a URL is unique, it is common practice to use one as part of the URI.

You can declare default or explicit namespaces. When a default namespace is used, all elements in the document are assumed to be from the same namespace. The following example shows how to add a default namespace to the previous example. Note that I removed an element to increase readability.

```
1 <? xml version="1.0" encoding="UTF-8"?>
2 <!-- Doc Version 2.0 Created 12/13/00 -->
3 <CompanyDirectory xmlns="www.DataDrivenWebSites.com-Corporate" _
                     updated="1/1/01">
4  <Company>
5   <name>DataDrivenWebSites.com, Inc.</name>
6   <businesstype>Corporation</businesstype>
7   <title="President">Garth Wells</contact>
8   <phonenumber>713.555.1212</phonenumber>
9  </Company>
10 </CompanyDirectory>
```

Line 3 is modified to add a namespace. The URI (www.DataDrivenWebSites.com-Corporate) is simply a unique identifier I created. All the elements in the document are assumed to belong to this namespace.

Explicit namespaces preface each element name with an alias that is associated with a namespace. You typically use this approach when document elements are based on two or more namespaces. The following code shows how to modify the previous example to add another namespace and aliases for each one referenced in the document. This example is for illustrative purposes only, as more than one namespace is not needed to describe this document.

```
1 <? xml version="1.0" encoding="UTF-8"?>
2 <!-- Doc Version 2.0 Created 12/13/00 -->
```

```
3 < cor:CompanyDirectory xmlns:cor="www.DataDrivenWebSites.com-Corporate" _
                          xmlns:gen="www.DataDrivenWebSites.com-GeneralUse" _
                          updated="1/1/01">
4   <cor:Company>
5   <cor:name>DataDrivenWebSites.com, Inc.</cor:name>
6   <cor:businesstype>Corporation</cor:businesstype>
7   <cor:title="President">Garth Wells</cor:contact>
8   <gen:phonenumber>713.555.1212</gen:phonenumber>
9   </cor:Company>
10 </cor:CompanyDirectory>
```

Schemas

A schema allows a developer to define how the elements in an XML document are processed. It provides mapping information that allows the parser to determine the relationship between an element in an XML document and a table/column in a database. The original way this type of functionality was implemented was with a DTD (Document Type Definition). Microsoft felt the DTD approach was not the most efficient way to add structure definition to a document because it is not based on XML syntax and does not allow for data type declarations. Microsoft created its own method for adding structure, and it is called XDR (XML-Data Reduced) language. XDR schemas are created and used later in the appendix.

One of the key factors for the long-term success of XML lies in the ability to create industry-specific schemas that are used as standards for conducting XML data transfer. Having standard schemas per industry will make implementing XML solutions easier because developers are not required to spend countless hours trying to create schemas that contain all the needed data elements. There are a number of organizations that promote the creation and use of these types of schemas. You can read about Microsoft's effort to promote standard schemas here: http:/www.biztalk.org/library/library.asp.

XSL

As I mentioned previously, XML does not contain language elements to support data display. When you need to produce formatted output for data in an XML document, you use XSL. Please note that you can also use CSS (cascading style sheets) to display XML data, but XSL is the preferred approach because it is based on the XML language. XSL allows you to pull data stored in an XML document and display it in a format like HTML. XSL uses the same syntax as XML, so there is no need to learn another language to add formatting to your data.

The examples presented in the appendix do not require XSL because they demonstrate how to modify a database based on the contents of an XML document; no data presentation is needed. I cover the term so you will be aware of its role in implementing XML-based solutions.

SQL/XML Primer

Now that you have a basic understanding of XML, I want to cover how to use SQL Server to process XML documents. There are two steps involved in implementing XML/SQL Server interaction. The first is to configure a virtual root on a Web site to communicate with SQL Server; the second involves writing the XML and SQL statements to interact with the database.

Configuring SQL/XML Support

XML integration with SQL Server is implemented with HTTP via IIS (Internet Information Server). The examples presented in this appendix use the IIS default Web site (inetpub\wwwroot) and the **CodeCentric** database. If you did not create the **CodeCentric** database with the example scripts in the Chapter 13 sample file (Ch13.sql), please do so before continuing.

The first thing to do when configuring SQL/XML is to create three subdirectories using Windows Explorer. On my computer the default Web site is installed on the C: drive, so I created the following subdirectories.

```
c:\inetpub\wwwroot\CodeCentric
c:\inetpub\wwwroot\CodeCentric\template
c:\inetpub\wwwroot\CodeCentric\schema
```

The CodeCentric subdirectory is used to create the virtual directory under wwwroot. I could have used any name in place of CodeCentric, but since the database we are working with is named CodeCentric this is a good name to choose. The template and schema directories hold files that facilitate XML/SQL integration. You can use other names in place of "template" and "schema," but given the types of documents they hold (templates and schemas), this makes the most sense.

Now that the subdirectories are in place, use the Configure SQL XML Support in IIS utility to create the virtual directory. The utility is located in the SQL Server group off the Programs option (Start>Programs>Microsoft SQL Server). Once the utility is open, complete the following steps:

1. Expand the server listing in the left pane.

2. Right-click Default Web Site, highlight New, and select Virtual Directory.

3. On the General tab, specify CodeCentric for the Virtual Directory Name and the path to the CodeCentric subdirectory in the Local Path input box.

4. Click the Security tab and supply a valid User Name and Password that has full rights to the **CodeCentric** database. If you do not have a user created, you can use the following statements to create a login that is member of the fixed-database role **db_owner** in **CodeCentric**.

```
USE CodeCentric
go
sp_addlogin @loginname='XMLUser',
            @passwd='password',
            @defdb='CodeCentric'

sp_grantdbaccess @loginname='XMLUser'

sp_addrolemember @rolename='db_owner' ,
                 @membername='XMLUser'
```

5. Click the Data Source tab; you will be prompted to verify the password.

6. On the Data Source tab, specify the name of the SQL Server on which **CodeCentric** is located. Use the default of (local) if IIS and SQL Server are on the same computer.

7. Click the down arrow on the Databases list box and select CodeCentric after the list box is populated. You can type the database name, but listing them ensures you can connect to SQL Server.

8. Click the Settings tab and click the check boxes for: Allow URL queries, Allow template queries, Allow XPath, and Allow POST.

9. Click the Virtual Names tab and click the New button. Specify Schema in the Virtual Name field, select Schema in the Type list box, and specify the CodeCentric\schema subdirectory in the Path field. Click Save to exit the dialog.

10. Click the New button again and specify template in the Virtual Name field, select template in the Type list box, and specify the CodeCentric\template subdirectory in the Path field. Click Save to exit the dialog.

11. Click the New button again and specify dbobject in the Virtual Name field and select dbobject in the Type list box. Path is not required for this entry. Click Save to exit the dialog.

12. Click Apply to save the settings for the virtual directory.

> **WARNING Host Headers Causes Error**
>
> *If you use host headers to support multiple sites off the same IP, the Configure SQL XML Support in IIS utility will not work. An error is generated that indicates the virtual directory could not be created. Host headers must be removed before the utility can complete successfully.*

Accessing Data via HTTP

As I mentioned earlier, XML data is transferred to SQL Server via HTTP. Now that the virtual directory is configured, you can communicate with the server via the address line in your browser. Execute the following statements in **CodeCentric** so you have data to query.

```
CREATE TABLE Customers
(
 Cus_UniqueID int IDENTITY PRIMARY KEY,
 Cus_Name varchar(30) NOT NULL,
 Cus_ConFName varchar(30) NOT NULL,
 Cus_ConLName varchar(30) NOT NULL
)
go
INSERT Customers VALUES ('Astros','Drayton','McLane')
```

In order to query the data via HTTP, you supply a valid SQL SELECT via the address bar in IE. The following URL retrieves all the data the **Customers** table.

```
http://ace/CodeCentric?sql=SELECT * FROM Customers _
                        FOR XML AUTO,ELEMENTS&root=root
```

The name of my server is "ace;" you need to modify the URL per your setup. The SELECT statement is passed into the virtual directory created previously, and the results are returned to the browser. I will cover the SELECT…FOR XML syntax in the next section, but for now let's look at the output shown in Figure D-2.

The data is retrieved from the database, and a structured XML document is created and written to the browser. If you look at the URL in Figure D-2, you will notice that it is not the same as the one listed previously. More specifically all the spaces have been replaced with '%20,' which is an escape sequence needed to pass a space to IIS. IIS doesn't handle URLs with spaces, so the string is encoded before it is passed to IIS

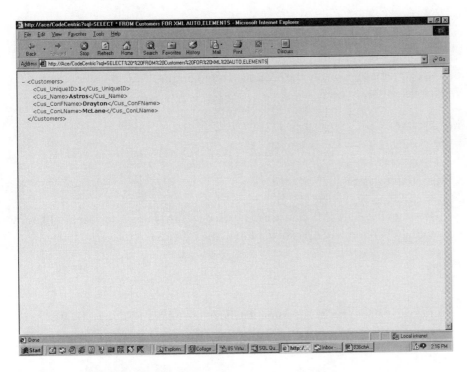

Figure D-2. XML output from customers

I am not going to use the URL approach to manipulate data stored in SQL Server. It's great for testing the initial configuration of the virtual directory, but it opens up too many security holes to use on an ongoing basis. Any valid SQL statement can be passed to the server via a URL when the Allow URL Queries option is enabled. There is nothing to keep anyone who knows the address of the virtual directory from sending DELETE or other destructive statements to the database. In order to eliminate this security hole, I suggest you use the Configure SQL XML Support in IIS utility to turn off the Allow URL Queries option. To turn off this option, complete the following steps:

1. Open the utility (it is probably still open from the previous exercise).

2. Right-click CodeCentric in the right pane and select Properties.

3. Click the settings tab and uncheck the Allow URL Queries option.

SELECT... FOR XML

The example I presented in the previous section used the FOR clause of the SELECT statement to create the XML structured output. The general syntax for the FOR clause is shown here.

```
FOR XML { RAW | AUTO | EXPLICIT }
    [ , XMLDATA ]
    [ , ELEMENTS ]
    [ , BINARY base64 ]
```

Note that the FOR XML clause can be used within Query Analyzer just like any other SELECT statement. An explanation of the clause's components follow.

XML

Returns resultset as an XML document. One of the RAW, AUTO, or EXPLICIT options must be specified when XML is used.

RAW

Transforms each row in the resultset into an XML element with a "row" generic identifier.

AUTO

Creates a nested tree structure of the resultset. Each table referenced in the SELECT is represented with an element and element attributes. Note that only the tables that return data are included in the output.

EXPLICIT

Allows the structure of the XML document to be specified in the SELECT statement using aliases. This is an advanced option and will not be covered in this appendix.

XMLDATA

Returns a document schema without a root element. The resultset is appended to the schema as an XML document.

ELEMENTS

Produces an XML document that is element-centric. The column values are
returned as sub-elements of the table elements.

BINARY64

Base-64 encoded format. Default mode when AUTO is specified.

FOR XML Examples

The best way to see how the various clauses of FOR XML work is by looking at a
series of examples. To show more meaningful examples, I need to create two more
tables to go along with **Customers**. The following statements create an **Orders** and
Products table and populate each with a minimal amount of data.

```
CREATE TABLE Products
(
 Pro_UniqueID int IDENTITY PRIMARY KEY,
 Pro_Desc varchar(30) NOT NULL,
 Pro_Price smallmoney NOT NULL
)
go
INSERT Products VALUES ('baseball',12.65)
INSERT Products VALUES ('basketball',80.00)
INSERT Products VALUES ('football',65.34)

CREATE TABLE Orders
(
 Ord_UniqueID int IDENTITY PRIMARY KEY,
 Cus_UniqueID int NOT NULL REFERENCES Customers(Cus_UniqueID),
 Ord_Date smalldatetime NOT NULL,
 Pro_UniqueID int NOT NULL REFERENCES Products(Pro_UniqueID),
 Ord_Quantity smallint NOT NULL,
 Ord_Price smallmoney NOT NULL
)
go
INSERT Orders VALUES (1,'12/13/00',1,100,12.65)
```

The following query demonstrates how to find the orders placed by a customer
and is used as the basis for the FOR XML examples.

```
SELECT a.Cus_Name,
       c.Pro_Desc,
       b.Ord_Quantity,
       b.Ord_Quantity*b.Ord_Price AS Ord_Cost
FROM Customers a
JOIN Orders b ON a.Cus_UniqueID = b.Cus_UniqueID
JOIN Products c ON b.Pro_UniqueID = c.Pro_UniqueID
--Results--
Cus_Name   Pro_Desc                            Ord_Quantity  Ord_Cost
---------- ----------------------------------- ------------- ------------

Astros     baseball                            100           1265.0000
```

The next set of examples demonstrates how to use the various FOR clause arguments.

FOR XML RAW

The first example shows the output produced by RAW argument.

```
SELECT a.Cus_Name,
       c.Pro_Desc,
       b.Ord_Quantity,
       b.Ord_Quantity*b.Ord_Price AS Ord_Cost
FROM Customers a
JOIN Orders b ON a.Cus_UniqueID = b.Cus_UniqueID
JOIN Products c ON b.Pro_UniqueID = c.Pro_UniqueID
FOR XML RAW
--Results--
XML_F52E2B61-18A1-11d1-B105-00805F49916B-----------------------------------------
<row Cus_Name="Astros" Pro_Desc="baseball" Ord_Quantity="100" _
     Ord_Cost="1265.0000"/>
```

Each column returned by the SELECT is placed as an attribute value for the "row" element. This output demonstrates the attribute-centric approach described earlier—all data is an attribute of an element.

FOR XML AUTO

The output produced with AUTO argument is shown here. Note that the results are formatted to increase readability. The actual output in Query Analyzer is one line of data.

```
SELECT Cus_Name,
       Pro_Desc,
       Ord_Quantity,
       Ord_Quantity*Ord_Price AS Ord_Cost
FROM Customers
JOIN Orders ON Customers.Cus_UniqueID = Orders.Cus_UniqueID
JOIN Products ON Orders.Pro_UniqueID = Products.Pro_UniqueID
FOR XML AUTO
--Results--
XML_F52E2B61-18A1-11d1-B105-00805F49916B
-----------------------------------------------------------------------------
<Customers Cus_Name="Astros">
 <Products Pro_Desc="baseball">
  <Orders Ord_Quantity="100" Ord_Cost="1265.0000"/>
 </Products>
</Customers>
```

The table aliases used in the previous example were removed to improve the structure of the output. When a table alias is used, it is listed in the tags instead of the table name (e.g., Customers = a).

FOR XML...XMLDATA

The XMLDATA argument can be used with both RAW and AUTO. It produces an inline schema of the document and then includes the data elements returned by the resultset. The format of the data section is a function of RAW or AUTO. The schema is defined between the <Schema...>...</Schema> tags and the XML document is appended immediately after. Please note the results shown below are heavily formatted to fit on a printed page. The actual output is on a single line and is 618 characters long.

```
SELECT Cus_Name,
       Pro_Desc,
       Ord_Quantity,
       Ord_Quantity*Ord_Price AS Ord_Cost
FROM Customers
JOIN Orders ON Customers.Cus_UniqueID = Orders.Cus_UniqueID
JOIN Products ON Orders.Pro_UniqueID = Products.Pro_UniqueID
FOR XML AUTO, XMLDATA
--Results--
XML_F52E2B61-18A1-11d1-B105-00805F49916B
-----------------------------------------------------------------------------
<Schema name="Schema2" xmlns="urn:schemas-microsoft-com:xml-data"
                       xmlns:dt="urn:schemas-microsoft-com:datatypes">
```

639

```
<ElementType name="Customers" content="eltOnly" model="closed" order="many">
 <element type="Products" maxOccurs="*"/>
  <AttributeType name="Cus_Name" dt:type="string"/>
   <attribute type="Cus_Name"/>
</ElementType>
<ElementType name="Products" content="eltOnly" model="closed" _
            order="many">
 <element type="Orders" maxOccurs="*"/>
 <AttributeType name="Pro_Desc" dt:type="string"/>
  <attribute type="Pro_Desc"/>
</ElementType>
<ElementType name="Orders" content="empty" model="closed">
 <AttributeType name="Ord_Quantity" dt:type="i2"/>
 <AttributeType name="Ord_Cost" dt:type="fixed.14.4"/>
  <attribute type="Ord_Quantity"/>
  <attribute type="Ord_Cost"/>
 </ElementType>
</Schema>
<Customers xmlns="x-schema:#Schema2" Cus_Name="Astros">
 <Products Pro_Desc="baseball">
  <Orders Ord_Quantity="100" Ord_Cost="1265.0000"/>
 </Products>
</Customers>
```

FOR XML...ELEMENTS

The ELEMENTS argument produces a document that has each column's value mapped to a sub-element. The results are formatted to increase readability.

```
SELECT Cus_Name,
       Pro_Desc,
       Ord_Quantity,
       Ord_Quantity*Ord_Price AS Ord_Cost
FROM Customers
JOIN Orders ON Customers.Cus_UniqueID = Orders.Cus_UniqueID
JOIN Products ON Orders.Pro_UniqueID = Products.Pro_UniqueID
FOR XML AUTO, ELEMENTS
--Results--
XML_F52E2B61-18A1-11d1-B105-00805F49916B
-------------------------------------------------------------------------------
<Customers>
 <Cus_Name>Astros</Cus_Name>
 <Products>
```

```
  <Pro_Desc>baseball</Pro_Desc>
  <Orders>
   <Ord_Quantity>100</Ord_Quantity>
   <Ord_Cost>1265.0000</Ord_Cost>
  </Orders>
 </Products>
</Customers>
```

This output conforms to the element-centric approach—the data values are associated with single elements.

The FOR option(s) you use are dependent on the schema used by the application. If the application uses a schema that cannot be produced with the options presented in the previous examples, you need to research the EXPLICIT option. For more information on this option, see the Books Online topic: Using EXPLICIT Mode.

OPENXML

OPENXML is a rowset provider that allows the data elements in an XML document to be manipulated as if they were held in a table. It can be used in the FROM clause of a SELECT just like a table or view. The syntax of OPENXML follows.

```
OPENXML(idoc int [in],rowpattern nvarchar[in],[flags byte[in]])
[WITH (SchemaDeclaration | TableName)]
```

The various clauses of the rowset provider are explained here.

idoc int [in]

The document handle of the internal representation of the XML document. The value is created with the **sp_xml_preparedocument** system stored procedure.

rowpattern nvarchar[in]

The XPath patterns that identifies the document nodes.

flags byte[in]

An optional indicator that determines the mapping between the XML data and the rowset. The valid values are shown in Table D-2.

Table D-2. Valid Flag Values

VALUE	DESCRIPTION
0	Attribute-centric mapping. This is the default value.
1	Attribute-centric mapping with XML_ELEMENTS
2	Element-centric mapping with XML_ATTRIBUTES
8	Data should not be copied to the @mp:xmltext overflow property

WITH (SchemaDeclaration | TableName)

The optional WITH clause specifies the schema used to format the resultset. To declare the schema explicitly within the SELECT, use the SchemaDeclaration option. You can also reference an existing table with the TableName if one exists whose structure mirrors the resultset.

When the WITH option is omitted, the resultset produced is in the form of an edge table. An edge table contains detailed information about the XML document and is used when custom formatting is required. Use this approach when the other WITH arguments do not create a document per the application's specification. The columns that compose an edge table are shown in Table D-1.

Table D-2. EdgeTable Columns

COLUMN	DESCRIPTION
id	Unique ID of the document node.
parentid	Parent ID of the document node.
nodetype	Node type. The valid values are: 1=element, 2=attribute, 3=text.
localname	Local name of element or attribute.
prefix	Namespace prefix of the node.
namespaceuri	Namespace URI of the node.
datatype	Data type of the element or attribute.
prev	XML ID of the previous sibling element.
text	The text form of the attribute value or element content.

sp_xml_preparedocument

To use the OPENXML rowset provider to process an XML document, the document must be internalized so its data can be exposed. The internalization process parses the text of the document using the XML Parser (MSXML.DLL) and stores the results in SQL Server allocated cache. A document is processed with the **sp_xml_preparedocument** system stored procedure, and a document handle is returned to the calling application. The syntax of the procedure is shown here:

```
sp_xml_preparedocument hdoc OUTPUT
[, xmltext]
[, xpath_namespaces]
```

The parameters of the procedure are listed next.

hdoc OUTPUT

An OUTPUT parameter that returns the handle to the calling application.

xmltext

The text of the XML document. The argument can be passed as a string or with a variable. The valid data types for a variable are: char, varchar, nchar, nvarchar, text, and ntext.

xpath_namespaces

The namespace URIs used in the XML document.

sp_xml_removedocument

The internal representation of the document remains in cache until it is explicitly removed with the **sp_xml_removedocument** system stored procedure. To remove a document, call the procedure with the document handle as shown here.

```
EXEC sp_xml_removedocument @idoc
```

OPENXML Examples

The examples presented in this section demonstrate how to use OPENXML to produce a resultset. The following shows the edge table produced when the WITH clause is omitted.

```
DECLARE @idoc int,
        @doc varchar(4000)
```

```
--Populate variable with XML document
SET @doc = '
<ROOT>
<Customer>
  <Cus_UniqueID>2</Cus_UniqueID>
  <Cus_Name>Texans</Cus_Name>
  <Cus_ConFName>Bob</Cus_ConFName>
  <Cus_ConLName>McNair</Cus_ConLName>
 </Customer>
<Customer>
  <Cus_UniqueID>3</Cus_UniqueID>
  <Cus_Name>Aeros</Cus_Name>
  <Cus_ConFName>Steve</Cus_ConFName>
  <Cus_ConLName>Watson</Cus_ConLName>
 </Customer>
</ROOT>'

--Obtain handle of internal document
EXEC sp_xml_preparedocument @idoc OUTPUT, @doc

--Produce resultset with schema declaration
SELECT *
FROM OPENXML (@idoc, '/ROOT/Customers',2)

--Remove document from cache
EXEC sp_xml_removedocument @idoc
--Results (partial)--
```

id	parentid	nodetype	localname	...
2	0	1	Customers	...
3	2	1	Cus_UniqueID	...
12	3	3	#text	...
...				

Note that the results of the example only show the first four of the nine columns of the resultset. The other columns are too wide to fit on a printed page. Use the descriptions listed in Table D-1 to understand the output.

The next example shows how to create a formatted output using the schema declaration argument of the WITH clause.

```
DECLARE @idoc int,
        @doc varchar(4000)

--Populate variable with XML document
SET @doc = '
```

```
<ROOT>
<Customer>
  <Cus_UniqueID>2</Cus_UniqueID>
  <Cus_Name>Texans</Cus_Name>
  <Cus_ConFName>Bob</Cus_ConFName>
  <Cus_ConLName>McNair</Cus_ConLName>
 </Customer>
 <Customer>
  <Cus_UniqueID>3</Cus_UniqueID>
  <Cus_Name>Aeros</Cus_Name>
  <Cus_ConFName>Steve</Cus_ConFName>
  <Cus_ConLName>Watson</Cus_ConLName>
 </Customer>
</ROOT>'

--Obtain handle of internal document
EXEC sp_xml_preparedocument @idoc OUTPUT, @doc

--Produce resultset with schema declaration
SELECT *
FROM OPENXML (@idoc, '/ROOT/Customers',2)
WITH (Cus_UniqueID  int,
      Cus_Name varchar(30),
      Cus_ConFName varchar(30),
      Cus_ConLName varchar(30))

--Remove document from cache
EXEC sp_xml_removedocument @idoc
```

Cus_UniqueID	Cus_Name	Cus_ConFName	Cus_ConLName
2	Texans	Bob	McNair
3	Aeros	Steve	Watson

The schema listed in the WITH clause is identical to the **Customers** table created earlier. Instead of specifying the schema in the WITH clause, the **Customers** table can be referenced instead. The following shows how to alter the SELECT to reference **Customers** for the schema. The SELECT produces the same output as the previous example.

```
SELECT *
FROM OPENXML (@idoc,'/ROOT/Customer',2)
WITH Customers
```

The examples so far have shown how to produce a resultset from the contents of an XML document. The real need, however, is to take the data in the document and populate one or more tables in the database. Because the resultset produced by OPENXML is the same as a table or view, the SELECT can be used with the INSERT statement. The following shows how to insert the data in the sample XML document into the **Customers** table.

```
DECLARE @idoc int,
        @doc varchar(4000)

--Populate variable with XML document
SET @doc = '
<ROOT>
<Customer>
  <Cus_UniqueID>2</Cus_UniqueID>
  <Cus_Name>Texans</Cus_Name>
  <Cus_ConFName>Bob</Cus_ConFName>
  <Cus_ConLName>McNair</Cus_ConLName>
 </Customer>
<Customer>
  <Cus_UniqueID>3</Cus_UniqueID>
  <Cus_Name>Aeros</Cus_Name>
  <Cus_ConFName>Steve</Cus_ConFName>
  <Cus_ConLName>Watson</Cus_ConLName>
 </Customer>
</ROOT>'

--Obtain handle of internal document
EXEC sp_xml_preparedocument @idoc OUTPUT, @doc

--INSERT data into Customers table
INSERT Customers
SELECT *
FROM OPENXML (@idoc, '/ROOT/Customer',2)
WITH (Cus_Name varchar(30),
      Cus_ConFName varchar(30),
      Cus_ConLName varchar(30))

--Remove document from cache
EXEC sp_xml_removedocument @idoc
--Results--

(2 row(s) affected)
```

As you can see, all I did was add an INSERT Customers before the SELECT. The following code shows the statement worked as expected.

```
SELECT *
FROM Customers
--Results--
Cus_UniqueID  Cus_Name  Cus_ConFName         Cus_ConLName
------------  --------  -------------------  -------------------
1             Astros    Drayton              McLane
2             Texans    Bob                  McNair
3             Aeros     Steve                Watson
```

Updategrams

An updategram is a process for using schemas to modify data in a SQL Server database. This functionality was not included with the first public release of SQL Server 2000; instead, it was released as a series of updates calls SQL Server XML and Internet Support. I use the Beta 2 release (December 2000) in the examples presented next. If the SQL Server 2000 service packs are available when you read this, you will want to check to make sure the updategram support is included. If no service packs are available, you'll need to go to http://msdn.microsoft.com/xml and download the latest version of SQL Server XML and Internet Support. The Beta 2 version was extremely easy to install and came with documentation that clearly explained how updategrams work.

Before updategrams were introduced, the only way to use an XML document to modify data in a SQL Server was to use the OPENXML approach I presented in the previous section. Updategrams streamline this type of data modification by allowing schemas to be used to modify data. The schemas map the XML data elements to corresponding tables and columns in the database and keywords are used to specify the type of modification to apply. After covering the updategrams examples presented in this section, I am sure you will conclude this approach is more efficient than OPENXML.

The general form of an updategram is shown next.

```
<ROOT xmlns:updg="urn:schemas-microsoft-com:xml-updategram">
  <updg:sync [mapping-schema= "XDRSchemaFile.xml"] >
    <updg:before>
      ...
    </updg:before>
    <updg:after>
      ...
    </updg:after>
  </updg:sync>
</ROOT>
```

The namespace in use is promulgated by Microsoft, but you can define your own if you wish. The key to updategrams lies in the second line of the code. The **mapping-schema** directive points to a schema file that maps the data elements in the XML document to columns in the database. As indicated by the brackets, the directive is optional, but for most real-world applications a schema is required. The `<before>`, `<after>`, and `<sync>` keywords perform the data modifications. The function each keyword performs is listed in Table D-2.

Table D-2. Updategram Keywords

KEYWORD	DESCRIPTION
<before>	The existing state of the data.
<after>	The post modification state of the data.
<sync>	Wraps a <before> and <after> to produce the modification

The examples presented in the next section will show how these work together to modify a database.

Creating an XDR (XML-Data Reduced) Schema

XDR schemas implement updategram functionality by providing mapping information from a source XML document to the target database table(s). Schemas are not required for simple updategrams where there is one-to-one mapping of element/attribute and table/column names. They are, however, useful when mapping multi-table relationships, or when the source XML elements/attributes do not have the same names as the target table/columns.

XDR schemas are fairly easy to understand because all they do is map data elements in XML documents to tables and columns within a database. XDR schemas consist of data element definitions and annotations that indicate which elements belong to a table in the database. When there is a one-to-one correspondence between element and table/column names, no annotations are required. The following shows the XDR schema (Customers.xml) for the **Customers** table referenced throughout the appendix. I have added line numbers to facilitate the explanation.

```
1 <?xml version="1.0" ?>
2   <Schema xmlns="urn:schemas-microsoft-com:xml-data" _
          xmlns:sql="urn:schemas-microsoft-com:xml-sql">
3
4     <ElementType name="Cus_Name" content="textOnly" />
```

```
5     <ElementType name="Cus_ConFName" content="textOnly" />
6     <ElementType name="Cus_ConLName" content="textOnly" />
7
8     <ElementType name="Customer" sql:relation="Customers">
9     <element type="Cus_Name" />
10    <element type="Cus_ConFName" />
11    <element type="Cus_ConLName" />
12    </ElementType>
13 </Schema>
```

Line 2 references Microsoft-promulgated namespaces, but you can use your own if you like. Lines 4–6 are references to the elements in the source XML document. The content="textOnly" indicates the document is structured without attributes (element-centric approach). Lines 8–12 define the mappings to the **Customers** table columns. Line 8 contains the only annotation in the schema. The sql:relation annotation maps the Customer root element of the source document to **Customers** table in the database. If the root element in the source document is named **Customers**, no annotation is required. There are no element-to-column annotations needed on Lines 9–11 because the element names are the same as the column names.

The following XDR schema shows the various annotations needed when the source element names do not match the column names in the target table. The schema is also structured to handle an attribute-centric source document.

```
1 <?xml version="1.0" ?>
2  <Schema xmlns="urn:schemas-microsoft-com:xml-data" _
          xmlns:dt="urn:schemas-microsoft-com:datatypes" _
          xmlns:sql="urn:schemas-microsoft-com:xml-sql">
3   <ElementType name="Customer" sql:relation="Customers" >
4    <AttributeType name="Name" />
5    <AttributeType name="ConFName" />
6    <AttributeType name="ConLName" />
7
8    <attribute type="Name" sql:field="Cus_Name" />
9    <attribute type="ConFName" sql:field="Cus_ConFName" />
10   <attribute type="ConLName" sql:field="Cus_ConLName" />
11  </ElementType>
12 </Schema>
```

Lines 3 and 11 wrap the Customer element and its attributes. Lines 4–6 reference the attributes in the source document. Lines 8–10 map the source attributes to columns in the **Customers** table. The attribute-centric approach will not be used in the examples in this section. I did, however, want to show you what it looks like so you will understand how it differs from the element-centric format.

The key to understanding annotated XDR schemas is knowing the various annotations that can be used. The examples presented here are fairly simple, so we can get by with just a few. For more information on all the annotations available, see the Books Online topic: Annotations to the XDR Schema.

XDR schemas used with updategrams are placed in the template subdirectory of the virtual directory bound to the database. For this example, Customers.xml is placed in c:\inetpub\wwwroot\CodeCentric\template. If you recall, the CodeCentric, schema, and template subdirectories were created in the Configuring SQL/XML Support section earlier in the appendix.

Inserting Data

Now that the Customers.xml schema is in place, I want to create an updategram that contains data to insert into **Customers**. The updategram will reference Customers.xml in order to map the data elements to the proper columns. The following updategram adds one row to **Customers**.

```
1  <ROOT xmlns:updg="urn:schemas-microsoft-com:xml-updategram">
2   <updg:sync mapping-schema="Customers.xml">
3    <updg:before>
4    </updg:before>
5    <updg:after>
6     <Customer>
7      <Cus_Name>Rockets</Cus_Name>
8      <Cus_ConFName>Les</Cus_ConFName>
9      <Cus_ConLName>Alexander</Cus_ConLName>
10    </Customer>
11   </updg:after>
12  </updg:sync>
13 </ROOT>
```

Lines 2 and 12 reference the <sync> tag, which acts as a wrapper for the <before> and <after> keywords. Line 2 also has the reference to the XDR schema created in the previous section. Lines 3 and 4 show the current state of the data. When data is being inserted this section does not contain data. Lines 5–11 contain the post-modification state of the data.

The document is saved as Customers_INSERT.xml in the templates directory under the CodeCentric virtual root. Once saved, it can be called via the address line in IE with the following (you need to change the reference to "ace" so it matches your computer name).

```
http://ace/CodeCentric/template/Customers_INSERT.xml
```

The following SELECT shows the updategram worked as expected.

```
SELECT *
FROM Customers
--Results--
Cus_UniqueID  Cus_Name     Cus_ConFName                    Cus_ConLName
------------- ------------ ------------------------------- -------------

1             Astros       Drayton                         McLane
2             Texans       Bob                             McNair
3             Aeros        Steve                           Watson
4             Rockets      Les                             Alexander
```

Updating Data

Updating data via an updategram is very similar to adding, but you are required to supply the before and after picture of the data. You also have to supply a primary key so the correct row is updated. The following shows the changes applied to the schema file (Customers2.xml) to accommodate **Cus_UniqueID**, the primary key needed for the update.

```
<?xml version="1.0" ?>
 <Schema xmlns="urn:schemas-microsoft-com:xml-data"
         xmlns:sql="urn:schemas-microsoft-com:xml-sql">

  <ElementType name="Cus_UniqueID" content="textOnly" />
  <ElementType name="Cus_Name" content="textOnly" />
  <ElementType name="Cus_ConFName" content="textOnly" />
  <ElementType name="Cus_ConLName" content="textOnly" />

  <ElementType name="Customer" sql:relation="Customers" >
   <element type="Cus_UniqueID" />
   <element type="Cus_Name" />
   <element type="Cus_ConFName" />
   <element type="Cus_ConLName" />
  </ElementType>
</Schema>
```

Now that the schema is updated, I can use the following code (Customers_UPDATE.xml) to change the contact name information for the row with a **Cus_UnqiueID** = 1.

```
<ROOT xmlns:updg="urn:schemas-microsoft-com:xml-updategram">
 <updg:sync mapping-schema="Customers2.xml">
  <updg:before>
   <Customer>
    <Cus_UniqueID>1</Cus_UniqueID>
   </Customer>
  </updg:before>
  <updg:after>
   <Customer>
    <Cus_ConFName>Garth</Cus_ConFName >
    <Cus_ConLName>Wells</Cus_ConLName >
   </Customer>
  </updg:after>
 </updg:sync>
</ROOT>
```

The primary key column is added to the <before> section, and the desired changes are placed in the <after> section. The updategram is called in IE with

```
http://ace/CodeCentric/template/Customers_UPDATE.xml
```

The results of running the updategram are shown here;

```
SELECT *
FROM Customers
--Results--
Cus_UniqueID  Cus_Name     Cus_ConFName         Cus_ConLName
------------  ------------ -------------------- -------------
1             Astros       Garth                Wells
2             Texans       Bob                  McNair
3             Aeros        Steve                Watson
4             Rockets      Les                  Alexander
```

Deleting Data

Deleting data using an updategram is easy. Specify the primary key in the <before> section and nothing in the <after> section. The following (Customers_DELETE.xml) shows how to delete the row with a **Cus_UniqueID** = 4.

```
<ROOT xmlns:updg="urn:schemas-microsoft-com:xml-updategram">
 <updg:sync mapping-schema="Customers2.xml">
  <updg:before>
   <Customer>
```

```
    <Cus_UniqueID>4</Cus_UniqueID>
   </Customer>
  </updg:before>
  <updg:after>
  </updg:after>
 </updg:sync>
</ROOT>
```

If you try to delete the first two Customers created, an error is generated. Recall that orders were added for these customers, so attempting to delete them produces a foreign key violation error.

Integrating ASP and XML

Now that you understand how updategrams work, the next logical step is to learn how to create a client application that uses the updategrams to modify the database. In this process, you simply modify the updategram to accept parameters. I will demonstrate both inserting and updating data in this section.

Insert Example

The following (Customers_INSERT2.xml) shows how to add parameters to the insert template created earlier. This file is placed in the template subdirectory under the CodeCentric virtual directory.

```
1 <ROOT xmlns:updg="urn:schemas-microsoft-com:xml-updategram">
2  <updg:header>
3   <updg:param name="Cus_Name"/>
4   <updg:param name="Cus_ConFName"/>
5   <updg:param name="Cus_ConLName"/>
6  </updg:header>
7
8  <updg:sync >
9   <updg:before>
10   </updg:before>
11   <updg:after>
12     <Customers Cus_Name="$Cus_Name"
13       Cus_ConFName="$Cus_ConFName"
14       Cus_ConLName="$Cus_ConLName"/>
15   </updg:after>
16  </updg:sync>
17 </ROOT>
```

Lines 2–6 contain the header information, which is where the parameter declarations are held. The parameters correspond to the <input> tag definitions used in the .asp file that gathers user input. Lines 12–14 associate the parameter values with elements in the XML document. The .asp used to capture the data and call the updategram is shown next. The .asp file should be placed in the wwwroot subdirectory.

```
<HTML>
 <BODY>
  <center>
  <FORM name="Customer" _
        action="http://ace/CodeCentric/template/Customers_INSERT2.xml" _
        method="POST">
   <input type=hidden name="contenttype" value="text/xml">
   <TABLE width="50%">
    <tr>
     <td>Company Name:</td>
     <td><input type=text name="Cus_Name" value=""></td>
    </tr>
     <td>Contact First Name:</td>
     <td><input type=text name="Cus_ConFName" value=""></td>
    </tr>
     <td>Contact Last Name:</td>
     <td><input type=text name="Cus_ConLName"></td>
    </tr>
    <tr>
     <td colspan=2 align="center"> <input type="submit" _
         value="Submit"></td>
    </tr>
   </TABLE>
  </FORM>
 </BODY>
</HTML>
```

As you can see, this is a simple .asp file similar to the ones covered in Appendix B and used in Chapters 13 and 14. The call to Customers_INSERT2.xml is defined in the <FORM> tag. Load the .asp page in your browser, populate the input fields, and click the Submit button. The values are passed to the updategram, which in turns adds them to the **Customers** table.

Update Example

If you recall from Chapter 14, my approach to editing data in an ASP application is to list the rows on one page and allow the user to click the row to be edited. The next example uses the same approach. The stored procedure creates the results for the listing page.

```
CREATE PROCEDURE ps_SELECT_Customers
AS
SELECT Cus_UniqueID,
       Cus_Name,
       RTRIM(Cus_ConFName)+' '+Cus_ConLName AS ContactName
FROM Customers
ORDER BY Cus_Name
FOR XML AUTO
Go
```

The formatted output generated by the stored procedure is shown here.

```
XML_F52E2B61-18A1-11d1-B105-00805F49916B
------------------------------------------------------------
<Customers Cus_UniqueID="3" Cus_Name="Aeros" ContactName="Steve Watson"/>
<Customers Cus_UniqueID="1" Cus_Name="Astros" ContactName="Garth Wells"/>
<Customers Cus_UniqueID="5" Cus_Name="Comets" ContactName="Les Alexander"/>
<Customers Cus_UniqueID="2" Cus_Name="Texans" ContactName="Bob McNair"/>
```

The listing page needs its own updategram to call the stored procedure. The following (Customers_SELECT.xml) code creates the updategram.

```
<root xmlns:sql="urn:schemas-microsoft-com:xml-sql">
 <sql:header>
 </sql:header>
 <sql:query>
  EXEC ps_SELECT_Customers
 </sql:query>
</root>
```

Now that the data portion is in place, I need an .asp page to call the updategram and list the results for the user's selection. The following code uses the MSXML parser to call the updategram and load the results into the DOM (Document Object Model). An explanation of the major components is listed in the code.

```
<% Option Explicit%>
<HTML>
 <%
  Dim objXML, objCustomer, i

  REM Call updategram and place data returned in DOM
  Set objXML=Server.CreateObject("MSXML2.DomDocument")
  objXML.async=False
  objXML.Load("http://ace/CodeCentric/template/Customers_SELECT.xml")
 %>

<BODY>
 <center>
 <FORM name="Customer" _
       action="http://ace/CodeCentric/template/Customers_UPDATE2.xml" _
       method="POST">
  <input type=hidden name="contenttype" value="text/xml">
  <TABLE width="50%">
   <tr>
    <td>Company Name:</td>
    <td>Company Contact:</td>
   </tr>
   <tr>
    <td colspan=2><hr></td>
   </tr>
   <%
    REM Loop through DOM to list data
    For i=0 to objXML.documentElement.childNodes.length-1
     set objCustomer=objXML.documentElement.childNodes.Item(i)
   %>
   <tr>
    <td>
     <a href="AppD_CusEdit.asp?ID=<%=objCustomer.attributes(0).value%>">
      <%=objCustomer.attributes(1).value%>
     </a>
    </td>
    <td><%=objCustomer.attributes(2).value%></td>
   </tr>
   <%
    Next
    %>
  </TABLE>
 </FORM>
</BODY>
</HTML>
```

The output produced by the code is shown in Figure D-3.

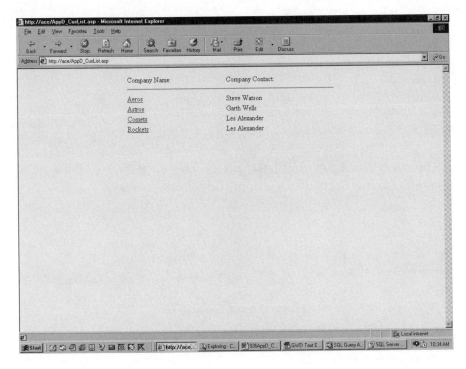

Figure D-3. Customer listing

When a user clicks a customer name, AppD_CusEdit.asp is called with the **Cus_UniqueID** value so the required data can be retrieved from the database. The stored procedure that returns the data per the unique ID is shown next.

```
CREATE PROCEDURE ps_SELECT_Customers_ByUnqiueID
@Cus_UniqueID int
AS
SELECT Cus_UniqueID,
       Cus_Name,
       Cus_ConFName,
       Cus_ConLName
FROM Customers
WHERE Cus_UniqueID = @Cus_UniqueID
ORDER BY Cus_Name
FOR XML AUTO
go
```

The updategram (Customers_SELECT2.xml) that calls the procedure follows.

```
<root xmlns:sql="urn:schemas-microsoft-com:xml-sql">
 <sql:header>
  <sql:param name="Cus_UniqueID"></sql:param>
 </sql:header>
 <sql:query>
  EXEC ps_SELECT_Customers_ByUnqiueID @Cus_UniqueID
 </sql:query>
</root>
```

The data retrieval portion is in place, so now I create the .asp page used to list the data for editing. The contents of AppD_CusEdit.asp follow.

```
<HTML>
 <%
  REM Use the unique ID value to retrieve data and load DOM
  Set objXML=Server.CreateObject("MSXML2.DomDocument")
  objXML.async=False
  objXML.Load("http://ace/CodeCentric/template/Customers_SELECT2.xml? _
              Cus_UniqueID=" & Request.querystring("ID") )
  set objCustomer=objXML.documentElement.childNodes.Item(0)
  On Error Resume Next
 %>

 <BODY>
  <center>
  <FORM name="Customer" _
        action="http://ace/CodeCentric/template/Customers_UPDATE2.xml" _
        method="POST">
   <input type=hidden name="contenttype" value="text/xml">
   <input type=hidden name="Cus_UniqueID" _
          value="<%=objCustomer.attributes(0).value%>">
   <TABLE width="50%">
    <tr>
     <td>Company Name:</td>
     <td><input type=text name="Cus_Name" _
                value="<%=objCustomer.attributes(1).value%>"></td>
    </tr>
     <td>Contact First Name:</td>
     <td><input type=text name="Cus_ConFName" _
                value="<%=objCustomer.attributes(2).value%>"></td>
    </tr>
     <td>Contact Last Name:</td>
```

```
      <td><input type=text name="Cus_ConLName" _
              value="<%=objCustomer.attributes(3).value%>"></td>
    </tr>
    <tr>
     <td colspan=2 align="center"> <input type="submit" _
         value="Submit"></td>
    </tr>
   </TABLE>
  </FORM>
 </BODY>
</HTML>
```

I modified the call to the updategram to accept and pass the unique ID parameter, but other than that it's the same logic as AppD_CusList.asp. The updategram (Customers_UPDATE2.xml) that posts the change to the database follows.

```
<ROOT xmlns:updg="urn:schemas-microsoft-com:xml-updategram">
 <updg:header>
  <updg:param name="Cus_UniqueID"/>
  <updg:param name="Cus_Name"/>
  <updg:param name="Cus_ConFName"/>
  <updg:param name="Cus_ConLName"/>
 </updg:header>

 <updg:sync >
  <updg:before>
   <Customers Cus_UniqueID="$Cus_UniqueID"/>
  </updg:before>
  <updg:after>
   <Customers Cus_UniqueID="$Cus_UniqueID"
              Cus_Name="$Cus_Name"
              Cus_ConFName="$Cus_ConFName"
              Cus_ConLName="$Cus_ConLName"/>
  </updg:after>
 </updg:sync>
</ROOT>
```

The key here is to add the Cus_UniqueID parameter to the <before> section so the proper row can be located and updated.

Additional Internet Resources

As a result of the popularity and expectations of XML, there are a number of Web sites that contain good information for learning this technology. The following sites will provide you with more than enough information to increase your awareness of the XML technologies in use today.

- `http://msdn.microsoft.com/XML`

- `http://www.w3schools.com/xml/`

- `http://msdn.microsoft.com/xml/articles/xmlguide.asp`

- `http://www.w3.org/XML/1999/XML-in-10-points`

- `http://msdn.microsoft.com/msdnmag/issues/1100/BeyondASP/BeyondASP.asp`

Before You Go

This primer covered the basics of XML and the features in SQL Server 2000 that facilitate XML integration. I covered the steps required to configure SQL/XML and presented examples that demonstrated how to produce an XML document from data stored in SQL Server. In addition, I showed two methods for updating a database based on the contents of an XML document.

Index

Special Characters

* (asterisk)

    using with SELECT in production code, 84

- (dash)

    using with LIKE operator, 93

-- (double dash)

    commenting single lines of code with, 15

/*...*/

    commenting lines of code with, 15

[ ] (brackets)

    using with LIKE operator, 94

A

<a>...</a>

    defining an anchor tag with, 540

ad hoc queries, 622

ADO command object

    interacting with a database with, 575–580

FOR [DELETE][,][INSERT][,][UPDATE]

    determining when the trigger is executed with, 388

AFTER trigger

    how it works, 219

    use of, 386–387

aggregate functions, 176–180

alerts

    firing event-based with SQLServerAgent service, 246–247

aliasing

    column, 98–99

    table, 97–98

[ALL | DISTINCT] optional keywords, 74

ALTER DATABASE arguments, 47

ALTER DATABASE statement

    changing database level collation with, 21

    modifying a database with, 47

    statement permissions, 48

ALTER FUNCTION statement, 208–210

    inline table-valued functions, 209

    multi-statement table-valued functions, 209–210

    scalar functions, 209

ALTER INDEX statement, 69

ALTER PROCEDURE statement

    syntax for, 337–338

ALTER TABLE statement

    changing column level collation with, 21

    making changes to tables with, 57

    permissions, 57

ALTER TRIGGER statement

    permissions for, 401

    syntax for, 400–401

L

LEFT function, 156

LEFT JOINS

and views, 232

LEN function, 156

LIKE operator, 93

examples of how to use, 96–97

wildcard characters for, 93–94

local temporary table

creating, 52

logical operators

examples of how to use, 94–97

testing for truth in a condition with, 92–94

LOG ON argument

CREATE DATABASE statement, 42

LOWER function, 156–157

LRU (least recently used) method, 324

LTRIM function, 157–158

M

mail profile

creating in SQL mail, 294–295

Manage Indexes dialog

accessing from Enterprise Manager, 68

accessing from Query Analyzer, 67

Manage Indexes/Keys icon

accessing in Table Designer, 68

mantissa

defined, 27

master database

installed with SQL Server, 242

system tables in, 244–245

materialized table. *See* derived tables

mathematical functions, 172–176

MAX function

returning the maximum value in an expression with, 178

MAXSIZE argument

using when creating a database, 44–45

MAXSIZE = max_size argument

FOR ATTACH argument, 43

Message Pane

in Query Window, 5

MIN function

returning minimum value in an expression with, 179

model database

installed with SQL Server, 242

MODIFY FILE <filespec>

ALTER DATABASE argument, 47

money and smallmoney data types, 26–27

money data type

description and storage size, 27

MONTH function

getting integer value of a month with, 171

msdb database

installed with SQL Server, 242

system tables in, 246–248

msg_id component

of RAISERROR statement, 373

msg_str component

of RAISERROR statement, 373

multi-parameter search screen

adding the interface, 415–420

N

V

varbinary[(n)] data type, 25

varchar[(n)] data type, 22

variant data types, 29–30

table

CREATE INDEX, 63

VIEW_COLUMN_USAGE

information schema view, 236

VIEW_METADATA argument

for CREATE VIEW statement, 215

view_name argument

for CREATE VIEW statement, 215

views, 213–238

altering in Query Analyzer, 231–232

creating and updating, 223–230

creating a non-clustered index on, 226

creating a unique clustered index on, 225–226

creating with Enterprise Manager, 222–223

creating within another view's definition, 225

creating with Query Analyzer, 220–221

defined, 214

dropping in Enterprise Manager, 235

dropping in Query Analyzer, 234–235

editing in Enterprise Manager, 233

VIEWS

information schema view, 236

views

and LEFT JOINS, 232

limitations, 216

requirements for creating an index on, 217

restrictions on executing INSERT or UPDATE statements on, 219

restrictions on indexing, 217–218

updating table data via, 227–230

views and clicks

example code for counting on www.Fine-Art.com, 440–447

VIEW_TABLE_USAGE

information schema view, 236

W

WAITFOR

control-of-flow keyword, 127

Web Assistant category

of system stored procedures, 251

Web Assistant procedures, 288–292

Web site

deciding on cross-browser compatibility of, 541

free and fee-based hosting providers, 536–537

information resources for developing, 553

maintaining a hosted, 534–537

Web stat counter

example code for custom, 447–456

WHERE clause

adding search_conditions to, 80–82

filtering SELECT statement resultsets with, 78–82

using with the DELETE statement, 146

[WHERE search_condition] argument, 74

WHILE

control-of-flow keyword, 123–126